Harrow June 20.th 1805

The Gentlemen of Harrow School request the
honour of trying their Skill at Cricket with the
Gentlemen of Eton, on Wednesday July 31.st at
Lords Cricket Ground. A Speedy answer, declaring
whether the time and place be convenient, will
oblige

LORD'S GROUND

(60p)

ETON v. HARROW

SATURDAY, 21st JUNE, 2014   (55 overs per side)

HARROW   Innings

#	Batsman	Dismissal	Runs
1.	F.W.A. Ruffell	b MacMillan	0
†2.	D.J. De Silva	c Watt b Fenwick	19
*3.	R.G. White	b Gnodde	45
4.	A. Rath	b Griffin	59
5.	D.G.A. Steward	c Russell b Gnodde	30
6.	R.S. Wijeratne	b MacMillan	40
7.	J.W. Grist	lbw b Fenwick	3
8.	M.C. Smith	b Griffin	1
9.	M.G. Kellock	c Russell b MacMillan	3
10.	H.W.A. Robyns	lbw b MacMillan	2
11.	M.J. Elworthy	not out	5

b 3, l-b 4, w 19, n-b , p ,   26

Total ....(51.3 overs)   233

FALL OF THE WICKETS

1—0   2—50   3—78   4—145   5—175   6—194   7—197   8—205   9—209   10—233

ANALYSIS OF BOWLING   Innings

Name	O.	M.	R.	W.	W.	N-b.
MacMillan	9.3	1	39	4	7	...
Griffin	11	0	40	2	3	...
Fenwick	11	0	46	2	1	...
Bouchier	5	0	33	0	...	...
Gnodde	9	1	30	2	1	...
Yerburgh	6	0	38	0	3	...

ETON   Innings

#	Batsman	Dismissal	Runs
1.	J.H. Watt	run out	0
2.	A.R. Treon	c White b Robyns	11
†3.	J.S.D. Gnodde	c White b Elworthy	73
*4.	A.D.L. Russell	c Kellock b Robyns	10
5.	H.A.S. Blake	lbw b Rath	1
6.	E.J. Collins	b Ruffell	0
7.	A.K. Bouchier	b Ruffell	7
8.	R.C. MacMillan	c Steward b Rath	33
9.	C.R.D. Griffin	b Ruffell	22
10.	C.A.G. Yerburgh	b Rath	5
11.	E.W.F. Fenwick	not out	0

b , l-b 3, w 4, n-b 1, p ,   8

Total ....(51 overs)   170

FALL OF THE WICKETS

1—2   2—43   3—59   4—71   5—72   6—91   7—111   8—148   9—169   10—170

ANALYSIS OF BOWLING   Innings

Name	O.	M.	R.	W.	W.	N-b.
Smith	6	3	15	0	...	...
Elworthy	7	1	29	1	1	...
Kellock	10	1	27	0	2	...
Robyns	8	2	24	2	...	1
Rath	10	1	30	3	...	...
Ruffell	10	0	42	3	0	...

Umpires—P.D. Nicholls & G. Frost   Scorers—J.G.E. Jarvis & G. Kitada

†Captain   *Wicket-keeper

Play begins at 11.00   Luncheon Interval 1.00-1.40   Tea Interval – after 25 overs of the side batting second

(Times may vary according to the state of the game)

Harrow won the toss   Harrow won by 63 runs

(60p)

ETON v. HARROW

SATURDAY, 20th JUNE, 2015   (55 overs per side)

HARROW — Innings

1.	F.W.A. Ruffell	c Harrington b Fenwick	10
2.	A.A. Copestick	lbw b Hardman	28
3.	A. Rath	c Treon b Fenwick	103
4.	Rahul Wijeratne	c MacDonagh b Hardman	40
†*5.	D.G.A. Steward	b Wilkinson	24
6.	Sachin Wijeratne	c Hardman b Whipple	9
7.	J.J. Cleverly	b Takavarasha	14
8.	S.J.S. Assani	not out	18
9.	M.G. Kellock		
10.	T.M. Nevile		
11.	A. Nazir		

b , l-b **7**, w **16**, n-b **4**, p ,   **27**

Total ....(7 wkts, 55 overs)   **273**

FALL OF THE WICKETS

1—22   2—58   3—145   4—212   5—232   6—237   7—273   8—   9—   10—

ANALYSIS OF BOWLING — Innings

Name	O.	M.	R.	W.	W.	N-b.
Whipple	11	1	39	1	...	...
Fenwick	11	1	60	2	2	...
Takavarasha	11	0	73	1	4	4
Hardman	11	0	40	2	4	...
Wilkinson	11	0	54	1	2	...
	...	...	...	...	...	

ETON — Innings

1.	E.J. Collins	c Steward b Assani	7
2.	A.R. Treon	not out	103
3.	J.H.R.I. Hardman	b Nazir	23
*4.	A.D.L. Russell	lbw b Nazir	13
†5.	W.R.C. Gordon Lennox	c R. Wijeratne b Nazir	19
6.	N.C. MacDonagh	not out	4
7.	N.R.J. Harrington		
8.	T.C.E. Wilkinson		
9.	J.M.P. Takavarasha		
10.	E.W.F. Fenwick		
11.	W.J.E. Whipple		

b , l-b **4**, w **11**, n-b **2**, p ,   **17**

Total .... (4 wkts, 35.5 overs)   **186**

FALL OF THE WICKETS

1—24   2—103   3—154   4—182   5—   6—   7—   8—   9—   10—

ANALYSIS OF BOWLING — Innings

Name	O.	M.	R.	W.	W.	N-b.
Ruffell	4	0	19	0	5	1
Assani	4	0	19	1	1	1
Copestick	6	1	19	0	...	...
Kellock	3	0	34	0	...	...
Nevile	5	0	25	0	1	...
Nazir	8.5	1	49	3	1	...
Rath	5	0	17	0	1	...

Umpires—L.R. Allan & D.A. Brooks   Scorers—F.A.S. Young & G. Kitada

†Captain   *Wicket-keeper

Play begins at 11.00   Luncheon Interval 1.00-1.40   Tea Interval – after 25 overs of the side batting second
(Times may vary according to the state of the game)

Eton won the toss and elected to field   **Eton won by 6 wickets (D/L method)**

MATCHES AT LORD'S 2015

APRIL

Sun.	12	**Middlesex v. Nottinghamshire** (LV=CC)	4 Days
Tue.	21	**M.C.C. v. Ireland "A"**	1 Day
Tue.	28	**M.C.C. Men's Regional Twenty20 – Final**	1 Day

MAY

Sat.	2	**Middlesex v. Durham** (LV=CC)	4 Days
Wed.	6	**M.C.C. v. M.C.C. Young Cricketers**	1 Day
Thur.	21	**ENGLAND v. NEW ZEALAND** (Investec Test Match)	5 Days
Thur.	28	† **MIDDLESEX v. KENT** (NatWest T20 Blast)	1 Day
Sun.	31	**Middlesex v. Warwickshire** (LV=CC)	4 Days

JUNE

Thur.	11	**Inter-Services Twenty20 Tournament**	1 Day
Sat.	13	* **J.P. Morgan International Cricket Cup**	1 Day
Thur.	18	† **MIDDLESEX v. HAMPSHIRE** (NatWest T20 Blast)	1 Day
Sat.	20	**Eton v. Harrow**	1 Day
Tue.	23	**M.C.C. Universities Challenge – Final**	1 Day
Sat.	27	**Oxford v. Cambridge**	1 Day
Sun.	28	**Middlesex v. Hampshire** (LV=CC)	4 Days

JULY

Thur.	2	† **MIDDLESEX v. SUSSEX** (NatWest T20 Blast)	1 Day
Thur.	16	**ENGLAND v. AUSTRALIA** (Investec Test Match)	5 Days
Tue.	21	**M.C.C. v. Melbourne C.C.**	1 Day
Thur.	23	† **MIDDLESEX v. SURREY** (NatWest T20 Blast)	1 Day

Sun.	26	**Middlesex v. Warwickshire** (Royal London One-Day Cup)	1 Day
Mon.	27	**M.C.C. v. Sydney Cricket Ground XI**	1 Day

AUGUST

Thur.	6	**Middlesex v. Nottinghamshire** (Royal London One-Day Cup)	1 Day
Fri.	7	**Middlesex v. Sussex** (LV=CC)	4 Days
Wed.	12		
Thur.	13	‡ *NatWest T20 Blast – Quarter-Final*	(2 Days)
Fri.	14		
or Sat.	15		
Mon.	17	**Middlesex v. Glamorgan** (Royal London One-Day Cup)	1 Day
Thur.	20	**M.C.C. v. Club Cricket Conference** (Centenary Match)	1 Day
Tue.	25		
Wed.	26	‡ *Royal London One-Day Cup – Quarter-Final*	(2 Days)
Thur.	27		
or Fri.	28		

SEPTEMBER

Sat.	5	**ENGLAND v. AUSTRALIA** (Royal London One-Day International)	1 Day
Sun.	6	‡ *Royal London One-Day Cup – Semi-Final*	(2 Days)
or Mon.	7		
Tue.	8	**M.C.C. Schools v. E.S.C.A.**	1 Day
Wed.	9	**Middlesex v. Yorkshire** (LV=CC)	4 Days
Sun.	13	**Davidstow National Village Cup – Final**	1 Day
Sat.	19	**ROYAL LONDON ONE-DAY CUP – FINAL**	(2 Days)

† Floodlit match   * Sponsor's Cricket Day   ‡ Dependent on Middlesex's progress in the competition and on the draw

(LV=CC) – LV= County Championship matches will be played in Division 1

Where the duration of a match is shown in parentheses the game is scheduled to be finished in one day, but the number of days shown has been set aside to allow for the possibility of bad weather.

Runs per over (use for Limited-overs matches)

1st Innings

1	2	3	4	5	6	7	8	9	10
11	12	13	14	15	16	17	18	19	20
21	22	23	24	25	26	27	28	29	30
31	32	33	34	35	36	37	38	39	40
41	42	43	44	45	46	47	48	49	50

2nd Innings

1	2	3	4	5	6	7	8	9	10
11	12	13	14	15	16	17	18	19	20
21	22	23	24	25	26	27	28	29	30
31	32	33	34	35	36	37	38	39	40
41	42	43	44	45	46	47	48	49	50

M.C.C MUSEUM AND TOURS OF LORD'S

The M.C.C. Museum, situated at the back of the Pavilion, houses a unique collection of cricket memorabilia, including the Ashes. The Museum is open on all match days. Admission charges are £3 for adults and £1 for concessions.

For those who would like the opportunity to see more of the Home of Cricket, the Lord's Tour is an exceptional experience. For further information, please visit the Tours Reception, opposite the Museum, or telephone 020 7616 8595.

ETON & HARROW
PAST & PRESENT

AT LORD'S

ROBERT TITCHENER-BARRETT

Robert Titchener-Barrett

Foreword by Matthew Fleming (Kent & England)

This book is dedicated both to the memory of my parents
and to my cricketing sons Dominic and Alexander.

Stet Fortuna Domus. Donorum Dei
Dispensatio Fidelis.

This book was first published in 1996
and now, revised and expanded, is published by
Woodstock Investment Management
Designed by Andrew Younger
and printed by
Woolnough Printers & Bookbinders
February 2006
Copyright Robert Titchener-Barrett

CONTENTS

M V FLEMING

Matthew Fleming played eleven one-day internationals for England, and 310 matches for Kent County Cricket Club between 1989-2003. He was captain of Kent from 1999-2003 and was named Kent Player of the Year in 2001. He was Chairman of the Professional Cricketers' Association from 1996-2001, since when he has been a Vice-President. Matthew is a trustee of The Lord's Taverners, a board member of the London Playing Fields Society and a member of the committee of Kent and M.C.C.

FOREWORD

MATTHEW FLEMING
(Eton, Combined Services, Kent and England)

I am delighted that Robert Titchener-Barrett has once again undertaken the arduous task of researching and updating his fine history of Eton and Harrow cricket in this its 200th Anniversary year, both from the perspective of its performers and what they have achieved in the wider context of the game and elsewhere, as well as in the oldest fixture still being played at Lord's since 1805.

Having myself played in the 1981/82 fixtures for Eton at Lord's and been lucky enough to achieve further success in the game at a higher level and play many times at Lord's, I know what a very special and unique ambience it has and how privileged I was, as is so for all who have played there. Long may the contest prosper and show all that is best in schoolboy cricket. Robert Titchener-Barrett has provided a fascinating insight into the feats of the participants from both schools, who are still providing representatives in the County game, the latest being Nick Compton of Middlesex, Alex Loudon of Kent and Warwickshire, and James Bruce of Hampshire. The book is even better illustrated than before and shows just how much the game of cricket owes to the many famous names who have learned their cricket on the playing fields of both these illustrious establishments, displayed their skills in the great match and, in many cases, have gone on to play and administer the game at the highest level.

Cricket has always been as much a test of character as technique and on the really big occasion even more so. May both schools continue to provide young men of the highest calibre that set an example for cricket in a wider context.

I am confident that the book will not only be of great interest to Etonians and Harrovians and particularly to those who played at Lord's, but will have a much broader appeal to all cricket enthusiasts, historians and lovers of our national summer game. I wish it the very greatest of success.

Matt Fleming

AUTHOR'S PREFACE

It is nearly ten years since I wrote Eton and Harrow at Lord's in 1996 and inevitably there has been a great deal of new material and photographs that have come to light in the intervening period. Since the 200th Anniversary of the fixture at Lord's in 1805 has just been celebrated it was suggested that I might like to do another edition. Inevitably in the last book there were some mistakes and omissions; this gives me a chance to correct these, add some new material, redesign the script and photographs to bring it right up-to-date. Again it has been an onerous task whilst trying to do a day job as well but worthwhile and rewarding. I have also tried to make it more appealing to cricket lovers everywhere although still wishing to retain the original flavour. The title has been changed slightly to *Eton & Harrow Past & Present* to reflect the huge contribution to the game that these two great institutions have made and the participants thereof in the past, present and, I believe, the future.

I would like to thank most sincerely the considerable help and co-operation I have received, in particular from Michael Meredith, the Eton College librarian, Adam Chadwick, the M.C.C. curator, Ralph Oliphant-Callum in charge of Eton cricket and his opposite number at Harrow Simon Halliday. Andrew Younger, my ever patient designer, Adam Fleming, Nick Forman Hardy and many other sponsors, and several Eton and Harrow families who have provided new material and last but not least my printer Paul Kidson also deserves my heartfelt thanks.

I am most grateful that Matthew Fleming, a very distinguished Eton, Kent and England cricketer of recent vintage, has agreed to write the Foreword and thank him for his kind support and encouragement.

I sincerely hope readers will get much pleasure and delight from the book into which I have put my heart and soul and produced it for the benefit and enlightenment of future generations of cricketers, particularly those from the two Schools.

An ode of Horace which begins *eheu fugaces, Postume, Postume, labuntur anni* ('Alas Postumus, Postumus, the years slip away in flight') aptly sums up the contribution our cricketers have made to the rich tapestry of England's heritage which is often forgotten but we need reminding of from time to time.

Robert Titchener-Barrett
February, 2006, London

Whatsoever thy hand findeth to do, do it with thy might.
Eton College Chronicle May 1905

THE YEARS BEFORE 1805

Cricket had been a serious game at both schools for some time before the challenge to Eton at Lord's in 1805. Several major games had been played at Lord's and elsewhere between 1791 and 1805 some of which are detailed in Henry Bentley's scores, the forerunner of Lillywhite's and Wisden's, the cricketer's bibles. Eton played England on 30th May 1791 which they lost by 6 wickets and also lost to M.C.C. on 23rd June 1791 by 6 wickets at Burley Park. It also appears some school matches were played as on 13th May 1793 Eton beat Westminster by 34 runs. At Harrow cricket replaced archery in 1772 and the famous picture of the Buxton family at play in the Harrow School Museum shows that it was enjoyed by the landed gentry of the day but very few official matches were played before 1805 and little in the way of records survive (except that of 1800, which in itself is pretty sketchy).

Thomas Lord in action, taken from a sketch by George Shepherd (1770-1842).

The 9th Earl of Winchilsea (1752-1826) considered to be the founder of M.C.C. and with Charles Lennox, later Duke of Richmond the guarantors of Thomas Lord.

As can be seen from these early scorecards liberal use seems to have been made of guest players but the Earl of Winchilsea, one of the great early Etonian patrons of the game was clearly a player of some ability with 54 and 8 v. England and 20 and 76 v. M.C.C. on wickets which were very far from satisfactory.

LORDS.—30TH MAY, 1791.

The Gentlemen of Eton against the Gentlemen of England.

ETON.

	1st Inns.		2d Inns.	
Earl Winchilsea	54	b Cumberland	8	b Cumberland
Earl Darnley	3	b ditto	7	b ditto
Hon. E. Bligh	25	b ditto	21	c Louch
Hon. H. Fitzroy	6	c Louch	41	Not out
A. Smith, Esq.	1	b Grange	4	c Talbot
R. Wyatt, Esq.	13	b Cumberland	32	st Lennox
Mellish, Esq.	1	c Thanet	0	b Cumberland
Leycester, Esq.	0	b Cumberland	6	st Lennox
Mr. Dupuis	6	b Grange	28	b Cumberland
Miller, Esq.	0	Run out	9	b ditto
Lord	4	Not out	5	b Louch
Byes	3		6	
	116		167	

ENGLAND.

	1st Inns.		2d Inns.	
Ld. Thanet	17	c Darnley	10	b Darnley
Col. Lennox	61	b Fitzroy		
G. Talbot, Esq.	1	b Lord	0	b Darnley
Capt. Cumberland	12	Run out	2	b Lord
Raye, Esq.	57	b Darnley		
G. Louch, Esq.	10	b Fitzroy		
R. Stewart, Esq.	17	c Smith	3	Not out
Pitcairn, Esq	34	b Lord	8	b Darnley
Nicol, Esq.	8	b Lord	7	Not out
G. Dehaney, Esq.	8	Not out		
Grange	6	b Lord		
Byes	20		3	
	251		33	

England won by six wickets.

BURLEY PARK.—23D JUNE, 1791.

Seven Etonians (with Four Picked Men) against Seven Gentlemen of the Mary-le-bone Club (with Four Picked Men).

ETON.

	1st Inns.		2d Inns.	
C. Anguish, Esq.	14	b Walker	6	Run out
Hon. H. Fitzroy	6	c Louch	4	b Cumberland
Earl Darnley	0	c Lennox	1	c Talbot
Sale, Esq.	0	b Walker	5	b Taylor
A. Smith, Esq.	1	b Cumberland	0	b Cumberland
Hon. E. Bligh	2	c Lennox	15	b Taylor
Ld. Winchilsea	20	b Cumberland	76	c Talbot
Brown	7	b ditto	1	Run out
Graham	0	b ditto	0	c Lennox
Purchase	7	Not out	0	b Cumberland
Bullen	0	b Cumberland	4	Not out
Byes	2		2	
	59		114	

MARY-LE-BONE.

	1st Inns.		2d Inns.	
C.Cumberland, Esq.	2	c Bullen	0	b Bullen
Welsh, Esq.	9	b Purchase	5	b ditto
Hon. W. Harbord	1	b ditto	10	c Purchase
G. Talbot, Esq.	3	Run out	17	b Bullen
Col. Lennox	8	b Fitzroy	4	Not out
G. Louch, Esq.	29	c Bullen	2	Ditto
J. Maddox, Esq.	0	b Fitzroy		
Towell	2	b Purchase		
Goldham	24	b Bullen		
T. Walker	31	Not out		
Taylor	18	b Fitzroy		
Byes	7		2	
	134		40	

Mary-le-bone won by 6 wickets.

LORD'S.—13TH MAY, 1793.

Five Gentlemen of Eton, with Six Players, against Five Gentlemen of Westminster, with Six Players.

ETON.

	1st Inns.		2nd Inns.	
Earl Winchilsea	9	b Nicoll	13	c Ray
A. Smith, Esq.	21	c Louch	2	b Fennex
Mellish, Esq.	3	b Fennex	0	b Cumberland
Walpole, Esq.	1	b Cumberland	0	c Nicoll
Tyson, Esq.	14	Run out	3	c Goldham
Sale	2	c Dehany	0	b Cumberland
Bullen	21	c Nicoll	27	c Welch
Lord	18	Run out	3	c Sylvester
Turner	2	b Cumberland	0	b ditto
Bedsworth	15	Not out	7	b Fennex
Graham	25	b Cumberland	0	Not out
Byes	6	Byes	1	
	137		58	

WESTMINSTER.

	1st Inns.		2nd Inns.	
Dehany, Esq.	5	c Bedsworth	22	b Lord
G. Louch, Esq.	1	b Lord	30	b ditto
Capt. Cumberland	9	b Bullen	15	b Winchilsea
Welsh, Esq.	7	Run out	4	c Walpole
Nicoll, Esq.	17	b Lord	0	Run out
Button	8	b Bullen	9	c Bedsworth
Goldham	0	b ditto	10	Not out
Freemantle	1	b Lord	1	c Lord
Fennex	1	Not out	3	b Bullen
Ray	1	b Lord	0	b ditto
Sylvester	0	c Bedsworth	11	b Lord
Byes	1	Byes	6	
	50		111	

Eton won by 34 runs.

Cricket exercised the minds of many famous men at this time and Thomas Gray, despite the human generosity of his Elegy, had a slight sneer at the game;

'There is my Lord Sandwich and Halifax, they are statesmen: do you not remember them as dirty boys playing at cricket?'

Although cautious in his terms he gave cricket a little more praise in his noble and original 'Ode on a distant prospect of Eton College':

> *Say Father Thames for thou hast seen*
> *Full many a sprightly race*
> *Disporting on thy margent green*
> *The paths of pleasure trace,*
> *Who foremost now delight to cleave*
> *With pliant arms thy glassy wave?*
> *The captive linnet which enthrall?*
> *What idle progeny succeed*
> *To chase the rolling circle's speed,*
> *Or urge the flying ball?*

THE EARLY YEARS
1805-1860

The original challenge to Eton from Harrow came on **20th June 1805**; the letter is still extant in the Eton College Library and reads thus;

> *The gentlemen of Harrow School request the honour of trying their skill at cricket with the gentlemen of Eton, on Wednesday July 31st at Lord's Cricket Ground, A speedy answer, declaring whether the time and place be convenient will oblige.*

A reply duly came back that the Etonians would accept and the match was set for August 2nd **1805**. There are notes in the margin of a collection of Eton verses and translations now in the Vaughan Library at Harrow of a match played in 1800 which Harrow were supposed to have won but since no names and scores are attached except that of Tom Lloyd, the brother of J.A. Lloyd the Harrow captain of 1805, who died shortly after this match of a cold, we must therefore assume this to be null and void and therefore 1805 to be the first legitimate contest between the two great schools. It subsequently proved a most convincing win for the Etonians by an innings and 2 runs. It was also famous because the poet Lord Byron played in the match with a club foot, although subsequent research shows that his foot had considerably improved by the time the match was eventually played on August 2nd, in that he was able to wear a common boot over a corrective inner shoe, although he still had difficulty in running between the wickets and his performance was barely improved as his scores of 7 & 2 indicated. His claim that he scored more runs, except for Viscount Ipswich and W. Brockman, than any other Harrovian in the match, namely 18, proved to be incorrect since the match and the scores are in the Upper Club record book of 1805 in the Eton College library and show the correct scores of 7 and 2. His captain J.A. Lloyd was not enamoured of him and wrote, *"Byron played in the match and very badly too. He should never have been in the XI if my counsel had been taken."* It has been suggested that Byron was something to do with the original challenge and therefore he probably insisted on playing although this has never been substantiated. However enjoyment seemed to be had by all, as he wrote in a letter to his old friend Charles Gordon on August 4th 1805, which the following extract showed.

"We played the Eton (sic) and were most confoundedly beat, however it was some comfort to me that I got 11 notches the first innings and 7 the second which was more than any of our side, except Brockman and Ipswich, could contrive to hit. Later... to be sure we were most of us rather drunk and went together to the Haymarket Theatre where we kicked up a row, as you may suppose when so many Harrovians and Etonians met at one place. I was one of seven in a single Hackney Coach, 4

Byron at the time he left Harrow for Trinity College, Cambridge in 1805. The poet cricketer achieved greatness and some notoriety later but his lack of mobility and scores of 7 and 2 did not help Harrow's cause.

Lord Ipswich (Later 5th Duke of Grafton) Harrow XI 1805. Played in the first match in 1805 when Lord's was at Dorset Square and top scored for Harrow in both innings with 10 and 21. Eton still won decisively by an innings and 2 runs.

4th Duke of Dorset Harrow XI 1807/8 played in winning matches where the records had been lost.

Viscount Palmerston, the great Victorian Prime Minister who was at Harrow with Byron followed the matches closely after 1805 and confirmed that 'we beat them afterwards' although no scores survived until 1818.

Eton and 3 Harrow fellows, we all got into the same box, the consequence was that such a devil of a noise arose that none of our neighbours could hear a word of the drama, at which not being highly delighted they began to quarrel with us and we nearly came to a battle royal etc."

Eton were rather pleased with themselves and sent the following epigram to Harrow after the match:

> *Adventurous 'boys' of Harrow School, of cricket you've no knowledge,*
> *Ye played not cricket but the fool with 'men' of Eton College.*

Eton received the following reply believed to have been composed by Byron:

> *Ye Eton wits to play the fool*
> *Is not the boast of Harrow School:*
> *No wonder then, at our defeat,*
> *Folly like yours could ne'er be beat.*

The match was played at Dorset Fields, the first home of Lord's which was to move once more before eventually settling on its current site at St. John's Wood in 1814. Viscount Harry Ipswich was top scorer for Harrow in both innings with 10 and 21 out of 55 and 65 respectively. A present day descendant left Harrow a few years ago and T. Dury who played for Harrow in this match was the forebear of several generations of Durys who have continued at Harrow ever since, two of whom played in subsequent Harrow XIs.

Stratford Canning who played for Eton in the 1805 match went into the Diplomatic Service after Cambridge and had a most distinguished career eventually becoming Ambassador to Constantinople from 1842 to 1858 at a time when the Eastern question was highly important in European politics. He was signally successful and died in 1880 at the age of 92 as Viscount Stratford de Radcliffe, a most respected and honourable man.

William Carter who was the son of the Vice-Provost of Eton kept the scorebook of 1805 and passed it on to his son R.H. Carter who was in the Eton X1 of 1859. He went into farming and for many years it was used as a farming log book by the Carter family until it was sold by descendants of the Carter family in 1952 at Sotheby's. Fortunately, it was bought by Eton College otherwise this priceless relic might have disappeared into the unknown.

The next match for which a score survives is that of 1818, although it is believed that there were some matches played between **1805** and **1818** but the records of these were either lost or destroyed. M.C.C. moved from Dorset Fields in 1811 to North Bank and thence to its current site in 1814. The first Lord's pavilion was destroyed by fire in 1825 and disastrously most of the original records and cricketana went with it, including records of various Eton and Harrow matches. Copies of the records were rather surprisingly not preserved at either school but the 4th Duke of Dorset who entered Harrow in 1802 stated that he had taken part in one and Palmerston in referring to the Eton success of 1805 observed, "But we beat them afterwards." In one of these matches, in about 1808 won by Harrow, the Duke and G. Claridge were the

A map showing the position of Thomas Lord's three grounds.

Two of the Eton heroes of the win over England in 1816. 'Squire' Osbaldeston was the finest all round sportsman of his generation and Ben Aislabie the first Secretary of M.C.C. from 1822/42.

leading bowlers for the winners. The 4th Duke of Dorset was the son of the 3rd Duke of Dorset who was one of the first great patrons of cricket in the early years and one of the backers of Thomas Lord's first ground in Dorset Square in 1787. He did not appear to continue his cricket seriously after Harrow since he does not appear in any of the major matches of the day. He died very young after leaving Christ Church, Oxford, falling off his horse on his estate in Ireland in 1815. On August 5th 1816 Eton played against the might of England at Lord's and succeeded in beating them by 10 wickets. Eton contained the famous George Osbaldeston and Ben Aislabie, a future Secretary of M.C.C. whilst England were represented by William Ward who scored 278 at Lord's for M.C.C which stood as the highest score there for over 100 years, and Henry Bentley the founder of the forerunner of Wisden.

Harrow succeeded in levelling the series in **1818**, winning by 13 runs after trailing in the first innings. The Harrow captain, Charles Oxenden, who arranged the match, also played a match-winning innings of 31 for Harrow in the second innings. He had previously been at Eton and it is the only known instance of such a changeover. In *Eton of Old*, a book of reminiscences by an Old Colleger W.H. Tucker, it was stated that there was something of a revolution at Eton against the Eton Head Master John Keate, an old Etonian himself who was known as a notoriously cruel flogger and had just expelled six boys from College. Two of these boys, including Oxenden, had taken a carriage over to Harrow and been admitted before the next morning's post gave formal notice of their expulsion. The 'Old Colleger' of this book was one W.H. Tucker who died in 1901 when nearly 99 years old. He wrote his book at the age of 88 and gave a most interesting account of how he himself came to play in the match of 1818. After various obstacles it was resolved to play the match at the beginning of the holidays. By this time most of the Etonians had made their

LORDS.—5TH AUGUST, 1816.

Eleven Gentlemen of Eton against Nine Gentlemen of England (with Robinson and H. Bentley.)

ENGLAND.

	1st. Inns.		2d. Inns.	
H. Lloyd, Esq.	0	b Barnard	11	Run out
J. Poulet, Esq.	3	c Osbaldeston	1	b Becket
A. Schabner, Esq.	9	c Woodbridge	15	b Barnard
Robinson	23	b Osbaldeston	15	b James
H. Bentley	24	b Barnard	6	bOsbaldestone
W. Ward, Esq.	0	b Becket	25	b James
C. Warren, Esq.	4	b ditto	12	b ditto
T. Vigne, Esq.	9	b ditto	1	c ditto
T. Burgoyne, Esq.	0	b Barnard	3	b ditto
Maj. Hesketh	0	Not out	1	st Barnard
W. Barton, Esq.	0	Absent	13	
Byes	3		10	
	75		113	

ETON.

	1st. Inns.		2d. Inns.	
D. James, Esq.	2	b Ward		
F. Woodbridge, Esq.	22	b Poulet	1	Not out
E. Woodbridge, Esq	13	c Ward		
Bache, Esq.	8	b Robinson		
G. Osbaldestone Esq	29	c Vigne		
T. Price, Esq.	9	b Ward	7	Not out
H Barnard, Esq.	40	b ditto		
T. Becket, Esq.	6	b Vigne		
B. Aislabie, Esq.	0	b ditto		
Dawson, Esq.	26	Not out		
Roberts, Esq.	22	Hit wicket		
Byes	4		0	
	181		8	

Eton won by 10 wickets.

H. Jenner, Eton XI 1822/3, Cambridge 1827 and Kent. Captain of Cambridge in the first university cricket match, he top scored with 47 out of 92 in a rain affected drawn match restricted to one day. This was in reply to Oxford's exceptional total of 258.

C. Wordsworth, Harrow XI 1822/5 and Oxford 1827 and 1829. A nephew of the poet, he captained Oxford in the first university cricket match in 1827 when he took 7/25 with his under arm off-breaks in a drawn match limited to one day by rain. In 1829 he made a pair but led Oxford to victory by 115 runs.

home travelling arrangements. Harrow had duly turned up with a full strength side but Eton had only three of their proper eleven, I.O. Secker, W. Pitt and D. Maclean. Four or five of Upper Club had come up to Lord's on the chance of filling vacancies, Tucker who had only reached second college and the remainder who had to be enrolled from the best material on the ground. Strangely a match had been played earlier in the term on April 13th and 14th, although the records do not state where this match which Harrow won by 26 runs was played. Harrow had scored 87 and 113, Eton in reply 79 and 95 but it is not regarded as one of the official series of results.

Sketch of Keate, the formidable Head Master of Eton from 1809-34.

In **1822/3** there appeared the great Herbert Jenner for Eton, one of the finest wicket-keepers of his day who was the last survivor of the first university cricket match in 1827 which he was largely responsible in founding with Charles Wordsworth. He died in 1904 at the age of 98. He was president of M.C.C. in 1833 at the very young age of 27 and went on playing club cricket till he was 74. Truly a Pitt of the cricket world! In the Harrow Sixth Form game of 1823/4 there were two future archbishops, Trench and Manning, three bishops, Perry, Charles Wordsworth and Oxenden, and one dean, Merivale. Harrow may have been holier but Eton's cricket was decisively better for several years to come. Harrow's first innings score of 24 in 1823 was the lowest total in the history of the match and they were duly routed by an innings and 33 runs (see colour section).

In **1824** there played for Eton E.H. Pickering who deserves to be remembered for a performance nearly 20 years later when he was an Eton master. His contribution in the great match was decidedly modest, 1 wicket and 2 not out. He made up for it, however, in **1825** taking 10 wickets in Eton's 7 wicket win and went on to captain Cambridge in 1829 after gaining a blue in the first university match of 1827. His claim to fame came later when he was sent for at very short notice to play for the Gentlemen v. the Players and departed for Lord's from Eton attired in a black suit, walked on to the field and made 19 and 20 on a rough Lord's wicket, against two of the best bowlers of the day, Messrs. Lillywhite and Hillyer. This was an event which not surprisingly was never to occur again.

After Jenner came several years without any particularly distinguished names. There was a sprinkling of archbishops and bishops and the famous Cardinal Manning for Harrow in 1825 who just avoided a pair by scoring one in the second innings before being bowled by Pickering. He was presented with a bat by the Harrow captain Charles Wordsworth and judging by the verse of thanks he sent to Wordsworth there was little indication that his batting got much better. Charles Wordsworth, a nephew of the poet, achieved the unique distinction of playing in the first university cricket match between Oxford and Cambridge in 1827, rowing in the first boat race of 1829 and again playing in the varsity cricket match of 1829.

Charles Chapman, the Eton captain of **1825/26**, created a record that will stand forever. He was at the College for over 12 years, longer than any boy either before or since, leaving at the age of 20. Wordsworth, largely responsible for the first Boat Race as well as the first Oxford and Cambridge cricket match, reflecting on these times 60 years later when Bishop of St. Andrew's wrote:

"I had a large acquaintance among cricketers who had gone off from Eton, Winchester, Rugby and Harrow to both Universities… nothing came of my wish to bring about a match between the Universities in 1826. But in 1827 the proposal was carried into effect. Though an Oxford man, my home was at Cambridge as my father was Master of Trinity and this gave me an opportunity to communicate with men of that University. In writing of the need for permission to leave Oxford in term time to play at Lord's, he continues: *"My conscience still rather smites me when I remember that in order to gain my end, I had to present myself to the Dean of Christ Church and tell him that I wished to go to London – not to play a game of cricket (that would not have been listened to) but to consult a dentist… at all events my tutor Longley, afterwards Archbishop of Canterbury was aware of it!"*

A picture of Robert Grimston at Lord's in the 1860s with his back to the field of play. He could not bear to watch the Eton and Harrow match because of the tension and spent the weekend in the country but popular belief was that he used to stand at Lord's during the match with his back to the field of play and this belief is reflected in the picture.

The second match took place at Oxford two years later immediately after Wordsworth had promoted and rowed in the first Boat Race at Henley. He contributed a few wickets with his left hand underarm off breaks in his side's handsome victory but got a pair in the batting; his hands were reputedly still so sore from rowing that he could hardly hold the bat. He was also a fine tennis, skating, football and rackets player. What a performer! He was also a very fine academic taking the top Oxford Latin prizes and recording a double first in Classics. As a Don he was Tutor to Cardinal Manning and William Gladstone, the future Prime Minister, and after ordination he taught at Winchester and was Warden of Glenalmond before becoming Bishop of St. Andrews. At all events he set the example for the true all rounder ideal which has been followed by generations of Etonians and Harrovians since, until more recent times when specialisation has been the fashion.

In **1827** two illustrious cricketers played for Harrow, the Hon. E.H. Grimston and C.J. Harenc. Grimston, who scored 49 in the first innings, and his brother Lord Grimston, who also made 49, combined to produce the main contribution to Harrow's first innings total of 155. In the second innings Lord Grimston scored 38 out of a total of 64, but it was not enough to save Harrow from defeat by 6 wickets. In one six-ball over Lord Grimston scored 3 fives and E.H. Grimston 3 threes and in a somewhat unusual occurrence stumps were drawn when Eton were four short of victory because of an error by the scorers. Although Harrow appealed to the M.C.C. committee the result of the match was upheld. Grimston was to play again in **1828** when his bowling was more successful than his batting but his seven wickets in the match failed to change the result and Eton won again by 6 wickets. Eleven years later Grimston played in a famous match for England against Kent in Fuller Pilch's benefit when England were just beaten by 3 runs. Needing only 80 runs to win England were bowled out by Hillyer and Mynn, two of the most famous bowlers in the country at that time. Grimston made the highest score in the first innings, a creditable 46 out of England's total of 130. Harenc was a Kentish man and although not asked to bowl in this match was complimented by the great John Lillywhite, no

R.J.P. Broughton Harrow XI 1832/5 and Cambridge 1836, 1838/9. His 13 wickets in 1834 with his slow bowling led Harrow home to a narrow victory by 13 runs. He batted with rather limited success at Cambridge and his bowling was rarely used.

less: *"I bowls the best ball in England and Mr. Harenc the next."* He was originally a fast under-arm bowler but changed to a slow round-arm bowler at this time.

After 1828 there was a gap until **1832** when Eton again had an overwhelming win by an innings and 156 runs. It was in this year that the Hon. Frederick Ponsonby, later Lord Bessborough, appeared for Harrow, one of the most famous and devoted of all Harrovians, and also R.J.P. Broughton. Bessborough's name will always be remembered by Harrovians with that of his great friend the Hon. Robert Grimston who was never in the Harrow XI but afterwards played for Oxford in 1838 and the Gentlemen. Bessborough certainly had a pretty depressing time of it at Lord's scoring two ducks in 1832 and one in 1833 and not being required to bat in Harrow's second innings when they at last achieved victory by 8 wickets, ending a barren run since 1822. Broughton had a great deal more success in his four years in the XI from 1832/5 taking 13 wickets in 1834 and scoring 19 runs in Harrow's second innings total of 97 when Harrow sneaked home by 13 runs. Dress was reasonably formal in these times and breeches were worn till 1830. Eton first adopted their famous light blue colours in 1831, believed to have been derived from their founder Henry VI. In 1834 Broughton and his Harrovian colleague W. Buckingham collided going for a catch at short leg and were both knocked out. They were carried into the pavilion and laid side by side on a table until they came round. The umpire informed the gathering that between them the ball had been held long enough to make a catch but no-one had appealed. Buckingham was unable to take any further part in the match but fortunately for Harrow Broughton was able to continue his match-winning spell. There were no drawn matches during these years mainly due to the fact that matches started at 10am and play continued with only a short adjournment for lunch and no tea interval until it became dark around 7.30 or 8.00. The wickets were also pretty rough and worn and it was not until 1860 that the first drawn match occurred. Broughton gained Cambridge blues in 1836 and 1838/39 as a batsman with rather limited success and his round-arm slow bowling was rarely used. Broughton was a member of the M.C.C. Committee for nearly 60 years and one of its original trustees. He was a lively hitter and a first rate fieldsman at cover point. He was probably never happier than in 1907 when his grandson R.B. Cowley scored 50 and 75 in M.C. Bird's famous match of 1907 for Harrow, thus playing a major part in their triumph by 79 runs. It was said his grandson wore the same Harrow colours his grandfather had worn 75 years previously. Bessborough was one of the three founders in 1845 of I. Zingari , the most famous of all wandering clubs, and Broughton was also one of the 25 original members. For many years Bessborough and Grimston made the journey from London to Harrow to coach the boys. Never was a memorial inscription to two men more fitting than that shown at Harrow:

"In memory of the Hon. Robert Grimston and Frederick Ponsonby, Earl of Bessborough, famous cricketers, loyal Harrovians, blameless gentlemen, whose

Hon F.G.B. Ponsonby (later Earl of Bessborough) Harrow XI 1832/3 & Cambridge Univ. 1836. He failed to score in his three innings at Lord's for Harrow but he was one of the most famous and devoted of all Harrovians. He played for the Gentlemen v the Players, coached the XI at Harrow for over 50 years and founded I. Zingari, the most prestigious wandering club in 1845 with his brother and J.L. Baldwin.

friendship begun in school days and cemented on fields of English sport, rendered more conspicuous the love they bore to Harrow, where through fifty summers while teaching skill in cricket, they taught manliness and honour."

J.C. Ryle, the Eton captain of **1834** issued a challenge to his Harrow counterpart R. J. P. Broughton, the Harrow captain on 6th May 1834 following the Harrow precedent of 1805 (see colour section). Harrow won narrowly for the second year running, mainly due to the fine slow bowling of the Harrow Captain. Ryle eventually became the first Bishop of Liverpool, the diocese of the late David Sheppard of Sussex & England fame.

An extremely rare Eton & Harrow billboard of 1836.

Eton were not without their famous players, the two most renowned in 1834 being C.G. Taylor and J.H. Kirwan. Taylor was regarded as the most polished and elegant amateur batsman of the time who played for England in the Fuller Pilch benefit of 1839 and was one of the first batsman to move to the pitch of the ball. He gained Cambridge blues in 1836 and 1838/9 captaining them in those years, and also played 38 matches for Sussex between 1838/54. J.H. Kirwan was a very fast round-arm bowler and created a unique record in his two appearances for Eton at Lord's. His ten wickets in 1834 were all bowled as were his thirteen wickets in 1835. This was in addition to taking all 10 wickets in an innings for Eton v. M.C.C. at Lord's. In 1836 he was to achieve another astonishing feat by taking 15 wickets in the match for Cambridge University v. Cambridge Town Club including 9 wickets in the first innings, all bowled. He gained his blue in 1839 and took 111 first-class wickets. Although no analyses were recorded, they were undoubtedly at low cost! Sadly he gave up cricket when he went into the church after leaving Cambridge – he would surely have been a force to be reckoned with. It was somewhat fortunate that there were no throwing laws at this time since he had a jerk in his action and it was recognised by the authorities in later years that he was probably the first 'chucker'.

The year **1835** marked the first of four appearances for Eton of T.A. Anson who, in the fourth and last of them in 1838, so exasperated one of the Harrow bowlers that he threw the ball at Anson's head. The cause of the exasperation it appears was Anson's habit of dancing for joy when the ball passed the wicket and putting the bowler off in his run up by throwing up his arms as if to stop him. He appears to have been a pretty good batsman, however, and appeared for Cambridge from 1839/42 captaining the side a record three times from 1840/42 – rivalled only at Oxford by the illustrious R.A.H. Mitchell, the father of Eton cricket, who captained them from 1863/5. Eton played their first round-arm bowler in 1835/6, R.W. Essington, but he had relatively limited success with 3 wickets in 1835 and none in 1836.

1838 was Anson's last year in the Eton XI but the first in which two remarkable performers were to appear for Eton, Emilius Bayley and W.B. Glyn. In his three years in the Eton XI Glyn took 28 wickets at Lord's, 23 of them clean bowled, and was largely responsible for Eton's three suc-

A fascinating letter in the Times from Emilius Bayley (Laurie) the previous record holder who scored 152 in 1841, an enormous score on the unpredictable wickets of those times.

Last Saturday, J. F. Marsh made the highest score ever obtained in the University match, and yesterday, in the Eton and Harrow, another, far older, record went by the board, D. C. Boles, the Eton batsman, playing an innings of 183, and thus beating the oft-quoted 152 made by Emilius Bayley in 1841. A more remarkable innings than Boles' we have never seen in a public school match. It was marked by the strongest possible contrasts, being steady to a degree in its early stages, but amazingly brilliant afterwards. The young batsman took an hour and three-quarters to get his first 20 runs, but ended by scoring 35 in two overs. After seeming a veritable Barlow, he revealed himself as a hitter of tremendous power, his driving being something that no one fortunate enough to be present will ever forget. The fact that he can play two such entirely different games shows that he has an extraordinary amount of self-control. One ex-

Emilius Bayley, his huge record score of 152 on a poor wicket lasted for 63 years.

cessive victories. In 1838 there were some strange happenings. G.D.W. Ommanney who was not a member of the Harrow XI, was allowed to bat for W.B. Trevelyan who was injured in the first innings, although this appeared to be strictly contrary to the laws of the game. It gained Harrow little, however, since Ommanney was out for a duck. Trevelyan batted in the second innings scoring 20 and Harrow lost by an innings and 30 runs. Harrow also had two other injuries which did not help their cause. E.M. Dewing was unable to play owing to a brick falling on his head and J.K. Fitzherbert had his foot severely cut by a glass bottle in 'Ducker', the Harrow outdoor swimming pool. H.S. Russell, who played at Lord's, had already left the school and was totally out of form scoring 7. O.G.J. Boudier who played for Eton from 1836/9 was the founder of Sixpenny, a club open to all lower boys at Eton. It was so named because the membership subscription was six pence and the ground was the scene of many famous fights including those between Arthur Wellesley, grandson of the famous Duke, and Percy Shelley, the equally famous poet.

It was in **1840** during a particularly exciting finish that Lord Drumlanrig, later the Marquess of Queensberry, could not bear to stay at Lord's to see the finish, and hired a cabman to drive him two miles from the ground and bring him back again. On his return, he found out that Eton had won by 31 runs. He then rode down Portland Place and Regent Street with the Eton captain Emilius Bayley cheering at the top of his voice – considered a strange form of exhibitionism at the time. Emilius Bayley, who derived his Christian name from his father's horse which won the Derby in the year of his birth, made himself immortal in his fourth and last appearance at Lord's and his second year as Eton captain by scoring a record 152 out of a total of 308, an enormous score in those times. In a chanceless innings he hit 4 fives, 11 fours, 14 threes, 19 twos and only 8 singles when all runs had to be run rather than hit to the boundary for four or six. A score of this magnitude on very poor wickets where shooters were a frequent batting hazard would have been equivalent to at least double on wickets of later years and it was not to be beaten until 1904 when D.C. Boles scored 183 – still the highest score in the match. It should be remembered that the lawn mower was not invented until 1830 and was not manufactured in a form for general use until some years later. Until then, grass was cut with scythes, probably using sheep for the outfield. Hence wickets were unpredictable up to 1840 at least. Also rollers were pulled by horses until well into the 1900s and even with soft shoes cannot have been very flat.

E.M. Dewing Harrow XI 1839/41 & Cambridge 1842/5. Harrow's captain in 1841 when they lost to Eton by an innings and 175 runs, the largest defeat in the history of the match. However, he was good enough to captain Cambridge for two years in 1844/5.

Viscount Drumlanrig later the Marquess of Queensberry, Scottish Peer, Patron of Boxing and originator of the Queensberry rules. Father of Lord Alfred Douglas and scourge of Oscar Wilde. His strange behaviour after the Eton triumph of 1840 was indicative of his mad streak.

Cricket in Marylebone Fields before the Marylebone Club and Thomas Lord linked the neighbourhood with cricket for all time. C1790.

The young Earl of Winchilsea. One of Eton's finest early players and the founder of M.C.C. in 1787. (see early scorecards)

The famous painting of Thomas Lord was presented by his last surviving descendant, Miss Florence Lord in 1930. It was on his ground in August 1805 at Dorset Fields that the famous series started.

The famous picture of the Buxtons, one of Harrow's oldest families playing cricket at Harrow in 1772. (Harrow School Museum.)

17

The challenge made by J.C. Ryle, the captain of the Eton XI in 1834 to the Harrow captain R.J.P. Broughton. Harrow narrowly won the match by 13 runs. Ryle became the first Bishop of Liverpool, the diocese of the late David Sheppard, Sussex, Cambridge Univ. and England.

A fine picture of the Etonian Courtenay brothers by Thomas Hudson (1701-1779) C1770 at Powderham Castle, Exeter, still owned by the family and whose descendant Lord Courtenay was recently at Eton.

Three-stump wicket, which was used at Lord's from 1798 until 1821. (Lord's Museum)

Harrow XI clothing of the 1830/40s, possibly presented by R.J.P. Broughton Harrow XI 1832/5 and Cambridge Univ. (one of the first trustees of M.C.C.) Lord's Museum.

Lord Byron's letter after the match in 1805 to his great friend Hon. Charles Gordon (scion of the Marquis of Aberdeen), another of Harrow's most distinguished families. (Vaughan Library, Harrow)

Cricket on college field, Eton by William Evans R.W.S. (1798-1877) c.1845 (Eton College collection) In this picture can be seen several games of cricket. It is interesting to note that as late as the middle of the 19th Century the umpires continued the old tradition of carrying bats. In the early days there was no square leg umpire and to score a run it was necessary to touch the bat which the umpires held. For this reason both umpires stood near the wicket. William Evans was an Etonian par excellence. Indeed he was known as William Evans of Eton. He was born in the town and educated at the college where in 1818 he followed his father Samuel Evans as drawing master. He represented the second of four generations to hold the position as drawing master at Eton.

The Wood children by Joseph Wright of Derby (1734-1797) signed and dated 1789, ancestors of Sir Samuel Hill-Wood (pre 1910 Wood) Eton and Derbyshire (capt. 1899/1901) and father of B.S.H. Hill-Wood Eton XI 1916/18 and Derbyshire, M.C.C. tour to Australia and New Zealand 1922/3. C.K.H. Hill-Wood Eton XI 1925/6, Oxford Univ. 1928/30 & Derbyshire. D.J.C.H. Hill-Wood Eton, Oxford Univ. 1928 & Derbyshire. A fine soccer player also, Oxford blue and chairman of Arsenal F.C. until 1982. W.W.H. Hill-Wood, Eton XI 1918/20, Cambridge Univ. 1922, Derbyshire & M.C.C. tour to Australia and New Zealand 1922/3. P.D. Hill-Wood Eton XI 1952/4 & son of D.J.C.H. chairman of Arsenal F.C. since 1982.

Cricket on the famous sixth form ground at Harrow by John Glover c.1887. The Earl of Bessborough, the architect with Hon. Robert Grimston of Harrow cricket for over 50 years is seen as umpire resplendent in top hat. The Field House Club and pavilion are seen in the distance much as today.

The new Lord's cricket ground c1830 showing the rather primitive nature of the ground when bowlers still bowled underarm, the pitch was rough, shooters were prevalent and breeches were worn by the players.

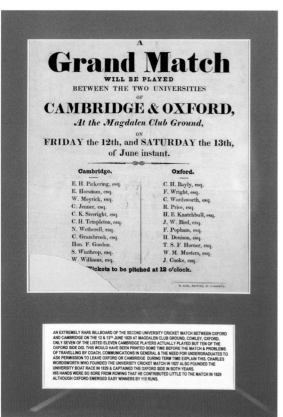

An extremely rare billboard of the second University cricket match between
Oxford and Cambridge on 23rd June 1829. The participants included five
representatives from the two Schools.

Albert Chevallier Tayler's painting of the 1886 match. It shows
the old Lord's 'A' enclosure and next to it the old Lord's pavilion
replaced in 1899 over which 'Buns' Thornton hit his famous six
in 1868.

A piece of metal work dedicated to
C.I. Thornton by an Eton boy Ingalton Drake in
1868 for his phenomenal feats of hitting.

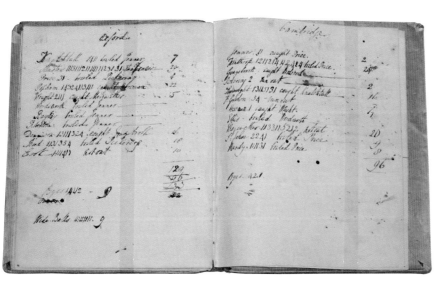

The Oxford and Cambridge scorebook of 1829, the second match of the series.

A fine Spy watercolour of the legendary 'Mitch' who was involved in a curious mix up of the bowling changes in 1871 with the Eton captain G.H. Longman.

The painting is dated 1842 and hangs at Stoneleigh Abbey. The painting includes Hon William Henry Leigh (aged 18) holding the cricket bat (Harrow 1838/42, 2nd Baron Leigh 1850-1905), Hon Sir Edward Chandos Leigh (aged 10) holding the stumps (Harrow XI 1850-1851 – Oxford Univ. XI 1852/1854, MCC President 1887) and Hon Julia Anna Eliza Leigh (aged 22) looking on (Lady Norton). Stoneleigh Abbey – © Stoneleigh Trust. See addenda on Edward Chandos Leigh.

Three early scorecards of the Eton and Harrow matches of 1864, 1865 and 1866, a hat trick of easy wins for Harrow by an innings.

The famous M.C.C. colours of red and yellow were adopted by the club from Nicholson Gin's colours in gratitude to William Nicholson who advanced the money to buy the ground in 1866 without which Lord's would not be here today (£18,666 equivalent in today's money to around £20m). Nicholson Harrow XI 1841/3 and the Gentlemen 1846/58.

THE ETON & HARROW BILLBOARDS FOR 1854 & 1855, BOTH MATCHES WON EASILY BY HARROW. K.E. DIGBY, THE HARROW CAPTAIN FROM 1853 TO 1855, THUS CREATED A UNIQUE ACHIEVEMENT ON BOTH SIDES. HE WAS ALSO IN THE WINNING HARROW XI FOUR YEARS RUNNING FROM 1852 TO 1855 CREATING ANOTHER RECORD. HE WAS A FINE WICKETKEEPER / BATSMAN & AN OUTSTANDING CAPTAIN WHO WENT ON TO GAIN OXFORD BLUES FROM 1857 TO 1859 BATTING WELL IN 1857 & 1858. BOTH MATCHES WERE WON DECISIVELY BY OXFORD.

The Lord's billboards of 1854/5, the last two years of Kenelm Digby's three years as Harrow captain, all Harrow wins and a record likely to remain.

The unknown Zingaro, dated June the 20th, 1866, since when the colours black, red and gold have appeared in I. Zingari's records. Founded by Harrovians, membership has always been much prized by Etonians and Harrovians down the ages.

Eton v Harrow – July, 31st 1823.

From Henry Bentley – An account of the principal matches played in 1823 and printed in the same year. This was the fourth recorded contest between the two schools and Harrow's first innings total of 24 is the lowest innings total in the history of the match. Charles Wordsworth who played for Harrow was Captain in 1824 & 1825. Wordsworth was a double blue at Oxford in 1829, rowing in the first boat-race against Cambridge and also played in the first cricket match against Cambridge in 1827. He went on to become Bishop of St. Andrews and died in 1892.

Herbert Jenner who played for Eton was a famous wicketkeeper and the last survivor of the first Oxford and Cambridge match in 1827, dying in 1904 aged 98.

The Henry Bentley scorecard of 1823 showing Harrow's lowest total ever of 24 in Eton's decisive win by and innings and 33 runs, all three innings finished in one day.

The three founders of I. Zingari. LEFT TO RIGHT: Fred Ponsonby, Earl of Bessborough, J.L. Baldwin seated and Hon. Spencer Ponsonby Fane. The most prestigious of all wandering clubs founded in 1845 and election only by invitation. Etonians and Harrovians have long formed the bulwark of the club and it still has its headquarters at Lord's.

Cyril Wells, Cambridge Univ. and Middlesex. Succeeded the famous 'Mitch' as cricket master at Eton in 1897 eventually stepping down in 1919. He was also a renowned rugby international and an expert on many other things besides as well as Gubby Allen's housemaster!

The three sons of the Earl of Dudley c.1883 by George Elgar Hicks (1824-1914). Viscount Ednam (LEFT), The Hon. John Ward (CENTRE) and the Hon. Robert (RIGHT). Robert Ward played in the Eton XI 1888/89 and John Ward in 1889. John Ward opened the bowling in 1889 and took 3/62 in the first innings v. Harrow and also took 8/92 in the match v. Winchester. Their brother Hon. Gerald Ward played in the Eton XI of 1896 again opening the bowling for Eton and taking 35 wickets at an average of 11 per wicket in the season and was killed in the great war at Zandvoorde in 1914.

The balls of 1865/6 celebrating M.H. Stow's Harrow wins as captain in both years. He had the remarkable record of never being on the losing side in seven appearances at Lord's for Harrow and Cambridge Univ.

The cup presented to W.O. Hewlett (Harrow) for the best catch in the 1862 match which Eton won by 54 runs on a treacherous wicket. This was some consolation for his poor performance with the bat, 1 run in three innings in the 1862/3 matches.

The two giants of Yorkshire cricket Lord Hawke, the patriarch – Eton Cambridge, Yorkshire (captain 1883/1910) and England and Wilfred Rhodes Yorkshire 1898/1930 and England. The outstanding cricketer of his era he became Harrow coach from 1930/6

The Hon. Charles Lyttelton Eton and Cambridge University (later Viscount Cobham). The eldest of the seven brothers who all played in the Eton XI, an all time record and one of four who gained blues at Cambridge.

The Rev. Sir Emilius Laurie (Bayley) wrote a fascinating letter to *The Times* in 1904 when the record was broken by Boles, mentioning that the joint totals of Harrow's two innings were 19 less than his own score, commenting on the superb bowling of Yonge and Marcon and the fact that the wickets were much more unpredictable – implying that a big score in those times was more of a feat than at the time his record was broken. In any event he had a very long life, changed his name from Bayley to Laurie in 1886 in order to inherit the estates of his great uncle and died in 1917 at the great age of 94. It was not surprising that Harrow subsided to overwhelming defeat by an innings and 175 runs, the largest margin ever recorded in the history of the match, especially as Eton had two terrifying fast bowlers in W. Marcon and Harvey Fellows. Both Marcon and Fellows had rather low deliveries somewhere between underhand and round-arm and Marcon needed two long stops to stem the number of byes and wides.

In **1841** it was again Marcon and another fast bowler G.E. Yonge who caused the damage and bowled Harrow out for 35 in their second innings. Harrow reversed the tide in 1842, winning by 65 runs helped by the massive number of extras in the match, 112, another record unlikely

W. Marcon Eton XI 1841/2, Oxford 1844. A fast roundarm bowler who took 8 wickets in Eton's win by an innings and 175 runs in 1841, the largest winning margin in the history of the match and scored 55 not out and took 6 wickets in the 1842 match which Harrow won by 65 runs. He was said to have broken a man's leg when playing for Oxford in 1844 but this was doubted by W.G. Grace as both a doctor and cricketer.

In addition to a number of family wreaths, a handsome tribute of chrysanthemums and other flowers was laid on the grave from the Harrow Cricket Eleven. This mark of remembrance from the famous school, was prompted by the recollection of the record cricketing feat achieved by the late Baronet in his Eton days, when, in 1841, he beat Harrow in one innings off his own bat with 152 runs, a performance unparalleled before or since. That the tribute should have come from the defeated side enhanced its interest in a very happy way. The wreath was tied with light blue and dark blue ribbon intertwined, the respective colours of Eton and Harrow, and a card bore the following words: — "Lords, July 30th-31st; August 1st, 1841. Emilius Bayley, caught T. Nicholson, bowled Agar, 152. In memory from the Harrow Eleven, 1917. —Guy Butler, captain."

The Harrow blue ribbon and message sent by the captain of the Harrow XI Guy Butler in 1917 on Emilius Bayley's death as a tribute to his memorable performance.

The M.C.C. 1st innings scores v Eton from the Upper Club record book of 1841 kept by Emilius Bayley and now in the possession of Sir Bayley Laurie, great grandson of Sir Emilius. Some famous names appeared for the M.C.C. including R.W. Keate, son of the notorious Dr Keate, Head Master of Eton, Roger Kynaston, an old Eton cricketer of 1823 and top scorer in the first innings with 40 not out in a total of 74 and secretary of M.C.C. from 1842-58, Lord Drumlanrig, later the Marquess of Queensbury, who had a poor match scoring 0 and 1, J. Walker, grandson of the founder of The Times newspaper and John Bayley, father of the two Bayleys in the Eton side and later Sir John Bayley, President of M.C.C. in 1844. The Eton team's batting order was Bayley, Bean, Ainslie, Fiske, Marcon, Yonge, Garth, Carter, Bayley mi, Fellows, Carlyon.

Arthur Haygarth, an eminent example of a man who fails to make a mark as a player - he was a deadly dull batsman for Harrow, MCC, the Gentlemen and other sides - but who makes a memorable contribution to the game in another way. Haygarth, who died in 1903, aged 77, devoted his lifetime, and considerable expenditure, to compiling the invaluable Cricket Scores and Biographies, 14 volumes of immensely detailed work for which cricket students will forever remain indebted.

A. Haygarth Harrow XI 1842/3, Middlesex 1850/1, M.C.C., Sussex 1843/60 (3 matches).

W. Nicholson Harrow XI 1841/3. The 'Gin King' and saviour of Lord's.

to be beaten and 85 in the two Harrow innings. Marcon was said to have broken a man's leg when bowling for Oxford in 1844 but the great W.G. Grace was sceptical as both a doctor and cricketer. Fellows was regarded as one of the fastest bowlers ever to appear in first-class cricket, particularly in 1848/9, but his pace thereafter was much reduced when he appeared for M.C.C. and Hertfordshire. In an exciting and fluctuating match in 1843 Harrow emerged victorious by 20 runs. Apart from Arthur Haygarth, the founding father of statisticians and author of *Scores and Biographies*, none of the other Harrow names are much recognised though they must have been a reasonable side. H.P. Long, who played for Harrow in 1843 was one of the founding members of I. Zingari and its first secretary in 1845. Harrow had done well as according to Ashley Cooper they had only 87 boys to choose from against the 600 of Eton. George Yonge who played in the Eton XI from 1841/3 was a fast round-arm bowler who bowled very straight with a good action and always kept both his feet behind the bowling crease. He was not quite as successful as he had been in 1841 but still took six wickets in 1842 and seven wickets in 1843 v. Harrow and went on to play for Oxford from 1844/8 achieving very good results in all his five years against Cambridge with 43 wickets overall. He also played for Gentlemen v. Players from 1847/52 and in a remarkable feat for M.C.C. against Eton in 1847 the school were bowled out for 12 against his bowling. William Nicholson, who was in the Harrow XI from 1841/3 and captain in 1843, was a fine wicket-keeper batsman and appeared for Gentlemen v. Players from 1846 to 1858. But his chief claim to fame was that he saved Lord's from the builders in 1866 when he lent M.C.C the money to buy the freehold from Mr. Moses for £18,333 when no one else would touch it. His family fortune came from Nicholson's Gin and he was also very generous to Harrow when he purchased a large piece of ground and presented it to the school in 1893.

Arthur Haygarth, who played in the two winning Harrow XI's of **1842/3**, was a remarkable man and the game of cricket owes much to his work of compiling statistics for over sixty years till his death in 1903. As a player he was defensive, but this proved very useful on the rough and bumpy wickets at Lord's when he wore down the bowling. When asked what his batting average was, he always replied *"One hour"* which was about the time he usually stayed at the wicket. He played for the Gentlemen v. Players on sixteen occasions between 1846 and 1859, never making very high scores but proving most consistent.

Only around 3,000 came to Lord's in those days and there were the usual rivalries between the two schools, in particular an annual fight between the two best known cads of the day, Picky Powell of Eton and Bill Warner of Harrow. The traditional beginning of Powell's affray was usually the same: *"All the good I see in 'Arrow is that you can see Eton from it, if you go into the churchyard."* Fists started flying and Powell being the bigger man usually won this annual encounter, but it never failed to arouse his courageous opponent. C.O. Eaton, the originator of the Harrow Goose Match in 1849 played at Harrow at the beginning of the winter term between the prospective Harrow XI and Old Harrovians with appropriately, a goose supper afterwards, represented the XI in 1844/5 with modest results. Another remarkable bowler appeared for Eton from 1845/7, E.W. Blore, who achieved 33 wickets in his three appearances against Harrow. He took 14 wickets in **1845**, 4 wickets in 1846 and 15 wickets in 1847, the highest individual number in the history of the match and the highest overall by an Etonian. He was regarded as the greatest schoolboy bowler of his day with his slow off-breaks and also took 35 wickets in his three matches against Winchester. He had considerable success at Cambridge gaining blues from 1848/51, captaining the side in 1851 and taking some 104 wickets. He also founded with F.H. Whymper, a fellow Etonian and Cambridge blue the Quidnuncs Cricket Club at Cambridge composed of the leading University cricketers and similar to the Oxford Harlequins. He retired from first-class cricket in 1855 after going into the church and afterwards played for Buckinghamshire. He subsequently became a tutor, fellow and junior dean of Trinity College, Cambridge. J.J. Hornby who opened the batting for Eton in 1845, subsequently became Headmaster of College, from 1868/84 and then Provost of Eton. It appeared at the time that there was a considerable crisis at Harrow since Christopher Wordsworth had vacated the headmastership at Christmas 1844 and had been succeeded by Dr Vaughan. At one time the number of boys at the school was down to 67, the lowest number ever known at Harrow. Haygarth wrote in his scores and biographies, *"The Harrow XI was perhaps the smallest that ever played at Lord's. They were all mere children except Messrs. Blayds and Currer."* Fortunately the great Vaughan turned the tide and numbers rose steadily at Harrow and with it comfortable wins for Harrow in 1848 and 1849 at Lord's.

E.W. Blore Eton XI 1845/7 and Cambridge 1848/51. The greatest schoolboy bowler of his day, he took 68 wickets against Harrow and Winchester in his three years in the Eton XI. He took 15 wickets in Eton's nine wicket win in 1847, the record for the match. His slow off breaks were successful at Cambridge too and he captained the side in 1851.

The Harrow XI of **1849**, when they won by 77 runs, was considered at the time to be the strongest Harrow XI up to that time by the experts of the day. The match was largely won by the medium round-arm bowling of R. Hankey who took 14 wickets in the match, Harrow's highest total in the series. It was his batting however which gained him blues at Oxford in 1853 and 1855 as captain in both winning years for Oxford and the reputation as one of the best amateur batsmen of his day. His most famous innings was for the Gentlemen v. Players in 1857, when he scored 70 on a difficult wicket at Lord's whilst feeling unwell against the best professional bowlers of the day Wisden, Willsher, Jackson, Caffyn and Parr. His appearances in first-class cricket thereafter were limited by business commitments although he later played a few games for Surrey and Oxfordshire. The old Harrow name of Torrens appeared in 1848/9 and was to be followed in due course by two further generations in the Harrow XI. H.M. Aitken who was in the Eton XI from 1846/9 and was captain in the last two years was highly regarded as a fast round-arm bowler with a good action which impressed Surrey so much that he was offered a place in their XI at the age of 15 and achieved 41 wickets in his four years against Winchester and Harrow. He gained his Oxford blue in 1853 when on the winning side they beat Cambridge by an innings and 18 runs but his contribution was only three wickets in the match.

R. Hankey Harrow XI 1849/50 and Oxford 1853 and 1855. His 14 wickets in 1849 largely won the match for Harrow by 77 runs, Harrow's highest total in the history of the match. At Oxford he was regarded as one of the best amateur bats of the day although his record was rather modest.

In **1850** when Eton won by 7 wickets there first appeared the famous Harrow names of Crawley and Walker. The Walker was A.H., the elder brother of the other three great Harrovian cricketers V.E., I.D. and R.D., G.B. Crawley was the uncle of H.E. and great-uncle of three other fine cricketers, A.S., C.S., and L.G. A.H. Walker was a useful middle order batsman and bowler who played a few matches for Middlesex before he badly broke a leg whilst playing football in 1862 which effectively ended his cricket.

In **1851** there began a record run for Harrow of eight wins in a row and the name of H.M. Butler appeared in the Harrow side. He scored a creditable 41 in Harrow's first innings, the second highest score, and helped his side to a comfortable 8 wicket win. He was somewhat fortunate at the start of his innings when one of the Eton bowlers hit him so hard on the knee that play had to be stopped and the Eton side crowded round with sympathy and remedies. When play eventually resumed, the umpire, one T. Sewell, whispered in Butler's ear, *"It's lucky for you sir that you was 'it so hard, as the bowler forgot to ask for leg before and you was clean out."* His father Dr G. Butler had been Head Master of Harrow from 1805 to 1829 and he was later to follow his father and become Head Master from 1860 to 1885 - astonishingly young for the times - before becoming Master of Trinity College, Cambridge, from 1886 to 1918. He was the father of E.M. and A.H.M. and grandfather of G.M., all Harrow XI cricketers at various times. The Hon. Edward Chandos-Leigh who was in the Harrow XI of 1850/51 and captained the winning Harrow side in 1851 came from an old Harrow family dating back to the middle part of the 18th century. He was the second son of the first Lord Leigh and gained Oxford blues from 1852/4. He afterwards became a most distinguished lawyer, was appointed the Speaker's Counsel from 1883/1907 and was President of M.C.C. in their centenary year of 1887. He learnt his cricket by means of a catapult he invented in 1848 which propelled the ball towards the batsman, a forerunner of the modern bowling machine!

Harrow's unprecedented run in the 1850s coincided with John Wisden, the well-known Sussex bowler and founder of the famous almanack in 1864, being taken on as the school professional in **1852**, the same year that the famous Harrow blue-and-white-striped caps were first worn at Lord's. Sir Kenelm Digby, who was captain of the Harrow XI for an unprecedented three years from 1853 to 1855, said of him: *"He had a very beautiful delivery and was very accurate in pitch with a fair amount of spin on the ball. He was very straight and moderated his pace cleverly but he seldom bowled a really difficult ball; it was his great accuracy which made him so successful. There were many bowlers who had a more difficult ball than Wisden."* Wisden was a most successful coach and initiated the system of professional bowlers at the school which continued at Harrow until fairly recent times. Dean, a Sussex team mate and great friend of Wisden's, was the first of these and a real character. He was a most ungainly figure, looking something like a broad half-filled sack and had a great beaming smile. Although he could not bat very well, having a rather awkward style which militated against scoring runs, he was often successful for Sussex and M.C.C. As a slow bowler he was very useful for practice and bowled remarkably straight. V.E. Walker who played for Harrow in 1853/4 told an excellent story about him: "An umpire was required at the Oval and a message was sent to Lord's asking that one should be sent. After a time old Jemmie Dean waddled on to the ground. He was of course asked at once, *"How's the match at Lord's going?"* to which he replied very gravely, *"Oh, capitally! Lord C (who was a sticker) and Mr ... as been in for 'arf an hour; they gets no runs but just as I left the ground his Lordship kicked a beautiful leg-bye!""* Others who followed Dean and came down to bowl before the Winchester and Eton matches were James Lillywhite, his father William Lillywhite and Nixon of Nottingham.

It was highly appropriate that a winning sequence for Harrow should start with a Butler and a Crawley in the side and for the next seven years they won the match, most of them by crushing margins. In 1852 two Walkers played for Harrow although C.H. was not related to V.E. of the famous seven Southgate brothers. It was V.E. who substituted for R.A. Fitzgerald and caught a catch. Fitzgerald who played for Harrow in 1852 went on to gain Cambridge blues from 1854/56 and after being admitted as a barrister in 1860 became Secretary of the M.C.C. from 1864/76 when he was forced to retire through ill health. He was very well liked by both the amateurs and professionals and the club became prosperous due to his efficient stewardship. He was also an amusing writer on the game.

In **1853** V. E. Walker was in the XI but batted poorly, getting a pair at Lord's, as did G.R. Dupuis, a very good Eton batsman who later played for Cambridge in 1857. Dupuis was the son of G.J. Dupuis who was a master at Eton and eventually Vice Provost of the College and nephew of the Eton captain of 1896/7, H. Dupuis. As an Eton master he was the first beak to stand as umpire on Upper Club and take a hand in the coaching of the XI. In 1854 V.E. Walker improved

V.E. Walker, Harrow XI 1853/4 and Middlesex. In 1860 he was rated as the best all-round amateur cricketer in England. Founder of Middlesex with his brother I.D. in 1864, he captained them from 1864/72.

Harrow XI 1852 & Cambridge University 1854/6, Secretary of MCC from 1863 to 1876, Bob Fitzgerald endeavoured to make Lord's the great centre of cricket, an ambition not always in tune with a Committee described as "deplorably lethargic and out of date". However, his overtures eventually led to Middlesex playing their home games at Lord's. In spite of criticism from some members, others found Fitzgerald "sagacious, cheery and amusing", and above all an excellent Secretary.

The Eton & Harrow billboards for 1854 & 1855, both matches won easily by Harrow. K.E. Digby, the Harrow captain from 1853 to 1855, thus created a unique achievement on both sides. He was also in the winning Harrow XI four years running from 1852 to 1855 creating another record. He was a fine wicketkeeper/batsman and an outstanding captain who went on to gain Oxford blues from 1857 to 1859 batting well in 1857 & 1858, both matches were won decisively by Oxford.

significantly on his performance of 1853 by scoring 29 and 16 and taking 7 wickets in the match. By 1860 he was considered the best all-round amateur cricketer in the country. Although he played for Middlesex from 1859, it was he who founded the modern club in 1864 with his brother I.D. His most famous performance was when playing for England v. Surrey at the Oval in 1859, he scored 20 not out and 108 as well as taking 10/74 and 4/17. He also took 10/104 for Middlesex V. Lancashire at Old Trafford in 1865 having achieved the same feat in 1864 for the Gentlemen of Middlesex v. Gentlemen of Kent at Maidstone and played for the club from 1859/77, captaining them from 1864/72.

In **1855** Walker handed on the torch to the two Lang brothers, G.L. and R., G.L. having the remarkable analysis of 7/17 off 11 overs, whilst H. Arkwright, a very good slow bowler, took 6/44 in the Eton second innings. R. Lang went on to gain Cambridge blues from 1860/2 after having a major part in the winning of the 1859 match for Harrow. Kenelm Digby's four years in the Harrow XI from 1852/5 all resulted in victories and three of them under his captaincy, a unique achievement almost certainly never to be equalled. He was not only a very good batsman and wicket-keeper but an outstanding captain. He went on to gain Oxford blues in 1857/9 batting well in the varsity matches and was also a fine scholar, gaining a first in mods. and greats at Corpus Christi College, Oxford. He became a tutor and fellow of the college before turning to the law as a career. He eventually became a circuit judge and Permanent Under-Secretary at the Home Office between 1895 and 1903.

The **1856** match was not played because Dr Goodford, the Head Master of Eton, would not give permission for the match at Lord's although he suggested it was played at Eton saying, *"You must not play in London but I shall be happy to see Harrow down here,"* which Harrow rejected. Doubts were expressed by the Eton captain, E.B. Fane, to the Harrow captain, W.S. Church, that once the fixture at Lord's was given up it would not be played again; fortunately this foreboding was not fulfilled.

Once again in **1857** Dr Goodford showed his tiresome obstinacy and would not allow any member of the Eton XI who had not left to play at Lord's and this excluded six of their team. It thus became an irregular contest between Eton under 21 v. Harrow under 20 and it has always been disputed whether this match should be regarded as part of the regular series. However, the extra year Eton were allowed did not help them and they went down conclusively by 10 wickets. Big crowds were still unknown at this time and only the boys playing and some of their relations attended. There were no boundary ropes and only some small stands here and there and every hit had to be run. For instance if Eton were fielding and the ball went into a group of Harrow boys the Eton fielders sometimes found it difficult to extricate the ball and vice versa. The batsmen profited on some occasions but on others they were decidedly hard done by.

Henry Arkwright who played in the Harrow XI of 1855/7 at first bowled fast underhand at Harrow but in 1853 changed to slow roundarm which, because he delivered the ball rather high and swung it, caused bewilderment amongst batsmen, resulting in many catches and stumpings. He achieved excellent results in the two matches against Eton in 1855 and 1857 and gained his Cambridge blue in 1858. In a 12-a-side match for the Gentlemen of M.C.C. v. Gentlemen of Kent in 1861 he took 18 wickets out of the 22 that fell and at the time of his death in 1866 he was A.D.C. to the Lord Lieutenant of Ireland. He was killed in an avalanche whilst climbing Mont Blanc and remarkably his body was eventually found in 1897 preserved in a glacier.

1858 was the first year in the Eton XI of the great R.A.H. Mitchell who was to have a huge influence on Eton cricket for 30 years. For his first two years in the XI he did nothing special

K.E. Digby (later Sir Kenelm Digby), Harrow XI 1852/5, Oxford 1857/9, pictured second from left in the front row. He created a unique record of captaining a winning Harrow side three years running from 1853/5 and playing in four successful Harrow XIs. He was a very good wicket keeper batsman who was also successful in the varsity matches.

but in 1860 he scored 70 out of Eton's first innings score of 98 on a difficult Lord's wicket before it eased out and the first draw in the series resulted. Although still having another year at Eton he was asked to play for the Gentlemen at Lord's, the youngest player ever before or since to do so, and at Oxford Mitchell established himself as the best amateur batsman of his time, captaining the university a record three times from 1863/5. Until W.G. Grace appeared on the scene in 1870 and put everyone else in the shade 'Mike', as he was known, was supreme. He became an assistant master at Eton in 1866 and for the next 30 years ran Eton cricket literally from the sidelines, rather as a football manager would do today. He would tell the Eton captain who to put on to bowl and where to place his field and this continued till relatively late in his reign. His first-class appearances after 1866 were limited but, when he did appear, spectators relished his powerful hitting and an average of 30 in his first-class career was very good going on the difficult wickets of those days.

Hon. C.G. Lyttelton, (later 8th Viscount Cobham), Eton XI 1858/60 and Cambridge 1861/4. One of the famous seven Lyttelton brothers who all played in the Eton XI and a hard hitting middle order batsman during his four years in the Cambridge XI. He averaged over 27 per innings, not far short of his better known brother Alfred.

In **1858** the first of the famous Lyttelton brothers and one of Eton's greatest sporting families down the ages appeared. C.G. Lyttelton was undoubtedly the best Eton batsman of the year and played in 1859/60, but was not considered in the family quite as good as his younger brother Alfred. Nevertheless he was excellent by most standards, especially at Fenners where he was in the Cambridge side for four years from 1861/4. The ubiquitous Arthur Hayward would say that there was no one to compare with Charles Lyttelton, including Mitchell, and his cutting especially was superb. This was high praise indeed from a Harrovian of earlier vintage!

In **1859** Harrow again had a very good side and won by an innings and 48 runs. Besides R. Lang and A.W.T. Daniel Harrow had two other good bats in R.D. Elphinstone and E.W. Humphreys who were the main contributors to Harrow's first innings total and also another Walker, R.D., not a stylish bat but a very effective one and a good bowler as well. On the Eton side was the first of the Lubbocks, Montague, who had a very good eye and faced the fast bowling of Lang without either pads or gloves and made top score of 12 and 22 for Eton with a very crooked bat in both innings. Both Lyttelton and Mitchell made ducks for Eton in the second innings as they had done in the first innings of the previous year. H.M. Plowden who was a fine slow

R.A.H. Mitchell Eton XI 1858/61, Oxford 1862/5 (captain 3 years running) Leicestershire & Warwickshire (before they became first-class). Regarded as England's finest amateur batsman till W.G. Grace arrived on the scene and the father of Eton cricket. Master in charge of Eton cricket 1866/96, his appearances were therefore limited but he averaged 30 in first-class cricket which was very good for the times.

R. Lang, Harrow XI 1855,58/9 and Cambridge 1860/2. A highly successful fast bowler at Harrow and Cambridge he was on the winning side at Lord's in all six years. In three matches for Cambridge at Lord's and the Oval in 1860 he took 19 wickets at a cost of four runs each.

bowler, did much of the damage to Eton in 1853 taking 9 wickets in the match but it was G.H. Hodgson, who was not rated as highly as Plowden or Lang, who achieved the amazing figures of 7/9 in 49 balls, all clean bowled in Eton's lowly total of 44 in the first innings. In those days play went on more or less irrespective of the weather and in Eton's second innings the Harrow fielders were drenched to the skin. Plowden went on to gain Cambridge blues from 1860/3, captaining the side in 1862/3, and was also a noted rackets player. He was regarded as deadly on slow wickets when spin bowling was quite uncommon. He was pretty successful in his four matches for Cambridge in the varsity match, Cambridge beating Oxford in all three years from 1860/2, but the toss played a large part in their defeat by 8 wickets in 1863 and Plowden took 7/25 in Oxford's first innings. His first-class career was very brief thereafter as he went into the legal profession and thence to India where as Sir Henry Plowden he became Judge of the Chief Court in the Punjab from 1877 to 1894. Robert Lang was a member of the Harrow XI from 1855 to 1859 and was captain in his last two years and played against Eton three times. In each of his three matches Harrow won by an innings and he took 12 wickets for 89 runs in aggregate. He will always be remembered for his tremendous pace bowling at Cambridge when he was on the winning side all three years from 1860/2. It was fortunate that Cambridge possessed an excellent long stop in Herbert Marshall otherwise his bowling would have been very expensive. In his three matches at Lord's and the Oval for Cambridge in 1860 he took 19 wickets at a cost of 4 runs each. In 1861 he was largely ineffective but in 1862 he took 10/26 for the University v. Surrey and 9/35 v. Oxford at Lord's. He appeared twice for the Gentlemen v. Players in 1860 and 1862 but on going into the church he gave up serious cricket after 1862.

Although **1860** was the first drawn match, A.W.T. Daniel distinguished himself as the first Harrovian to make a century at Lord's with 112 not out. He was a very good bat and fielder and accomplished at all sports particularly rackets, football and athletics. He gained Cambridge cricket blues from 1861/4 as well as representing the university at rackets, athletics and football. He was to play 16 matches for Middlesex between 1861/9 but died young in 1873 of consumption. Although there was no result in 1860, two very good sides fought out an exciting match. Lyttelton had bowled out four of the first five Harrow batsmen including Walker and Daniel without a run between them. There were as previously mentioned, two superb innings played in the match from Mitchell and Daniel. Daniel was lucky not to have been caught first ball, however as Lyttelton had forgotten to set a deep slip for him. The great I.D. Walker made his first appearance for Harrow, as did W.F. Maitland, and these two were both a fixture in the Harrow side for four years. The unselfish Philip Norman of Eton was called for a short single by Mitchell but gave his wicket away to save Mitchell. Eton needed 259 to win and managed 221/8 before time was called. It was very hot, Harrow were extremely tired and Eton believed they could have pulled it off had time allowed. It was the first occasion a large crowd came to Lord's to watch the Eton and Harrow match and what they saw did not disappoint them. It was the start of the great social attraction that it became until the beginning of the Second World War and was not to be missed by those society hostesses who wished to parade their daughters before suitable young men.

A.W.T. Daniel, Harrow XI 1858/60, Cambridge 1861/4 and Middlesex. Harrow's first centurion in the series with 112 not out in the drawn match of 1860, the first of many to come. He was a fine all-round sportsman representing Cambridge at athletics and rackets also but died of consumption in 1873.

The inscription on the bat with which A.W.T. Daniel scored Harrow's first century.

THE GOLDEN YEARS

1861-1918

Eton were the decided favourites in **1861**, considered to be a very good side and Harrow a poor one. Nonetheless Harrow performed creditably at Lord's gaining a first innings lead of 29 and having none the worse of the draw. They were much indebted to G.E Reid and E.W. Burnett who had a remarkable last wicket stand of 63 in their first innings total of 164. This turned the match much in the manner of the last wicket stand between Adams and Richardson for South Africa in the test series v. England in early 1996. Harrow had three fine players in C.F. Buller, Walker and Maitland, but they were still relatively immature. They were all there the following year with C.L. Hornby, brother of the famous A.N. "Monkey" Hornby the future Lancashire and England cricketer. Harrow had the worst of the game in **1862** and were bowled out by Eton's two pace bowlers, A.S. Teape, who took 9 wickets in the match and J.St.J. Frederick, who was very fast and dangerous in short spells and finished with 6/28. Maitland, despite his immaturity, scored a very fine 73 in Harrow's second innings and it was considered by many, given the high class bowling and the condition of the wicket, to be one of the finest innings ever seen in this match. For the first time organised coaching was introduced at Eton by Frederick Bell of Cambridge. The Harrovians not to be outdone had the famous John Lillywhite who took over from John Wisden. It was also the first time Eton had beaten Harrow since 1850.

Two very strong teams contested the **1863** match captained by two famous names, Alfred Lubbock for Eton and I.D. Walker for Harrow. It was interesting to note that J.H. Dark, the proprietor of Lord's, discontinued the practice in 1863 of charging 7/6d to each boy who played in the great match! E.W. Tritton's knock of 91 for Eton out of 184 was the best of the match and Lubbock's 80 in Eton's second innings was careful and patient as he had made a duck in the first innings. Harrow's innings of 268 was much inflated by 56 extras, largely byes and wides due to the Eton long stop who was unable to cope with the unpredictable Lord's outfield. Lubbock had scored 174 not out v. Winchester that year and was regarded for a few years after as one of the best young players around. He was a particularly good fielder, especially at cover point. His finest year was probably 1867 when he made 129 for England v. Middlesex at Lord's and 107 not out for the Gentlemen v. Players at the Oval. There were no test matches at that time but at his best, particularly in 1867, he would almost certainly have been picked for England. He was compared favourably with W.G. Grace who was just starting and it is interesting to note that when he scored his 129, Grace aged 19 was in the same side and made 75. Lubbock went to Eton when he was under 9 in 1854 and left in 1863 when he was only 17; in theory he could have stayed for another two years. Alfred Lubbock's own account

I.D. Walker, Harrow XI 1860/3 and Middlesex. The founder with his brother of Middlesex C.C.C. in 1864, captain from 1873/84 and founder also of Harrow Wanderers in 1870. One of the leading batsman in the country throughout his first-class career.

A. Lubbock, Eton XI 1861/3. The Eton captain of 1863 scored 80 in the second innings to save his side from defeat. For a few years he was regarded as one of the best bats in the country, particularly in 1867 when he made 129 for England v Middlesex at Lord's. Founded Eton Ramblers in 1862 with other members of the XI.

of the match, taken with his account of the match against Winchester a fortnight earlier, sheds its own light on the manners of the day. The Winchester fixture was a two-day match and when stumps were drawn on the first day, he was not out 130. That evening, as was the custom, both XIs had to dine with the Headmaster Balston. He asked to be excused as he was so tired, and Balston said, *"Certainly, Lubbock sir, you must be tired."* He intended to go to bed early but a 'sock supper' at his tutor's with some claret revived him and, instead of going to bed early, he sat out in his tutor's garden with a few Old Etonians who had come to supper till way past one o'clock, smoking big cigars! His fellow centurion, E.W. Tritton, and himself both had heavy hangovers the next morning but still managed to thrash the Wykehamists by an innings and 194 runs. Lubbock was presented with 40 bats, some from his school friends, some from Old Etonians whom he hardly knew, and two from "Fat" Powell, the Eton bat-seller at that time, and one from the Provost and Fellows of the College. His room was more like a bat-maker's shop than anything else. Half of them he gave away and the rest, which he thought were the best, he kept.

Lubbock's description of the Lord's match against Harrow is also most interesting. He was caught off his very first ball by I.D. "Donny" Walker, who kept wicket for Harrow. It was a bad ball on his legs and ought to have gone for four but he hit it a little too soon and it caught the back of the bat and bobbed up in the air for an easy catch by I.D. It was a humiliating end for the Eton Captain from whom so much was expected, walking back into the pavilion amidst a dead silence having scored a duck. He was very annoyed with himself because it was the only time his father had come to see a match and he had taken a great deal of trouble to get him a good seat in the front row. He made up for it with his 80 in the second innings but there was a tremendous amount of noise from the Etonians, who were trying to put off the Harrow bowlers so much so that play was stopped on several occasions. This only made the Etonians shout even more and it probably put the batsmen off as much as the bowlers and eventually the match was drawn without Harrow going in again. For grace and style he could hardly be surpassed and he played eight times for the Gentlemen between 1866/71 averaging 30, a very good performance in those times. It was in 1862 that with other members of the Eton XI he founded Eton Ramblers and chose their famous colours. He was very much the leading light of the club until he gave up playing relatively young at the age of 28 due to his profession as a banker. I.D. "Donny" Walker, who led the Harrow side, kept wicket when he was not bowling and this was also the last year of the four Walker brothers of Southgate who played for Harrow. I.D. was arguably the best known of the seven brothers who all played for Middlesex and he it was who founded the club with his brother V.E. Walker in 1864. He played for the county from 1862/84 and remained one of the leading batsmen throughout his first-class career, captaining the side from 1873 to 1884. Even in his last season at the age of 40 he scored 674 runs at just over 28. He also founded Harrow Wanderers in 1870 and led them on their Northern Tour which still survives to this day, till his death in 1898. W.F. Maitland, who had been more of a batsman than a bowler at Harrow, developed into a very fine slow bowler who was able to get an exceptional amount of spin on the ball. He gained blues at Oxford from 1864/7 and often got wickets with deliveries which top batsmen regarded as too wide to be

The Hon. F.G. Pelham (later Earl of Chichester), Eton XI 1863, Cambridge 1864/7 & Sussex. Captained Cambridge in 1866/7 and took 26 wickets in his four matches v. Oxford. (Picture courtesy of Richard Pelham).

dangerous. He played county cricket for Essex (pre-first-class), and Oxfordshire and was a very fine athlete who represented the university in the high jump and long jump as well as rackets. He became M.P. for Breconshire from 1875 to 1895. The Hon. F.G. Pelham, who played in this match for Eton, was a very slow roundarm bowler. He had little success in this match but improved considerably thereafter and gained blues at Cambridge from 1864/7, captaining the XI in 1866 and 1867 taking 26 wickets in his four matches v. Oxford and also representing the university at athletics. He later succeeded as the 5th Earl of Chichester in 1901 and was the grandfather of A.G. Pelham, the hero of Eton's success at Lord's in 1930.

E.W. Tritton, the Eton opening batsman was the best, apart from Alfred Lubbock, of a very strong group of Eton batsmen at that time. His scores of 130 v. Winchester and 91 and 58 v. Harrow in 1863 proved his class. On going up to Christ Church, Oxford he gained blues in all four years from 1864/7 and was certainly one of the key members of the famous Oxford sides of 1864 and 1865 captained by his fellow Etonian R.A.H. Mitchell. His best knock was in 1865 when he scored 114 v. M.C.C. who had a very strong bowling attack of Wootton, Grundy, Alfred Shaw and the amateurs S.C. Voules and R.D, Walker, the finest of their day. He played a few matches for Middlesex from 1864/7 without quite fulfilling the expectations that were formed of him at Eton.

W.B. Money, Harrow XI 1865/7 & Cambridge 1868/71. A famous lob bowler he took 10/80 in Harrow's win by an innings and 51 runs in 1865 followed by 9/50 in the win by an innings and 136 runs in 1866 and was a competent middle-order batsman. He had considerable success in the first-class game before giving up in 1871 when he went into the church.

Large crowds came to Lord's in **1864** and saw the Harrow run of victories start once again. Around 16,000 people turned up on the two days and a record £570 was taken in gate receipts on Friday, the first day. Harrow were a particularly good side with C.F. Buller, M.H. Stow and A.N. Hornby to bat and two reasonable bowlers in Hon. J.G.H. Amherst and C.L. Arkwright who were good enough to bowl out an unusually poor Eton side twice and gain a handsome victory by an innings and 66 runs. The Prince and Princess of Wales were present on both days and the two captains, W.S. Prideaux and C.F. Buller, were complimented on their fine play. Buller, who scored 61 in this match, was a most stylish middle-order batsman and went on to play 24 matches for Middlesex between 1865/77 scoring 3,140 runs in his short first-class career. His exceptional wrist power served him well in 1865 when he made 105 not out for Middlesex v. Surrey at the Oval and 106 for M.C.C., v. Sussex at Lord's. Two important changes to the game came in 1864, the first being the introduction of over-arm bowling by M.C.C., before this time the arm was only allowed to be extended to the shoulder. The second

A.N. Hornby, Harrow XI 1864/5 & Lancashire. The patriarch of Lancashire C.C.C., he played from 1867/99 and was captain from 1880/93 and 1897/8. Capped three times for England he also played rugby for his country. His son A.H. Hornby also captained Lancashire from 1908/14 but never got in the Harrow XI.

F.C. Cobden, Harrow XI 1866 and Cambridge 1870/2. His very fast 'yorkers' had much to do with Harrow's overwhelming win by an innings and 136 runs in 1866 - he took eight wickets, of which seven were clean bowled. His most famous feat was in bowling the last three Oxford batsmen in successive balls in 1870 to win the match for Cambridge by two runs in the last over. He afterwards played for Shropshire and Herefordshire.

important change was that boundary ropes were recognised and for six years these hits counted as three until becoming four runs in 1870. Even the newspapers had begun to realise the importance of the contest and *The Times* declared on the morning of the 8th July, the first day of the match, that the annual encounter was the Derby day of the cricketing year. This was a golden age, until the end of the century, for the number of blues from both schools and those who represented the Gentlemen v. the Players. By the Monday morning the ground had been so ridden over and trodden down by the horses (which were then the main means of transport) that Lord's had nearly assumed the appearance and character of a highway road.

The lobs of W.B. Money who took 10 wickets in the match, skittled out Eton to a second innings defeat in **1865**. He also had a major impact in 1866 when he took another 9 wickets at low cost, particularly in the Eton second innings of 42 when he took 7/32 off 14.5 overs. Harrow had achieved a hat-trick of innings wins. A.N. "Monkey" Hornby, the Harrow opening batsman of 1864/65, was the leading light at Lancashire for many years as both player and administrator. He played 292 matches for Lancashire between 1867/99 and 437 first-class matches scoring 16,109 runs at an average of over 24 with a highest score of 188. He played in three tests v. Australia in 1878/9 and 1884 and would have played in many more had tests been played whilst he was in his prime but he failed to do himself justice in the three he played. He captained Lancashire from 1880/93 and in 1897/8, while his best season was in 1881 when he scored 1,534 runs at an average of 40.56. "Monkey", as he was nicknamed, played his last first-class game at the age of 59 for an England XI in 1906 and was a fine rugby player who was capped nine times for England between 1877 and 1882 as well as being a very good boxer and athlete. He was president of Lancashire for over 25 years until his death in 1925. His son A.H. did not make the Harrow XI but was a most effective middle-order batsman for Lancashire between 1899/1914, scoring 9,781 runs at an average of 25. He captained the side from 1908/14 and his best season was in 1913 when he hit 1,336 runs at an average of over 28. J.M. Richardson, the Harrow middle-order batsman of 1864/5, went on to gain a blue as a freshman and played in the Cambridge side from 1866/8. He was a brilliant all round sportsman and as a famous amateur jockey won the Grand National in 1873 and 1874. A pavilion was erected in his memory after his death in 1912 on the philathletic ground at Harrow in 1914 which has only recently been renovated in 2004.

F. A. MacKinnon failed to get into the Harrow XI as a steady, middle order batsman but gained an unexpected blue for Cambridge in 1870 and followed this with 78 matches for Kent between 1875/85. An extremely modest record of 16 per innings did not prevent him going on Lord Harris's (his Kent captain) tour to Australia in 1878/9 where he played in the one Test match and scored 5 in his two innings. Surely not a case of favouritism? He afterwards became the 35th Head of the MacKinnon clan and was a familiar figure at the Canterbury Festival until his death in his 99th year in 1946 (see photograph on next page).

Although Money had a major influence on Eton's crushing defeat in **1866** it was F.C. Cobden who was the most frightening with his very fast yorkers and he bowled out eight Etonians at low cost, seven clean bowled. Cobden, who left Harrow early, was also a hard-hitting lower order batsman, but it was his fast straight bowling which made him famous in 1870 while playing for Cambridge in the varsity match. Oxford needed four off the last over of the day with three wickets standing and looked certain to win. A single was scored off the first ball but then Cobden struck. The last three Oxford batsmen were clean bowled in successive deliveries to leave Cambridge winners by 2 runs. He was immortalised by the verse of 1870 which read:

> *Cobden whose name in Cambridge halls*
> *That feat until this day recalls*
> *Three wickets with the last three balls,*
> *To win the match by two.*

M.H. Stow, the Harrow captain of 1865/6, had a highly successful cricket career for both Harrow and Cambridge, never losing a match in his seven appearances at Lord's. In his four appearances for Harrow from 1863/6 his scores were as follows: 3 run out, 54, 32 not out and 50 run out, the last three contributing to the three innings wins for Harrow. C.I. Thornton was a great hitter for Eton from 1866/8 with his most effective stroke being the drive when he

M.H. Stow, Harrow XI 1863/6, Cambridge 1867/9. In his seven successive appearances at Lord's he was never on the losing side, captaining Harrow successfully in 1865 & 1866 and Cambridge in 1869.

Kent C.C.C. captained by Lord Harris and including F.A. MacKinnon, a test cricketer of doubtful provenance, 1876.
STANDING - *Henty, Hearne (G.G.), Thompson, W.B. Pattisson, W. Foord-Kelcey, F.Penn, F.A. Mackinnon, V.K. Shaw.* SITTING - *W. Yardley, Lord Harris, C.A. Absolom, Major Fellowes, R.E.*

A drawing by A.C. James of the unusual stance of Edgar Lubbock, Eton XI 1864/6 and brother of the famous Alfred. Eton lost by a massive margin under his captaincy in 1866, by an innings and 136 runs.

moved down the wicket to meet the ball in contrast to the usual firm-footed methods of his contemporaries. In 1866 he backed himself in the Winchester match to hit the ball out of the old Winchester ground and succeeded in doing so twice, the first off the first ball he received. In Harrow's overwhelming victory of 1866 there was a controversial incident when the Eton captain Edgar Lubbock, brother of the great Alfred, drove a ball at high speed off the pacy Cobden and a small boy jumped up and fielded the ball inside the boundary ropes, threw it to the chasing fielder who hurled it in to the wicket-keeper. His partner J.W. Foley was out of his ground and given run out by the umpire. Lubbock lost his temper and, although the Harrow captain Stow suggested that Foley should be reinstated, cricket was abandoned for the day. The crowd was so incensed by the incident that the Princess of Wales was driven away in disgust. Edgar Lubbock, the youngest of eight celebrated brothers all at College, was known as Quintus by his friends because when he came to Eton in 1857 four of his elder brothers were still in the school and he stayed for nine years. This was unusual even in those days and his sporting record at Eton was remarkable. His uncharacteristic bad manners at Lord's did not affect him in after life and at the time of his death in 1907 he was a director of Whitbread and Co. and Deputy Governor of the Bank of England.

In 1867's inconclusive match Money's lobs were again feared but, after bowling the Eton opener Hay for a duck first ball, he was hit out of the match by the formidable Thornton and only took one more wicket in the match. The **1867** Harrow captain Money, who was also a more than competent batsman, gained blues for Cambridge from 1868/71 as well as rackets. His most successful year was 1870 when he made 134 for Cambridge v. Surrey and 70 and 109 not out for the Gentlemen v. the Players and also took 10/66 with his lobs in a representative match. After going into the church in 1871 he gave up serious cricket although he did appear occasionally for Suffolk. Eton had the advantage in the number of boys at this time, 815 to Harrow's 481, but whether this had any effect on the depth or quality of their cricket is hard to say. In the event results soon started to turn Eton's way with Mitchell's influence on the coaching particularly noticeable.

Thornton was to achieve a feat of hitting that was phenomenal even by his own standards in **1868**. After hitting the Harrow opening bowler C.T. Giles over the ropes on the on side he proceeded to hit the last ball of the over clean over the old pavilion at Lord's, which was a gigantic hit and according to John Lillywhite the finest straight drive he had ever seen in his life. In those days of frequent shooters Giles was to gain his revenge when he bowled Thornton with one after he had scored a rapid 44. The wickets at Lord's were still inconsistent and in a relatively low scoring match Harrow had a fairly easy win by 7 wickets with C.W. Walker, no relation of the Southgate Walkers, achieving 10 wickets in the match.

C.I. Thornton, Eton XI 1866/8, Cambridge 1869/72, Kent & Middlesex. The greatest hitter of his day. He hit a ball over the old pavilion at Lord's in 1868, in practice at Brighton 168 yards and in a county match at Canterbury 152 yards. A founder of the Scarborough Festival.

Thornton was an extraordinary character and went on to gain Cambridge blues from 1869/72, captaining the side in 1872. He also played for Kent from 1867/72 and Middlesex from 1875/85. Among his astonishing cricketing feats were hits of 168 yards and 162 yards in practice at Brighton and in a match for Kent at Canterbury, a 152 yard carry. What was even more astonishing was that he never wore pads and very seldom gloves except on the worst pitches. He was also for many years a leading figure at the Scarborough Festival which he had been largely instrumental in founding. He once hit upon the idea of playing an innings 'ball by ball' in the manner of a certain well known batsman. It was an ingenious exercise but one which foundered all too swiftly. For the master mimic was out first ball when, according to contemporary sources ' leaving the ball alone in the customary manner of a certain defensive player'. Apart from his legendary hitting previously mentioned he is reputed to have hit a ball into the sea at Scarborough off Tom Emmett and when playing at the Oval in the early 1870s struck a delivery from Surrey's James Southerton so far that the wicket-keeper Edward Pooley exclaimed 'So 'elp me God Jimmy, I believe it's gone on to Brixton Church'.

He got his nickname 'Buns' at Eton when fielding at long leg in a school match and feeling hungry he called out to a vendor with his cart of ices, cakes and buns and proceeded to eat a jam-filled bun on the field. Many of his most remarkable hits were at Scarborough although there was one incident which unlike his mighty blow into the North Sea he probably preferred to forget. As he strode out to the middle he could hear a band playing in the background. Disregarding any enjoyment the music may have provided for holidaymakers Thornton did not wish to be distracted from his art and immediately ordered the band to stop playing. The command was obeyed but Thornton was out for a duck anyway! Hours later he was still blaming his dismissal on the band.

Thornton's style of batting was aptly described by W.J. Ford in his book *'The Cambridge University Cricket Club 1820-1901'*. 'He was wonderfully quick on his feet, and as a rule went boldly in to meet the bowling whatever its pace: and if he hit the ball fair, it was a boundary, or over it, like a streak of lightning. It was no fun to field even on the boundary as his low

C.J. Ottaway Eton XI 1867/9. Scored 108 in 1869, Eton's first hundred since Emilius Bayley in 1841. Gained rackets, tennis, athletics and soccer blues as well as cricket and played twice for England at football.

S.E. Butler Eton XI 1868/9, Oxford 1870/3. His most famous feat was taking 10/38 in Cambridge's first innings of the varsity match of 1871 at Lord's, a unique achievement.

skimming hits came humming and twisting among the grass blades like a bumblebee while if he lifted the ball it went clean out over everything.' In his reminiscences of 1921, he tells of his time at Eton, in 1865 some of the Upper Club boys noticed his hitting propensities and he was summoned to Upper Club to practise with Fred Bell, the professional engaged to coach the boys.

'Our ideas did not coincide as I hit all his best balls into the trees and as he had to fetch them he didn't like it. I think I would have been in the Eton XI in 1865 if it had not been for him but as it was about the worst eleven Eton ever had I did not miss much. However I got in for the next three years although I was never on the winning side even though I made over 50 runs each time'.

He tells an amusing story about W.G. Grace at Scarborough. Farrands the umpire gave him out l.b.w., a decision W.G. disagreed with (not for the first time) and told him so. Tim O'Brien a fellow amateur and Thornton concocted a letter from Farrands saying how surprised he was at Dr W.G. impugning his decision and speaking to him as umpire in the way he did etc. and got the butler to give it to W.G. at dinner. The old man took it all in and was most concerned as Farrands said he was going to report the matter to M.C.C. They let W.G. know later and he said *'Chairly* (as he called Thornton in his Gloucestershire burr) *you took me in this time, proper'*.

W.H. Hadow, who played for Harrow in 1866/7, had a stance with his legs far apart similar to another famous Harrovian A.J. Webbe and thus did not make use of his height. He did little for Oxford in his three varsity matches from 1870/2 but was more successful for Middlesex for whom he played between 1870/9. Among his notable scores were 217 v. M.C.C. in 1871 at Lord's, 140 v. Notts also at Lord's in 1878 and 97 for the Gentlemen v. the Players in 1871. His 217 at Lord's was particularly notable as no innings of over 200 had been scored in a major match at Lord's since William Ward's 278 for M.C.C. v. Norfolk in 1820. Eton had some fine players in their side besides Thornton including C.J. Ottaway, the Hon. G.R.C. Harris (later Lord Harris), and S.E. Butler but having done well in previous matches were overconfident of winning at Lord's.

It was a different story in **1869** and Eton's convincing win by an innings and 19 runs was very much due to the gifted Ottaway whose 108 was the first hundred at Lord's for Eton since Emilius Bayley in 1841. Ottaway was a sound defensive batsman and successful wicket-keeper but had a relatively short but distinguished first-class career. He gained blues all four years he was at Oxford from 1870/3 and also represented the university at rackets, real tennis, athletics and soccer. He is the only Oxford undergraduate to have gained five full blues sports matched on the Cambridge side by the Hon. Alfred Lyttelton who gained blues in the same five sports as Ottaway. He was also good enough to play for England in the forward line in two international soccer matches. He played for Kent in 1869/70 and Middlesex in 1874 and 1876. In 1869 he averaged 76 for Eton and scored nine centuries in the season for Eton, Kent and in other fixtures. He was adjudged by Mitchell, who was intimately acquainted with all Etonian batsmen over 30 years as the most talented defensive batsman he had ever coached at Eton. Among his notable scores in 1876 when he averaged 89 in his four matches were 112 v. Surrey and 106 v. Notts at Prince's, Hans Place where Middlesex were playing at the time before settling at Lord's, and he represented the Gentlemen v. the Players in 1870, 1872 and 1876. After being called to the bar in 1877 he retired from serious cricket but was to die shortly afterwards in 1878 from a heart condition. S.E. Butler, the Eton opening bowler had been converted by 'Mitch' from a slow bowler to a fast bowler and took seven wickets in the match with a match-winning performance of 5/25 in the first innings when Harrow were bowled out for 91. He gained blues all four years at Oxford and undoubtedly his finest performance was in the university match of 1871 when he took all ten wickets for 38 in the Cambridge first innings, a feat unique to this day in the varsity match and finished with 15/95 in the match. On the strength of this performance he was drafted into the Gentlemen v. Players match at both Lord's and the Oval. F.E.R. Fryer who played in the Harrow XI 1867/8 but was dropped in 1869 was a most graceful batsman who gained Cambridge blues from 1870/3 and was captain in 1873. He was, however notably unsuccessful in his four varsity matches v. Oxford at Lord's, his highest score being 46 and in Cambridge's matches v. M.C.C. at Lord's even more so. He was more successful on truer wickets elsewhere particularly at Fenners and the Oval where his vulnerable defence was not so exposed; he was very much a front foot player, particularly on the leg side. He was responsible for holding a superb catch in the famous 1870 varsity match off C.J. Ottaway of Oxford at short leg when he was threatening to win the match for Oxford off his own bat. This paved the way for Cobden's famous hat-trick in the last over for Cambridge which won the match by two runs. He afterwards played for Suffolk until 1883 before he took up golf with great success. Spencer Gore who captained the Harrow XI in 1869 was a very fine all round athlete and became England Lawn Tennis Champion in 1877.

Hon G.R.C. Harris (later Lord Harris), Eton XI 1868/70, Oxford 1871/2, 1874 Kent and England. A leading light in Kent and M.C.C. affairs for over 50 years, captain of Kent from 1871/89, a stickler for the laws of the game and a fearsome opponent when crossed.

The Hon. G.R.C. Harris, later the famous Lord Harris, captained Eton to a narrow and exciting win by 21 runs in **1870** and it was clear that Mitchell's organisation and coaching was beginning to pay off. The captain did little in this match but caused uproar in the crowd when he ran out one of Harrow's leading batsman backing up, C.A. Wallroth on 30, and curiously he was run out by Harris again in the second innings from deep slip. This and the Harrow opening batsman being given out off his elbow in the second innings tipped the balance Eton's way and G. Macan's 10/50 in the match for Harrow failed to change the result. Despite not being bowled at Cambridge, he gained blues in 1874/5 and was a useful lower order batsman. Harris was undoubtedly one of the most influential personalities in the game, particularly for Kent and M.C.C., right up until his death in 1932. An Oxford blue in 1871/2 and 1874 he played for Kent on and off from 1870/1911, captaining the side from 1871, when its fortunes were at a very low ebb till 1889. He scored nearly 10,000 runs in his first-class career at an average of 27 with a best year of 1884 when he scored 1,417

George Macan. Harrow XI 1869-71, Cambridge University 1874/5. A fine all round match in 1870 with 10/50 and 42 for once out.

runs at an average of 34. He captained England in the four tests in which he played including the first test match ever played against Australia in this country. After 1884 his first class cricket was restricted by various political offices including Under-Secretary for India and later Under-Secretary for War. He also spent five years in India as Governor of Bombay from 1890/5.

He was a stickler for the spirit and laws of the game and was the prime mover in the stamping out of throwing which plagued cricket in the 1880s. Although he was a fair minded person he had a hot temper which made him a fearsome opponent when crossed.

Such large crowds assembled for the Eton and Harrow match in 1870 that for the first time no one was allowed into the ground on horseback and the enormous sum for the times of £1,450 was taken for admission into the ground on the two days. A.W. Ridley's stylish knock of 117 and 4/32 in Harrow's second innings, well supported by G.H. Longman's 68, went a long way to explaining Eton's success by an innings and 77 runs in **1871**. A most amusing incident happened in the match when Mitchell's management of the bowling got slightly confused and his original message to his captain, G.H. Longman, of 'no change' became 'put on Napier Miles' who was a very occasional bowler. The Eton captain who had been considerably annoyed by this request was astonished when the Harrow No.3, E.P. Baily, was bowled by a dead shooter from Miles in his first over. It seemed nothing could go right for Harrow after this and they succumbed to Eton's high class bowling attack. Ridley went on to play for Oxford from 1872/5 captaining them in 1875 and also played for Hampshire and Middlesex. His most notable innings were 103 for the Gentlemen v. the Players in 1876 and 136 for Middlesex v. Surrey in 1883 and his excellent lob bowling was a decisive factor in Oxford's six-run victory over Cambridge in 1875. His 222 first-class wickets at an average of 15 proves the point.

F.M. Buckland Eton XI 1871/3, Oxford 1875/7. He had three highly successful years in the Eton XI at Lord's as a leg break bowler with figures of 5/36, 12/77 & 9/117 respectively. At Oxford he converted to medium pace round arm bowling and was a most useful batsman with highly creditable figures at both.

G.H. Longman, the Eton captain of 1871 and a most refined opening bat, played for Cambridge from 1872/5 and for Hampshire thereafter. He was a more than useful footballer who represented Middlesex and afterwards was Treasurer and President of Surrey C.C.C. E.P. Baily, the Harrow batsman wicket-keeper from 1868/70, gained Cambridge cricket blues in 1872 and 1874 and also played non-first-class cricket for Somerset in 1880. His son R.E.H., who was also a wicket-keeper batsman, played for Harrow from 1901/4, gained a Cambridge blue in 1908 and played a few games for Surrey.

F.M. Buckland's superb leg break bowling was largely the difference between the two sides in **1872** and he finished with match figures of 12/77 in Eton's six-wicket win. There were three Lyttelton brothers in the Eton side of 1872, R.H. being joined by his illustrious brothers Edward and Alfred. Alfred's 19 not out in Eton's second innings was a foretaste of greatness to come. Harrow reversed the tide when they got home by 5 wickets in **1873**, the two Lyttletons, Edward and Alfred, making little impact for Eton and despite the fine bowling once again of Buckland who took 9/117 in the match. In his three years against Harrow

Hon. A. Lyttelton Eton XI 1872/5, Cambridge 1876/9, Middlesex & England. The greatest of the seven Lyttelton brothers, an outstanding all round sportsman he gained blues for football, athletics, rackets & real tennis as well as cricket, playing for England at both football and cricket.

and Winchester he had taken 62 wickets at a cost of 461 runs and was also a batsman of no mean ability in the fine, forward Etonian style advocated by "Mitch". At Oxford where he gained blues from 1875/77 he converted to a medium pace line and length bowler with some success and scored a superb 117 not out v. Cambridge in the varsity match of 1877. In the face of a Cambridge total of 134 Oxford had lost 6 wickets for 31 runs and the position looked desperate. At this point Buckland was joined by H.G. Tylecote and they completely turned the match by putting on 142 runs and Oxford eventually won by 10 wickets. Buckland's magnificent driving that day was remembered by all and he also took 7/50 in the match. F.L. Shand, Harrow's left-arm fast bowler, played a decisive part in Harrow's win, taking 8 wickets in the match as well as scoring a vital 36 not out in the first innings following his 6/45 in the 1872 match. In the opinion of many he would have gone far had he stayed in this country and not emigrated to Ceylon now Sri Lanka. He was somewhat erratic but sent down the occasional unplayable ball and had taken 8/14 for Harrow against a very powerful Harlequins side earlier in the year.

An average Eton team managed to overcome a modest Harrow side with the exception of A.J. Webbe in **1874**. The Harrow captain played two marvellous knocks of 77 and 80 and got the Eton captain Edward Lyttelton out in the second innings for nought after 58 in the first innings with a sensational catch at deep mid-off. It was not quite enough however, and the Etonians got home by 5 wickets. Lyttelton and 'Webby' were to play against each other for seven years running at Lord's. Edward Lyttelton gained Cambridge blues from 1875/8, captaining the Cambridge side in 1878 when they won eight first-class matches including victory v. the Australians by an innings and when playing for Middlesex in the same year v. the Australians scored 113. He excelled also at football,

The Lord's match of 1872 which was won comfortably by Eton due to the superb leg break bowling of F.M. Buckland who took 12/77 in the match. Most of the spectators seemed to have a rather bored expression on their faces as though expecting a Harrovian defeat!

AT LORD'S CRICKET-GROUND: THE ETON AND HARROW MATCH.
SEE PAGE 61.

A.J. Webbe and I.D. Walker. The two main architects of Harrow & Middlesex cricket in the second half of the 19th Century.

The aristocracy at play in the 1870s during the Lord's match.

Alfred Lyttelton (left, with Arthur Balfour, Prime Minister and brother-in-law) was a wicketkeeper-batsman (and sometime lob bowler) for Eton, Cambridge, Middlesex, Worcestershire, the Gentlemen, and England. Business at the Bar and in politics took him from the first-class game after 1887, though he took on the presidency of MCC in 1898. A superb tennis and rackets player, he also played football for England, and stood for all that was admirable in a sportsman. After dismissal by a lightning piece of stumping by Lancashire professional Dick Pilling he sought out the wicketkeeper after play and pressed £1 into his hand with a word of congratulation. He was perhaps the most distinguished member of a highly distinguished family, youngest of eight brothers. He became a bencher of the inner Temple in 1899 and QC in 1900, and was successively legal private secretary to Sir Henry James (Attorney-General), Recorder of Hereford, Recorder of Oxford, and Chancellor of the Diocese of Rochester. He entered Parliament in 1895 as Member for Leamington, and was Colonial Secretary from 1903 to 1905. Yet in popular memory he is recalled as the wicketkeeper who took off his pads in a Test match at The Oval in 1884 and took 4 for 19 with underarm lobs. All eleven England players bowled in that Australian innings of 551. Cricket may have caused Lyttelton's death, in 1913, at the age of 56. He scored 89 in a match against Bethnal Green Tradesmen - Tom Hayward played, too, three days before making his hundredth century - and a blow from the ball caused an internal abscess. He died, after an operation, eleven days later, having whispered to one of his brothers, 'Don't let them make too much of the cricket ball - just a piece of bad luck'.

fives and athletics, representing the university at these sports too. He later became Head Master of Eton from 1905 to 1916 and died in 1942 at the age of 86. Whenever invited to preach he could not resist viewing the aisle of a strange church and speculating as to whether or not it would take spin. An interesting postscript to 1872 was that the three Lytteltons in the Eton XI, R. H., Alfred and Edward were given a dinner at the White Hart by their five elder brothers, four of whom had previously been in the Eton side. A record of seven brothers in the Eton XI is extremely unlikely ever to be beaten on either side, the nearest being the six Studd brothers, who achieved fame a short while later. Edward Lyttelton, the Eton captain of 1874, described some of his recollections of that year and how "Mike" had been down to watch the Harrow XI and had returned to Eton with the warning, *"Most of the team are nothing in partic-ular, but you may have trouble with Webbe, the best bat Harrow has produced for years"*, and so it proved. He makes mention of an extremely fine catch to dismiss "Webby" in this match off an occasional bowler Wakefield in the first innings, but an astonishing one by "Webby" to dis-miss him in the second innings. He was facing Percy Crutchley, second wicket down, whom he perceived to be a rather indifferent bowler, and in the first ball of the second over hit it deep over the bowler's head, swerving away from "Webby". Like a man inspired he ran twenty yards to the ball where it was coming low and hard to him but away to the right, and could not believe it when his right hand shot out and held it inches above the ground. He saw many great catches in his time but believed this was the finest ever. The two were to see a lot of each other in the next few years opposing each other at the two great Universities, "Webby" for Oxford and Lyttelton for Cambridge, captains both in 1878.

Edward Lyttelton's captaincy of Cambridge in 1878 started a sequence of nine Etonian captains till 1887 interrupted only by A.G. Steel of Lancashire and England in 1880 whose son A.I Steel subsequently played for Eton in 1910/11 including the famous Fowler's match and who were related to the Lyttelton's by marriage.

"Webby" was one of the finest cricketers Harrow has ever produced with the possible exceptions of Jackson and MacLaren. An Oxford blue from 1875/8 he effectively took over from the Walkers as the decisive influence on Middlesex's affairs. He played for them from 1875/1900, was captain from 1885/98 and also acted as honorary secretary for 25 years there-after. His two most famous knocks were in August 1887 when opening the batting for Middlesex. He hit 192 not out v. Kent at Canterbury and followed it up with 243 not out v. Yorkshire at Huddersfield - not surprisingly this was his best season with 1,244 runs at an aver-age of 48. He played one test for England when he went on Lord Harris's tour in 1878/9 to Australia and scored 14,465 runs in his first-class career. He was also a fine rackets and football player who represented Oxford at both sports. W.H. Grenfell who played in the Harrow XI of 1873/4 rowed in the Oxford boat for two years and ran the three miles, becoming President of both rowing and athletics. He was afterwards to become Tory M.P. for Wycombe and the first Lord Desborough in 1905.

Eton captained by the great Alfred Lyttelton just failed to pull off a decisive victory in **1875**

A.J. Webbe Harrow XI 1872/4, Oxford 1875/8, Middlesex & England. He played for Middlesex from 1875/1900, captaining them from 1885/98. They were joint leaders in his last season and he gained his one test cap on Lord Harris's tour to Australia in 1878/9. An all time Harrow 'great' with Jackson and MacLaren.

H. Whitfeld, Eton XI 1875/7, Cambridge 1878/81 and Sussex. An exceptional all round athlete, Eton were unlucky not to win in 1877 when he was captain and he captained Sussex in 1883/4. He represented Cambridge at athletics, soccer and in the tennis doubles with Ivo Bligh as well as cricket.

Hon. Ivo Bligh, Eton XI 1876/7, Cambridge 1878/81, Kent and England. His first-class career was relatively short due to ill health but he is especially remembered for recapturing the Ashes in 1882/3 for England.

mainly due to an unfinished seventh wicket stand of 70 in Harrow's second innings from C.A.D. Tyssen and L. Chater with Harrow only 63 runs ahead with four wickets to fall at the close. The Eton captain top-scored with 59 but probably erred tactically when taking the extremely fast J. Wakefield off after he had clean bowled four Harrovian batsmen but had then bowled four wides. Alfred Lyttelton, the best known of the brothers, was an outstanding all-round sportsman and a quite brilliant wicket-keeper batsman. He gained Cambridge blues from 1876/9, captaining them in 1879, and played for Middlesex from 1877/87. He represented England in four tests v. Australia in 1880, 1882 and 1884 and his batting was described by the connoisseurs as the champagne of cricket. He also gained blues at rackets, real tennis, athletics and soccer at which he represented England in 1877 and the Old Etonians in the cup final of 1876. He was M.P. for Warwick from 1895 to 1906 and from 1906 till his death in 1913 for St George's, Hanover Square. He retired from first-class cricket at the early age of 30 due to his work at the bar.

The Eton captain W.F. Forbes had a major impact on the **1876** match opening the batting and scoring a brilliant 113 out of 150 in 105 minutes, hitting 22 fours and also taking six wickets in the match. He opened the batting with J.E.K. Studd the first of the famous six Studd brothers who all played for Eton, four of whom went on to gain Cambridge blues. G.H. Portal, Eton's left-arm fast bowler and a scion of the well known banknote company, took 5/20 in Harrow's second innings to secure an easy win for Eton by an innings and 24 runs. Although Forbes went on to play for the Gentlemen v. the Players in 1882 and 1885 he did not play any first-class county cricket.

An exceptionally strong Eton team in **1877** containing three Studds, Herbert Whitfeld and the Hon. Ivo Bligh were probably denied a win when they were set 187 to win and had scored 78/1 when rain fell heavily and the match had to be abandoned. Whitfeld the Eton captain, batted exceptionally well in the match and was unbeaten in both innings with 63 not out and 19 not out. He went on to gain blues in all four years at Cambridge from 1878/81 and played 39 matches for Sussex between 1878/85 captaining them in 1883 and 1884. A most distinguished all-round athlete he represented Cambridge at athletics, soccer and in the tennis doubles with Ivo Bligh. J.E.K. Studd gained Cambridge blues from 1881/4 captaining them in 1884 succeeding his two brothers in 1882/3. In 1881 he made his highest first-class score of 154 for Cambridge v. the Gentlemen of England and performed very well v. the Australians in 1882 and 1884, also playing a few matches for Middlesex. He was largely responsible for the founding and running of the London Polytechnic and was President from 1903 till his death in 1944 at the age of 85. A leading light in the Merchant Taylors' company he was Lord Mayor of London in 1928/9 as Sir Kynaston Studd. The Hon. Ivo Bligh who made little impact for Eton in 1876 or 1877, became the 8th Earl of Darnley in 1900 and was most famous for recapturing the Ashes for England in Australia in 1882/3. He had a relatively short first-class career due to ill health but played 47 matches for Kent between 1877 and 1883. After Australia had beaten England for the first time in 1882, the Sporting Times printed a mock obituary notice lamenting the death of English cricket and adding that 'the body will be cremated and the ashes taken to Australia'. When in the following winter the Hon. Ivo Bligh took a team to Australia and reversed the result, certain ladies burned a stump, sealed the ashes in an urn and presented it to him. In his will Lord Darnley bequeathed the urn to M.C.C. on his death in 1927. The Ashes do not however change hands and are kept permanently in the Lord's Museum, a priceless relic. W.H. Patterson who opened the batting and bowling for Harrow in 1877 was to prove a most distinguished cricketer thereafter. He gained Oxford blues in 1880/1, played for Kent between 1880 and 1900 as joint captain from 1890/3, although unable to play regularly due to his profession. He afterwards became President of Kent C.C.C. and served on the M.C.C. committee, dying in 1946 at the age of 87.

P.J.T. Henery Harrow XI 1877/8, Cambridge 1882/3 & Middlesex. His seven wickets in 1878 did much to win a close match by 20 runs. He played for Middlesex from 1879/94 but his overall record was disappointing.

The **1878** match was exceedingly well contested by two equally matched sides and in the closest match since 1870 Harrow squeezed home by 20 runs. Only the matches in 1818 and 1834 had been closer. A.C. Cattley, the Eton opening bowler, had a very strange first over: 4 wides, the fifth ball of the over got a wicket as the Harrow opener W.H. Heale was caught off the back of his bat at long-stop and the seventh was hit for four. There was little to choose between the two sides in the first innings with Harrow ahead by two runs but fine contributions from P.J.T. Henery, 45, and E.M. Lawson, 66, enabled Harrow to set Eton 227 to win in the second innings. This was a formidable task in those faraway days but C.T. Studd's 56, well supported by E.K. Douglas's 53, took them very close. Henery bowled well in the match and particularly so in the second innings to finish with seven wickets. He went on to gain Cambridge blues in 1882/3 and played some 72 matches for Middlesex between 1879/94. Robert Grimston, Harrow's greatest supporter and coach who very rarely watched the match because he found the tension

All conquering Cambridge defeated MCC, Oxford and the Australians at Lord's in 1878. LEFT TO RIGHT (STANDING): *Hon. Ivo Bligh, Hon. Alfred Lyttelton, D.Q. Steel, L.K. Jarvis, A.F.J. Ford.* (SITTING): *F.W. Kingston, A.P. Lucas, Hon. Edward Lyttelton, P.H. Morton.* (FRONT): *H. Whitfeld, A.G. Steel. The Lyttelton's and Steel's were brothers in law. The XI contained 4 Etonians and 1 Harrovian in the side and was captained by Edward Lyttelton, future Head Master of Eton from 1905/16.*

A warm-up before play by W.H. Patterson, a 'natural' whose career as a solicitor allowed him little cricket until the second half of the summer. All elegance, from his necktie to his smart footwork, he went from Harrow to Oxford, and played for Kent for twenty years to 1900, excelling on wet wickets and surprising constantly with his ability to do well without practice.

unbearable, was persuaded to be present on the second day as Harrow seemed to have the game well in hand. When at last Harrow had won Grimston took off his well-known broad-brimmed hat, mopped the perspiration from his brow and exclaimed, *"Well I do think they might have spared me that hour's agony."*

G.B. Studd, Eton XI 1877/8, while not as gifted as his famous brother, C.T., played for Cambridge from 1879/82, captained them in 1882, the first year of three in which Studds captained the side, and appeared in 29 matches for Middlesex. He made 120 for Cambridge in the varsity match of 1882 and was a brilliant fielder. He, like his brother C.T., went on Bligh's triumphant Ashes tour to Australia in 1882/3 playing in all four tests but with limited success. He gave up cricket in 1886 to join his brother C.T. in China as a missionary and later went to India and America. Punch magazine gave the three Studd brothers the nickname *"The set of Studds"* and there was a banker who went one better than Punch. He had three gold studs for his evening dress shirt engraved with the initials of the three brothers. Whichever made top score on the day when all three were playing went top in the shirt that night. Undoubtedly Charlie Studd was one of the greatest all rounders of any era in the game. It was characteristic of his sincere Christian beliefs that the large sum of money left to him by his father Edward Studd when he reached twenty five, was given away to Christian causes within a few weeks in January 1887. In his own words he had invested in the Bank of Heaven. Henceforward his life was devoted to good works and teaching the gospel in China, India and Africa.

1879 was one of the wettest cricket seasons on record and the Lord's match proved to be no different. The wicket had not recovered from previous rain on the Friday and it was heavy and difficult to bat on. It duly turned out to be a very low scoring game and was finally abandoned on Saturday at five o'clock with Harrow, needing 118, on 69/4 and the game fairly evenly poised. As expected the bowlers had the edge throughout with R.C. Ramsay, the Harrow opening bowler, taking 10/63 in the match and C.T. Studd, the Eton captain and leading all rounder, bowling beautifully to take 8/46 in the unfinished match. P.J. de Paravicini, whose brother H.F. had played the previous year for Harrow, also performed well for Eton with his excellent slow bowling. The legendary C.T. Studd, Eton XI 1877/9, played for Cambridge from 1880/83 and Middlesex from 1879/84. His great years were 1882 and 1883 when he topped the first-class batting averages in 1882 and was second in 1883 and did the 'double' in both years with 131 wickets in 1883. His scores of 118 for Cambridge v. the Australians, 100 for the Gentlemen v the Players at Lord's and 114 for M.C.C. and Ground v. the Australians indicated what a magnificent cricketer he was against the top opposition of the day. He played five tests for England v. the Australians and toured with his brother on Ivo Bligh's England tour of 1882/3. He was a great public hero at the time and never was a

The three famous Studd brothers from left to right J.E.K., C.T. and G.B. Captains of Cambridge three years running 1882/4.

J.E.K., Eton XI 1876/7 Cambridge 1881/4 and Middlesex. He was not as gifted as his two brothers but still a fine cricketer. Founder of the London Polytechnic and Lord Mayor of London in 1928/9 as Sir Kynaston Studd.

C.T., Eton XI 1877/9 Cambridge 1880/3, Middlesex and England. The most talented of the six Studd brothers he topped the first-class batting averages in 1882 & was second in 1883 while still at Cambridge performing the double in both years. After gaining 5 caps for England he gave up cricket to become a missionary in China.

G.B., Eton XI 1877/8 Cambridge 1879/82 Middlesex and England. His four tests on Ivo Bligh's tour of 1882/3 were not a great success but he was a very good middle-order batsman and brilliant fielder. (Picture courtesy of Lady Studd).

P.J. de Paravicini, Eton XI 1878/81 Cambridge 1882/5 and Middlesex. An excellent cricketer but an even better footballer. He played for Cambridge and England and in two FA Cup finals for the Old Etonians. He was on the winning side against Blackburn Rovers in 1882. His less talented brother H.F. played for the Harrow XI in 1877/8 with little success.

player more missed. Ill-health forced him home from China but he went out to India in 1900 to do similar work and later to the Belgian Congo where he remained for the rest of his life despite several illnesses and considerable hardship. The Hon. Martin Hawke, later Lord Hawke, Eton XI 1878/9 and the patriarch of Yorkshire for many years, did not appear with great distinction in these two years but more than made up for it afterwards and devoted most of his life to the game. After playing for Cambridge in 1882/3 and captaining them in 1885 he played for Yorkshire for 30 years from 1881/1911 and as captain from 1883 onwards. He scored 16,749 runs in his career and played five tests for England, three in 1895 and two in 1898 v. South Africa. From the start of his presidency of Yorkshire in 1898 to his death in 1938 he virtually controlled the county's affairs. He introduced winter pay for the professionals and at the same time sacked those whom he thought were heavy drinkers (including the great Bobby Peel) and thus a bad influence. It was largely at his instigation that test selectors were introduced for home internationals and his influence was much in evidence in the modernisation of first-class cricket.

The next two years, **1880** and **1881**, belonged to Harrow and they had comfortable wins by 95 runs and 112 runs respectively, despite the remarkable bowling performance of Eton's Percy Paravicini with match figures of 12/92 and 12/99 in the two years. His total of 31 wickets against Harrow was the fourth highest in the series, only beaten by E.M. Dowson (Harrow) 1895/99 with 35 wickets, E.W. Blore (Eton) with 33 wickets 1845/47 and H.M. Aitken (Eton) with 32 wickets 1847/9. His overall tally of wickets against Harrow and Winchester combined

M.C. Kemp Harrow XI 1879/80, Oxford 1881/4 & Kent. An excellent wicketkeeper batsman who captained Oxford in 1883/4. 'Bishop' was cricket beak at Harrow for over 30 years from 1888 onwards and had a profound influence on Harrow cricket. He also excelled at rackets, soccer and athletics.

over four years was even more remarkable, 62 wickets at nine runs apiece. In later years he was to prove a hard-hitting batsman and a good outfielder for Cambridge from 1882/5 and in his 62 matches for Middlesex. In all he scored 2,699 runs in his first-class career but his bowling rather faded away. He was an even better footballer and represented the university and England. He appeared in two F.A. Cup finals for the Old Etonians and was on the winning side against Blackburn Rovers in 1882.

In both Harrow's two winning years they were indebted to the fine batting of E.M. Hadow who scored 77 for once out in 1880 and a magnificent 94 in Harrow's second innings of 1881. He was a useful player for Middlesex from 1883/93 with his hard-hitting batting, useful bowling and fielding and was also a noted rackets player. F.G.L. Lucas's high-pitched slow bowling proved effective against Eton batsmen lacking in footwork and he finished with 7/37 in the first innings of 1880. M.C. "Bishop" Kemp, the Harrow wicket-keeper batsman of 1879/80 and captain in 1880, went on to achieve great things for Oxford from 1881/4 as captain in 1883 and 1884 and Kent from 1880/95. He captained Oxford University to a famous victory over the strong Australian touring team in 1884 by 7 wickets scoring 63 not out

Society picnicking at the Eton & Harrow match on 16th July 1881.

opening the batting in the second innings to clinch the match. He also excelled at rackets, soccer and athletics. He returned to Harrow in 1888 as a master and presided over the cricket at the school for nearly 30 years. He was rightly described as "one of the patron saints and tutors of Harrow cricket, and its most agonised spectator". It is a moot point whether he or Lord Grimston were the more agonised! "Bishop" was one of four brothers who all played in the Harrow XI, C.W.M. 1874/5, H.F. 1875/6 and A.F. 1880/1. A.E. Newton, the free-hitting lower order batsman and Eton wicket-keeper of 1879/81, gained a blue for Oxford in 1885 and made his debut for Somerset in 1880 before they became a first-class county and played from 1891 to 1914 when they were first-class. Thus his county career lasted a remarkable 35 years and he went on playing club cricket till he was 81, dying in 1952 at the ripe old age of 90 in his native county.

H.W. Bainbridge Eton XI 1879/82, Cambridge 1884/6, Surrey & Warwicks. Captain of Warwickshire from 1888/1902.

Three drawn matches followed in **1882**, **1883** and **1884**, that of 1882, 1884 in Harrow's favour and 1883 in Eton's, all in one way or another affected by the weather. H.W. Bainbridge who played four years in the Eton XI from 1879/82 became a better player after school and gained blues at Cambridge from 1884/86, played for Surrey in 1883/5 and after-

Middlesex C.C.C. 1884, the last year in which I.D. 'Donny' Walker captained the side. A.J. Webbe, on his right, his fellow Harrovian captained Middlesex from 1885/98. Three Etonians were in the side Hon. A. Lyttelton, P.J. de Paravicini and J.E.K. Studd. LEFT TO RIGHT (STANDING): *G. Burton, Sir T.C. O'Brien, J.E.K. Studd, W.C. Clarke.* (SITTING): *P.J. de Paravicini, T.S. Pearson, Hon. A. Lyttelton, I.D. Walker, A.J. Webbe, J. Robertson, G.F. Vernon.*

F. Marchant Eton XI 1882/3, Cambridge 1884/7 & Kent. Scorer of 93 in the drawn match of 1883 when Harrow were forced to follow on in a rain affected match. He played for Kent from 1883/1905 as a stylish middle order batsman although his record was relatively modest.

H. T. Hewett Harrow XI 1882/3, Oxford 1886 & Somerset. Hard hitting left hand opening batsman he captained Somerset from 1891/3 when he resigned due to a dispute with the Somerset committee. He scored 201 v Yorkshire at Taunton in 1892 who had one of the strongest attacks in the game and he was a great loss to county cricket.

wards for Warwickshire from 1886 to 1902, although they only became a first-class county in 1894. He was skipper from 1888 to 1902 and after retirement he became Hon. Secretary of the county in 1903. His best season was in 1895 when he scored 1,162 runs at an average of over 34. F. Marchant who appeared for Eton in 1882/3 was a brilliant hitter especially in front of the wicket on the leg side and was a delight to watch. His 93 in the 1883 match out of 115 in 95 minutes was the feature of the Eton innings, well supported by a useful 64 from A.H. Studd, another of the brothers, and this enabled Eton to enforce the follow-on. His stylish play gained him Cambridge blues from 1884/7 and he made 226 appearances for Kent from 1883 to 1905. His 9,124 first-class runs would have been considerably more had he been able to turn out more regularly. The Hon. A.E. Parker, Eton's fast right-hand opening bowler, performed a remarkable feat in the Harrow first innings of 1883 when he took 8/37 including the last six wickets for seven runs in 18 balls. Harrow were saved as much by T. Greatorex as by the weather with his two calm knocks of 37 not out and 40 not out in the match and he averaged 57 for Harrow that year. It was said that a broken finger at Cambridge in 1884 deprived him of his blue that year. B.A.F. Grieve who opened the bowling for Harrow in 1883 and took 4/61 in Eton's only innings, toured South Africa with Major Warton's team in 1888/9 and appeared in the two Tests which were the first played on South African soil and also his earliest appearance in first class cricket. Although a member of M.C.C. for many years he never represented a first class county.

H.T. Hewett, the Harrow left-handed middle-order batsman of 1882/3, did little in the two Lord's matches but afterwards became a very hard-hitting batsman for Oxford in 1886 and Somerset from 1884/93. He captained Somerset from 1891/93 when he resigned because he felt his authority had been unjustifiably overruled by the Somerset Committee against the Australians and did not play first-class cricket for the county again. This was a great loss to the game as he was one of the most remarkable hard-hitting batsman of his day. His highest score was 201 v. Yorkshire who had one of the strongest bowling attacks of the time at Taunton in 1892 when he and L.C.H. Palairet made 346 for the first wicket together, then a record for first-class cricket and still the Somerset record partnership. This was also his best season when he scored 1,407 runs at an average of over 35. He hated the rain with a venom and this was the cause of his downfall. Hewett watched from the pavilion as rain wiped out the first day's play between Somerset and the Australians in July 1893. The second day saw more rain but the weather gradually improved and play was able to begin eventually resulting in a victory for the visitors in a low-scoring game. In truth the decision to play at all was that of the Somerset committee against the wishes of Hewett and the umpires who had deemed the conditions unplayable. So outraged was Hewett by the decision to play that he resigned the captaincy on the spot. In September 1895 Hewett was chosen to lead an England XI v. Yorkshire at the Scarborough Festival. Once again the start was delayed becasue of rain and when the reluctant Hewett finally led his men out he was subjected to abuse and derision from the crowd, a scene described by Wisden as a 'most unseemly demonstration'. This was too much for the

Highest first wicket partnership of 346 between H.T. Hewett (left) and L.C.H. Palairet for Somerset v Yorkshire at Taunton in 1892, still the record Somerset partnership.

Kent's indispensable amateur bulwark in 1887. STANDING: *Leslie Wilson, Frank Marchant Eton XI 1882/3.* SEATED: *W.H. Patterson Harrow XI 1877, Lord Harris Eton XI 1868/70, M.C. Kemp Harrow XI 1879/80.* ON GROUND: *W. Rashleigh.*

"How could I spend the best years of my life in living for the honours of this world, when thousands of souls are perishing every day?" – C.T.Studd

GENTLEMEN OF ENGLAND, 1884

Back—A. P. Lucas, Lord Harris, C. T. Studd
Centre—W. E. Roller, A. W. Ridley, Dr. W. G. Grace, E. J. Diver, A. G. Steel
Front—F. T. Welman, W. W. Read, S. Christopherson

H. Philipson Eton XI 1884/5, Oxford 1887/9, Middlesex & England. A good all round sportsman representing Oxford at soccer, rackets and tennis he played for England in five tests as a wicketkeeper batsman on two tours to Australia in 1891/2 & 1894/5.

E.M. Butler Harrow XI 1883/5 & Cambridge 1888/9. E.M. Butler's crucial 48 not out led Harrow to victory by three wickets in 1885. Later followed his father as Head Master of Harrow. G.M. Butler Harrow XI 1916/17. He followed his father as a fine all round sportsman and was president of Cambridge athletics in 1920/1.

The two Harrow Centurions of 1885 A.K. Watson 135 & E. Crawley 100 who put on 235 for the second wicket and had a large part in Harrow's success that year in a thrilling match by three wickets.

temperamental Hewett who promptly stormed off the pitch, out of the ground and indeed out of first-class cricket! For the remaining twenty six years of his life he never again lifted a bat in anger. All due to a couple of rainy days!

C.D. Buxton, who was in the Harrow XI as a middle order batsman in 1883/4, played for Cambridge from 1885/8 captaining the side in 1888 and played for Essex from 1883/91 when they were a non first-class county. He was an excellent rackets player and won the Public Schools Doubles in 1883 and 1884 going on to represent Cambridge in the rackets and tennis doubles from 1886/8 and also Amateur Rackets champion in 1888. A pavilion was erected at Harrow in his memory after his death in 1892.

Two very high quality XIs contested the **1885** match. Eleven of the twenty-two participants subsequently played first-class cricket, seven of them Etonians and Eton started the match as slight favourites. The match was won by an outstanding partnership in Harrow's first innings of 235 for the second wicket between Harrow's two centurions Arthur Watson, 135, and Eustace Crawley, 100, in reply to Eton's more than respectable score of 265. Harrow's 59-run lead was crucial and on a wearing wicket Eton were bowled out in their second innings for 151. Harrow were left with a relatively simple task of scoring 93 for victory with two hours to get them. But they had reckoned without the very fine slow bowling of E.G. Bromley-Martin who had a good match in 1884 taking 8 wickets. Bromley-Martin who had bowled 42 overs in the first innings to take 6/88 once again got to work reducing Harrow to 65/6 and then 73/7. E.M. Butler, the Harrow captain and later Head Master of Harrow following his legendary father, batted on coolly to take his side home to victory with a crucial 48 not out with only three minutes to spare. Bromley-Martin's 10 wickets in the match for 137 runs had nearly caused an upset but it had been an enthralling match and one of the most exciting till the famous 'Fowler's match' of 1910. Bromley Martin played in various trials at Oxford without playing any first-class matches and represented Worcestershire before they became a first-class county and in 1899/1900 when they did. He became Hon. Secretary to the county in the 1890s.

H.R. Bromley-Davenport Eton XI 1886/9 Cambridge 1892/3, Middlesex & England. A fine left arm fast bowler and lower order right hand batsman he appeared in four tests in South Africa during two tours from 1895/6 & 1898/9.

Six other Etonians played first-class cricket with varying degrees of distinction: Hylton Philipson, the Eton wicket-keeper batsman of 1884/5, scored 53 and 27 in 1885 and was good enough to play for England in 5 tests on two Australian tours in 1891/2 and 1894/5. He took 150 victims in his first-class career for Oxford 1887/9, Middlesex 1895/8 and England. His batting was modest but he had several notable performances in his first-class career including 150 for Oxford v. Middlesex at Chiswick Park in 1887 and he played for the Gentlemen v. the Players from 1887/92. He was a fine all-round sportsman and represented Oxford at rackets, tennis and also soccer. F. Freeman-Thomas, the Eton captain of 1885, was a Cambridge blue from 1886/9 and played for Sussex from 1886/90 and undertook two tours to India in later years. He had a most distinguished political and diplomatic career, being M.P. for Hastings and then Bodmin and Junior Lord of the Treasury from 1909 to 1912. His diplomatic career ranged from Governor-General of Bombay and Madras to Governor-General of Canada and finally from 1931 to 1936 as Viceroy of India. He was created the first Lord Willingdon in 1910.

H.W. Forster, Eton's slow left-arm bowler of 1884/5, gained Oxford blues from 1887/9 and played 5 matches for Hampshire. He had reasonable success with his bowling, taking 135 wickets at under 22 per wicket, but his batting rather went off although he was an excellent fielder. He was M.P. for Sevenoaks from 1892/1919 and then became Governor-General of Australia in 1919 when he was created the first Lord Forster of Lepe. Lord George Scott who top scored with 32 in the drawn contest of 1884 and played in 1885 for Eton was to distinguish himself later when brought in at the last minute for Oxford in the varsity match. He scored 100 and 66 v. Cambridge at Lord's in 1887 and went on to captain the side in 1889. Whilst serving in the Army during the Boer War he flew the Union Jack over Bloemfontein when the town was captured. Harrow did not let their supporters down with four future blues in their side and

C. Heseltine - another forgotten cricketer who prospered after Eton, playing 52 matches for Hampshire as a fast bowler and going on 3 overseas tours, playing 2 tests in South Africa and taking 5/38 in one of them during 1895/6. He achieved soccer blues at Cambridge in 1891/2.

two others who played representative first-class cricket, although in the case of W.A.R. Young, the Harrow slow bowler of 1883/5, it was only two matches for Somerset. His batting and bowling in the three great matches, however, were more than reasonable: 4/48 in 1883, 23 not out and 35 not out in 1884 and 7 wickets plus 11 and 15 not out in 1885. A.K. Watson, the joint Harrow hero of 1885, got his blue for Oxford in 1889 and played 15 matches for Middlesex between 1890/4 with limited success, averaging just under 15, and he later played for Suffolk and then Norfolk. E.M. Butler, the Harrow captain of 1885, gained Cambridge blues in 1888/9 and also represented the university at tennis, rackets and athletics, winning the 100 yards at the varsity sports in 1885. His results were rather modest on the cricket field however and he averaged only 18 per innings. C.H. Benton, the Harrow middle-order batsman of 1885, played 29 matches for Lancashire between 1892/1901 with limited success. He also played for Cheshire and was on the M.C.C. committee but sadly committed suicide in 1918.

Eton caused an upset in **1886** when their young, inexperienced side overcame the might of Harrow by 6 wickets for their first win in 10 years. Eustace Crawley's fine innings of 40 and 69 were unable to offset the penetrating left-arm fast bowling of H.R. Bromley-Davenport who took 9 wickets in the match. Eton's first innings was dominated by a very classy innings from C.P. Foley who scored 114 out of 202 and, although Harrow fought hard in the second innings, Eton made it with something to spare. H.J. Mordaunt, the Eton captain of 1886, gained Cambridge blues in 1888/9 scoring 127 in the varsity match of 1889, his highest first-class score. He also played a few matches for Middlesex between 1889/93 but his overall average was a little disappointing. Eustace Crawley's brilliant school-boy career rather belied his performances in the first-class game. Although gaining Cambridge blues from 1887/9 he only averaged 16 in 17 matches. He was however one of only two batsmen who have scored centuries in the Eton and Harrow match and the varsity match. He scored 103 not out for Cambridge v. Oxford in 1887 to add to his 100 in the 1885 Eton and Harrow match. It was not until 1934 that this was equalled by A.W. Allen of Eton in the varsity match for Cambridge v. Oxford. Crawley afterwards played occasional county cricket for Herts. and Worcestershire before they became first-class and was a very good tennis player. M.J. Dauglish, the Harrow captain and wicket-keeper from 1884/6, gained Oxford blues in 1889/90 and played a few matches for Middlesex. Although a splendid wicket-keeper he was rather a poor bat and averaged under 8 in his 24 first-class knocks.

F.W. Milligan, Yorkshire & England. A Yorkshire iron master's son, he didn't play for Eton but was a great success for Yorkshire between 1894/8. Two Tests v. South Africa in 1898 but killed in action on March 31st 1900 at Mafeking.

Eton had seven old choices as opposed to Harrow's three in **1887** but appearing in Harrow colours for the first time were two of the greatest cricketers Harrow have ever produced, F.S. Jackson and A.C. MacLaren, future England captains both. Harrow had an astonishing collapse in their first innings from 84/1 to 101 all out of which MacLaren, only 15, made 55. Eton were indebted to Lord Chelsea, who had been chosen at the last moment, for a brilliant hitting innings of 72 not out which turned the match and gave Eton a first innings lead of 104. Once again Harrow batted badly in the second innings with the exception of MacLaren who scored 67, hooking the short ball magnificently. Eton only needed 101 to win but without R.C. Gosling's 56 not out, a splendid knock in the circumstances of the match, Eton might well not have got home. Chelsea's family owned Prince's ground in Hans Place where Middlesex had their headquarters for a short time before they moved to Lord's on a permanent basis. Lord Chelsea played little cricket thereafter but became M.P. for Bury St. Edmunds from 1892/1900 and Private Secretary to Arthur Balfour, the Conservative Prime Minister and brother-in-law of Alfred Lyttelton, dying in 1908.

C.P. Foley, the defensive Eton opening batsman of 1886/7, gained Cambridge blues from 1889/91 and played 57 matches for Middlesex between 1893/1906 and went on Brackley's tour to the West Indies in 1904/5. His overall average of 17 in 123 first-class matches was a little disappointing. He was primarily a soldier, took part in the Jameson Raid of 1895 and later fought in both the Boer War and First World War. W.D. Llewelyn, the Eton middle-order batsman of 1886/7, played very well for his Oxford blues in 1890/1 and represented Glamorgan before they became a first-class county. He died as a result of a shooting accident at Swansea in 1893 when he was 25. Gosling, who was in the Eton XI from 1885/7, went on to gain Cambridge blues from 1888/90 but had relatively limited success with the bat. He also won his blue for soccer in 1890 and went on to play for England five times and was the donor of the Arthur Dunn Cup in memory of his old friend presented to the winners of the old boys soccer competition. As in 1886 the bowling of T.W. Brand, the Eton captain, and Bromley-Davenport had been crucial to Eton's success with 7 and 8 wickets respectively.

C.P. Foley EtonXI 1886/7, Cambridge 1889/91 & Middlesex. Defensive opening batsman who scored 114 in Eton's six wicket win of 1886. He fought in three major wars and played 57 matches for Middlesex. He wrote a chatty book of reminiscences, 'Autumn Foliage', and revealed a fascination towards the 'golden-hearted' W.G. Grace and the way he said 'Glasstershire' and dropped an occasional 'h'.

After the two Eton victories of 1886 and 1887 the tide turned back to Harrow once again in **1888**. After two low-scoring first innings totals the match was won for Harrow by the superb batting of R.B. Hoare, 108, and the magnificent all-round capabilities of Jackson, who scored 59 with Hoare in the Harrow second innings. More important was his excellent medium-fast bowling which brought him match figures of 11/68. Eton collapsed dramatically in their second innings and were all out for 52. At one time Jackson had taken five wickets for five runs, all clean bowled, before a ninth wicket partnership of 36 gave the Eton innings a semblance of respectability. Harrow's comprehensive victory by 156 runs inspired the famous Harrow song *'A Gentleman's a bowling'* by the Harrow master E.E. Bowen. Jackson's all-round performance overshadowed the fine individual bowling performance of Eton's opening bowler H.W. Studd, one of the famous Studd brothers, who took 14/99 in the match. This was the highest number of wickets in the match since proper bowling analyses were recorded in 1854 and still stands, although Charles Robins came close in 1951 with thirteen wickets. Jackson had only recently recovered from illness and was promised by his father, the well-known politician who

A.M. Miller - He didn't make the Eton XI but captained Wiltshire for 25 years and went on Hawke's Tour to South Africa in 1895/6 playing in 1 Test scoring 24 runs without being dismissed and dying in 1959 at the age of 90.

The classical batsmanship of F.S. Jackson - for Harrow, Cambridge (1890/93), Yorkshire and England - is well caught in this Chevallier Tayler picture dated 1905, Jackson's heroic year.

became Lord Allerton in 1902, a sovereign for every wicket he took and a shilling for every run. Despite his huge achievements he was always a modest man and congratulated afterwards on his performance he replied, *"I don't care so much for myself, but it'll give the guv'nor such a lift."*

Jackson brought his triumphant schoolboy career to a close captaining Harrow to a nine-wicket win in **1889**. He again played a significant part with 68 out of 272 in Harrow's first innings and five vital wickets. Eton, following on 103 behind, were only just bowled out in time in their second innings and Harrow got the 50 runs they needed with 15 minutes to spare. Strangely Archie MacLaren was unsuccessful again and was bowled out four times by Studd in 1888 and 1889 for low scores, the last time as Studd wrenched his knee and did not bowl in the match again. Studd played in the Freshmen's match of 1890 but played no first-class cricket at Cambridge although he played a few matches for Hampshire in 1898. His bowling rather went off but he became a more than competent middle-order batsman and averaged over 27 in his limited first-class cricket due to his successful army career where he became a Brigadier-General. Bromley-Davenport, who played four years in the Eton XI from 1886/9, was more successful with his left-arm fast bowling in the first two years but thereafter he relied more on his batting. He achieved Cambridge blues in 1892/3 and played 28 times for Middlesex between 1896 and 1898. He had two successful tours to the West Indies in 1894/5 and 1896/7 when he topped the bowling averages both times. He played in four test matches on Lord Hawke's Tours of South Africa in 1895/6 and 1898/9 when his batting was more successful than his bowling. His 187 first-class wickets were gained at the very good average of under 18 and he was one of the few players at this time who played cricket in glasses. H. R. Bromley-Davenport who took 17 wickets in his two matches for Eton in 1886/7 was extremely highly rated by both MacLaren and Jackson and according to Jackson the best boy bowler ever seen at Lord's, high praise indeed from the future England captain.

Jackson showed his true greatness as a cricketer in his 20 home tests v. Australia when he scored 1,415 runs at an average of 49, phenomenal for the times and even exceeding the greatest cricketer of the time W.G. Grace, who had scored 1,098 runs in 22 tests at an average of 32. He never played for England overseas and only had two full seasons of county cricket – in 1898 when he made 1,566 runs and took 104 wickets and in 1899 when he made 1,847 runs. His annus mirabilis was undoubtedly 1905 when he captained England v. Australia and dominated the series with scores of 82 not out, 144 not out, 113 and 76 averaging over 70 and also took 13 wickets at 15 apiece. He played for Cambridge from 1890/3 captaining them in 1892/3, Yorkshire from 1890/1907 and was highly influential in the administration of the game until his death in 1947. He was Tory M.P. for the Howdenshire Division of Yorkshire from 1915 to 1926, Financial Secretary to the War Office in 1922 and Chairman of the Unionist Party in 1923 and later Governor of Bengal. He truly represented the golden age of cricket in the Victorian/Edwardian era.

The **1890** match was dominated by the weather and a magnificent innings under very difficult conditions by Archie MacLaren, the Harrow captain. There was no play on the first day and Eton after being 59/1 collapsed to 108 all out as the wicket became more difficult. MacLaren's 76 out of 133 in Harrow's innings showed his extraordinary capacity to play an attacking innings under the most difficult circumstances and was a foretaste of greatness to come. The wicket then eased and Eton played out time in their second innings to finish on 120/3. Eton had a poor XI in 1890, and there was only one member of the previous year's XI left, G. B. Gosling, and he was ill for the whole of the summer term and never came back. Lewin Cadogan was the first of the Upper Club choices but was considered unsuitable by Mitchell

F.S Jackson (later the Rt. Hon. Sir Stanley Jackson) Harrow XI 1887/9, Cambridge 1890/3, Yorkshire & England. One of the most brilliant all round cricketers of his generation. He was particularly successful in his 20 Tests v. Australia and averaged 49 although he never toured there because of business commitments.

A.C. MacLaren, Harrow XI 1887/90, Lancashire and England. He and Jackson were the finest batsmen Harrow has ever produced. He played in 35 tests for England and batted brilliantly on his three tours of Australia. The holder of the top score in English first-class cricket with 424 in 1895 until Brian Lara broke his record with 501 in 1994.

("Mike"), the master in charge of cricket, and so a sixteen-year-old R.C.Norman was chosen as captain who was by his own admission a moderate cricketer. He was captain again in 1891 but even more unlucky than in the two rained-off fixtures of 1890 against Winchester and Harrow in that he collided with the Winchester captain and was seriously ill at Lord's, and unable to bat in the second innings during Eton's heavy defeat by seven wickets. He was the last Etonian to wear brown boots at Lord's or elsewhere when playing for the XI and apparently never had

Defiant, imperious, aware of both his appearance and his importance, Archie MacLaren, captain of Lancashire and England, gives the photographer a view of himself similar to that 'enjoyed' by bowlers. He was fit enough at 51 to score a double-century during a tour of New Zealand in 1922/3.

a white pair. He could have stayed on in 1892 to captain the XI for the third year running as he was only seventeen, but decided his time had passed. He became a director of Martin's Bank and Chairman of L.C.C. in 1918/19. MacLaren of course was to become one of the dominant personalities of the game for many years to come. He made 108 for Lancashire v. Sussex at Hove on his debut for them in August of that year, an astonishing feat for a schoolboy. He played for his native county from 1890/1914, twelve of these years as captain, and in 35 tests for England between 1894/5 and 1909. His greatest performances were his 424 v. Somerset at Taunton in 1894, a county record until Brian Lara broke it in 1994 with his 501 for Warwickshire v. Durham, and his three magnificent tours of Australia when he made 2,696 runs, at an average of over 50 including twelve centuries, seven of them at Sydney. He captained the 1897/8 and 1901/2 sides to Australia

and was hailed by the Australian public as one of the greatest batsman ever seen. He was a superb tactical expert but, unlike his great Yorkshire contemporary Jackson, was rather an autocratic captain who did not tolerate lightly others less talented than himself and he was criticised for some of the selections of the England teams. He silenced his critics, however, in 1921 when he raised and captained an amateur side that defeated Warwick Armstrong's previously invincible Australian side by 28 runs at Eastbourne in August of that year. He was never such a prolific scorer in England as he was in Australia due to the climate in England which aggravated his lumbago. He took a team to Australia and New Zealand in 1922/3 where he was still scoring runs and taking catches in the slips. This was to be his swan song.

The Taunton ground during Somerset's match against Lancashire in July, 1895. The visitors made 801, Archie MacLaren scoring 424, and won by an innings and 452 runs. The impact of MacLaren's innings, which lasted almost eight hours, was enormous. The public had not become accustomed to huge individual scores, as they were to become during the twentieth century, when Ponsford, Bradman, Hammond and others reached the heady heights of 300, even 400, with some regularity. MacLaren, aged only 23, scored one six, 62 fours, 11 threes, 37 twos, and 63 singles, and added 141 for the first wicket with Albert Ward (64) and 363 for the second with A.G. Paul (177), and the first-class record he beat was W.G. Grace's 344, made in 1876.

Jackson and MacLaren had set the tone for Harrow and they again triumphed over a modest Eton side in **1891** by 7 wickets. The Eton opener, G.R. Brewis, batted well in both innings to score 70 and 41 but a first innings lead of 116 was too much for Eton to overcome, especially as their captain, R.C. Norman, was unable to bat in the second innings due to concussion received in the Winchester match the week before. It was a relatively simple task to knock off the 71 needed for victory with the loss of three wickets. C.G. Pope, the Harrow opening bowler, took 7/64 in the match and also scored 44 and 12 not out. He gained a Cambridge blue in 1894 for his bowling and afterwards played for Bedfordshire from 1892 to 1901. He returned to teach at Harrow and became House

Master of the The Grove. This was the first year that the Eton XI followed the example of their opponents by appearing in white boots.

Harrow again got the better of a strong Eton batting side, including five future blues, in **1892**, although Harrow had the better of the wicket. A first innings lead of 70 proved decisive as Harrow were bowled out for 116 in the second innings. Eton set to score 187 runs to win succumbed to the pace of C.S. Rome and C.J.L. Rudd and lost by 64 runs. Rudd nearly did not play as he had an injured hand which severely handicapped him but his seven wickets in the match vindicated his selection. The match had started sensationally with D.H. Forbes, the Eton captain, bowling the first two Harrow batsmen with the first two balls of the match. His 60 not out in the Eton second innings out of 122 failed to save the day and none of his team were able to stay with him. His fine fast bowling gained him an Oxford blue in 1894 and in his twelve first-class matches he took 44 wickets including 6/100 for Oxford Past and Present v. the Australians in 1899 at Portsmouth. Harold Arkwright, the Eton opening bowler, had the reputation of bowling the odd unplayable ball and he duly gained an Oxford blue in 1895, taking a more than useful 71 wickets in his 23 appearances. R.A. Studd, the Eton opening bat from 1890/2 and the last of the six Studd brothers to play for Eton, had little success in his three Lord's matches but gained a blue for Cambridge in 1895 and averaged 27 in his 14 first-class matches. B. N. Bosworth Smith, son of a Harrow House Master, who made top score of 31 in Harrow's second innings of 1892, wrote of Harrow's teachers of the game at this time.

C.C. Pilkington, Eton XI 1892/5 Oxford 1896. He was regarded as an extremely gifted all rounder but played very little first class cricket. The opening attack of Pilkington and Cunliffe in 1895 was regarded by the experts as the finest yet seen at Eton and they took over 100 wickets in the season despite Pilkington missing several fixtures.

> *"In those days at Harrow professional coaching and bowling were unknown and not really needed for every day of the summer term. The great I. D. Walker was present at nets or watching the game, to play his lobs was a cricket education in itself. I. D's devotion was ably backed up by a host of other famous Harrow cricketers. M. C. Kemp as a master, A. J. Webbe as often as County Matches allowed and dear old Lord Bessborough still came down. Under such guidance it was easy to learn the spirit in which the game should be played and in both my years the XI were successful at Lord's".*

It was accepted wisdom that Eton had a much stronger side than Harrow in **1893** and would have beaten them on any type of wicket: a sound batting side with no tail, a strong bowling attack in depth and a good fielding side. F.H.E. Cunliffe was a very good left-arm medium-pace bowler, C.C. Pilkington right-handed with good length and direction who could move the ball both ways; P.W. Cobbold was a steady leg-break bowler; and H.R.E. Harrison was quick with a fine slinging action. This was all too much for Harrow and they succumbed in both innings without much of a fight. Harrison was the leading wicket-taker with 9/55 in the match off 27 overs as Harrow went down by 9 wickets. Cobbold earned a Cambridge blue in 1896 with his accurate leg-break bowling and played for Suffolk from 1902, captaining the county for some years and also representing Cambridge at rackets and tennis.

Notes at the match of 1894. The whole of the first day was lost to rain and Eton having bowled out Harrow for 129 and 80 would undoubtedly have won if time had allowed. Two very fine Eton opening bowlers in Cunliffe and Pilkington were the difference between the two sides.

The result would probably have been the same in **1894** had the weather not wiped out the whole of the first day's play. Eton arguably had a better side than in 1893 and both Cunliffe, with his left-arm medium-pace and Pilkington had improved markedly from 12 months before. Harrow won the toss and batted very slowly on the second day in quagmire conditions with Cunliffe bowling off just three paces instead of his usual long approach. Towards the end of the Harrow innings the ball began to bite and Cunliffe finished with 7/54 in 33.2 overs. Eton fared no better and but for Pilkington's 33 and Cunliffe's 32, would have been in even worse trouble. There was just time to bowl Harrow out a second time for 80 just before 7 o'clock with the two Eton heroes once again to the fore, Cunliffe taking 6/40 and Pilkington 4/19 in 19 overs. Cunliffe's remarkable match figures of 13/94 were the second equal highest number of wickets in the match since proper bowling analyses were recorded. He played for Oxford from 1895/8, captaining them in 1898 and appeared for Middlesex between 1897 and 1903. Cunliffe's bowling was most effective in first-class cricket and he took 235 wickets in his 56 first-class matches at an average of 21.78 per wicket with a best of 8/26. He was a distinguished military historian and became a Fellow of All Souls, Oxford, before being killed in the Great War in 1916 after inheriting the family baronetcy. G.E. Bromley-Martin, the Eton captain of 1893/4, gained Oxford blues in 1897/8 and played for Worcestershire between 1899/1904. He averaged 22 in his 48 first-class matches including two centuries. Cunliffe took 60 wickets in school matches during 1894 at 9 per wicket and Pilkington who missed several matches through injury also took 40 wickets at not much more.

A remarkable match in **1895** resulted in Harrow just saving the day when they finished on 75/9 needing 218 to win in their second innings. H.B. Chinnery, the Eton opening batsman, scored 75 and 64 enabling Eton to gain the batting advantage, although they were 66 behind on the first innings. J.H. Stogdon's splendid innings of 124 was the feature of the Harrow first innings, well supported by A.S. Crawley's 78. There was some fine bowling from E.M. Dowson in the first of his five appearances at Lord's with his left-arm slow bowling and he finished with eight wickets in the match. Pilkington once again bowled well for Eton and finished with eight wickets in the match. This was the last year that the Harrow XI wore stiff-fronted shirts, fastened at the chest with the XI button in the form of links and starched cuffs (see team photograph).

Pilkington was regarded as a most gifted all-rounder and played two matches for his native Lancashire in 1895 with some success. He went on to gain an Oxford blue in 1896 but appeared very rarely in first-class cricket. He averaged 25 in his 13 first-class appearances but did little with his bowling. H.B. Chinnery, the stylish Eton opening bat of 1894/5, played for both Surrey and Middlesex between 1897/1904 but was unable to make the Oxford side. He averaged 25 in his 66 first-class appearances, including four centuries, carried on playing after he retired from first-class cricket till 1914 and was killed in the Great War in 1916. Stogdon never achieved as much in first-class cricket as his promise as a schoolboy had indicated, probably because his defence at the higher level was not quite good enough and there was a certain stiffness in his play caused by a broken left arm. He gained blues at Cambridge from 1897/9 and played a few matches for Middlesex between 1899/1907 but his results were rather modest.

B.J.T Bosanquet (Eton, Oxford University, Middlesex and England) in Oxford cricket gear. The 1904 South Africans were soon sick of the sight of Bosanquet. He took nine wickets in an innings against them for MCC, then hit a century for Middlesex a few weeks later.

Eton's daunting total in **1896** was dominated by their two finest batsmen in contrasting styles. H.C. Pilkington played with natural grace and charm for his 101 and B.J.T. Bosanquet in his slightly uncouth style hit immensely hard for his 120. H.J. Wyld's 81 saved Harrow from total disaster against the wiles of F.H. Mitchell's lobs but they still followed on 168 behind. Some fine off driving from the rackets player W.F.A. Rattigan, the father of the famous playwright Terence Rattigan who played for Harrow in 1929, with 72 saved Harrow from an innings defeat and they finished 87 runs ahead with 2 wickets standing. Bosanquet was originally a fast bowler at Eton and most of the time he was in the Oxford side from 1898/1900 but he will always be remembered as the inventor of the googly still often called 'the Bosie' in Australia. He initially developed this on the billiard table and tried it first at Lord's in 1900. For a few years he had much success with it despite its inaccuracy from time to time and he went on to play 7 tests for England between 1903 and 1905. His two match-winning performances with the ball were in 1904 in Sydney when he took 6/51 and 8/107 at Trent Bridge in 1905. After 1905 he abandoned regular first-class cricket having just scored two hundreds in a match for the second time, 103 and 100 not out v. Sussex at Lord's, as well as taking 11 wickets in the match. This followed his 136 and 139 v. Leicestershire at Lord's in 1900. His career as an effective bowler ceased after 1905 but he was to play irregularly for Middlesex until 1919 as an attacking batsman on both sides of the wicket, effectively what he had always been and usually producing his best form despite lack of first-class practice. He had a marvellous season in 1908 when he headed the first-class averages with 1,081 runs at over 54 per innings. In one famous knock he hit 214 in 195 minutes for the Rest of England v. the Champion County at the Oval. He topped 1,000 runs in a season six times and achieved his only double in 1904 when he took 132 wickets. He was a considerable all-round athlete, representing Oxford at athletics and billiards and was also an accomplished ice-hockey player! He was the father of the late television newsreader and personality Reginald Bosanquet. R.F. Vibart, the Harrow middle-order batsman who had played in the XI for four years, made up for his disastrous double duck in 1895 to score 42 and 35 in the match as well as taking two useful wickets.

Bernard Bosanquet, the innovator. His googly caused fun and anguish, won many a match, and attracted disciples in all countries. Though the dearth of English wrist-spinners today would doubtless have appalled 'Bosie', he would have approved of Shane Warne.

Yorkshire won nine County Championships between 1893 and 1912, establishing a narrow lead over Surrey by the First World War that was extended massively after. The 1894 team pictured are: BACK ROW – H.Turner (scorer), T. Wardall, L. Whitehead, M. J. Dodsworth (vice president), J. Mounsey, H. Draper (umpire); SEATED – J. Tunnicliffe, R. Peel, Lord Hawke (captain), Hon. F. S. Jackson, E. Wainwright; FRONT – J. T. Brown, D. Hunter, G. H. Hirst. Nine of the eleven players were professionals and the other two were of course Lord Hawke (Eton) and Hon. F. S. Jackson (Harrow).

The Eton and Harrow match in 1895. Lunch interval showing the fashions and the stands on the north side of Lord's.

An Oxford University Past & Present XI who were soundly beaten by the Australians in 1899 by 10 wickets. Three Etonians represented Oxford in this match H.C. Pilkington, D.H. Forbes who took 6/100 in Australia's first innings & F.H.E. Cunliffe seated second from left in front row. Cunliffe Eton XI 1893/4, Oxford 1895/8 & Middlesex was an excellent left arm medium pace bowler with 235 first-class wickets in 56 matches. His 13/94 for Eton in 1894 nearly took his side to victory in a severely rain affected match reduced to one day. The great C.B. Fry is second to the right in the front row.

T.G.O. Cole Harrow XI 1895/7 & Derbyshire. His great knock of 142 in 1897 gave Harrow the better of a drawn match. He was a disappointment in the first class game & averaged under 16 but went on Brackley's tour to the West Indies in 1904/5.

Harrow had the better of yet another draw in **1897** which resulted in the suggestion that the match should be played over three days instead of two. This was supported by Welldon, the Head Master of Harrow, and the M.C.C. committee but was eventually vetoed by Warre, the Head Master of Eton, on the grounds that this would interfere with academia and in any case Henley was just as important to Eton. E.M. Dowson in his third match in the XI for Harrow bowled beautifully with his left-arm spinners to take eight wickets in the match and also score 25 and 64. In the first innings particularly, he had Eton in trouble bowling his fast yorker without any discernible change of action and he achieved 6/51, all clean bowled. F.H. Mitchell, the son of the great 'Mitch', whose lob bowling had caused problems for Harrow the year before, turned to leg-breaks with great effect taking 7/64 in Harrow's first innings and 11/156 in the match. Mitchell played three matches for Oxford in 1898 without gaining a blue and represented Buckinghamshire for a few years. A notable golfer he gained blues at Oxford and played for England. As Sir Frank Mitchell he was assistant private secretary to George VI. T.G.O. Cole, the Harrow opener of 1895/7, played a very great knock in the second innings to score 142, only ten short of Emilius Bayley's 152 in 1841 well supported by Dowson's 64. He played a few matches for Cambridge, Lancashire, Derbyshire and Somerset and went on a tour of the West Indies in 1904/5 but never quite made the grade at first-class level, his average being very modest at under 16 per innings. Eton were left to get 324 in 240 minutes but were never equal to the task and finished on 208/7 with Mitchell top scoring on 48. P.R. Johnson, son of an old Cambridge blue, G.R. of 1855/7, made his one appearance in the Eton and Harrow fixture but afterwards became a most stylish opening batsman for Cambridge, where he gained a blue in 1901, and Somerset between 1901 and 1927. He made nearly 12,000 first-class runs at an average of 26 with eighteen centuries and went on several international tours, including Lord Hawke's side to Australia and New Zealand in 1902/3 and M.C.C. to New Zealand in 1906/7, without getting a test cap. His most notable innings were 164 and 131 for Somerset v. Middlesex at Taunton in 1901 and 117 v. Hampshire in 1908, considered to be one of the finest knocks of the year.

Neither team was considered to be very strong in **1898** but both sides had two outstanding players in H.C. Pilkington, the Eton captain, and E.M. Dowson, the Harrow captain. Harrow won the toss and batted first; this proved crucial as the wicket started to wear as time went on. Harrow's significant total of 386 was based round W.S. Medlicott's 87,

F.H. Mitchell, Eton XI 1896/7. Highly successful with his lob and leg break bowling in his two appearances at Lord's. A fine golfer, he played for England and was Assistant Private Secretary to George VI as Sir Frank Mitchell. The youngest of 'Mitch's' 3 sons, all Eton XI cricketers.

P.R. Johnson Eton XI 1897, Cambridge 1901 & Somerset. A stylish opening right hand batsman he had a long career with Somerset playing from 1901/27, went on several overseas tours without gaining a test cap and scored nearly 12,000 runs.

Eton v. Harrow in the 1890s. "A Close Run" by Francis Barraud

Smart fielding and backing up by Eton with the old pavilion in the background.

The highly successful Oxford XI of 1900 which was unbeaten and won five of their nine first class matches. It contained three Etonians, H.C. Pilkington far right back row, B.J.T. Bosanquet far right seated and C.H.B. Marsham right on the ground. H.C. Pilkington Eton XI 1896/8 & Oxford 1899/1900. Scored 101 in the drawn match of 1896. The brother of C.C. and likewise regarded as a very stylish middle order batsman at Oxford.

well supported by Rattigan, 69, A.S. Drew, 59, and the captain, 47. Eton were once again put on the rack by Dowson's accurate slow bowling and Eton followed on 163 behind with Dowson taking 6/54. Eton fought hard to save the day and might have done so with a little more luck. Pilkington, aided by some useful supporting knocks took Eton to 215 in their second innings and Harrow knocked off the 53 runs for victory with 14 minutes to spare and 9 wickets in hand. Rattigan repeated his success of 1896 with 69 and 18 not out and Dowson finished with 9 wickets in the match. W.S. Medlicott, Harrow's steady middle-order batsman of 1897, played for Oxford in 1901/2, gaining a blue in 1902 with satisfactory performances and afterwards played for Wiltshire. The Harrow wicket-keeper of 1896/8, W.P. Robertson, who had played very well in 1897, went on to prove a most reliable wicket-keeper batsman for Cambridge, for whom he got a blue in 1901 and Middlesex whom he represented between 1900/19 in 99 matches, averaging 26 with the bat – exceptional for a wicket-keeper at this time. There was a curious phenomenon in the Eton second innings when Eton were 40/0 – Pilkington 39 not out, C.H.B. Marsham 0, no-balls 1 and Marsham was then missed off the next ball. Marsham who opened the batting in 1897/8 for Eton was the son of Rev. C.D.B. Marsham, in his time the best amateur bowler in England. His father had gained blues for Oxford from 1854/8, unusual in itself, and C.H.B. also achieved the same from 1900/02, captaining the side in 1902, and played for Kent from 1900/22, although his appearances after 1908 were limited. He was captain of the county from 1904/08 leading Kent to their first championship win in 1906. His great year for Oxford was in 1901 when he saved the game for them v. Cambridge with 100 not out after Oxford had lost seven wickets for 145 runs in attempting to

C.H.B. Marsham Eton XI 1897/8, Oxford 1900/2 and Kent.

E.M. Dowson, Harrow 1895/9, Cambridge University and Surrey. an exceptional all rounder who took 35 wickets in his five appearances at Lord's for Harrow.

W. Findlay Eton XI 1898/9, Oxford 1901/3 and Lancashire. A more than useful wicketkeeper batsman he played for Lancashire between 1902/6 including the championship winning side of 1904. Secretary of M.C.C. from 1926/36.

get 327 to win in the last innings. He played as he had never done before and in his three hour innings he scored his runs off 33 strokes including 20 fours. He was essentially an off-side player and was a most popular captain of both the University and Kent. 1898 marked the death of I.D. Walker and the Harrow flag was duly at half-mast during the match at headquarters. He had done so much for the coaching of Harrow cricket and, as well as founding Middlesex C.C.C. with his brother in 1864. Like his brother, C.C., the Eton captain H.C. Pilkington was a most gifted and stylish batsman regarded as the best Eton batsman since C.T. Studd who gained Oxford blues in 1899/1900 and played a few matches for Middlesex in 1903/4, but he was never able to play regularly which was a great loss to the first-class game.

On a typical fast Lord's wicket which Eton were probably better prepared for than Harrow due to their new wicket on Agar's Plough, the batting in **1899** on both sides was too good for the moderate bowling and Eton were unable to force a result in Harrow's second innings. There were some fine batting performances from the two Eton openers – H.K. Longman with 44 and 81 and F.O. Grenfell with 28 and 81 who were well supported by O.C.S. Gilliat with 53 and 54 not out, J. Wormald 43 and G.E. Lambert 40. E.M. Dowson, the Harrow captain for the second year running and his fifth in the XI, finished on a high note with 6/108 in Eton's first innings and 87 not out in Harrow's first innings total of 283 which just topped Eton's score of 274. In retrospect Eton did not leave themselves enough time to bowl out Harrow in their second innings and Harrow easily achieved the draw with five wickets in hand.

H.J. Wyld, the Harrow middle-order batsman from 1896/9 who had had considerable success for Harrow at Lord's, scored 24 and 57 in this match and gained blues for Oxford from 1901/3 and also played a few matches for Middlesex in 1900/1. He was only moderately successful but he had a second string to his bow as he represented the university at soccer. W. Findlay, the Eton wicket-keeper of 1898/9, gained blues for Oxford from 1901/3 captaining the side in 1903 and played 58 matches for Lancashire from 1902/6, including the championship-winning side of 1904. He was also a steady middle-order batsman averaging nearly 20 in his first-class career and taking 167 victims. He then followed a long career in the administration of the game as Secretary of Surrey from 1907/19, Assistant Secretary of M.C.C. from 1919/26 and Secretary from 1926/36 and headed the 'Findlay Commission' into the problems of County Cricket.

"Toddles" Dowson, the son of Edward who had played 54 matches for Surrey between 1860/70, took 35 wickets in his five Eton and Harrow matches, the all-time record and almost certain to remain so. Although his bowling never quite reached the peaks it once promised at the higher level he was to prove a very fine batsman for Cambridge, for whom he gained blues from 1900/03, and Surrey in 44 matches between 1900/03. He went on several overseas tours including Lord Hawke's tour to Australia and New Zealand in 1902/3 without gaining a test cap. He averaged over 29 in his first-class career and took 357 wickets at 24 per wicket. After 1903 he played very little first-class cricket but second only to Stanley Jackson he was probably the finest all-round cricketer Harrow has ever produced. He wrote a delightful account of his experience on his first match at Lord's in 1895:

"I was very young at the time of this match but acquainted with cricket from 1886, having been born in 1880, my father taking me regularly to the best matches at the Oval until I went to school in 1890 and then in the holidays. I think this gave me the opportunity of discriminating the finer points of the game earlier than most. Personally I had a few words at the Pavilion entrance on asserting I was a 'player'. Perhaps this was not to be wondered at considering I was only five foot high and in an Eton suit, the fashion of going up to Lord's in lounge suits came in later. Furthermore this was the last year the Harrow side wore stiff-fronted shirts fastened at the chest with the XI button in the form of links and starched cuffs. I then distinguished myself by giving Mr. George Robey, the famous actor, two bob for bowling to me at the nets though I had noticed his flannels looked somewhat immaculate for a ground bowler. Like a sahib he took the coin without comment thereby saving me a great deal of embarrassment, innocent though I was at that moment."

E.G. Whateley Eton XI 1900/1. His fine hat-trick failed to save Eton from a 1 wicket defeat in 1900.

He said little of his performance in the match but the scorebook shows that the boy of fifteen, very small and doubted as a player by the doormen of the Pavilion was put on first to bowl, took 8 wickets in the match and saved Harrow from defeat with stubborn defence. P. R. Johnson of the Eton XI of 1897, and afterwards of Cambridge and Somerset, wrote of the 1897 match and Dowson's bowling to him *"left-handed, slow medium with a good flight and spinning the ball; then a fast yorker without any change of action and the stumps on the ground"*.

A poignant moment from the match of 1899. Is this the start of a new romance?

G.M. Buckston Eton XI 1900, Cambridge 1903 and Derbyshire. A wicketkeeper who took over the captaincy of Derbyshire in 1921 at a time of great difficulty for the county and served them well.

Lord Dalmeny Eton XI 1900, captain of Surrey 1905/7. A fierce hitter of the ball and forthright leader.

An overall record in his five matches of 281 runs for an average of 46 and 35 wickets at 21 could "ne'er be beat" as Byron would have said in earlier times!

G. Howard-Smith who played for Eton in 1898/99 as a fast bowling all-rounder finally achieved a Cambridge blue in 1903 and later played for Staffordshire. He was more outstanding as an athlete and won the high jump against Oxford three years running from 1901/3 clearing over 6ft., a considerable feat at the time, and also represented the university in the hurdles in 1901/2 becoming President of Athletics in 1903. He was another unfortunate victim of the Great War and died of his wounds in 1916.

A breathtaking match in **1900** finished just after seven o'clock on the second day between two very strong sides with Harrow the narrow winners by 1 wicket. This was the most exciting game since the start of the series in 1805 and only bettered by 'Fowler's match' in 1910. A perfect wicket and a very hot day resulted in two high scores in the first innings. Eton's main contributors in their first innings of 294 were Lord Dalmeny, 52, G.E. Lambert, 46, and G.M. Buckston, 45. Harrow replied with 388 and fine innings came from G. Cookson, the Harrow opener, with 88, F.B. Wilson, 79, and H.S. Kaye, 60. The match looked certain to be a draw when Eton were 188/2 but two wickets fell at the same score and the fireworks started. K.M. Carlisle was then put on to bowl his slow-medium off-breaks and immediately found a rough spot. A.A. Tod, the Eton opener who had batted brilliantly for 96, was bowled by a ball which pitched on off stump and hit the top of the leg stump, shades of an earlier Shane Warne, the current great Australian leg break bowler. Carlisle eventually finished with 5/15 in just over ten overs, all bowled, as Eton's innings collapsed to 218 all out. Harrow, left 125 to win with plenty of time in hand, seemed to have the match sewn up. Cookson and E.W. Mann took the score to 34 before he was bowled by A.C. Bernard and in the next over E.G. Whately did the hat-trick finding the same spot as Carlisle had done, bowling out Mann, Kaye and Bewicke. Wickets fell at regular intervals and F.B. Wilson was run out for the second time in the match for 24. Harrow were then 104/8 and the game was very much in the balance. R.H. Crake, who had played well for his 47 in the first innings, joined Carlisle and they reached 118 before Carlisle was l.b.w. to Bernard. In came A.Buxton, a famous Harrow name at such a time of crisis with Harrow on 118/9. However Crake was the man of the moment with a four and single to level the scores. The match was very nearly a tie as Whately beat both the bat and pad of Crake, the ball going a fraction over the top of the middle stump before Crake hit the next ball for four to win the match. Crake finished on 21 not out and his 68 runs in the match had proved vital – the ovation he received was indeed deserved.

H.K. Longman, the Eton opener of 1898/1900, gained a Cambridge blue in 1901 and played for Surrey and Middlesex in 1919/20 with limited success. J. Wormald, the Eton middle-order batsman, played 22 matches for Middlesex between 1910/12 and also played for Norfolk. G.M. Buckston, the Eton wicket-keeper, gained a Cambridge blue in 1903 and played for Derbyshire but much of his first-class cricket was in 1921 when he was appointed captain of the county at a time of great problems for the club, and served them well. Lord Dalmeny played for Middlesex in 1902 and Surrey from. 1903/8, captaining them from 1905 to 1907. In 1905 Surrey were fourth in the county championship, in 1906 third and 1907 again fourth. Much credit was due to Dalmeny's forthright leadership and in a strong batting side his fierce hitting made him worth his place on his own merits. In two of his years he exceeded 1,000 runs and proved himself a good judge of form when he gave Jack Hobbs his county cap in 1905 within two weeks of making his first-class debut. He was to put this judgement to good use as a legend in the racing world which he dominated for most of his very long life until his death in 1974 at the age of 92. F.B. Wilson, the Harrow middle-order batsman, captained Cambridge in 1904 after blues in 1902/3 and averaged 27 in his 27 first-class matches. He became a well known sporting journalist, first with the *Daily Mirror* and then with *The Times* after the First World War.

Arthur Haygarth, the well known cricket statistician who had played in two winning Harrow XI's in 1842/3, produced a famous verse addressed to all Harrovian cricketers past, present and future which goes thus:

> *Ye cricketers of Harrow School, who long years since did play –*
> *Men famous in the times of yore, men famous in my day;*
> *Ye cricketers of future fame, whose star is rising fast,*
> *Remember now the laurels won by Harrow in the past.*
>
> *Near sixty years have passed away since I first struck a ball,*
> *But still the Harrow pluck and skill will all the world enthrall*
> *Let not the Bay Leaves fade: Perchance, by terrors vext,*
> *Ye make a 'duck's egg' in your first; make fifty in your next.*
>
> *In 'forty two and 'forty three, when first I played at Lord's,*
> *The critics said the School must fall before the Eton hordes:*
> *But yet we won, and won with ease, though Eton was so strong*
> *With bowlers fast and terrible with Fellows, Marcon, Yonge.*
>
> *Then fairly play; nor flinch before the best and fastest ball*
> *That e'er was hurled by Eton's sons with action to appal.*
> *And when the victory is gained - defeat may heav'n forfend!*
> *For you in calm and happiness the century shall end.*
>
> *Long live the Queen, long live the School, and long live Eton, too,*
> *Until the time when each has done the task that he can do.*
> *Victors and vanquished then shall meet together in one hall,*
> *Where there is no more struggle, no bitterness nor gall.*

Arthur Haygarth

Harrow XI 1842-43

The Gentlemen of 1901, who lost to the players by 221 runs. BACK (L-R): *W.M.Bradley, A.O.Jones, R.E.Foster, J.R.Mason.* MIDDLE: *D.L.A.Jephson, K.S.Ranjitsinhji, Gregor MacGregor, C.M.Wells (mentor of Eton cricket 1897-1919, Oxford Univ. and Middlesex), C.B.Fry.* FRONT: *G.L.Jessop, P.F.Warner.*

The 1905 Surrey XI captained by Lord Dalmeny (later Earl of Rosebery). The young Jack Hobbs is first on the left in the back row. A shrewd judge of form as he was to prove later on the turf, he awarded Hobbs his county cap two weeks after he made his first class debut!

They could pass for a school (or whatever the collective term may be) of detectives, but they are merely the amateur members of the M.C.C. team which set out to tour New Zealand at the end of the 1902 summer. FROM THE LEFT: *B.J.T.Bosanquet (Eton, Oxford, Middlesex & England), A.E.Leatham, F.L.Fane, P.R.Johnson (Eton, Cambridge and Somerset), E.M.Dowson (Harrow, Cambridge and Surrey), T.L.Taylor, J.N.Tonge, C.J.Burnup, P.F.Warner (captain).*

There were no doubts about the result in **1901** when Harrow were convincing winners by 10 wickets despite the efforts of the Eton captain E.G. Whately, who scored 45 and 40 and took 4/118, although he bowled innocuously on the second day. Eton had beaten a strong Winchester side a fortnight earlier and had expected to do better but were lacking in bowling strength as the following verse indicates, written in the *Eton College Chronicle* of 16th May 1901:

> *Captain wielder of ball and bat,*
> *Upper Club's mighty controller,*
> *If you want to knock Harrow into a cocked hat,*
> *You'll have to find Eton a bowler.*

After winning the toss Eton lost their first five wickets for 50 but respectability was restored by F.W.B. Marsham, 61, and the lower order batsmen who took the score to 239. Harrow had 100 up with only one man out and Harrow's five future blues all did well except C.H. Eyre, the 1906 Cambridge captain. R.E. Lambert, 71, C. Bewicke, 48, and R.E.H. Baily, 45, all gave the Eton bowling a fearful pasting on the Saturday morning to take Harrow to a first innings lead of 137. The surprise of the match was A. Buxton, an inconsistent leg-break bowler, who had the Eton batsman all at sea in the second innings when he found the right length and took 6/38 off 25.4 overs including four bowled. As G. W. Lyttelton tells us *'the pavilion was full of old gentlemen demonstrating with walking-sticks how leg breaks should be played.'* Eton succumbed to 140 and one ball smashed for four was enough to see Harrow home. Six of the victorious Harrow XI came from the same House Elmfield, regarded by many as the most establishment house on the Hill and the choice of the discerning. The Hon. M.R.H.M. Herbert, the best batsman on the Eton side, who made 35 in the match, played for Notts before term began, scoring 65 v. Middlesex against the formidable bowling of Albert Trott and the two Hearne brothers, Alec and J.T. He went on to play for Oxford in 1904 without gaining a blue and played 31 matches for Somerset between 1903/24 with disappointing results. E.W. Mann, the Harrow opener of 1899/1901, who made 69 in the 1901 match, gained Cambridge blues from 1903/5 and played six matches for Kent in 1902/3, achieving the more than respectable average of over 25 in his 43 first-class matches. K.M. Carlisle, the middle-order Harrow batsman of 1899/1901, who had been one of the match winners of the great 1900 match, went on to gain Oxford blues from 1903/5 and although his figures were respectable enough he played no first class cricket afterwards due to his subsequent career in the Argentine.

Harrow achieved a hat-trick in **1902**, helped by a disastrous decision to bat first on a drying wicket by the Eton captain R.G. Gregson-Ellison which did little to help their cause. Heavy overnight rain had made the wicket somewhat tricky and Eton were bowled out before lunch for a paltry 72. G. MacLaren, the third of the brothers to play for Harrow, took 3/27 and G.A. Phelips, the grandson of Sir Spencer Ponsonby-Fane and nephew of the Earl of Bessborough, two of the distinguished Harrovian founders of I.Zingari, took 4/10 off 12 overs. Harrow's reply put the advantage firmly in their court mainly due to the 'Jessopian' hitting of F.J.V. Hopley, a South African, 74, supported by G.G.M. Bennett's 52 not out. A first innings lead of

F.R.R. Brooke Harrow XI 1902, the Army & Lancashire. A hard hitting batsman and wicket-keeper, he played little county cricket because of his military career but was one of the mainstays of the Army side for many years and averaged 26 in his first class career.

169 put Harrow in the driving seat and after the two Eton openers, R.V. Buxton, 74, and K.I. Nichol, 50 – the two best batsman in the side – had put up a good fight the rest of the side rather fell apart and were finished off by M.M. Carlisle's leg-breaks, 4/10 off eight overs. Harrow only needed 60 to win which they achieved with the loss of two wickets and the Harrow captain C.H. Eyre, hit 32, his highest score in five innings at Lord's for Harrow, always a disappointment to him, though he had the consolation of appearing in three winning Harrow XIs. He gained Cambridge blues in 1904/6, captaining the side in 1906 and was sadly killed in action in 1915. F.J.V. Hopley, the Harrow all-rounder of 1901/2, gained a Cambridge blue in 1904 and was also a fine rugby footballer, representing Cambridge and later England. He was regarded as the best amateur heavyweight boxer of his day and played cricket for Western Province in 1909/10, eventually settling in Rhodesia where he died in 1951. G.A.C. Sandeman who played for Eton in 1901/2 as a left-arm swing bowler took 5/73 in the Harrow first innings in 1902. He had achieved the astonishing feat that year of taking 16/46 v. Winchester and all ten for 22 in the first innings in Eton's 4 wicket win. He could be rather inconsistent and did not achieve the success he should have done at Oxford and was killed in the Great War during 1915. F.R.R. Brooke, the hard hitting batsman and wicket-keeper of Harrow's 1902 side, played 29 matches for Lancashire in 1912/13 but because of his military career was unavailable thereafter. He was one of the mainstays of the Army side for many years averaging 26 in his 62 first-class matches and still good enough to be selected for the Army until 1929.

Eton avenged themselves decisively in **1903** for their three losses in succession when they triumphed by an innings and 154 runs, the third highest margin of victory in history. The match was lost in the first two hours of play when Harrow, having won the toss and batted, lost their first six wickets for 78 and were all out for 115. Much credit was due to the slow left-arm bowling of C.E. Hatfeild who took 12/91 in the first of his four matches for Eton at Lord's. Eton laid into Harrow's rather poor bowling attack and by the end of the first day had run up a massive total of 425 with E.N.S. Crankshaw 100, P.F.C. Williams 89, W.N. Tod 59 and K.I. Nicholl 44, all hitting hard and putting Harrow to the sword. Apart from the Harrow wicket-keeper, R.E.H. Baily, 61, and W.S. Bolton there was little resistance from Harrow on the second day. Hatfeild took 7/58 in the second innings and they subsided to 156 all out. Despite the incapacity of two of their players, Harrow had failed to do themselves justice and this was Eton's first victory since 1893. P.F.C. Williams, the attractive middle-order Eton batsman of 1902/3, went on the M.C.C. tour of New Zealand in 1906/7 but was unable to gain a place in the Oxford side. He played in 112 matches for Gloucestershire after the First World War from 1919/25 with fairly modest results but had a very successful career as a banker becoming Sir Philip Williams.

Harrow were bowled out cheaply once again in **1904** on the first morning of the match, the only serious resistance coming from W.S. Bolton who scored 64 out of the Harrow total of 109. D.C. Boles, the Eton opener, smashed the weak Harrow attack to all parts of the ground and recorded the highest number of runs in an innings, 183, beating Emilius Bayley's record of 152 which had stood since 1841. It was an innings of curious contrasts. Eton had lost three wickets for not many runs, his first twenty runs took 105 minutes, his fifty 160 minutes and then after reaching his hundred added 50 more in 35 minutes finishing with 35 off two overs and hitting 27 fours. This is still the highest score in an Eton and Harrow match and with the advent of the one day match in 1982 is unlikely to be beaten unless a Bradman or a Lara emerges from one of the two schools! Boles was well supported by W.N. Tod, 84, and H.C. Cumberbatch, 53 not out. Harrow put up a much better showing in the second innings led by the Harrow captain wicket-keeper for the second year running, R.E.H. Baily, who made 72 despite being hit in the eye whilst keeping wicket, and good supporting knocks from E.H. Crake, 55, and D.R. Brandt, 53. Once again the mainstay of the Eton attack was Hatfeild who finished with 6/71 in the match. There was no doubt which was the better side and Harrow went down by an innings and 12 runs. M.C. Bird made the first of his four appearances in this match without any great distinction but was to make up for it later in no uncertain fashion. D.C. Boles, the hero of the Eton side, would surely have made an impact in first-class cricket had he not gone into the army and served overseas. He played briefly for Devon and later became M.P. for Wells for many years. R.E.H. Baily, the Harrow wicket-keeper batsman of 1901/4 and captain in 1903/4 played five matches for Surrey from 1904/6 and gained his blue for Cambridge in 1908. He was the son of E.P. Baily, the Harrow wicket-keeper of 1869/71 who had gained blues for Cambridge in 1872 and 1874.

N.E. Haig Middlesex & England. A nephew of Lord Harris, he failed to make the Eton XI but was a permanent feature of the Middlesex side from 1912/34 as a splendid all rounder. He captained Middlesex from 1929/34 and gained 5 Test caps, the last at the age of 43.

1905 was one of the great matches of the series, ranking closely with the matches of 1900 and 1910 and certainly one of the most exciting drawn matches. In a closely fought contest between two high-quality sides containing nine future first-class cricketers there was no place for the Eton all-rounder Nigel Haig, the nephew of Lord Harris and a future Middlesex and England cricketer. The advantage went from one side to the other. Harrow batting first on a good wicket were dismissed once again by the superb bowling of Hatfeild, who took 5/45 in 23.5 overs, for 199. Eton's first innings lead of 78 seemed to put the advantage their way and

but for a remarkable innings from J. Reunert, 92, one of two South African brothers playing for Harrow, would probably have won. He was last out and Eton were left to score 216 in 210 minutes. Three disastrous run outs did not help Eton's cause and with 120 minutes to play six wickets were down for 56. Eton still needed 130 runs with two wickets left in the last 90 minutes and it seemed Harrow would triumph. Hatfeild was then dismissed and there remained 30 minutes to capture the last wicket. The Hon. P.A. Methuen and N.C. Tufnell managed to survive despite Methuen's wicket having been hit and the bails not being dislodged. Eton were 79 runs short at the close of play but they had escaped by the skin of their teeth. N. C. Tufnell wrote of the last over:

Men of the centuries - "Plum" Warner, Harry Lee, J.W. Hearne and Nigel Haig. - Middlesex 543-4 dec. v Sussex in 1920. The first four batsman all scored centuries, a unique achievement in first class cricket at that time. Lee also took 11/68 in Middlesex's overwhelming win by an innings and 130 runs in two days.

N.C.Tufnell, Eton XI 1904-06, Cambridge 1909-10 and England.

"I looked at the clock and realised that we must survive six more balls. A heavy storm was brewing, thick black clouds rolled up behind the pavilion and as Methuen bent to take the first ball a low growl of thunder sounded in the distance. The first ball was outside the off stump and Methuen ignored it. Suddenly it seemed to strike him that he would infinitely prefer me to play the rest of the over and, having hit the next ball to extra cover between two silly points he called me to run which I did somewhat reluctantly and just managed to get home. I looked around me. The Harrow field had closed in like an impenetrable wall. It was nearly 7.30 and four more balls to play. Owing to the impending storm it was becoming ever more difficult to see the ball and I had not been at that end for over 20 minutes. How, where and at what pace those balls came or passed I have no recollection whatever but somehow I managed to survive them and the match was saved."

C.V. Baker, the Harrow middle-order batsman, played 31 matches for Middlesex between 1906 and 1912 but with very limited success. The strength of the Eton team was shown by the omission of Nigel Haig as he was not only a talented cricketer but an extremely good all-round games player at tennis, rackets, squash and golf. He played for Middlesex from 1912 to 1934 captaining them from 1929 to 1934 and played in five tests. He hit 1,000 runs in a season six times with a best of 1,552 runs in 1929. He was also a very useful fast-medium bowler who achieved the double three times, took over 100 wickets in a season five times with a best of 129 wickets in 1929. Four of his five test caps were gained on the England tour to the West Indies in 1929/30 when he was 43, a remarkable achievement.

C.E. Hatfeild Eton 1903/6. Oxford University & Kent. Another of the many fine cricketers lost to the Great War.

On a very fast Lord's surface in **1906** Harrow did not make enough runs in their first innings to really test the strong Eton batting and once again did not get to grips with Hatfeild who, in the last of his four appearances at Lord's, took 5/56 in the first innings with E.H. Crake, Harrow captain for the second year running, top scoring with 68 out of Harrow's first innings 230. Eton's P.J.S. Pearson Gregory, 90, and K.L. Gibson, 77, were outstanding in their total of 365. Although Hatfeild did not bowl quite as well in the second innings, Harrow's score of 229, with only M. Falcon, 79, making a major contribution did not seem enough to test Eton in their second innings and they were left with only 96 to win. However, Harrow put up a great fight and had not D.R. Brandt dropped J.M. Naylor when Eton were 38/5 could have even lost the match. Eton eventually sneaked home by 4 wickets. Hatfeild had taken 30 wickets in his four appearances at Lord's but never really fulfilled his outstanding schoolboy promise. He got his blue as a batsman at Oxford in 1908, scoring 25 and 35 not out in Oxford's two wicket win over Cambridge, but afterwards appeared with some distinction as an all-rounder for Kent in 45 matches between 1910 and 1914, cut short by the war years at the end of which he was killed in action in 1918 like so many others of his generation. N.C. Tufnell, the Eton wicket-keeper of 1904/6, gained Cambridge blues in 1909/10 and went on the M.C.C. tour to New Zealand 1906/7 and South Africa 1909/10, where he gained his only test cap. He was a very fine wicket-keeper taking 99 catches and stumpings in his brief first class career but a modest bat. Pearson-Gregory, the hero of 1906 for Eton with 90 and 45, was the son of T.S. Pearson who had played 66 matches for Middlesex between 1878/85 and had also represented Oxford at rackets and real tennis.

Lord's Pavilion.
80° in the shade.
1905

Lord's Pavilion, July, 1905, 85 degrees in the shade. A sketch given to Philip Norman by A.C.James. Four Eton Ramblers watching the match in the intense heat (l-r) J.C.Heathcote, Eton X1 1859 with whiskers of the Dundreary type, only more so. Lord Cobham (Hon. C.G.Lyttelton Eton XI 1858-60 Cambridge University 1861/4) though retaining his topper had otherwise unclothed himself as far as decency would allow, E.C.Austen-Leigh Eton X1 1857 and a most distinguished Lower Master at Eton had discarded not only his hat but the hair on top of his head and sought comfort with the help of a big cigar, the fourth unknown.

Golden days at Lord's as Edwardian society turns out in splendour in 1905.
"The schools' match ended in a draw," Wisden recorded, "but even if a definite result had been arrived at, the finish could not have been more exciting, Eton just avoided defeat after it had seemed any odds they would be beaten." Their last pair, N.C.Tufnell and Hon.P.A.Methuen, held out for 33 minutes in fading light to deny Harrow victory.

Morice Bird in a very chivalrous tribute to Pearson Gregory's 90 wrote:-

"Pearson Gregory was the Eton hero and I only wish he had made his century. He was a great player and would confirm what I am now writing. When he had scored 90 he said to me 'Let me get a hundred Morice'. I said, 'When you get 96 I will bowl you a full toss to leg'. I tried my hardest not to let him make 96 and bowled him four yorkers running, the fourth got underneath the bat and bowled him."

Pearson-Gregory played in the Freshman's and Senior's match at Oxford without getting in the side, whilst in his three matches for Nottinghamshire averaged 60 with a highest score of 71 and was unlucky not to play more. D.R. Brandt, the Harrow wicket-keeper of 1905/6 and opening batsman, got an Oxford blue in 1907 but was unable to retain his place when his batting declined somewhat.

The Eton and Harrow match of 1906 which was eventually won by Eton after a late scare by four wickets.

1907 will always be known as M.C. Bird's match. The captain of Harrow in his fourth appearance at Lord's performed the unique feat of a century in both innings, 100 not out and 131, as well as taking five wickets opening the bowling. Bird was very well supported by R.B. Cowley, grandson of R.J.P. Broughton the Harrow captain in 1834/35, who scored 50 and 75 and Hon. R. Anson, 73 not out in the second innings, which enabled Bird to declare on 382/8, setting Eton 314 to get in 200 minutes. Eton, to their credit, went for the runs but G.F. Earle and Bird bowled well enough to enable Harrow to win the match by 79 runs with 10 minutes to spare. It was a most fitting end to Morice Bird's Harrow career since it was their only win during his four years in the XI. Bird was the son of the old Middlesex cricketer George and played five matches for Lancashire in 1907 and 127 matches for Surrey between 1909/21, captaining them from 1911/13. He gained ten test caps on his two tours of South Africa in 1909/10 and 1913/14 and, although his record on the tours was modest, he did make his highest first-class score of 200 v. Orange Free State on the 1913/14 tour. He scored nearly 7,000 first-class runs, topping 1,000 runs in a season four times with a best of 1,404 in 1919. K.L. Gibson, the Eton wicket-keeper batsman of 1906/7, played 36 matches for Essex between 1909/12 taking 73 victims and scoring just under 1,000 runs with a top score of 75. Michael Falcon, the Harrow all-rounder of 1906/7, became a very fine cricketer who gained blues for Cambridge from 1908/11, captaining them in 1910. He played for the Gentlemen v. the Players on eight occasions and had a very good record in first-class cricket as an all-rounder, scoring 3,282 runs and taking 231 wickets. It was always said he would have played for England if he had played more regular first-class cricket but instead became one of the greatest Minor Counties cricketers of all time, representing Norfolk from 1906/46 and was captain from 1912/46 when he stepped down at the age of 58. One of his best feats was his six wickets for Archie MacLaren's England XI v. Warwick Armstrong's Australian tourists in 1921 which enabled them to beat the previously unbeaten Australians by 28 runs in the second last match of their tour at Eastbourne. He was M.P. for East Norfolk for many years. The Hon. H.G.H. Mullholland the Eton middle-order batsman and slow bowler who had scored 40 and 25 in this match, gained Cambridge blues from 1911/13, captaining them in 1913 and was due to play in the 1914 varsity match but stood down in deference to an agreement made some fifty years before. He had a most successful record in his four years at Cambridge, scoring 1,642 runs with a top score of 153 and also taking 51 wickets. He afterwards became an M.P. and Speaker of the Northern Ireland House of Commons from 1929 to 1945 as Sir Henry Mulholland.

There could be no doubt about the hero of Harrow's convincing victory by 10 wickets in **1908**. G.E.V. Crutchley batted superbly on a slow soft wicket to make 74 with beautiful wristy strokes, well supported by T.E. Lawson-Smith who finished undefeated on 79 out of Harrow's total of 210. Eton who had batted on hard wickets all year were undone in both innings by the medium-pace swing bowling and cutters of Crutchley who took 8/46 in the match and was particularly devastating in the first innings when his analysis was 4/13 off 11 overs and Eton were bowled out for 71. They fared little better in their

M.C.Bird Harrow XI 1904/7 Surrey & England. A Harrow legend and the only double centurion in the history of the match.

M. Falcon Harrow XI 1906/7 and Cambridge 1908/11. An enormously gifted all rounder he would probably have played for England if he had appeared more often in first-class cricket. One of the greatest Minor Counties cricketers, he played for Norfolk from 1906/46 captaining them from 1912 to 1946 in his 58th year! He was also MP for East Norfolk for many years.

G.E.V Crutchley, Harrow XI 1908/9 Oxford 1912 and Middlesex. He was the chief instigator of Harrow's convincing win by 10 wickets in 1908 with 74 opening the batting and match figures of 8/46. In the drawn fixture of 1909 he took 7/33 in the match. In the 1912 university match he was 99 not out overnight but was taken ill with measles and compelled to retire from the match. He played for Middlesex from 1910/30 and became President of the club.

second innings when following on and lost their first six wickets for 42 runs in 50 minutes, only W.A. Worsley, 42, Hon. A. Windsor Clive, 38, and Hon. Lionel Tennyson, 26, enabled Eton to attain a degree of respectability in reaching 152. Eton had a very strong side that year and were unlucky to have the worst of the wicket, but on the day Crutchley was a thorn in their side. The Hon. Lionel Tennyson, who played for Eton in 1907/8 as an all-rounder, was the grandson of the famous poet and became a cavalier cricketer. He played for Hampshire from 1913/35 in 247 matches, captaining them from 1919/33, and played nine tests for England, three as captain. He made 16,828 first-class runs with a top score of 217 for Hampshire v. West Indies in 1928 and hit 1,000 runs in a season seven times with a best of 1,335 runs in 1925. He was a much-loved character who inspired great devotion from his professionals and one of his greatest feats was a 139 yards hit over the pavilion at Southampton in 1920, reminiscent of another Etonian of earlier years, C.I. Thornton. He also won a very large bet with a friend in 1920 when odds were laid of 1,000-1 that he would never captain England. Brought into a depressed England side at Lord's in 1921 he attacked the Australian bowlers with such verve that the England selectors appointed him captain for the next match at Leeds where his heroic one-handed batting after an injury in the field when he scored 63 and 36 did much to restore England's pride. He went on to gain honourable draws in the last two matches of the series.

There were many legendary stories about Lord Tennyson as he now was, when he was captaining Hampshire. He was assisted in this respect by Walter Livsey who in addition to being the Hampshire wicketkeeper from 1913/1929 was also his lordship's personal manservant. Tennyson's instructions to Livsey when the latter was packing his cricket bags summed up his philosophy to the game – make sure there were sufficient bottles of champagne to celebrate victory or drown defeat. Livsey was supremely loyal to his captain and master. On one occasion when Tennyson's appeal against the light had been rejected by the umpires Livsey the next man in called out on approaching the wicket *'Where are you my lord? I can hear you but I cannot see you'*.

Tennyson liked to keep in touch with his batsman and when the umpires began objecting to his constant flow of messages to his batsmen he resorted to sending his instructions by telegram. One Hampshire batsman struggling to lay bat on ball was alarmed to see a boy in a blue uniform trotting out with a small orange envelope. The content revealed a terse inquiry as to what the recipient thought his bat was for. Tennyson's unique brand of man management showed itself on numerous occasions. One morning he found himself stranded in London after a particularly heavy night when required for a home game at Southampton. He took a taxi to Southampton and ordered the secretary of the club to pay the fare. The secretary had to go round the turnstiles and collect all the admission money to pay this off!

The Hon. L. H. (later Lord) Tennyson, a dashing captain of Hampshire between the wars.

The tour de force was the game with Warwickshire at Edgbaston in June 1922. Tennyson travelled up from Southampton in the company of a young amateur batsman Harold Day who played for Hampshire from 1922/31 with some success and was also a fine rugby player who played for Leicester and England as a wing threequarter. Adopting his usual routine Tennyson paused for refreshment at a number of inns en route with the result that the pair did not get to bed until dawn. *'Don't worry'* said Tennyson *'I'll win the toss'.* Sure enough he did and duly put the opposition in. But in reply to Warwickshire's total of 223, Hampshire were skittled out for 15 in half an hour. At the end of the first day the Warwickshire captain the Hon. F.S. Calthorpe, grandfather of Henry Blofeld, Eton XI 1955/6, Cambridge 1959 and the well known commentator was naturally in an optimistic mood after Hampshire were 186/6 in their second innings and suggested to Tennyson that as the game was bound to finish early the next day they should have a game of golf. Tennyson took exception to this and, in language that would have done credit to a barmaid, bet Calthorpe £10 (a large sum in those days) at 500-1 that Hampshire would win the match. Other bets were placed at very long odds by Tennyson and his team. The aforementioned Livsey coming in at No.10 batted out of his skin to score 110 not out, the highest score of his career in 455 knocks, adding 177 for the ninth wicket and 70 for the tenth. Hampshire's second innings total of 521 was followed by a Warwickshire collapse to 158 all out earning the visitors an unlikely 155 run victory. The Hampshire players returned South considerably richer.

In view of this cavalier attitude it was something of a surprise when Tennyson was named captain of England v. The Australians in 1921, no more so than to Tennyson himself. He certainly played a captain's innings, after injuring his left hand in the field, he went out to bat one handed with England in dire straits. Eight wickets were down and 92 runs still needed to avoid

SCORE **WARWICKSHIRE** CARD
° COUNTY °
CRICKET CLUB

Commence first day 12, other days 11.30 Lunch Interval 1.30-2.10. Stumps drawn 6.30

WARWICKSHIRE		1st Innings		2nd Innings	
1 Bates		c Shirley b Newman	3	c Mead b Kennedy	1
2 Smith		c Mead b Newman	24	c Shirley b Kennedy	41
3 Hn.F.S.G. CalthorpeCapt		c Boyes b Kennedy	70	b Newman	30
4 Quaife, W G		b Newman	1	not out	40
5 F R. Santall		c McIntyre b Boyes	84	b Newman	0
6 Rev E F Waddy		c Mead b Boyes	0	b Newman	0
7 B. W. Quaife		b Boyes	0	c & b Kennedy	7
8 Fox		b Kennedy	4	b Kennedy	0
9 Smart J.		b Newman	20	b Newman	3
10 Smart C.		c Mead b Boyes	14	c & b Boyes	15
11 Howell, H.		not out	1	c Kennedy b Newman	10
		Extras	2		10
		Total	**223**		**158**

| 1 wkt. for 3 | 2 36 | 3 44 | 4 166 | 5 177 | 6 184 | 7 184 | 8 200 | 9 219 | 10 223 |
| 1 wkt for 2 | 2 77 | 3 85 | 4 85 | 5 85 | 6 89 | 7 113 | 8 143 | 9 147 | 10 158 |

Bowling Analysis	O.	M.	R.	W	Wd.	Nb.	O.	M.	R.	W.	Wd.	Nb.
Kennedy	24	7	74	2								
Newman	12 3		70	4								
Boyes	16	5	56	4								
Shirley	3		21									

HAMPSHIRE.		1st Innings		2nd Innings	
6. Kennedy		c Smith b Calthorpe	0	b Calthorpe	7
5. Bowell		b Howell	0	c Howell b Quaife W. G.	45
2 H. V L Day		b Calthorpe	0	c Bates b Quaife W. G.	15
7 Mead		not out	6	b Howell	24
1 Hon. L. H. Tennyson		c Calthorpe b Howell	4	c Smart C. b Calthorpe	45
4 Brown		b Howell	0	b Smart C.	172
8 Newman		c Smart C. b Howell	0	c & b Quaife	12
10 W R Shirley		c Smart J. b Calthorpe	1	lbw b Fox	30
3 A. S. McIntyre		lbw b Calthorpe	0	lbw b Howell	5
9 Livsey		b Howell	0	not out	110
11 Boyes		lbw b Howell	0	b Howell	29
		Extras	4		27
		Total	**15**		**521**

Scorers-G. Austin & L. Sprankling   Umpires-A. J. Atfield & B. Brown.

| 1 wkt. for 0 | 2 0 | 3 0 | 4 5 | 5 5 | 6 9 | 7 10 | 8 10 | 9 15 | 10 15 |
| 1 wkt for 15 | 2 65 | 3 81 | 4 127 | 5 152 | 6 177 | 7 262 | 8 274 | 9 451 | 10 521 |

Bowling Analysis	O	M	R	W	Wd	Nb	O	M	R	W	Wd	Nb
Howell	45	2	7	6	-	-	53	10	156	3	-	1
Calthorpe	4	3	4	4	-	-	33	7	97	2	1	-
Quaife					-	-	49	8	154	3	-	-
Fox					-	-	7		30	1	-	-
Smart J					-	-	13	2	37	-	-	-
Santall					-	-	5		15	-	-	-
Smart C					-	-	1		5	1	-	-

A. REDMAN, Head Groundsman, Outfitter to Warwickshire County Cricket Club
Sole right of sale on ground of Cricket requisites. Good selection on view main entrance

Printed & Published by A G Barclay, 18 Clarence Avenue, Handsworth, Birmingham

"**Cadbury**" SEE THE NAME ON EVERY PIECE OF CHOCOLATE

The famous Scorecard of the Hampshire v. Warwickshire match on 14th, 15th & 16th June 1922. Arguably the greatest upset of all time in a first class county match which included two Etonians, Lionel Tennyson & W.R. Shirley on the Hampshire side.

The Hon Lionel Tennyson (later Lord Tennyson) batting one handed in the Test Match for England v Australia at Leeds in 1921.

the follow on and without Jack Hobbs with appendicitis. Wielding the bat like a tennis racket (see photograph) he battered the Australian attack for 63 in just over an hour including 10 fours and saved the follow on. In the Manchester Guardian Neville Cardus, the supreme cricket writer and journalist of the 20th Century wrote:-

"Tennyson showed us that a man can drive one handed if he gets himself quickly into the right position for driving. He rose high on his toes to the fast bowler's bumpers and played them down with a left elbow beautifully up. Tennyson returned to the pavilion at the end of his fine adventure to the wildest cheering one has heard on a cricket ground for many a long day."

Although still injured he made another 36 in the second innings and took a catch but in spite of these heroics England still lost the match by 219 runs.

G.H.G.M. 'Buns' Cartwright, who opened the Eton bowling in **1907/8** and was also a hard-hitting middle-order batsman, took eight wickets in 1907 and 5/44 in the first innings of 1908. He had extensive trials for Oxford in 1909/10, scored 523 runs and took 32 wickets in first class matches and in many years would have got a blue. He was a most formidable character and Secretary of Eton Ramblers from 1919 to 1955 and President from 1955 till his death in 1976 at the age of 87. The Hon. Rupert Anson, who had played a decisive part in Harrow's two victories at Lord's in 1907 and 1908, played 30 matches for Middlesex between 1910/14 with reasonable success.

1909 was a strange match in that all the play was confined to the first day. 37 wickets fell in 6 hours for 370 runs on a wicket which was not considered that difficult. The batting on both sides was most disappointing and it was a quirk of fate that rain on Friday night and Saturday morning prevented any further play with Harrow in a strong position, needing to take three more wickets to win with Eton 53 runs behind. R. St.L. Fowler with his off-breaks and cutters showed in ample measure what a scourge he would be to Harrow in 1910 and finished with match figures of 11/79 including 7/33 in Harrow's miserly second innings total of 76. Crutchley once again bowled beautifully to take 7/33 in the match, although his batting failed him on this occasion. He played for Oxford from 1910/12 gaining his blue in 1912 and played some 54 matches for Middlesex between 1910/30 with a top score of 181. He was most unlucky in the varsity match of 1912 when he was 99 not out at the close of play on the first day. He contracted measles overnight and was unable to take any further part in the match. He was a prisoner of war in Germany for nearly four years in the First World War and afterwards became President of Middlesex C.C.C., dying in 1969. R.H. Twining, the wicket-keeper who opened the batting for Eton from 1907/9, gained blues at Oxford from 1910/13 captaining them in 1912 and played 32 matches for Middlesex between 1910/28. He was a long-time administrator of M.C.C. and Middlesex, was President of M.C.C. in 1964 and Middlesex from 1950/57, dying in 1979 at the age of 89. W.A. Worsley, the Eton batsman of 1908/9, did not play any first-class matches while he was at Oxford but was brought in to captain Yorkshire in 1928/9 which he did with some success. He played in 59 matches for the county, holding his own with the bat. A scion of a very old Yorkshire landowning family, he was the father of the current Duchess of Kent. A.H. Lang, the Harrow wicket-keeper batsman of 1906/9, gained a Cambridge blue in 1913 and played in 13 matches for Sussex between 1911/13. He took 33 victims and batted well in his 22 first-class matches. His career was cut short by the First World War and he was killed in action in January 1915.

The **1910** Eton and Harrow match was one of those cricket matches that stick in the memory forever and there has never been a more exciting turnaround in the long history of the fixture described in more depth in the match report. Fowler had shown the year before what a fine cricketer he could be and now as Eton captain he produced his finest hour. Harrow were a pretty good side, had not been beaten all year and were confident of victory but knew Fowler was the man to be feared. Harrow's total of 232 seemed only adequate, but when Eton were bowled out for 67 in the first innings and followed on 165 runs behind, Harrow seemed to have the match in their pocket. When Eton again batted poorly in the second innings apart from Fowler's 64 they were only four runs ahead with the last pair at the wicket and all seemed lost. J.N. Manners and W.G.K. Boswell, the Eton last wicket pair, in desperation then hit out at everything and put on 50 in very quick time before Boswell was bowled by Earle for 32. Harrow's target of 55 seemed a foregone conclusion but what followed turned logic on its head. Fowler then produced a spell of bowling which until this day makes him immortal in the annals of Eton cricket and the fixture itself. In the space of 35 minutes keeping a perfect line just outside the off stump and varying his pace and spin cleverly, he had Harrow in desperate trouble at 32/9 with Fowler taking eight of the wickets, five clean bowled. O.B. Graham and

R.St.L. Fowler Eton XI 1908/10, the Army and Hampshire. A legend in Eton cricket history pictured in 1921. Famous for bowling out Harrow for 45 in 1910, he took 8/23 and won the match by nine runs. He also took 11/79 in the drawn fixture of 1909. An outstanding all round cricketer his military career prevented him from appearing much in first-class cricket but he was due to take the M.C.C. team to the West Indies in 1925/6 when he became ill and died in June 1925.

Hon. R.H.L.G. Alexander held out for a while and put on 13 before Alexander was caught in the slips off A.I. Steel for 8 and Eton had won by 9 runs, surely one of the most amazing recoveries in the history of the game and never to be forgotten by those present. There is no doubt that the heavy roller on the soggy, unsunned pitch changed the whole nature of the match. The late Charles Eyre the 1902 Harrow captain and Cambridge blue of 1904/6 was once asked at what moment he began to doubt Harrow's victory and answered, *'At Fowler's very first ball in the last innings. It looked to break a yard and came off the pitch like a rattlesnake.'*

No hero of fiction or film ever swayed events with more triumphant mastery than Fowler did on this day and for many a year the almost impossible splendour of his achievement coloured Eton cricket. Throughout the next decade and beyond the general feeling of Eton XIs was that if the first five did not get runs the last five would and this confidence produced victory after victory against both Harrow and Winchester and in other matches. C.M.Wells the old Oxford and Middlesex cricketer who had taken over the running of Eton cricket from the great Mitch in 1897, instilled in Etonian cricketers an admirable toughness and spirit, with only a sprinkling of outstanding players, until he retired in 1919 to be replaced by R.A.Young the former Cambridge, Sussex and England player.

Eton was also fortunate to have two outstanding coaches during this period of unprecedented success from 1909 to 1939 when they never lost to Harrow. Mat Wright who could only be described as a moderate cricketer began a period of devoted service to Eton cricket from 1885 to 1919 in the course of which he became one of the most familiar and beloved figures at Eton particularly with his famous bat shop (see illustration). In 1920 George Hirst of Yorkshire and England fame, whose legendary all round feat in 1906 will never be beaten (see illustration) stepped easily into his shoes. Eton cricketers learnt how the game should be played in every sense and his geniality, wisdom and quiet force of character impressed all who knew him. A balanced man on all occasions whether you had been bowled first ball or scored a century, he restored your confidence with the kindliest twinkle and a few direct but never harsh words. *'How did that happen, George?'* asked the Eton captain of 1932 N.E.W. Baker in 1931 after an unexpected defeat. *'Well, sir, you bowled too long'* – a pause – *'and you bowled too bad'* No one could resent that and Baker grinned. Two weeks later he bowled superbly at Lord's against Harrow and took 9/60 in the match to lead Eton to an innings win. It was no surprise that the tide of results in Eton's favour only changed when Hirst retired at the end of the 1938 season and Harrow won for the first time in 31 years in 1939 just before the declaration of war.

Fowler was the best-known man in town at a time when 20,000 people a day came to watch the Eton and Harrow match at Lord's and the fixture was a notable social occasion as impor-

It is given to few to have their names bestowed upon a cricket match, but Robert St. Leger Fowler will be forever associated with the Eton v Harrow game of 1910. He captained Eton, who made only 67 to Harrow's 232 and were only four runs ahead even with Fowler's 64, when the ninth wicket fell in the follow-on. The Hon. J. N. Manners (killed in the war) hit 40 not out, putting on 50 for the last wicket, and Harrow needed a mere 55 to win. Fowler, bowling accurate off-breaks on a soft Lord's pitch, then took 8 for 23 in 10 overs to bring his side a sensational nine-run victory. The Army later claimed him and he played very little first-class cricket.

tant as Ascot and Wimbledon are today. A telegram sent from his home in Ireland addressed to 'Fowler's mother, London' was actually delivered to her at her hotel. Fowler henceforth became something of a legend in the cricket world and afterwards went into the Army serving in the 17th Lancers during the Great War and winning the M.C. His military career prevented him playing much first-class cricket and he mostly appeared in Army and club cricket but he was persuaded by T.O. Jameson, a fellow Irishman and serving officer who had played against him in the 1909/10 Harrow XI, to play for Hampshire in 1924. He played well enough as an all-rounder to be appointed captain of the M.C.C. tour to West Indies in 1924/5. The tour was postponed until the following winter by which time Fowler had become seriously ill and he was to die on June 13th 1925 at the age of 34, much loved by all who knew him. In his handful of first-class matches he scored 957 runs with a top score of 92 not out and took 59 wickets with a best of 7/22. It was ironic that his father, Robert, who had played one first-class match for Cambridge in 1876, did not die until one month short of his 100th birthday in 1957. His fellow officer and friend T. O. Jameson who played much army cricket with him, wrote a cricketer's epitaph:

> *'Bob Fowler! What pleasant memories his name will always bring back to those who had the fortune to play cricket with or against him, as well as to hundreds more who loved to see cricket as Bob played it! Our match of 1910 will no longer be quoted as an example of the glorious uncertainty of cricket, but will stand as an everlasting memorial to that most modest and sporting cricketer whose death was mourned by all lovers of the game'.*

His partner in the glories of the Harrow match, John Nevile Manners, eldest son of Lord and Lady Manners was killed in action in France near Villiers Cotterets on September 1914. T.O. Jameson, the Harrow middle-order batsman of 1909/10 and Fowler's great friend and fellow Irish army officer, was a very fine all-round games player who played for Hampshire when available from 1919/32 and went on several overseas tours, including M.C.C. to West Indies in 1925/6 and with Tennyson to India in 1937/8. He scored 4,675 runs in his 124 first-class matches at an average of 27 and captured 252 wickets with his leg-breaks and googlies. He was a splendid

W. Monckton, Harrow XI 1910 (later Viscount Monckton of Brenchley). A more than useful wicketkeeper batsmen he was Attorney General at the time of Edward VIII's abdication. He became President of M.C.C. in 1956, Surrey from 1950/2 and 1959 until his death in 1965.

T.O. Jameson, Harrow XI 1909/10 and Hampshire. A fine hard-hitting batsmen and leg break bowler for Hampshire between 1919/32 he went to several major overseas tours. He won the British amateur squash title twice and was Army rackets champion three times.

Hon. H.R.L.G. Alexander (later Field Marshal Earl Alexander of Tunis). Harrow XI 1910. Played in the famous Fowler's match of 1910 and went on to become an outstanding allied military commander in World War II.

rackets and squash player, winning the Army rackets singles championship three times and the British Amateur squash title twice.

G.F. Earle, who had played for Harrow from 1907/10 and was the unfortunate Harrow captain in 1910, was primarily a very fast schoolboy bowler but became more of a hard-hitting middle-order batsman in later years. He played four matches for Surrey before turning to Somerset for whom he played 152 matches from 1922/31 and went on two M.C.C. tours to India and Ceylon in 1926/7 and New Zealand and Australia in 1929/30. He scored 5,810 runs in his first class career and took 104 wickets. His most celebrated feats were a score of 59 in 15 minutes v. Gloucestershire at Taunton and 98 in 40 minutes for M.C.C. v. Taranaki on the New Zealand tour in 1929/30. A motor-cycle accident on Martineau's tour to Egypt in 1932 forced him to retire from first-class cricket.

Two other famous alumni played in the 1910 match for Harrow who afterwards distinguished themselves in their fields. Walter Monckton was a wicket-keeper batsman who was somewhat unlucky to play only one first-class match whilst at Oxford when he scored 72 runs for once out and kept wicket for a Combined Oxford and Cambridge University side in 1911. He had a most successful career as a barrister and politician and was Attorney General at the time of Edward VIII's abdication. He was President of M.C.C. in 1956 and of Surrey from 1950/2 and 1959 until his death in 1965. He attained several other political offices and was a legendary cricket after-dinner speaker. The Hon. Robert Alexander became an outstanding commander of the Allied troops in the Second World War and was ennobled as Field Marshal Earl Alexander of Tunis.

W.S.Cornwallis (later Lord Cornwallis) (1892-1982), Kent. He did not make the Eton XI for the famous Fowler's match of 1910 but at his best was fast and effective. He captained Kent from 1924-26.

W. S. Cornwallis (later Lord Cornwallis) somewhat surprisingly did not make the Eton XI in 1910 but more than made up for it by representing Kent from 1919 to 1926 after serving in the Great War. He had a good action and when fit was genuinely quick. As he had played comparatively little for some years he was somewhat injury prone and in his 3 years as Captain from 1924 to 1926 only bowled 560 overs in all. He had two splendid performances against Lancashire in 1920 and the Australians in 1921. A most distinguished man in every sense of the word he was Lord Lieutenant of the County, leader of Kent County Council, President of M.C.C., Kent C.C.C. and a notable businessman at various times in his life dying in 1982 at the age of 90.

Fowler's Match

SIR—I much enjoyed Mr Michael Melford's description of Fowler's Match (Aug. 5).

The Eton-Harrow contest at Lord's in 1910 was indeed one of the classic encounters, equal in excitement to Botham's Match. I tried to do some justice to it in my book "The Golden Age of Cricket," But one small side-light came to my notice too late, when the book was with the printers.

Harrow in their second innings were so confident of an easy win that no. 10 in the batting order decided that he could relax in one of the tents set up at the Nursery end of the ground. He was indulging in the luxury of a cream bun when a breathless colleague burst into the tent to tell him that the Harrow wickets were falling like ninepins and that he might be needed at any moment.

He raced along the ground, stuffing the cream bun into his mouth as he ran, and reached the Pavilion just in time to buckle on his pads and get to the crease to take part in a last, but forlorn, effort to save the match for Harrow.

This story was told to me by the gallant bun-loving cricketer himself — the late Field-Marshal Lord Alexander of Tunis.

PATRICK MORRAH
Brighton.

W.D. Eggar, a well-known Eton beak at the time, composed the following verse in Fowler's honour which goes as follows:

If so be your chance to call
Heads and straight away tails shall fall,
Do not make a fruitless fuss,
Do not say 'Twas ever thus'
Exercise some self-control,
Cultivate a steadfast soul.

If you're safest drop a catch
Do not say 'there goes the snatch!'.
If so be one ball in six
Beat the bat and beat the sticks,
Still proceed your best to bowl,
Still possess your patient soul.

If when now your turn is nigh,
Clouds in darkness fill the sky,
'Ere the hour of six have struck,
Say not sadly 'just our luck'
Strive to keep your wicket whole,
Set your teeth, O steadfast soul.

If they make you follow on,
Do not say 'all hope is gone'
What though sky and fortune frown,
We may slowly wear them down.
Sure 'twill mitigate the pain
Just to put them in again.

Samuel Johnson late, like you,
Found his fame, his Boswell too.
'Manners maketh man', Got wot!
Manners maketh 'forty not'
Put them in? Why, man alive,
Put them in for fifty-five!

Birds may 'scape the Fowler's snare;
Just as well no Bird is there.
Harrow's turn to scrape for runs
Less like Birds than furry ones.
Joy we all the same to feel
Foeman worthy of our Steel.

Swift reward for patient pluck;
Not to every man such luck
One who cursed remains to bless
Eton may'st thou still possess,
When still deeper waters roll,
Thy 'unconquerable soul'.

Eton went into the match of **1911** as strong favourites and their XI was generally regarded as one of the best produced for many years and they had only been beaten by a very strong M.C.C. side during the term. Harrow did not approach the match with a great deal of confidence and this seemed to be borne out on the first morning when they were bowled out before lunch for 127 with T.B. Wilson, the Harrow opener in a patient knock of 46, providing the only real resistance. A.I. Steel, the son of the great Cambridge, Lancashire and England cricketer A.G. Steel, did much of the damage and took 4/41 off 14 overs with his slow bowling. Eton nearly passed the Harrow total with only one wicket down due to a fine partnership between D.G. Wigan, 79, and G.R.R. Colman, 74, and they eventually gained a lead of 143. Harrow fared better in the second innings with good defiance once again from

The sixth (1909-10) English team to tour South Africa, pictured in their glamorous M.C.C. blazers at Durban. BACK ROW – *G.J.Thompson, W.Rhodes, F.E.Woolley, J.B.Hobbs, H.Strudwick;* SEATED – *G.H.Simpson-Hayward, Capt.E.G.Wynyard, H.D.G.Leveson Gower (captain), D.Denton, C.P.Buckenham, M.C.Bird;* FRONT – *N.C.Tufnell, F.L.Fane, C.Blythe. In spite of the handful of top-class players, England lost the series 2-3, with Faulkner achieving wonders with bat and ball for South Africa and Vogler taking 36 wickets with leg-breaks and googlies. Eton are represented by N.C. Tufnell and Harrow by M.C. Bird.*

T.B. Wilson, 45, J.H. Falcon, 46, and K.B. Morrison, 42, to reach 254. Eton were left with what seemed a relatively easy task of scoring 112 to win on a fast and true wicket. However, when Eton lost their first two wickets for nine runs there were visions of Harrow revenge for the famous match of the previous year. Eton were steadied by their captain C.W. Tufnell who played better than he had done all year, having been bowled first ball in the first innings by Morrison, and by the time he was run out for 54 the match was very nearly won. Soon afterwards W.G.K. Boswell the Eton No.9 hit the winning runs and Eton were home by 3 wickets – a most courageous recovery by Harrow but not quite enough runs to play with.

G.R.R. Colman, the Eton No.3 batsman whose 74 had done much to win the match for Eton, gained blues for Oxford in 1913/14, averaging 25 in his 23 first-class matches and afterwards played for Norfolk until 1930 when he was forced to retire because of ill health. W.G.K. Boswell, the Eton batsman and change bowler of 1910/11, gained Oxford blues in 1913/14, batted with great success averaging over 30 in his fourteen first-class matches and took 14 wickets. He died in 1916 of wounds in France during the Great War and would undoubtedly have been an asset in county cricket had he survived. K.A. Lister-Kaye, the Eton left-arm medium-pace bowler of 1910/11, played a few matches for Oxford, Yorkshire and the Europeans, taking 37 wickets in his twelve first-class matches before emigrating to South Africa. A.I. Steel who had played in the two winning Eton XIs of 1910/11, had a fine record with his slow bowling in his two years taking 42 wickets at an average of 12.7 in 1910 and 47 wickets at 14.5 in 1911. It was said that he modelled his action on that of his famous father A.G. and was improving rapidly as a batsman which he would most likely have shown to good purpose had he decided to go up to Cambridge instead of taking a business appointment in India. He played two matches for Middlesex in 1912 before he went to India and after joining the Coldstream Guards was tragically killed in the Great War during 1917.

R.T. Stanyforth, the Eton 12th man of 1911 and lower order wicket keeper batsman captained M.C.C. on the 1927/8 tour to South Africa and led England in four Tests. This was a most unusual appointment since he had never appeared in first-class county cricket as most of his cricket was for the Army. He afterwards played three matches for Yorkshire in 1928 and went on the M.C.C. Tour to the West Indies in 1929/30. He averaged just over 17 in his 61 first class matches and took 93 victims behind the stumps. His Test record was less impressive although he was an excellent captain.

Eton once again had a powerful side in **1912** and after their two victories in the previous years were confident of another. They had an exceptionally strong batting side with no tail and a fast bowler in J. Heathcoat-Amory well above schoolboy level. On a fast and true wicket Harrow proved no match for Eton in either sphere. Heathcoat-Amory bowled very well throughout the match and particularly so in the Harrow first innings of 188 when he took 5/48 off 19.3 overs. Eton batted forcefully throughout to gain a first innings lead of 152 with the Eton captain D.G. Wigan, 64, G.S. Rawstorne, 64 not out, and G.L. Davies, 59, the main contributors. Once again Harrow made a spirited comeback in the second innings with C.H.B. Blount scoring 137 supported by a plucky effort from the Harrow opener U.W. Dickinson, 59. A total of 295 in their second innings left Eton to score 144 in under 120 minutes and they swept home to victory with some ease for the loss of only four wickets, their third victory in succession. Blount, the hard-hitting, middle-order batsman of Harrow's XI from 1910/12, played 10 first-class matches for the Services from 1920/24 and the R.A.F. 1927/30, averaging a highly creditable 34 per innings. He had an outstanding career in the R.A.F. and went on to become an Air Vice Marshal. He was killed in an air crash at Hendon in 1940 at the start of the Second World War.

A disastrous collapse by Harrow in **1913** after being put in to bat by the Eton captain, Heathcoat-Amory, in the first 90 minutes of play on the first morning against the Eton pace attack of Heathcoat-Amory, F.J.L. Johnstone and G.K. Dunning left Harrow struggling to make a match of it. Eton ran up a tremendous total of 383 on a near perfect wicket led by a fine knock from Johnstone, 94, aided by the captain's 61. A first innings lead of 308 left Harrow with little chance but Geoffrey Wilson with a superb innings of 173, the second highest score in the history of the match after D.C. Boles's 183 in 1904, supported by R.K.

C.H.B. Blount (later Air Vice Marshal). Harrow XI 1910/12. Services and RAF. Scored 137 in 1912 when Eton won by six wickets. Hard-hitting middle order batsman who averaged 34 in first-class cricket, he also played for Suffolk. He was killed in an air crash in 1940.

G.Wilson, Harrow XI 1912/14 Cambridge 1919 and Yorkshire. Played in three losing Harrow sides but had the distinction of scoring 173 in 1913 – still Harrow's highest score in this match. He went on to play for Yorkshire from 1919/24, captained them from 1922/24 and toured with the M.C.C. team to Australia and New Zealand in 1922/3.

Prince Henry William Frederick Albert Duke of Gloucester (1900-1974), the current Duke of Gloucester's father, with The Earl of Chesterfield at the Eton and Harrow cricket match 1914.

Makant's 46, gained Harrow a measure of respectability and saved them from an innings defeat. After the Eton opener had been run out for 0 the Light Blues cruised to victory by 9 wickets, a fourth defeat for Harrow in successive years. G.L. Jackson, the Harrow captain and opener of 1912/13 and brother of G.R. who played in 1914, represented Oxford and Derbyshire in 1914 before being killed in the Great War in 1917. Heathcoat-Amory played a few matches for Oxford in 1914 and Devon whom he captained for seven years. His final first-class match was for the Minor Counties in 1928.

Harrow put a much better showing in **1914** in what was to be the last official contest before the Great War and if they had batted a little better in their second innings would probably have won. Harrow batted first for the twelfth year in succession and were indebted to Geoffrey Wilson, the Harrow captain with 65, and G.R. Jackson, the future Derbyshire captain, 59, in a fine fourth wicket stand for their total of 232. Johnstone once again bowled very well for Eton to take 7/66 off 26.2 overs with his fast swinging yorkers. By the end of the first day Harrow had bowled out Eton for 146, a first innings lead of 86, and looked in a good position to win.

The 16-year-old left-arm fast-medium bowler N.A. Jessopp performed admirably for Harrow in taking 4/44 off 15 overs. A Harrow collapse on the second morning of the match despite another fine innings from the Harrow captain with 58, changed the situation dramatically. R.A.C. Foster, the Eton off-spinner, was largely responsible for this, taking 4/16 off 7 overs. Eton were set to get 233 runs in 270 minutes and despite a skilful innings of 77 by C.J. Hambro the game was still wide open when Eton were 188/6. However showing great coolness under pressure, T.S.D.'A. Hankey and F. Anson took Eton home to victory with 15 minutes to spare without being parted. This was a fifth victory in succession for the Etonians. Geoffrey Wilson, the Harrow captain, gained a Cambridge blue in 1919 and played for Yorkshire in 92 matches from 1919/24, captaining them from 1922/4, and went on the M.C.C. tour to Australia and New Zealand in 1922/3. His overall career average of 16 was rather disappointing and he only scored one century in 129 first-class knocks. Guy Jackson who was in the 1914 Harrow XI was a mainstay of Derbyshire for many years. He played 260 matches for Derbyshire between 1919/36 and captained them between 1922/30. He scored 10,291 runs in his first-class career and was chosen to captain the M.C.C. team to South Africa in 1927/8 but was forced to turn it down through ill health. M.B. Burrows, the Eton batsman and fast-medium bowler, played for Oxford before and after the Great War and was a mainstay of the Army side. In his 28 first-class matches he averaged over 32 and took 85 wickets, very respectable figures by any standards, and he eventually became a Lieutenant General. G.A.I. Dury, who played in the Harrow XIs of 1913/14, was the great-grandson of T. Dury who played in the Harrow XI of 1805, the first official contest between the two schools but without any success in either match. However the family connection with Harrow has continued to the present day.

1928, Robin Buckston (2nd left at back) on his debut for Derbyshire. G.R. Jackson, Harrow XI 1914 captained Derbyshire from 1922 to 1930. Two other Eton cricketers are in the front row, the two Hill-Wood brothers, both Oxford blues. Denis Hill-Wood did not get in the Eton XI but was an outstanding footballer and later chairman of Arsenal F.C. Charlie Hill-Wood is on the right of Jackson.

Guy Butler Harrow captain in 1917 but better known as an Olympic runner talking to competitors at White City on 3rd April 1934. He was both son and grandson of two famous Harrow Head Masters.

2d. Lord's MCC Ground.

OXFORD v. CAMBRIDGE.

MONDAY, TUESDAY & WEDNESDAY, JULY 4, 5, 6, 1921.

CAMBRIDGE.

	First Innings.		Second Innings.
1 J. L. Bryan	c and b Stevens	62	
2 C. A. F. Fiddian-Green	c Lowndes, b Stevens	17	
3 G. Ashton ....(Capt)	c Bettington, b Price	12	
4 H. Ashton	c Bickmore, b Price	118	
5 A. P. F. Chapman	c Bettington, b Jardine	45	
6 C. T. Ashton	b Bettington	48	
7 M. D. Lyon	st Neser, b Bettington	9	
8 A. G. Doggart	b Jardine	45	
9 C. H. Gibson	not out	43	
10 R. G. Evans	not out	0	
11 C. S. Marriott	Innings closed.		
	B 9, l-b 2, w 1, n-b 4, 16		B , l-b , w , n-b ,
	Total	415	Total

FALL OF THE WICKETS.

1-44	2-68	3-113	4-188	5-287	6-299	7-321	8-405	9-	10-
1-	2-	3-	4-	5-	6-	7-	8-	9-	10-

ANALYSIS OF BOWLING.

Name.	1st Innings.						2nd Innings.					
	O.	M.	R.	W.	Wd.	N-b.	O.	M.	R.	W.	Wd.	N-b
Price	30	3	107	2	1	1	...	...	...	...	...	...
Robertson-Glasgow	27	6	75	0		3	...	...	...	...	...	...
Lowndes	8	2	25	0			...	...	...	...	...	...
Stevens	20	3	75	2			..	...	...	...	...	...
Bettington	31	6	90	2			...	...	...	...	...	...
Jardine	10	3	27	2			...	...	...	...	...	...

OXFORD

	First Innings.		Second Innings.	
1 D. R. Jardine	c Chapman, b Gibson	5	l b w, b Evans	18
2 A. F. Bickmore	b Gibson	6	b Doggart	57
3 R. L. Holdsworth	c F.-Green, b Marriott	45	c Lyon, b Gibson	9
4 W. G. Lowndes	c Lyon, b Evans	4	c Chapman, b Bryan	3
5 H. P. Ward	c Doggart, b Evans	29	c F.-Green, b C. Ashton	39
6 L. P. Hedges	c G. Ashton, b Gibson	36	l b w, b Bryan	26
7 G. T. S. Stevens	b Marriott	0	c Evans, b Gibson	21
8 R. H. Bettington	b Marriott	8	c Lyon, b Gibson	31
9 V. H. Neser	c Evans, b Marriott	2	c E.-Green, b Marriott	10
10 V. R. Price ......(Capt)	b Marriott	12	l b w, b Marriott	8
11 R. C. Robertson-Glasgow	not out	0	not out	1
	B 9, l-b 6, w , n-b , 15		B 1, l-b 4, w , n-b 1, 6	
	Total	162	Total	229

FALL OF THE WICKETS.

1-6	2-25	3-30	4-74	5-125	6-125	7-141	8-143	9-155	10-162
1-64	2-78	3-82	4-108	5-141	6-156	7-201	8-206	9-228	10-229

ANALYSIS OF BOWLING.

Name.	1st Innings.						2nd Innings.					
	O.	M.	R.	W.	Wd.	N-b.	O.	M.	R.	W.	Wd.	N-b
Gibson	21	7	44	3	...	...	25	14	43	3	...	1
Evans	7	0	35	2	...	...	15	4	42	1	...	...
Marriott	26.4	7	44	5	...	...	29.4	8	67	2	...	...
Chapman	5	1	10	0	...	...	6	0	23	0	...	...
Doggart	6	2	14	0	...	...	5	0	22	1	...	...
Bryan	...	...	...	...	...	...	3	0	18	2	...	...
C. Ashton	...	...	...	...	...	...	3	0	8	1	...	...

Umpires—Moss and West.   Scorers—W. H. Slatter and Wainwright.

The figures on the Scoring Board show the Batsmen in.

Play commences at 11.30 each day.

Luncheon at 1.30.   Stumps drawn at 6.30 p.m.

TEA INTERVAL—There will probably be a Tea Interval not later than 5 o'clock but it will depend on the state of the game.

The Oxford and Cambridge XIs of 1921. Cambridge won convincingly by an innings and 24 runs. C.H. Gibson had an impressive match with 6/87 and 43 not out, W.G. Lowndes of Oxford with 4 and 3 not so impressive. TOP CAMBRIDGE, TOP ROW, LEFT TO RIGHT: *A.G. Doggart, M.D. Lyon, C.A.F. Fiddian-Green, J.L. Bryan.* MIDDLE ROW: *C.S Marriott, H.Ashton, C.H. Gibson, A.P.F. Chapman.* BOTTOM ROW: *C.T. Ashton, R.G. Evans.* Bottom. OXFORD, LEFT TO RIGHT TOP ROW: *A.F. Bickmore, H.P. Ward, R.C. Robertson-Glasgow, W.G. Lowndes.* MIDDLE ROW: *J.T.S. Stevens, R.L. Holdsworth, V.R. Price, R.H. Bettington, D.R. Jardine.* BOTTOM ROW: *V.H. Neser, L.P. Hedger.*

THE GREAT WAR YEARS

1914-1918

The onset of the Great War resulted in no match being played in **1915**, but throughout the War Years a series of home and away matches were played between **1916** and **1918**. Eton had the better of the first five contests and it was only in the sixth and last encounter on Agar's Plough that Harrow sneaked home in a very low-scoring game by 7 runs. Harrow were indebted to E.G. Hoyer-Millar who opened the batting and scored 46 out of the Harrow total of 98 on a very heavy ground. None of these contests counted in the official series but several very fine cricketers emerged during these years for Eton such as W.G.L.F. Lowndes who played in 1916, C.H. Gibson from 1916/19, twice as captain, and B.S. Hill-Wood from 1916/18. Lowndes gained an Oxford blue in 1921 after scoring 216 for the University v. Leveson-Gower's XI at Eastbourne. He played for Hampshire between 1924/35, captaining them during 1930/34 when Tennyson was unavailable. He scored 140 for Hampshire in a fourth wicket stand of 280 with Philip Mead against the powerful Australian touring side including Bradman in 1934. This was a record fourth wicket stand against the Australians until recently. B.S. Hill-Wood, the Eton fast medium bowler of 1916 and 1918, did not appear in any first-class matches whilst he was at Cambridge but played for Derbyshire between 1919/25 with modest results although he was a useful lower-order batsman.

ETON DOMINATION

1919-1939

The cessation of hostilities brought no respite for Harrow in **1919** and they were annihilated in different styles by the magnificent fast bowling of Eton captain Clem Gibson and the slow right-arm bowling of W.W. Hill-Wood who bowled Harrow out for 76 and 41 to win the match by 202 runs. There was no doubt that this Eton side was one of the strongest ever produced by the Light Blues with eight future first-class cricketers led by Clem Gibson, Gubby Allen, Ronnie Aird and the Hon. David Brand. Harrow's batting was feeble throughout the match and Gibson finished with match figures of 9/30 and Hill-Wood an

W.A.R. (later Sir William) Collins is introduced as Harrow captain to King George V, 1919. Two generations of Collins have since played for Eton.

impressive 11/69. Gubby Allen, in the first of his three matches against Harrow showed glimpses of his future greatness with 69 not out of 143 in Eton's second innings after being run out for 0 in the first innings without facing a ball. His bowling skills were to come later. Gibson gained Cambridge blues in 1920/1 and went on to the M.C.C. tour to Australia and New Zealand in 1922/3. He played for Sussex between 1919/26, although his appearances in county cricket were limited by his career in the Argentine. In his 84 first-class matches he took 249 wickets at 28 per wicket and was a more than useful lower-order batsman. There was little doubt that he was one of the finest fast bowlers Eton has ever produced and ranking closely with Gubby Allen. He was the main architect of the defeat of Warwick Armstrong's all conquer-

C.H. Gibson Eton XI 1916/19, Cambridge 1920/21 and Sussex. One of the best fast bowlers Eton has ever produced and would have played for England had he not spent most of his life in Argentina. His 6/64 in the Australian second innings was largely responsible for defeating Warwick Armstrong's previously invincible Australian tourists by 28 runs at Eastbourne in 1921, the penultimate match of their tour.

HARROW REQUIRED 244 RUNS TO WIN AND WE MUST SAY THAT MR. I. G. COLLINS NEVER LOOKED LIKE GETTING THEM —

MR. COLLINS REFUSED TO HIT WITH THE RESULT THAT HE HAD A VERY CROWDED EXISTENCE UNTIL HE WAS BOWLED.

AT 36 FOR 9 A HARROW BOY LEAVES THE GROUND WITH A "ONE OF THESE DAYS I SHALL RETURN" EXPRESSION.

A FEW YOUNG BLOODS FROM ETON CARRIED THEIR CAPTAIN OFF AT THE FINISH.

AFTER THE CRICKET WAS OVER WE HAD THE REAL ETON AND HARROW MATCH.

COME ALONG NORMAN — YOU CAN'T GIVE THE WEIGHT AWAY

OLD HARROW BOY.

FOND MOTHER SAVING THE

SUNSET AT ST JOHNS WOOD JULY 12th 1919.

(IT IS REALLY MUCH SAFER TO PLAY IN THE MATCH.)

An amusing cartoon of the 1919 match when top hats were not so expensive and topper fights were considered part of the tradition of the match!

ing Australian tourists in the penultimate match of their tour at Eastbourne in 1921 by 28 runs with Gibson taking 6/64 in the Australian second innings after the England XI had been bowled out for 43 in the first innings. Michael Falcon, the Harrovian of earlier vintage, also distinguished himself in this match by taking 6/67 in the first innings. The great Archie MacLaren discovered the irreproachable Sydney Barnes in the nets and put him instantly into the Lancashire XI, then proceeded to pick him for an England tour to Australia. He thus showed himself to be a pretty good judge of fast bowling and described Clem Gibson thus:

'With his perfect action, peculiar height and variation of pace and irreproachable length, he has everything that a high class bowler should possess and I have no fears about his success against any class of batsman.'

This was high praise indeed and it is probable that he would have played for England on a regular basis had his career been in this country. The useful Eton all-rounder of 1917/19 W.R.de la C. Shirley, who featured prominently in the 1918 fixture on the Harrow Sixth Form

Clem Gibson shakes hands with Sir Palham Warner, captain of the M.C.C. tour to South America in 1926/27 and one of the games 'greats'.

ground with 6/31 and 37, took Eton to a 56 run victory and went on to gain a Cambridge blue in 1924. He played 49 matches for Hampshire between 1922/5, scoring 1458 runs and taking 81 wickets in his first-class career. He also played for Hampshire as one of two Etonians who played in the famous match versus Warwickshire in 1922 described elsewhere.

There were some very fine players on both sides in **1920** but Harrow put themselves at a considerable disadvantage when they were bowled out for 85 in their first innings before lunch on the first day. W.W. Hill-Wood, the Eton captain, caused most of the damage once again and took 4/23 off 18 overs with Gubby Allen bowling the first two batsmen. Eton fared little better against the pace of H.J. Enthoven who took 5/25, but a lively last wicket stand took them to a lead of 56. Apart from C.T. Burnett's 64 and the last wicket stand of 60 between I.G. Collins and F.O.G. Lloyd, 44, Harrow would hardly have put up a showing at all. As it was, Eton raced to their target of 119 when Hill-Wood, 75 not out, and R. Aird, 44 not out, batted brilliantly against some loose Harrow bowling to win by 9 wickets. Hill-Wood gained a Cambridge blue in 1922 and played 35 matches for Derbyshire between 1919/36. He went on the M.C.C. tour to Australia and New Zealand in 1922/3, Archie MacLaren's last tour, and his best season was coincidentally 1923 when he hit 1,082 runs at an average of over 36.

W.W. Hill-Wood, Eton captain 1920. Eton XI 1918/20, Cambridge 1922 and Derbyshire, leading out the Eton XI of 1920. In 1919 he took 11/69 and scored 43 opening the batting and in 1920 scored 26 and 75 not out and took 6/85. He appeared irregularly in first-class cricket for Derbyshire until 1936 because of business commitments but when he did was well worth his place. He went on the M.C.C. tour to Australia and New Zealand in 1922/3.

R. Aird Eton XI 1919/21, Cambridge 1923 & Hampshire. Stylish batsman and brilliant cover point, he played for Hampshire from 1920/38. He was a much loved secretary of M.C.C. from 1953/62 and President in 1968/9.

The Prince of Wales, the future King Edward VIII and Duke of Windsor comes to Lord's in 1921 for the great match.

Two of the strongest sides for many years contested the Lord's match of **1921**. Harrow were rather unlucky to bat first on a damp wicket caused by too much watering. They never recovered from losing their first three batsmen to the outstanding Eton fast bowler G.O. Allen, all bowled, collapsing ignominiously to 64 all out. The Hon. J.B. Coventry took 4/9 in 10.2 overs with his slow left-arm bowling. Eton batted steadily against the less varied Harrow attack to gain a first innings of 174 with Tommy Enthoven taking 6/56 for Harrow. Harrow were given some hope by a fine free-hitting innings of 103 from L.G. Crawley, supported by lesser knocks from C.T. Bennett, the Harrow captain in his fifth year in the XI, Enthoven, P.H. Stewart-Brown and G.C. Kinahan, eventually totalling 295. Eton thus needed 122 to win and did so with relative ease thanks to a fine fourth wicket partnership between P.E. Lawrie, 67 not out, who had scored 53 in the first innings, and G.K. Cox, 30 not out, cruising home by 7 wickets. The superb wicket-keeping of M.L. Hill for Eton was a contributory factor to their success in 1921 as in 1920. He was the son of V.T. Hill, the Oxford blue of 1892, who had played for Somerset from 1891/1912 in 121 matches. He himself played for Cambridge in 1923/4 without gaining

Old Etonians v. Old Harrovians July 12th, 13th, 1920 at Lord's. The scorecard of the match between two exceptionally strong sides but once again the Etonians had the upper hand.

TOP ROW (LEFT TO RIGHT):
M. Falcon, C.H.B. Blount, R. St. L. Fowler, T.O. Jameson, G.H.M. Cartwright, M.B. Burrows, R. Anson, A.C. Wilkinson, F.R.R. Brooke, C.H. Gibson.
MIDDLE ROW (LEFT TO RIGHT):
L.H. Tennyson, M.C. Bird, N. Haig, R.H. Twining, E.W. Mann, H.K. Longman, W.P. Robertson, P.W. Cobbold,
FRONT ROW:
N.A. Jessop, G.E.V. Crutchley, G. Wilson, P.F.C. Williams.

Old Etonians v. Old Harrovians July 12th, 13th 1920 at Lord's. A fascinating photograph showing the strength of Eton and Harrow cricket at the time. All 22 cricketers had played first class cricket including two who did not get into the Eton XI. Nigel Haig was one of these and he went on to play for Middlesex and England; he is sitting in the middle row with two other England players Lionel Tennyson and Morice Bird.

The late great Gubby Allen showing the perfect side on action for a fast bowler against the West Indies in 1936.

a blue and in 42 matches for Somerset between 1921/32 also going on the M.C.C. tour to India and Ceylon in 1926/7. C.T. Bennett, the Harrow opening batsman of 1917/21 and captain in 1921, never lived up to his schoolboy promise but gained Cambridge blues in 1923 and 1925 and played a few games for Surrey and Middlesex with little success. He went on the M.C.C. tour to the West Indies in 1925/6. P.E. Lawrie, the Eton middle-order batsman of 1920/1, played for Oxford in 1922/4 without gaining his blue and also in 28 matches for Hampshire between 1921/8 with modest success averaging just over 21 in his 53 first-class innings. Hon. J.B. Coventry, the Eton slow left-arm bowler and lower-order batsman of 1920/21, played for Worcestershire between 1919/35 in 75 matches with rather average results but captained the county in 1929/30. Hon. D.F. Brand, the Eton all-rounder, went on the M.C.C. tour to New Zealand and Australia in 1922/3 but gave up first-class cricket after this and played for Hertfordshire in the minor counties championship. Ronnie Aird, the stylish middle-order batsman of 1919/21, gained a Cambridge blue in 1923 and played 108 matches between 1920/38 for Hampshire scoring 4,482 runs at an average of 22 per innings and was a brilliant cover point. He became a much-loved Secretary of M.C.C. between 1953/62 and was President of M.C.C. in 1968/9.

Gubby Allen (Middlesex) drives a ball from F.R.Brown (Surrey, Northants and England) during their match at the Oval on 12th August 1939. England captain's both.

Although never a regular county cricketer due to his career as a stockbroker, Gubby Allen was regarded between the two World Wars as one of the finest fast bowlers in the game as well as being a hard-hitting middle-order batsman. He gained Cambridge blues in 1922/3 and appeared in 146 matches for Middlesex between 1921/50. He was controversially selected for the Ashes tour to Australia in 1932/3 but more than justified his selection and went on the 1936/7 tour as captain when England were beaten 3-2 after being 2-0 up in the series. On his day he was quite outstanding as when he took all 10 wickets v. Lancashire at Lord's in 1929, a unique achievement at Lord's in county cricket, and his 788 first-class wickets at 22

Gubby Allen Eton, Cambridge University, Middlesex and England. His face portrays the sheer honesty and determination of this great cricketer and upholder of the traditions of cricket.

Gubby Allen (Middlesex and England) signing autographs on July 16th 1937 in the presence of the famous Jack Hobbs (Surrey and England) and Wavell Wakefield, one of the greatest England rugby players of all time and later long serving Conservative M.P.

Much has been said about Sir Alec Douglas-Home's cricketing prowess. But "Gubby" Allen never forgot one incident in which Sir Alec was less than a hero.

"We were both playing for Eton in the Eton-Winchester match of 1921," so "Gubby" recalled. "Lord Dunglass, as he then was, missed a possible catch off my first ball in the second innings. The batsman then went on to make 278 runs. I've never stopped pulling Alec's leg about it since.

"But he was a pretty fine cricketer. I would say good club standard. He didn't get his Blue at Oxford, but he did go on an MCC tour of South America in 1926, and did pretty well."

The scorer of the 278 for Winchester was John Guise and the next highest scorer in the innings was 21. He went on to gain blues at Oxford in 1924/5 and played 57 matches for Middlesex between 1922/34 averaging over 26.

per wicket and 9,232 runs at 29 per innings puts him well up the league of great all-rounders. He was a highly influential figure in the administration of cricket for many years right up until his death in 1991 and his offices included chairman of the England selectors from 1955/61, Treasurer of M.C.C. and Chairman of Middlesex. Very few important decisions regarding the game's future were decided without Gubby's wise counsel throughout his long life.

Alec Douglas-Home at the start of his political career, in his autobiography *The way the wind blows* tells an amusing story about Stanley Baldwin the Prime Minister of the day, who was a keen cricket enthusiast, particularly of the Eton and Harrow match and also wrote the foreword to *Eton and Harrow at the Wicket* in 1926 by Bernard Darwin. Baldwin, a passionate Harrovian, congratulated Bridgeman, the old Etonian Home Secretary on the quelling of a serious riot in one of the prisons.

> *'How did you do it Home Secretary?' 'Oh Prime Minister it was very easy. I just told the Governor to order the prison band to play '40 years on' and the prisoners stood to attention and quietly returned to their cells.'*

Harrow had their strongest XI for many years and were confident that this might be their year at last in **1922** but rain prevented play on the first day and the match only started at midday on the second day. This was on a new wicket on the north side of the ground that was wet and the outfield very slow. Enthoven once again bowled well for Harrow in taking 4/50 and the main contributors to Eton's total of 190 were the cautious innings of E.W. Dawson, 43, and Lord Dunglass's attacking 66. There was just time to complete Harrow's innings before the close of play when they were all out for 184 with the two main contributions coming from L.G. Crawley, 53, and his cousin C.S., 67 not out. Lord Dunglass showed what a useful all-round cricketer he was when he took 4/37 off 18 overs with his medium-pace away-swingers. Lord Dunglass, later Sir Alec Douglas-Home, played some ten first-class matches for Oxford and Middlesex, going on the M.C.C. tour to South America in 1926/7. He thus became the only Prime Minister in history to have played first-class cricket. I.G. Collins, the Harrow batsman of 1919/22, broke his leg in his first year at Oxford which prevented him from playing cricket but he went on to gain half blues for golf and tennis, representing Great Britain in the Davis Cup.

H.J Enthoven, the Harrow captain of 1922, went on to gain Cambridge blues from 1923/6, captaining the side in 1926 and played 123 matches for

Sir Alec Douglas Home (later Lord Home) Eton XI 1921/2, Oxford University and Middlesex batting for the Lord's and Commons at the Oval on 18th June 1951 wearing the famous Harlequins cap. The only Prime Minister to have played first class cricket.

H.J. 'Tommy' Enthoven 1919/22, Cambridge 1923/6 & Middlesex. A fine all round cricketer he captained Cambridge in 1926 and played for Middlesex from 1925/36 captaining the side with Nigel Haig in 1933/4.

L.G. Crawley Harrow XI 1920/2, Cambridge 1923/5 and Essex. The most gifted of the celebrated Crawley family and an outstanding all round sportsman. He scored 103 in 1921 and 53 in 1922 for Harrow and would have played for England had he been available more regularly. He played four times for England in the Walker Cup, was a very fine rackets player between the wars and a long serving golf correspondent of the Daily Telegraph.

Middlesex between 1925/36, captaining the side jointly with Nigel Haig in 1929/30. He scored 7,362 first-class runs with nine centuries and took 252 wickets at 32 per wicket. Leonard Crawley, the Harrow centurion of 1921, was regarded as one of the most talented cricketers of his generation but sadly was not able to play regular first-class cricket. When he did play he was a joy to watch as he was a very hard hitter of the ball befitting a top-class rackets player. A Cambridge blue for three years between 1923/5, he played 56 matches for Essex between 1926/36 and went on the M.C.C. tour to the West Indies in 1925/6. His highest score was 222 for Essex v. Glamorgan in 1928 at Swansea and he totalled 5,227 first-class runs at an average of over 31. He was a highly talented golfer, which he preferred to cricket, and appeared four times in the Walker Cup; he was the long-time golf correspondent of the Daily Telegraph. Hamer Bagnall gained a Cambridge blue in 1923 but was unable to retain his place thereafter and played 64 matches for Northants from 1921/8. He was a good player of fast bowling on true wickets but too often failed against the slow bowlers.

In 1921 and 1922 the standard of cricket at both schools was very high. Eton were described in Wisden as undoubtedly the best school side of the year in 1921 and of first-class school sides in 1922 Harry Altham wrote:

"I am tempted to plump unequivocally for Harrow as the best of them all."

Both schools had strong batting sides in **1923**, Eton particularly so, but were lacking in bowling talent. Even so Harrow had a struggle to save the match and were indebted in their first innings to a great last wicket stand of 93 by J.N.H. Foster, 75, and G.O. Brigstocke, 47 not out, to take Harrow to a respectable score of 322 on a very good wicket. Eton's only innings score of 502 was the highest in the history of the match and will stand for all time. Harrow's poor bowling attack was smashed to all parts of the ground by the Eton opener E.W. Dawson, 159, R.H. Cobbold, 100, and G.C. Newman, 82 not out, all future blues and county cricketers. Harrow did not help their cause by missing Dawson off the first ball of the match. Eton were unable to bowl Harrow out in their second innings, partly because R.G.M. Kennerley-Rumford, the Eton opening bowler, strained his back in his first over and was unable to bowl again. Harrow finished on 216/7 and just succeeded in saving the game due to a flawless knock from P.H. Stewart-Brown, Harrow's wicket-keeper captain, 102 not out – he just completed his century before the close of play. Stewart Brown had finished his four years in the Harrow XI from 1920/23 on a high note and went on to get Oxford blues in 1925/6 averaging 28 in his 17 first-class matches.

Edward Dawson, the Eton opener of 1922/3, went on to justify his high promise as a schoolboy recognised by his county Leicestershire

The record second wicket partnership of 301 between E.W. Dawson 113 and F.G.B. Arkwright 175 for Eton in the drawn match of 1923 v. Winchester.

Archie's last stand: A.C. MacLaren's final M.C.C. tour to Australia and New Zealand at the age of 51 containing five Etonians: Hon. D.F. Brand, C.H. Gibson, W.W. Hill-Wood, J.F. Maclean and A.C. Wilkinson and two Harrovians A.C. MacLaren and G. Wilson. Neither J.F. Maclean, a wicket-keeping batsman nor A.C. Wilkinson, a hard hitting opener, made the Eton XI but afterwards became fine cricketers for Worcestershire and the Army respectively.
TOP ROW: *H. Tyldesley, C.H. Titchmarsh, T.C. Lowry, W.W. Hill-Wood.* MIDDLE ROW: *W. Ferguson, Hon. D.F. Brand, A.P.F. Chapman, J.F. MacLaren, C.H. Gibson, A.P. Freeman.* FRONT ROW: *Dr R.J. Pope, A.C. Wilkinson, Lieut-Colonel J.C. Hartley, A.C. MacLaren (capt), Hon. F.S.G. Calthorpe, G.Wilson, H.D. Swan.*

The Cambridge side of 1924, which contained three Harrovians in C.T. Bennett, L.G. Crawley and H.J. Enthoven and two Etonians in E.W. Dawson and W.R. Shirley, although Bennett did not play at Lord's v. Oxford.
TOP ROW: *C.T. Bennett, A.H. White, H.M. Austin, W.R. Shirley, R.J.O. Meyer.* MIDDLE ROW: *H.B. Sherwell, P.A. Wright, G.C. Lowry, H.J. Enthoven, L.G. Crawley.* FRONT ROW: *J.E.F. Mann, E.W. Dawson.*

Two pairs of twins, Edward and George Ward and the two Ward sisters, at Lord's to see Eton play cricket against Harrow in July 1923. (Scions of the Earl of Dudley).

E.W. Dawson Eton XI 1922/3, Cambridge 1924/7 Leicestershire and England. Scored 159 in Eton's massive total of 502 in 1923, the record score for the series. Played for Leicestershire between 1922/34 captaining the side in 1928/9, 1931 and 1933 and scored 1,909 runs in 1929. He played five times for England on his two M.C.C. tours to South Africa and Australia in 1927/8 and 1929/30.

Etonians buying the famous light blue carnation from flower sellers at Lord's cricket ground, 1924, during the annual Eton and Harrow cricket match.

The Eton openers of 1926. Hope, captain in 1926 became 9th Duke of Newcastle. Cazalet Eton XI 1925/6, Oxford 1927 scored 100 not out for Eton in 1926 and also represented Oxford at rackets, lawn tennis and squash. He was a superb steeplechase jockey until a fall ended his career in 1938 and was the Queen Mother's racing trainer for 25 years.

whom he represented at 17 and gained five test caps on his two M.C.C. tours of South Africa in 1927/8 and Australia and New Zealand in 1929/30. He gained Cambridge blues from 1924/7, captaining them in 1927, and played 174 matches for Leicestershire between 1922/34, captaining them in four seasons during these years. He scored 12,598 runs in his first-class career with his best season being 1929 when he hit 1,909 runs at over 31 per innings, one of six players who scored over 1,000 runs for Leicestershire that season. George Newman, who had been so successful in his one innings for Eton at Lord's became an extremely useful middle-order batsman for Oxford, where he gained blues in 1926/7, and Middlesex in 50 matches from 1929/36 averaging 29 in 116 first-class innings. He was a fine athlete and represented Oxford in the high jump and hurdles.

There was a more interesting contest in **1924** and the bowling on both sides was of a much higher quality than in 1923. The first innings was evenly matched when the wicket was fast and true with fine innings on the Eton side from Lord Hyde, 86, and J.E. Tew, 58, R.E.C. Butterworth bowled well for Harrow to take 5/66. Harrow finished 39 behind on first innings but batted far too slowly. J.C. Butterworth, the brother of R.E.C., top scored with 72. On a deteriorating wicket Eton struggled for runs in their second innings although once again Tew batted very well for his 54 not out in a total of 143/6 declared and Butterworth took his tally in the match to eight wickets for Harrow. Harrow were set 183 runs in 120 minutes and little attempt was made to score the runs, the match fizzling out into a draw for the third year running. R.E.C. Butterworth, the Harrow all-rounder of 1923/4, gained an Oxford blue in 1927 and played 14 matches for Middlesex between 1935/7 with rather disappointing results. He averaged 19 with the bat and his 50 wickets cost 42 runs each. He was sadly killed in action in 1940. J.E. Tew, the Eton middle-order batsman who had scored 112 runs for once out at Lord's, played a few first-class matches for Oxford in 1927/8 with only limited success. H.A. Caccia, the Eton off-spin bowler, became a most distinguished diplomat and headed the Foreign Office during the 'sixties and early 'seventies. He was a highly popular Provost of Eton in his later years as Lord Caccia.

In Affectionate Remembrance
OF
ENGLISH CRICKET,
WHICH DIED AT THE OVAL
ON
29th AUGUST, 1882,
Deeply lamented by a large circle of sorrowing
friends and acquaintances.

R.I.P.

N.B.—The body will be cremated and the
ashes taken to Australia.

The Hon. Ivo Bligh's victorious Ashes tour to Australia in 1882/3 which contained three Etonians in Ivo. Bligh and the two Studd brothers. LEFT TO RIGHT BACK ROW STANDING: *W. Barnes, F. Morley, C.T. Studd, G.F. Vernon, C.F.H. Leslie,* SEATED: *G.B. Studd, E.F.S. Tylecote, Hon I. Bligh (capt.) A.G. Steel, W.W. Read,* ON THE GROUND: *R.G. Barlow, W. Bates.*

X-ray showing the damage to the stem of the Ashes urn

The Ashes urn bequeathed to M.C.C. by the Earl of Darnley on his death in 1927. (MCC Collection.)

Hylton Philipson's 2nd tour of Australia captained by W.G. Grace in 1894/5. He played for Eton 1884/5, Oxford Univ. 1887/9, Middlesex and England. He is in the back row on the left hand side.

The urn's velvet bag.

A collage of the all conquering Cambridge XI of 1878 captained by Edward Lyttelton, one of the famous seven brothers who played for Eton and future Head Master of Eton 1905/16.

Lord Hawke, Eton, Cambridge Univ., Yorkshire and England. The patriarch of Yorkshire till his death in 1938 and seen here in his I.Z. finery.

Oscar Wilde, Lord Alfred Douglas and The Marquis of Queensberry – leading players in a Victorian cause célèbre. His slightly mad streak manifested itself after the exciting match of 1840 when Eton won by 31 runs.

The 1885 Harrow Centurions A.K. Watson and E. Crawley gave Harrow a crucial advantage in the first innings and they just won by 3 wickets. E.M. Butler, the Harrow captain and future Head Master of Harrow took them home to victory with 48 not out.

Th. Th. Cricket Ground. Oxford.

GRAND MATCH.

AUSTRALIANS V. OXFORD UNIVERSITY.

May 15th, 16th & 17th, 1884.

AUSTRALIAN ELEVEN.

P. G. McDonell, c Nicholls, b Whitby	5	st Kemp, b Nicholls	36
A. C. Bannerman, c Haycock, b Whitby	32	c Nicholls, b Bastard	0
W. L. Murdoch, c Nicholls, b Whitby	11	b Bastard	0
G. Giffen, c Nicholls, b Page	14	c Cobb, b Bastard	9
G. J. Bonnor, c Nicholls, b Whitby	2	c Nicholls, b Page	11
J. McC. Blackham, b Whitby	20	c & b Bastard	18
W. Midwinter, c Asher, b Whitby	20	c Brain b Whitby	45
H. J. H. Scott, not out	6	c Kemp b Whitby	21
G. E. Palmer, b Page	12	c O'Brien b Page	7
H. F. Boyle,	5	not out	8
F. R. Spofforth,	6	c Key b Bastard	3
b n b	15	b 8 l b 1 n b	10
Total	**148**	**Total**	**168**

UNIVERSITY ELEVEN.

M. C. Kemp, run out	13	not out	63
T. R. H-Haycock, c Boyle, b Spofforth	0	not out	25
A. R. Cobb, b Palmer	0	c Alexander, b Boyle	6
J. H. Brain, c Giffen, b Spofforth	8		
T. C. O'Brien, b Boyle	92	b Spofforth	13
H. V. Page, b Palmer	33	c Palmer, b Boyle	1
A. G. G. Asher, run out	2		
K. J. Key, b Scott	30		
E. B. Nicholls,	16		
H. O. Whitby, c Bonnor, b Boyle	10		
E. W. Bastard, b Palmer	0		
b l b 2 n b	5	b 1 l b 1 n b	2
Total	**209**	**Total**	**110**

Umpires—Webb and Greenwood.

Printed by permission of the O.U.C.C., by H. Beesley, 4. Cowley Road, Oxford.

M.C. Kemp, Harrow, Oxford University and Kent, the second patriarch of Harrow cricket from 1890/1920 showing Oxford's great win in 1884 when he was captain. 'Bishop' scored 63 not out in their 7 wicket triumph.

The Hon. Ivo Bligh (later the Earl of Darnley). Eton, Cambridge University, Kent and Engand. He will always be remembered for his Ashes victory in Australia 1882/3.

Hon. F.S. Jackson (1870/1947). Harrow, Cambridge Univ., Yorkshire and England. At his best a brilliant all rounder, his Test average of 49 was up with the greats in an era when wickets were not always easy to bat on.

Francis Stanley Jackson was born in 1870. He came to Harrow (The Head Master's) in 1884. He was in the Cricket Eleven from 1887 to 1889 and Captain in 1889. He went to Trinity College, Cambridge, and was in the Cambridge Cricket Eleven from 1890 to 1893, and Captain in 1892 and in 1893. He played for England against Australia in Test Matches from 1893 to 1905, as Captain in 1905. He played for Yorkshire and for the Gentlemen V. the Players between 1890 and 1907.

Batting Record

	Total Runs	Highest Score	Average
Harrow V. Eton 1887–1889	152	68	30·40
Cambridge XI 1890–1893	1,649	123	26·59
England V. Australia 1893–1905	1,415 (including 5 centuries)	144 (not out)	48·68
First Class Cricket 1890–1907	16,251	160	33·00

Bowling Record

	Wickets	Average
Harrow V. Eton	20	10·65
Cambridge	153	17·73
England V. Australia	24	33·00
First Class Cricket	834	19·00

In 1898 he scored 1566 runs and took 104 wickets.

He served in the South African War in the King's

A.C. MacLaren, Harrow XI 1887/90 Lancashire and England. Outstanding batsman and tactician.

Hon. F.S. Jackson, Harrow XI 1887/9. Cambridge Univ., Yorkshire and England. Who could deny his greatness as a man and cricketer.

Stanley Jackson's outstanding career. His performances v. Australia were amazing, beating W.G. Grace by a mile.
His average of 49 in test matches on difficult wickets would probably have only been beaten by Don Bradman.

*Original Spy watercolour of Fred, Earl of Bessborough.
Harrow XI 1832/3 and Cambridge Univ. 1836.
A depressing time at Lord's but with Robert Grimston
the patriarch of Harrow cricket for over 50 years.*

*Hon. Edward Lyttelton. Eton XI 1872/4, Cambridge
1875/8 captained the Cambridge side in 1878 when
they won eight first class matches including victory by
an innings v. The Australians. He was a fine all round
games player excelling at fives, football and athletics
and became Head Master of Eton from 1905/16.*

*Father and sons who have captained Harrow XI's at Lord's. Spelling mistakes do
not just occur in books! (Bailey should be Baily).*

The gargoyles on the pavilion at Lord's depicting Spencer Ponsonby Fane of Harrow and Lord Harris of Eton, both very influential in the affairs of M.C.C. till their deaths in 1915 and 1932 respectively.

The five survivors of the 1858 Harrow XI at Lord's which Harrow won by an innings and 7 runs. The picture presented to M.C.C. in 1905. BACK: *H.M. Upcher and S. Hoare.* FRONT: *G.H. Hodgson, R. Lang and H.M. Plowden.*

A collage of the Eton XI in 1900 captained by H.K. Longman which narrowly lost by 1 wicket. A Cambridge blue in 1901, he played for Surrey and Middlesex between 1901/20.

The great Lord Harris, Eton, Oxford Univ., Kent and England. The patriarch of Kent and the most influential man in the game till his death in 1932.

A delightful caricature of the 1880 match from the Illustrated London News.

The hat-trick ball presented to E.G. Whateley for Eton in 1900 by Lord Harris.

Eton and Harrow C1889 by Albert Ludovici Jnr. (1852-1932). A charming impression embued with the spirit of the belle époque.

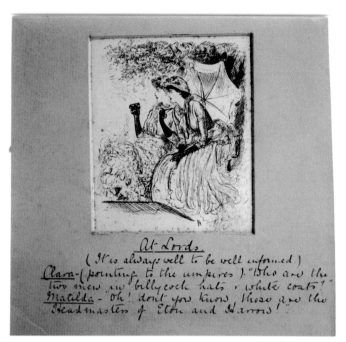

An amusing pen and ink drawing from the Eton and Harrow match in 1884 which appeared in the Punch edition of 19th July 1884. by George du Maurier (1834-1896) showing that fashion was as much part of the proceedings as the match itself. Ignorance is bliss! (Peter Beckwith collection)

The celebrated performance of F.S. Jackson in 1888, the balls presented to him by the Earl of Bessborough and the occasion which is celebrated in the famous Harrow song 'A Gentleman's a bowling' by Edward Bowen, the patron saint of Harrow Songs.

Hylton Phillipson, Eton XI 1884/5 in his elegant Eton gear.

On Saturday July 9th 1898 a presentation was made to R.A.H. Mitchell, the patriarch of Eton cricket from 1866 to 1897 at Lord's.

All the Eton captains from 1865 to 1897 were present except E.O.H. Wilkinson, captain in 1872 who was killed in the Zulu war.

Lord Harris gave the speech expressing their sincere appreciation and affection for 'Mitch' who will always remain a legend as player and coach in Eton history.

*The Eton fan of 1875. Eton were captained by the famous Alfred
Lyttelton who scored 59 in a drawn match very much in Eton's favour.*

*A miniature bat celebrating four Harrow centurions, two Crawleys,
Peter Studd in 1935 and Robert Tindall, son of Mark in 1976.*

*The miniature bat presented to T.G.O. Cole (Harrow) in
1897 on his 142 in a drawn match very much in
Harrow's favour.*

The Harrow fan of 1873. A closely fought match which Harrow won by 5 wickets.

A.N. 'Monkey' Hornby (1847-1925). Harrow, Lancashire and England. Captain of Lancashire from 1880/93 and 1897/8 he also played 9 times for England at Rugby football. An enormously influential figure in the game, his son A.H. Hornby Harrow and Lancashire also captained the county from 1908/14 with success.

Hylton Philipson (1866-1935). Eton, Oxford Univ.. Middlesex and England. A top class wicketkeeper, his batting never quite reached the heights. A very fine all round sportsman he gained blues in four sports and ranks with Alfred Lyttleton and C.J. Ottaway as the finest of Etonian Corinthians.

A cartoon of the match in 1921, Eton's eighth win in a row by 7 wickets despite Leonard Crawley scoring 103 for Harrow in their second innings. Harrow never recovered from a disastrous 64 all out in the first innings.

ABOVE: *M.C. Bird's remarkable performance in 1907, the only double centurion in the history of the match.* LEFT: *The bat he used in 1907*

D.C. Boles, Eton XI 1903/4. His 183 in 1904 stills remains the record score in Eton and Harrow matches.

Letter from Robert Hamilton Dundas (at Eton 1897-1903), describing a fight at the end of the 1900 match – '1/2 an hour, far better than last year.' 'Somebody would have an Eton flag, 10 Harrovians rushed to the rescue, whack on each others hats; hats crushed to shapeless wrecks over heads...very amusing.' He also mentions the playing of the 'excellent Whately'.

A bail from the 1939 match, Harrow's first victory for 31 years presented by G.F. Anson who scored a vital 76 in the first innings.

Charles Blount's very fine 137 in Harrow's second innings failed to save them from defeat by 6 wickets. He later became an Air Vice Marshall in the R.A.F. and was killed in 1940 at Hendon.

The tea interval at Lord's in 1929 by Jaques Emile Blanche (1861-1942) which shows the pavilion and the old grandstand rebuilt in 1931.

N.S. Hotchkin's superb 153 paved the way for Eton's decisive win by an innings and 16 runs in 1931. A record first wicket stand of 208/0 was achieved with A.W. Allen 112 on the first day before lunch.

A fine Ape Cartoon of the magnificent Alfred Lyttelton. The most talented of the seven brothers and with C.J. Ottaway Eton's greatest all round sportsman with five Cambridge blues and a soccer international as well.

WHO ARE YOU PUTTING ON TO BOWL NOW, CAPTAIN?

OH! YOU HAVE A TRY!

UMPIRE

The practice of bowling changes being managed from the boundry by R.A.H. Mitchell for Eton and I.D. Walker for Harrow continued until late into 1880's and was caricatured by this amusing cartoon.

Gubby Allen's 10/40 for Middlesex v. Lancashire in 1929.
A unique achievement in county cricket at Lord's.

Games. 1921

Date	Averages in — overs	maidens	runs	wkts	My Runs	How Out
Sat, April 30th	9	2	21	1	19	ct Broad, b Renshaw
Tues, May 3rd	—	—	—	—	35	ct Ship, b Baird (a wide)
Thurs, May 5th	14	3	26	0	5	bld Cubitt
Sat, May 7th	6	2	12	0	93	bld Dawson
Thurs 12th, XIII v XX	16	4	32	2	0	ct Bucknill, b Cubitt (a fine catch, if it ...)
Tues, May 17th, XII v XIII	—	—	—	—	6	ct Barrett, b Bridgeman (left-handed low catch ...)
Thurs, 19th DRAWN	8	4	17	1	45*	not out
Tues, May 31st	—	—	—	—	11	st Hill, b Cubitt (stumped ...)
M,T,W,T June 13-16th XI v XII DRAWN	—	—	—	—	13	ct Greg, b Hartley (caught between his legs)
Tues, June 21st (exp of gm)	8	0	24	4	25	ct Davies, b Hirst (caught off bottom edge of bat)
Tues, June 28th (end of w)	15	6	42	5	83*	not out (134 for 1st wkt with Hill 36)
Tues, July 5th (Final match)	—	—	—	—	13	bld Douglass (2nd innings)
					11	st Davies, b Barrett (2nd innings)
	76	21	176	13	359	

Bowling Average: 76 overs ... runs, 13 wkts = 13.54

Batting Average: 13 inns, 2 T.N.O, 359 runs, 93 H.S = 32.64

Gubby Allen's Upper Club record book of 1921 in his own handwriting.

A charming watercolour of the Eton and Harrow match in the 1920s by Septimus Scott (1879-1962).

Lord Dunglass (Alec Douglas Home) with his younger brother at Lord's in 1921.

The Eton and Harrow Cricket number of the Field magazine in 1930 showing Victor Rothschild opening the batting for Harrow in 1929. Victor Baerlein is the Eton wicketkeeper.

The front page of the Eton v. Harrow souvenir programme of 1906. The amount of advertising and detail in the programme shows what an important occasion it was considered to be.

A.G. Pelham, the hero for Eton in 1930 with 11/44 in the match. Cambridge Univ. 1934 and Sussex, he bowled well to take 34 wickets for Cambridge in 1934. Grandson of F.G. Pelham (later 5th Earl of Chichester).

1939.

M.C.C. v. WEST INDIES
MAY 13th, 15th, & 16th.

MIDDLESEX v. WEST INDIES
JUNE 3rd, 5th & 6th.

MINOR COUNTIES v. WEST INDIES
JUNE 14th, 15th & 16th.

ENGLAND v. WEST INDIES
JUNE 24th, 26th & 27th.

OXFORD v. CAMBRIDGE
JULY 1st, 3rd & 4th.

ETON v. HARROW
JULY 14th, & 15th.

The privilege of introducing the Ladies and Children (under 14) of a Member's household to the Ground, without payment, is withdrawn on the above-mentioned occasions.

R. S. RAIT KERR, Lieut.-Col.
Secretary, M.C.C.

The Hon. F.G Pelham (later Earl of Chichester), Eton XI 1863, Cambridge 1864/7 and Sussex. Captained Cambridge in 1866/7 and took 26 wickets in his four matches v. Oxford.

COMPLIMENTARY TICKET.

H   **123**

ETON v. HARROW,
JULY 14th and 15th, 1939.

Admit

MEMBER OF HARROW SCHOOL.
TO MEMBERS' ENCLOSURES—BLOCKS C, D, E, F, G, AND THE ROOFS OF LUNCHEON ROOMS (BLOCKS, O & P).
This Ticket does not admit at the Gate, but must be retained by the holder as a voucher for his seat, and must be shown at any time when demanded.

A 1939 ticket. Harrow's first win since 1908 with M.C.C.'s programme of matches showing Eton and Harrow's standing with M.C.C. 1939. The match was still important enough for M.C.C. to merit payment at the gate for member's relatives.

The social scene at lunchtime on the first day in 1926.

N.M. Ford Harrow XI 1924/6, Oxford 1928/30 & Derbyshire. The son of the legendary Harrow Head Master the Rev. Lionel Ford he captained Harrow in 1925/6. He did not enforce the follow on in 1925 when Harrow should have won. He averaged 38 for Oxford and Derbyshire in 1930 and was a fine rackets and Eton fives player gaining half blues for both at Oxford.

Harrow should really have won the match in **1925**, although Eton had started as favourites. Harrow only batted adequately on a true Lord's wicket except for E.W.E. Mann's 61 and a courageous last-wicket stand by K.R.M. Carlisle, 45, and D. Wormald, the Harrow wicket-keeper, 23 not out. It was something of a surprise that Eton's strong batting line-up collapsed against the modest Harrow bowling attack for 112, leaving Harrow with a lead of 119. A.C. Raphael, the Harrow opening bowler and middle-order batsman, bowled better than he had done all season to take 7/30 off 16 overs with his out-swingers. He was considerably aided by Wormald who took the record number of catches by a wicket-keeper in one innings, namely six. N.M. Ford, the Harrow captain, decided not to enforce the follow-on because of his weak attack which in retrospect was probably a mistake. Harrow batted too slowly in their second innings and the declaration was far too cautious; Eton were left to score 355 in 200 minutes. After the first hour Eton had lost five wickets and looked destined to lose the match but a fine sixth wicket partnership between H.P. Hunloke, 45, and J.P.T. Boscawen, 66, saved the day, Eton finishing eight wickets down and 134 runs short of the target. R.H. Cobbold, the Eton middle-order batsman and off-break bowler of 1923/5, captain in 1925 and one of the centurions of 1923, scored 42 and 65 in 1925, played for Cambridge in 1926/7, and gained a blue in 1927 with more than respectable results. He averaged 27 in his 14 first-class matches but his bowling was little used.

Mat Wright's Bat shop at Eton 1926. Etonians choosing cricket bats. Mat Wright played for Bucks from 1891-1913 and was a highly popular coach of the College from 1885 to 1919.

Famous British photographer Cecil Beaton arriving with his sisters for the Eton and Harrow match at Lord's, 1927.

Leicestershire had the unusual number of six batsmen who made over 1,000 runs in 1928: (LEFT TO RIGHT) *L.G. Berry, W.E. Astill, E.W. Dawson (Eton, Cambridge Univ., Leics. & England) in his first year as captain of the county, A.W. Shipman, N.F. Armstrong and T.E. Sidwell.*

Both teams were long on batting and experience in **1926** and as it turned out rather too cautious. Eton batted for five hours and Harrow rather longer to obtain a first innings lead of 64. A.M. Crawley, the most outstanding batsman in the Harrow XI, scored 87 in reasonable time but his example was not followed by his colleagues. R.C.C. Whittaker, in a mammoth spell for Eton with his slow left-arm deliveries, took 5/99 off 56 overs. Harrow had rather ruined the match and it was left to P.V.F. Cazalet to score 100 not out, batting with great style as befitted a rackets player, to show Harrow how it should be done. Eton finished on 200/6 in their second innings. H.E.H.P.C. Hope, the Eton captain of 1926 who had batted well throughout the season for Eton, went on to Freshmens' and Seniors' trials at Cambridge but made no further progress. He succeeded as 9th Duke of Newcastle in 1941 and died in relative obscurity in 1988, the ducal stately home Clumber Park and estate near Worksop having been sold off to pay death duties. Peter Cazalet gained an Oxford cricket blue in 1927 and played four matches for Kent averaging 22 in his 22 first-class matches. He also represented Oxford at rackets, lawn tennis and squash and became a notable steeplechase jockey until a bad fall ended his career in 1938. Subsequently he was the Queen Mother's trainer for 25 years till shortly before his death in 1973.

Aidan Crawley, the Harrow opening batsman of 1924/6, was one of the outstanding amateur batsmen of his generation gaining blues in all four years at Oxford between 1927/30 and, when time allowed in a busy journalistic career, played 33 times for Kent between 1927/47. His career record in first-class cricket compares favourably with all but the very best and in his 87 first-class matches he scored 5,061 runs at an average of 38. His best season was 1928 when he averaged 49 and in 1929 he made his highest score of 204 for Oxford v. Northants at Wellingborough. There is little doubt that had time and money allowed he might well have played for England. A very well-known journalist and author he also had two stints in Parliament on opposite sides as Labour M.P. for Buckingham from 1945/51 and Conservative M.P. for West Derbyshire between 1962/7. Neville Ford, the Harrow captain of 1925/6, was also a most distinguished cricketer of a well known Repton cricketing family and son of the great Harrow Head Master Lionel Ford. He gained Oxford blues from 1928/30 and played 31 matches for Derbyshire between 1926/34. He averaged just over 26 in his 75 first-class matches which included five centuries and a top score of 183. His most notable innings for Oxford were 151 v. Notts, 155 v. Kent, 183 v. Free Foresters and 180 v. Surrey when he added 276 for the fourth wicket with P.G.T. Kingsley in just under three hours and toured Canada with M.C.C. in 1937. He was afterwards a director of Wiggins Teape, the paper manufacturers, for some 35 years. His grandson Edward Grylls a well known Etonian explorer became the youngest Briton to climb Mount Everest a year before Ford's death in 2000 aged 93.

C.K.H Hill-Wood Eton XI 1925/6, Oxford 1928/30 and Derbyshire.

C.K.H. Hill-Wood, the Eton left-arm fast medium bowler of 1925/6 proved to be a very good bowler for Oxford and Derbyshire from 1928/30, gaining his blue in all three years and playing 18 matches for Derbyshire in these years. He took 185 wickets in his 58 first-class matches at an average of just under 30 and was a more than useful lower-order batsman, averaging 20 in 77 innings. He had an amazing bowling action, which puzzled many batsmen. His approach to the wicket was light, quick and springy. About three yards from the bowling crease his left arm reached forward and his head inclined sharply over to his shoulder. Then the left arm whizzed over and delivered the ball off the wrong foot from as high as he could reach, handicapped as he was by his bent body. He undoubtedly saved the varsity match for Oxford in 1928 when, with Oxford set 335 in 215 minutes, he batted 100 minutes for 20 not out after taking 6/79 in Cambridge's first innings. Hill-Wood and Benson, the Oxford last pair, batted for the last half hour to save the day and finished on 227/9. In any event he had a most creditable bowling and batting record for Oxford during his three years with 1929 being his best year when he took 51 wickets at a cost of 25. The pressure of business did not enable him to continue his highly promising first-class career.

C.K. Hill-Wood, Eton XI 1925/6, Oxford 1928/30 and Derbyshire. A most unusual left arm medium fast bowler and useful lower order batsman he took 185 wickets in his three years for Oxford and Derbyshire. Business prevented him from playing serious cricket thereafter, a great loss to the game.

123

R.H.R. Buckston Eton XI 1927 and Derbyshire. Son of the Eton wicket-keeper of 1900 G.M. Buckston and former Derbyshire captain he fulfilled the same role as captain from 1937/9.

Arriving at Lord's 1927.

Eton very narrowly failed to win in **1927** but Harrow had much the worst of the wicket. They still batted extremely slowly and took 7½ hours to score 252 runs in the two innings. R.C.C. Whittaker, the Eton captain, bowled very well in the match to take 9/98 and Harrow were never able to get to grips with his subtle variations of line and length. G.N. Capel-Cure's 65 was the feature of Eton's 225 in reply and it was left to Harrow to scrape a draw after two hours were lost to rain on the second morning. This they did but only just and when stumps were drawn nine wickets were down and Harrow only 27 runs ahead. W.E. Harbord, the Eton opening batsman, played a few matches for Oxford in 1930 and 16 matches for Yorkshire between 1929/35. He went on the M.C.C. tour to the West Indies in 1934/35 but his overall results were somewhat disappointing. He was a long-standing member of the Yorkshire Committee and managing-director of John Smith's, the well-known Tadcaster brewer for many years. C.W.C. Packe, the Eton middle-order batsman, played 21 times for Leicestershire between 1929/34 captaining the side in 1932 and averaging 25 with the bat. His appearances were very much restricted by his Army career and he was killed on active service in Normandy in 1944. R.H.R. Buckston, the Eton wicket-keeper and son of G.M., the Derbyshire captain of 1921, followed his father in playing 72 matches for Derbyshire between 1928/39, captaining them from 1937/9. Although a most popular captain his record was modest.

The Hon. C. J. Lyttelton (later 10th Viscount Cobham) was a scion of the famous cricketing family, the Lyttelton's. Cobham's grandfather and his six brothers all played for Eton and four for Cambridge yet at Eton he was nowhere near the XI and for some years afterwards was only a respectable club cricketer but study, practice and application improved his technique and he became a more than useful County cricketer. He was Vice-Captain of the M.C.C. Tour to New Zealand and Australia in 1935/6 and Captain of Worcestershire from 1936/9. He had the happy knack of getting runs when they were most wanted. His best score was 162 v. Leics at Loughborough in 1938 but his most valuable was his 48 in 35 minutes on a bad wicket to enable the County to beat Yorkshire in 1936 for the first time since 1909 and 50 and 35 as an opener against the 1938 Australians. He was a superb Committee man with his blend of humour and common sense, President of M.C.C. in 1954 and Governor of I. Zingari till his untimely death in 1975.

Both teams seemed determined to secure a win in **1928** after six years without a result and it proved to be one of the most exciting matches for many years. Eton who had batted well all season were more than surprised to be bowled out for 126 on a good wicket. The balance tilted Harrow's way when they secured a first innings lead of 106 but this was restored by a magnificent chanceless knock of 158 from Eton's I. Akers-Douglas and 69 from the Eton captain, E.R. Sheepshanks.

W.O'B Lindsay, Harrow XI 1926/8 and Oxford 1931. Determined right-hand opening batsman and wicket-keeper. He had a very good season in 1928 and was unlucky to gain a blue in only one year.

The 10th Viscount Cobham (formerly Charles Lyttelton), who brought zest and humour to many occupations from the captaincy of Worcestershire to the Governor-Generalship of New Zealand.

A charming photograph of Ian Akers-Douglas with his parents and sister in 1928.

When the declaration came with eight wickets down Harrow were left to score 308 in 210 minutes, a formidable target. Harrow to their credit chased the target all the way and very nearly succeeded, going down by 28 runs with 15 minutes to spare. A.G. Hazlerigg's clever variations of flight and spin tempted Harrow all the way and he finished with 5/73 including three stumpings. Akers-Douglas was most unlucky not to get his blue at Oxford, representing them in 1929/30 and scoring centuries in the Freshmens' trials in 1929 and the Seniors' match of 1930. He played 48 times for Kent between 1929/38 with reasonable success and was a very fine rackets player, representing Oxford and winning the British Open in 1933. He was sadly killed in a shooting accident in 1952. J.KN. Mayhew, the Eton wicket-keeper of 1928, was somewhat fortunate to get an Oxford blue in 1930 and afterwards played for Buckinghamshire. W.O'B. Lindsay, the Harrow opening batsman and wicket-keeper of 1926/8, played for Oxford from 1929/32 gaining his blue in 1931 and averaging 20 with the bat. He was afterwards to have a distinguished career in the Sudan, as Sir William Lindsay, becoming Chief Justice.

Harrow were somewhat lucky to avoid a second defeat in **1929** and after Eton had led by 29 runs in the first innings K.F.H. Hale in the innings of the match made 109 in 75 minutes, hitting 15 fours all round the wicket, well supported by his captain, A.G. Hazlerigg, with 71. The attendance on both days reached an all time record, some 22,000 came on the first day and 25,000 on the second day. In retrospect Eton were far too cautious in setting Harrow a target of 294 in 145 minutes. Harrow never looked like getting anywhere and struggled to keep the Eton bowlers, particularly J.H. Nevinson, out, finishing on 108/6. Lord Dalmeny, the Eton batsman who had scored 65 in this match and son of the legendary Lord Rosebery died of blood poisoning in his second year at Oxford after playing one match for Oxford in 1930 and two matches for Middlesex, following his father who had captained Surrey from 1905/7. It was

George Hirst (Yorkshire and England). A much loved Eton coach for 19 years from 1920/38 after an outstanding career for Yorkshire from 1889 to 1929. He will always be remembered for his 2,385 runs and 208 wickets in 1906, a record that one can safely say will never be broken.

Arthur Hazlerigg Eton XI 1927/9, Cambridge 1930/2 & Leicestershire. A good example of the gifted amateur and a very fine man to boot.

A.G. Pelham, Eton XI 1930, Cambridge 1934 and Sussex. An outstanding bowling performance of 11/44 in the match led Eton to victory by 8 wickets in 1930. Grandson of the Hon. F.G. Pelham (later 5th Earl of Chichester, who also played for Cambridge and Sussex) he bowled well to take 35 wickets in 1934 for Cambridge.

a tragedy that his father was said to have never got over. J.H. Nevinson, the Eton opening bowler of 1928/9, played a few first-class matches for Oxford in 1929/31 and six matches for Middlesex in 1933 but proved expensive as his 21 wickets cost 53 runs each. A.G. Hazlerigg, the Eton captain of 1929 and son of Sir Arthur Hazlerigg who captained Leicestershire between 1907/10, gained Cambridge blues from 1930/2, captaining them in 1932, and played 34 matches for Leicestershire between 1930/4, captaining the side in 1934 before having to give up first-class cricket for his career as a chartered surveyor. He averaged 26 in his 66 first-class matches and took 112 wickets. Arthur Hazlerigg had an extremely good war record gaining the M.C. and retiring as a Colonel in the Artillery. In thanking him for the magnificent support provided by his battery which had saved many lives, the commanding officer of the operation paid Hazlerigg the compliment of saying *'Arthur you shoot guns even better than you play cricket.'* A passionate golfer he retained his enormous zest for life into great old age and was still playing at the age of 85 finally dying in 2002 at the age of 92. He had succeeded his father in 1949 as the second Lord Hazlerigg.

Victor Rothschild, Harrow's stylish right-hand opening bat, represented Northants in 10 county matches between 1929/31 before giving up the game to concentrate on his academic career. He was an extremely eminent scientist and chairman of the Government think-tank on scientific policy in the 1970s. After inheriting the Rothschild barony in 1937 at the age of 27 he became a key figure in the Allies' war effort as director of military intelligence. After the war he became a director of several large companies including Shell and the family bank, N.M. Rothschild & Sons. A distinguished author of several books and scientific papers on a wide variety of subjects, he was also a fine golfer. Terence Rattigan was in the Harrow side of 1929 but did not play in the 1930 match at Lord's, although he had played throughout the season, because of an altercation with the Harrow authorities. He afterwards became one of the most famous playwrights of his generation.

Eton were indebted to an outstanding bowling performance from A.G. Pelham for their convincing win by 8 wickets in **1930**. None of the Harrow batsmen, apart from J.M. Stow with 64 in the Harrow first innings of 199, could get to grips with his immaculate length and variations in pace and movement off the wicket. He deservedly finished with match figures of 11/44, an average of 4 per wicket and the lowest cost in the series. J.C. Atkinson-Clark took full advantage of a simple dropped catch early on during his innings to punish the Harrow attack in his 135. Eton knocked off the 46 they needed with relative ease and the match was finished by 4.45 on the second day. A.G. Pelham went on to gain a Cambridge blue in 1934 and played 10 matches for Sussex from 1930/3 taking 84 wickets in his 35 first-class matches. A.S. Lawrence, the Harrow captain of 1930, went on to get a Cambridge blue in 1933, averaging 26 with the bat, but he died young at the age of 28 in 1939.

The Gentlemen's XI of 1931 captained by Douglas Jardine, containing the gifted Aidan Crawley, arguably the best of the 12 Crawley's who have played for Harrow. Aidan Crawley is standing fourth in the back row next to Freddie Brown of Surrey, Northants and England. Walter Robins Middlesex & England is in the front row on the right and father of Charles Robins Eton XI 1950/3 & Middlesex.

A.W. Allen Eton XI 1929/31, Cambridge 1933/4 and Northants. Scored 112 in the great opening partnership of 208 in 1931 with Neil Hotchkin, the highest first wicket stand in the history of the match. He was regarded as one of the most brilliant amateur cricketers of his generation and it was a great loss to Northants that he gave up serious cricket after leaving Cambridge and went into Lloyd's.

A very experienced Eton side with eight old colours overwhelmed a rather weak Harrow side in **1931** by an innings and 16 runs. On an easy-paced wicket Eton achieved the second highest score in the history of the match and the highest first wicket partnership of 208 before lunch on the first day between A.W. Allen, 112, and N.S. Hotchkin, 153. Harrow were bowled out in three hours for 245 and followed on 186 behind. They fared better in their second innings and when they were 144/1 with M. Tindall in his first Lord's scoring 77, there seemed to be some hope of saving the game but a brisk collapse against the medium-paced seam bowling of N.E.W. Baker erased all hope and Harrow were out for 170 with Baker taking 5/14 and 9/60 in the match. Allen, Eton's brilliant right-hand opening batsman of 1929/31, gained Cambridge blues in 1933/4 and played a handful of games for Northants between 1932/6. It was unfortunate that he virtually gave up serious cricket after he left Cambridge because he was good enough to have made a considerable impact on the game. He is the only Etonian to have scored centuries against Harrow, Winchester and Oxford. Atkinson-Clark, the Eton centurion of 1930 and captain in 1931, played eight matches for Middlesex between 1930/2 but had little success due to his inexperience at the higher level. A. Benn, the Harrow middle order batsman, went on to play for Oxford in 1934/5 gaining his blue in 1935 and averaging 19 in his 12 first-class matches.

Harrow for once were favourites to win the **1932** contest as Eton had only two of the all-powerful 1931 side left, but some splendid batting from N.S. Hotchkin saved Eton from

Neil Hotchkin leading out the Eton XI of 1933

N.S. Hotchkin Eton XI 1931/3, Cambridge 1935 & Middlesex. The outstanding schoolboy batsman of his generation. His record at Lord's v. Harrow was phenomonal 153, 109, 96, 88 & 12 and it was surprising that his record in first-class cricket was so modest. It was interrupted by the war years and he afterwards played a few games for Middlesex with a view to succeeding George Mann as captain. His career as a stockbroker militated against this.

M. Tindall Harrow XI 1931/3. Cambridge 1935/7 & Middlesex. A most elegant batsman he captained Harrow & Cambridge but never came to terms with the first-class game & his record was disappointing given his talent. A much loved Harrow House Master & cricket beak from 1946/59.

defeat. He went very close to equalling M.C. Bird's feat of 1907 in scoring two centuries in the match with 109 and 96. Harrow's 66-run lead owed much to R. Pulbrook's 104 and Eton finished 150 runs ahead at the close of play. F.E. Covington, the left-handed Harrow batsman of 1930/2 and captain in 1931/2, played a few matches for Cambridge and Middlesex with relatively limited success averaging 18 with the bat. Attendance at the match was still considerable and nearly 30,000 people paid for admission at Lord's in 1932. N.E.W. Baker, the Eton captain and opening bowler, played three first-class matches for Cambridge in 1934/5, taking 11 wickets at 17 per wicket and was probably rather unlucky not to be given a further trial. He afterwards played for Berkshire.

Once again in **1933** the Harrow captain, M. Tindall, tried hard to achieve a Harrow victory but did not quite have the bowling strength to get Eton out twice. Harrow owed much to a very fine innings from J.H. Pawle who just missed his century on 96 out of a total of 237 and N.S. Hotchkin, the Eton captain, was responsible for 88 out of Eton's total of 195. Harrow batted far too slowly in their second innings and setting Eton a target of 189 to win in 95 minutes was unrealistic. When Eton lost wickets quickly, including Hotchkin for 12 - his only failure in five innings at Lord's - the match quietly subsided into a rather dull draw. Hotchkin's record at Lord's in his five innings was both impressive and unprecedented: 153, 109, 96, 88 and 12, at an average of 92. He gained a blue at Cambridge in 1935 and played a few games for Middlesex between 1939/48 with a view to taking over the captaincy from George Mann. His career as a stockbroker in the city unfortunately prevented this but he never quite fulfilled his outstanding schoolboy promise, averaging only 21 in his 23 first-class matches. Mark Tindall, the Harrow captain of 1933, although a most elegant batsman, found it hard to adapt to first-class cricket. He was a Cambridge blue for 3 years from 1935/7, captaining the side in 1937, and he played 16 matches for Middlesex between 1933/8. Mark Tindall scored a century against M.C.C. in 1933 and made 80 against Nottinghamshire including the great England fast bowlers Larwood and Voce on his debut for Middlesex in the same year. It was a remarkable achievement for a schoolboy and there was no doubt he was one of the best players of fast bowling around but was nowhere near so comfortable against slow bowling and a first class average of 25 did not do justice to his great ability. J.M. Brocklebank, the Eton leg-break bowler of 1933 who was a nephew of F.S. Jackson, gained a Cambridge blue in 1936 and played four games for Lancashire in 1939. He was selected for the M.C.C. tour to India in 1939/40 but this was cancelled owing to the War. He took 68 wickets in his 21 first-class matches and after the War played for Cheshire. He became chairman of Cunard, the family shipping company, and as Sir John placed the order for the QE2. He died in 1974 at the age of 59. Roger Pulbrook, the Harrow centurion of 1932, went on to gain Oxford blues for rackets, lawn tennis and squash between 1933/6.

Both captains distinguished themselves in **1934** in what was to prove a rather uninspiring match. The Eton captain, A.N.A. Boyd, scored 100 in Eton's first innings total of 306, but it was not of the same calibre as his opposite number and Harrow dropped three catches off him in his long knock. J.P. Mann's leg-breaks soon had Harrow in trouble and they followed on 137 behind with Mann taking 5/66. Harrow made a much better showing in their second innings due to a magnificent knock from their captain, J.H. Pawle, who made one of the most unselfish acts of all in this series by declaring the Harrow innings closed when he was on 93 not out. It proved to be a fruitless exercise since after losing three quick wickets in a vain

J.M. Brocklebank (later Sir John Brocklebank Bt). Eton XI 1933, Cambridge 1936 & Lancashire. Pictured third from left in the back row of the Gentlemen XI of 1939 captained by Wally Hammond. A nephew of F.S. Jackson and medium pace leg break bowler who was chosen for the M.C.C. tour in 1939/40 to India which was subsequently cancelled because of the war. Afterwards he became chairman of the family shipping line Cunard and placed the order for the Q.E.2.

J.H. Pawle Harrow XI 1933/4, Cambridge 1936/7 & Essex. Scorer of 96 & 93 not out in 1933 and 1934 respectively at Lord's he was a very fine striker of the ball as befitted a top class rackets player who was British amateur champion from 1946/9 and twice challenger for the World title. His career was also interrupted by the war years and he afterwards played for Hertfordshire. After a long career as a stockbroker he became a successful artist in retirement.

M.A.C.P. Kaye Harrow XI 1933/5 and Cambridge University 1938. The second of three generations of Harrow XI cricketers.

P.M. Studd (later Sir Peter Studd). Harrow XI 1933/5, Cambridge 1937/9. The Harrow captain of 1935 scored 100 not out in the even draw of that year. Captain of Cambridge in 1939 his first class career was halted by the war. He became director of De La Rue after the war and a highly successful Lord Mayor of London in 1970/1.

attempt to score 107 runs in 50 minutes, Eton promptly shut up shop. Pawle went on to gain Cambridge blues in 1936/7 and also played a few games for Essex. He averaged over 28 in his 34 first-class matches with three centuries, he was also a superb rackets player, representing the university in all three years, and was Amateur Singles champion from 1946/9, beating D.S. Milford narrowly three times by 3-2 on each occasion, and doubles champion in 1939 and 1946. 1934 was the first year the two Mann brothers appeared, F.G. and J.P., sons of the famous J.T. Mann, a former captain of Middlesex and England.

An evenly matched game between two well balanced sides eventually resulted in yet another draw in **1935**, but it was still an interesting contest. W.R. Rees-Davies, the Eton opening bowler who was compared favourably to Gubby Allen, took 5/66 in Harrow's 249 and M.A.C.P. Kaye's 6/91 in Eton's 298 was also a fine performance. P.M. Studd, the Harrow captain of 1935 and a relation of the famous Etonian Studds made no mistake in securing his century and declared the Harrow innings when on 100 not out, setting Eton a target of 156 in 105 minutes. Eton made an attempt but the Harrow bowling was too accurate and they were forced to hold out for a draw and finished on 94/6, 62 runs short. Peter Studd gained Cambridge blues from 1937/9, captaining the side in 1939, and but for the War years would probably have played more first-class cricket. He averaged 26 in his 28 first-class matches for Cambridge with a top score of 80 not out. He was a director of Thomas De La Rue till his retirement in 1981 and a most distinguished Lord Mayor of London in 1970/1. M.A.C.P. Kaye, the Harrow medium-pace opening bowler of 1933/35 and hard hitting lower-order batsman, gained a Cambridge blue in 1938, averaged 18 with the bat and took 31 wickets at the relatively high cost of 40 per wicket. After being wounded in the War he became A.D.C. to the Queen from 1969/71 and a deputy Lieutenant of West Riding. W.R. Rees-Davies, the Eton opening bowler of 1934/5, gained a Cambridge blue in 1938 but was a little too inconsistent to be successful at the higher level. His 33 wickets cost over 43 each but his cricket career was cut short by the loss of his arm in the War. He went on to become a well-known barrister after his father who was a former Chief Justice of Hong Kong and Liberal M.P. for Pembroke. He himself became Conservative M.P. for the Isle of Thanet from 1953/83 but his acerbic Welsh temperament militated against ministerial office despite his undoubted ability.

A severely rain-affected match in **1936** resulted in only the Harrow innings being completed. F.G. Mann, the Eton captain in the last of his three appearances at Lord's, had little opportunity to show his great ability which manifested itself after the War years. He gained Cambridge blues in 1938/9 but his 54 appearances for Middlesex between 1937/54 were somewhat limited by the pressures of the family brewing business which became Watney Mann. His overall first-class batting average of 26 in 166 first-class matches was only adequate but he excelled

The captains of England and South Africa toss at Newlands, Cape Town before the start of the Third Test on 7ᵗʰ January 1949. George Mann (Eton, Cambridge, Middlesex & England) was an outstanding choice as captain and won the series 2/0. Dudley Nourse was the South African captain.

W.R.Rees – Davies Eton XI 1934/5, Cambridge 1938. A fine schoolboy fast bowler who was compared favourably with the great Gubby Allen. A little too inconsistent at Cambridge but he had a good action as can be seen here.

Five members of the Eton XI in 1936, all from the same House, R.M. England, F.G. Mann, R.A. Walker, J.P. Mann, A.J.B. Marsham.

himself as captain and batsman in his seven test matches, particularly so on the successful tour of South Africa in 1948/9. His test batting average of 38 was good enough for him to hold his place as a player and there is little doubt that he would have remained England captain for several more years had business allowed, such was his concern for and popularity with his players. He became an extremely influential administrator of the game as both chairman of the T.C.C.B. and Middlesex and the Governor of I. Zingari following Lord Home. D.H. Macindoe, the Eton swing bowler of 1935/6, showed a glimpse of his great ability in this match with figures of 6/50 in Harrow's modest total of 180. Eton finished on 26/0 and in all probability had the game gone the full course Harrow would have lost. Macindoe achieved blues from 1937/9 bowling with great success and after the War captained Oxford in 1946. He took 152 first-class wickets in his 42 matches and was also a more than useful lower-order batsman. David Macindoe was a highly respected master in charge of cricket from 1949/60 at Eton before becoming a House Master and ending his career at Eton as Vice Provost of the College. He was the great grandson of G. R. Dupuis Eton XI 1851/3 and the first master at Eton to supervise the cricket. B.D. Carris, the Harrow right-hand opening batsman of 1933/6 and captain in 1936, was the brother of H.E. Carris who had gained Cambridge blues for cricket and rugby in 1929 and 1930 respectively and went on to play 36 matches for Middlesex between 1928/33. Bertie Carris gained Cambridge cricket blues in 1938/39 as well as a rugby blue in 1936 and a golf blue in 1939. He was a highly talented sportsman and played 12 matches for Middlesex from 1937/39 but his overall first-class average of 23 in 32 matches did not reflect this. As with so many of his generation his career was cut short by the War and he was wounded in the Scots Guards. He afterwards emigrated to South Africa where he was in business for many years.

B.D. Carris Harrow XI 1933/6, Cambridge 1938/9 and Middlesex 1937/39. A fine all-round sportsman with blues for cricket, rugby & golf.

J.P. Mann Eton XI 1934/7 and Middlesex. The winning Eton captain of 1937 with 57 and 32 not out to take his side to victory by 7 wickets. He was initially regarded as more talented than his brother F.G. and extremely unlucky not to get a blue at Cambridge in 1939. The war years again cut short a promising first class career.

R.A.A. Holt Harrow XI 1936/8. An exceptional schooolboy cricketer, he scored 111 in 1937 when Eton won by 7 wickets and would have led Harrow to certain victory in 1938 had not rain intervened. He scored 910 runs in 1938 at an average of 101, only recently beaten in 2004 by Martin Walters. He played five matches for Sussex in 1938/9 without making any impact and was a very fine rackets player winning the British Amateur Doubles in 1947 & 1949.

In the first definite result since 1931 Eton were indebted to their captain J.P. Mann, the younger son of the great Frank Mann, in his fourth year in the XI for guiding them to victory by 7 wickets with 15 minutes to spare in **1937**. Harrow's captain, M.D. Watson, could also claim credit for setting Eton a competitive target of 156 in 95 minutes after a brilliant knock from R.A.A. Holt with 111 enabled Harrow to reach 211/5 in their second innings after both teams had batted poorly in their first with the exception of Mann, 57, and J.F. Boughey, 61, for Eton. S.M.A. Banister, the Eton off-break bowler, was largely responsible for Harrow's collapse to 118 in the first innings with figures of 6/32, the last four with successive deliveries and the first hat-trick since E.G. Whately for Eton in 1900. Mann played a few games for Cambridge in 1938/9 with limited success and was most unlucky not to get a Cambridge blue in 1939 before war interrupted his studies. He played 15 matches for Middlesex between 1939/47 with some success. As a schoolboy he was judged more talented than his brother George but afterwards there was little comparison. A.J.B. Marsham, the Eton leg-break bowler and left-handed lower-order batsman of 1936/7, came from a strong cricketing background. His grandfather C.D.B. Marsham was an Oxford blue for five years from 1854/8 and was widely regarded as the best amateur bowler of his day, appearing ten times for the Gentlemen v. the Players at Lord's with a best performance of 9/64 v. The Gentlemen of England in 1855. His father C.H.B., who played in the Eton XI of 1897/8, gained Oxford blues from 1900/2 and played 141 matches for Kent between 1900/22, captaining the side from 1904/8 and leading them to the Championship in 1906. He also had two great uncles who had gained cricket blues for Oxford. He himself gained an Oxford blue in 1939 and after the War played six matches for Kent in 1946/7. His record was modest - he took 35 wickets at over 39 per wicket and averaged 16 with the bat. F.F.T. Barnardo, the Eton middle-order batsman of 1936/7 who scored 62 not out in 1937 to lead Eton home to victory by 7 wickets, was unlucky only to play one match for both Cambridge and Middlesex, scoring 75 and two 0s, but was killed in the War at El Alamein in 1942.

In **1938** Harrow were denied an almost certain victory by the weather, which interrupted play on both days. They needed only 149 to win in 145 minutes when rain stopped play with 135 minutes to go and Harrow on 16/1. R.A.A. Holt, the Harrow centurion of 1937 and captain in 1938, was cruelly robbed of victory after a magnificent season in which he had scored 910 runs at an average of 101, the record number of runs and average in a Harrow season until 2004 when Martin Walters beat this with 1204 runs at an average of 109. Holt was a fine all-round sportsman whose sporting career was cruelly cut short by the War. He played five matches for Sussex in 1938/9 with little success and represented Cambridge at rackets in 1939. He played very little serious cricket after the War when he became a solicitor and chairman of the Hutchinson Publishing Group. He won the British Amateur Rackets Doubles in 1947 and 1949 with A.R. Taylor. D.R. Hayward, the Harrow leg-break and googly bowler of 1937/8, who had been largely responsible for bowling out Eton for 118 in their second innings with an analysis of 5/40, played nine first-class games for Oxford and Middlesex in 1939 taking 20 wickets at 30 per wicket but was killed in a flying accident in April 1945.

A record number of years without a Harrow win (1909/39) was finally ended in **1939** when Harrow at last achieved victory after the unlucky result in 1938. It was appropriate that the two main architects of the Harrow victory were E. Crutchley, 115, and G.F. Anson, 74, son and nephew respectively of the two heroes of Harrow's last win in 1908: G.E.V. Crutchley and Hon. R. Anson. Harrow, left to score 131 to win in plenty of time were led home to victory by the Harrow captain, A.O.L. Lithgow, with 67 not out. Frenzied scenes ensued reminiscent of the first match after the Great War in 1919 when warnings were issued by Lord's about fighting between the two schools' supporters and such a warning would probably have been issued once again but for the commencement of the War. The press cuttings of the day reveal a scene of total chaos: top hats were smashed in, ties torn and trousers ripped off. One very distinguished Old Etonian punched an Old Harrovian who was a pillar of the Church. Immediately two other Old Harrovians set upon the Old Etonian, threw him to the ground and tore off his trousers. Schoolboys soon joined in amidst the carnage, noses bled, eyes were blackened and the police intervened.

Crutchley looked destined to follow in his father's footsteps for Middlesex and Oxford had not the War intervened. He played for Oxford during the War against Cambridge but had no luck in his two matches for Middlesex in 1947. The demands of his stockbroking career meant he

E. Crutchley Harrow XI 1939/40. It was somewhat appropriate that his match winning innings of 115 was the main reason why Harrow were victorious in 1939, their first win since 1908 when his father G.E.V. was the hero with bat and ball. A war time blue at Oxford he was wounded in the war and afterwards became a stockbroker.

The Oxford XI of 1939 containing D.H. Macindoe front row, left, Eton XI 1935/6 and Oxford 1937/9 and 1946. An extremely accurate medium-pace swing bowler he took 6/50 in the rain affected match of 1936. He played successfully for Oxford from 1937/9 and returned after the war to captain the side in 1946. He took 152 first-class wickets in his four years at Oxford and was an outstanding master in charge of cricket at Eton from 1949/60. He became Vice Provost of Eton after his retirement as a House Master. A.J.B. Marsham, back row far left, Eton XI 1936/7, Oxford 1939 and Kent. He came from a long line of distinguished cricketers and was in the winning Eton XI of 1937 and Oxford in 1939. LEFT TO RIGHT, BACK ROW: A.J.B. Marsham, R. Sale, P.H. Blagg, S. Pether, J. Stanning, G. Evans. FRONT ROW: E.D.R. Eagar, D.H. Macindoe, E.J.H. Dixon, J.M. Lomas, R.B. Proud.

was unable to play any more serious cricket thereafter. G.F. Anson, who played in the Harrow XIs of 1939 and 1941 but was ill in the 1940 season, was an attacking right-hand batsman who played in the wartime Cambridge side of 1942 and returned to Cambridge in 1946 after serving in the Coldstream Guards during the War. He looked certain to gain his blue in 1947 but left the university to take up a colonial appointment. He played seven matches for Kent in the same year and averaged 26 in his 10 first-class matches.

Class divisions in 1937. Harrovians Peter Wagner (left) and Thomas 'Timmy' Dyson come under the scrutiny of local lads George Salmon, Jack Catlin and George Young as they wait outside the gates for Dyson's parents. But a family tragedy haunts Bert Hardy's famous social commentary of toffs and urchins. The following year, 1938, Dyson travelled to India to join his parents for the summer holidays, caught diphtheria on the ship out and died shortly after arriving. His father, Lt-Colonel George Dyson, MC, himself an Old Harrovian, died in Korea in 1942 while a prisoner-of-war of the Japanese.

THE WAR YEARS

1940-1945

The single innings wartime matches played from **1940/5** alternated between Eton and Harrow and went very much Eton's way apart from 1943 when the match was abandoned. The first contest in **1940** at Harrow was by far the most exciting when Eton scraped home by 1 wicket. The performances of A.V. Gibbs for Eton with 7/43 and D.F. Henley for Harrow with 6/38 were the features of the match although the Eton captain D.W.J. Colman's knock of 92 was an excellent one. There is little doubt that Eton produced the more distinguished cricketers during this period of whom the best were the Hon. L.R. White, Eton XI 1943/4, P.D.S. Blake, Eton XI 1943/5 and captain in 1945, C.R.D. Rudd, Eton XI 1944/6 and captain in 1946, and W.G. Keighley, Eton XI 1941/3 and captain in 1943.

Harrow had two future blues in D.F. Henley, Harrow XI 1939/41, M.H. Wrigley, Harrow XI 1942, and very little else. Notable performances by Harrovians were few and far between in these years apart from M.N. Garnett's 82 not out in 1945 when Harrow were still beaten by 6 wickets due to an outstanding innings from Blake with 76 not out. Among other fine performances for Eton during these years, not already mentioned, were C.M. Wheatley's 7/31 and 48 not out in 1941, T.H. Marshall's 7/24 in 1942 and Hon. L.R. White's 76 in 1944.

D.F. Henley, Harrow's opening bowler from 1939/41 gained Oxford cricket and golf blues in 1947. In his 17 first-class matches for Oxford he was more successful with the bat than the ball, averaging over 21 with the bat and taking 23 wickets at over 40 apiece and he later played for Suffolk. White, Eton's middle order batsman of 1943/4, was undoubtedly a highly talented cricketer who would have achieved more but for the War years. He scored 102 for the Public

Hon. L.R. White (later Lord Annaly) Eton XI 1943/4. A highly talented schoolboy cricketer he scored 102 for the Public Schools v. Lord's XI and played in the victory test for England v. Australia in 1945. After a year at Cambridge he served in the RAF for five years and then went into the city. A great loss to the first class game.

P.D.S. Blake, Eton XI 1943/5, Oxford 1950/2 and Sussex. One of Eton's best schoolboy batsmen with five centuries in his last year. Stylish middle order batsman and captain of Oxford in 1952. His decision to go into the church meant an early retirement from the first class game in 1953.

Schools v. Lord's XI, captained by R.W.V. Robins, the Middlesex and England captain, and 77 for a joint Middlesex and Essex side v. Kent and Surrey and played in the victory test for England v. Australia in 1945 during his one year at Cambridge. This was a very fine achievement for an 18-year-old schoolboy. He served in the R.A.F. for 5 years and his first-class cricket was limited to three matches for Middlesex in 1946/7 with little success. He later went into the city and became a partner in W. Greenwell, the well-known stockbroking firm.

M.H. Wrigley, the Harrow right-arm fast-medium bowler of 1942, gained an Oxford blue in 1949 and took 48 wickets at an average of 22 per wicket in his 16 first-class matches for the university and the Combined Services, a creditable achievement.

B. H. Farr, Harrow's right arm medium pace bowler of 1942, played for Cambridge University in 1943 and six matches for Notts between 1949/51 with best figures of 5/96. He was Managing Director of the family owned Home Brewery in Nottingham for many years before it was taken over by Scottish & Newcastle Breweries.

Alistair McCorquodale the the Harrow left arm fast bowler of 1943/4 played 3 matches for Middlesex in 1951 and went on the M.C.C. Tour to Canada in 1951. He was better known as a fine sprinter and the 'fastest white man in the world', coming fourth in the 1948 Olympic Games at White City. He afterwards became Chairman of the family printing company McCorquodale's for many years before it was taken over.

W.G. Keighley, Eton's sound opening right-hand batsman, gained Oxford blues in 1947/8 and played for Yorkshire from 1947/51 in 35 matches. He went on the M.C.C. tour to Canada in 1951 and scored 2,539 runs in his first-class career at an average of 27. Geoffrey Keighley still holds the second wicket partnership record of 226 in the Varsity match made with Tony Pawson in 1947. He was the first to unravel the magic of West Indian bowling 'magician' Sonny Ramadhin as he watched his original bowling action through binoculars. He then successfully showed the combined Minor Counties team, which he captained, how to combat the new sensation. He was later approached to captain M.C.C., Yorkshire and Middlesex but by then he had decided to emigrate to Australia for cattle farming. He stood on the New South Wales Legislative Council for 13 years and died in 2005 at the age of 80.

P.D.S. Blake, Eton's stylish middle-order batsman and captain in 1945, scored nearly 800 runs in the season for Eton with five centuries and was the best schoolboy cricketer of the year, averaging over 86 per innings. He went on to gain Oxford blues from 1950/2, captaining the side in 1952 and playing 23 matches for Sussex between 1946/51. He scored 2,067 first-class runs at an average of over 22. His decision to go into the church cut short his highly promising cricket career thereafter.

C. R. D. Rudd won an Oxford Blue as a freshman in 1949 in a talented XI that had beaten Yorkshire and Middlesex but lost to Cambridge at Lord's by 7 wickets, in the 'surprise of the season' as Wisden put it. He toured Canada with M.C.C. under R. W. V. Robins in 1951 and although failing to score heavily proved his all round ability by taking 14 wickets at an average of 9 and taking some excellent close catches. He afterwards returned to South Africa to work for the Anglo-American Corporation, of whom his family were one of the founders in 1952 and died in 1997.

W.G. Keighley Eton XI 1941/3, Oxford 1947/8 and Yorkshire. Here seen opening the batting with the great Len Hutton at Bramall Lane, Sheffield for Yorkshire v. South Africa in 1951. The pair put on 169 for the first wicket of which Geoffrey Keighley scored 51.

Field Marshal the Lord Bramall KG GCB OBE MC JP Eton XI 1941/2 & Combined Services. A fine cricketer and outstanding soldier who led the British troops in the Falklands War.

11th July 1940. Patsy Hendren coaches two Harrovians in the week before their match against Eton. Though they look vastly superior they must have taken some of his advice. In the match D. F. Henley (CENTRE) 'struck a brilliant streak of bowling' (Wisden) and finished with 6 for 36. J. F. Godsell (LEFT) took 2 for 49 but Eton won by 1 wicket. The great Middlesex and England cricketer coached at Harrow between 1937-47.

C.R.D. Rudd, Eton XI 1944/6 and Oxford 1949. BACK ROW, SECOND LEFT: Eton's captain in 1946 when he should have enforced the follow on. He was in a strong Oxford XI in 1949 which won six first class matches but lost the varsity match by 7 wickets. M.H. Wrigley, Harrow XI 1942, Combined Services and Oxford 1949. Back row third right, he took a creditable 48 wickets in his 16 first-class matches for Oxford and Combined Services at 22 per wicket and was somewhat unlucky to lose his place in the Oxford side of 1950. LEFT TO RIGHT, BACK ROW: M.B. Hofmeyer, C.R.D. Rudd, G.H. Chesterton, M.H. Wrigley, I.P. Campbell, B. Boobbyer. LEFT TO RIGHT, FRONT ROW: P.A. Whitcombe, C.E. Winn, C.B. Van Ryneveld, A.H. Kardar, D.B. Carr.

THE POST-WAR YEARS

1946-2005

Official contests started again at Lord's in **1946** after the end of hostilities and Eton might well have won had the Eton captain C.R.D. Rudd, son of the old Oxford and Olympic runner controversially not enforced the follow-on when Harrow were 123 behind on first innings after being bowled out for 190. He was severely criticised by Etonians, even more so when Rudd's generous declaration with two wickets down in their second innings failed to produce the result they deserved and Harrow finished 45 short with seven wickets down. Rudd went on to play for Oxford from 1949/51, but given his talent results were somewhat modest in his 21 first-class matches. W.N. Coles's 107 in the first innings for Eton was a useful knock but he made no further progress whilst at Cambridge.

Both sides were stronger in batting than bowling in **1947** and on an easy-paced wicket Eton probably batted on too long to have a realistic chance of bowling their opponents out in the second innings and the match finished in a rather tame draw with Harrow still six behind with four wickets down. There were fine innings on the Harrow side from R.H. Thompson, 71, and R. La T. Colthurst, 51, and two centuries for Eton in T. Hare, 103, and S.D.D. Sainsbury, 100. A most tragic death was to befall Thompson in the summer of 1948 whilst he was still at Harrow. Academically bright and a fine all-round games player, he was the son of R.W. Thompson, the Old Harrovian Headmaster of Aysgarth, the well-known preparatory school in North Yorkshire and there was no doubt that a golden future awaited him. It was one of the saddest events in Harrow's history.

Harrow just avoided defeat in **1948** with only one wicket remaining in their second innings and 42 runs short of victory. R.G. Marlar, the Harrow off-spinner in his second appearance at Lord's, showed glimpses of the promise that was to manifest itself in later years with 5/78 in Eton's second innings and there was a fine innings of 66 by A.S. Day, in his fourth year in the XI, in Harrow's second innings which effectively saved the day for his side. G.C. Hoyer-Millar the Harrow wicket-keeper captain of 1947/8, gained an Oxford rugby blue in 1951, played in two first class cricket matches and gained a boxing blue in 1952, and was capped for Scotland at rugby in 1953. He was afterwards Sainsbury's property director until his retirement. Both his father E.G. in 1918 and his son C.G. in 1976 played for Harrow.

Bobby Jacques Harrow X1 1947/50. The finest bowler of his generation, he would have done well in any company.

In **1949**'s low-scoring match, where conditions aided the bowlers, Eton deservedly won their first victory at Lord's since 1937 by 7 wickets, largely due to some good bowling performances from their opening bowler M.G.C. Jeffries with 4/7 in the Harrow first innings and 6/56 from their slow off-spin bowler J.S. Guthrie in the second innings. Marlar once again bowled well for Harrow in taking 6/60 during Eton's first innings score of 176 but Harrow's poor second innings performance left Eton an easy task and the match was all over by 3.30 p.m. on the second day. Marlar gained Cambridge blues from 1951/3, captaining the side in 1953 and played for Sussex between 1951/1968, although after 1959 his appearances were very limited. He took 970 first-class wickets and achieved 100 wickets in a season four times with a best of 139 in 1955 at an average of 21.55. He captained Sussex from 1955/59 and his best bowling performance in an innings was 9/46 v. Lancashire at Hove in 1959. He founded a management consultancy company and was the well-known cricket correspondent of the *Sunday Times* for over 40 years till the end of 1995. He was recently President of Sussex, a member of the M.C.C. Committee and the President of M.C.C. in 2005/6. I.R. Lomax, the Eton hard-hitting batsman and opening bowler of 1948/9, played most of his county cricket for Wiltshire but in 1962 played six matches for Somerset with some success before he fell out with them and did not play again. P.H. Ryan who played for Harrow in 1949 gained a Cambridge rugby blue in 1952 and later played for Richmond and England in 1955.

Royal box: the scene at the Eton and Harrow match of July 1946. From the left, Mrs. David Bowes Lyon, Princess Elizabeth, The Queen, Lord Harcourt, Lt. Philip Mountbatten, R. N., W. W. Hill-Wood, The King, Miss Sharman Douglas, Princess Margaret, Mr. Hugh Wyld, Sir Pelham Warner, Miss Davina Bowes Lyon, Hon. L. H. White, Mrs. Hugh Wyld. The royal engagement had been announced the previous day. Co-host Gubby Allen is out of the picture.

12th July 1946. Eton supporters arrive for the game at Lord's against Harrow. As at Ascot the game was on austerity lines and missing from the display were the familiar Eton top hats and straw hats of Harrow.

3D LORD'S MCC GROUND 3D

ETON v. HARROW
FRIDAY & SATURDAY, JULY 8, 9, 1949. (2-day Match)

HARROW

		First Innings		Second Innings	
1	B. G. O. Wilenkin	b Jeffreys	5	b Aird	0
2	G. S. O. Colthurst	c Aird b Jeffreys	2	b Guthrie	10
3	A. Falcon	b Jeffreys	5	l b w b Guthrie	11
†4	A. S. Day	b Guthrie	29	b Lomax	5
5	J. D. Thicknesse	b Lomax	2	c Wadham b Lomax	6
*6	R. M. Spiro	b Lomax	2	b Guthrie	22
7	J. W. E. Bleackley	b Guthrie	9	st Brooks b Guthrie	4
8	P. H. Ryan	b Guthrie	7	b Guthrie	38
9	R. G. Marlar	b Aird	45	b Jeffreys	0
10	M. Kok	l b w b Jeffreys	12	not out	0
11	R. A. Jacques	b Guthrie	0	l b w b Guthrie	4
		B 7, l-b 2, w 1, n-b	10	B 5, l-b 11, w 1, n-b 2	19
		Total	128	Total	151

FALL OF THE WICKETS

1—6 2—15 3—18 4—27 5—37 6—58 7—65 8—80 9—128 10—128
1—1 2—24 3—59 4—59 5—73 6—75 7—91 8—92 9—133 10—151

ANALYSIS OF BOWLING

Name	1st Innings O. M. R. W. Wd. N-b						2nd Innings O. M. R. W. Wd. N-b					
Jeffreys	10	4	7	4			10	4	15	1		2
Aird	4.2	0	11	1			10	1	30	1		
Lomax	7	3	21	2	1		13	3	39	2	1	
Wadham	3	0	13	0			1	1	0	0		
Guthrie	9	3	48	3			15.5	3	56	6		
Bailey	4	0	18	0			2	0	11	0		

ETON

		First Innings		Second Innings	
1	D. H. Clegg	b Marlar	27	c Thicknesse b Jacques	0
*2	R. A. Brooks	c and b Marlar	44	c Wilenkin b Marlar	3
3	I. R. Lomax	l b w b Thicknesse	17	b Kok	31
4	M. D. Sellar	c and b Marlar	7	not out	32
5	A. C. Ingleby-Mackenzie	b Marlar	17	not out	24
6	R. S. Napier	b Kok	12		
7	N. C. Wadham	not out	7		
†8	J. A. Bailey	b Kok	9		
9	M. G. C. Jeffreys	b Kok	0		
10	J. S. Guthrie	c Falcon b Marlar	12		
11	A. S. Aird	l b w b Marlar	6		
		B 21, l-b 2 w 1 n-b 1	23	B 14 l-b 2 w , n-b 1	17
		Total	176	Total	107

FALL OF THE WICKETS

1—51 2—76 3—97 4—108 5—139 6—139 7—139 8—141 9—159 10—176
1—0 2—21 3—58 4— 5— 6— 7— 8— 9— 10—

ANALYSIS OF BOWLING

Name	1st Innings O. M. R. W. Wd. N-b						2nd Innings O. M. R. W. Wd. N-b					
Jacques	7	1	15	0		1	8	2	29	1		
Kok	14	1	48	3	1	1	9	0	36	1		1
Marlar	19.5	3	69	6			14.2	5	27	1		
Thicknesse	6	0	13	1			3	0	8	0		
Falcon	6	1	18	0								

Umpires—Mavins & Watkins

Robin Marlar's off-breaks so impressed in his freshman year at Cambridge in 1951 that he was invited to join the Gentlemen at Lord's. 'Experienced batsmen faced him with respect,' Wisden noted. In an outstanding game of cricket in 1953 Cambridge won the Varsity match by 2 wickets with Marlar taking 12/143 in the match. President of M.C.C in 2005/6

This card does not necessarily include the fall of the last wicket

Surrey County Cricket Club 3D.
KENNINGTON OVAL
Y. A. of SURREY v. Y. A. of MIDDLESEX
Saturday, 30th August, 1947 (Two Day Match)

Y. A. of MIDDLESEX

		First Innings		Second Innings	
*1	P. Kelly	c Edes, b Bailey	128		
2	M. E. J. Fitzgerald	c Turton, b Nathan	45		
3	R. D. Owen	b Turton	35		
4	M. Hardy	b Wilkin	8		
5	T. Hare	c Riley, b Bailey	0		
6	P. D. J. Johnston	c Nathan, b Connell	15		
†7	G. Hoyer-Millar	c Nathan, b Turton	12		
8	M. P. Brooks	not out	73		
9	L. K. Lewis	b Turton	36		
10	Peter Kelly	lbw b Connell	10		
11	D. H. K. Rata				
		B 17, l-b4 , w2 , n-b1	24	B , l-b , w , n-b	
		Total (9 wkts)	386	Total	

FALL OF THE WICKETS

1—99 2—192 3—214 4—215 5—236 6—248 7—273 8—359 9—386 10—
1— 2— 3— 4— 5— 6— 7— 8— 9— 10—

BOWLING ANALYSIS

	First Innings O. M. R. Wd. N-b					Second Innings O. M. R. W. Wd. N-b					
Connell	18	1	60	2							
Bailey	21	5	59	2							
Wilkin	12	2	43	1							
Rendall	7	2	37	0							
Nathan	7	0	60	1							
Turton	15	1	56	3	2						
Millen	11	2	47	0							

Y. A. of SURREY

		First Innings		Second Innings	
*1	J. M. Edes	c Hoyer-Millar, b Rata	75	b Hardy	64
*2	G. S. F. Wilkin	c Rata, b Hardy	59	c Peter Kelly, b Johnston	4
*3	P. G. Nathan	st Hoyer-Millar b Rata	0	b Peter Kelly	0
5	B. G. de Clive-Lowe	lbw b Lewis	88	b Rata	10
6	J. A. Bailey	b P. Kelly	14	c Hoyer-Millar, b Hardy	9
7	A. S. J. Riley	b Johnston, b P. Kelly	90	c and b Hardy	2
8	P. H. Turton	c Hoyer-Millar, b P. Kelly	13	st Hoyer-Millar, b Hardy	6
9	A. J. Millen	st Hoyer-Millar, b Rata	0	b Rata	
10	D. A. Connell	not out	6	not out	
11	S. D. Rendall	b Rata	11	lbw b Hardy	17
†3	R. A. Russell				
		B 1 , l-b 5 , w , n-b2	8	B 5 , l-b , w , n-b 1	
		Total	359	Total	117

FALL OF THE WICKETS

1—113 2—113 3—144 4—177 5—186 6—218 7—238 8—248 9—244 10—256
1—13 2—15 3—42 4—61 5—99 6—99 7—108 8—111 9—117 10—11

BOWLING ANALYSIS

	First Innings O. M. R. Wd. N-b					Second Innings O. M. R. W. Wd. N-b					
Lewis	12	2	42	2							
Peter Kelly	16	2	71	0	2	4	0	11	1		
Rata	20	5	71	4		10.3	4	26	3		
Owen	2	0	17	0							
Hardy	8	3	27	1		9	3	30	5		
P. Kelly	6	2	23	3		9	3	30	0		
Johnston						6	1	29	1		
Brooks						3	1	24	0		

*Captain †Wkt.-keeper Toss won by MIDDLESEX

Umpires—J. Scott and G. H. Beet Result—Middx won by an innings and 10 runs

HOURS OF PLAY—

1st Day 11.30—6.30. Lunch 1.30. 2nd Day 11.0—6.0 or 6.30 Lunch 1.15.

LIST OF FIXTURES ON BACK OF CARD CUSHIONS MAY BE HIRED 6d. EACH PER DAY

OFFICIAL SCORE CARDS ARE NOT SOLD OUTSIDE THE GROUND

Loudspeaker Equipment by R. G. JONES & Co., Morden, Surrey.

Printed on the Ground by the Surrey County Cricket Club Printing Department

A.C.D. Ingleby-Mackenzie Eton XI 1949/51 and Hampshire. He scored 81 and 52 in 1951 when Harrow were desperately lucky to avoid defeat. A most popular and enterprising captain of Hampshire from 1958/65 he led them to the championship in 1961 and was president of M.C.C for two years from October 1996/8.

G.C. Hoyer-Millar, Harrow XI 1946/8. A talented wicketkeeper batsman who captained Harrow in 1947/8 as can be seen from the county representative game scorecard where he took seven victims. He went on to gain an Oxford rugby blue in 1952 and Scottish rugby caps in 1953 as well as representing Oxford behind the stumps.

Harrow were probably rather unlucky not to win in **1950** when needing only 103 runs to win in 112 minutes. An hour's play was lost to rain and Harrow, in their desperate attempt to score the runs in 52 minutes, only succeeded in losing five of their wickets for 34 runs before the close of play. R.A. Jacques, the Harrow captain and opening bowler in his fourth year in the XI, so nearly pulled it off for Harrow with seven wickets in the match to gain a decisive 45-run advantage on the first innings. His 57 wickets in the season for Harrow was a record until 1975 when it was broken by A.C.S. Pigott with 58 and his 149 wickets in his four years in the XI still remains the record. He was a very unusual bowler by all accounts. His opening partner Myron Kok in 1950 described it thus, *'the ball used to move straight down the pitch from his hand, curling round at the very last moment most viciously, rather like the handle of a walking stick'*. He also bowled off the wrong foot and therefore must have been very difficult to read and was also exceptional in the field. It seemed a huge waste of talent that he went no further in the game through lack of encouragement and opportunity and became a Civil Servant.

The 16 year old King Faisal of Iraq who was at Harrow spectating at the 1951 match. He was assassinated in 1958.

Eton were desperately unlucky not to win the **1951** match and Harrow were totally outplayed in both batting and bowling. They had two outstanding schoolboy cricketers in A.C.D. Ingleby-Mackenzie, whose 81 and 52 showed promise of much to come, and the superb leg spin bowling of R.V.C. Robins, son of R.W.V. the Middlesex and England captain, whose match figures of 13/91 were the second highest in the match after H.W. Studd's 14/99 in 1888. Harrow just managed to hang on for a draw with 9 wickets down, 104 runs short of the Eton target. As a schoolboy Ingleby-Mackenzie was outstanding at all sports and after national service in the Navy was to prove a fine attacking middle-order batsman between 1951/65 for Hampshire and an inspiring captain. He played in 309 matches for Hampshire, averaged over 24 in his first-class career and went on seven unofficial overseas tours. His annus mirabilis was 1961 when he led Hampshire to the County Championship with a series of improbable results. He was chairman of Holmwoods, the leading schools' insurance broker, has served on many M.C.C. and Hampshire committees and was President of M.C.C. for two years from 1996/8. B.C.G. Wilenkin, the Harrow middle-order batsman of 1949/51, gained a Cambridge blue in 1956 and scored 661 runs in his 28 first-class knocks at an average of 25.

Colin Ingleby-Mackenzie was very much in the mould of Lionel Tennyson, the former Hampshire captain, an attacking batsman who enjoyed the lighter side of the game and the social aspects of it. In his book *Many a Slip*, written in 1962 after Hampshire's championship success in 1961, he comes up with some extremely amusing cricketing stories and his legendary wit and humour come through in abundance. Whilst playing for Combined Services v. The Australians in 1953, during his national service in the Navy, Keith Miller pushed an easy catch straight through the legs of the rather portly Major Parnaby who was fielding at short leg. This infuriated Freddie Trueman who was fielding down at long leg. *'Why is the Major occupying my Yorkshire and England position?'* he demanded, in his usual blunt Yorkshire fashion. His fury increased as Miller went on to score a double century and then he completely lost interest in the game. At the end of the match, a senior official approached him and said,

'Trueman you'll never play for Combined Services again' to which Freddie replied, *'you're bloody right I won't. I'm being demobbed tomorrow!'*

In Colin's bachelor days he shared a flat in Lexham Gardens, Kensington with his old Eton friend Donald Marr Eton XI 1952, a very fine golfer and Oxford blue. Godfrey Evans, the superb Kent and England wicketkeeper who had not met Donald came to stay with them late one night and was up bright and early in the morning to play golf. Godfrey was one of those impossible characters who greeted the day with laughter and song and soon he was in close harmony with Housewife's Choice. Colin hushed him saying *'For heavens sake shut up Godders. You'll wake up Marr.'* Godfrey obeyed instantly but a little later when Marr appeared Godfrey exclaimed *'Marr! I thought you said Ma. I expected to see your mother bearing down on me with a rolling pin, curlers and all!'*

After a Commonwealth tour of South Africa in 1959/60 Colin was met at the airport by Charles Robins Eton XI 1950/3 and Middlesex who was returning his car which he had borrowed. He wondered why he had taken such pains to park the car rather tightly against the wall but he discovered next day when he saw an enormous scratch all down one side. Next day he joined up with Denis Compton who had captained the tour to discuss their recent trip. After lunch with Denis and a Turkish bath they went for a drink at the house of some friends. At about 8:30 Dennis suddenly realised that he was expected home for dinner and would be in trouble with his wife Valerie if he did not return home to Gerrards Cross forthwith. *'You can borrow my car'* said Colin *'and if you can write it off so much the better. I need a new one.'* Next morning he was awakened by a telephone call from his father the Admiral. *'Have you seen the papers this morning?'* he asked *'Have a look at the front page of the Daily Express.'* There was a smiling picture of Denis and a story, the heading of which was 'It must have been slippery'. Sure enough Denis had smashed Colin's car on his way home, careering off the road near

A.C.D. Ingleby-Mackenzie, captain of Hampshire being congratulated on winning the County Championship in 1961 by Desmond Eagar, his immediate predecessor.

Sir Pelham Warner, Middlesex and England cricketer and administrator/writer. Sir Pelham arrives at Lord's, for the annual Eton v Harrow cricket match, 11th July 1952.

Denham and dropping 30ft, coming to rest a yard or two from the river. Luckily the Compton luck held and Denis had stepped out of the wreck unharmed, save for a tiny scratch on his finger. Denis rang up cheerfully shortly afterwards and said *'I've done the job for you. It's a write off.'* He did not sound like a man who had just had a near escape from death!

The fine Eton and Oxford University cricketer David Macindoe who was in charge of Eton cricket from 1949/60 summed Colin up well in one of his reports *'consistent industry and discreet in his slumbers!'*

In **1952**, Harrow achieved their first win at Lord's since 1939 mainly due to an outstanding bowling performance from D.J. Hulbert who cut the ball both ways at medium pace and achieved match figures figures of 12/64. At the end of the first innings Harrow had achieved a small first innings lead of six and the match appeared to be wide open. A spectacular collapse occurred in Eton's second innings and they were bowled out in 95 minutes for 73 with Hulbert taking 4/31 and H.A. Clive, his opening partner, 4/18. Eton were severely handicapped all season by Robins being unable to bowl his legbreaks because of a hand injury. He was unable to stop Harrow winning by 7 wickets despite taking the first three wickets with off-breaks. He was to gain his revenge most decisively the following year. C.R.J. Hawke, the Harrow wicket-keeper of 1951/2, had an excellent season with the bat and behind the stumps. He had one first-class match for Oxford in 1953 with some success and it was a little surprising that he was not given any further opportunities.

R.V.C. Robins, son of the great R.W.V. Eton XI 1950/3 and Middlesex. Seen here batting for Middlesex v. Northants in 1955 at Lord's. A superb schoolboy cricketer he was less successful in the first class game than expected. Jack Webster Cambridge 1939 and Northants, master-in-charge of cricket at Harrow from 1960/70 is fielding at slip.

A.R.B. Neame, Harrow XI 1952/5 & Kent. Here seen batting in the 1953 match which Eton won by 10 wickets. A fine schoolboy cricketer he captained Harrow in 1954/5, his 11/77 with his off-breaks in 1954 was decisive in Harrow's nine wicket win and he achieved 8/81 in a close match when Harrow lost by 38 runs in 1955. He also achieved a hat trick, the first in the match since 1937 and only the third this century. He had talent with the bat too but his four games for Kent in 1956/7 were rather unsuccessful with both bat and ball.

The two heroes of the previous two years met up as captains of their respective sides in **1953**, Robins for Eton and Hulbert for Harrow. Although Hulbert again bowled well for Harrow, taking 5/73 in Eton's first innings total of 238, Robins's contribution in the match was to prove decisive. He was let off the hook by some poor Harrow catching and took full advantage in scoring 102 to take his side to a respectable 238 after a bad start. Harrow's reply was disastrous and R.A. James, the Eton opening bowler, had the remarkable analysis of 5/13 off 14 overs as Harrow collapsed to 82 all out. D.R. Maclean, his opening partner, also bowled well to take 4/32. After a good opening partnership in the second innings Harrow again collapsed aided by James bowling three Harrow batsman for two runs in eight deliveries. A total of 158 left Eton the formality of scoring three runs for victory and they duly triumphed by 10 wickets. Although Robins was without question one of the most outstanding schoolboy bowlers Eton has ever produced, he never really fulfilled his potential thereafter for Middlesex, which was a considerable disappointment to his father R.W.V., the old Middlesex and England player. He played 44 times for Middlesex between 1953/60 and in 60 first-class matches his overall record was mildly

A.R.B. Neame, Harrow XI 1952/5 left and D.J. Hulbert, Harrow XI 1951/2 right, walking out during the 1953 match. Dennis Hulbert's fast medium cutters proved deadly in 1952 and he won the match for Harrow with 12/64, Harrow's highest equal analysis this century. He bowled well again in 1953 as captain but Harrow were never in the match and lost decisively.

disappointing 107 wickets at 34 per wicket and his batting even more so. He averaged 13 in 92 first-class knocks. He has given considerable service on the administrative side as the past chairman of both Middlesex C.C.C. and the General Purposes Committee of M.C.C. G.M. Challenor who played for Harrow in 1953 was the son of the great West Indian and Barbados Test cricketer George Challenor who came on three tours of England in 1906, 1923 and 1928. His best year was 1923 when he scored 1556 runs at an average of 52 and his highest score was 237 not out for Barbados v. Jamaica at Bridgetown in 1924/5. The family are very influential in Barbados as one of the founding families of the Barbados Shipping & Trading Companies, one of the largest enterprises on that fair island.

A.R.B. Neame, the Harrow captain of **1954**, had much to do with Harrow's win by 9 wickets. He had an outstanding match with figures of 11/77 overall and a useful 49 in Harrow's first innings total. Eton were bowled out for 168 in their first innings mainly due to R.B. Bloomfield's 5/27, with only C.T.M. Pugh's 76 providing stout resistance. Harrow's lead after the first innings of 53 was to prove decisive and in a fine display of off-spinning in Eton's second innings Neame took 7/30 and Eton were all out for 119. Harrow's relatively easy task of scoring 69 to win was achieved as they romped home to win by 9 wickets. C.A. Strang, the Harrow batsman of 1952/4, won Cambridge rackets blues in 1955/6 and golf blues in 1956/7. C.H. Gibson, the son of Clem Gibson, Eton captain in 1918/19 and the fine Sussex and Cambridge cricketer, turned the tables on Harrow in **1955** when in a low scoring game Eton won by 38 runs. It was a disappointing end for Neame in his second year as captain of the Harrow XI and his fourth appearance at Lord's since he had another good match with figures of 8/81 overall. He achieved only the second hat-trick since 1900 after S.M.A. Banister did so for Eton in 1937 when he took four wickets in four balls. E.J, Lane-Fox with his cunningly flighted slow left-arm bowling took Eton to a first innings lead of 56 which ultimately proved decisive. Harrow, who needed 223 to win in their second innings, were undone by the left-arm

The 1959 Cambridge XI which lost by 85 runs to Oxford. Henry Bloefeld Eton XI 1955/6 is third from the left in the back row and Simon Douglas-Pennant second from the right back row. Blofeld, an outstanding schoolboy cricketer would probably have reached the top levels of the game but for his unfortunate accident in 1957 at Eton.

Henry Blofeld, Eton XI 1955/6 & Cambridge 1959. A phenomonal performance in the representative game at Lord's in 1956, 179 runs for once out. He remains a witty commentator and writer on the game.

seam bowling of S. Douglas-Pennant who bowled extremely well with clever variation to take 7/33 as Harrow succumbed for 184.

C.T.M. Pugh, the Eton opening batsman of 1954/5, played for Gloucestershire between 1959/62, captaining the side in 1961/2. A competitive all-round sportsman he was a somewhat controversial choice which Tom Graveney, the leading Gloucestershire and England batsman, was unable to agree with and this persuaded Graveney to change his allegiance to Worcestershire. In retrospect this did Graveney a favour since he matured greatly as an international cricketer after his move to Worcester. Despite Pugh's somewhat modest record - he averaged 19 in 80 first-class matches with a highest score of 137 - he proved a good leader and Gloucestershire's record was considerably better under him than in previous years and for some time afterwards. He was unlucky to be replaced after the 1962 season since they had just finished fourth in the Championship table. There was little doubt that his batting had been affected by a bad injury when he was hit on the head by the Northants and England fast bowler David Larter. He remained a fine rackets player for many years. Neame, the Harrow captain of 1954/5, appeared to have an outstanding future ahead of him. Sadly he did not have the application to really work at his game and his bowling rather faded away. He played four games for Kent in 1956/7 and only averaged 13 in his ten first-class matches with the bat and with the ball his 4 wickets cost 43 per wicket. The family brewery Shepherd Neame, of which his brother has been chairman for many years, have had a long connection with Kent cricket.

C.T.M. Pugh Eton XI 1954/5 and Gloucestershire scored 76 in 1954 when Harrow won decisively. This competitive sportsman was a controversial choice as captain of Gloucestershire in 1961/2 but although his record was modest the results were better under his captaincy than before and until recently with their outstanding record in one day cricket.

The **1956** match was badly affected by rain and Eton had reached 157/8 before the weather washed out half the day's play but not before R.S. Miller had knocked the stuffing out of the Eton batting with a fine display of swing bowling to take 6/38. Eton declared at the start of the second morning and Harrow had 120 minutes batting before the rain once again finished play with Harrow in a good position on 94/1 and the Harrow captain, J.M. Parker, showing fine form in his 51 not out. Parker, Harrow's captain and opening left-hand batsman in his fourth year in the XI, was a most talented cricketer and captained the Public Schools XI at Lord's v. Combined Services. He was certainly good enough to play first-class cricket but not the necessary application and as with many left-handers got out far too often flashing outside the off stump. The outstanding player on the Eton side was their 16-year-old wicket-keeper, H.C. Blofeld, in his second year in the XI. Prodigiously talented he scored 179 runs in the two schools representative games for only once out, including a century. But for a most unfortunate road accident at Eton in 1957, when he was captain of the XI but unable to play at Lord's, it is reasonable to assume he would have reached the very highest levels of the game. As it was he was good enough to gain a Cambridge blue in 1959 and played for his native Norfolk. In his 17 first-class matches he scored 758 runs at an average of over 24 with a top score of 138 and took eleven victims behind the stumps. He has since become a well-known cricket journalist and broadcaster with a most distinctive style. He was well connected on his mother's side as his grandfather was the Hon. Frederick Calthorpe, the well-known Warwickshire and England cricketer who captained the side from 1920/29, hence his second name Calthorpe. The left-arm fast medium Eton bowler Simon Douglas-Pennant, who played in 1955/6, gained a

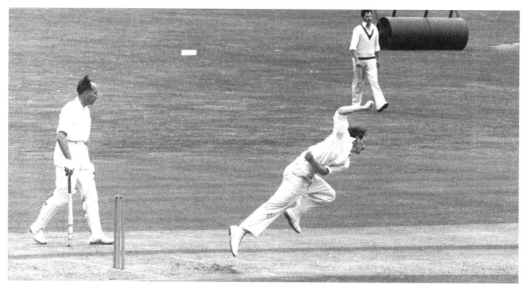

S.Douglas-Pennant, Eton XI 1955/6 and Cambridge 1959. A fine left-arm round the wicket seam bowler he played a large part in Eton's 1955 victory by 38 runs with 7/33 in Harrow's seccond innings. Here he demonstrates a near perfect follow through.

Cambridge blue in 1959 bowling consistently well throughout the season and was somewhat unlucky not to retain his place in 1960/1. He tended to be a little on the expensive side but took 83 wickets in his 35 first-class performances with a best analysis of 7/56. F.E.R. Butler who played for Harrow in 1956 gained Oxford rugby blues in 1959/60 and was head of the Civil Service and Cabinet Secretary under Margaret Thatcher, John Major and Tony Blair. He is now Master of University College, Oxford and chaired the Butler report on the war in Iraq as Lord Butler of Brockwell.

Rain again interfered with both days of the match in **1957** and the feature of the Harrow innings was a stylish innings of 50 from the left-handed J.D.C. Vargas and some shrewd left-arm off break bowling from E.J. Lane-Fox who had taken over the captaincy of the Eton XI from the stricken Blofeld. Eton looked to be in a strong position when rain came down once again and were 21 runs ahead with four wickets in hand. The bulk of the Eton runs were scored by their two fine strikers W.G.A. Clegg, 77, and A.R.B. Burrows, unbeaten on 68. Lane-Fox was an elegant left-handed middle-order batsman who played for a number of years for his native Oxfordshire with some success, representing the Minor Counties against the West Indies and Indian tourists on two occasions. His bowling was affected by severe knee trouble and he gave up serious cricket relatively young. Vargas returned to teach at Harrow and became a House Master and Second Master of the School. He has since become Director of the Harrow Association. Laurie Champniss, the Harrow captain of 1957 was a devastating leg break bowler off the wrong foot and on his day virtually unplayable. He was very successful for Buckinghamshire between 1971/77 and in club cricket very few batsman could read him.

The **1958** match was one of the poorest in quality for many years with Harrow undoubtedly the weaker of the two sides. In a low scoring match Harrow were fortunate to avoid defeat and had Eton not taken 5 hours to score 170 runs in their first innings there is little doubt that they would have won with relative ease. Harrow were bowled out for 96 in their first innings and set 185 in 165 minutes never made any attempt to go for them and finished on 81/7. A.B. Cable, the Harrow captain in his fourth year in the XI had a disastrous year and was unfortunate enough to make a 'pair' at Lord's and found it difficult to inspire a rather moderate side.

W.J. Foster Harrow XI 1950/2 an elegant middle order batsman just regains his ground for the Navy v. R.A.F. in 1961 at Lord's. Two well known cricketers look on, Joe Hardstaff at point, son and grandson of two famous Notts & England cricketers hits the wicket whilst Maurice Fenner of Kent, R.A.F. & Combined Services is the keeper.

Eton once again had the better of the **1959** match but just failed to bowl Harrow out in their second innings. Eton were in a strong position when they batted first and scored 270/5 declared, mainly due to a fine innings from their opening batsman/wicket-keeper J. Baskervyle-Glegg with 75 and some hard hitting from their captain, M.L. Dunning, 79, in his fourth year in the Eton XI. Harrow just avoided the follow-on by 5 runs and Eton went hard for the runs in their second innings. A target of 202 runs in 165 minutes was too much for the Harrow batsman and when half the side were out for 48 Harrow looked well beaten. They managed to hold on, however, and finished 44 runs short with eight wickets down. Both M.L. Dunning and J. Baskervyle-Glegg went into the Army and represented the Combined Services at first-class level. M.J.H. Weedon, the Harrow opening bowler from 1957/9, gained a Cambridge blue in 1962 and took 45 wickets in his 17 first-class matches at 36 per wicket. Robert Fellowes, the Eton batsman of 1957/9 became a most distinguished Private Secretary to the Queen and was enobled as Lord Fellowes.

Harrow had the better of a rapidly worsening wicket in **1960** but deservedly won by 124 runs with 90 minutes to spare largely due to their strong, three-man spin attack. In retrospect Harrow's 216, batting first, was more than enough and a first innings lead of 63 proved decisive. Eton never looked likely to score 207 runs to win and their innings collapsed in disarray on a sharply turning wicket against C.M.S. Kaye, son of M.A.C.P. and grandson of H.S., and C.B.N. Rome, son of D.A.M. and grandson of C.S., and they were all out for 82. Kaye's 3/12 and Rome's 4/26 in the innings proved crucial for Harrow. B.S. Raper, the Harrow captain and opening bowler, was an inspiring captain throughout the season although his bowling went off slightly due to a back injury and he failed to retain his place in the Public Schools side v. the Combined Services. M.A. Rogerson, Eton's elegant middle-order batsman who had scored 690 runs in the season, was unlucky not to be selected for the representative schools games, he ran a well-known preparatory school, Cottesmore in West Sussex for many years.

R.C.S. Titchener-Barrett Harrow XI 1961/2 Middlesex & Oxfordshire. A formidable pace bowler he won the match for Harrow in 1961 with 12/76 by an innings and 12 runs, their first innings win since 1866 and was largely responsible for Eton following on in 1962. He was just short of the top level due to knee problems but nonetheless at his best a fine bowler and the only taker of five wickets in five balls at Lord's. He took Oxfordshire's only hat trick of the century in an analysis of 8/58 v. Devon in 1964 and took an England Counties XI tour to the West Indies in 1975 which was unbeaten.

Harrow won by an innings in **1961** for the first time since 1866 due to some fine batting from J.R. Hodgkinson, 94, and C.J.A. Jamieson, 72, and some outstanding fast bowling from R.C.S. Titchener-Barrett, whose 12/76 in the match proved decisive. Harrow were stronger all round and very well led by M.J.B. Wood in his third year in the XI. The only real resistance came from the 16-year-old N.C. Pretzlik, who played very well for his 63 and 36. Eton followed on 148 behind after Titchener-Barrett had wrecked the Eton innings, taking 7/37 off 20 overs. Once again in Eton's second innings, bowling fast and straight and moving the ball into the bat, Titchener-Barrett swept away the Eton resistance and finished with 5/39 off 21 overs. Eton were all out for 136 and Harrow had won by an innings and 12 runs by 4.15 on the second day.

Harrow should have achieved a hat-trick of wins in **1962** when they bowled out Eton for 110 in their first innings and followed on 137 behind. When Eton lost their first five wickets for 134, Harrow looked in a strong position but easy dropped catches off M.C.T. Prichard, the Eton captain, and J.A. Cornes, the eccentric Eton wicket-keeper in his third year in the XI, let Eton off the hook and in the end they saved the match fairly easily, with Prichard's 95 and Cornes's 61 proving crucial. Prichard, who was the grandson of Agatha Christie, was given the rights to *The Mousetrap* which continues in the West End to this day as a considerable money spinner for its owner. Titchener-Barrett opened the bowling for the Public Schools at Lord's and played for Middlesex II and Oxfordshire during the summer holidays. He was to remain a fine fast bowler for many years and achieved several outstanding feats including five wickets in five balls for Cross Arrows v Middlesex Young Cricketers in 1963 at Lord's, the only bowler ever to have done so at headquarters, and 8/58 for Oxfordshire v. Devon, including a hat-trick in 1964. He took an England Counties XI tour to the West Indies in 1975 which was unbeaten. He appeared against the full might of Barbados and took 5/25 in their second innings in a side which included two outstanding fast bowlers, Joel Garner of West Indies fame, and Gregory Armstrong of Barbados and Glamorgan.

The three Pilkington Brothers - continuing the long line of Pilkington cricketers who have played for Eton. T.C. 1957/9, R.A. 1962/3 and G.W. 1964/5.

In a rain-ruined fixture Eton had much the better of the match in **1963** and were in a strong position to register their first win since 1955. A fine innings from R.C. Daniels, 84, was the main contributor to Eton's 202/9 and Harrow were in deep trouble when they finished on 79/5 at the end of the first day against the lively bowling of J.P. Consett, 3/17, and the flighted leg-breaks of G.R.V. Robins, the younger son of the Middlesex and England cricketer R.W.V. Robins and brother of R.V.C., Eton's hero of 1951 and 1953. Only 15 minutes play was possible on the second day before play was abandoned for the day and the match drawn. Both the Harrow captain, R.J. Pelham, and N.C. Pretzlik, the Eton left-hander, distinguished themselves with good performances for the Schools XI v. The Combined Services at Lord's. Pretzlik especially could have gone on to achieve greater honours but after playing for Hampshire II for two years with some success he gave up the game soon after to run his family printing business; he tragically died of a heart attack in 2004.

Eton thoroughly deserved their first victory over Harrow for nine years in **1964** by 8 wickets, despite a considerably less experienced side and only two old colours, even though R.C. Daniels, the Eton captain, and J.P. Consett, the opening bowler, were easily the best players on the two sides and had a major part in their victory. Harrow batted poorly in both innings and but for R.J. Clover-Brown, the son of C. Clover-Brown, the Harrow opening batsman of 1925/7, with 90 and 51, would have been in even deeper trouble against the pace of Consett, who took 4/36 in the first innings, and R.M. Whitcomb, 4/28 in the second. Daniels batted well for the second year running to score 84, the same as he had done in 1963. This was a disappointing end for D.W.W. Norris, the Harrow wicket-keeper in his fourth year in the XI, and, although a fine wicket-keeper, he never really fulfilled his batting potential. He went on to gain Cambridge blues in 1967/8, but his contributions with the bat were distinctly modest and he only averaged 10 in his 33 first-class innings. R.C. Daniels was an outstanding school-boy cricketer who did very well in the schools representative matches but when it came to first-class cricket he lacked confidence and his technique was simply not good enough against pace bowling particularly of the short-pitched variety as he tended to back away to square leg. In 14 first-class knocks for Oxford in 1965/66 he averaged 7 and his off-spin bowling was hardly used.

In one of the best contested matches since the War, Harrow gained their revenge in **1965** by 48 runs with only five minutes to spare, largely due to a deadly late spell of fast bowling from C.A. Holt, the son of R.A.A. Holt and Harrow captain in 1938, who took Eton's last five wickets in three overs for one run. Harrow's victory had been set up by two fine innings from A.H. Crawley, the son of A.M., the Kent and Oxford cricketer, with 62 and 73 but until Holt's dramatic spell a Harrow victory had looked unlikely. Like his brother Randall and father Aidan, Crawley was an excellent rackets player and tragically killed with his brother in a plane crash over Italy in 1988. The tall Harrow opening bowler of 1965/6, P.R. Dunkels played three first-class matches for Warwickshire and Sussex with little success but performed very well for Devon in the Minor Counties. He had several outstanding performances for the county and with his great height he was able to gain steepling bounce on occasions which disconcerted many batsmen.

Viscount Crowhurst (later, The Earl of Cottenham) Eton X1 1966-67.
A fearsome fast bowler for Northants 2nd XI who could easily have played first-class cricket had the desire been there. A stalwart of the Arabs and Eton Ramblers for many years.

Eton had much the better of the **1966** match and Harrow made no attempt to go for the runs in their second innings, the game ending with Harrow a long way short and five wickets down. The Eton innings was dominated by their captain and opening batsman, D.M. Smith, who scored 106 to record the first century in this match since R.V.C. Robins in 1953. Harrow's opening batsman R.E. Lindsay, the son of Sir William Lindsay, Harrow XI 1926/8 and Oxford blue of 1931, was unbeaten in the match with 72 not out and 27 not out and without him Harrow would have been in dire straights against the quick bowling of Eton's C.A. Lawrie who recorded 6/31 in Harrow's first innings total of 149. P.G. Lowndes, the son of W.G. Lowndes, the Hampshire and Oxford blue of 1921, played in 1965/6 as a hard-hitting batsman and medium-pace bowler of some talent. He afterwards played for Berkshire and is currently President of Eton Ramblers and Senior Partner of Lane Fox, the estate agents. C.E.G. Lyttelton, the son of Viscount Cobham (formerly Charles Lyttelton), opened the bowling for Eton in 1965 and thus continued the long line of Lyttelton cricketers who have played for Eton at Lord's. A.R.T. Peebles, the son of the brilliant Middlesex and England leg-spin bowler Ian Peebles, also played for Eton in 1966 as a leg-spin bowler. R. H. G. Fulton, the Eton off-spinner and father of J.A.G., captain of Eton in 1995/96 and Oxford in 1998 afterwards captained the Navy and played for Combined Services. He is now head of the Royal Marines at Portsmouth.

Eton's strong batting put the Harrow bowling to the sword in **1967** with some fine stroke play from B.L.H. Powell, 79, and M.J.J. Faber, 53, in their declared total of 274/6. Harrow were 84 behind on the first innings and only a fine innings from the 15-year-old left-hander, P.J.E. Needham, 53, saved them from following on. In the end Harrow were fortunate to avoid defeat, finished 7 wickets down in their second innings and 68 runs short of their target. Eton were captained by their tall fast bowler Viscount Crowhurst, who succeeded his father as the Earl of Cottenham in 1968. He was a fearsome fast bowler who played for Northants II for two years with some success and matched David Larter the England pace bowler for speed. Charles Cottenham toured the West Indies with the Duke of Norfolk's XI in 1970 and became a notable cross country rider representing England abroad and competing at Badminton and Burghley before setting up a string of Language schools which proved highly successful before his untimely death of a heart attack in 2000 at the age of 51.

M.J.J. Faber Eton XI 1967/8, Oxford 1972 and Sussex. A most talented all round sportsman he scored 100 in 1968, gained his blue in 1972 and played 57 matches for Sussex between 1973/76. A grandson of Harold Macmillan, his overall performance with Sussex was a shade disappointing given his ability. He won the Public Schools rackets doubles three years running and gained rackets blues at Oxford. He died most tragically at the age of 42 of a blood clot in 1991.

Despite a strong Eton side in **1968** with several quality players, including M.J.J. Faber, V.A. Cazalet, the son of P.V.F. Cazalet, the Queen Mother's racing trainer, the wicket-keeper and captain R.C. Kinkead-Weekes and J.R.T. Barclay, the 15-year-old off-spinning all-rounder, Harrow succeeded in defying the odds largely due to an outstanding performance from their Sri Lankan captain I. Coomaraswamy, who had match figures of 12/92 with his slow left-arm off-spin. He was making his fifth appearance at Lord's, only achieved by four other Harrovians since 1805 and he registered the third best Harrow analysis since proper bowling analyses were recorded from 1854 onwards. There were some good performances from both sides. As befitted two very fine rackets players, Faber, 100, and V.A. Cazalet, 62, played with great style in Eton's first innings of 210, but their colleagues were unable to counter Coomaraswamy's clever flight and spin and he finished with 7/42 in the innings. Harrow's first innings lead of 50 was to prove crucial with A.P. Webster's 90 giving Harrow a very good start. Barclay, in the first of his four appearances for Eton, showed his outstanding promise with 6/100 in the Harrow innings off 31 overs. Eton were again flummoxed in their second innings by Coomaraswamy and the only real resistance came from the Eton opener D.J.B. Wood with 69. The relatively simple task for Harrow of scoring 92 for victory in 120 minutes was achieved for the loss of three wickets but not without some anxious moments. A.P. Webster, the Harrow all-rounder of 1966/8 and son of the Harrow cricket master from 1960/70 J. Webster, the Cambridge blue of 1939 and Northants medium-pace bowler, played for Northants II with some success and gained a Cambridge rugby blue in 1971. Faber, the elegant Eton batsman of 1967/8 and grandson of Harold Macmillan, was an outstanding rackets player and won the Public Schools

I. Coomaraswamy, Harrow XI 1964/8. The only player of the last century from both schools to have made five appearances at Lord's in peacetime. He won the match for Harrow in 1968 by 7 wickets against a strong Eton side taking 12/92 with his left arm spin bowling. Unlucky enough to be at Cambridge during Phil Edmonds residence, he would surely have gained a blue in other times.

Fred Goldstein's 1967 half-century was an hors d'oeuvre for the 155 he served up a year later as Oxford captain. The varsity match of 1967 featuring the wicketkeeper for Cambridge D. W. W. Norris Harrow X1 1961/64 and Cambridge University 1967/68.

J.R.T. Barclay Eton XI, 1968/71, showing the fine potential in the 1968 match which he continued with Sussex from 1970/86.

Eton had stellar support in 1969. Queen Elizabeth the Queen Mother and Actress Elizabeth Taylor were among the party Peter Cazalet invited to Lord's when his son, Victor, captained the eleven. Cazalet had been training horses for Her Majesty for twenty years. With them are Lord Gage, Victor's younger brother Anthony and their sister, Sheran Hornby. The match was drawn, after Victor Cazalet's cultured 49 and subsequent declaration set Harrow to score 208 in two and a half hours.

Three fine Eton cricketers in traditional pose, Victor Cazalet, Ronnie Aird and Sir Alec Douglas-Home at the 1968 match. On this occasion it failed to produce the desired result and Harrow got home by 7 wickets against a strong Eton side.

Doubles three years running and the singles twice. He played cricket for Oxford from 1970/2, gaining his blue in 1972, and afterwards had a stint with Sussex from 1973/6 with some success. His best season was 1975 when he scored 1,060 runs at an average of 31 and won a Gillette Cup winners medal in the one day competition at Lord's. He also represented Oxford at rackets for three years. It was often said he was the last of the Corinthian games players and talented at most sports he played. In the years before his untimely death from a blood clot in 1991 he had taken up golf and was part of the winning Eton Halford-Hewitt side. R.C. Kinkead-Weekes, the Eton wicket-keeper of 1966/8, gained an Oxford blue in 1972 and played in two matches for Middlesex in 1976 before a broken finger unluckily put him out of action for the rest of the season when a long run in the side was his for the asking as the Middlesex keeper Nigel Ross had suffered a similar injury. In his six first-class matches he took ten victims and averaged 11 with the bat. Coomaraswamy played two first-class matches for Cambridge in

1972 without bowling but was unfortunate to be in residence at the same time as Phil Edmonds, the Middlesex and England left-arm spin bowler. In many other years he would probably have made the Cambridge side and continues to be a successful club cricketer.

Harrow were indebted to an outstanding all-round performance from S.A.F. Mitchell for their avoidance of defeat in **1969**. Eton, captained by V.A. Cazalet, had much the better of the game and deserved to win. Mitchell's match figures of 11/113 restricted Eton in both innings with sustained accuracy and when Harrow were 52/6 in their second innings they looked likely to lose. But an aggressive 50 from Mitchell led them to safety and they finished on 136/8 and 71 behind at the close. Cazalet had a very good season and was unlucky not to be chosen for representative honours, like his colleague Johnny Barclay, in the first of his three appearances for M.C.C. Schools, a remarkable achievement. Cazalet went on to Oxford but a rackets blue was his only honour, although he played a few Kent II games.

1970 was the first time in peacetime since 1805 that this famous fixture was not played at Lord's since the ground had been reserved for a Middlesex Gillette Cup tie which never took place as Middlesex had already been knocked out. Eton deservedly won on Harrow's Sixth Form

P.J.E. Needham captain of the Harrow XI 1969/70, tries to run out A.E. Martin-Smith, the Eton opener who scored 60 in the first innings in 1969, whilst S.A.F. Mitchell looks on. In a drawn match favouring Eton, Mitchell scored 50 and took 11/113, a fine performance.

Ground in a relatively low-scoring game which gave all the bowlers a little help and took increasing spin later on. After another fine bowling performance from Mitchell with 6/64 in Eton's first innings of 165, Harrow were unable to cope with the medium pace 'induckers' of the tall H.M. Wyndham, who bowled most effectively in both innings for match figures of 10/83. Eton proved worthy winners by 97 runs with six minutes to spare. Barclay, the Eton captain of 1970 had a magnificent season all round and broke the College batting record with 897 runs. He was within a whisker of taking all ten wickets in an innings at Lord's for the Schools v. E.S.C.A. but eventually finished with all nine wickets that fell for 57 runs. P.J.E. Needham, the left-handed Harrow captain for the second year running, played one match for Glamorgan against the tourists in 1975 and had a lengthy run in the 2nd XI with modest results. Sadly his technique was not good enough at this level and like many other left-handers he was caught outside the off stump flashing too many times without getting his feet to the ball. He has since proved an effective administrator as a past Chairman of Glamorgan's Cricket Committee and on the M.C.C. Committee.

J.R.T. Barclay Eton XI 1968/71. A most popular captain of Sussex from 1981/86 here seen with the John Player Sunday League Trophy in 1982.

Fortunately the match returned to headquarters in **1971** after much protestation from Etonians, Harrovians and others loth to see the oldest fixture at Lord's removed from its rightful venue. It proved to be a somewhat lacklustre affair and the two teams sparred with each other but without much purpose. Eton were greatly handicapped throughout the season by a back injury to Barclay in his second year as captain and Wyndham, the match-winner of the previous year, who had jaundice for much of the term. The two captains both made their mark in this match, J. Halliday, 58 for Harrow and Barclay, 66 for Eton, in their respective first innings. It was somewhat surprising that Eton made little attempt to go for a target of 137 runs in 77 minutes and finished on 70/4 in a rather tame draw. Barclay went on to captain the Young England side in the West Indies in 1972 and proved an outstanding success as both player and captain in a side that included the young Graham Gooch and Bill Snowden, the Cambridge Blue and future Harrow cricket master from 1984/94. Barclay's outstanding ability as a schoolboy was never entirely fulfilled in his 265 first-class matches for Sussex and between 1970/86 he scored 9,677 first-class runs at an average of 25 and took 324 wickets with his off-breaks at 31 per wicket. His best season was in 1979 when he scored 1,093 runs at 32 and came close to an overseas tour but he was a very popular captain of Sussex from 1981/6. 'Trout', as he was nicknamed by the pros, always seemed reluctant to bowl when he was captain due to his natural modesty and surprising lack of confidence in his own ability. Since retiring from the first-class game he has run the Arundel indoor cricket centre with great aplomb and was manager of the highly successful England 'A' tour to India in 1994 and deputy manager of the

England tour to South Africa in 1995/6 and the World Cup following in India and Pakistan under Ray Illingworth. He was appointed manager of the England tour to Zimbabwe and New Zealand in 1997 but his lack of business experience and unwillingness to promote himself would appear to limit further progress in English cricket administration. M. Thatcher, the son of the Conservative Prime Minister, Margaret Thatcher played in 1971 but was more known for his rackets and won the Public Schools Singles in 1971. His career since has been plagued by poor publicity and controversy much to the chagrin of his famous mother.

Harrow had the better of the drawn match in **1972**, the batting and bowling in general being stronger than their illustrious opponents. Eton, set 193 to get in 140 minutes, never looked in the hunt against some tight Harrow bowling and when five wickets had fallen for 34 runs they were in danger of defeat but in a timely rearguard action were saved by P.J. Remnant and the Eton wicket-keeper captain, I. MacDonald. Eton finished on 106/6 and a long way short of the target at the close. W.R. Worthy, the Harrow seam bowler, finished with eight wickets in this match and had a good season overall. He afterwards played a few 2nd XI games for Essex but failed to make his mark. He has been a stalwart of Ealing C.C. for many years as a slow bowler who can bat lower down the order.

The 1970s were a rather barren period for Eton cricket except for 1977, when Harrow threw the match away when seemingly well on top, and it was not reversed until 1986 when John Claughton, the Oxford University and Warwickshire cricketer, took over the running of Eton cricket with John Rice, the old Hampshire all-rounder as coach.

Once again Harrow had the better of a drawn game in **1973** and after a long delay for rain on the second day Eton never made any serious attempt at a stiff target of 159 runs in 80 minutes, finishing on 63/3 at the close. Two well-known names captained the Eton and Harrow XIs in 1973: the Marquis of Bowmont, the Eton middle-order batsman of 1972/3 and scorer of 53 not out in Eton's second innings, succeeded his father as the 10th Duke of Roxburghe in 1974 and inherited the superb Scottish stately home of Floors Castle, Kelso. Guy Roxburghe won the Sword of Honour at Sandhurst in 1974 and graduated from Cambridge in 1980 after a spell in the Royal Horse Guards/1st Dragoons and has since been most successful on the turf; C.D. Gilliat, the Harrow leg-break bowler of 1971/3, was a cousin of the Hampshire and Oxford captain Richard Gilliat and had an excellent season with the ball taking 45 wickets at a cost of under 12 per wicket.

M.K. Fosh Harrow XI 1973/5, Cambridge 1977/8 and Essex. Harrow's captain in 1975 and the scorer of Harrow's second highest individual total since the start of the series in 1805 with 161 not out. Harrow's overwhelming victory by an innings and 151 runs was their greatest margin of victory in the history of the match.

Eton were demolished in **1974** after the first day's play had been totally wiped out. J.H. Morrison, the Harrow opening bowler who had match figures of 6/50 in 1973, was largely responsible for Eton being bowled out for 90 with Morrison taking 5/25 in 14 overs and bowling four of his victims. Harrow ambled to victory in 37 overs for the loss of two wickets with the young A.C.S. Pigott in his first year in the XI showing promise with the bat rather than the ball in scoring 37 not out.

R.M. Tindall Harrow XI 1975/7 and Northants, Son of M. Tindall, the Harrow, Cambridge and Middlesex cricketer he had an outstanding match in 1976 with 151 and 5/39 when Eton just saved the match. He played 14 matches for Northants in 1980/1 but suffered from a lack of confidence and was a nervous starter.

A.C.S. Pigott Harrow XI 1974/6, Sussex, Surrey and England. Harrow's only England player since the war. An outstanding schoolboy fast bowler with 127 wickets in his three years in the Harrow XI. He played in one test during the M.C.C. tour of New Zealand in 1984 and was a gallant servant of Sussex from 1978/93 and Surrey from 1994/96.

Harrow overwhelmed Eton in **1975** with their strongest XI for many years and the margin of victory by an innings and 151 runs was Harrow's greatest since the start of the series in 1805. Harrow were captained by the left handed M.K. Fosh, son of Arthur Fosh the Harrow captain of 1943 and arguably Harrow's most outstanding schoolboy batsman since the War with the recent exception of Martin Walters, the Border under 19 cricketer in 2004. He demolished the weak Eton bowling and scored 161 not out with fine attacking shots, partnered by the elegant R.C. Compton with 63. This was the second highest Harrow individual innings in the history of the match after Geoffrey Wilson's 173 in 1913 and it is likely that he would have beaten D.C.

Boles of Eton's 183 in 1904 as the all-time record had he not declared the Harrow innings closed on 303/2. If he had known how close he was to the record one suspects Fosh might have gone on batting for another three or four overs. The equally weak Eton batting was demolished by the pacy Pigott who took 5/31 in Eton's first innings 96, well supported by F.J. McMullen, the accurate medium-pace swing bowler, with the remarkable figures of 4/3. In their second innings Eton fared even worse and were bowled out for a derisory 56, their lowest score since 1866 when they totalled 42. Pigott and McMullen were again the main destroyers and McMullen's figures of 7/13 in the match merited a glass or two of their famous beer. Fosh's aggregate of 778 runs in the season at 71 per innings was a Harrow record since the War until recently broken in 2004 and second only to R.A.A. Holt in 1938 who scored 901 runs. It has only been beaten at both schools since the War by Johnny Barclay's 897 runs in 1970, an Eton all-time record. Pigott also broke the Harrow School bowling record with 58 wickets in the season at 10.5 per wicket. Fosh went on to represent England Young Cricketers and gained Cambridge blues in 1977/8. He played in 14 first-class matches for Essex from 1976/8 and averaged just over 23 in 30 first-class matches which did little justice to his great talent. If he had stuck at it a glittering first-class career and the potential captaincy of Essex beckoned. It was a sad loss to the game when he gave up early but in any case it is doubtful that he would have lasted since he suffered from knee trouble. He was also a talented rugby player at fly-half and gained a Cambridge blue in 1977 but once again knee problems caused an early retirement from the game. He became a successful derivatives trader in the city before selling out and is now Managing Director of SVB Holdings, a Lloyds reinsurance broker.

Harrow, captained by A.C.S. Pigott in **1976**, were most unlucky not to achieve a hat-trick of wins when Eton finished only four runs ahead in their second innings with only one wicket remaining chasing the Harrow innings total of 328/9. Harrow had posted a first innings lead of 108. The innings of the match came from R.M. Tindall, the son of Mark Tindall, captain of Harrow in 1933 and the old Cambridge and Middlesex cricketer who was in charge of Harrow cricket from 1946/59, with 151 in a display of left handed elegant stroke play. His left arm spin bowling was also more than useful and he took five wickets in Eton's second innings and so nearly took Harrow home to victory. Once again Pigott had an outstanding season for Harrow with the ball taking 57 wickets in the season and his overall total of 127 wickets in his three years in the Harrow XI was impressive. Pigott was a distinguished player for Sussex from 1978/93 and Surrey for three years thereafter with nearly 700 first-class wickets and a best season in 1988 of 74 wickets at an average of 28 per wicket. He was fortunate to play one test for England in New Zealand on the tour there in 1984 when England suffered a spate of injuries. He was somewhat controversially called up for the second test when playing domestic cricket in that country and on honeymoon. He failed to make an impact and did not appear again. His batting had always looked promising but never materialised into anything significant. He only scored one first-class hundred in 18 years of first-class cricket. He was a natural all-round games player and fine rackets and squash player who won the Public Schools rackets in 1976. He was afterwards chief executive of Sussex for a short spell before being ousted by Dave Gilbert, the former Australian fast bowler.

T.M.H. James, Harrow XI 1976/8. Son of R.M. the old Cambridge blue he scored 112 not out in 1978 when Harrow just failed to win. He was also a more than useful seam bowler who played for Berkshire for several years.

Eton were extremely fortunate to win the **1977** match, their first since 1970 when Harrow at the end of the first day appeared to have the match in the bag when they had declared at 225/7 and taken seven Eton wickets for 93. Eton were bowled out for 127 on the following morning leaving Harrow a first innings lead of 98. Harrow made very slow progress in the second innings and when the declaration came at 94/5, Eton were set a relatively generous 193 to score in 160 minutes. The way that Eton had batted in the first innings made it unlikely that Eton would score the runs against Harrow's relatively experienced attack. R.H.M. Raison, Eton captain for the second year running seized his chance and in a partnership with J.L. Rawlinson of 101 turned the game for his side. He finished on 73 not out and took his side to victory with one ball to spare by 6 wickets. J.L. Rawlinson's 61 was his second major score in the match following his 53 in the first innings and he had an excellent season overall. He went on to play nine first-class matches for Oxford in 1979/80 but in 16 innings only managed to average 8 per innings.

R.M. Tindall, the Harrow captain, played for Northants from 1978/81 and played 14 first-class matches in 1980/1 and scored 330 runs with a highest score of 60 not out, averaging 18 overall. His useful off-spin bowling was rarely used and this part of his game fell away somewhat. He seemed to suffer from a lack of confidence in his own ability and like many left-handers was a rather poor starter. If he had been able to tighten up his defensive game he could well have been a more than useful county cricketer, brilliant on occasions when well set.

Harrow were most unlucky not to win the **1978** match when, after bowling Eton out for a derisory 112, they piled on a big total of 341/6 against a weak Eton bowling attack. The Harrow innings was dominated by their captain, T.M.H. James, with an outstanding knock of 112 not out well supported by W.J. Haggas, 65. In hindsight Harrow probably went on slightly too long and Eton following on, finished 10 runs behind with their last pair together. James, the son of R.M. James who taught at Harrow for a few years and scored a century for Cambridge v. the Australian tourists in 1956, had a good season with both bat and ball for Harrow and was a very powerful hitter of the ball for a schoolboy. He played for Berkshire for several years with considerable panache and would probably have succeeded at the higher level such was his ability and determination.

1979 was notable for a most unselfish act by Harrow's captain, W.J. Haggas, when he declared Harrow's innings closed on 211/2 and himself on 87 not out in reply to Eton's 261. It was reminiscent of John Pawle's similar action in 1934 when he was captain and on 93 not out. Haggas thus deprived himself of one of those feats which are treasured for life, a century at Lord's in an important match. Sadly it was to no avail as Harrow's accurate seamers did not enable Eton to set Harrow a sensible target. R.J. Compton-Burnett, the Eton batsman of

1977/9 and captain in 1979, was the son of A.C. Burnett, a beak at Eton, Cambridge blue of 1949 and Glamorgan cricketer. He played well for his 66 in Eton's first innings and was possibly unlucky to get only one first-class opportunity for Cambridge in 1981 as he had considerable ability. E.C. Gordon-Lennox, the hard-hitting middle-order batsman for Harrow in 1978/9 and son of Major-Gen. Bernard Gordon-Lennox, Eton XI 1950 came from a long line of Etonian soldiers, was an extremely hard hitting batsman and useful seamer and went on to captain the Army and Combined Services. He was offered the opportunity to play first-class cricket on several occasions but turned it down. He looked to have an excellent Army career ahead of him after winning the Sword of Honour at Sandhurst but decided to leave midway through his career due to lack of opportunity and now works for Whitbread, the brewers.

W.J. Haggas, scion of a well-known Yorkshire textile family, had an outstanding Lord's in 1978/9 and captained Harrow through an unbeaten season. He has been a successful breeder and trainer at Newmarket for some years, son-in law of the great Lester Pigott and winning trainer of the Derby winner Shaamit in 1996 a marvellous feat for a 35-year-old at that time of his career. A highly talented cricketer he was reckoned by Fred Trueman to be a *'certain future captain of Yorkshire'* and would more than likely have made an impact in the game.

Harrow again had much the better of proceedings in **1980** and forced Eton to follow on 140 runs behind. When rain ended play two hours early on the second day Eton were only one run

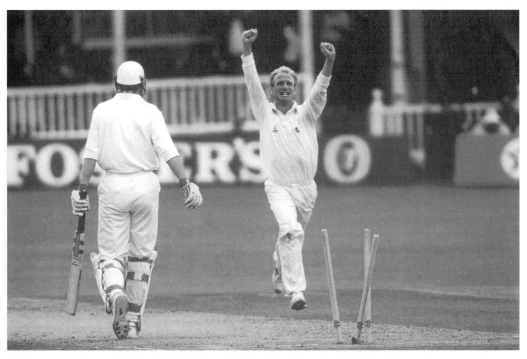

M.V. Fleming, Eton XI 1981/2, Combined Services, Kent & England celebrating a wicket in the semi-final of the Benson & Hedges Cup. Kent went on to lose the final against Lancashire at Lord's in 1995. A great striker of the ball, useful seam bowler and magnificent cover fielder.

Champion show: Kent captain Matthew Fleming leads his side's celebrations with the Norwich Union trophy in 2001. Andrew Symonds the Australian Test Player stands behind Fleming.

ahead with six wickets in hand. S.E. Haggas, the 16-year-old brother of the previous year's Harrow captain, scored a fine 75, well supported by his captain C.L. Feather, son of the victorious Harrow captain of 1952, R.L. Feather. O.F.O. Findlay had two remarkable spells of bowling in Eton's two innings to finish with match figures of 7/25. H.T. Rawlinson, the Eton captain, gained Oxford blues in 1983/4 with his useful seam bowling and sound batting, but he was fortunate to be up when the standard of Oxford cricket was fairly poor. His record for Oxford in 16 first-class matches was rather modest 156 runs in 21 innings at an average of 9 and his 23 wickets cost over 61 per wicket with a best of 5/123. J.A.G.H. Stewart who played for Harrow in 1979/80 had the unusual distinction for a cricketer of gaining an Oxford rowing blue in 1984. Harrow's batsman M.L. Sealy was the nephew of G.M. Challenor, Harrow XI 1953.

Sadly **1981** was to be the last of the two day fixtures between the two schools and again the result was inconclusive, although once more very much in Harrow's favour. Harrow's first innings lead of 83 was put to good use by their captain Haggas who again performed well for his 63 not out in their second innings 148/2. The target set for Eton of 232 in 150 minutes proved too much for them and the match petered out into a tame draw with Eton on 94/1 at the close. Haggas went on the ground staff at Lord's for two years and had the necessary ability to become a serious cricketer but decided not to take up the challenge. Arguably he was not as talented as his brother but a trial with Yorkshire was on the cards and success was possible if the determination had been there.

1982 proved to be a watershed in several respects for this fine old fixture. Owing to the pressures of the academic timetable and congestion on the fixtures at Lord's the authorities decided to reduce the match to a one-day fixture for the first time except for the War years. This was regrettable in many respects but the match had lost some of its lustre and there had only been three results in 15 years, all in Eton's favour. This also proved the first year when the balance of power which had been in Harrow's favour through the 1960s and 1970s turned decisively back to Eton. Harrow struggled throughout the game in 1982 and after Eton had declared on 216/3 they looked to be in danger of defeat when Harrow were 45/5 but were saved by an undefeated partnership of 63 from J.D.R. Field and a 15-year-old Sri Lankan, D.R. Nirmalalingham. M.V. Fleming who played for Eton in 1981/2 and scored 52 in this match had a fine all-round season with bat and ball and was unlucky not to get selected for the representative matches. A scion of the Fleming banking family he went on to captain the Combined Services and play for Kent between 1989 and 2003, captaining them from 1999/2003 and playing 11 one day 'internationals' for England. He was a cavalier attacking batsman, more than useful medium pace bowler and superb fielder. Limited overs cricket was made for him and he was Kent player of the year in 2001 when they won the Norwich Union Sunday League title. He was Chairman of the Professional Cricketers Association between 1996-2001 and is now Managing Director of Fleming Media and on the M.C.C. and Kent Committees.

Harrow probably had the edge in **1983** but were unable to force a result with Eton finishing 64

The last of the Eton and Harrow coaches at Lord's in 1984. The Rome family coach represented three generations of the Rome family in the Harrow XI, C.S. Harrow XI 1891/3, D.A.M. Harrow XI 1926/9 and C.B.N. Harrow XI 1960. A.S.R. Winlaw Harrow XI 1955/6 is on the left at the end and C.B.N. Rome is in the middle.

behind Harrow with seven wickets down. The situation was reversed in 1984 and Eton very much had the edge in yet another drawn match.

Harrow had a strong opening attack in **1984** for the first time since the Pigott era of 1974/6 in D.B.M. Fox who took 5/36 and J.J. Pethers, 4/55, in Eton's modest total of 166. Harrow had 180 minutes in which to get the runs and a Harrow victory was feasible However, Harrow batted so poorly against the accurate seam attack of C.G.M. Redmayne and A.G. Butterwick that in the end they struggled to avoid defeat and finished on 73/6.

In a low-scoring match in **1985** Eton achieved victory by the narrowest of margins and it proved to be a tense and absorbing contest throughout. They were much indebted to a fine all round performance from F.N. Bowman-Shaw who scored a vital 42 in Eton's 141 and then proceeded to take 7/38 with his medium paced seamers from the pavilion end. When Harrow were 98/9 it looked all over but a most courageous last-wicket stand of 40 between R.A. Hills, the Harrow wicket-keeper, and M.R. Middleton, the slow left-arm bowler and No.11 batsman, took Harrow up to 138. In what would have been the winning hit Hills was caught most unluckily high on the short deep square leg boundary for 46 and Eton had won by 3 runs. This was probably the most thrilling finish since the War but not of the highest quality. It was, though, the closest finish in the history of the match and matched in closeness only by the contests of 1900 when Harrow won by 1 wicket and 1910 when Eton won by 9 runs. J.J. Pethers,the Harrow opening bowler, achieved the record number of wickets in a season for Harrow with 59 victims beating Tony Pigott's 58 in 1975. Once again he bowled well in this match to take 6/87. Middleton gained somewhat a fortunate blue for Cambridge in 1987 when a last minute injury enabled him to take his place in the line-up at Lord's but has proved a more than useful slow bowler for M.C.C. and first division league cricket.

Overnight rain which delayed the start until three o'clock was partly responsible for Harrow's poor showing in **1986** and they were lucky to get away with a draw in the fifth lowest total in the history of the match, 37, and their lowest since 1847 when Harrow mustered 27 including 10 extras! All four Eton bowlers shared the wickets though J.D. Norman had the most remarkable figures: 6 overs, 5 maidens, 1 run, 3 wickets. Further rain later in the afternoon prevented the formality of Eton scoring the necessary 38 runs for victory. R.A. Pyman who had the ignominy of captaining Harrow in this match became a much improved cricketer after he left Harrow and put up some useful performances for Cambridge with bat and ball which were good enough to persuade Mike Atherton to give him a blue in 1989 and he again did well enough to appear against Oxford again in 1990. He also appeared for Dorset in the Minor Counties championship but his results were somewhat erratic. He was an unorthodox batsman who bowled medium-pace off the wrong foot, but needed to play more regularly to achieve good results. He is now managing director of Singer and Friedlander private banking. It was noticeable that there was a lot more steel in Eton's cricket from 1986 onwards when John Claughton, the old Oxford and Warwickshire cricketer took over the running of cricket at Eton - in particular their fielding and catching improved considerably.

The moral victory was Eton's in **1987** when they batted 30 overs less than Harrow and finished only 28 runs short of victory. A record Harrow first-wicket stand of 116 between H. Boralessa and M.B.T. de Souza Girao in 150 minutes was a pale shadow compared to the great Eton opening stand of 208 between A.W. Allen and N.S. Hotchkin in the same time in 1931 but nevertheless a record of sorts. A Harrow collapse after this left Eton a stiff target to pursue and a fine knock from their Captain R.D.O. Macleay 70 not out, took them close. Eton had one of their strongest sides for several years and were unbeaten in the season. D.C. Manasseh, the son of Maurice Manasseh, the old Oxford and Middlesex player, in his fourth year in the Harrow XI, was a disappointment as both captain and player with both his batting and left arm spin bowling going off markedly. He is now a sports agent handling the affairs of cricketers such as Brian Lara, Waquar Younis and Wasim Akram with some success. Rory Macleay played for Durham University with success and was an extremely useful league cricketer and captain of the Eton Ramblers Cricketer Cup side which won in 2001.

Harrow batted so slowly in their innings that they gave themselves little chance of bowling

Eton out in the 48 overs left for play in **1988**. The chief culprit was the Harrow opener H. Boralessa who took more than three hours over his 42, although Harrow's South African captain C. Keey and J.K. Bourne, 67, tried hard to atone for his sluggishness. Eton made a valiant attempt to score the 216 they needed and when C.H.G. St. George, 84, and J.E. Carr, 51, put on 123 together they were in with a chance. In the end Eton finished just short on 197/6 although they deserved to win, being much the more positive of the two sides. Chris Keey had a fine year for Harrow scoring 703 runs, the third highest aggregate of runs for Harrow at the time since the War. After representing Durham University for 3 years he went up to Oxford as a post-graduate and gained Oxford blues in 1992/3, playing with some success, scoring 111 v. Northants in 1992 and three half centuries in 1993 v. Middlesex (2) and Notts. J.E. Oppenheimer, the Harrow opening bowler of 1988 and grandson of Harry Oppenheimer, the former South African mining magnate and De Beers Chairman, gained a somewhat fortunate Oxford blue in 1991 but failed to take many wickets and those he did at a relatively high cost. Rob Nelson, the Harrow off spin bowler of 1987/8 was a highly successful Captain of Brondesbury, the strong Middlesex League side for several years winning the Middlesex League and Evening Standard Cup and also doing the double in 1999, a unique occurence.

Brondesbury captain Rob Nelson Harrow XI 1987/8 celebrates winning the Evening Standard Cup for Brondesbury in 1999.

After the Harrow captain, C. Raper, son of the Harrow captain in 1960 B.S. Raper, had put Eton in to bat on a slow wicket in **1989**, Eton set about the modest Harrow attack and there were some fine innings from E.R. Lush, 89, the Eton opener, and later S.R.B. Martin with 71. J.T. Trusted, the Eton captain and wicket-keeper, set Harrow a fair target of 227 runs in 175 minutes. After a reasonable start from their openers Harrow were eventually struggling to avoid defeat and finished on 171/6. C.H.G. St. George, the attacking Eton batsman of 1988/9, was the leading Army and Combined Services batsman for several years, captaining both sides in 1996.

All credit to Eton in **1990** when they won a most convincing victory by 7 wickets, the first result since the 3-run win by Eton in 1985. They successfully chased 220 runs in 153 minutes, achieving this in the last over with four balls to spare. Harrow batted very slowly in their innings, particularly against the slow left-arm spin of J.M.S. Whittington, and when they declared at 219/8 Eton appeared to have only a slim chance of success. They needed 121 off the last 20 overs and were indebted to W.R.G. Sellar and N.R.G. Hagen primarily for taking them home to victory. M.E.D. Jarrett, the Harrow captain of 1990, gained Cambridge blues in 1992/3 and, after a rocky start in the first-class game, became a much improved batsman, especially in his last year when he had gained more confidence. He finished his medical studies at Oxford where he was somewhat unlucky not to get a blue in 1995 and was twelfth man in the varsity match at Lord's. He became a superb cover fielder and a more than useful wicket-keeper where he performed in several first-class matches for Oxford in 1995 and represented Oxford again in 1996 without gaining a blue in an exceptionally strong Oxford batting side.

M.M.J. Hawkins Harrow XI 1991/2. He had two fine bowling performances for Harrow in 1991/2 with 5/50 and 5/35 respectively against Eton. Harrow should have won easily in 1992 but caution prevailed and Eton finished a long way behind with seven wickets down.

(25p) LORD'S MCC GROUND (25p)

OXFORD v. CAMBRIDGE

Tuesday, Wednesday & Thursday, June 30 & July 1, 2, 1992   (3 day Match)

OXFORD		First Innings	Second Innings
1 R. R. Montgomerie..	Worcester	c Pearson b Johnson ... 16	not out 45
2 J. E. R. Gallian	Keble	b Jones b Johnson 1	st Arscott b Wight 66
3 A. C. Storie	Keble	c Johnson b Hooper..... 5	
†4 G. B. T. Lovell	Exeter	c Crawley b Pitcher ... 32	
5 C. L. Keey	Keble	l b w b Pearson 33	
6 H. R. Davies	Christ Church	l b w b Abington 39	
7 M. P. W. Jeh	Keble	c Pearson b Johnson ... 8	Innings closed
8 R. H. MacDonald	Keble	not out 8	
9 D. J. Anderson	St. Edmund Hall	not out 8	
*10 C. J. Townsend	Brasenose	Innings closed	
11 B. S. Wood	Worcester		
		B 15, l-b 11, w 6, n-b , 32	B , l-b 3, w 1, n-b , 4
		Total 182	Total 115

FALL OF THE WICKETS

1—14   2—21   3—35   4—66   5—130   6—149   7—166   8—   9—   10—
1—115   2—   3—   4—   5—   6—   7—   8—   9—   10—

ANALYSIS OF BOWLING

Name	1st Innings						2nd Innings				
	O.	M.	R.	W.	Wd.	N-b	O.	M.	R.	W.	Wd. N-b
Johnson	18	4	62	3	5	...	6	0	22	0	1 ...
Pitcher	17	5	36	1	1	...	11	0	39	0	...
Pearson	14	4	37	1	...	...	8	0	31	0	...
Hooper	5	2	6	1	...	...					
Wight	11	5	14	0	...	...	4	0	13	1	...
Abington	2	1	2	1	...	...	2	0	7	0	...

CAMBRIDGE		First Innings	Second Innings
1 A. M. Hooper	St. John's	c Montgomerie b Gallian	b Jeh 17
2 G. W. Jones	Gonville & Caius	c Townsend b Gallian... 12	l b w b Macdonald 18
†3 J. P. Crawley	Trinity	c Gallian b Jeh 1	not out 106
4 R. M. Wight	Trinity Hall	c Storie b Jeh 5	not out 62
5 J. P. Carroll	Homerton	c Townsend b Wood ... 7	
*6 J. P. Arscott	Magdalene	c Gallian b Macdonald 14	
7 M. E. D. Jarrett	Girton	not out 7	c Anderson b Gallian ... 22
8 S. W. Johnson	Magdalene	c Anderson b Macdonald 14	
9 C. M. Pitcher	Selwyn		
10 R. M. Pearson	St. John's		
11 M. B. Abington	Homerton	Innings closed	
		B , l-b 3, w , n-b 5, 8	B 3, l-b 4, w 4, n-b 2, 13
		Total 60	Total 238

FALL OF THE WICKETS

1—5   2—11   3—24   4—25   5—35   6—37   7—60   8—   9—   10—
1—25   2—56   3—72   4—   5—   6—   7—   8—   9—   10—

ANALYSIS OF BOWLING

Name	1st Innings						2nd Innings				
	O.	M.	R.	W.	Wd.	N-b	O.	M.	R.	W.	Wd. N-b
Jeh	8	1	15	2	5	...	6	0	27	1	... 2
Gallian	8	4	10	2	...	...	18	1	49	1	1 ...
Wood	6	0	19	1	...	...	12.5	0	56	0	1 ...
Macdonald	5.4	3	13	2	...	...	12	3	30	1	2 ...
Anderson							4	0	29	0	...

Umpires—J. D. Bond & V. A. Holder
Scorers—G. S. Gordon, R. May & E. Solomon
† Captain   * Wicket-keeper
Play begins 1st & 2nd days at 11.30, 3rd day at 11.00
Luncheon Interval 1st & 2nd days 1.30—2.10, 3rd day 1.00—1.40
Tea Interval 1st & 2nd days 4.10—4.30, 3rd day 3.40—4.00
Stumps drawn 1st & 2nd days at 6.30, 3rd day at 5.30 or 6.00
(Timings may be varied according to state of game)

Oxford won the toss

Cambridge won by 7 wickets

(25p) LORD'S MCC GROUND (25p)

OXFORD v. CAMBRIDGE

Wednesday, Thursday & Friday, June 30 & July 1, 2, 1993   (3 day Match)

OXFORD		First Innings	Second Innings
1 R. R. Montgomerie	Worcester	run out 1	c Cake b Pearson 23
†2 J. E. R. Gallian	Keble	c Cake b Whittall 115	not out 53
3 G. I. Macmillan	Keble	c Cake b Whittall 63	not out 15
4 G. B. T. Lovell	Exeter	c Haste b Pitcher 114	
5 C. L. Keey	Keble	b Pearson 33	
6 C. M. Gupte	Pembroke	not out 43	
*7 C. W. Lyons	Keble	run out 2	
8 R. S. Yeabsley	Keble	not out 20	
9 M. Jeh	Keble		
10 R. H. MacDonald	Keble	Innings closed	
11 P. W. Trimby	Worcester		
		B 2, l-b 5, w , n-b 2, 9	B 4, l-b 1, w 4, n-b , 9
		Total 400	Total 100

FALL OF THE WICKETS

1—3   2—170   3—186   4—276   5—356   6—371   7—   8—   9—   10—
1—59   2—   3—   4—   5—   6—   7—   8—   9—   10—

ANALYSIS OF BOWLING

Name	1st Innings						2nd Innings				
	O.	M.	R.	W.	Wd.	N-b	O.	M.	R.	W.	Wd. N-b
Pitcher	27	3	90	1	...	...	1	0	13	0	4 ...
Charlesworth	35.5	4	104	0	1	...					
Pearson	30	10	77	1	...	...	9	1	31	1	...
Haste	13	1	61	0	...	...					
Whittall	20	0	61	2	...	...	8.2	2	31	0	...

CAMBRIDGE		First Innings	Second Innings
†1 J. P. Crawley	Trinity	l b w b Jeh 63	l b w b Gallian 49
2 G. W. Jones	Caius	c Trimby b Macmillan 39	l b w b Gallian 2
3 M. E. D. Jarrett	Girton	b Trimby 22	c Lyons b Trimby 26
4 R. Q. Cake	St. John's	c Macmillan b Trimby 0	b MacDonald 0
5 G. M. Charlesworth	Hughes Hall	l b w b Jeh 49	b Macmillan 17
6 J. P. Carroll	Homerton	c Lovell b Macmillan ... 0	b Gallian b Jeh 21
*7 J. P. Arscott	Magdalene	c Keey b Macmillan ... 0	c Gupte b Trimby 14
8 N. J. Haste	Pembroke	l b w b Yeabsley b Jeh 36	c Gallian b Trimby 0
9 R. M. Pearson	St. John's	l b w b Yeabsley b Jeh 1	not out 37
10 C. M. Pitcher	Selwyn	l b w b Trimby 0	c Lovell b Jeh 31
11 A. R. Whittall	Trinity	not out 0	c Macmillan b Yeabsley 40
		B 4, l-b 8, w 1, n-b 18, 31	B , l-b 8, w 5, n-b 16, 29
		Total 241	Total 255

FALL OF THE WICKETS

1—95   2—136   3—144   4—168   5—168   6—168   7—229   8—238   9—241   10—241
1—44   2—67   3—67   4—103   5—138   6—138   7—138   8—181   9—185   10—255

ANALYSIS OF BOWLING

Name	1st Innings						2nd Innings				
	O.	M.	R.	W.	Wd.	N-b	O.	M.	R.	W.	Wd. N-b
Jeh	14	2	61	4	...	14	18	2	90	2	... 14
Gallian	15	5	41	0	1	2	16	2	52	3	3 2
Yeabsley	5	0	40	0	...	...	1	1	0	1	...
Trimby	24.2	8	79	3	...	...	15	1	72	3	...
MacDonald	10	2	22	0	...	2	8	3	23	1	...
Macmillan	8	5	13	3	...	...	2	1	10	0	2 ...

Umpires—G. I. Burgess & G. Sharp
Scorers—G. S. Gordon, A. R. May & K. Bird
† Captain   * Wicket-keeper
Play begins 1st & 2nd days at 11.30, 3rd day at 11.00
Luncheon Interval 1st & 2nd days 1.30—2.10, 3rd day 1.00—1.40
Tea Interval 1st & 2nd days 4.10—4.30, 3rd day 3.40—4.00
Stumps drawn 1st & 2nd days at 6.30, 3rd day at 5.30 or 6.00
(Timings may be varied according to state of game)

Cambridge won the toss and elected to field

Oxford won by 9 wickets

C.L. Keey Harrow XI 1987/8 and Oxford University 1992/3 and M.E.D. Jarrett Harrow XI 1989/90 both Harrow captains on opposing sides in the Varsity matches of 1992/3. Cambridge won by 7 wickets in 1992 and Oxford gained revenge in 1993 winning by 9 wickets.

There was a much closer contest in **1991** and, although Eton won by 3 wickets, Harrow made them fight all the way. Harrow struggled in their innings against the accurate Eton attack and only C.G. Hill's 54 prevented the innings from total disintegration. Despite a target of only 143 to win Eton made very hard work of it, especially against M.M.J. Hawkins, the Harrow opener, who bowled particularly well in his second spell to take 5/50, but Eton just sneaked home. Whittington, the Eton captain and slow left-arm spinner, had a good season and gained selection for the Schools XI at Lord's v. E.S.C.A. and Combined Services. He played one first-class match for Middlesex v. Cambridge in 1992 but bowled without taking a wicket and has since given up after going to Durham University.

Harrow should have won the **1992** match easily against a very inexperienced Eton side containing no old colours, the first time in their history this had ever happened. Harrow's poor start made them over-cautious and although H.St.J.R. Foster, 102 not out, and J.J. Renshaw, 80 not out, put on 196 in an unbroken fourth wicket partnership, it took them nearly four hours and Harrow had batted for 87 overs in all. Hawkins again bowled beautifully for Harrow to take 5/35 and put Eton on the rack. However, having left themselves only 44 overs to bowl

H.St. J.R. Foster, Harrow XI 1992/3. Here seen in action during his 102 not out in 1992, Harrow's first century since 1978. The son of D.R.J. Foster Harrow XI 1957/9 and grandson of J.H.N. Foster Harrow XI 1923. In 2005 he won the World Rackets Championship.

Eton out they had only themselves to blame when Eton finished on 137/7 at the close and salvaged a draw.

Harry Foster, the Harrow batsman of 1992/3, son of D.R.J. and grandson of J.H.N. distinguished himself by winning the World rackets Championship in 2005. A century at Lord's and World Rackets Champion is certainly a most coveted and unusual 'double' which he has achieved through hard work and dedication.

Eton had much the better side in **1993** and would surely have won easily but for inate caution. Harrow paid dearly for a lost run out opportunity against H.V. Machin in the seventh over of the day when he went on to make 150 not out, the sixth highest Eton score in the history of the match, well supported by his captain, TA. Simpson, 52, an England Schools representative. They put one of the weakest Harrow attacks ever seen at Lord's to the sword and it was a merciful release when the declaration came at 254/2, leaving Harrow a target of 255 in 180 minutes. Harrow never looked likely to get anywhere near the target and were saved by their captain, J.J. Renshaw, who, having not scored many runs all season, batted 130 minutes for his 57 not out to save the dark blues from an ignominious loss. Simpson had a very fine season for Eton scoring 835 runs, the second highest total since the War (after J.R.T. Barclay's 897 runs in

J.A.G. Fulton Eton XI 1994/6. A centurion in 1994 in Eton's gallant attempt to score the runs and their captain in 1995/6. He was somewhat fortunate to represent M.C.C. Schools in 1996 since he had a relatively modest season. Oxford University 1997/8 but 12th man in 1999.

1970) and leading them in an unbeaten season with nine straight wins. He has become an extremely useful club cricketer for Brondesbury whom he currently captains but in former times would have played for Middlesex.

Harrow were put in to bat by Eton in **1994** in a vain attempt to force a result and were saved by a useful partnership of 160 by O.H. Chittenden, 96, and S.F. Roundell, 89, to take Harrow to 235/6 after 81 overs. The Harrow captain P.A.J. Montgomery, who had taken 2 wickets all season set Eton a run rate of over five per over to win. They very nearly achieved it against some rank bad Harrow bowling with the honourable exception of their tall South African opening bowler, M.S. Rayner, who took 4/47. A magnificent 112 from 16-year-old J.A.G. Fulton, well supported by J.C.S. Hardy, 75, only just failed to take Eton home to a deserved victory and they finished just seven runs short. It was clear that Harrow had gone into the match with several passengers in their side including the captain and a bowling attack (apart from Rayner) which was woefully weak and fielding at best moderate.

Eton were dismissed for the first time in 10 years in **1995** by some fine swing bowling from T. D.de M. Leathes who took 6/19 in 16 overs and would surely have lost but for a creditable defensive knock of 100 from H.H. Dixon, son of M.H. Dixon (Eton XI 1960/1) and grandson of G.H. (Eton XI, 1932/4). Harrow were fortunate to get the Eton captain, J.A.G. Fulton out early, but bowled and fielded creditably to get Eton out for 219 and although Harrow had 30 overs less than Eton to score the runs, strove manfully but finished 43 runs short with three wickets in hand. The match reflected well on a young Harrow team with only two old flannels. Much of the credit for this was due to Mark Williams who had taken over the running of Harrow cricket from Bill Snowden. R.G. MacAndrew, the Harrow wicket-keeper, scored 775 runs, at that time the second highest total of runs in a season since the War, and also took 30 victims behind the stumps, including five at Lord's, second only to D. Wormald who took six in 1925.

Two strong batting sides contested the **1996** match with Eton having the edge in their bowling attack. Harrow strove hard for a result and declared their innings closed on 236/8 after 63.3 overs. Eton were shocked to lose their first three wickets for 23 runs and afterwards made little attempt to go for the runs. They finished on 139/4 after 57 overs with some of the Harrow bowling being less than distinguished, including 24 overs of fairly innocuous spin. This did less than justice to two reasonably strong sides and was a disappointing end for John Claughton to finish his stewardship of Eton cricket from 1986/96 on, particularly as he had done so much to improve the competitiveness of their cricket. He has since become a distinguished Headmaster of Solihull and recently Chief Master of K.E.S. Birmingham his old school, and has also joined the Warwickshire C.C.C Committee, his old county.

Hugo Loudon, the Eton captain, finished an outstanding cricket career at Eton with 807 runs at an average of 90 in **1997**. He went on to have a season with Hampshire before representing Durham University from 1999/2001. He was not given the chance he should have had to make an impact at Hampshire; in other times it might have been very different. His opening partner David Kay-Shuttleworth, son of Lord Shuttleworth, also performed very well, scoring 499 runs at an average of 71. Eton also had the distinction of three Blues in the Oxford University side which drew the Varsity match against Cambridge in 1997, a highly creditable achievement in an egalitarian world. All three: J.G. Fulton, the freshman and Eton captain in 1996, C.G.R. Lightfoot and P.G. Morgan had their moments, particularly Fulton with four first-class fifties

The 1997 Oxford & Cambridge scorecard showing a considerable degree of success by the three Etonian representatives

J. A. G. Fulton. Eton XI 1994-96, Oxford University 1997 and captain in 1998.

C. G. R. Lightfoot. Eton XI 1992-94, Oxford University, 1997-98.

P. G. Morgan. Eton XI 1991, Oxford University 1997.

J. R. S. Redmayne, Eton XI 1997, Oxford Blue 2000 and 2002. A fine footballer, double Oxford blue also.

in the season. Oxford beat the eventual County Champions Glamorgan with their captain M. A. Waugh of Warwickshire scoring two hundreds in the match and P. G. Morgan, 63 in the first innings. James Redmayne, the Eton middle order batsman of 1997, scored useful runs for Oxford University in their handful of first class matches in 2000 and gained a cricket blue to add to his soccer blue. He was 12th man in 2001 and regained his place in 2002 with a fine 75 not out v. Cambridge in the varsity match to save Oxford from defeat.

Alex Loudon, the younger brother of Hugo, captained the Eton XI in **1998** and 1999 and also the E.C.B under 17 and under 19s side. A highly talented all-rounder he scored 374 runs at 53 per innings and took 35 wickets with his off spinners at 15 per wicket in 1998 and captained the England under 19 side at the 2000 World Cup. After Durham University and Kent, where he had begun to show his prowess, particularly in 2004 he moved to Warwickshire in 2005, after disillusionment with the Kent management. Form with both bat and ball is beginning to show through and if he

Alex Loudon Eton XI 1997/9. Durham University, Kent & Warwickshire. The first Etonian to go on a test tour since George Mann in 1948/9.

can continue to improve, the future could be bright with an England place as an all-rounder distinctly possible. He represented Warwickshire in the Cheltenham and Gloucester Final at Lord's in September 2005, Warwickshire losing to Hampshire by 18 runs in a high scoring contest. After a reasonable first season with Warwickshire he was chosen for the Test Tour of Pakistan in November 2005, the first Etonian to be picked for a major Test Tour since George Mann captained England in South Africa in 1948/9. He has taken his batting average to 33 and achieved two 5 wicket hauls in county cricket with his off spinners, helped by a 'doosra' that moves away from right handers. He delivers it using his fingers rather than rolling it out from the back of the wrist, making it a more legitimate delivery than that of certain sub-continent spinners. His future will be followed with huge interest by all concerned and clearly if he continues to make progress could be a future England captain in the making a few years down the line.

Alex Titchener-Barrett, the Harrow opener of 1997/8, represented Middlesex under-19s in 1998, as did Sam Stevens in 1999, scoring 66 on debut but it is as a Rackets player he is likely to achieve fame. A double Foster Cup winner, the first Harrovian to do so, he is now No. 4 in the world and within touching-distance of the World Singles Title within the next two years, currently held by another Harrovian, Harry Foster, the Lord's centurion of 1992.

Alex Titchener-Barrett, Harrow XI 1997/8, a more than useful cricketer but a superb rackets player. Can he achieve the World Title in 2007?

Sebastian FitzGerald the Eton opener of 1998, besides being a Balliol Scholar, succeeded in gaining Oxford rugby blues from 2000/2002 as a stand off half, unusual for an Etonian since rugby has only recently been taken as a serious rival to football.

Gurrick Maan, the Eton seam bowler of 1998/9 took 48 wickets at 10 in the 1999 season, including 8/27 v. Winchester, and also scored 406 runs in what was an extremely strong Eton side in 1999 with ten wins and a tie in their matches.

James Bruce, the Eton seam bowler of 1997/8, who bowled superbly in the Eton and Harrow match of 1998, taking 6/40 off 16 overs, represented Durham University and in 2004/5 played several games for Hampshire, showing some promise. He will, however, need to quicken up a yard or two if he is to make any real impact at this level.

Nick Compton, the Harrow opening batsman, grandson of the great Denis Compton of Middlesex and England and captain in 2001 topped the batting and bowling averages in 2000 and scored 685 runs in 2001 at 49. He also made a one-day debut for Middlesex. His progress has not been so fast since; he has played a handful of County Championship games without making a real impact. A certain arrogance is not helping his chances but he undoubtedly has ability and could well make it in the big time. If he can achieve a small measure of what his famous grandfather did it will be well worth waiting for.

Luke de Rougemont Harrow XI 1997/2000. Arguably Harrow's best wicketkeeper batsman since the war, an outstanding talent but sadly not continued in county cricket.

The two captains at Lord's in 2003 Peter Dunbar, Harrow (LEFT) and Ben Thompson, Eton (RIGHT)

WOOLDRIDGE

Even Denis would have struggled to succeed in these days of neglect

OUR beloved Chancellor really missed a trick this week when he used the undoubtedly very clever Laura Spence as the human detonator to explode another class war.

Railing vehemently against the decision by Magdalen College, Oxford, not to admit her as a student — and asserting wrongly that this was because she came from a state school on Tyneside — he went absolutely bonkers about old boy networks and old school ties.

If he was really intent on stirring up social strife all he had to do, instead of embarrassing this girl who anyway is going to Harvard University on a £65,000 scholarship, was to slide away from the Palace of Westminster in his ministerial chauffeur-driven car and proceed in a north-westerly direction to Lord's Cricket Ground.

There, by heavens, on the very day he was ranting on at a Trades Union reception, he would have witnessed a scene that could well have induced genuine apoplexy. It was the Eton-Harrow cricket match.

This fixture was first played in 1805 and on Thursday, having survived the Reform Bill, the Peterloo Riots, Keir Hardie, two World Wars and, so far, Mr Blair's administration, the latest instalment started a little late due to early morning rain.

Eton won the toss, put Harrow into bat on a dampish pitch and claimed their first wicket with only two runs on the board. Enter now a young batsman with the inevitable three initials who assisted in a second-wicket stand of 68 which actually

won the match. He was out, bowled while attempting to sweep to leg, for 20.

It was sheer deja vu. Known as Nick to his mates he was listed as N.R.D. Compton. No mention that he is the grandson of the great Denis Compton, whose sweeping, driving, cutting and eccentric running between the wickets for Middlesex and England enthralled millions in the world's most famous cricket ground for decades.

Nick is the son of Richard, Denis's son from his second marriage. Richard lives in South Africa and has so prospered in the media business that he can afford to send his lad to Harrow. Privileged by his father's success, no doubt about it. But that is not the point of this story.

Grandfather Denis, founder of the dynasty, came from a very different background: sound working-class family in north London. His privilege was simply that he went to a state school where sport was an essential on the curriculum, where excellent playing fields existed, where schoolmasters stayed behind long after hours to coach the promising.

Denis was so promising that, aged 12, he captained his school team and was chosen to play for North London Schools v South London Schools. He

One for future: grandson Nick Compton starred at Lord's

scored 88 on his first appearance at Lord's. His next visit was two years later when, at 14, he captained London Elementary Schools against a Public Schools' XI. Denis scored 114 and took two for five to win the match. He was taken on to the Lord's groundstaff to bowl to MCC members and sell scorecards on big match days. Meanwhile, having played football for England Schoolboys against Wales, he was signed by Arsenal and went on to play in the winning 1950 FA Cup Final side.

'Lucky,' Denis used to say. 'Went to a decent school, you see.' It wasn't a posh school, it wasn't a public school. But where are those schools today? A few full of good intent still exist because I get letters from state schoolmasters despairing of playing

fields sold to industry, the ludicrously short time allotted to sport and the inanities of political correctness which decree that kids with enormous talent must not be encouraged to the limit because it makes contemporaries feel deprived and inferior.

Don't tell me there is not raw, brilliant intuitive talent of the Denis Compton class out there somewhere. But until we provide the facilities to find and nurture it we shall continue to import mercenary foreign footballers to entertain us and have a third-world cricket team.

Mr Chancellor Brown's rhetoric contained one remark with which we would all concur: 'It is about time we had an end to the old Britain, where all that matters is the privileges you were born with, rather than the potential you actually have.'

Dead right, pal. Speaking as one whose old school tie wouldn't be recognised at five paces by one of my contemporaries, I wonder what he's going to do about it?

i.wooldridge@dailymail.co.uk

Daily Mail, Saturday May 27, 2000.

Harrow at last won in **2000**, their first win in 25 years, albeit a short-ened version of the new format of 55 overs, in 40 overs. Never had the match been played so early in the season and in a low-scoring match the result was in doubt until near the end, when Eton, not helped by three run-outs, succumbed by 19 runs. Luke de Rougemont, Harrow's captain and wicket-keeper batsman of 1997/2000 was a class act all through his schooldays but more is the pity that he has not gone on to further honours. In former times Counties would have cried out for players of his calibre. Tom Dunbar, the sound Harrow opener of 1999/2000, created a unique record by winning the Foster Cup Rackets singles and doubles, The Public Schools Fives and Golf in one year as well as batting pretty well in a winning Lord's XI, scoring 46 out of Harrow's total of 143. David Ferreira, the Eton captain/wick-et-keeper of 1999/2000 also looked a fine player and was easily top scorer with 38 in Eton's score of 124. He certainly looks capable of representative honours.

An abandoned match in **2001** was sad because both sides were strong and the unofficial game at Eton two weeks later showed that it could have been a thriller. Ben Thompson, in the first of his three years in the Eton side, showed a huge talent and was extremely unlucky in **2002** with 98 at Lord's not to get the century he deserved, followed by 50 in **2003**. Eton's three victories in succession by varying margins, the first treble since 1921, was a tribute to the fine coaching of their longstanding professional John Rice, formerly of Surrey and Hampshire. Thompson was undoubtedly the Eton hero in **2002** when they won easily by 66 runs and had much to do with their success in 2003 with his all round capabilities and leadership skills when they got home by 36 runs. Thompson has a big future ahead in the game and

M.D. Walters, a controversial one year choice for Harrow in 2004. Phenomonal record of 1204 runs at 109, an all time Harrow best.

already Warwickshire and Gloucestershire have shown interest. Ed Nissen, the Eton captain of **2004** played one of the most remarkable innings ever in an Eton and Harrow contest of 124 not out in 82 balls out of a total of 239/6 after a moderate season and was the match winner over a very strong Harrow side which should probably have triumphed but lost a thrilling struggle by 20 runs after losing their two star batsman Morrison and Walters at a crucial time to brilliant catches by Ed Bruce.

Martin Walters, the Border under-19 cricketer from South Africa was only at Harrow for two terms and many people other than Etonians thought this was bending the rules a little too much. In any case, he relished the easy pickings of schools cricket, scoring five 100s and seven 50s in a total of 1,204 runs at an average of 109, easily beating the school batting record that had stood since 1938 by nearly 300 runs. I quote a piece in the Eton College Chronicle in June 2004, which probably summed up Etonian feelings on the subject:

'Eton cricketers were delighted to see how well Martin Walters has settled into the Harrow XI (100 vs Radley; 79 vs Charterhouse; 84 vs Free Foresters; 104 vs Wellington) and were sorry not to have joined in his nineteenth birthday celebrations back in March. Many will know that Marty was in the South African Under 15 World Cup side in 2000.

While at Harrow he will be managing cricket commitments at both school and club level as well as putting himself through the rigours of an AS course - a demanding timetable - for even the toughest of antipodeans. But he is sure to recover quickly when he returns to South Africa in December.

We therefore wish him every success with his single AS module and a very happy twentieth birthday next March.'

He also proved a more than useful seam bowler with a very good line just outside off stump and clearly has a big future in the game back in South Africa or should he decide to return to England. It would not surprise anyone if he became an international cricketer in the next five years.

The 200th Anniversary in **2005** of the first fixture at Lord's in 1805 proved to be Eton's nemesis. An extremely strong Harrow side, which went through the season unbeaten with 13 wins, was much too good for an Eton side that had too many weaknesses and they won by seven wickets with 16 overs to spare. This was arguably the best Harrow side since the middle 1970s when they had Pigott, Fosh and Tindall, and the fielding and catching were superb. The Harrow players who caught the eye were Sam Northeast, in his second year in the XI with three more to go, Glenn Querl, the Zimbabwean, who had a very fine Lord's with 65 not out and 4/26, Will Spencer, the opener and leg spinner, and Mumtaz Habib, the Afghani all-rounder. It would be surprising if all four did not make an impact somewhere in the game. Special mention should be made of Northeast, who scored 627 runs at 53 in the season, has a very good temperament, is technically sound and has a passion for the game. He could be a possible England player of the future; Glenn Querl, also for Zimbabwe if there is a level playing field but certainly for a county with international possibilities. Eton's Alex Ball, who opened the innings for three years, has a lot of class and is likely to go up to Oxford in 2006 and has also represented Hampshire under-19s. Guy George, the Eton wicket-keeper batsman, looks a fine prospect and his two superb stumpings in the 2004 match come to mind. Ed Bruce, the fourth of the Bruce brothers to have represented Eton, is a combative all-rounder, who should do well both at Durham University and with Hampshire, where he has played at under-19 level.

Ben Thompson Eton XI 2001/3. He has the ability to go a long way in the game.

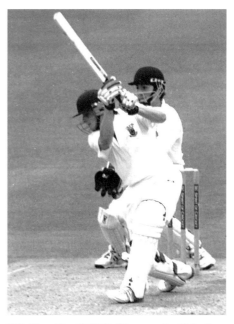

Eddie Nissen Eton XI 2002/4. If he can produce his Lord's form he should go for it.

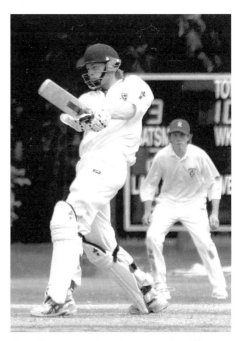

Alex Ball Eton XI 2003/5. A classy opener who could make an impact at Oxford.

Ed Bruce Eton XI 2003/5. A combative all rounder who could turn out to be the best of the Bruce brothers.

The expectation is that Harrow are likely to have the upper hand in these matches for the next few years with increasingly strong sides aided by a sports scholarship system which will tempt highly talented cricketers to Harrow. It appears that Eton do not want to go down this route for understandable reasons, mainly that this changes the ethos and traditions of the school which is neither necessary nor needed. However, it must be hoped that the matches will remain competitive in the best spirit possible and that Harrow will not lose sight of the fact that the winning is not everything and gaining an unfair advantage is not in anyone's interest for the long-term future of this magnificent contest.

It is an interesting exercise to analyse the results since the match begun in 1805. There were lengthy periods of domination on both sides up until the first drawn match in 1860 with Harrow's being the greatest, eight wins in succession up to 1859 with no fixture in 1856. Results were achieved up to this time principally for two reasons: first, the unpredictable nature of the wickets at Lord's, where the bounce at best was uncertain and shooters were inevitable; secondly play started much earlier in those times than was the fashion after 1860 when it became more of a social event. Play commenced at 10 o'clock in the morning with only a short break between innings and continued until the light became uncertain, usually about 8 o'clock, and it was extremely rare to stop for rain or bad light. As wickets and batting techniques improved, draws became more likely but up until 1909 wins still predominated, with Harrow retaining the edge with 19 wins, Eton 13 wins and 18 draws. Eton reversed this with a vengeance and Harrow were unable to force a win between 1909/1938, the longest period without a victory from one side in history. There is no doubt that Eton had in general stronger sides and thus played the better cricket during this period and won 12 matches with Harrow's only win being in 1939, the last year before the Second World War, with 13 draws during this period.

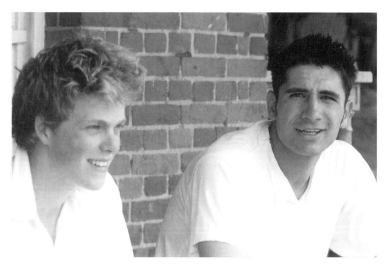

Sam Northeast Harrow XI 2004/5, LEFT, *a huge talent for the future. Has a possible three years to go and scored 677 runs at 53 in 2005. A potential England cricketer in the making? Mumtaz Habib,* RIGHT, *Afghan sports scholar at Harrow and more than useful allrounder.*

Lord's 2004…. Martin Walters bowling in the 2004 match for Harrow and the conclusion of an extremely fine match narrowly won by Eton, their third win in a row.

W. Spencer Harrow XI 2004/5. An exceptional leg-spinning all rounder with 1056 runs and 58 wickets over two years with a possible two more years to go.

Glenn Querl (Harrow) the man of the match with 4/26 and 65 not out in 2005, likely to play for Zimbabwe in the under 19 World Cup and has two more years in the Harrow XI. Likely to be a scourge to Eton in the next two years.

Since the Second World War there have been only 22 results out of 57 contests with 12 wins to Eton and 10 to Harrow with 3 matches abandoned without a ball being bowled in 1997, 1999 and 2001. However, since the game became a one day fixture in 1982 and reverted to the limited overs format of 55 overs per side in 2000 after a short experiment with an overs limit for the side batting first, Harrow won narrowly for the first time in 25 years in 2000, and Eton in 2002, 2003 and 2004 – the first hat-trick of wins since 1921, Harrow won by 7 wickets in the 200th Anniversary match in 2005.

There is no doubt that outstanding cricketers on both sides who have gone on to play county cricket since the Second World War have been few and far between due to the game turning totally professional in 1962 and the need to make a choice between playing cricket for a living or going straight into a profession or career. At the same time, Oxford and Cambridge, the two ancient Universities are not playing the part they should be because of academic pressures. This has been recognised by the fact that the University match between Oxford and Cambridge over 3 days is no longer played at Lord's but is a one day limited overs match. A 4 day match is played alternatively at Oxford and Cambridge but nevertheless a fixture that goes back to 1827 at Lord's has been cast aside needlessly in the opinion of many.

Durham University has taken up the role with enthusiasm. Cricket for the first time for many years is becoming more popular with the general public as shown by the huge enthusiasm for the recent success of England in the home Ashes series of 2005 and Public School and University cricketers are now staying in the game and doing well, Andrew Strauss of Radley Durham University, Middlesex and England, Alex Loudon of Eton, Durham University and Warwickshire, James Bruce of Eton, Durham University and Hampshire and

Nick Compton of Harrow and Middlesex being good examples. There is now more money available in first class cricket and a decent living to be earned by diligence and hard work. The former amateur cricketer is now being wooed and cultivated since the State Schools are not producing the talent for reasons which are obvious i.e. lack of teachers, coaches and proper facilities, all of which private schools have in abundance.

Harrow look set to have some good years ahead in the foreseeable future and at least two or three potential first class cricketers in Sam Northeast, Will Spencer and Glenn Querl. Time will tell but golden opportunities are there for the successful and talented and the media opportunities are endless. It is clear that Oxford and Cambridge even with the help of the new Universities are not producing the cricketers they should and although Eton and Harrow - particularly Eton - have had a remarkably high percentage of Blues, there has been a substantial decline over the last fifty years. This is a great shame but until admission policies are reviewed this will not change for the gifted sportsman, who will go elsewhere. Eton and Harrow can still set the example for the game as a whole and fortunately the interest at both schools in representing their teams at Lord's is as high as ever; more encouragement is being given and opportunities for going further up the ladder are even greater.

The well known Eton verse by Denis Buxton is appropriate to both schools:

You saw the vision glorious
And strove to bring that vision true,
To have your Eton live in us,
As all our Eton lives in you.

or as Hilaire Belloc so succinctly put it:

"There's nothing worth the wear of winning,
but laughter and the love of friends?"

THE CRAWLEY
CONNECTION

It would be remiss not to mention the unique record of the Crawley family, an unbroken five generations of Crawleys have represented Harrow at Lord's from G. B. Crawley in 1850 to Spencer Crawley, who played in the 200th Anniversary of the fixture in 2005, scoring the winning runs in his 54 not out. All told, twelve of the family have played with varying degrees of distinction, beating two other distinguished Etonian familes, the Hoares of banking fame with ten representatives, and the Lytteltons with ten also. Six of the Crawleys played first-class cricket but undoubtedly the two most famous and gifted were Aidan Crawley, the well-known politician and journalist, and Leonard Crawley who was probably better known for his golf but was an outstanding batsman. Both were easily good enough to play for England had they concentrated purely on cricket. A special match was played in 1965, which contained on one side members of the Crawley family v. The Household Brigade at Burton Court, Chelsea. [Photograph: 1965]

SCORES OF THE CRAWLEY FAMILY

in the Eton and Harrow match at Lord's.

G. B. Crawley	*1850*	23 & 0	*1851*	1 & 18★		
C. D. Crawley	*1853*	3 & 0	*1854*	18 & 6		
H. E. Crawley	*1882*	9 & 22★	*1883*	3		
E. Crawley	*1885*	100 & 7	*1886*	40 & 69		
A. S. Crawley	*1894*	11 & 3	*1895*	78 & 11		
C. S. Crawley	*1920*	1 & 7	*1921*	1 & 3	*1922*	67★
L. G. Crawley	*1920*	18 & 0	*1921*	1 & 103	*1922*	53
K. E. Crawley	*1922*	4	*1923*	3 & 7	*1924*	11 & 4
A. M. Crawley	*1924*	8 & 10	*1925*	25 & 12	*1926*	87
A. H. Crawley	*1964*	10 & 13	*1965*	62 & 73		
R. S. Crawley	*1966*	13 & 16	*1967*	6 & 18		
S. H. Crawley	*2005*	54★			★Not Out	

Spencer Crawley, The fifth generation of Crawley's to represent Harrow at Lord's. He didn't let them down with a fine 54 not out and the winning runs in a 7 wicket win. Will he go further and achieve success at a higher level? Time will tell.

Emilius Bayley Eton XI 1838/41 & Kent

W. Marcon Eton XI 1841/2 Oxford Univ. & Somerset

E.W. Blore Eton XI 1845/7 & Cambridge Univ.

R. Hankey Harrow XI 1849/50 Oxford Univ. & Surrey

V.E. Walker Harrow XI 1853/4 & Middlesex

Hon. C.G. Lyttelton Eton XI 1858/60 & Cambridge Univ.

R.A.H. Mitchell Eton XI 1858/61 Oxford Univ. & Leicestershire

A.W.T. Daniel Harrow XI 1858/60 Cambridge Univ. & Middlesex

A. Lubbock Eton XI 1861/3 & Kent

W.B. Money Harrow XI 1865/7 & Cambridge Univ.

A.N. Hornby Harrow XI 1864/5 Lancashire & England

F.C. Cobden Harrow XI 1866 & Cambridge Univ.

C.I. Thornton Eton XI 1866/8 Cambridge Univ. Kent & Middlesex

C.J. Ottaway Eton XI 1867/9 Oxford Univ. & Middlesex

S.E. Butler Eton XI 1868/9 Oxford Univ. & Somerset

Hon G.R.C. Harris Eton XI 1868/70 Oxford Univ. Kent & England

F.M. Buckland Eton XI 1871/3 Oxford Univ. & Middlesex

Hon. A. Lyttelton Eton XI 1872/5 Cambridge Univ. Middlesex & England

A.J. Webbe Harrow XI 1872/4 Oxford Univ. Middlesex & England and I.D. Walker Harrow XI 1860/3 & Middlesex

H. Whitfeld Eton XI 1875/7 Cambridge Univ. & Sussex

Hon. Ivo Bligh Eton XI 1876/7 Cambridge Univ. Kent & England

Hon. M.B. Hawke Eton XI 1878/9 Cambridge Univ. Yorkshire & England

P.J. de Paravicini Eton XI 1878/81 Cambridge Univ. & Middlesex

M.C. Kemp Harrow XI 1879/80 Oxford Univ. & Kent

H.W. Bainbridge Eton XI 1879/82 Cambridge Univ. & Warwickshire

F. Marchant Eton XI 1882/3 Cambridge Univ. & Kent

H.T. Hewett Harrow XI 1882/3 Oxford Univ. & Somerset

H. Philipson Eton XI 1884/5 Oxford Univ. Middlesex & England

H.R. Bromley-Davenport Eton XI 1886/9 Cambridge Univ. Middlesex & England

C. Heseltine Eton Hampshire & England

F.W. Milligan Eton
Yorkshire & England

C.P. Foley Eton XI 1886/7
Cambridge Univ. &
Middlesex

A.M. Miller Eton
Captain of Wiltshire for
25 years & England

F.S. Jackson Harrow XI
1887/9 Cambridge Univ.
Yorkshire & England

A.C. MacLaren Harrow XI
1887/90 Lancashire
& England

C.C. Pilkington Eton XI
1892/5 Oxford Univ.
& Middlesex

B.J.T Bosanquet Eton XI
1896 Oxford Univ.
Middlesex & England

C.H.B. Marsham Eton XI
1897/8 Oxford Univ.
& Kent

E.M. Dowson Harrow
1895/9 Cambridge Univ.
& Surrey

W. Findlay Eton XI
1898/9 Oxford Univ.
& Lancashire

Lord Dalmeny
Eton XI 1900 Middlesex
& Surrey

N.E. Haig Eton
Middlesex & England

D.C. Boles Eton 1903/4
The Army & Devon
highest score 183

C.E. Hatfeild Eton
1903/6 Oxford Univ.
& Kent

N.C. Tufnell Eton X1
1904/6 Cambridge Univ.
& England

M.C. Bird Harrow XI
1904/7 Surrey
& England

M. Falcon Harrow XI
1906/7 Cambridge
& Norfolk

G.E.V. Crutchley Harrow XI
1908/9 Oxford Univ.
& Norfolk

The Hon. L. H.Tennyson
Eton XI 1907/8
Hampshire & England

R.St.L. Fowler Eton XI
1908/10 The Army
& Hampshire

T.O. Jameson Harrow XI
1909/10 Hampshire &
MCC to West Indies

W.S.Cornwallis
1892-1982 Eton & Kent

C.H.B. Blount Harrow XI
1910/12 & Combined
Services

G.Wilson Harrow XI
1912/14 Cambridge Univ.
& Yorkshire

W.W. Hill-Wood Eton XI
1918/20, Cambridge
Univ., Derbyshire & MCC
Tour to Australia & New
Zealand 1921/2

R. Aird Eton XI
1919/21 Cambridge Univ.
& Hampshire

G.O. Allen Eton XI
1919/21 Cambridge Univ.
Middlesex & England

Sir Alec Douglas-Home
Eton XI 1921/2
& Middlesex

H.J. 'Tommy' Enthoven
Harrow XI 1919/22
Cambridge Univ.
& Middlesex

L.G. Crawley
Harrow XI 1920/2
Cambridge Univ.
& Essex

N.M. Ford Harrow XI
1924/6 Oxford Univ.
& Derbyshire

A.M. Crawley Harrow XI
1924/6 Oxford Univ.
& Kent

C.K.H. Hill-Wood Eton XI
1925/6 Oxford Univ.
& Derbyshire

Hon. C. Lyttelton
Eton & Worcestershire

A.G. Hazlerigg Eton XI
1927/9 Cambridge Univ.
& Leicestershire

A.G. Pelham Eton XI
1930 Cambridge Univ.
& Sussex

N.S. Hotchkin Eton XI
1931/3 Cambridge Univ.
& Middlesex

M. Tindall Harrow XI
1931/3 Cambridge Univ.
& Middlesex

J.H. Pawle Harrow XI
1933/4 Cambridge Univ.
& Essex

M.A.C.P. Kaye Harrow XI
1933/5 & Cambridge
Univ.

P.M. Studd Harrow XI
1933/5 & Cambridge
Univ.

B.D. Carris Harrow XI
1933/6 Cambridge Univ.
& Middlesex

F.G. Mann Eton XI
1934/6 Cambridge Univ.
Middlesex & England

R.A.A. Holt Harrow XI
1936/8 & Sussex

E. Crutchley Harrow XI
1939/40 & Middlesex

W.G. Keighley Eton XI
1941/3 Oxford Univ. &
Yorkshire

Hon. L.R. White Eton XI
1943/4 & Middlesex

R.A. Jacques Harrow X1
1947/50

R.G. Marlar Harrow XI
1948/50 Cambridge Univ.
& Sussex

A.C.D. Ingleby-Mackenzie
Eton XI 1949/51
& Hampshire

R.V.C. Robins Eton XI
1950/3 & Middlesex

C.T.M. Pugh
Eton XI 1954/5
& Gloucestershire

J.R.T. Barclay
Eton XI 1968/71
& Sussex

M.K. Fosh Harrow XI
1973/5 Cambridge Univ.
& Essex

A.C.S. Pigott Harrow XI
1974/6 Sussex, Surrey
& England

M.V. Fleming Eton XI
1981/2 Kent & England

A.G.R. Loudon Eton XI
1997/9 Durham Univ.
Kent & Warwickshire

B.R. Thompson
Eton XI 2001/3

M.D. Walters
Harrow XI 2004

S.A.Northeast
Harrow XI 2004/5

The three outstanding cricketers of the future

Peter Blake Eton XI 1943/5 Oxford University 1950/2 and Hants.
A most stylish batsman whose entry into the Church cut short his
cricket career in 1952.

1956 Henry Blofeld batting for Eton, the Harrow
wicketkeeper is A.B. Cable, Harrow XI 1955/8 and
M.J.H. Weedon, Harrow XI 1957/9 and Cambridge
University 1963 is at slip.

Geoffrey Keighley Eton XI 1941/3, Oxford
Univ. 1947/8 and Yorkshire playing for
Yorkshire v. Middlesex at Lord's in 1950.
He and Frank Lowson put on 137 for the first
wicket of which his contribution was 60.

Field Marshall Lord Bramall, Eton
XI 1941/2 and Combined Services,
President of M.C.C. 1988/9. Eton's
most distinguished soldier/cricketer
since the Second World War.

Harrow XI 1956. BACK ROW: *R.F.C. Webster, A.S.R. Winlaw, M.L. Maydon, F.E.R. Butler, J.D.C. Vargas,*
R.F.S. Miles. FRONT ROW: *L.J. Champniss, G.D. Massy, J.M. Parker (Capt.), R.S. Miller, A.B. Cable. In a match*
badly affected by rain Harrow were very unlucky not to win. Robin Butler (now Lord Butler) became cabinet
secretary to three P.Ms and Dale Vargas a much loved senior master at Harrow.

Tony Pigott Harrow XI 1974/6, Sussex. Surrey and England. Harrow's only test player since the war in fine appealing form for Sussex.

BACK ROW: *M.G. Howat, N.F.M. Popplewell, A.R. Dewes, S.J. Gardiner, D.J. Littlewood, A.M. Mubarak,* FRONT ROW: *M.K. Fosh, P.W.G. Parker, A.J. Hignell, M.E. Allbrook, I.A. Greig. Matthew Fosh, Harrow XI 1973/5, Cambridge Univ. 1977/8 and Essex, in the Cambridge Univ. XI of 1978. He went on an England under 19 tour to the West Indies in 1976. Several other well known names are in the picture, Nigel Popplewell Somerset and son of Sir Oliver Popplewell Camb. Univ. 1949/51, Paul Parker of Sussex, Durham and England, Alistair Hignell of Gloucestershire and noted rugby international and Ian Greig, brother of Tony, Sussex and England.*

Rex Neame's hat trick in 1955 for Harrow failed to prevent Eton winning by 38 runs.

Ball presented to the author by M.C.C. on his 12/76 for Harrow v. Eton at Lord's in their win by an innings and 12 runs in 1961.

Ball presented to the author by Oxfordshire on his 8/58 including a hat trick v. Devon in the minor counties championship in 1964, the first for Oxfordshire in the century.

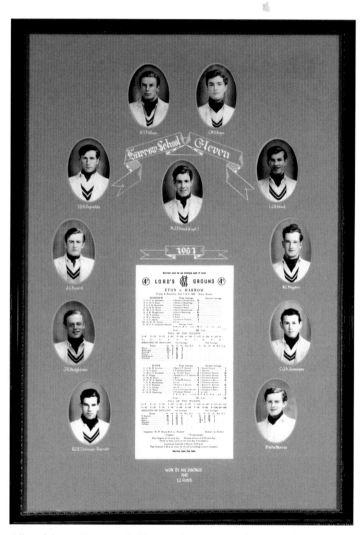

A fine image of the Eton and Harrow match from a private collection of postcards of the 1960s showing the style of the 1920s.

Bill and Ned Metaxa, sons of Alec Metaxa Eton XI 1950, Ned Eton XI 1979/81 and Bill, Eton 12. Fine footballers both, Oxford and Cambridge blues respectively in their distinctive blazers.

Collage of the 1961 Harrow XI which beat Eton by and innings and 12 runs, their first innings win since 1866. The author took 12/76 in the match! Left to right from top: H.T. Pelham, C.M.S. Kaye, I.S.R. Reynolds, M.J.B. Wood (capt.) L.G.R. Wood, J.C. Beard, R.C. Maydon, J.R. Hodgkinson, C.J.A. Jamieson, R.C.S. Titchener-Barrett, D.W.W. Norris.

One of Matthew Fleming's nine victims in the Kent v. Durham match during 1997, the highest match analysis of his career. John Morris, the Derbyshire, Durham and England player is the victim here.

The strong Durham Univ. side of 2001 which just lost the BUSA trophy at Lord's by 7 runs to Loughborough. The side contained three Etonians in Hugo and Alex Loudon and James Bruce. Coached by Graeme Fowler of Lancashire and England it also contained five other players who represented their counties including James Foster, the wicketkeeper of Essex and England.
BACK ROW, LEFT TO RIGHT: *J.S. Foster, T.J. Phillips, J.TY.A. Bruce, A.G.R. Loudon, M. Thorburn, C.G. Van der Gucht, R.S. Ferley, G. Fowler (coach).* FRONT ROW, LEFT TO RIGHT: *R.A. Stead, J.C.R. Rowe, M.J. Banes (captain), H.J.H. Loudon, M.J. Brown.*

Matt Fleming here seen appealing for England in the one day internationals at Sharjah in 1999 where he played with great success as an all rounder.

Matt Fleming showing the fine hitting style for which he was renowned. Here he scores 138 v. Essex at the Canterbury Festival in 1997.

The Oxford University XI of 1997 captained by Mark Wagh of Warwickshire and containing three Etonians Charles Lightfoot (FRONT ROW FAR RIGHT), *James Fulton* (BACK ROW LEFT) *and Peter Morgan* (THIRD FROM RIGHT BACK ROW). *They distinguished themselves by beating Glamorgan, the county champions that year.*

Alex Titchener-Barrett the Harrow opener being dismissed by James Bruce of Eton in 1998's drawn match. He finished a superb display with 6/40 off 16 overs in the innings and has gone on to play for Durham Univ. and Hampshire.

Alex Loudon, Eton XI 1997/9, Durham Univ., Kent and Warwicks. Training with Michael Vaughan, the England Captain, on the recent Test tour of Pakistan in November 2005. A possible future England captain who would be the first Etonian since George Mann in 1948/9 if he makes it. He didn't get a test cap and is currently on the England 'A' tour of the West Indies.

Robin Marlar Harrow XI 1947/9, Cambridge University 1951/3 and Sussex 1951/68. A fine off-spinner but controversial choice as President of M.C.C. in 2005/6.

The three Harrow stars of the future

Sam Northeast, Harrow XI 2004/5, England under 16 squad, fine attacking batsman.

Glenn Querl, Harrow XI 2005 and Zimbabwe under 19s. Superb attacking batsman and fast bowler.

Will Spencer, Harrow XI 2004/5 and Middlesex under 16 squad, leg spinning all rounder.

All three are capable of playing first class cricket and representing their country in due course if they continue to make progress allied with their natural talent.

The Harrow Keeper G.I. Matthey taking a fine catch to dismiss Ed Bruce for 11 in 2005. He didn't let any byes through either. Sadly it appears he doesn't want to continue in the game because he has the talent to be successful at a higher level.

Ben Thompson Eton XI 2001/3 showing his versatility as a cricketer with some useful seambowling in the 2003 match.

Alex Ball, Eton XI 2003/5 showing the elegant style which could make him a force to be reckoned with at Oxford in the coming years.

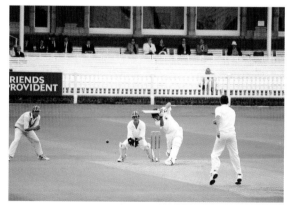

Eddie Nissen Eton XI 2002/4 in fine attacking form during his superb 124 not out in 2004 which did much to win the game for Eton.

Lord's 2005. The end of a superb day's cricket for Harrow, a win by 7 wickets and the two unbeaten batsmen Glenn Querl and Spencer Crawley returning to the pavilion.
(Reproduced courtesy of Xin Pang Walker.)

An Irish George III penny was used for the toss as M.C.C. were unable to purchase an English 1805 coin because of their extreme rarity. This was due to the war with France resulting in our famous victory at Trafalgar in October 1805.

LORD'S
THE HOME OF CRICKET

SATURDAY 18th JUNE, 2005
ONE-DAY MATCH

ETON
v
HARROW

200th ANNIVERSARY
OF THE FIRST MATCH AT LORD'S

GATES OPEN 10.00 am   PLAY BEGINS 11.00 am

ADMISSION   Ground admission price includes Gate and Stand Entry   **£13**

Eton and Harrow billboard for the 200th Anniversary match.

A
DINNER
TO CELEBRATE
THE 200th ANNIVERSARY
OF THE
FIRST ETON v HARROW MATCH
AT
LORD'S

FRIDAY, 17 JUNE 2005
THE NURSERY PAVILION
LORD'S

The menu of the dinner celebrating the 200th Anniversary of the first Eton and Harrow match at Lord's, attended by some 350 participants of both schools.

Eton v. Harrow
Saturday 18th June 2005

200th Anniversary of the first Eton v. Harrow match at Lord's

£5

The souvenir programme celebrating the 200th Anniversary match.

200TH ANNIVERSARY OF FIRST ETON v. HARROW MATCH AT LORD'S

The 2005 M.C.C. members pass depicting the crests of Eton and Harrow in celebration of the 200th anniversary.

THE MATCHES
PLAYED

BETWEEN 1805 & 2005

MATCH REPORTS

2nd Innings   Harrow

Ld Ipswich	02221113221	b. Hewson	21
Farrer	111	c. Bradley	3
Lloyd	0	b. Carter	0
Boulton	0	b. Heaton	0
Brockman	10	b. Heaton	10
Shakespear	5	run out	5
Dyne	6	st. Heaton	6
Erskine	0	b. Heaton	0
Ld Byron	2	b. Carter	2
Stanley	7	c. Canning	7
Asheton	0	not out	0
		Byes	3
			65

Byes - 111

The Harrow were beat in one Innings by 12
Notches easy —

Hurra

Exeunt Omnes

A page from the Eton Upper Club scorebook, 1805. This clearly had no significance for a later owner of the book who used it to record his tenants tithe accounts! Harrow's team included the poet Lord Byron, who had a runner because of his lameness, and Lord Ipswich, who succeeded as 5th Duke of Grafton in 1844. Among the Eton players was Stratford Canning, from 1852 Viscount Stratford de Redcliffe, Ambassador to Constantinople 1841-1858. The book was taken by another of the players, William Carter, (whose son Richard was in the XI of 1859) and was purchased by the College in 1952 at Sotheby's.

THE MATCH REPORTS

The first match played at Lord's Ground, Dorset Fields.

1805 August 2   *Eton won by an innings and 2 runs*

Harrow	55	
	65	
Eton	122	(G. Camplin. 42)

The famous first match in which Lord Byron played and recorded in the Eton Upper Club record book of 1805. He was sportingly allowed a runner by the Etonians as he had a club foot but this did not improve his rather poor performance. The Harrow Captain J.A. Lloyd who was so scathing in his comments on Byron fared no better and was bowled twice for nought.

1818 July 29, 30   *Harrow won by 13 runs*

Harrow	53	
	114	
Eton	74	
	80	(W. Pitt 37)

This match was arranged by the Harrow captain Charles Oxenden at the end of term, he had previously been at Eton and the light blues were not representative having only three of their regular team. One of them, William Pitt, was by far the most successful with 37 runs in the second innings and eight wickets in the match, but Harrow just sneaked home.

1822 August 1, 2   *Harrow won by 87 runs*

Harrow	99	(J.C. Clarke 32)
	105	
Eton	65	
	52	(Barnard 21 C. Wordsworth 5 wickets)

Charles Wordsworth, the nephew of the poet, took eight wickets in the match and played in the first of his four appearances at Lord's for Harrow, the last two as captain. An interesting detail of these early matches was that wickets were not credited to the bowler but quite often to the catcher or the stumper and according to these scores even l.b.ws were not accredited to the bowler!

1823 July 31   *Eton won by an innings and 33 runs*

Harrow	24	
	91	
Eton	148	(G.W. Barnard 42)

Harrow made the lowest score in the history of the match, 24, with a highest score of eight and five batsmen scoring ducks in the first innings with no extras, unusual for these times. Eton replied with 148, G.W. Barnard scoring 42 and T. Hand 33, and then bowled Harrow out again for 91 to win by an innings and 33 runs, all in one day! The pitches of those days, particularly Lord's, were rough and uncovered and under these conditions it was a considerable feat to bat for any length of time (scorecard in colour section).

1818

ETON *v.* HARROW, at Lord's, 29, 30 July

Harrow won by 13 runs

1st Innings	HARROW		2nd Innings	
J. W. Methold, run out	. . 2	not out	. .	6
J. S. Forbes, b Secker	. . 0	b Secker	.	0
G. T. Vigne, b Pitt	. . 2	c Pitt	. .	30
G. Wyndham, b Secker	. . 7	c Townsend	.	1
C. T. Robinson, b Pitt	. . 6	b Pitt	. .	3
C. Oxenden,* st Maclean	. . 0	b Pitt	. .	31
J. P. Byde, st Maclean	. . 20	c Maclean	. .	2
A. J. Lewis, hit wicket	. . 16	run out	. .	8
S. G. Gunning, b Pitt	. . 0	run out	. .	14
H. B. Cooke, b Pitt	. . 0	c Howard	.	2
H. Davidson, not out	. . 0	b Pitt	. .	13
		Byes	. .	4
	—			—
	53			114

1st Innings	ETON		2nd Innings	
F. Cuthbert, c Oxenden	. . 10	c Davidson	. .	1
— Howard, c Davidson	. 6	c Davidson	.	0
D. Maclean, st Vigne	. . 13	c Oxenden	. .	11
W. Pitt, b Wyndham	. . 7	c Davidson	. .	37
R. E. A. Townsend, st Vigne	. 4	not out	. .	0
I. O. Secker, c Oxenden	. . 10	b Robinson	. .	3
G. A. Bushby, b Oxenden	. 8	b Robinson	. .	7
W. H. Tucker, b Wyndham	. 0	c Forbes	. .	5
R. J. Monypenny, st Vigne	. 5	b Robinson	. .	4
H. M. Wagner, not out	. . 10	c Forbes	. .	12
G. Wear, c Oxenden	. . 1	c Oxenden	. .	0
	—			—
	74			80

Only three of the regular Eton XI being present (Maclean, Pitt and Secker), eight substitutes played in above match.

1822

ETON *v.* HARROW, at Lord's, 1, 2 August

Harrow won by 87 runs

1st Innings	HARROW		2nd Innings	
R. Martin, b Battye	. . 0	b Young	. .	0
C. Perry, b Battye	. . 1	b Chapman	. .	8
G. Prendergast,* c Barnard	. 7	b Battye	. .	21
F. Calvert, b Chapman	. 1	run out	. .	16
Chas. Wordsworth, c Jenner	. 15	lbw	. .	6
J. Davidson, st Barnard	. 6	b Young	. .	17
J. C. Clarke, run out	. . 32	run out	. .	2
J. A. Gardner, b Chapman	. 9	c Battye	. .	17
J. Neeld, c Jenner	. . 11	run out	. .	0
O. J. A. Fuller, run out	. 8	not out	. .	5
E. H. Handley, not out	. 2	b Battye	. .	2
Byes	. . . 7	Byes	.	11
	—			—
	99			105

1st Innings	ETON		2nd Innings	
H. Jenner, b Wordsworth	. 2	b Wordsworth	. .	0
G. W. Battye, b Davidson	. 0	c Wordsworth	. .	2
C. Chapman, b Wordsworth	. 21	b Davidson	. .	3
G. W. Barnard,* c Clarke	. 7	b Calvert	. .	21
W. Gurdon, b Wordsworth	. 2	c Neeld	. .	4
J. Dolphin, b Davidson	. 0	b Wordsworth	. .	0
J. Antrobus, b Clarke	. 5	not out	. .	1
D. D. Sampson, b Clarke	. 20	b Davidson	. .	0
R. W. Shaw, c Calvert	. 6	c Perry	.	14
H. Young, not out	. . 0	b Wordsworth	. .	0
T. Hand, st Davidson	. 0	c Wordsworth	. .	1
Byes	. . . 2	Byes		6
	—			—
	65			52

G.T.LOWTH'S MATCH

1824 July 30 31   *Eton won by 9 wickets*

Harrow	103	(G.T. Lowth 7 wickets)
	71	(G.T. Lowth 7 wickets)
Eton	123	(C. Chapman 41, R.C. Pollard 37)
	52-1	(R.C. Pollard 29 not out)

G.T. Lowth's 14 wickets in the match was the highest in the series so far and was only beaten by E.W. Blore's 15 wickets in 1847. Little was heard of him afterwards and he spent his career in the Diplomatic Service. Eton were indebted to R.C.Pollard who scored a large percentage of their runs in both innings but died less than two years later in March 1826.

1825 July 29, 30   *Eton won by 7 wickets*

Harrow	90	(E.H. Pickering 6 wickets)
	91	
Eton	76	(J. Frere 37)
	106-3	(H. Snow 41 not out)

Henry Manning, later Cardinal Manning, was presented with a bat by Charles Wordsworth, subsequently Bishop of St. Andrew's. Manning sent the following verse to Wordsworth.

> *That bat that you were kind enough to send,*
> *Seems (for as yet I have not tried it) good:*
> *And if there's anything on earth can mend*
> *My wretched play, it is that piece of wood*

His subsequent career in the Church was far more successful. He became Archbishop of Westminster in 1865 and a Cardinal in 1875.

1827 August 3, 4   *Eton won by 6 wickets*

Harrow	144	(Hon. E.H. Grimston 49, Lord Grimston 49)
	64	(Lord Grimston 38, C.H.Jenner 5 wickets)
Eton	166	(H. Dupuis 56)
	50-4	

In a six ball over Lord Grimston scored three fives and E.H. Grimston three threes off A. Broadhead, the Eton bowler. Eton were four short of victory when stumps were drawn owing to a mistake by the scorers. Harrow appealed to the M.C.C. committee but Eton were awarded the game.

1828 July 31   *Eton won by 6 wickets*

Harrow	68	
	53	
Eton	78	(Hon. E.H. Grimston 5 wickets)
	45-4	

A match notable only for the very low scores on both sides and which was finished in one day. Hon. E.H. Grimston who had done well the previous year took seven wickets in the match and top scored in Harrow's first innings of 68 with a modest 17. The second son of the 1st Earl of Verulam, he gained an Oxford blue in 1836, scoring 33 in the first innings of Oxford's win by 121 runs in the varsity match. C.J. Harenc, the Harrow captain of 1828, top scored in Harrow's second innings with 17 out of 53. He later played for the Kent XI and was considered the best gentleman bowler of his day.

1832 August 3, 4   *Eton won by an innings and 156 runs*

Harrow	49	(J.W. Dolignon 5 wickets)
	44	
Eton	249	(J.W. Dolignon 52)

Two of the founder members of I.Zingari, the Hon. F.G.B. Ponsonby and R.J.P. Broughton, were on the Harrow side. Neither did very well, Ponsonby failing to score in either innings and Broughton only managing three in the first innings. J.W. Dolignon took eight wickets for Eton in the match as well as scoring 52 runs in Eton's one innings.

1833 August 2, 3   *Harrow won by 8 wickets*

Eton	86	
	57	(C. Horrocks 33)
Harrow	118	(C. Horrocks 5 wickets)
	27-2	

The Hon F.G.B. Ponsonby, later the Earl of Bessborough, again failed to score in Harrow's first innings and extras were the highest total in this innings, 25. An easy win for Harrow would have been overwhelming but for Horrock's 50 runs and 5 wickets in the match for Eton.

R.J.P. BROUGHTON'S MATCH

1834 July 31, August 2   *Harrow won by 13 runs*

Harrow	69	(J.H. Kirwan 5 wickets)
	97	(J.H. Kirwan 5 wickets)
Eton	103	(R.J.P. Broughton 6 wickets)
	50	(R.J.P. Broughton 7 wickets)

During the intervening day, August 1st, Eton played Winchester and won by 13 runs whereas Harrow had lost a very low scoring match on July 30th by 1 wicket. This was the first year a match was played between the Old Etonians and Old Harrovians. Harrow just got home thanks to Broughton's fine bowling in the Eton second innings and finished with 13 wickets in the match.

J.H. KIRWAN''S MATCH

1835 July 30, 31   *Eton won by 165 runs*

Eton	111	
	149	(G. Wagner 47)
Harrow	48	(J.H. Kirwan 7 wickets)
	47	(J.H. Kirwan 6 wickets)

J.H. Kirwan created a unique record in this match when all his 13 wickets were clean bowled to add to his 14 wickets v. Winchester, 13 bowled in an Eton win by 5 wickets. He represented Cambridge from 1836/42 but only gained a blue in 1839 which given his great success that year was surprising.

1836 July 28, 29   *Harrow won by 9 wickets*

Eton	49	(C.A. Denison 5 wickets, Hon. T. Edwardes 5 wickets)
	68	
Harrow	97	(W Massey 32, J. Walter 6 wickets)
	21-1	

In a relatively low scoring match the bowlers on both sides predominated. The Hon. T. Edwardes, son of 2nd Baron Kensington and landowner of much of Kensington at that time, took 5 wickets in Eton's first innings and J. Walter, grandson of the founder of *The Times*, took 6 wickets in Harrow's first innings. In the Eton v. Winchester match at. Lord's that followed, he took 14 wickets and Eton won by 2 wickets. Harrow's easy 9 wicket win showed how unpredictable cricket was in those days as they had lost to Winchester two days earlier by an innings and eight runs in one day.

1837 August 3, 4   *Eton won by 8 wickets*

Harrow	89	
	62	(W.P. Pickering 7 wickets)
Eton	104	(H.G.G. Duff 8 wickets)
	48-2	

All H.G.G. Duff's wickets in Eton's first innings were clean bowled. W.P. Pickering who captained the two victorious Eton XI's of 1837/8 was known as 'Bull' Pickering and reputed to be the greatest cover point of the day who could throw in with either hand. He gained Cambridge blues in 1840 and 1842 and appeared occasionally for Surrey over a period of four years being one of the original members of the club.

1838 August 3, 4 *Eton won by an innings and 30 runs*

Eton	157	(H.G.G. Duff 5 wickets)
Harrow	56	(W De St. Croix 6 wickets)
	71	(W. De St. Croix 5 wickets)

G.D.W. Ommanney, who was not a member of the Harrow XI, was allowed to bat in Harrow's first innings for W.B. Treveleyan who was absent injured. W. De. St Croix, who took 11 wickets for Eton in the match, played for Cambridge from 1839/42, taking 24 wickets from 1840/2 in three Cambridge wins v. Oxford. Cambridge also won in 1839 on his first appearance by a massive innings and 125 runs.

1839 August 1, 2 *Eton won by 8 wickets*

Harrow	59	(W.B. Gwyn 6 wickets)
	65	(WB. Gwyn 5 wickets)
Eton	104	
	22-2	

G.J. Boudier, Eton XI 1836/9 and captain in 1839 top scored with 35, the next highest score being 16. He was a fine striker of the ball with the bat over the shoulder and excelling at the cut shot.

1840 July 30, 31 *Eton won by 31 runs*

Eton	122	
	86	(Lord Y.H.A. Loftus 7 wickets)
Harrow	58	
	119	(WB. Gwyn 5 wickets)

W.J. Farrer, a member of the prestigious family firm of solicitors Farrer and Co. top scored for Eton with 27 in their first innings total of 122. Lord Henry Loftus, son of 2nd Marquess of Ely, took 7 wickets in Eton's second innings and played in the Oxford XI of 1841, but it was not enough to save Harrow from defeat. John Nicholson, the brother of William Nicholson and saviour of M.C.C., top scored for Harrow in their second innings with 25 and went on to play in the Oxford Xl of 1845.

J.R.L.E. BAYLEY'S MATCH

1841 July 30, 31, Aug 2 *Eton won by an innings and 175 runs*

Eton	308	(J.R.L.E. Bayley 152)
Harrow	98	(G.E. Yonge 5 wickets)
	35	(G.E. Yonge 6 wickets)

This was the largest winning margin in the history of the match and J.R.L.E. Bayley's score of 152 was the highest score in the match until 1904 when D.C. Boles hit 183 for Eton, still the highest score to this day. In a chanceless innings he hit 4 fives, 11 fours, 14 threes and only 8 singles. G.E. Yonge took 11 wickets for Eton in the match and W. Marcon 8 wickets. This was also the first match played over three days.

1842 July 29, 30 *Harrow won by 65 runs*

Harrow	141	(WA. Commerell 33, extras 53, byes 38, wides 15)
	121	(W.A. Commerell 37, W.Nicholson 35)
Eton	79	
	118	(W. Marcon 55 not out, the Hon. H.W.E. Agar 6 wickets)

Extras were easily the highest component of Harrow's first innings total and in the second innings 32 out of 121 runs were extras – a record 85 for the two innings which cost Eton the match. W. Marcon, primarily a fearsome fast bowler, easily top scored in Eton's second innings with 55 not out as well as taking 6 wickets in the match.

1843 August 5, 7 *Harrow won by 20 runs*

Harrow	99	(C. Randolph 5 wickets)
	52	(G.E. Yonge 5 wickets)
Eton	36	(A.H. Farmer 7 wickets)
	95	(A.H. Farmer 4 wickets)

In the second closest match of the series so far, Eton were bowled out twice by A.H. Farmer who had previously been at Eton. G.E. Yonge, the Eton captain of 1843, took 5 wickets in Harrow's second innings but was unable to prevent Harrow winning by 20 runs.

1844 August 2, 3   *Eton won by an innings and 69 runs*

Harrow	60	(Hon. L. Neville 6 wickets)
Eton	91	
	920	(S.T. Abbot 59, J.C. Patterson 50)

L.H. Bayley, captain of the Eton XI in 1844 and brother of Emilius Bayley, captain in 1841 and scorer of 152, led his side to another convincing victory. The bowling of Hon. L. Neville and E. Macniven for Eton, with 8 wickets and 7 wickets respectively, was decisive. Macniven was unusual in that he gained blues for both cricket and rowing at Cambridge.

E.W. BLORE'S MATCH

1845 August 1, 2   *Eton won by an innings and 174 runs*

Eton	261	(E. Macniven 49. M. Jones 6 wickets)
Harrow	32	(E.W. Blore 7 wickets)
	55	(E.W. Blore 7 wickets)

J.J. Hornby, who opened the Eton batting, subsequently became Head Master of Eton from 1868/84 and Provost of the College in 1884. He also rowed for Oxford in 1849 and 1851. E.W. Blore achieved the second highest total of wickets before proper analyses were recorded in 1854 which he was subsequently to beat in 1847 with 15 wickets. He went on to play for Cambridge from 1848/ 51, captaining the side in 1851.

H.M. AITKEN'S MATCH

1846 July 30, 31, August 1   *Eton won by an innings and 135 runs*

Eton	279	(F.J. Coleridge 69, W.S. Deacon 51)
Harrow	62	(H.M. Aitken 5 wickets)
	82	(H.M. Aitken 7 wickets)

The Eton captain of 1846, F.J. Coleridge, top scored with 69 in Eton's total of 279. He and his brother C.E., who played in the same match, both appeared for Oxford in 1850, C.E scoring 43 in Oxford's win by 127 runs and taking 8 wickets in the match. H.M. Aitken, who took 12 wickets for Eton with his fast round-arm deliveries in this match, achieved 32 in his four matches v. Harrow from 1846/9.

E.W. BLORE'S MATCH

1847 July 31, August 2   *Eton won by 9 wickets*

Harrow	27	(E.W. Blore 7 wickets)
	103	(E.W. Blore 8 wickets)
Eton	119	(M. Jones 5 wickets)
	12-1	

Eight Harrovians failed to score in the first innings, the most ever recorded in one innings of this match. E.W. Blore's 15 wickets in the match was the highest ever recorded in Eton and Harrow matches before proper analyses were recorded in 1854. Harrow's first innings total of 27 was also the second lowest total on record and included ten extras.

T.D. PLATT'S MATCH

1848 Aug 4, 5, 7   *Harrow won by 41 runs*

Harrow	100	(H.M. Aitken 7 wickets)
	66	(T.D. Platt 8 wickets)
Eton	68	(T.D. Platt 5 wickets)
	57	

H.M. Aitken gained an Oxford blue in 1853 and T.D. Platt, who took 13 wickets in the match, was the first player on either side to play five years v. Eton at Lord's, subsequently equalled by three other Harrovian cricketers but none by Eton. His record apart from 1848 was rather modest and he only succeeded in taking one wicket in the previous four encounters, although he was Harrow captain for two years and also took 11 wickets v. Winchester, a match which Harrow won by 18 runs at Lord's in a three day match

---

R. HANKEY'S MATCH

1849 August 3, 4   *Harrow won by 77 runs*

Harrow	157	(C. Thackeray 5 wickets)
	111	
Eton	112	(R. Hankey 7 wickets)
	79	(R. Hankey 7 wickets)

R Hankey, who took 14 wickets in this match, the record for Harrow in the series, gained Oxford blues in 1853 and 1855, represented the Gentlemen v. the Players and was regarded as one of the best amateur bats of his day when his bowling faded. H. Vernon, the Harrow captain, equalled T.D. Platt's record of playing in five Eton v. Harrow matches at Lord's. After gaining blues at Cambridge from 1850/52 and playing with only modest success he died very young at the age of 26.

I850 August 2, 3   *Eton won by 7 wickets*

Harrow	100	
	108	(C. Thackeray 5 wickets)
Eton	105	(G.F. Ashton 7 wickets)
	104-3	

After Hankey's success the previous year, he was unable to repeat his feats as captain and Eton won comfortably by 7 wickets mainly due to C. Thackeray's 8 wickets and 24 and 37 in the match. This was the first year of a Crawley appearing for Harrow, G.B., who top scored with 23 in the first innings but made a duck in the second.

I85I August 1, 2   *Harrow won by 8 wickets*

Eton	126	(A.M. Curteis 5 wickets)
	92	(Hon. D. Campbell 6 wickets)
Harrow	184	(Hon. E. Chandos-Leigh 42, T.O. Reay 5 wickets)
	35-2	

H.M. Butler, who scored 41 in the Harrow first innings, subsequently became Head Master of Harrow and Master of Trinity College, Cambridge. This was the first of a record-winning sequence of eight Harrow victories in a row, only equalled by Eton's run from 1910/21 (there were no regular contests during the Great War).

S. AUSTEN-LEIGH'S MATCH

I852 July 30, 31, August 1   *Harrow won by 71 runs*

Harrow	215	(S. Austen-Leigh 85 not out, Hon.D. Campbell 50, H.N. Hoare 5 wickets)
	108	(Hon D. Campbell 36 not out)
Eton	142	
	110	(T.O. Reay 43)

Spencer Austen-Leigh's fine free-hitting 85 not out in Harrow's first innings and 5 wickets in the match were the decisive factors in Harrow's win by 71 runs. The Hon. Dudley Campbell, son of the 1st Baron Campbell, also performed very well, scoring 50 and 36 not out after his 9 wickets in 1851. Harrow's unique blue and white striped caps were worn for the first time.

I853 July 29, 30   *Harrow won by 3 wickets*

Eton	58	
	79	(Hon. R. Stewart 4 wickets)
Harrow	55	
	85-7	

This was the start of K.E. Digby's unique three-year reign as Harrow captain, the only player in the history of the match to have captained three winning sides and played in four winning elevens. V. E. Walker also made his debut for Harrow, one of seven remarkable cricketing brothers from Southgate, four of whom were at Harrow and played in the eleven. He and his brother, I.D. Walker, founded Middlesex County Cricket Club in 1864. He bagged a pair in this match but made up for it by taking 4 wickets.

I854 Aug 5, 7, 8   *Harrow won by 98 runs*

Harrow	130	(A.H.A. Morton 5/33)
	128	(K.E. Digby 53)
Eton	71	
	89	

There was an unusual occurence when two brothers, Lord Garlies and Hon. Randolph Stewart, Sons of 9th Earl of Galloway opened the batting for Harrow in 1853 and 1854 with little success. Randolph Stewart was more successful with the ball however and took 7 wickets in 1853 and 6/46 in 1854, a vital component of Harrow's two wins in these years. They went on to succeed as 10th and 11th Earls of Galloway respectively. This was the first year that proper bowling analyses were recorded. V. E. Walker took 7/46 in the match and the captain, K.E. Digby, easily top-scored in the match with 53, the next highest score in the Harrow second innings being 16.

1855 August 3, 4 *Harrow won by an innings and 66 runs*

Eton	35	(G.L. Lang 7/17)
	90	(H. Arkwright 6/44)
Harrow	191	

This was Eton's lowest score in the history of the match and the last year of K.E. Digby's great winning run as Harrow captain. Eton were completely overwhelmed by the pace of G.L. Lang, brother of R., in the first innings with 7/17 off 11 overs and H. Arkwright's slow round-arm high-pitched deliveries with 6/44 off 24.4 overs in the second.

The ball presented to Kenelm Digby in recognition of his three years as Harrow captain from 1853/5 when he led them to victory against Eton and Winchester in all six matches, a unique performance unlikely ever to be repeated.

1857 July 29, 30 *Harrow won by 10 wickets*

Eton

(under 21)	70	(H. Linton 6/37)
	59	(H. Linton 5/29, H. Arkwright 5/27)

Harrow

(under 20)	118	(J. Carpenter 41)
	12-0	

The ages of the participants make it questionable whether this match should be counted but Harrovians always dispute the first match in 1805 so the results of both these matches have been included. F.H. Norman, the Eton captain of 1857, had little success in his matches v. Harrow and Winchester between 1854 and 1857 but was much more successful in his three years for Cambridge between 1858 and 1860, the last as captain, and for Kent between 1858/64.

1857
ETON v. HARROW, at Lord's, 29, 30 July
Harrow won by 10 wickets

1st Innings	ETON		2nd Innings	
T. E. Bagge, c and b Arkwright.	0		b Arkwright	3
E. G. Hornby, b Linton	5		b Arkwright	1
E. C. Austen-Leigh, b Linton	17		c and b Linton	4
F. H. Norman,* c Carpenter, b Arkwright	23		b Linton	11
B. Field, b Arkwright	0		c Arkwright, b Linton	8
E. B. Fane, c Church, b Linton	8		c Kington, b Arkwright	2
A. H. Thesiger, run out	3		c Church, b Arkwright	10
G. B. Davy, b Linton	4		b Linton	2
R. Rawlinson, b Linton	1		c Moncreiff, b Linton	13
R. D. Cleasby, c and b Linton	0		not out,	2
W. K. Mott, not out	1		hit wkt, b Arkwright	0
Byes 4, lb 4	8		Byes 1, lb 1, w 1	3
	70			59

1st Innings	HARROW		2nd Innings	
C. Barclay, hit wkt, b Thesiger	2		not out	9
C. I. Strong, b Mott	0		not out	1
A. E. Northey, c Rawlinson, b Mott	4			
J. Carpenter, b Field	41			
R. W. Monro, c Mott, b Thesiger	1			
W. M. N. Kington, c Davy, b Mott	1			
H. Linton, b Field	14			
H. Arkwright,* b Mott	12			
W. S. Church, c and b Thesiger	4			
C. Weguelin, b Thesiger	11			
H. J. Moncreiff, not out	6			
Byes 4, lb 3, w 14, nb 1	22		Wides 2	2
	118			12

This match does not count, owing to boys who had left taking part in it.

HARROW BOWLING	B.	R.	W.	B.	R.	W.		ETON BOWLING	B.	R.	W.	B.	R.	W.
Arkwright	92	25	3	68	27	5	Thesiger		80	31	4	8	9	0
Linton	88	37	6	68	29	5	Mott		60	44	4	5	1	0
							Field		36	5	2			
							Bagge		20	8	0			
							Hornby		20	8	0			

1858
ETON *v.* HARROW, at Lord's, 9, 10 July
Harrow won by innings and 7 runs

1st Innings	ETON		2nd Innings	
A. Austen-Leigh, b Plowden	.	0	b Plowden	2
B. M. Davies, b Hodgson	.	8	b Hodgson	7
Hon. C. G. Lyttelton, b Hodgson	.	0	b Plowden	6
F. N. Langham, c Hoare, b Plowden	.	10	b Plowden	3
J. B. Dyne,* b Hodgson	.	2	c Upcher, b Plowden	8
C. L. Sutherland, b Plowden	.	8	b Hodgson	3
R. A. H. Mitchell, b Hodgson	.	0	b Lang	24
W. H. Stone, b Hodgson	.	2	b Lang	4
J. H. Gibbs, b Hodgson	.	0	c Lang, b Plowden	9
W. M. Hoare, not out	.	4	not out	10
G. F. Dawson, b Hodgson	.	4	c Lang, b Plowden	6
Byes 4, lb 1, w 1	.	6	Byes 5, w 9, nb 1	15
		44		97

HARROW

E. W. Humphreys, b Dyne	.	4
H. M. Upcher, b Lyttelton	.	21
H. M. Plowden, b Stone	.	1
E. C. Prichard, b Stone	.	5
W. C. Clayton, b Stone	.	34
R. Clayton, b Lyttelton	.	0
A. W. T. Daniel, c Davies, b Stone	.	16
G. H. Hodgson, b Lyttelton	.	2
R. Lang,* st Austen-Leigh, b Mitchell	.	26
J. D. Burnett, not out	.	8
S. Hoare, b Lyttelton	.	4
Byes 6, lb 7, w 14	.	27
		148

HARROW BOWLING					ETON BOWLING			
	B.	R.	W.	B. R. W.		B.	R.	W.
Plowden	48	29	3	103 49 6	Dyne	115	32	1
Hodgson	49	9	7	76 16 2	Stone	169	52	4
Lang				50 14 2	Mitchell	20	12	1
Prichard				12 3 0	Lyttelton	75	25	4

The ball with which G.H. Hodgson took 7/9 off 49 deliveries, all bowled in Eton's first innings of 44 and set Harrow up for victory by an innings and 7 runs.

G.H. HODGSON'S MATCH

1858 July 9, 10   *Harrow won by an innings and 7 runs*

Eton	44	(G.H. Hodgson 7/9)
	97	(H.M. Plowden 6/49)
Harrow	148	

G.H. Hodgson achieved one of the finest analyses in the history of the match with 7 wickets for 9 runs off 49 deliveries on a wet surface in Eton's first innings, all clean bowled in Eton's fourth lowest score in this match. W.C. Clayton, the Harrow wicket-keeper stood up very well to the two fast bowlers Bob Lang and Hodgson conceding very few byes and top scoring with 34 in the Harrow innings of 148.

1859 July 8, 9   *Harrow won by an innings and 48 run*

Harrow	242	(E.W. Humphreys 63)
Eton	91	(R. Lang 5/33)
	103	

This was the last of Harrow's winning sequence of eight wins in a row and equalled only by Eton's run from 1910/21. The wicket was hard this year and Bob Lang's expresses came into their own and he finished with 9/66 in the match. He was fortunate in having a very good long stop in Sam Hoare who stopped a large number of extras being added to the total.

Harrow XI 1859 which won by an innings and 48 runs.
LEFT TO RIGHT BACK ROW: *R.D. Walker, R.Lang (Capt), A.W.T. Daniel, Hon. E. Stanhope, J.D. Burnett, E.W. Humphreys, Hon. H Strutt.*
FRONT ROW: *R.D. Elphinstone, G.N. Marten, H.M. Rogers, S. Hoare.*

1859

ETON *v.* HARROW, at Lord's, 8, 9 July

Harrow won by innings and 48 runs

HARROW

Hon. E. Stanhope, b Lyttelton .	17
R. D. Walker, c Hornby, b Lyttelton . . .	28
R. D. Elphinstone, b Mitchell .	43
E. W. Humphreys, c and b Mitchell	63
A. W. T. Daniel, b Mitchell .	4
R. Lang,* b Lyttelton . .	1
G. N. Marten, b Mitchell . .	6
Hon. H. Strutt, c Hornby, b Lyttelton . . .	33
H. M. Rogers, c Dyne, b Hornby	18
J. D. Burnett, run out . .	10
S. Hoare, not out . . .	6
Byes 3, lb 8, w 2 . .	13
	242

1st Innings	ETON		*2nd Innings*	
A. Austen-Leigh, b Lang . .	6	run out	22
F. N. Langham, c Lang, b Walker	9	b Lang . . .	5
J. B. Dyne,* b Lang . . .	0	c Humphreys, b Rogers	16
R. A. H. Mitchell, st Strutt, b Walker	10	st Strutt, b Walker .	0
Hon. C. G. Lyttelton, b Lang .	9	b Lang . . .	0
R. H. Carter, c Lang, b Walker .	7	c Lang, b Rogers .	1
M. Lubbock, c Strutt, b Walker .	12	run out . . .	22
W. M. Hoare, b Lang . .	6	b Lang . . .	3
P. Norman, b Lang . . .	5	not out . . .	5
W. M. Young, not out . .	5	b Walker . . .	0
C. R. Hornby, run out . .	9	b Lang . . .	8
Byes 11, lb 1, w 1 . .	13	Byes 15, lb 3, w 3 .	21
	91		103

ETON BOWLING

	B.	R.	W.
Lyttelton	167	72	4
Mitchell	124	70	4
Hornby	96	62	1
Dyne	12	25	0

HARROW BOWLING

	B.	R.	W.	B.	R.	W.
Lang	104	33	5	92	33	4
Walker	100	45	4	60	28	2
Rogers				30	21	2

Harrow XI 1860, the first drawn match.
LEFT TO RIGHT: *R.D. Walker, R.H.L. Burton, A.J. McNeile, W.F. Maitland, H.R.T. Alexander, A.W.T. Daniel, R.D. Elphinstone, Lord Acheson, I.D. Walker, G. Upton, G.H. Fillingham.*

1860 July 13, 14   *Match Drawn*

Harrow	83	(Hon C.G. Lyttelton 5/31)
	274	(A.W.T. Daniel 112 not out, R.D. Elphinstone 66)
Eton	98	(R.A.H. Mitchell 70 R.D. Walker 5/37)
	221-8	(D. Pocklington 41 not out)

This was the first drawn match in the series and A.W.T. Daniel scored Harrow's first century in this match with a magnificent 112 not out in the second innings. I.D. Walker, the founder of Middlesex & Harrow Wanderers, played the first of his four matches for Harrow scoring 20 not out and R.A.H. Mitchell, the father of Eton cricket and in his third year in the Eton eleven, played a superb knock of 70 in Eton's first innings 98 on a difficult wicket and was summoned to play for the Gentlemen v. the Players with a year to go at Eton, the youngest player ever to appear for the Gentlemen.

1861 July 12, 13   *Match Drawn*

Eton	135	(I.D. Walker 4/27)
	229	(H.W. Hoare 51, I.D. Walker 5/78)
Harrow	164	(S. Smith 5/44)
	53-2	

This was a disappointing match for Eton as they undoubtedly had the stronger and more experienced side with Mitchell as captain and several other excellent schoolboy bats, including Hon. T. de Grey, A. Lubbock, G. H. Tuck and A. S. Cleasby.

Eton were taken aback to be bowled out for 135 in their first innings by the Harrow captain H.R.T. Alexander, 4/43 and I.D. Walker, in his second year in the XI, 4/27. Harrow's first innings lead of 20 was largely due to a last wicket stand of 63 by C.F. Reid and E.W. Burnett although this was not without controversy as Reid was immediately out, caught behind by G.H. Tuck, the Eton wicket-keeper but given not out by the umpire. This was later admitted by Reid in 1880 so even in those days it was not always customary to walk. It changed the whole nature of the game and in retrospect probably saved Harrow from defeat. A better showing by Eton in the second innings left Harrow to score 201 to win with time of academic importance. The Lord's wicket was very rough then and Harrow had no realistic chance of getting the runs but Eton could well have bowled them out. It rained hard on Saturday afternoon when Harrow were 53/2 and soon after it was agreed to draw the match the weather cleared. Eton regretted their haste since they could still have had time to bowl Harrow out. It was also unfortunate that they had not included the fast bowler A.S. Teape in their side as he proved how deadly he was the following year and for Oxford thereafter.

1862 July 11, 12   *Eton won by 54 runs*

Eton	97	(E.W. Burnett 4/27)
	155	(E.W. Burnett 4/33)
Harrow	56	(A.S. Teape 5/28)
	142	(W.F. Maitland 73, A.S. Teape 4/50)

Eton won by virtue of the fact that they had two very good pace bowlers in A.S. Teape and J.St.J. Frederick, who was very fast and dangerous in short spells. Harrow had some good players in I.D. Walker, C.F. Buller and W.F. Maitland, who easily made the highest score of the match considered by the pundits at the time as one of the best knocks played in this match against good bowlers on a most difficult wicket. Frederick, the Eton opening bowler took 3 wickets for 6 runs in the first innings and 6 wickets for 28 runs in the match and also scored a crucial 33 in Eton's second innings of 155, second highest score after G.H.Tuck's 43 not out. This was Eton's first win since 1850. Teape also bowled superbly throughout for his analysis of 9/78 in the match.

1863 July 10, 11   *Match drawn*

Eton	184	(E.W. Tritton 91)
	285	(A. Lubbock 80, E.W. Tritton 58, C.F. Buller 6/57)
Harrow	268	(C.L. Hornby 68, Extras 56)

By most standards these were two very high quality sides and the Eton eleven contained four future blues in Tritton, Pelham, G.W.S. Lyttelton and Frederick, whilst Harrow were captained by the famous I.D. Walker and contained fine players in M.H. Stow, who captained Cambridge in 1869, C.F. Buller, W.F. Maitland and W.E. Grimston. Tritton's 91 for Eton in their first innings was a classical one and the Harrow first innings contained 56 extras, the highest number in a Harrow innings ever, of which 24 were no balls.

1863 Harrow XI which had slightly the better of a drawn fixture. LEFT TO RIGHT BACK ROW: *W. Fuller Maitland, W.E. Grimston, E.W. Burnett, H.G. Phipps, I.D. Walker, W.O. Hewlett, C.F. Buller, W.E. Mirehouse.* SEATED LEFT TO RIGHT: *C.L. Hornby, M.H. Stow, W. Richardson.*

The victorious Eton XI of 1862 which won by 54 runs. LEFT TO RIGHT BACK ROW: *G.H. Tuck, A. Lubbock, S.F. Cleasby (Capt) W.S. Prideaux.* SEATED: *Hon. H.B. Sutherland, L. Garnett, Hon. N.G. Lyttelton, E.W. Tritton, L.W. Dent, A.S. Teape.* ON GROUND: *J.St.J. Frederick.*

Eton XI 1863. LEFT TO RIGHT BACK ROW: *E.W. Tritton, Hon G.W. Lyttelton, C.A. Teape, A. Pepys.* SEATED LEFT TO RIGHT: *E.P. Bovill, W.S. Prideaux, A. Lubbock (Capt.), J.St.J. Frederick. Hon N.G. Lyttelton, H.B. Sutherland and Hon F.G. Pelham.*

1864 July 8, 9   *Harrow won by an innings and 66 runs*

Harrow 242   (C.F. Buller 61, M.H. Stow 54)
Eton   63   (C.L. Arkwright 5/34)
        113   (Hon. G.W.S. Lyttelton 50,
               C.L. Arkwright 6/29)

Harrow under the captaincy of C.F. Buller overwhelmed Eton and the captain himself top-scored with 61, well supported by M.H. Stow, 54. Eton were bowled out by C.L. Arkwright who took 11/63 in the match, supported by Hon. J,G.H. Amherst who took 8/69.

This was A.N. Hornby's first year in the Harrow eleven, always nicknamed 'Monkey' by his contemporaries, and as the picture of him indicates he weighed under six stone with a bat in his hand. He afterwards played highly successfully for Lancashire for many years. This was the first year that boundary ropes were introduced.

1864 Harrow XI which won by an innings and 66 runs. A.N. Hornby later of Lancashire and England was the smallest boy who ever appeared at Lord's being only 5ft 3ins and weighed under six stone with bat in hand. LEFT TO RIGHT BACK ROW: *WT. Phipps, J.M. Richardson, Hon. J.G.H. Amherst, C.F. Buller, A.N. Hornby (on shoulders) C.L. Arkwright, M.H. Stow, H.G. Phipps.* SEATED LEFT TO RIGHT: *F.W. Smith, W Evetts, H.H. Montgomery.*

Two of the earliest printed scorecards by Fred Lillywhite from 1864 & 1865, both easy wins for Harrow.

1865 July 14, 15 *Harrow won by an innings and 51 runs*

Harrow	248	(Hon J.G.H. Amherst 85)
Eton	86	(W.B. Money 4/27)
	111	(W.B. Money 6/53)

Harrow had a very strong side that year captained by M.H. Stow and including A.N. Hornby, Hon. J.G.H. Amherst and W.B. Money. Amherst's batting in the first inning was outstanding and Money bowled his lobs very well for a match analysis of 10/80 with Amherst also bowling well in both innings to take Harrow home to a convincing victory.

W.B. MONEY'S MATCH

1866 July 13, 14 *Harrow won by an inning an 136 runs*

Harrow	302	(M.H. Stow 50)
Eton	124	(C.I. Thornton 46 n.o. F.C. Cobden 5/37)
	42	(WB. Money 7/32)

Harrow, again under the captaincy of M.H. Stow, were a powerful side and once more overwhelmed Eton, their third innings win in a row. The Eton second innings total was their third lowest ever. F.C. Cobden, with his very fast yorkers took 5/37 in the first innings, all clean bowled and had a match analysis of 8/47. Money once again bowled very well to take 7/32 in Eton's second innings and 9/50 in the match. He was the outstanding lob bowler in the game for several years. Apart from C.I. Thornton's 46 not out for Eton in the first innings it was a dismal batting performance by the light blues. There was an unpleasant incident when the Eton Captain E. Lubbock hit a ball towards the seats and a small boy jumped up and fielded the ball throwing it into the chasing fielder. The fielder then hurled it to the Harrow wicket-keeper who took the bails off and the umpire gave J.W. Foley the other Eton batsman out. Lubbock lost his temper and refused to go on with the game although the Harrow captain generously suggested that Foley should stay. Cricket was abandoned for the day and did not recommence till next morning. As Eton were in a hopeless position it would have made little difference in any case.

The powerful Harrow XI of 1866. LEFT TO RIGHT BACK ROW: *H.H. Montgomery, T. Hartley, W.B. Money, C.J. Smith.* SEATED: *F.C. Cobden, J.H. Ponsonby, R. Digby, W.H. Hadow, M.H. Stow (capt.), E. Mathews, J.H. Gibbons.*

1867 July 19, 13   *Match drawn*

Eton	208	(R.J. Graham 6/44)
	221	(C.I. Thornton 47)
Harrow	173	(F.G. Templer 50 not out)
	78-1	

W.B. Money captained Harrow in the absence of C.J. Smith, who was injured and F.G. Templer who came in as the last choice top scored in the Harrow first innings with 50 not out. Money was not as effective as in previous years, being hit out of the attack by that formidable striker of the ball C.I. Thornton and finished with only two wickets in the match. It is interesting to note that the creases were still not painted at this time but were cut and brushed out with a broom between innings.

1868 July 10, 11   *Harrow won by 7 wickets*

Eton	116	(C.I. Thornton 44)
	123	(C.W. Walker 6/40)
Harrow	179	
	62-3	

Eton had only won once in 11 years but were moderately confident of success, particularly since the great Eton and Oxford cricketer, R.A.H. Mitchell had come to the school as a master and was considered a brilliant coach. There were eight future blues playing in this match, five on the Eton side, Harris, Thornton, Longman, Maude and Ottaway and three on the Harrow side, F.E.R. Fryer, S. Pelham and W. Law, so these were both strong sides. The feature of the match was a ball hit over the old pavilion by the Eton captain, C.I. Thornton who top scored with 44 out of the Eton first innings total of 116. This was only done again twice by H.E. Meek, the Harrow captain, in 1876 till Albert Trott hit a ball over the new pavilion in 1899 for Middlesex, a feat that has never been achieved since. F.E.R. Fryer played two fine innings for Harrow with 31 and 33 not out and did most towards winning the match. These were the days of constant shooters and batting could at times be quite dangerous. G.H. Longman of Eton and a future Cambridge captain in 1874 and 1875 had his cap taken off with a ball that came straight at his head and was constantly hit in the ribs while batting – which left him with a large lump on his left side in later life (see illustration below).

An early example of mediaeval cryccet in the 14th century. Bumpers were not unknown even in those days!

1869
ETON v. HARROW, at Lord's, 9, 10 July
Eton won by innings and 19 runs

ETON

G. H. Longman, b Giles	. .	15
A. S. Tabor, b Giles	. .	7
C. J. Ottaway, b Gore	.	108
F. W. Rhodes, c and b Law	.	11
Hon. G. R. C. Harris, c Crake, b Walker	. .	0
F. P. U. Pickering, c Gore, b Walker	.	9
W. C. Higgins,* c and b Walker		32
J. P. Rodger, c Crake, b Macan		24
S. E. Butler, b Gore	.	13
Lord Clifton, run out	.	3
J. Maude, not out	.	1
Byes 10, lb 1, w 3	.	14
		237

1st Innings	HARROW		*2nd Innings*	
C. W. Walker, c Tabor, b Butler	23	b Butler	. .	16
W. P. Crake, run out	16	b Maude	.	13
E. P. Baily, c Rhodes, b Butler	1	b Maude	.	0
F. A. Currie, b Higgins	4	c Higgins, b Maude	.	4
S. W. Gore,* run out	4	c and b Maude	.	41
A. A. Apcar, c Longman, b Clifton	13	c Rhodes, b Maude	.	12
W. Law, b Clifton	0	b Maude	.	1
A. J. Begbie, c Harris, b Butler	15	c Rodger, b Clifton	.	18
W. E. Openshaw, b Butler	3	b Maude	.	9
G. Macan, c Higgins, b Butler	1	c Clifton, b Butler	.	0
C. T. Giles, not out	4	not out	.	3
Byes 3, lb 4	7	Byes 6, lb 3, w 1		10
	91			127

HARROW BOWLING	B.	R.	W.						
Walker	244	74	3						
Giles	252	69	2						
Macan	88	28	1						
Law	100	31	1						
Gore	76	21	2						

ETON BOWLING	B.	R.	W.		B.	R.	W.
Higgins	80	38	1		40	23	0
Butler	64	25	5		116	50	2
Clifton	36	13	2		48	8	1
Maude	24	8	0		128	36	7

C.J. OTTAWAY'S MATCH
1869 July 9, 10   *Eton won by an innings and 19 runs*

Eton	237	(C.J. Ottaway 108)
Harrow	91	(S.E. Butler 5/25)
	127	(J. Maude 7/36)

C.J. Ottaway made the first 100 for Eton against Harrow since Emilius Bayley's 152 in 1841 and was in all respects a most distinguished athlete. S.E. Butler, who was converted by R.A.H. Mitchell from a slow bowler to a fast bowler bowled very well in the first innings to take 5/25 and J. Maude the slow bowler took 7/36 in the second innings to take Eton to a convincing victory by an innings, their first victory since 1862. The Harrow captain Spencer Gore in his third year in the XI was the only batsman to make an impression with a top score of 41 in Harrow's second innings total of 127.

1870 July 8, 9   *Eton won by 21 runs*

Eton	189	(G. Macan 5/25)
	151	(A.S. Tabor 50, G.Macan 5/25)
Harrow	205	(E.P. Baily 76)
	114	(M.A. Tollemache 5/48)

This was one of the most exciting and closest matches in the series since 1805. Eton were captained by the great Lord Harris of Kent and England fame and Harrow by C.W. Walker, no relation of the famous Southgate brothers. No fewer than nine future blues appeared in this match: Harris, Longman, Tabor and Ridley for Eton and Baily, Law, Wallroth, Macan and Dury for Harrow. Harrow gained a lead on first innings of 26 runs, mainly due to a very fine innings by E.P. Baily of 76. There was a strange incident when C.A. Wallroth, who had made 30 for Harrow, was run out backing up by Harris which caused a considerable furore. He was also run out in the second innings for 0 by Harris, this time from deep slip. G. Macan bowled very well for Harrow to gain match figures of 10/50, but M.A. Tollemache, who was considered an extremely good bowler by Harris, took 9/83 in the match for Eton to take them home to a narrow victory. Law, the Harrow opener, was mistakenly given out caught off his elbow by the Eton keeper Longman, in the second innings which would possibly have made a difference to the eventual result.

The two XI's of 1870 containing nine future blues contested an exciting match which Eton won narrowly by 21 runs.

ETON XI 1870 LEFT TO RIGHT:

J.P. Rodger, A.W. Ridley, F.W. Rhodes, Hon A.T. Lyttelton, A.S. Tabor, Hon. M.A. Tollemache, G.H. Longman, Hon. G. Harris, F. Pickering, Lord Clifton, G.H. Cammell.

HARROW XI 1870 LEFT TO RIGHT:

E.P. Baily, G. Rivett-Carnac, W. Law, W.P. Crake, W.E. Openshaw, G. Macan, C.W. Walker, C.A. Wallroth, T.S. Dury, E.P. Parbury, A.C. Lucas.

Eton XI 1871. Hon. R.H Lyttelton, Hon. F.J. Bruce, E.O.H. Wilkinson, G.H. Cammell, A.W. Ridley, A.G. Bovill, A.S. Tabor, C.N. Miles, G.H. Longman, F.M. Buckland, Hon. M.A. Tollemache.

A.W. RIDLEY'S MATCH

1871 July 14, 15   *Eton won by an innings and 77 runs*

Eton	308	(A.W. Ridley 117, G.H. Longman 68, A.A. Hadow 5/96)
Harrow	133	(A.A. Hadow 20 not out)
	98	(A.A. Hadow 34)

Eton had an overwhelming win largely due to A.W. Ridley's 117 and G.H. Longman's 68. There was a strange incident relating to the then prevailing custom of the bowling being managed from the pavilion by R.A.H. Mitchell for Eton and I.D. Walker for Harrow. When Harrow's captain, E.P. Baily, came in to bat the instruction was relayed to G.H. Longman, the Eton captain, put on 'Napier Miles' which he duly did and to his utter astonishment Miles bowled Baily with a shooter in the first over. He then received a message from Mitchell that either he must manage the bowling or Mitchell. The first message should have been no change but had somehow become 'Napier Miles' by the time it reached Longman! A.A. Hadow had a good match for Harrow with 5/96 in Eton's first innings total of 308 and also scored 20 not out and 34 in Harrow's second innings of 98, easily the top score.

F.M. BUCKLAND'S MATCH

1872 July 12, 13   *Eton won by 6 wickets*

Harrow	125	(F.M. Buckland 6/35)
	111	(F.M. Buckland 6/42)
Eton	110	(F.L. Shand 6/45)
	127-4	

Eton won the match comfortably largely because of the magnificent leg-break bowling of F.M. Buckland with match figures of 12/77. There were three Lytteltons in the Eton side, including the famous Alfred Lyttelton, who went on to play for Cambridge, Middlesex and England, and A.J. Webbe, a long time Middlesex cricketer who had his first match for Harrow, went on to captain Cambridge and Middlesex and play one test for England v. Australia in 1878. W. Blacker played well for Harrow to score 45 in Harrow's first innings of 125 but was then bowled by the familiar shooter. F.L. Shand bowled fast and straight to take 6/45 in Eton's first innings of 110.

Eton XI 1872. Left to right, back row: E. Hanbury, H.E. Whitmore, C.N. Miles, Hon. F.J. Bruce, Hon. R.H. Lyttelton, Hon F. Lyttelton, seated: T.M.F. Parkyns, F.M. Buckland, E.O.H. Wilkinson, Hon. Alfred Lyttelton, W.W. Whitmore.

1873 July 11, 12   *Harrow won by 5 wickets*

Eton	145	
	166	(F.L. Shand 5/65)
Harrow	146	(F.L. Shand 36 not out)
	168-5	(P.F. Hadow 54 not out, P.E.Crutchley 49, F.M. Buckland 5/54)

In a close fought encounter Harrow squeezed home. F.L. Shand bowled well in both innings for match figures of 8/116 and hit a very useful 36 not out to take Harrow to a one-run lead on first innings. Once again F.M. Buckland of Eton bowled beautifully to take match figures of 9/117 and batted well in their first innings for 37. In his three years in the eleven he finished up with 26 wickets against Harrow and gained Oxford Blues from. 1875/7. H.E. Whitmore of Eton achieved the hat-trick in Harrow's first innings, bowling G.B. Walker, A.J. Layard and H. Leaf in successive deliveries. F.H. Leyland of Harrow was considered by Webbe to be very quick and took 6/44 in the match. P.E. Crutchley was the first of three generations of Crutchley's to play in the Eton and Harrow match, all three in winning teams. G.E.V. Crutchley, his nephew, played in the winning 1908 Harrow eleven and E. Crutchley his son played in the first Harrow victory since then in 1939. Crutchley was promoted to go in first wicket down and played well for 49 and P.F. Hadow's fine 54 not out wore down Buckland's admirable bowling and took Harrow to victory. Shand would have gone far as a bowler had he stayed in England. He was slightly erratic but occasionally sent down the unplayable ball. He achieved distinction that year by taking 8/14 for Harrow against a very powerful Harlequins side.

A.J. WEBBE'S MATCH

1874 July 10, 11   *Eton won by 5 wickets*

Harrow	155	(A.J. Webbe 77, W.F. Forbes 5/21)
	145	(A.J. Webbe 80)
Eton	143	(Hon. E. Lyttelton 58, H.E. Meek 7/45)
	159-5	(H.E. Whitmore 61 not out)

The match was a contest between an average Eton team and a colossus representing Harrow, A.J. Webbe the Harrow captain. He performed brilliantly to score 77 and 80, half Harrow's runs in both innings, and was undoubtedly the best bat Harrow had produced for many

years. He was caught in the first innings by a brilliant catch at long leg by E. Lyttelton, the Eton captain. Lyttelton, after scoring a useful 58 in the first innings, had the position reversed in the second innings and was caught off a magnificent catch by 'Webby' in the deep over the bowler Crutchley's head for a duck. H.E. Whitmore's patient and wise innings of 61 not out took Eton home to victory by 5 wickets, Crutchley taking 4/44 of the five wickets that fell.

1875 July 9, 10   *Match Drawn*

Eton	202	(Hon. Alfred Lyttelton 59)
Harrow	110	(L. Chater 30 not out E.W.B. Denison 5/45)
	155-6	(L. Chater 35 not out)

This was the first time that the wicket at Lord's was covered before the match and Eton had the advantage since the Harrow bowlers were forced to run on wet ground and Eton put on 60 in the first half-hour. The Eton captain, Alfred Lyttelton, batted well for 59 and W.F. Forbes for 47, H.E. Meek the Harrow bowler finishing with 4/34 after his 7/45 in the Eton first innings of 1874. Eton would probably have won if their fast bowler, J. Wakefield, had not been taken off after bowling four wides, although he had taken 4/33, all clean bowled. In the opinion of many he was one of the finest schoolboy fast bowlers that had been seen up to this time.

W.F. FORBES'S MATCH

1876 July 14, 15   *Eton won by an innings and 24 runs*

Eton	308	(W.F. Forbes 113, L. Bury 72, L.K. Jarvis 5/77)
Harrow	157	
	127	(G.H. Portal 5/20)

W.F. Forbes gave the Harrow bowlers a real pasting during his 113 in 90 minutes striking 22 fours, aided by L. Bury with 72, mostly on the leg side, in Eton's total of 308. L.K. Jarvis, the only future first-class cricketer in the Harrow side, bowled tidily to record 5/77. H.E. Meek, the Harrow captain, achieved the remarkable feat of hitting the ball twice over the old pavilion and scoring 25 off six consecutive balls before getting out. The pavilion at Lord's then was much lower in height than it is now but C.T.

Eton XI 1876 which won by an innings and 24 runs, the Eton captain W.F. Forbes had much to do with their success scoring 113 runs and taking six wickets. LEFT TO RIGHT BACK ROW: *J.E.K. Studd, F.P. Gervais, C.W. Foley (capt.), H.C. Goodhart.* SEATED: *Hon. Ivo Bligh, E.J. Ruggles-Brise, W.F. Forbes, H. Whitfeld, L. Bury.* ON GROUND: *G.H. Portal, C.M. Smith.*

Thornton is the only other player to have achieved the feat in this match. Harrow were bowled out for 157 and 127 with Forbes taking 4/40 in the first innings and G.H. Portal 5/20 in the second to give Eton a convincing innings win.

1877 July 13, 14   *Match Drawn*

Harrow	157	(H.E. Meek 58, G.H. Portal 5/45)
	193	(F.C.C. Rowe 82)
Eton	163	(H. Whitfeld 63 not out)
	78-1	

Eton produced a very strong side this year containing three Studds, H. Whitfeld and Ivo Bligh, all first-class cricketers and Cambridge blues, whilst Harrow only had W.H. Patterson who played for Kent and the Gentlemen and P.J.T. Henery the Cambridge blue of 1882/3. The match was well contested and there was little to choose between the sides after the first innings. H.E. Meek, the Harrow captain, batted well for 58 and G.H. Portal, despite a damaged bowling finger, took 5/45 for Eton. In Eton's first innings only Whitfeld batted proficiently for 63 not out from a total of 163. The outstanding innings of the match was the left-hander F.C.C. Rowe's 82 for Harrow in the second innings and there was the prospect of an exciting finish when Eton set 187 to win had scored 78-1 before rain fell heavily and the match was abandoned as a draw.

1878 July 12, 13   *Harrow won by 20 runs*

Harrow	119	
	224	(E.M. Lawson 66, C.M. Smith 6/59)
Eton	117	
	206	(C.T. Studd 56, E.K. Douglas 53)

This was the most exciting game since 1870, only two previous matches (those of 1818 and 1834) having been closer, both narrow wins by 13 runs. Two Paravicini brothers, H.F. for Harrow and the great P.J. for Eton, were playing on opposing sides and the schools had seven future blues on both sides. Eton included C.T. and G.B. Studd, Hon. Martin Hawke, the future Lord Hawke of Yorkshire and England fame, and P.J. de Paravicini, the outstanding Cambridge and Middlesex cricketer. The Harrow team included F.C.C. Rowe, P.J.J. Henery and R. Spencer. Harrow's first innings started strangely with four wides from A.C. Cattley who then took the Harrow opener W.H. Heale's wicket for 0 in the same over. C.T. Studd and C.M. Smith bowled too well for Harrow with the exception of C.J.E. Jarvis who scored 40 and J.H. Stirling 30, Studd taking 4/48 and Smith 3/24 in Harrow's 119. Eton replied with 117, only Hawke, 32, and S.W. Cattley, 32, made runs. Henery and E.M. Lawson, 66, had

The strong Eton XI of 1977 which contained five future Cambridge blues, the three Studds, Herbert Whitfeld and Ivo Bligh. LEFT TO RIGHT BACK ROW: *G.H. Portal, C.M. Smith, A.B. Ridley, C.T. Studd, A.J. Chitty.* SEATED: *H.C. Goodhart, Hon. Ivo Bligh, H. Whitfeld, J.E.K. Studd.* ON GROUND: *G.B. Studd, L.W. Matthews.*

The two very strong sides of 1878 produced the most exciting match since 1870 with Harrow just prevailing by the narrow margin of 20 runs. There were seven future blues in the two sides and three future England players in C.T. and G.B. Studd and Hon. Martin Hawke for Eton. HARROW (ABOVE), LEFT TO RIGHT BACK ROW: *H.F. de Paravicini, M.F. Ramsay, C.J.E. Jarvis, P.J.T. Henery, J.H. Stirling.* SEATED: *W.H. Heale, F.W. Leaf, F.C.C. Rowe, E.M. Lawson, T.G.H. Moncreiffe.* ON GROUND: *R. Spencer.* ETON (BELOW), LEFT TO RIGHT BACK ROW: *R.W. Byass, Hon. M.B. Hawke, A.C. Cattley, E.K. Douglas.* SEATED: *S.W. Cattley, G.B. Studd, C.M. Smith, C.T. Studd, C.H. Polhill-Turner.* ON GROUND: *P.J. de Paravicini, R. Durant.*

a very good stand to give Harrow a reasonable total of 224 in their second innings, with C.M. Smith taking 6/59 for Eton. Eton were set a formidable target for those days of 227 to win but with C.T. Studd making 56 and E.K. Douglas 53 they were in with a chance. Amidst great excitement Henery bowled particularly well, backed up by good fielding, to take 4/73 in Eton's narrow defeat. Polhill-Turner was the last Eton man out on 22, hitting the ball high in the air and the Harrow captain Jarvis had the presence of mind to call to the wicket-keeper Rowe to take the catch.

1879 July 11, 12   *Match Drawn*

Eton	99	(R.C. Ramsay 6/37)
	85	
Harrow	67	(C.T. Studd 6/28)
	69-4	

1879 was a particularly wet season from start to finish and the wicket at Lord's had not recovered on the Friday morning from the previous day and it was no surprise when J.H. Stirling, the Harrow captain, put Eton in to bat. Although no rain fell on Friday, Saturday proved a different story and the wicket was very difficult throughout the match, hence the very low scores of both sides and a top score in the match of 34 not out from T.G.H. Moncreiffe of Harrow in the second innings. Both teams had two pairs of good bowlers, Studd and Paravicini for Eton and the two Ramsay brothers for Harrow, RC, medium pace, and M.F, slow. Harrow were left 118 to win and after 4 wickets had fallen quickly rain came and made the wicket easier. It looked as though Moncreiffe and M.C. Kemp might have pulled it off for Harrow had time allowed.

In those days the umpires were not empowered to decide when play was possible and C.T. Studd, the Eton captain, led his team in and out when showers kept appearing. Eventually the game was abandoned at 5 o'clock with Harrow slight favourites. The bowlers, however, were dominant throughout the match as their analyses indicate. Eton's C.T. Studd had figures of 8/46, Paravicini 5/69. Harrow's R.C. Ramsay's 10/163 and M.F. Ramsay 7/76, yet both sides were reasonably strong in batting.

P.J. PARAVICINI'S MATCH
1880 July 9, 10   *Harrow won by 95 runs*

Harrow	148	(P.J. de Paravicini 5/50)
	142	(P.J. de Paravicini 7/42)
Eton	107	(F.G.L. Lucas 7/37)
	88	

A heavy thunderstorm on the first morning of the match made the wicket treacherous and the medium and slow bowlers held the ascendancy throughout. R.C. Ramsay and A.F. Kemp, the brother of the Harrow captain, M.C, played well, but a moderate total seemed likely until E.M. Hadow, batting at 9 scored 28 not out. He was helped by

Harrow XI 1880. LEFT TO RIGHT: BACK ROW: *R.C. Ramsay, P.H. Martineau, M.C. Kemp, R.J. McNeill, F.G.L. Lucas.* SEATED: *F.W. Pember, F.W. Stancomb, A.F. Kemp, J. Dunn, W.E.T. Bolitho.* ON THE GROUND: *E.M. Hadow.*

a missed catch at point and made the same score as Ramsay to take Harrow to 148 all out. Eton fared even worse with 107 and only P.J. de Paravicini's 35 provided resistance. F.G.L. Lucas bowled steadily for Harrow to take 7/37 but Eton's batsmen failed to take advantage of his high trajectory by moving their feet and making many deliveries into simple full-tosses. Hadow again played very well for a match-winning 49 out of 142 and Harrow were in a strong position on a poor wicket. Eton succumbed for 88, bowled out by Ramsay, Kemp and Lucas with some ease. Paravicini, the Eton captain, bowled superbly throughout the match for figures of 12/92 which he was to repeat the following year, notwithstanding his lone batting effort in the first innings.

1881 July 7, 8   *Harrow won by 112 runs*

Harrow	140	(P.J. de Paravicini 6/42)
	202	(E.M. Hadow 94, P.J. de Paravicini 6/57)
Eton	64	(G.H. Shakerley 5/30)
	166	(J.E.A. Greatorex 5/35)

Harrow, captained by A.F. Kemp, brother of the previous year's captain, again had an easy victory largely due to the brilliant hitting of E.M. Hadow with 94 out of 202 in Harrow's second innings, supported by 28 and 44 from W.E.T. Bolitho and some good bowling from G.H. Shakerley with 5/30 in the Eton first innings and J.E.A.

Greatorex with 5/35 in the second. Once again Paravicini was the giant of the Eton side with 12/99 in the match, supporting a poor Eton side. In his four years in the Eton eleven he had taken 31 Harrow wickets only exceeded by two other Etonians before proper analyses were recorded.

Harrow had an easy win for the second year running by 112 runs in 1881 mainly due to a brilliant knock of 94 from E.M. Hadow. LEFT TO RIGHT: BACK ROW: *R. Moncreiffe, P.H. Martineau, G.H. Shakerley, E.M. Hadow.* SEATED: *W.E.T. Bolitho, J.E.A. Greatorex, D.G. Spiro, A.F. Kemp, M.T. Baines, Hon. E.W.H. Ward.* ON THE GROUND: *L.A. Routledge.*

Eton XI 1881. LEFT TO RIGHT, BACK ROW: *W.F. Cave, R.J. Lucas, J. Hargreaves, Hon. C. Trefusis, Hon. D.H. Lascelles,* SEATED: *Hon. C.M. Knatchbull-Hugessen, H.W. Bainbridge, P.J. de Paravicini, A.E. Newton,* ON THE GROUND: *R.H. Rawson, A.C. Richards.*

1882 July 14, 15   *Match Drawn*

Harrow	187	(T. Greatorex 48, I.F. Jardine 5/68)
	141	
Eton	140	(R. Moncreiffe 5/54)
	132-7	(W.F. Cave 49)

This appeared to be a rather uneventful and low-scoring match with no outstanding performers on either side. Harrow undoubtedly had the better of the match gaining a first innings lead of 47 and nearly bowling Eton out in the second innings, Eton finished 56 short with three wickets left. W.F. Cave with 49 and J. Hargreaves, 25, saved the game for Eton. The general standard of fielding, particularly by Eton, was rather poor and the Eton batsman F. Marchant, later to play for Cambridge in four successive years and captain Kent, dropped five catches fielding at point.

1883 July 13, 14   *Match Drawn*

Eton	231	(F. Marchant 93, A.H. Studd 64)
Harrow	120	(T. Greatorex 37 not out, Hon. A.E. Parker 8/37)
	76-1	(T. Greatorex 40 not out)

In a rain affected match the outstanding feature was F. Marchant's innings of 93, scored in 90 minutes out of 115, a remarkable exhibition of hard, clean hitting. He should have been run out when he was 0 but made up for his poor performance in the field in 1882 by taking a very fine, one-handed catch low down off H.E. Crawley on 3. C.D. Buxton and T. Greatorex batted well for Harrow before a devastating spell of fast bowling from A.E. Parker caused a complete collapse, his last six wickets only costing seven runs, with six of his eight victims bowled. Greatorex again batted well for Harrow in the follow on to remain undefeated on 40 for the second time in the match before a couple of severe thunderstorms prevented any chance of a definite result.

1884 July 11, 12   *Match Drawn*

Harrow	126	(E.G. Bromley-Martin 6/46)
	152-6	
Eton	82	(C.D. Buxton 4/12)

This match was again ruined by rain and, although the Eton side was a reasonably strong one, with six future blues in the side, they failed dismally, only Lord George Scott with 32 batting sensibly against a moderate Harrow attack. W.A.R. Young batted stubbornly for Harrow and finished not out in both innings for an aggregate of 58. Had it not rained for the whole of the second day Harrow probably would have won and were 196 ahead with four wickets standing when the game was abandoned.

Eton XI 1884. LEFT TO RIGHT, BACK ROW: *H.J. Mordaunt, H. Philipson, T.H. Barnard, Lord George Scott, C.E. Murdoch, F.A. Soames,* SEATED: *F. Freeman-Thomas, R.J. Lucas, H.W. Forster,* ON THE GROUND: *E.G. Bromley-Martin, W.C. Bridgeman.*

Harrow XI 1884. LEFT TO RIGHT, BACK ROW: *A.K. Watson, A.D. Ramsay, C.D. Buxton, C.H. Dent, C.E. Kindersley,* SEATED: *A.R. Cox, F.H. Oates, E.M. Butler, W.H. Dent, W.A.R. Young,* ON THE GOUND: *M.J. Dauglish.*

Harrow were fortunate to scrape home by 3 wickets in 1885 on a wearing wicket against a high quality Eton side. HARROW (ABOVE) LEFT TO RIGHT, BACK ROW: *J.T. Sanderson, G.B. Bovill, E.M. Butler, H.F. Kemp, A.D. Ramsay.* SEATED: *A.K. Watson, M.J. Dauglish, W.A.R. Young, E. Crawley, W.H. Dent.* ON GROUND: *C.H. Benton.* ETON (BELOW) LEFT TO RIGHT, BACK ROW: *H. St. G. Foley, S.E. Forster, T.H. Barnard, Hon. T.W. Brand.* SEATED: *Lord George Scott, H.W. Forster, F. Freeman-Thomas, H. Philipson, E.C. Bromley-Martin.* ON GROUND: *R.C. Gosling, H.J. Mordaunt.*

A.K. WATSON'S MATCH

1885 July 10, 11   *Harrow won by 3 wickets*

Eton	265	(H. Philipson 53)
	151	
Harrow	324	(A.K. Watson 135, E. Crawley 100,
		E.G. Bromley-Martin 6/88)
	96-7	(E.M. Butler 48 not out
		E.G.Bromley-Martin 4/49)

This was another exciting match between two high-quality sides with eleven future first-class cricketers on the two sides. Eton won the toss on a good wicket and only made a fair score in the circumstances. Harrow with two brilliant knocks from A.K. Watson, 135, and E. Crawley, 100, gave the dark blues a commanding advantage. Harrow wickets fell rapidly the next morning and Eton went in a

second time with a deficit of only 59. The wicket was wearing fast and Eton only managed 151 with a top score of 27 from H. Philipson, the Eton opener, who had also top scored in the first innings. Harrow had a relatively easy task of scoring 93 to win but E.G. Bromley-Martin again bowled well for his 4/49, and had Harrow in some trouble. A run out was missed at a critical time for Eton, but E.M. Butler, the Harrow captain with 48 not out, and W.A.R. Young took Harrow to victory with three minutes to spare. There were considerable scenes of jubilation and despair from supporters of both schools in front of the pavilion at the conclusion of the game.

C.P.FOLEY'S MATCH

1886 July 9, 10   *Eton won by 6 wickets*

Harrow	133	(H.R. Bromley-Davenport 5/79)
	220	(E. Crawley 69, J. St. F. Fair 61)
Eton	202	(C.P. Foley 114)
	154-4	

The Harrow side was a strong one and it was undoubtedly an Eton victory against the odds with only two of the side left from 1885, H.J. Mordaunt and the Hon. T.W. Brand. H.R. Bromley-Davenport bowled well for Eton in the two Harrow innings and Eustace Crawley again showed powerful defensive batting for Harrow in both innings to make 40 and 69. In the second Harrow innings J.St.F. Fair supported Crawley well for his 61 and Bromley-Davenport finished with 9 wickets in the match for Eton. The outstanding innings for Eton in their first innings was C.P. Foley's 114 out of 202. A target of 152 in the fourth innings was completed with some ease by Eton with 6 wickets to spare, their first victory over Harrow for 10 years. There were six future blues playing on both sides, a benchmark of the quality of both teams.

1887 July 8, 9   *Eton won by 5 wickets*

Harrow	101	(A.C. MacLaren 55, H.R. Bromley-Davenport 6/44)
	204	(A.C. MacLaren 67)
Eton	205	(Lord Chelsea 72 not out)
	101-5	(R.C. Gosling 56 not out)

This was the start of the golden years of F.S. Jackson and A.C. MacLaren for Harrow, probably the two greatest cricketers Harrow has ever produced, both to be future England captains. A.C. MacLaren, only fifteen, played two of the finest knocks seen at Lords, 55 out of 101 after Harrow had been 84-1, and 67 out of 204 in Harrow's second innings on a difficult wicket. For a small boy he had great confidence and his hooking of the short ball was magnificent. Bromley-Davenport again performed very well for Eton to take eight wickets in the match to follow his nine of the previous year. Lord Chelsea, a last minute choice remarkable hitting knock of 72 not out that had a great deal to do with Eton winning the match. He never again made runs and little was known about his cricket thereafter.

Jackson failed both times with the bat, only scoring 3 and 1 and his bowling was not utilised enough in the first innings otherwise the Eton score would probably have been somewhat less. R.C. Gosling played a very composed innings of 56 not out in Eton's second innings to take the light blues home to victory by 5 wickets.

Harrow XI 1887. LEFT TO RIGHT. BACK ROW: *E.G. Raphael, W.M. Torrens, T.B.A. Clarke,* SEATED: *A.C. MacLaren, H.D. Watson, J.A. MacLaren, J.St.F. Fair (capt.), N. Ramsay, P. Ashworth, F.S. Jackson.* ON GROUND: *A.C.S. Barchard.*

Eton XI 1887. A remarkable hitting knock of 72 not out in the first innings from Lord Chelsea who was a last-minute choice had much to do with Eton's win by 5 wickets in 1887. LEFT TO RIGHT, BACK ROW: *Hon. M.G. Tollemache, Lord Chelsea, L.C. Maclachlan, C.A. Field, W.D. Llewelyn, F.R.G. Hervey-Bathurst.* SEATED: *Hon. H.T. Coventry, R.C. Gosling, Hon. T.W. Brand (capt), C.P. Foley, H.R. Bromley-Davenport.*

1888 July 13, 14

F.S. JACKSON & R.B. HOARE'S MATCH
Harrow won by 156 runs

Harrow	80	(H.W. Studd 6/27)
	234	(R.B. Hoare 108, F.S. Jackson 59, H.W. Studd 8/72)
Eton	106	(F.S. Jackson 6/40)
	52	(F.S. Jackson 5/28, R.B. Hoare 4/21)

Eton appeared to have the initiative after the first innings when they were ahead by 26 runs on a slow, difficult wicket with the bowlers on both sides, particularly H.W. Studd for Eton with 6/27 and F.S. Jackson for Harrow with 6/40, well on top. In Harrow's second innings they had lost three quick wickets when R.B. Hoare and Jackson came together for the last ninety minutes and batted superbly on a still difficult wicket. They went on to score the majority of Harrow's runs, Hoare with 108 and Jackson 59 in Harrow's total of 234, despite the splendid bowling of Studd with fast off-cutters, who finished with match figures of 14/99. This was the highest total of wickets in the Eton and Harrow match since proper analyses were recorded in 1854 and only beaten by E.W. Blore of Eton's all-time record of 15 wickets in 1847. It was never to be beaten again. Jackson followed up his 6 wickets and 59 runs with another superb performance in the Eton second innings taking the first 5 wickets for 5 runs, all clean bowled, well supported by Hoare once again with 4/21. Eton were bowled out for 52 and Harrow had achieved a heroic victory.

Harrow XI 1888. The superb all-round performances of R.B. Hoare and F.S. Jackson, particularly Jackson's magnificent bowling in both Eton Innings, led to Harrow's decisive victory in 1888 by 156 runs. 'A Gentleman's a bowling', the famous Harrow song was composed in his honour by Edward Bowen. LEFT TO RIGHT, BACK ROW: *N.Ramsay, R.D. Cheales, H.D. Watson, C.E. Gilroy, W.J.F. Giffard.* SEATED: *G.W. Roffey, R.B. Hoare, J.A. MacLaren (capt), F.S. Jackson, A.C. Maclaren.* ON GROUND: *W.E. Greaves.*

The strong Harrow XI of 1889 captained by the legendary F.S. Jackson and including A.C. MacLaren which triumphed by nine wickets. The only occasion when two England captains have appeared in the same side from both schools. LEFT TO RIGHT, BACK ROW: *A.H.M. Butler, W.B. Anderson, H.M. Peebles, C.G. Pope, J.Gowans (12th man).* SEATED: *D.R. Napier, A.C. MacLaren, F.S. Jackson (capt), R.B. Hoare, C.P. Wills.* ON GROUND: *R.S. Chaplin, A. Neame.*

1889 July 12, 13   *Harrow won by 9 wickets*

Harrow	272	(F.S. Jackson 68, C.P. Wills 50)
	50-1	
Eton	169	
	152	

Harrow won the toss and batted on a good wicket. F.S. Jackson, the Harrow captain and C.P. Wills were the main contributors to Harrow's respectable 272. Rain on the wicket did not help Eton in their innings and they were bowled out by the accurate Harrow attack for 169 with Jackson taking 3/33. They fared little better in the second innings when following on 103 behind and only H.R. Bromley-Davenport made much of a showing with useful knocks of 31 and 42, although his left-handed swing bowling was not as good as in previous years. Jackson and W.B. Anderson both bowled well in Eton's second innings to dismiss them for 152 and left Harrow the simple task of scoring 50 runs to win, which they duly did in 35 minutes, Studd of Eton having wrenched his knee in bowling Archie MacLaren for the fourth time in two matches. This was some feat against a player of his quality.

1890 July 11, 12   *Match Drawn*

Eton	108	(H.M. Peebles 4/27)
	120-3	
Harrow	133	(A.C. MacLaren 76, D.H. Forbes 5/68)

There was no play on the first day as the ground was waterlogged with further rain in the afternoon. Eton flattered to deceive when after a prompt start at 10.30 they collapsed from 59/0 on a featherbed wicket to 108 all out, the main wicket-takers being H.M. Peebles and C.G. Pope. A.C. MacLaren batted brilliantly for his 76 but the Harrow captain was the only batsman that played D.H. Forbes the Eton fast bowler with any confidence in Harrow's 133. With no chance of a result Eton plodded on to 120/3 at the close.

1891 July 10, 11   *Harrow won by 7 wickets*

Eton	125	(G.R. Brewis 70)
	187	
Harrow	241	(J.C. Bevington 71, M.Y. Barlow 58)
	72-3	

Harrow won the toss and put Eton in on a soft wicket not fully recovered from recent heavy rain and only G.R Brewis with 70 made runs, driving and pulling to square leg after R.A. Studd, his opening partner, had been run out for 9. The wicket improved steadily and Harrow's score was respectable enough at 241 with J.C. Bevington, M.Y. Barlow and C.G. Pope all batting well after Pope's 4/22 in the Eton first innings. Eton suffered from the loss of their captain, R.C. Norman, who was absent ill suffering from concussion after being hit in the Eton and Winchester game the week before and unable to bat in the second innings. Eton only fared slightly better in their second innings and Harrow had to score 72 to win which they did with relative ease for the loss of only three wickets. This was the first year that the Etonians followed the Harrovian example and appeared in white boots.

1892 July 8, 9   *Harrow won by 64 runs*

Harrow	214	
	116	(E. Lane-Fox 4/18)
Eton	144	(G.E. Bromley-Martin 68, C.J.L. Rudd 4/22)
	122	(D.H. Forbes 60 not out)

On a fairly placid wicket Harrow batted first and scored what seemed a modest 214 pinned down by an accurate Eton attack. This proved to be good enough and only G.E. Bromley-Martin with 68 made any significant contribution against C.J.L. Rudd who was playing with an injured hand and very nearly did not play. Eton were bowled out for 144 with Rudd taking 4/22 and the last four Eton wickets fell at the same score. Harrow made a mess of their second innings but apart from the Eton captain D.H. Forbes 60 not out, bowled well enough in Eton's second innings to gain a comfortable victory by 64 runs. Forbes bowled the first two Harrovians with the first two balls of the match.

1893 July 14, 15   *Eton won by 9 wickets*

Harrow	125	(H.R.E. Harrison 6/29)
	105	
Eton	199	(H.F. Meeking 50)
	32-1	

Eton were undoubtedly a much stronger side than Harrow with a good batting line-up and no tail but their chief strength lay in the bowling. F.H.E. Cunliffe was a very fine left-arm medium pace bowler, C.C. Pilkington a medium right-hand bowler with immaculate length, P.W. Cobbold a good leg-break bowler and H.R.E. Harrison a bowler of above-average pace which unsettled schoolboy batsmen. It was a very slow and easy-paced Lord's wicket with the light somewhat uncertain. Harrison bowled superbly on a wicket which hardly suited him to end up with 6/29 off 11.4 overs. Eton batted very slowly in their first innings with Hon F.W.G. Egerton and H.F. Meeking putting them in a strong position and Pilkington and Cobbold batting well at the end, A lead of 74 was more than the moderate Harrow batting could cope with and they finished up 105 all out in their second innings. J.H. Stogdon, who went on to gain blues at Cambridge from 1897/9, was dismissed for a pair. Harrison again bowled well to take nine wickets in the match with Cunliffe taking 3/23 in the second innings. Eton were comfortable victors by nine wickets.

F.H.E. CUNLIFFE'S MATCH

1894 July 13, 14   *Match Drawn*

Harrow	129	(F.H.E. Cunliffe 7/54)
	80	(F.H.E. Cunliffe 6/40)
Eton	127	

The whole of the first day was lost to rain and on the Saturday Harrow decided to bat after winning the toss on a very slow, wet wicket and for the first 90 minutes the wicket played easily. Harrow batted very slowly with only J.H. Stogdon, 32 out of a total of 129, making a respectable score. F.H.E. Cunliffe and C.C. Pilkington bowled very well, especially Cunliffe with 13/94 in the match. Towards the end of the Harrow innings the ball began to stop and cut sharply as the pitch dried out. In the Eton innings the pitch became very difficult and had it not been for the two outstanding bowlers, Cunliffe and

Despite the loss of the whole of the first day in 1894 Eton bowled out Harrow twice on the second day mainly due to the outstanding left arm fast bowling of F.H.E. Cunliffe with a match analysis of 13/94. Although a draw Eton did enough to suggest that they would have won had time allowed. LEFT TO RIGHT, BACK ROW: *A.M. Hollins, A.W.F. Baird, A.B. Lubbock, R.W. Mitchell.* SEATED: *H.W. Kettlewell, C.C. Pilkington, G.E. Bromley-Martin (capt), F.H.E. Cunliffe, I.D. Gosling.* ON GROUND: *T.D. Pilkington, H.B. Chinnery.*

Pilkington with 32 and 33 respectively, Eton would have been in a much worse state. There was no hope of a result but Eton did enough to suggest, having bowled Harrow out for 80 in the second innings just before 7 o'clock, that had they won the toss and batted they could probably have won. Cunliffe and Pilkington were reckoned to be one of the finest pairs of schoolboy opening bowlers ever seen. Cunliffe took sixty wickets in school matches at just over nine per wicket while Pilkington claimed forty wickets having missed several matches owing to injury. Cunliffe's 13/94 in the match was not to be equalled again till 1951 when R.V.C. Robins achieved 13/91.

1895 July 12, 13		*Match Drawn*
Eton	260	(H.B. Chinnery 75, E.M. Dowson 5/90)
	283-9 dec.	(A.B. Lubbock 66, H.B. Chinnery 64)
Harrow	326	(J.H. Stogdon 124, A.S. Crawley 78)
	75-9	(C.C. Pilkington 5/30)

This was another poor performance by the Harrow batsmen in the second innings and they were very lucky to avoid a heavy defeat. They collapsed to 75-9 at the close, 142 runs behind. If Eton had batted more briskly in the second innings or declared slightly earlier it would have been a foregone conclusion. H.B. Chinnery batted very well for Eton in both innings with 75 and 64, as did A.B. Lubbock with 66 in the second innings. E.M. Dowson, in the first of his five years in the Harrow eleven, took 5/90 in the Eton first innings and eight wickets in the match. Harrow's first innings of 326 contained a fine innings of

124 from J.H. Stogdon and a good supporting one from the rackets player, A.S. Crawley, of 78. Harrow set 218 to win batted atrociously and only just held out with 9 wickets down for 75. The Eton destroyers were C.C. Pilkington who took 5/30 off 30 overs and R.W. Mitchell, one of the three cricketing sons of R.A.H. 3/7.

1896 July 10, 11		B.J.T. BOSANQUET'S MATCH Match Drawn
Eton	386	(B.J.T. Bosanquet 120, H.C. Pilkington 101)
Harrow	218	(H.J. Wyld 81, F.H. Mitchell 6/44)
	255-8	(W.F.A. Rattigan 72, E.B.T. Studd 50)

Eton won the toss and batted first on a good wicket with the weather hot and fine throughout the two days. There were two exceptionally high-class knocks, both very different in their way, in the Eton first innings of 386. H.C. Pilkington's was an extremely classy knock of 101. He always seemed destined for the highest honours but never fulfilled his true potential. B.J.T. Bosanquet's 120 was full of powerful strokes way beyond his years and it was strange that this was his only year in the Eton eleven. He was to make up for this with a vengeance in later years representing Oxford, Middlesex and England with great distinction and invented the famous googly ball, formerly known as the 'Bosie' after him. Apart from H.J. Wyld's 81 and R.F. Vibart's 42 Harrow's innings was a disappointment. F.H. Mitchell's lobs caused consternation and he finished with 6/44. Harrow batted better in the second inning with W.F.A. Rattigan, the rackets player and father of Terence Rattigan the famous playwright and future Harrow eleven player in 1929/30, scoring 72, well supported by E.B.T. Studd's 50 in a match-saving stand that left Harrow on 255-8.

T.G.O. COLE'S MATCH

1897 July 9, 10   *Match Drawn*

Harrow	236	(W.P. Robertson 50, F.H. Mitchell 7/64)
	248-4 dec.	(T.G.O. Cole 142, E.M. Dowson 64)
Eton	160	(E.M. Dowson 6/51)
	208-7	

Two reasonably strong sides failed to get a positive result with Eton playing out the last half-hour to save the game. In Harrow's first innings of 236 W.P. Robertson batted very well for 50 with good contributions from T.G.O. Cole, 36, and W.S. Medlicott, 35. The feature of Eton's bowling attack was F.H. Mitchell the best of the three cricketing sons of the great R.A.H. who changed from lobs to leg-break bowling with remarkable results taking 7/64 and 11/156 in the match. Only H.C. Pilkington with 41 out of 160 managed to cope with Harrow's E.M. Dowson – left-handed slow-medium spinners and faster yorker. He well deserved his 6/51, his wickets all clean bowled. In Harrow's second innings T.G.O. Cole played with superb timing to score 142 and was well supported by E.M. Dowson with 64 to take Harrow up to 248-4 dec. and leave Eton a target of 324 in 240 minutes. With 30 minutes of time left Eton were seven wickets down but

---

Lord's Ground. ETON v. HARROW.
FRIDAY and SATURDAY, JULY 9, 10, 1897.

HARROW.	First Innings.		Second Innings.	
1 P. T. Maw, Esq. (Capt.)	c Lubbock, b Mitchell	7	c Browning, b Mitchell	4
2 T. G. O. Cole, Esq.	b Penn	36	b Mitchell	142
3 W. S. Medlicott, Esq.	b Legard	35		
4 W. P. Robertson, Esq.	c Browning, b Mitchell	50	c Johnson, b Mitchell	28
5 E. B. T. Studd, Esq.	b Mitchell	14		
6 H. J. Wyld, Esq.	b Penn	1		
7 E. M. Dowson, Esq.	b Mitchell	25	c Legard, b Mitchell	64
8 W. F. A. Rattigan, Esq.	c Marsham, b Mitchell	31	not out	5
9 A. S. Drew, Esq.	st Browning, b Mitchell	18		
10 J. F. Wilkes, Esq.	l b w, b Mitchell	0	[Innings closed.]	
11 S. F. A. A. Hurt, Esq.	not out	7		
	B 11, l-b , w 1, n-b ,	12	B 2, l-b , w 1, n-b 2	5
	Total	236	Total	248

FALL OF THE WICKETS.
1-17 2-61 3-124 4-140 5-145 7-199 9-219 10-236
1-8 2-203 3-216 4-248

ANALYSIS OF BOWLING.

Name.	1st Innings O.	M.	R.	W.	Wd.	N-b.	2nd O.	M.	R.	W.	Wd.	N-b
Tryon	14	3	34	...			6	1	34	0		
Mitchell	38.1	15	61	7	...	...	8.4	6	92	4	1	1
Legard	19	9	31	1	1		19	7	49	0		1
Robarts	15	8	29	0			8	2	27	0		
Penn	21	9	46	2			7	1	41	0		

ETON.	First Innings.		Second Innings.	
2 R. Lubbock, Esq.	c and b Cole	27	l b w, b Dowson	13
8 C. H. B. Marsham, Esq.	b Dowson	29	c Robertson, b Wyld	8
3 H. C. Pilkington, Esq.	c Dowson, b Wyld	41	b Wyld	12
1 A. D. Legard, Esq. (Capt.)	b Dowson	0	run out	35
4 F. H. Mitchell, Esq.	b Dowson	3	l b w, b Dowson	48
5 E. F. Penn, Esq.	run out	0	b Dowson	22
9 P. R. Johnson, Esq.	b Dowson	5	not out	13
10 G. Robarts, Esq.	b Dowson	22	b Drew	30
6 G. L. Tryon, Esq.	b Dowson	7		
11 Hon. W. G. Cadogan	b Wyld	9	not out	10
7 C. H. Browning, Esq.	not out	5		
	B 5, l-b 5, w 1, n-b 1	12	B 4, l-b 6, w 3, n-b	17
	Total	160	Total	208

FALL OF THE WICKETS.
1-43 2-96 3-97 4-103 5-103 6-109 7-112 8-125 9-134 10-160
1-15 2-35 3-42 4-88 5-162

ANALYSIS OF BOWLING.

Name.	1st Innings O.	M.	R.	W.	Wd.	N-b.
Dowson	49.3	25	51	6		
Cole	14	1	38	1	1	
Hurt	31	19	39	0		
Maw	5	1	14	0		
Wyld	9	5	6	2		

Umpires—W. Hearn and Titchmarsh.   Scorers—Clayton and G. G. Hearne.

ONE PENNY.   The figures on the scoring board show the batsmen in.   Stumps will be drawn at 7.30 p.m.   Two-day Match.

Eton XI 1897 captained by A.D. Legard which managed to hold out for a draw. On the far left seated is F.H. Mitchell, Eton XI 1896/7. The son of R.A.H. Mitchell he achieved match figures of 11/156 in 1897 with his leg-breaks after bowling lobs in 1896. A notable golfer who played for Oxford and England he was afterwards assistant private secretary to George VI as Sir Frank Mitchell. LEFT TO RIGHT, BACK ROW: *P.R. Johnson, E.F. Penn, G.T.L. Tryon, C.H.B. Marsham.* SEATED: *F.H. Mitchell, R. Lubbock, A.D. Legard (capt.), H.C. Pilkington, C.H. Browning.* ON GROUND: *W.G. Cadogan, G.R. Robarts.*

Harrow XI of 1897. LEFT TO RIGHT, BACK ROW: *A.S. Drew, W.S. Medlicott, P.T. Maw (capt.), J.F. Wilkes, S.F.A.A. Hurt.* SEATED: *W.F.A. Rattigan, E.B.T. Studd, T.G.O. Cole, W.P. Robertson, E.M. Dowson.* ON GROUND: *H.J. Wyld.*

P.R. Johnson a future Cambridge University and Somerset player and Hon. W.G.S. Cadogan held out. There were six future blues playing in the two sides, three on each side of Pilkington, Johnson and Penn for Eton and Robertson, Wyld and Dowson for Harrow.

The three Harrow heroes of 1897 in a drawn fixture which was very much in Harrow's favour. LEFT TO RIGHT: *E.M. Dowson, W.P. Robertson, T.G.O. Cole.*

E.M. DOWSON'S MATCH

1898 July 8, 9   *Harrow won by 9 wickets*

Harrow	385	(W.S. Medlicott 87, W.F.A. Rattigan 69, A.S. Drew 59)
	53-1	
Eton	222	(C.H.B. Marsham 53, E.M. Dowson 6/54)
	215	(H.C. Pilkington 58)

Harrow won the toss and batted first on a very good wicket and kept Eton in the field till 70 minutes before the close on the first day. A score of 385 was a formidable one with W.S. Medlicott making 87, W.F.A. Rattigan 69, A.S. Drew 59 and the captain E.M. Dowson 47. Eton, after a long day in the field, lost 3 wickets for 55 before the close of the first day. Thereafter on the second day it was only a question of whether Eton could save the day. C.H.B. Marsham, the future Kent and Oxford captain, with 53 and G. Howard-Smith batting 10 on 49, failed to save Eton from following on. Dowson again bowled very well to take 6/54 in Eton's total of 222. In their second innings the other outstanding player in the match, H.C. Pilkington, the Eton captain, batted beautifully for his 58 and scored the first 39 runs out of a total of 40 before his opening partner Marsham bothered the scorer. Harrow bowled Eton out for 215 in the second innings and Harrow had the formality of scoring 53 to win which they did by 9 wickets but with only 10 minutes to spare at 7.20. The Harrow captain's contribution of 47 and 9 wickets in the match proved crucial.

The Harrow XI of 1898, including W.F.A. Rattigan, father of the playwright Terence Rattigan, which defeated a strong Eton XI by 9 wickets with only 10 minutes to spare. LEFT TO RIGHT, BACK ROW: G. Cookson, E.B.T. Studd, E.M. Dowson (capt.), J.F. Wilkes, W.S. Medlicott. SEATED: A.S. Drew, W.P. Robertson, W.F.A. Rattigan, H.J. Wyld, S.F.A.A. Hurt. ON GROUND: C.R. Kennaway.

The Eton XI of 1898, captained by H.C. Pilkington which lost by 9 wickets. LEFT TO RIGHT, BACK ROW: G. Howard Smith, P. Loraine, E.G. Martin, H.K. Longman. SEATED: W. Findlay, C.H.B. Marsham, H.C. Pilkington, Lord F. Scott, N.E.T. Bosanquet. ON GROUND: C.V. Fisher-Rowe, C.M. Macnaghten.

Harrow XI 1899. LEFT TO RIGHT BACK ROW: F.B. Wilson, E.G. M'Corquodale, H.J. Wyld, C.P. Goodden. E.W. Mann. SEATED: P.C.F. de Paravicini. G. Cookson, E.M. Dowson (capt.), K.M. Carlisle, W.D. Black. ON GROUND: H.S. Kaye.

E.M. DOWSON'S MATCH

1899 July 14, 15   *Match drawn*

Eton	274	(O.C.S. Gilliat 53, E.M. Dowson 6/108)
	264-2 dec.	(H.K. Longman 81, F.O. Grenfell 81, O.C.S. Gillliat 54 not out)
Harrow	283	(E.M. Dowson 87 not out)
	133-5	(H.J. Wyld 57)

Harrow were on paper the stronger side and the wicket played fast and true in dry weather throughout the two days. There were eight future blues in the two teams, four on each side, and Eton put up a good performance throughout the match. O.C.S. Gilliat batted well for his 53 and forties from three other players took Eton to 274 in their first innings. E.M. Dowson, the Harrow captain in his fifth year in the eleven, one of only six Harrovians in the history of the schools to have achieved this feat, again bowled admirably for his 6/108 and batted superbly for his 87 not out to gain Harrow a narrow first inning lead. He was well supported by forties from G. Cookson and E.W. Mann. Eton batted beautifully in their second innings with Longman, Grenfell and Gilliat to the fore. Gilliat with 107 in the game for once out had a particularly good match and Harrow were left 256 to win in 150 minutes. Harrow had little chance of winning and even less so when five wickets fell for 116 runs before Dowson and Kaye played out time. H.J. Wyld's 57 was crucial in Harrow saving the game. Eton's ground fielding and catching were infinitely superior to Harrow's which had been indifferent, especially in Eton's second innings. E.M. Dowson's 35 wickets in his five Eton and Harrow matches stands as the record number in this contest and is almost certain to remain so for all time.

1900
ETON v. HARROW, at Lord's, 13, 14 July
Harrow won by 1 wicket

1st Innings	ETON		2nd Innings	
A. A. Tod, c Eyre, b McCorquodale	33	b Carlisle . . .	96
H. K. Longman,* b Wilson	36	c and b Buxton .	40
D. J. Cassavetti, b Buxton	20	c McCorquodale, b Buxton . . .	1
J. Wormald, c Crake, b Wilson .	29	c Crake, b Kaye .	46
E. G. Whately, c Eyre, b Kaye .	13	b Kaye . . .	0
C. E. Lambert, c Bewicke, b Wilson	46	c Crake, b Buxton .	4
Lord Dalmeny, c Mann, b Kaye .	52	b Carlisle . . .	1
Hon. G. W. Lyttelton, c Kaye, b McCorquodale . . .	0	b Carlisle . . .	5
G. M. Buckston, c Lyon, b Wilson	45	b Carlisle . . .	4
W. Payne-Gallwey, b McCorquodale . . .	8	b Carlisle . . .	5
A. C. Bernard, not out . .	6	not out . . .	4
Lb 4, nb 2 . . .	6	Byes 7, lb 2, w 1, nb 2 . .	12
	294		218

1st Innings	HARROW		2nd Innings	
G. Cookson,* b Bernard . .	88	b Bernard. . .	19
E. W. Mann, c Dalmeny, b Payne-Gallwey . . .	4	c Dalmeny, b Whately	16
C. H. Eyre, c Cassavetti, b Payne-Gallwey . . .	9	b Whately . .	6
H. S. Kaye, b Bernard . .	60	b Whately . .	0
C. Bewicke, b Whately . .	42	lbw, b Whately .	0
K. M. Carlisle, c Lyttelton, b Whately . . .	16	lbw, b Bernard . .	24
F. B. Wilson, run out . .	79	run out . . .	24
E. G. McCorquodale, b Payne-Gallwey . . .	0	lbw, b Bernard . .	5
H. F. Lyon, b Bernard . .	25	c Lyttelton, b Whately	3
R. H. Crake, c Bernard, b Whately	47	not out . . .	21
A. Buxton, not out . .	1	not out . . .	1
Byes 10, lb 4, w 1, nb 2 .	17	Byes . . .	9
	388		128

HARROW BOWLING								
	O.	M.	R.	W.	O.	M.	R.	W.
McCorquodale	25	2	117	3	19	4	60	0
Buxton	17	1	60	1	17	3	64	3
Wilson	27	11	55	4	15	5	25	0
Carlisle	11	1	31	0	10·1	5	15	5
Kaye	9	1	20	2	12·4	4	42	2
Lyon	1	0	5	0				

ETON BOWLING								
	O.	M.	R.	W.	O.	M.	R.	W.
Bernard	27	4	93	3	24	4	60	3
P.-Gallwey	24	3	92	3				
Tod	15	1	45	0				
Whately	16·1	1	66	3	24·3	8	59	5
Lambert	5	0	34	0				
Dalmeny	4	0	24	0				
Lyttelton	2	0	13	0				
Longman	1	0	4	0				

1900 July 13, 14   *Harrow won by 1 wicket*

Eton	294	(Lord Dalmeny 52)
	218	(A.A. Tod 96, K.M. Carlisle 5/15)
Harrow	388	(G. Cookson 88, F.B. Wilson 79, H.S. Kaye 60)
	128-9	(E.G. Whately 5/59)

This was probably the most exciting match in the history of the series apart from Fowler's match of 1910. Both teams were regarded by the pundits as very strong with six future blues in the two sides, Harrow having the distinction of four, three of whom were captains of Cambridge in successive years. F.B. Wilson in 1904, E.W. Mann in 1905 and C.H. Eyre in 1906. H.K. Longman of Eton and G. Cookson of Harrow, the two captains, were both regarded as the outstanding schoolboy players of their year. Lord Dalmeny and G.M. Buckston hit hard for Eton and Harrow were lucky to get their opponents out for 294. In Harrow's innings of 388 Cookson batted beautifully for 88 until bowled by A.C. Bernard and was well supported by F.B. Wilson, 79, and H.S. Kaye, 60. At lunch on the second day, Eton were still two behind with eight wickets to fall. A draw seemed certain with Eton on 188/2. Then wickets fell at the same score and there followed a remarkable spell of bowling from K.M. Carlisle. A slow medium off-break

A thrilling match in 1900 between two quality sides resulted in a narrow win for Harrow by 1 wicket. Harrow (above) LEFT TO RIGHT, BACK ROW: *A. Buxton, K.M. Carlisle, G. Cookson (capt), C.H. Eyre, H.F. Lyon.* SEATED: *R.H. Crake, F.B. Wilson, E.W. Mann, H.S. Kaye, E.G. McCorquodale.* ON GROUND: *C. Bewicke. Eton (below)* LEFT TO RIGHT, BACK ROW: *E.G. Whately, Lord Dalmeny, Hon. G.W. Lyttelton, D.J. Cassavetti, G.M. Buckston.* SEATED: *C.E. Lambert, A.C. Bernard, H.K. Longman (capt), J. Wormald, A.A. Tod (absent - W.D. Barber and W.T. Payne-Gallwey).*

bowler he had the reputation of always being able to spin the ball but his length was usually the problem. On this occasion he found the spot at once and managed to use it. A.A. Tod, the Eton opener, was bowled on 96 by a ball which pitched outside the off stump, came quickly off the pitch and hit the leg stump. Carlisle finished with the remarkable figures of 5/15 off 61 balls, all bowled. Harrow appeared to have an easy task with only 125 to win. After Cookson was out for 19 with the total on 34, E.G. Whately, the Eton spinner, caused panic in the Harrow ranks with a hat-trick, capturing E.W. Mann, H.S. Kaye and C. Bewicke with successive balls. He had found the same spot which Carlisle had used so successfully and the whole game suddenly changed. C.H. Eyre was bowled on 55 by Whately and then Wilson joined Carlisle and made 24 in even time. A bad call by Carlisle saw Wilson run out by a couple of yards and then E.G. McCorquodale and H.F. Lyon were bowled out cheaply to leave Harrow on 104/8. Harrow then had 21 to win and it was anybody's game. R.H. Crake who had scored 47 in the first innings started off confidently and took the score to 118 before Carlisle was l.b.w. This brought the last man, A. Buxton, to the wicket. Crake made the match-winning runs with a pull off the middle stump to mid-wicket but not before the previous ball had beaten him all ends up and went a fraction over the top of the middle stump. Whately had bowled superbly to take 5/59 off 24.3 overs but Harrow had just made it.

1901 July 12, 13   *Harrow won by 10 wickets*

Eton	239	(F.W.B. Marsham 61)
	140	(A. Buxton 6/38)
Harrow	376	(R.E. Lambert 71, E.W. Mann 69)
	4-0	

Harrow had a pretty good side in 1901 with five future University blues under the captaincy of E.W. Mann, but Eton undoubtedly performed disappointingly after having beaten a strong Winchester side a fortnight earlier. Eton, under the captaincy of E.G. Whately, won the toss and batted first.

After the first five batsmen were out for 50, they achieved the respectability of 239 largely due to a partnership between F.W.B. Marsham, 61, and Whately, 45. Harrow had 100 up with only one man out and Mann played really well for his 69 and K.M. Carlisle less well for his 49. Harrow hit out boldly on Saturday morning with R.E. Lambert, 71, C. Bewicke, 48, and R.E.H. Baily, 45, to the fore. Whately who had bowled steadily on Friday was innocuous on Saturday and Harrow finished 137 ahead on first innings. Eton batted very poorly in their second innings, especially against A. Buxton, Harrow's leg-break bowler, who, although not usually a very consistent performer, found a good length and placed his field well. He finished with 6/38 off 26 overs, a fine achievement that left Eton with no chance. Harrow had only 4 runs to win the match which was hit off the first ball, appropriately enough off the Eton captain Whately.

The strong Harrow XI of 1901 which won by 10 wickets contained six members of the same house Elmfield, regarded by many as the best house at Harrow.

1902 July 11, 12   *Harrow won by 8 wickets*

Eton	72	(G.A. Phelips 4/10)
	228	(R.V. Buxton 74, K.I. Nichol 50,
		M.M.Carlisle 4/10)
Harrow	241	(F.J.V. Hopley 74, G.G.M. Bennett
		52 not out, G.A.C. Sandeman 5/73)
	60-2	

R.C. Gregson-Ellis, the Eton captain, decided to bat on a drying wicket which was to prove a major blunder. Eton duly paid the price by being bowled out before lunch for 72. Geoffrey MacLaren kept one end going for most of the innings and took 3/27 off 21 overs and G.A. Phelips supported him well with 4/10 off 14 overs. F.J.V. Hopley's 'Jessopian' hitting in his 74 and G.G.M. Bennett's sound 52 not out enabled Harrow to gain a substantial first innings lead of 169. Eton's R.V. Buxton, 74, and K.I. Nichols, 50, made a big dent in Harrow's lead but the rest of the Eton team failed to make any significant contribution and M.M. Carlisle cleaned up with 4/10 off eight overs. Harrow easily achieved their target of 60 with 8 wickets to spare, C.H. Eyre, the Harrow captain, contributing 32. This was his highest score in three appearances at Lord's.

The Harrow XI of 1902, captained by C.H. Eyre, which won for the third year running by 8 wickets. Eyre gained Cambridge blues from 1904/6, the last as captain, and was killed in 1915 during the Great War. LEFT TO RIGHT, BACK ROW: *G.G.M. Bennett, W.S. Bolton, C.H. Eyre, R. Gorell Barnes, A.H. Macan.* SEATED: *G.A. Phelips, R.E.H. Baily, G. MacLaren, M.M. Carlisle, F.J.V. Hopley.* ON GROUND: *F.R.R. Brooke.*

The Eton XI of 1903, which won by an overwhelming innings and 154 runs. LEFT TO RIGHT, BACK ROW: *E.N.S. Crankshaw, G. Aspinall, R.B. Scholfield, W.N. Tod.* SEATED: *A.F. Lambert, G.C. Campbell, K.I. Nicholl (capt), P.F.C. Williams, D.C. Boles.* ON GROUND: *C.E. Hatfeild, C.E. Lucas.*

C.E. HATFEILD'S MATCH

1903 July 10, 11   *Eton won by an innings and 154 runs*

Harrow	115	(C.E. Hatfeild 5/33)
	156	(R.E.H. Baily 61, C.E. Hatfeild 7/58)
Eton	425	(E.N.S. Crankshaw 100, P.F.C. Williams 89,
		W.N. Tod 59)

Eton reversed the trend of Harrow victories and draws with a vengeance. This was their first victory since 1893 and only their second since 1887 whilst Harrow had won eight times. Harrow won the toss and never recovered from a disastrous start. Six wickets went down for 78 and the innings folded to 115 in two hours. C.E. Hatfeild bowled extremely well from the pavilion end making the ball swing and turn just enough to beat the bat, and claimed 5/33 off 22 overs, all bowled. Eton went in with their tails up and on a very hot day ran up a big total of 425 before the close of play. E.N.S. Crankshaw, 100, P.R.C. Williams, 89, W.N. Tod, 59, and K.E. Nicholl, 44, all played fine knocks, hitting with great power. Harrow thus had no chance of winning on the second day and only a slight chance of saving it. Only the Harrow captain, R.E.H. Baily, 61, and W.S. Bolton, 37, played Hatfeild with any confidence and the innings collapsed feebly for 156. Eton, were thus worthy winners by a massive margin. Hatfeild again bowled magnificently in the Harrow second innings to take 7/58 and 12/91 in the match.

D.C. BOLES'S MATCH

1904 July 8, 9   *Eton won by an innings and 12 runs*

Harrow	109	(W.S. Bolton 64)
	285	(R.E.H. Baily 72, E.H. Crake 55, D.R. Brandt 53)
Eton	406	(D.C. Boles 183, W.N. Tod 84, H.C. Cumberbatch 53 not out, R.O. Morris 5/93)

Once again this was a very one-sided contest against a strong Eton side. Harrow were bowled out for a paltry 109 and only W.S. Bolton showed any real resistance with 64. C.E. Hatfeild with 3/25 off 16 overs and J.N. Horlick 3/30 were the main destroyers. Eton then proceeded to amass a very big total with D.C. Boles outstanding on 183, still the highest score in the history of the match. He plastered the weak Harrow bowling all over the ground and W.N. Tod, 84, H.C. Cumberbatch, 53 not out, both joined in. Harrow had an almost impossible task in the second innings but made much more of a fight of it. They eventually achieved respectability with a total of 285 but still went down by an innings and 12 runs. Hatfeild with 3/46 and Horlick 3/60 were again the main Eton bowlers.

The record scoring Etonian D.C. Boles (left) coming into lunch in the 1904 match with C.G.E. Farmer (right).

The 1904 Eton XI which won by an innings and 12 runs. LEFT TO RIGHT, BACK ROW: *J.J. Astor, H.C. Cumberbatch, C.E. Severne, C.G.E. Farmer.* SEATED: *C.E. Hatfeild, D.C. Boles, G.C. Campbell, W.N. Tod, J.N. Horlick.* ON GROUND: *N.C. Tufnell, A.G. Turner.*

1905 July 14, 15   *Match Drawn*

Harrow	199	(C.E. Hatfeild 5/45)
	293	(J.R. Reunert 92, C.V. Baker 57, W.N. Tod 5/103)
Eton	277	(W.N. Tod 77, R.O. Morris 5/82)
	136-9	

Harrow won the toss and batted first on a very good wicket and apart from D.R. Brandt, 45, and M.C. Bird, 36, were once again thwarted by C.E. Hatfeild with 5/45 off 24 overs, a very fine performance indeed on such a good track. W.N. Tod, the Eton captain, batted stylishly for his 77 in their reply to gain his side a first innings lead of 78. Harrow started badly in their second innings and lost their opener, Brandt, bowled by Tod for 0 but C.V. Baker, 57, and R.E. Eiloart, 32, made a good stand to put Harrow back in the game. Four wickets then fell quickly and it looked odds on that Eton would not have too many to make. J.R. Reunert, batting at No. 8. for Harrow, then turned the match on its head hitting all the Eton bowlers to the boundary with the utmost contempt. It was not till the last Harrow man had been in for some time that he was eventually out for a magnificent 92, so nearly a

```
                    1905
        ETON  v. HARROW, at Lord's, 14, 15 July
                  Match drawn
    1st Innings      HARROW            2nd Innings
D. R. Brandt, c H. S. Hatfeild,
  b Methuen  .    .    .    .  45  b Tod   .    .    .   0
M. C. Bird, lbw, b Chinnery  .  36  c Tufnell, b Methuen .  20
R. E. Eiloart, c Astor, b Methuen  16  c  Finch-Hatton,   b
                                         Chinnery  .    .  32
C. V. Baker, c Gold, b Methuen .  22  lbw, b Tod   .    .  57
E. H. Crake,* b C. E. Hatfeild .   2  b Methuen   .    .  11
C. Reunert, run out .    .    .  15  c Astor, b Tod  .    10
M. A. C. Halliday,  b  C. E.
  Hatfeild    .    .    .    .  11  c Astor, b Tod  .    29
J. Reunert, b C. E. Hatfeild  .  20  c  Finch-Hatton,   b
                                         Chinnery  .    .  92
G. Pike, b C. E. Hatfeild  .    .  12  b C. E. Hatfeild   .   2
R. O. Morris, not out   .    .   0  c Astor, b Tod  .    .   4
G. H. Watson, b C. E. Hatfeild .   0  not out   .    .    .  10
  Byes 11, lb 4, w 4, nb 1  .  20     Byes 9, lb 4, w 4,
                                         nb 9   .    .    .  26
                              ___                            ___
                              199                            293
    1st Innings       ETON            2nd Innings
H. S. Hatfeild, lbw, b Morris  .  11  run out   .    .    .  15
J. J. Astor, b J. Reunert  .    .  43  run out   .    .    .   5
E. F. Chinnery,  st Brandt,  b
  Morris  .    .    .    .    .  40  c Brandt, b J. Reunert   5
C. A. Gold, c Brandt, b Pike  .  25  b Pike    .    .    .  16
W. N. Tod,* c and b Morris  .  77  run out   .    .    .   9
B. J. Blackett, c Eiloart, b Morris  10  b Morris  .    .    .   0
Hon. D. G. Finch-Hatton, c Bird,
  b C. Reunert  .    .    .    .  10  c Pike, b C. Reunert  .  25
H. C. Dunell, lbw, b J. Reunert  10  b C. Reunert   .    .  13
C. E. Hatfeild, c Morris, b Pike .   4  c Brandt, b Watson  .   6
N. C. Tufnell, not out   .    .  16  not out   .    .    .  20
Hon. P. A. Methuen, c Eiloart,
  b Morris  .    .    .    .    .  10  not out   .    .    .   2
  Byes 10, lb 8, w 1, nb 2  .  21     Byes 15, lb 1, w 1,
                                         nb 3   .    .    .  20
                              ___                          ___
                              277                  For 9 wkts 136
```

ETON BOWLING	O.	M.	R.	W.	O.	M.	R.	W.
C. E. Hatfeild	23·3	8	45	5	24	2	80	1
Tod	17	2	51	0	23	3	105	5
Chinnery	8	1	45	1	6·2	1	22	2
Methuen	20	8	37	3	13	1	54	2
Finch-Hatton	2	1	1	0	1	0	8	0

HARROW BOWLING	O.	M.	R.	W.	O.	M.	R.	W.
Pike	25	7	72	2	19	13	18	1
Morris	31·4	7	82	5	18	6	29	1
J. Reunert	18	7	31	2	11	4	32	1
Watson	6	1	23	0	10	6	8	1
C. Reunert	8	1	29	1	17	8	25	2
Bird	4	0	19	0	3	0	3	0
Halliday					4	3	1	0

The Eton XI of 1905 which just succeeded in holding out for a draw. LEFT TO RIGHT, BACK ROW: *Hon. D.G. Finch-Hatton, O.H.C. Dunell, Hon. P.A. Methuen, C.A. Gold.* SEATED: *N.C. Tufnell, C.E. Hatfeild, W.N. Tod, J.J. Astor, E.F. Chinnery.* ON GROUND: *H.S. Hatfeild, B.J. Blackett.*

The Harrow XI of 1905 which deserved to win an exciting match. LEFT TO RIGHT, BACK ROW: *G.H. Watson, G.Pike, R.O. Morris, M.A.C. Halliday, C.V. Baker.* SEATED: *M.C. Bird, D.R. Brandt, E.H. Crake, R.E. Eiloart, J. Reunert.* ON GROUND: *C. Reunert.*

match-winning knock. At four o'clock on the last day Eton went in with 216 to win in 210 minutes. Eton started very cautiously and calamity followed with the two openers, H.S. Hatfeild and J.J. Astor both run out for very few runs and the same fate befell Tod. Six wickets had fallen for 56 and Harrow were very much in the driving seat. Eton's score of 96/8 with 90 minutes to play left them struggling to avoid defeat. N.C. Tufnell playing in his first match at Lord's held out for 55 minutes with C.E. Hatfeild before Hatfeild was caught behind the wicket off G.H. Watson, a very slow leg break bowler. P.A. Methuen the last Eton batsman came in with 35 minutes to play amidst extreme tension. Despite being clean bowled by Watson, the bail failed to come off and he and Tufnell managed to hold out and achieve a draw for Eton, still 80 runs short of the target.

P.J.S. PEARSON-GREGORY'S MATCH

1906 July 13, 14   *Eton won by 4 wickets*

Harrow	230	(E.H. Crake 68, R.E. Eiloart 54, C.E. Hatfeild 5/56)
	229	(M. Falcon 79)
Eton	365	(P.J.S. Pearson-Gregory 90, K.L. Gibson 77, C.A. Gold 57)
	96-6	(P.J.S. Pearson-Gregory 45)

Once again Harrow won the toss and batted first on a fast wicket. The Harrow captain, E.H. Crake, played well for his 68 with good support from RE. Eiloart, 54, and later H.E.C. Biederman, 32, but Harrow never got on top of the Eton attack and should have made a much greater score than 230. C.E. Hatfeild, the Eton captain, finished with 5/56 and H.M. Sprot's two wickets at the start with his slow leg-breaks to dismiss D.R. Brandt and M.C. Bird, Harrow's two best bats, was crucial for Eton. P.J.S. Pearson-Gregory and K.L. Gibson batted beautifully for Eton and completely mastered the Harrow attack. At the end of the first day Eton were very much on top and C.A. Gold, 57, and H.S. Hatfeild, 37, consolidated the position next morning, followed by a punishing innings from R.L. Benson, 33. At 12.45, when the last Eton wicket fell, they were 135 ahead on first innings. Harrow's second innings start was again marred by Sprot's two wickets in the first twenty minutes but M. Falcon, 79, and D.R. Brandt batted well until Brandt was bowled by D.G. Finch-Hatton the Eton pace-bowler. It was only when A.W.M.S. Griffin, coming in at No.10, hit out fiercely for 40 before being caught and bowled by C.E. Hatfeild that Harrow finally achieved the respectability of 229. Eton's target of 96 should have been a simple one but M.C. Bird and Eiloart bowled steadily on a dusty and wearing wicket to take three wickets each and give Eton a major fright. Pearson-Gregory once again batted with great skill for his 45 to add to his 90 in the first innings and was Eton's main match winner in their four wicket win.

M.C. BIRD'S MATCH

1907 July 12, 13   *Harrow won by 79 runs*

Harrow	222	(M.C. Bird 100 not out, R.B. Cowley 50)
	382-8 dec.	(M.C. Bird 131, R.B. Cowley 75, Hon.R. Anson 73 not out, G.H.G.M.Cartwright 5/114)
Eton	291	(R.L. Benson 74, T.L.C. Curtis 64 not out)
	234	(H.S.E. Bury 65)

M.C. Bird, the Harrow captain in his fourth year in the eleven, achieved the remarkable feat of a century in both innings, the only double centurion in the history of the match. This, added to his five wickets in the match opening the bowling and shrewd captaincy, made for a truly outstanding performance. He was well supported by R.B. Cowley, in both innings with 50 and 75, the grandson of R.J.P. Broughton, captain of Harrow in 1834/5 and R. Anson with 73 not out in the second innings after Eton had taken a first innings lead of 69. Eton were set to get 324 in 200 minutes and went after the runs. Bird and G.F. Earle with 4/60 to add to his 4/67 in the first innings bowled shrewdly for Harrow to take them to victory with 10 minutes to spare by 79 runs. This was quite a strong Eton side containing Hon. Lyonel Tennyson, the future Hampshire and England cricketer, G.H.H. Mulholland, captain of Cambridge in 1913, R.H. Twining, the Middlesex and Oxford captain, and G.H.G.M. Cartwright, the Eton opening bowler who took eight wickets in the match and became the long time secretary and President of Eton Ramblers. Harrow's debt to Morice Bird over four years was immense and never to be forgotten.

1907
ETON v. HARROW, at Lord's, 12, 13 July
Harrow won by 79 runs

HARROW

1st Innings		2nd Innings	
M. Falcon, b Cartwright	1	c Cartwright, b Sprot.	7
J. E. Mumm, b Sprot	16	b Cartwright	9
R. B. Cowley, b Hatfeild	50	c Gibson, b Cartwright	75
M. C. Bird,* not out	100	c Sprot, b Tennyson	131
Hon. R. Anson, b Hatfeild	0	not out	73
A. H. Lang, b Cartwright	19	c Sprot, b Cartwright	5
J. S. Royle, lbw, b Cartwright	1	c Benson, b Cartwright	5
J. V. Adair, b Curtis.	1	c Twining, b Tennyson	40
G. F. Earle, b Hatfeild	24	not out	20
F. M. Carlisle, c Naylor, b Hatfeild	3		
A. V. Makant, lbw, b Sprot	0	b Cartwright	0
Byes 5, lb 2	7	Byes 13, lb 1, w 1, nb 2	17
	222	For 8 wkts †	382

† Innings declared.

ETON

1st Innings		2nd Innings	
R. L. Benson, c Mumm, b Carlisle	74	b Falcon	43
R. H. Twining, c Lang, b Bird	5	c Lang, b Earle	30
K. L. Gibson, b Earle	28	b Bird	0
Hon. H. G. H. Mulholland, c Adair, b Carlisle	40	c Bird, b Falcon	25
H. S. E. Bury, b Earle	4	c Anson, b Carlisle	65
J. M. Naylor, b Bird.	33	c Anson, b Earle	17
T. L. C. Curtis, not out	64	run out	23
H. S. Hatfeild,* lbw, b Earle	21	c Lang, b Earle	8
H. M. Sprot, c Lang, b Falcon	5	c Lang, b Bird	4
G. H. M. Cartwright, c Lang, b Earle	9	not out	4
Hon. L. H. Tennyson, c Lang, b Bird	1	c Lang, b Earle	1
Byes 4, lb 2, nb 1	7	Byes 8, lb 5, w 1	14
	291		234

ETON BOWLING

	O.	M.	R.	W.	O.	M.	R.	W.
Cartwright	26	8	69	3	33	7	114	5
Tennyson	16	6	44	0	22	1	88	2
Sprot	7·4	2	15	2	34	3	102	1
Curtis	13	2	53	1	17	3	41	0
Hatfeild	9	3	34	4	6	1	17	0
Mulholland					1	0	3	0

HARROW BOWLING

	O.	M.	R.	W.	O.	M.	R.	W.
Bird	18·5	5	60	3	18	5	41	2
Makant	11	0	48	0	7	0	31	0
Carlisle	16	1	68	2	9	0	42	1
Earle	18	2	67	4	22·1	5	60	4
Anson	3	0	21	0	7	1	16	0
Falcon	3	1	20	1	11	3	30	2

G.E.V. CRUTCHLEY'S MATCH

1908 July 10, 11
Harrow won by 10 wickets

Harrow	210	(T.E. Lawson-Smith 79, G.E.V.Crutchley 74, G.H.G.M. Cartwright 5/44)
	14-0	
Eton	71	(G.E.V. Crutchley 4/13, Hon R. Anson 4/3 1)
	152	(G.E.V. Crutchley 4/33)

Both sides had played on hard wickets throughout the summer but the weather broke just before the match and the wicket became soft. The winning of the toss was crucial to Harrow and G.E.V. Crutchley, 74, batted beautifully for Harrow with wristy, graceful strokes, well supported by T.E. Lawson-Smith. Eton did not bowl particularly well apart from G.H.G.M. Cartwright, with his right-arm medium pace off cutters, who took 5/44. Eton came up to Lord's with a strong batting side used to true wickets but made a mess of things on a wicket which became more difficult as time went on. At the end of the first day curtailed by rain Eton had lost six wickets for 37. Crutchley bowled particularly well with his late swing to

The Harrow captain M.C. Bird's unique achievement of two centuries in the match had much to do with Harrow's win by 79 runs in 1907. LEFT TO RIGHT, BACK ROW: *J.V. Adair, G.F. Earle, M. Falcon, F.M.M. Carlisle, A.V. Makant.* SEATED: *Hon. R. Anson, A.H. Lang, M.C. Bird, J.S. Royle, J.E. Mumm.* ON GROUND: *R.B. Cowley.*

The 1908 Eton XI, which lost decisively by 10 wickets to Harrow. There were some fine cricketers in the side however particularly the Hon Lionel Tennyson, R.H. Twining, W.A. Worsley & G.H.M. Cartwright. 'Buns', second from left seated, was successful in his two appearances at Lord's with eight wickets in 1907 and 5/44 in Harrow's first innings of 1908, both Harrow wins. He was somewhat unlucky not to get an Oxford blue in 1909/10 but afterwards became the leading light of Eton Ramblers, was secretary from 1919/55 and President till his death in 1976. LEFT TO RIGHT, BACK ROW: *R.St.L. Fowler, G.W. Cattley, R.O.R. Kenyon-Slaney, W.A. Worsley.* SEATED: *Hon. L.H. Tennyson, G.H.G.M. Cartwright, R.L. Benson (capt), R.H. Twining, Hon. A. Windsor-Clive.* ON GROUND: *F.W.L. Gull, E.W.S. Foljambe.*

The Harrow XI of 1908, which won convincingly by 10 wickets mainly due to the outstanding all round performance of G.E.V. Crutchley, who scored 74 out of Harrow's 210 in their first innings and took 8/46 in the match.
LEFT TO RIGHT, BACK ROW: *V. Routledge, T.E. Lawson-Smith, A.V. Makant, W.L. Everard, G.E.V. Crutchley.* SEATED: *G.F. Earle, F.M.M. Carlisle, A.H. Lang, Hon. R. Anson, G.A. Laverton.* ON GROUND: *S.St.M. Delius.*

take 4/13 off 11 overs and Eton's last four wickets fell quickly on Saturday morning and Eton were all out for 71, following on 139 behind. Eton again batted badly in their second innings losing their first six wickets for 42 runs in 50 minutes. W.A. Worsley, the future Yorkshire captain, batting eight for Eton, scored 42 but the result was never in doubt and they were bowled out for 152, Harrow winning by 10 wickets. Crutchley had an outstanding match with his 74 on a dead wicket and 8/46 in the match.

1909 July 9, 10 — *Match Drawn*

Harrow	135	(R.O.R. Kenyon-Slaney 5/47, R. St. L. Fowler 4/46)
	76	(R.St.L. Fowler 7/33)
Eton	92	(G.E.V. Crutchley 4/15, W. Falcon 4/17)
	67-7	(G.E.V. Crutchley 3/18)

This was rather a strange contest as play was confined to the first day owing to a downpour on Friday night and further rain on Saturday which prevented any further play, but even so there was very nearly a result for Harrow on the Friday. The wicket was never really difficult but the batting was disappointing on both sides. In Harrow's first innings only T.L.G. Turnbull, 40, playing in only his second match and T.B. Wilson, 32, did themselves justice, although R.O.R. Kenyon-Slaney with 5/47 and R.St.L. Fowler, 4/46, bowled penetratively. Fowler's clever variations of spin with his cut and turn made him difficult to play. Eton's first innings was a procession with G.E.V. Crutchley taking 4/15, once again extremely effective helped by W. Falcon, 4/17. Harrow's second innings was just as disappointing although Fowler again bowled magnificently to take 11/79 in the match. Eton never looked like getting the 120 they needed to win, despite a fifth wicket partnership of 30, and they finished on 67/7 at 7 o'clock on the first day, 53 runs short of the target, a moral victory for Harrow.

The 1909 Eton XI, captained by R.H. Twining, which achieved a somewhat fortunate draw. Twining, Eton XI 1907/9, Oxford 1910/13 and Middlesex was a most useful wicket-keeper batsman who played spasmodically for Middlesex between 1910/28 and was afterward President of Middlesex and M.C.C. in 1964. W.A. Worsley, Eton XI 1908/9, captained Yorkshire in 1928/9 and was the father of the current Duchess of Kent. LEFT TO RIGHT, BACK ROW: *R.H. Lubbock, E.W.S. Foljambe, J. Kekewich, W.T. Birchenough.* SEATED: *W.A. Worsley, Hon. A. Windsor-Clive, R.H. Twining, R.St.L. Fowler, R.O.R. Kenyon-Slaney.* ON GROUND: *J.C. Hollins, Hon. V.D. Boscawen.*

The 1909 Harrow XI which was unlucky not to win a match restricted to one day, mainly due to some fine bowling once again from G.E.V. Crutchley.
LEFT TO RIGHT, BACK ROW: *W. Falcon, J.M. Hillyard, G.F. Earle, A.C. Straker, T.L.G. Turnbull.* SEATED: *G.W.V. Hopley, G.E.V. Crutchley, A.H. Lang (captain and an excellent wicket-keeper batsman), T.B. Wilson, T.O. Jameson.* ON GROUND: *K.G. de Jongh.*

The Eton XI of 1910, which achieved the most remarkable turnaround in the history of the match to win by nine runs.
LEFT TO RIGHT, BACK ROW: *A.B. Stock, D.G. Wigan, G.C.T. Giles (12thman), W.G.K. Boswell, K.A. Lister-Kaye.* SEATED: *C.W. Tufnell, R.H. Lubbock, R.St.L. Fowler (capt), W.T. Birchenough, A.I. Steel.* ON GROUND: *Hon. J.N. Manners, W.T.F. Holland.*

R.St.L. FOWLER'S MATCH

1910 July 8, 9   *Eton won by 9 runs*

Harrow	232	(J.M. Hillyard 62, T.B. Wilson 53, A.I. Steel 4/69)
	45	(R.St.L. Fowler 8/23)
Eton	67	
	219	(R.St.L. Fowler 64)

This was undoubtedly the most famous match in the history of the series and certainly the most extraordinary turnaround ever seen. Harrow succeeded in making what should have been an easy victory into an inglorious defeat. Harrow had proved themselves a good side all year and were unbeaten. G.F. Earle, the Harrow captain and J.M. Hillyard were two first-rate opening bowlers, especially Earle who was very quick, and Harrow also had competent batsmen and good fielders. They came to Lord's confident of victory but knew R.St.L. Fowler, the Eton captain, was the danger man. How right they were! Harrow batting first made the respectable total of 232 with J.M. Hillyard 62 and T.B. Wilson 53. Eton's first innings was a disaster, only Fowler with 21 out of a total of 67 showing fight, but he was caught off a rank long hop from T.O. Jameson and there the resistance ended. In

The strong Harrow XI of 1910 which was unlucky to be bowled out in their second innings by the legendary Fowler when the match was firmly in their grasp. G.F. Earle, the Harrow captain, was a hard hitting middle-order batsman for Somerset between 1922/31 and went on two M.C.C. tours to India in 1926/7 and Australia/New Zealand in 1929/30. LEFT TO RIGHT, BACK ROW: *W.T. Monckton, A.C. Straker, G.W.V. Hopley, O.B. Graham, C.H.B. Blount.*
SEATED: *T.O. Jameson, T.L.G. Turnbull, G.F. Earle (capt.), J.M. Hillyard, T.B. Wilson.* ON GROUND: *Hon. H.R.L.G. Alexander.*

the follow on three wickets fell for 20 before Fowler joined W.T. Birchenough who was then out off a remarkable catch at short-leg by T.L.O. Turnbull off Jameson for 29. Fowler continued to bat well until he was out for 64 but with nine wickets down Eton were only 4 runs ahead and looked doomed to easy defeat. J.N. Manners and W.G.K. Boswell, the last wicket pair, hit out at everything and put on 50 in very quick time. Boswell was finally bowled by Earle for 32 and Harrow were left with the relatively simple task of scoring 55 to win the match. What followed defied imagination. Fowler, bowling a perfect length just on or outside the off stump, had Harrow in real trouble from the start. Wilson was bowled for 0 in his first over, Hopley and Turnbull in the second. Earle, the Harrow captain, tried to make the runs quickly but was then caught in the slips for 13. Within half an hour Harrow had collapsed to 32/9 and Fowler had taken eight wickets, five clean bowled. The last pair, O.B. Graham and R.H.L.G. Alexander, strove to save the game, putting on 13 runs, but eventually Alexander was caught in the slips off A.I. Steel, to leave Eton winners by 9 runs. Fowler had taken 8/23 in the innings, and 12/113 in the match, and also top scored in both Eton innings with 21 and 64. Never was there a more joyous 'hoisting' when the Eton eleven returned to College later that evening.

1911 July 7, 8   *Eton won by 3 wickets*

Harrow	127	
	254	
Eton	270	(D.G. Wigan 79, GR.R. Colman 74)
	112-7	(C.W. Tufnell 54)

Eton came to Lord's with one of the best elevens they had produced for many a year and had only been beaten by a very strong M.C.C. side. Harrow were considered to be very much the underdogs. This appeared to be borne out

The Eton XI 1911 which won a closely fought contest by 3 wickets. LEFT TO RIGHT, BACK ROW: *Hon G.J.A. Mulholland, G.R.R. Colman, R.T. Staynforth (12th man) D.G. Wigan, Hon. G.F. Freeman-Thomas.* SEATED: *W.F.T. Holland, A.I. Steel, C.W. Tufnell (capt.) K.A. Lister-Kaye, W.G.K. Boswell.* ON GROUND: *E.F. Campbell, R.A. Persse.*

Harrow XI. 1911. LEFT TO RIGHT, BACK ROW: *H.G. Gregson, K.B. Morrison, T.B. Wilson, V.P. Trew, C.S. Wilson.* SEATED: *G.L. Jackson, C.H.B. Blount, T.L.G. Turnbull (capt.), J.H. Falcon, L.A. de Jongh.* ON GROUND: *E.T. Buller.*

Lord's Ground.

ETON v. HARROW.

FRIDAY & SATURDAY, JULY 8, 9, 1910. (Two-Day Match.)

HARROW.	First Innings.		Second Innings.	
1 T. O. Jameson	c Lubbock, b Fowler	5	b Fowler	2
2 T. B. Wilson	b Kaye	53	b Fowler	0
3 G. W. V. Hopley	b Fowler	35	b Fowler	0
4 T. L. G. Turnbull	l b w, b Fowler	2	c Boswell, b Fowler	0
5 G. F. Earle .... (Capt.)	c Wigan, b Steel	20	c Wigan, b Fowler	13
6 W. T. Monckton	c Lubbock, b Stock	20	b Fowler	0
7 J. M. Hillyard	st Lubbock, b Fowler	62	c Kaye, b Fowler	0
8 C. H. B. Blount	c Holland, b Steel	4	c and b Steel	5
9 A. C. Straker	c Holland, b Steel	5	b Fowler	1
10 O. B. Graham	c and b Steel	6	not out	7
11 Hon. R. H. L. G. Alexander	not out	0	c Holland, b Steel	8
	B 18, l-b 2, w , n-b l, 21		B 1, l-b , w , n-b , l	
	Total	232	Total	45

FALL OF THE WICKETS.

| 1-15 | 2-84 | 3-88 | 4-121 | 5-133 | 6-166 | 7-191 | 8-201 | 9-216 | 10-232 |
| 1-0 | 2-8 | 3-8 | 4-21 | 5-21 | 6-21 | 7-26 | 8-29 | 9-32 | 10-45 |

ANALYSIS OF BOWLING.

Name.	1st Innings.						2nd Innings.				
	O.	M.	R.	W.	Wd.	N-b.	O.	M.	R.	W.	Wd. N-b.
Fowler	37.3	9	90	4	...	...	10	2	23	8	... ...
Steel	31	11	88	4	...	...	6.4	0	12	2	... ...
Kaye	12	5	23	1	...	l	3	0	9	0	... ...
Stock	7	2	12	1	...	i	...	...	...	...	... ...
Boswell	8	4	17	0	...	...	...	...	...	...	... ...

ETON.	First Innings.		Second Innings.	
1 R. H. Lubbock	l b w, b Earle	9	c Straker, b Hillyard	9
2 C. W. Tufnell	b Hillyard	5	l b w, b Alexander	7
3 W. T. Birchenough	c Hopley, b Graham	5	c Turnbull, b Jameson	22
4 W. T. Holland	c Hopley, b Hillyard	2	st Monckton, b Alexander	5
5 R. St. L. Fowler ...... (Capt.)	c Graham, b Jameson	21	c Earle, b Hillyard	64
6 A. I. Steel	b Graham	0	c Hopley, b Hillyard	6
7 D. G. Wigan	c Turnbull, b Jameson	8	b Graham	16
8 A. B. Stock	l b w, b Alexander	2	l b w, b Earle	0
9 Hon. J. N. Manners	c Graham, b Alexander	4	not out	40
10 K. Lister Kaye	c Straker, b Alexander	0	c Jameson, b Earle	13
11 W. G. K. Boswell	not out	0	b Earle	32
	B 10, l-b , w l, n-b , 11		B 2, l-b , w 3, n-b , 5	
	Total	67	Total	219

FALL OF THE WICKETS.

| 1-16 | 2-16 | 3-26 | 4-34 | 5-36 | 6-57 | 7-62 | 8-64 | 9-66 | 10-67 |
| 1-12 | 2-19 | 3-41 | 4-47 | 5-86 | 6-107 | 7-164 | 8-166 | 9-169 | 10-219 |

ANALYSIS OF BOWLING.

Name.	1st Innings.						2nd Innings.				
	O.	M.	R.	W.	Wd.	N-b.	O.	M.	R.	W.	Wd. N-b.
Earle	...	...	...	...	...	...	17.3	3	67	3	i i
Hillyard	19	9	38	2	...	...	23	7	85	3	i ...
Graham	9	1	3	2	...	...	18	12	33	1	... ...
Jameson	9	...	7	2	...	...	9	1	26	1	... ...
Alexander	4.1	1	7	3	...	...	14	4	33	2	i i
Wilson	...	...	...	...	...	...	2	2	0	0	... ...

Umpires—Moss and Whiteside.   Scorers—G. G. Hearne and Newman.

ETON WON BY 9 RUNS.

The silk scorecard presented to Bob Fowler by M.C.C. for his outstanding performance at Lord's for Eton in 1910. He top scored in both innings with 21 and 64 and took 12/113 in the match with 8/23 in the dramatic second innings.

by Harrow's performance in the first innings when they were all out before lunch on the first day for 127, T.B. Wilson with a patient 46 being the only feature. A.I. Steel, the Eton slow bowler and son of the famous A.G. Steel the Lancashire and England cricketer, bowled well to take 4/41 off 14 overs. D.G. Wigan, 79, and G.R.R. Colman, 74, had a very productive partnership of 150 but two run outs left Eton with a lead of 143 although less than it probably should have been. Harrow made a better fist of things in the second innings with T.B. Wilson, 45, and H.G. Gregson, 33, putting the hundred up in just over 60 minutes. The main feature on the second morning was a stand of 86 between J.H. Falcon, 46, and K.B. Morrison, 42 batting No 9, to take Harrow to a total of 254. Eton were not taking anything for granted, especially after Fowler's matchí in 1910, but on a fast and easy track 112 was not a difficult task and although wickets kept falling the Eton captain C.W. Tufnell kept his head and hit the bad balls in a knock of 54. When he was finally run out the match was all but over, W.G.K. Boswell hitting the winning runs for a 3 wicket victory. Steel, the best bowler on the two sides, finished with 8/106 in the match.

1912 July 12, 13   *Eton won by 6 wickets*

Harrow	188	(J. Heathcoat-Amory 5/48)
	295	(C.H.B. Blount 137, U.W. Dickinson 59)
Eton	340	(D.G. Wigan 64, G.S. Rawstorne 64 not out, G.L. Davies 59)
	144-4	

Eton had a powerful batting side all – capable of making runs down to No.11, as they subsequently proved. J. Heathcoat-Amory, the Eton fast bowler who had performed well all summer, fully sustained his reputation to take 5/48 in Harrow's inadequate total of 188 on a hard, fast wicket in ideal conditions. D.G. Wigan continued his good form of the previous year with 64, well supported by G.S. Rawstorne, 64 not out, and G.L. Davies, 59, in Eton's total of 340 against the moderate Harrow bowling. C.H.B. Blount scored 137 in Harrow's second innings helped by a certain amount of good fortune with good support from U.W. Dickinson, 59, a patient left hander in their total of 295. One of the features of both Harrow innings was the large number of extras, 74 in total. Eton hit off the 144 runs they needed to win in very confident fashion and were worthy winners by 6 wickets. G.S.

Rawstorne finished on 26 not out to add to his undefeated 64 of the first innings.

The Eton XI of 1912 which gained a relatively easy victory by 6 wickets. LEFT TO RIGHT, BACK ROW: *C.S. Rawstorne, L.C. Leggat, D.R. Heaton (12th man), C.H.B. Chance, M.B.Burrows.* SEATED: *J. Heathcoat-Amory, E.F. Campbell, D.G. Wigan (capt), Hon. G.F. Freeman-Thomas, G.L. Davies.* ON GROUND: *R.E. Naylor, G. Hamilton-Fletcher.*

1913 July 11, 12   *Eton won by 9 wickets*

Harrow	75	(G.K. Dunning 4/17)
	324	(G. Wilson 173)
Eton	383	(F.J.L. Johnstone 94, J. Heathcoat-Amory 61)
	17-1	

Harrow put in to bat by the Eton captain J. Heathcoat-Amory on a very good wicket collapsed so badly that they were all out in 90 minutes before lunch on the first day. Eton went after the Harrow bowlers from the start of their innings with F.J.L. Johnstone, 94, and HeathcoatAmory, 61, the two opening bowlers, being particularly fierce. G. Wilson batted superbly for his 173 in the Harrow second innings, Harrow's highest score in the history of the match, with R.K. Makant, 46, giving good support, but it was nowhere near enough. Eton knocked off the 17 they needed to win with ease but not before G. Hamilton-Fletcher was run out for 0 to record his second duck of the match. The vagaries of cricket!

The strong Eton XI of 1913 once again overwhelmed Harrow by 9 wickets despite Geoffrey Wilson's 173, Harrow's highest score in the history of the match. This was their fourth victory in a row.
LEFT TO RIGHT, BACK ROW: *G.K. Dunning, L.C. Leggatt, G.D. Pope (12th man), T.E.G. Nugent, R.A.C. Foster.* SEATED: *G. Hamilton-Fletcher, M.B. Burrows, J. Heathcoat-Amory (capt), R.E. Naylor, G.S. Rawstorne.* ON GROUND: *F.J.L. Johnstone, R.C. Gull.*

The Eton XI of 1914. The last contest before the First World War. A much closer match but still the same result, an Eton win by 4 wickets - their fifth victory in a row. LEFT TO RIGHT, BACK ROW: *C.J. Hambro, F. Anson, O.W.H. Leese (12th man), F.C. Letts, C.S. Vane-Tempest.* SEATED: *R.A.C. Foster, F.J.L. Johnstone, G.S. Rawstorne (capt), T.E.G. Nugent, T.S.D'A Hankey.* ON GROUND: *B.R.F. Christy, R.D. Crossman.*

1914 July 10, 11   *Eton won by 4 wickets*

Harrow	232	(G. Wilson 65, G.R. Jackson 59 F.J.L. Johnstone 7/66)
	144	(G. Wilson 58, R.A.C. Foster 4/16)
Eton	146	
	233-6	(C.J. Hambro 77)

At the end of the first day, when Harrow led on the first innings by 86 runs, it looked as though they had a good chance of success but poor Harrow batting and a fine piece of bowling from R.A.C. Foster, 4/16, left Eton with 231 to win in 240 minutes. Harrow's bowling attack fought hard and though C.J. Hambro, 77, and R.D. Crossman 39, played with great skill, Eton were 188-6 and the match could have gone either way. However T.S.D.'A. Hankey and F. Anson played with great calmness and took Eton home to victory. F.J.L. Johnstone, the Eton hero of 1913, bowled particularly well in the Harrow first innings to take 7/66 and his fast swinging yorkers were particularly lethal, four of his seven victims being clean bowled. There was some fine catching on both sides and it was an enthralling match.

The Harrow XI of 1914 put up a good showing despite losing by 4 wickets. Led by Geoffrey Wilson, Harrow's highest scorer in the history of the match with 173 in 1913. The future Derbyshire captain Guy Jackson, front row, scored 59 in the first innings. LEFT TO RIGHT, BACK ROW: *W.K. McClintock, G.F. Marsden-Smedley, R.K. Makant, L.H.K. Gregson, N.A. Jessop.* SEATED: *H.N.L. Renton, G.A.I. Dury, G. Wilson (capt), R.G.D. de Uphaugh, G.R. Jackson.* ON GROUND: *R.A.B. Chancellor.*

THE GREAT WAR MATCHES

The wartime matches were not counted as part of the regular series between the two schools

SIXTH FORM GROUND, HARROW

1916 July 4   *Eton won by 88 runs*

Harrow	112	(C.H. Gibson 5/31)
Eton	200	(N.A. Jessopp 5/86)

In the first of the wartime matches Harrow were put in to bat on a slow wicket. Although losing G.M. Butler without scoring, Harrow progressed steadily to 96/3 with catches being dropped off H.G. Patterson and N.A. Jessopp before he had scored. At this point there was a startling collapse and Harrow lost their last seven wickets for 16 runs. The 15-year-old C.H. Gibson showed glimpses of the very fine cricketer he was to become when he took five wickets for four runs in three overs. The Eton captain, N.A. Pearson, also bowled well to take 3/16 off eight overs. Eton still had to fight hard for their runs and only passed Harrow's score with five wickets down. Pearson and W.N. Roe, 41, who put on 45 together, largely determined the result of the match and Eton then went on batting till the close.

G. Akroyd & Lord Kingsborough, son of the Earl of Kingston opening the batting for Eton in 1916, the first of the Great War matches which Eton won by 88 runs.

AGAR'S PLOUGH, ETON

1916 July 15   *Eton won by 27 runs*

Harrow	128	(E.O. Bleackley 42, N.A. Pearson 4/22)
Eton	155	(W.G.L.F. Lowndes 44, L.H.K. Gregson 4/58, N.A. Jessopp 4/62)

In the return match on their own ground Eton again prevailed in a much closer contest. Harrow were once again put in to bat and they made a poor start losing their first four wickets for 25 runs. A useful stand of 56 by E.O. Bleackley, 42, and N.S. Stevenson-Moore, led to some recovery by Harrow but only A.H.M. Jackson of the later batsman made much impression and the innings subsided to 128. Once again the Eton captain bowled well for his 4/22, well supported by B.S. Hill-Wood with 3/30 off 16 overs. Eton fared little better, losing their first four wickets for 36 runs. However a crucial partnership between W.G. Lowndes, 44, and T.E. Halsey of 63 largely determined the game, although Eton oniy headed the Harrow total with seven wickets down and were seven runs ahead when the ninth wicket fell. Harrow had bowled well, led by N.A. Jessopp and L.H.K. Gregson, but their fielding let them down at the crucial time.

The Eton XI of 1916 which won both home and away contests in the first of the Great War matches by 88 runs and 27 runs respectively. The young C.H. Gibson first emerged, here, and other good cricketers of note at this time were B.S. Hill-Wood (Derbyshire) and W.G.L.F. Lowndes (Oxford and Hampshire). LEFT TO RIGHT, BACK ROW: *C.J. Wilson, H.F. Wilkinson, Sir A. Baillie (12th man), R.H.R. Palmer, G. Akroyd.* SEATED: *W.N. Roe, T.E. Halsey, N.A. Pearson (capt), W.G.L.F. Lowndes, Lord Kingsborough.* ON GROUND: *C.H. Gibson, B.S.Hill-Wood.*

SIXTH FORM GROUND, HARROW

1917 June 26   *Eton won by 86 runs*

Harrow	154	(C.H. Gibson 4/32)
Eton 240/4 dec.		(C.J. Wilson 80, A.G. Barker 66 not out)

There was no doubt that Eton were much the stronger of the two sides and were heavy favourites after Harrow had lost to Winchester and Charterhouse the previous week. Harrow were put in to bat and when they were 100/4 a reasonable total seemed on the cards but once again the accuracy of Gibson, with 4/32 off 23 overs, and some good support bowling led to Harrow being all out for 154. When Eton lost their first two wickets for 23 it seemed they might have a fight on their hands but C.J. Wilson, 80, and A.G. Barker, a left hander, 66 not out, attacked the weak Harrow bowling with relish and victory was assured when Wilson was out on 147. When the Harrow target had been passed Eton batted on and some fierce hitting came from Wilson and T.A.L. Brocklebank, 47 not out, before the innings was declared. Eton had scored their 240 in 140 minutes and rain then prevented any further cricket.

AGAR'S PLOUGH, ETON

1917 July 14   *Eton won by 46 runs*

Eton	150	(A.H.M. Jackson 6/44)
Harow	104	(E.B.Hoare 5/38)

In the return contest Harrow put up a much better showing after they had put Eton in to bat. Eton found runs hard to score against some accurate bowling from A.H.M. Jackson, 6/44 off 20 overs, and W.A.R. Collins, 3/50 off 18 overs. Some excellent Harrow fielding was capped by J.J. Dalal who took three fine slip catches, two of them absolutely brilliant. W.R. de la C. Shirley's 37 in 90 minutes was in the circumstances a match winning innings. Once again the greater strength of Eton's bowling attack led them to victory and the first six Harrow wickets went down for 38 runs. Although it was E.B. Hoare who took most wickets, 5/38 off 24.3 overs, it was Gibson's great accuracy and control which was as much to do with Harrow's demise and he finished with 3/22 off 27 overs. Although there was some measure of recovery Harrow were still short of the Eton score and went down by 46 runs.

SIXTH FORM GROUND, HARROW

1918 June 25   *Eton won by 56 runs*

Harrow	142	(W.R. de la C.Shirley 6/31)
Eton	198	(W.A.R. Collins 4/74)

Although the scores would suggest that Eton's margin of victory was not so great, it was a misleading impression and Eton were undoubtedly much the better side. Harrow were unable to cope with the fast Eton opening bowler Shirley, and he bowled superbly to take 6/31 off 13 overs to bowl Harrow out for 142. He was also top scorer with 37 in Eton's total of 198. The game was continued with an ignominious performance by Harrow in their second innings when they were 79/9, only 23 runs ahead of Eton's single innings.

AGAR'S PLOUGH, ETON

1918 July 13   *Harrow won by 7 runs*

Harrow	98	(E.G. Hoyer-Millar 46, W.R.de la C. Shirley 5/16, A.C.Gore 4/35)
Eton	91	(W.A.R. Collins 5/38, J.R.M. Matson 4/28)

On a slow and heavy pitch Harrow achieved some consolation in the return fixture. It was a somewhat pyrrhic victory however as Eton were without two of their most dependable members, B.S. Hill-Wood and T.Bevan, due to influenza. Harrow were bowled out for 98 and would have been in even more dire straights without the fighting qualities of E.G. Hoyer-Millar, 46, who batted for 120 minutes. Once again Shirley bowled exceptionally well to take 5/16 off 6.3 overs, well supported by A.C. Gore 4/33 off 18 overs, and the Eton captain, C.H Gibson. Eton found batting just as difficult and lost wickets steadily to W.A.R. Collins, the Harrow captain, and J.R.M. Matson. So much so that they lost their ninth wicket at 74 and, despite a last wicket stand of 17 between C. Cokayne-Frith and A.C.C. Gore Harrow scraped home by 7 runs. Play continued for another two hours and Eton just had time to bowl Harrow out for 68 in their second innings before stumps were drawn. Collins finished with 5/38 off 18.2 overs and 4/28 off 17 overs.

RESUMPTION OF OFFICIAL MATCHES

W.W. HILL-WOOD and C.H. GIBSON'S MATCH

1919 July 11, 12   *Eton won by 202 runs*

Eton	176	(Hon D.F. Brand 50 not out)
	143-9 dec.	(G.O. Allen 69 not out)
Harrow	76	(C.H. Gibson 6/18, W.W. Hill-Wood 4/40)
	41	(W.W. Hill-Wood 7/29, C.H. Gibson 3/12)

The official series of matches continued at Lord's after the war years when one day matches were played at Eton and Harrow from 1916/18. Eton were particularly strong in batting with four future county and blues players in G.O. Allen, R. Aird, C.H. Gibson and W.W. Hill-Wood and a dangerous pair of opening bowlers in Gibson (fast) and Hill-Wood (spin). The match started sensationally when Allen was run out backing up off the third ball of the match without facing a ball. Eton lost wickets steadily until D.F. Brand joined Hill-Wood and took Eton to respectability, helped by a good tail-end knock from G.H.B. Fox who had been chosen for his fielding. R.O. Ramsey, 4/46, and W.S. Miles, 4/33, bowled well for Harrow in Eton's total of 176. Harrow batted badly in their first innings and only managed 76 with Gibson, 6/18, and Hill-Wood, 4/40, taking full advantage. In Eton's second innings of 143/9 only Allen's, 69 not out,

saved them from a much lower total helped by another useful tail-end knock from Fox. Rain delayed the start on the second day till 3 o'clock but Harrow were again routed by Hill-Wood, 7/29, and Gibson, 3/12. They managed to score only 41 in their second innings to lose the match by 202 runs, their sixth lowest score in the history of the match. Clem Gibson the captain's 9/30 in the match was an exceptional performance and at times he was unplayable.

W.W. HILL-WOOD'S MATCH

1920 July 9, 10   *Eton won by 9 wickets*

Harrow	85	(WW. Hill-Wood 4/23)
	174	(C.T. Bennett 64, Hon D.F. Brand 5/38)
Eton	141	(H.J. Enthoven 5/25)
	121-1	(W.W. Hill-Wood 75 not out, R.Aird 44 not out)

For the second year running Harrow batted badly and the Eton captain and hero of 1919, W.W.Hill-Wood took 4/23 in 18 overs in their total of 85 which would have been even less if the tail-enders P.H.Stewart-Brown, I.G.Collins and F.O.G.Lloyd had not struck out. Eton fared only slightly better in their first innings with only Hill-Wood 26 and the tail enders in a lively last wicket stand enabling

The immensely strong Eton XI of 1919 captained by Clem Gibson which demolished Harrow by 202 runs in the first post-war contest at Lord's. LEFT TO RIGHT: *J.P. Dewhurst, G.H.B. Fox, R. Aird, G.J. Yorke, W.R. Shirley, C.H. Gibson (capt), W.W. Hill-Wood, Hon. D.F. Brand, G.O.B. Allen, R.S. Chance, C.T.W. Mayo.*

The Eton XI of 1920 in traditional pose. LEFT TO RIGHT: *G. Cox, P.E. Lawrie, Hon. J.B. Coventry, G.O. Allen, Hon. D.F. Brand, W.W. Hill-Wood (capt), R. Aird, J.P. Dewhurst, C.T.W. Mayo, M.L. Hill, H. Surtees.*

them to reach 141. H.J. Enthoven bowled particularly well to take 5/25.

Harrow fared slightly better in their second innings with C.T. Bennett scoring 64 in a classy knock and the last wicket pair of I.G. Collins and F.O.G. Lloyd with 18 not out and 44 putting on 60 with attacking methods to reach 174. Eton batted brilliantly in their second innings to reach their winning target of 121 with ease after Gubby Allen was out early. Once again Hill-Wood distinguished himself with 75 not out partnered by R. Aird on 44 not out. Winchester had an exceptionally strong side in 1920 beating Harrow by 202 runs and Eton by 131 runs despite Gubby Allen taking 9/34 in their first innings.

1921 July 8, 9

P.E. LAWRIE'S MATCH
Eton won by 7 wickets

Harrow	64	(Hon. J.B. Coventry 4/9, G.O.Allen 3/24)
	295	(L.G. Crawley 103)
Eton	238	(P.E. Lawrie 53, H.J. Enthoven 6/56)
	125/3	(P.E. Lawrie 67 not out)

The standard of the combined sides was of the highest quality, the top four Harrow batsmen, C.T. Bennett, H.F. Bagnall, H.J. Enthoven and L.G. Crawley, all gained Cambridge blues, but Eton had the outstanding bowler in G.O. Allen the future Cambridge, Middlesex and England fast bowler and hard hitting middle-order batsman. Allen started the Harrow collapse by clean bowling Bennett, Enthoven and Crawley, Harrow's three best bats, and Hon. J.B. Coventry in a very steady spell had the remarkable analysis of 4/9 in just over 10 overs to bowl Harrow out for a paltry 64. Eton's innings featured a brief elegant

innings from D.F. Brand, a useful 53 from P.E. Lawrie and a sound knock from Allen, 34, to reach 238. Harrow's bowling attack was steady but lacking the variety of their opponents, although H.J. Enthoven again bowled well to take 6/56 off 19 overs. Harrow fared very much better in the second innings, Crawley playing in his usual attacking style and driving fiercely to score 103 with good support from Bennett, Enthoven, P.H. Stewart-Brown and G.C. Kinahan. A total of 295 for Harrow was not enough and Eton, after an early setback when three wickets fell cheaply, were guided home by another good innings from P.E. Lawrie, 67 not out, and G.K. Cox, 50 not out. As in 1920 one of the features of the match was the very fine wicket-keeping of M.L. Hill, the Eton keeper who impressed all, particularly with his takes on the leg side.

The Eton XI of 1921 which defeated a strong Harrow side by 7 wickets. LEFT TO RIGHT, BACK ROW: *T.C. Barber, P.E. Lawrie, E.W. Dawson (12th man), G.K. Cox, Lord Dunglass.* SEATED: *M.L. Hill, R. Aird, Hon. D.F. Brand, G.O. Allen, Hon. J.B. Coventry.* ON GROUND: *M.R. Bridgeman, H.D. Sheldon.*

The 1921 Harrow XI being led out by C.T.Bennett - Harrrow XI 1917/21 and Cambridge 1923 and 1925.
A most promising schoolboy cricketer who played for five years in the Harrow XI, but he failed to make his mark
in the first class game.

The Eton captain of 1921 the Hon. D.F. Brand.
Regarded as a gifted all rounder, he gave up first-
class cricket after his M.C.C. Tour to Australia
and New Zealand in 1922/3.

The Eton XI going out to field at Lord's in 1921 led by their captain, the Hon. D.F. Brand (later
Viscount Hampden), and Ronny Aird, Gubby Allen is right, in the background.

2d. Lord's Ground.

ETON v. HARROW.

FRIDAY (no play) & SATURDAY, JULY 14, 15, 1922. (2-Day Match.)

ETON.

		First Innings.		Second Innings.
1	E. W. Dawson	c S.-Brown, b Anderson	43	
2	J. E. Hurley	b Enthoven	3	
3	Lord Dunglass	b Anderson	66	
4	F. G. B. Arkwright	st S.-Brown, b Lloyd	22	
5	G. K. Cox ....Capt.	c Anderson, b Enthoven	13	
6	N. Llewelyn Davies	c K. E. Crawley, b Lloyd	13	
7	G. S. Incledon-Webber	b Enthoven	5	
8	W. P. Thursby	c Enthoven, b Lloyd	3	
9	R. G. M. Kennerley-Rumford	not out	4	
10	N. R. Barrett	b Enthoven	12	
11	M. R. Bridgeman	Innings closed.		

B l, l-b , w , n-b 5, 6   B , l-b , w , n-b ..

Total 190   Total ....

FALL OF THE WICKETS.

1-6   2-109   3-120   4-150   5-151   6-167   7-170   8-172   9-190   10-

1-   2-   3-   4-   5-   6-   7-   8-   9-   10-

ANALYSIS OF BOWLING.

Name.	1st Innings.						2nd Innings.				
	O.	M.	R.	W.	Wd.	N-b.	O.	M.	R.	W.	Wd. N-b.
Enthoven	27	7	50	4	...	5					
Anderson	21	4	56	2	...	...					
Powell	4	0	15	0	...	...					
Lloyd	13	2	53	3	...	...					
C. S. Crawley	4	0	10	0	...	...					

HARROW.

		First Innings.		Second Innings.
1	I. G. Collins	c and b Bridgeman	7	
2	H. J. Enthoven	b Bridgeman	14	
3	H. F. Bagnall	c Davies, b Bridgeman	0	
4	L. G. Crawley	l b w, b Dunglass	53	
5	P. H. Stewart-Brown	c Dawson, b Dunglass	11	
6	C. S. Crawley	not out	67	
7	R. H. Baucher ....Capt.	b Dunglass	1	
8	K. E. Crawley	c Bridgeman, b Dunglass	4	
9	M. Powell	b Cox	8	
10	F. O. G. Lloyd	l b w. b Cox	0	
11	W. E. Anderson	c K.-Rumford, b Cox	1	

B l1, l-b , 5, w 2 n-b , 18   B , l-b , w , n-b ,

Total 184   Total ....

FALL OF THE WICKETS.

1-24   2-24   3 49   4-78   5-105   6-108   7-116   8-170   9 174   10 184

1-   2-   3-   4-   5-   6-   7-   8-   9-   10-

ANALYSIS OF BOWLING.

Name.	1st Innings.						2nd Innings.				
	O.	M.	R.	W.	Wd.	N-b.	O.	M.	R.	W.	Wd. N-b.
Bridgeman	17	8	48	3	1	...					
Cox	13.3	5	45	3	...	...					
Dunglass	18	9	37	4	1	...					
Incledon-Webber	3	0	20	0	...	...					
Kennerley-Rumford	3	0	8	0	...	...					
Hurley	5	1	8	0	...	...					

Umpires—Moss and West.   Scorers—Burton and Wainwright.

The figures on the Scoring Board show the Batsmen in.

Luncheon at 1.30.   Play commences at 11 each day   Stumps drawn at 7 (half-an-hour extra if necessary

TEA INTERVAL—If there is a Tea Interval it will be not later than 5 o'clock but it will depend on the state of the game.

The Eton XI of 1922 captained by G.K. Cox, which drew a rain affected match. Lord Dunglass (later Lord Home of the Hirsel), Eton XI 1921/2 scored 66 and took 4/37 in this match. He played a few first-class games for Oxford and Middlesex and was of course a much respected Foreign Secretary in two terms of Government, as well as Prime Minister in 1963/4. He is the only Prime Minister to have played first-class cricket. LEFT TO RIGHT, BACK ROW: *F.G.B. Arkwright, R.G.M. Kennerley-Rumford, W.G. Worthington (12th man), G.S. Incledon-Webber, J.E. Hurley.* SEATED: *E.W. Dawson, Lord Dunglass, G.K. Cox (capt), M.R. Bridgeman, N. Llewelyn-Davies.* ON GROUND: *N.R. Barrett, W.P. Thursby.*

1922 July 14, 15   *Match Drawn*

Eton   190-9   (Lord Dunglass 66)

Harrow   184   (C.S. Crawley 67 not out, L.G. Crawley 53, Lord Dunglass 4/37)

This was a disappointing match especially from Harrow's point of view since they had one of their best elevens for a long while, although Eton had in E.W. Dawson, the future Cambridge, Leicestershire and England player, an outstanding cricketer. It rained heavily for most of the first day and cricket started at midday on the second morning and only then on a new wicket high up on the north side of the ground. The pitch was very wet, the outfield heavy and slow. Eton won the toss and decided to bat. After H.J. Enthoven, the Harrow captain, bowled the Eton opener, J.E. Hurley, early, E.W. Dawson, 43, and Lord Dunglass, 66, put on 103 for the second wicket. Enthoven continued to bowl well for an analysis of 4/50 and Eton declared at 190/9 leaving Harrow a token innings batting. The two Crawley's L.G., 53, and C.S., 67 not out, batted well for Harrow but there was little support otherwise in their total of 184. M.R. Bridgeman, the Eton captain bowled tidily for his 3/48 as did the future Prime Minister to take 4/37 off his 17 overs. The Eton fielding was particularly good but the match was rather a let down for Harrow in the circumstances.

1923 July 13, 14   *Match Drawn*

Harrow   322   (J.N.H. Foster 75, R.E.C. Butterworth 56)

       216-7   (P.H. Stewart-Brown 102 not out)

Eton   502   (E.W. Dawson 159, R.H. Cobbold 100, G.C. Newman 82 not out, W.P. Thursby 57)

Both sides had strong batting, particularly Eton, but were weak in bowling. Harrow did not help themselves by their three best batsmen being run out but a record last wicket stand of 92 between J.N.H. Foster, 75, and G.O. Brigstocke, 47 not out, eventually helped Harrow to the respectability of 322. Eton amassed the enormous score of 502, the record total for these matches. P.H. Stewart-Brown did not help the Harrow cause by dropping E.W. Dawson off a difficult catch first ball and he went on to score 159, G.C. Newman, 82 not out, and W.P. Thursby, 57, in Eton's formidable total aided by some poor Harrow bowling. Stewart-Brown made up for his catching lapse

This card does not necessarily include the fall of the last wicket.

2d. Lord's ⚜ Ground.

ETON v. HARROW.

FRIDAY & SATURDAY, JULY 13, 14, 1923. (Two-day Match.)

HARROW.

		First Innings.		Second Innings.	
1	K. E. Crawley	b Kennerley-Rumford ...	3	c and b Incledon-Webber	7
2	J. V. Hermon	run out	28	cK.-Rumford,bI.-Webber	0
3	J. C. Butterworth	run out	13	b Bridgeman	12
†4	P. H. Stewart Brown	run out	14	not out	102
5	R. E. C. Butterworth	c Hurley, K. Rumford ..	56	c Cobbold, b Bridgeman..	22
6	M. F. Kemp	c Thursby, b Bridgeman	22	cK.-Rumford,bI.-Webber	18
7	I. Bulloch	b Kennerley-Rumford ...	10	c I.-Webber, b Newman .	30
8	J. H. N. Foster	c Dawson, b I.-Webber...	75	c Cobbold, b Newman ...	10
9	F. M. Bucher	c Cobbold, b Bridgeman .	19	not out	2
10	C. M. Andreae	b Cobbold	22	
11	G. O. Brigstocke	not out	47	
		B 11, l-b 1, w , n-b 1,	13	B 11, l-b 1, w 1, n-b ,	13
		Total	322	Total	216

FALL OF THE WICKETS.

1-3   2-36   3 56   4-69   5-143   6-147   7-163   8-188   9-230   10 322
1-7   2-14   3-27   4 82   5-119   6-184   7 204   8-   9-   10-

ANALYSIS OF BOWLING.

Name.	1st Innings.					2nd Innings.				
	O.	M.	R.	W.	Wd. N-b	O.	M.	R.	W.	Wd. N-b
Bridgeman	22	5	60	2	... ...	24	9	53	2	... ...
Kennerley-Rumford	14	1	75	3	... ...	1	0	9	0	... ...
Bateson	12	5	23	0	... ...	5	1	16	0	... ...
Cobbold	17	2	71	1	1 ...	11	2	26	0	... ...
Incledon-Webber	6.4	2	29	1	... ...	21	3	77	3	1 ...
Newman	7	0	46	0	... ...	8	3	13	2	... ...
Hurley	1	0	5	0	... ...	5	1	9	0	... ...

ETON.

		First Innings.		Second Innings.
1	E. W. Dawson	b Brigstocke	159	
2	W. P. Thursby	cJ.Butterworth,bAndreae	57	
3	F. G. B. Arkwright	c and b Crawley	31	
*4	G. M. Crossman	st S.-Brown, b Crawley ..	4	
5	G. S. Incledon-Webber	b Crawley	8	
6	J. E. Hurley	c and b Bucher	1	
7	R. G. M. Kennerley-Rumford	c Foster, b Brigstocke	23	
8	R. H. Cobbold	c and b Andreae	100	
9	G. C. Newman	not out	82	
†10	M. R. Bridgeman	b Andreae	0	
11	D. M. Bateson	c S.-Brown, b Brigstocke	5	
		B 17, l-b 1, w 4, n-b 4,	32	B , l-b , w , n-b ,
		Total	502	Total

FALL OF THE WICKETS.

1-111   2-171   3-179   4-197   5-206   6-235   7 380   8-458   9-458   10 502
1-   2-   3-   4-   5-   6-   7-   8-   9-   10-

ANALYSIS OF BOWLING.

Name.	1st Innings.					2nd Innings.				
	O.	M.	R.	W.	Wd. N-b	O.	M.	R.	W.	Wd. N-b
Hermon	17	2	49	0	... ...					... ...
R. E. C Butterworth	26	2	93	0	1 ...					... ...
Andreae	30	4	102	3	... ...					... ...
Bucher	14	4	44	1	... ...					... ...
Brigstocke	27.4	3	82	3	3 3					... ...
Crawley	22	6	66	3	... ...					... ...
Stewart-Brown	4	0	23	0	... ...					... ...
Bulloch	1	0	11	0	... ...					... ...

Umpires—Moss and West.   Scorers—Wainwright and Attewell.

The figures on the Scoring Board show the Batsmen in.

Play commences at 11 each day.

Luncheon at 1.30.   † Captain.   * Wicket-keeper.   Stumps drawn at 7

—○—

TEA INTERVAL—If there is a Tea Interval it will be not later than 5 o'clock but it will depend on the state of the game.

The Eton XI of 1923 achieved the highest score in the history of the match, 502, with three centuries. Harrow managed to bat out a draw in their second innings. G.C. Newman (right, seated on the ground) Eton XI 1923, Oxford 1926/7 and Middlesex, scored 82 not out in the 1923 match, also playing for Middlesex between 1929/36 and averaging 29 in his 73 first-class matches. He was also a notable athlete and represented Oxford in the high jump and hurdles. LEFT TO RIGHT, BACK ROW: *G.M. Crossman, F.G.B. Arkwright, H.P.C. Hope (12th man), W.P. Thursby, D.M. Bateson.* SEATED: *G.S. Incledon-Webber, E.W. Dawson, M.R. Bridgeman (capt), J.E. Hurley, R.G.M. Kennerley-Rumford.* ON GROUND: *R.H. Cobbold, G.C. Newman.*

later by batting flawlessly for 102 not out in Harrow's second innings to save them from defeat and finish on 216/7. The Eton fielding had been very good all through the match but the bowling was a different story.

The record last wicket of 92 between J.H.N. Foster 75 and G.O. Brigstocke 47 not out for Harrow in 1923. Note the old grandstand built in 1867, demolished in the winter of 1929/30 to make way for another new grandstand which was itself replaced in 1998 by the current much acclaimed grandstand.

1924 July 11, 12   *Match Drawn*

Eton	290	(Lord Hyde 86, J.E. Tew 58, R.E.C. Butterworth 5/66)
	143-6 dec.	(J.E. Tew 54 not out)
Harrow	251	(J.C. Butterworth 72, D.M. Bateson 5/40)
	87-3	

Harrow were much criticised in this match for being far too defensive. Eton batting first on a very good wicket did not begin too well and half their wickets fell for 105 before Lord Hyde, 86, and J.E. Tew, 58, played excellently for their side and took the total to a satisfactory 290. Harrow paid the price for their lack of enterprise and what should have been a reasonable lead at one time turned into a deficit of 39, not helped by a collapse in the later order. The earlier Harrow batsmen took far too long to score their runs, J.C. Butterworth, the Harrow opener, for instance took 240 minutes to score 72. In the Eton second innings Tew once again came to the rescue and played well for his 54 not out partnered by G.W. Norris, 30 not out, to take Eton on to 143/6 leaving Harrow to score 183 to win in 120 minutes – a total Harrow made little attempt to score. Once again D.M. Bateson and R.H. Cobbold bowled steadily for Eton after their very long spells in the first innings – Bateson took 5/40 off 45 overs, and Cobbold 4/54 off 54 overs. Harrow finished a disappointing 87/3 at the close of play.

Eton XI 1925 captained by R.H. Cobbold. He scored a century in 1923 and gained a Cambridge blue in 1927. LEFT TO RIGHT, BACK ROW: *P.V.F. Cazalet, D. Lomax, D.W.A.W. Forbes (12th man) E.V. Hill, R.C.C. Whittaker.* SEATED: *L.R. Percival, H.P.C. Hope, R.H. Cobbold, Lord Hyde, H.P. Hunloke.* ON GROUND: *C.K. Hill-Wood, J.P.T. Boscawen.*

A.C. RAPHAEL'S MATCH
1925 July 10, 11   *Match Drawn*

Harrow	231	(E.W.E. Mann 61)
	235	(A.C. Raphael 54, R.C.C. Whittaker 6/64)
Eton	112	(A.C. Raphael 7/30)
	221-8	(J.P.T. Boscawen 66, R.H. Cobbold 65)

Harrow batted first on a very good Lord's wickets and did not make as many as they should have done although E.W.E. Mann, 61, and a useful last wicket stand of 53 between K.R.M. Carlisle, 45, and D. Wormald, the Harrow keeper, 23, helped them to 231. A.C. Raphael bowled really well for Harrow to take 7/30 in Eton's total of 112 and only R.H. Cobbold, the Eton captain with 42, played him with any confidence. Wormald distinguished himself by taking six catches behind the stumps, an innings record by a wicket-keeper in this series.

C.K. Hill-Wood, Eton XI 1925/6, Oxford 1928/30 and Derbyshire. A rare picture of Charlie Hill-Wood's most unusual bowling action. A left-arm medium fast bowler and useful lower-order batsman, he took 185 wickets in his three years for Oxford and Derbyshire, a creditable achievement. Business prevented him from playing serious cricket thereafter, a great loss to the game.

Controversially the Harrow captain, N.M. Ford, the future Oxford and Derbyshire cricketer, did not enforce the follow on and Harrow batted rather too slowly in the second innings, particularly A.C.L. Wills in his not out 44, although Raphael played a significant innings of 54. R.C.C. Whittaker bowled well for Eton to take 6/64 off 35 overs. Eton were left to get 355 to win in 180 minutes and when Eton lost 5 wickets in an hour for 75 runs and Lord Hyde was out for a duck for the second time in the match after his 86 the previous year it seemed Harrow would win. Cobbold again saved his side with 65 and J.P.T. Boscawen, 66, and Hunloke, 45, who put on 115, together saw Eton home to safety. Harrow were rather unlucky not to win and Eton finished on 221/8 at the close. Raphael had an excellent match for Harrow, with 10 wickets and 54 runs, which deserved to give Harrow the win they so desperately wanted.

The Eton XI of 1926, captained by H.P.C. Hope, the future Duke of Newcastle. LEFT TO RIGHT, BACK ROW: *M. de S.C. Ward, M.H. De Zoete, F.W.H. Loudon, (12th man), D.H. Studley-Herbert, D.W.A.W. Forbes.* SEATED: *R.C.C. Whittaker, P.V.F. Cazalet, H.P.C. Hope, D. Lomax, C.K. Hill-Wood.* ON GROUND: *L. Cecil, G.N. Capel-Cure.*

1926 July 9, 10   *Match Drawn*

Eton	312	(M.H. de Zoete 73)
	204-6 dec.	(P.V.F. Cazalet 100 not Out)
Harrow	376	(A.M. Crawley 87, K.R.M. Carlisle 62,
		C.M. Andreae 54, R.C.C.Whittaker 5/99)

Both teams appeared to be fairly strong in batting and experience, Eton with five old choices and Harrow six, but both displayed undue caution and only M.H. de Zoete after lunch on the first day played attacking cricket for Eton to score 73 but he tended to hit the ball too much in the air and was eventually out to a skyer at mid-off. Eton's innings lasted five hours and Harrow took almost exactly the same time to obtain the lead. A.M. Crawley, the outstanding player on the Harrow side, scored 83 out of 118 before stumps were drawn on the first day but was out early on the second day for 87. K.R.M. Carlisle, 62, C.M. Andreae, 54, D.A.M. Rome, 41, and G.E.M. Pennefather, 41, all batted well for Harrow but they went on too long, batting for 5¾ hours which rather ruined the match. R.C.C. Whittaker bowled a very accurate length for Eton throughout once again and finished with 5/99 off 56 overs with his slow, left arm deliveries. Eton went in at 4 o'clock on the second day and P.V.F. Cazalet scored 100 not out and batted with great aplomb for 160 minutes placing the ball beautifully rather than hitting it hard. Eton saved the game with ease but the feature of the match was the superb fielding of both sides.

The Harrow XI of 1926, captained by Neville Ford for the second year running, which was strong in batting and experience, but failed even so to achieve a result. A.M. Crawley, second from left in the front row, was the leading schoolboy batsman of the year. LEFT TO RIGHT, BACK ROW: *G.L. Raphael, R.H. Palmer (12th man) C.M. Andreae, W.O'B. Lindsay, A. Atha.* SEATED: *K.R.M. Carlisle, A.M. Crawley, N.M. Ford (capt), G.E.M. Pennefather, C. Clover-Brown.* ON GROUND: *D.A.M. Rome, J.F. Robinson.*

Robin Buckston keeping wicket during the 1927 match for Eton.

2d. Lord's ◈ Ground.

ETON v. HARROW.

FRIDAY & SATURDAY, JULY 8, 9, 1927. (Two-day Match.)

HARROW.	First Innings.		Second Innings.	
*1 W. O'B. Lindsay	c and b Whittaker	9	c Greville, b Whittaker	20
†2 C. Clover-Brown	c Capel Cure, b Ward	14	c and b Harbord	6
3 C. G. Shuckburgh	c and b Whittaker	46	c and b Ward	13
4 D. A. M. Rome	c Sheepshanks, b Harbord	4	c Gosling, b Capel-Cure	20
5 K. R. M. Carlisle	c Harbord, b Capel Cure	12	b Harbord	6
6 R. H. G. Calthorpe	b Whittaker	31	c Capel-Cure, b Whittaker	5
7 M. J. Lindsay	c Hazlerigg, b Ward	10	c Greville, b Whittaker	0
8 T. A. S. O. Mathieson	b Whittaker	4	b Whittaker	0
9 G. L. Raphael	b Whittaker	0	not out	20
10 R. H. Palmer	c Capel Cure, b Ward	2	b Ward	0
11 J. F. Robinson	not out	0	not out	3
	B 5, l-b 1, w , n-b 1,	7	b 17, l-b 3, w , n-b ,	20
	Total	139	Total	113

FALL OF THE WICKETS.

| 1 24 | 2 24 | 3 45 | 4 62 | 5 104 | 6 133 | 7 137 | 8 137 | 9 139 | 10 139 |
| 1 14 | 2 43 | 3 43 | 4 59 | 5 64 | 6 79 | 7 79 | 8 97 | 9 134 | 10 |

ANALYSIS OF BOWLING.

Name.	1st Innings.						2nd Innings.					
	O.	M.	R.	W.	Wd.	N b.	O.	M.	R.	W.	Wd.	N b.
Ward	37.2	20	34	3	...	1	47	30	27	2	...	...
Whittaker	41	20	47	5	...	...	43	22	51	4	...	...
Harbord	6	2	5	1	...	...	5	4	1	2	...	...
Capel Cure	10	2	32	1	...	...	4	2	8	1	...	...
Hubbard	2	0	14	0	...	...	4	2	6	0	...	...

ETON.	First Innings.		Second Innings.	
1 W. E. Harbord	b Palmer	18		
2 C. W. C. Packe	c Rome, b Robinson	18		
3 M. de S. C. Ward	c Palmer, b Rome	8		
4 R. C. Greville	c Mathieson, b Rome	42		
5 A. G. Hazelrigg	l b w, b Mathieson	7		
6 G. N. Capel-Cure	l b w, b Mathieson	65		
7 E. R. Sheepshanks	c M. J. Lindsay, b Raphael	30		
8 C. H. Gosling	st W. Lindsay, b Rome	1		
9 R. A. Hubbard	b Palmer	12		
†10 R. C. O. Whittaker	not out	3		
*11 R. H. R. Buckston	c Palmer, b Mathieson	3		
	B 11, l-b 3, w 2, n-b 2,	18	B , l-b , w , n-b ,	
	Total	225	Total	

FALL OF THE WICKETS.

| 1 26 | 2 48 | 3 50 | 4 88 | 5 107 | 6 183 | 7 191 | 8 213 | 9 217 | 10 225 |
| 1- | 2- | 3- | 4- | 5- | 6- | 7- | 8- | 9- | 10- |

ANALYSIS OF BOWLING.

Name.	1st Innings.						2nd Innings.					
	O.	M.	R.	W.	Wd.	N b.	O.	M.	R.	W.	Wd.	N t.
Palmer	21	3	56	2	1	1						
Raphael	22	7	66	1	1							
Robinson	14	3	33	1	...							
Rome	22	10	30	3	1	...						
Mathieson	14.4	6	22	3	...							

Umpires—King and Young. Scorers—Caldicott and Atfiel!

The figures on the Scoring Board show the Batsmen in

Play commences at 11 each day.

Luncheon at 1.30.   † Captain.   *Wicket-keeper.   Stumps drawn at 7 p.m. Half-an-hour extra if necessary.

1927 July 8, 9   *Match Drawn*

Harrow   139   (R.C.C. Whittaker 5/47)

113-9

Eton   225   (G.N. Capel-Cure 65)

The match was drawn for the sixth year in succession with Eton having much the better of the game throughout. Harrow were only 27 runs on with one wicket remaining when stumps were drawn at 7.15 on Saturday evening. It was fair to say that Harrow had much the worst of the wicket in both innings but still batted excruciatingly slowly, taking seven and a half hours to score their 252 runs in the match. The two Eton left-hand opening bowlers, M.deS.C. Ward and R.C.C. Whittaker, bowled a very good line and length, well supported by smart and accurate ground fielding. Whittaker, the Eton captain, put Harrow in to bat and C. Clover-Brown, the Harrow captain, and W.O.'B. Lindsay started so slowly that only 24 runs had come in 70 minutes with both batsmen out. Only C.G. Shuckburgh, 46 in nearly two hours, and R.H.A.G. Calthorpe, 31, made much of a showing and after lunch six Harrow wickets fell for 38 runs in 70 minutes. Whittaker finished with 5/45 and Ward 3/34 off 37.2 overs, a fine piece of bowling. Eton did not start off much better in improved conditions for batting and despite R.C. Greville batting well for 42 Eton were 107/5. However G.N. CapelCure, 65, and E.R. Sheepshanks, 30, produced the best partnership of the match and added 72 in 75 minutes to leave Eton 40 runs on at the end of the first day.

Rain fell heavily during Saturday morning, play not starting till one o'clock, and Harrow then disposed of the last five Eton wickets for 46 runs in 85 minutes. Harrow were then 86 behind with more than four hours left to play on a drying wicket against two redoubtable bowlers and con-

The Eton XI of 1927 who narrowly failed to win the match decisively. LEFT TO RIGHT, BACK ROW: *A.G. Hazlerigg, R.C. Greville, F.J.R. Coleridge (12th man), R.A. Hubbard, C.H. Gosling.* SEATED: *R.H.R. Buckston, M. de S.C. Ward, R.C.C. Whittaker (capt), G.N. Capel-Cure, W.E. Harbord.* ON GROUND: *E.R. Sheepshanks, C.W.C. Packe.*

centrated their energies on stubborn defence. They just succeeded in thwarting the two Eton bowlers, Whittaker taking 4/51 off 43 overs and Ward 2/27 off 47 overs. The two hours lost to rain on Saturday proved vital and Eton could rightly claim they were the moral victors.

1928 July 13, 14

I. AKERS-DOUGLAS'S MATCH
Eton won by 28 runs

Eton	126	(J.F. Robinson 4/13)
	415-8 dec.	(I. Akers-Douglas 158, E.R. Sheepshanks 69, I.A. de H. Lyle 67)
Harrow	234	(W.M. Welch 70 not out)
	279	(W.O.'B. Lindsay 68, A.G.Hazlerigg 5/73)

The match proved to be one of the most exciting and fluctuating for many years and was the first conclusive result for seven years. Most of the cricket was of a very high standard and Saturday in particular was enthralling. Eton who had batted well all season won the toss and decided to bat on a good track, but in two hours were dismissed for 126. C.G. Ford the Harrow opening bowler took the first three Eton wickets for 30 runs, then I. Akers-Douglas and C.H. Gosling put on 48 for the fourth wicket in 25 minutes, but when Akers-Douglas was dismissed for 42, stumped off the wicket-keeper's pads, the last six wickets fell for 49 runs in just over an hour. Harrow's first innings started poorly and six Harrow wickets went down for 100 runs. The seventh Harrow wicket should have fallen at 107 when W.M. Welch gave a difficult chance on eight but he then went on to score 70 not out with good support from W.M. Deas, 19, and A.R. Ramsay, 31. Harrow had thus secured a very useful lead of 108. R.H. Jelf bowled well for Eton, taking 4/48 off 23 overs with his slow left-arm bowling. At the start of Saturday's play Eton were still 64 in arrears with two wickets down and Harrow were marginal favourites to win. Two magnificent knocks from Akers-Douglas, 158, and E.R. Sheepshanks, the Eton captain, 69, turned the game in their favour. Akers-Douglas made runs all round the wicket, giving no discernable chances and hitting twenty-six fours in an innings lasting 195 minutes. Sheepshanks declared the Eton innings closed at 3.30 having hit 371 runs for the loss of six wickets in 220 minutes, a remarkable average of over 100 runs an hour. Harrow were thus set to get 308 runs in 210 minutes. Despite a fine second wicket partnership of 97 between W.O'B. Lindsay, 68, and W.M. Welch,

The victorious Eton XI of 1928 that won a fluctuating and exciting match by 28 runs - the first conclusive result for seven years. Ian Akers-Douglas's 158 was the feature of the match. LEFT TO RIGHT, BACK ROW: *Lord Dalmeny, J.H. Nevinson, Keville Davies (12th man), I.A. de H. Lyle, L. Monroe-Hinds.* SEATED: *I. Akers-Douglas, A.G. Hazlerigg, E.R. Sheepshanks (capt), C.H. Gosling, A.R.C. Southby.* ON GROUND: *R.H. Jelf, J.F.N. Mayhew.*

The fine Harrow XI of 1928 led by W.O'B. Lindsay which narrowly lost by 28 runs in a superb match. LEFT TO RIGHT, BACK ROW: *A.R. Ramsay, W.J. Riddell, G.L. Raphael, W.M. Deas, W.M. Welsh.* SEATED: *C.G.S. Shuckburgh, D.A.M. Rome, W.O'B. Lindsay (Capt.), J.F. Robinson, A.S. Lawrence.* ON GROUND: *C.G. Ford.*

2d. Lord's Ground.

ETON v. HARROW.

FRIDAY & SATURDAY, JULY 13, 14, 1928. (Two-day Match.)

ETON.

	First Innings.		Second Innings.	
1 A. G. Hazlerigg	c Lindsay, b Ford	8	c Riddell, b Ford	0
2 A. R. C. Southby	c Welch, b Ford	1	b Ford	2
3 I. Akers-Douglas	st Lindsay, b Rome	42	c Lindsay, b Ford	158
†4 E. R. Sheepshanks	b Ford	13	c Robinson, b Deas	69
5 C. H. Gosling	c and b Welch	22	c Rome, b Ford	41
6 I A. de H. Lyle	b Welch	9	b Ramsey	67
7 L Monroe-Hinds	c sub, b Robinson	5	lbw, b Robinson	6
*8 J. F. N. Mayhew	c Deas, b Robinson	7	not out	25
9 Hon. A. R. Primrose	c Raphael, b Robinson	4	c Riddell, b Robinson	19
10 R. H. Jelf	c sub, b Robinson	1	Innings closed.	
11 J. H. Nevinson	not out	1		
	B 7, l-b 1, w 5, n-b	13	B 24, l-b 3, w , n-b l	28
	Total	126	Total	415

FALL OF THE WICKETS.

1 5	2-14	3 30	4-87	5 104	6 111	7-119	8 120	9-125	10-126
1 0	2 7	3 156	4 245	5 297	6 316	7 378	8-415	9-	10-

ANALYSIS OF BOWLING.

Name.			1st Innings.						2nd Innings.				
	O.	M.	R.	W.	Wd	N-b.		O.	M.	R.	W.	Wd.	N-b.
Ford	10	4	28	3	4	...		17	2	58	4	...	...
Raphael	3	0	12	0	...	...		13	2	44	0	...	1
Lawrence	3	0	11	0	...	...		5	0	42	0	...	...
Deas	7	2	27	0	1	...		6	0	24	1	...	...
Rome	4	0	19	1	...	...		5	1	25	0	...	...
Welch	5	4	3	2	...	...		13	0	77	0	...	...
Robinson	5.1	1	13	4	...	...		24.1	3	108	2	...	...
Ramsay	...	...	...	...	...	...		2	0	9	1	...	...

HARROW.

	First Innings.		Second Innings.	
1 G. L. Raphael	b Jelf	17	run out	13
†*2 W. O'B. Lindsay	b Primrose	22	l b w, b Jelf	68
3 C. G. S. Shuckburgh	c Mayhew, b Jelg	22	b Hazlerigg	9
4 D. A. M. Rome	c Southby, b Hazlerigg	4	c Sheepshanks, b Hazlerigg	21
5 A. S. Lawrence	c Mayhew, b Primrose	12	l b w, b Nevinson	46
6 W. M. Welch	not out	70	st Mayhew, b Hazlerigg	36
7 W. J. Riddell	c Mayhew, b Nevinson	11	st Mayhew, b Hazlerigg	32
8 W. M. Deas	c Mayhew, b Jelf	19	st Mayhew, b Hazlerigg	4
9 A. R. Ramsay	l b w, b Jelf	31	b Nevinson	0
10 J. F. Robinson	b Hazlerigg	8	not out	1
11 C. G. Ford	b Primrose	11	b Nevinson	11
	B 2, l-b 2, w 2, n-b l	7	B 35, l-b 2, w , n-b l	38
	Total	234	Total	279

FALL OF THE WICKETS.

1 23	2 53	3 64	4-70	5-81	6 100	7-135	8-185	9-204	10-234
1-42	2 137	3-161	4 162	5 194	6-241	7-241	8-253	9 264	10 279

ANALYSIS OF BOWLING.

Name.			1st Innings.						2nd Innings.				
	O.	M.	R.	W.	Wd.	N-b.		O.	M.	R.	W.	Wd.	N-b
Nevinson	24	6	56	1	...	...		23	5	58	3	...	...
Primrose	18	6	56	3	2	1		8	1	31	0	...	...
Jelf	23	9	48	4	...	...		13	4	58	1	...	...
Hazlerigg	17	3	67	2	...	...		16.3	0	73	5	...	1
Lyle	...	...	...	...	...	...		3	0	18	0	...	...
Akers-Douglas	...	...	...	...	...	...		2	0	5	0	...	...

Umpires—Morton and King.   Scorers—Caldicott and Atfield.

The figures on the Scoring Board show the Batsmen in Play commences at 11 each day.

36, Eton had the advantage when Harrow were 5 wickets down and still had 114 to make with only 70 minutes left. However A.S. Lawrence, 46, and W.J. Riddell, 32, came together and put on 47 after a shaky start and at this juncture Harrow needed 67 runs to win in 40 minutes with five wickets in hand and an improbable Harrow victory seemed in sight. However the last four Harrow wickets fell for 38 runs and they were all out for 279 at 7.15, losing by the narrow margin of 28 runs. A.G. Hazlerigg, the Eton slow bowler, played a vital part taking 5/73 including three stumpings. The delightful weather ensured a big crowd on both days and more than 34,000 people paid for admission, both sides playing in the most sporting and attacking spirit. Akers-Douglas went on to score 111 for the Lord's Schools v. The Rest and 51 for the Public Schools v. The Army. Harrow were represented by Lindsay, Harrow's wicket-keeper captain who scored 715 runs in the season and averaged 55 as did D.A.M. Rome.

N.M.V. Rothschild (later Lord Rothschild), Harrow XI 1929 and Northants, here seen batting during the 1929 match. A stylish opening batsman, he gave the game up in 1932 to concentrate on his academic career at Cambridge. An eminent scientist and chairman of a Government 'think tank' on scientific policy in the 1970's. (See colour section)

K.F.H. HALE'S MATCH

1929 July 12, 13   *Match Drawn*

Eton	347	(Lord Dalmeny 65, L. Monroe-Hinds 61, J.C. Atkinson-Clark 57,C.G. Ford 5/50)
	264-5 dec.	(K.F.H. Hale 109, A.G.Hazlerigg 71)
Harrow	318	(D.A.M. Rome 74, J.H. Nevinson 6/85)
	108-6	(C.G.S. Shuckburgh 53)

Eton batting first on a very good wicket scored 347 runs in 240 minutes showing the typical Eton style. Fierce driving from L. Monroe-Hinds 61, J.C. Atkinson-Clark, 57, and Lord Dalmeny, 65 – especially Dalmeny with 12 fours in his knock – were the feature. Harrow still bowled steadily and also fielded well. C.G. Ford the Harrow opening bowler, used his 6ft 3 inches height to good effect and made the ball gather pace from the pitch taking a creditable 5/50 off his 22 overs. When Harrow went in N.M.V. Rothschild batted well for 43 out of 68 before he was dismissed and Harrow reached 107 without further loss. However a collapse followed. J.H. Nevinson, the Eton fast bowler, was largely responsible for the dismissal of half the Harrow side for 133, making the ball come quickly off the pitch from the pavilion end. D.A.M. Rome, the Harrow captain, batted sensibly for 150 minutes for his 74, well supported by C.H. Liddell, 43, to take Harrow within 29 runs of the Eton total. When Eton batted a second time A.G. Hazlerigg, the Eton captain, made 71 out of 94 in 80 minutes hitting 12 fours. K.F.H. Hale carried on the good work by scoring 109 after his 46 in the first innings. He and J.C. Atkinson-Clark, 42 not out, took advantage of two dropped catches to score at a very fast rate, putting on 154 in 70 minutes. Hale's 109 was completed in 75 minutes. When the declaration came at 5.05 Harrow were set 294 runs to win in 145 minutes. All chance of Harrow attaining the target disappeared almost at once when they lost two wickets quickly for six runs. Despite C.G. Shuckburgh's 53, batting in spirited fashion for Harrow, it was left to the captain Rome to save them from defeat. He was undefeated with 27 not out after batting 75 minutes and Harrow were left on 108/6, a long way short of the target. J.H. Nevinson, the Eton fast bowler, bowled well in both innings taking 6/85 off 30 overs in the first innings and 1/31 off 18 overs in the second. He took 44 wickets for Eton during the term. Rome, the Harrow captain, averaged over 69 in the season.

The 1929 Eton XI, captained by Arthur Hazlerigg, which had much the better of a drawn match. LEFT TO RIGHT, BACK ROW: *B.M.F. Franks, L. Monroe-Hinds, E. Ford (12th man), K.F.H. Hale, J.C. Atkinson-Clark.* SEATED: *Lord Dalmeny, A.R.C. Southby, A.G. Hazlerigg, J.H. Nevinson, R.H. Jelf.* ON GROUND: *A.M. Baerlein, A.W. Allen.*

A.G. PELHAM'S MATCH

1930 July 11, 12   *Eton won by 8 wickets*

Harrow	199	(J.M. Stow 64, A.G. Pelham 7/21)
	130	(A.G. Pelham 4/23)
Eton	284	(J.C. Atkinson-Clark 135)
	46-2	

Eton owed their convincing victory to an outstanding bowling performance from A.G. Pelham with 11/44 in the match and an attacking knock from J.C. Atkinson-Clark, 135, the twenty-seventh three-figure score obtained in these matches. The right-handed medium paced Pelham, with his variations of pace and movement off the seam with immaculate length, rarely bowled a bad ball throughout the match and had Harrow in all sorts of trouble. His figures in the first innings were 21 overs, 12 maidens, 21 runs, 7 wickets and in the second innings 21.1 overs, 12 maidens, 23 runs, 4 wickets and only J.M. Stow, 64, and W.M. Welch, 48, made any impression against him for Harrow. Only Atkinson-Clark batted convincingly for Eton and he took full advantage of a simple dropped catch at deep extra-cover on the second morning of the match to attack the Harrow bowling forcefully and Eton achieved a first innings lead of 85. Harrow made an even

A.G. Pelham, Eton XI 1930, Cambridge 1934 and Sussex. An outstanding bowling performance of 11/44 in the match led Eton to victory by 8 wickets (see colour section).

worse mess of things in the second innings and were all out for 130, with Pelham taking 4/23 and R. Page 4/28. Eton were left the simple task of scoring 46 to win which they did with ease and the game was over by a quarter to five with eight wickets to spare. T.M. Rattigan who had played in the 1929 side for Harrow was forbidden to play at Lord's due to an altercation with the authorities but had played in the Harrow eleven throughout the season until then which undoubtedly affected the morale of the side.

The Eton XI of 1930, which won by 8 wickets, taking the field led by their captain K.F.H. Hale, who scored 109 in the previous year's contest.
C.E.W. Sheepshanks   T.F. Hanbury   N.E.W. Baker
M.S. Gosling   J.N. Hogg
A.G. Pelham   R. Page   J.C. Atkinson-Clarke   K.F.H. Hale A.W. Allen
A.M. Baerlein (Wkt)

N.B. Clive (Harrow), bowled by A.G. Pelham for 8 during Harrow's 1st innings, one of his 11 victims in 1930. A.M. Baerlein is the Eton wicket-keeper.

N.S. HOTCHKIN and
N.E.W. BAKER'S MATCH

1931 July 10, 11   *Eton won by an innings and 16 runs*

Eton	431-5 dec.	(N.S. Hotchkin 153, A.W. Allen 112)
Harrow	245	(N.E.W. Baker 4/46)
	170	(M. Tindall 77, N.E.W. Baker 5/14)

Eton on an easy-paced wicket achieved the huge total of 431-5 dec., the second highest total in the history of the match after Eton's 502 in 1923, in 285 minutes with the openers N.S. Hotchkin scoring 153 and A.W. Allen 112 from some wayward Harrow bowling. Eton achieved the distinction of the largest total ever before lunch on the first day, 208-0, and the highest 1st wicket stand by some way and still the record with Allen also scoring a century before lunch. Eton were 368-3 at tea on the first day and the declaration duly came at 5.15. Harrow were bowled oul. for 245 in their first innings in 180 minutes and followed on 186 behind. At. 3.45 on Saturday, when Harrow in their second innings were 144-1, they had some hopes of saving the match but the superb medium-paced bowling of N.E.W. Baker once again ruined their hopes and they were all out by 5 o'clock for 170. Baker finished with

A.W. Allen on-driving during his innings of 112, and the record first wicket partnership of 208 before lunch for Eton with N.S. Hotchkin in 1931.

5/14 in the innings and 9/60 in the match. One of the features of the Harrow innings was the large number of extras, 46 in the first innings and 18 in the second. Eton were pretty strong with eight of the previous year's eleven whilst Harrow were comparatively inexperienced. Only M. Tindall in his first year for Harrow did himself justice and scored 77 out of 170 in the second innings.

1931 A.W. Allen and N.S. Hotchkin going out to bat in the record opening partnership of 208 for Eton before lunch on the first day.

The very strong Eton XI of 1931 which thrashed Harrow by an innings and 16 runs. LEFT TO RIGHT, BACK ROW: *T.F. Hanbury, J.H.L. Aubrey-Fletcher, J.H. Lane-Fox (12th man), M.S. Gosling, N.E.W. Baker.* SEATED: *J.N. Hogg, A.W. Allen, J.C. Atkinson-Clark (capt), A.M. Baerlein, R. Page.* ON GROUND: *N.S. Hotchkin, A.M. Hedley.*

2d. Lord's Ground

ETON v. HARROW.

FRIDAY & SATURDAY, JULY 10, 11, 1931. (Two-day Match.)

ETON.	First Innings.		Second Innings.
1 A. W. Allen	c Covington, b Clive	112	
2 N. S. Hotchkin	l b w, b Las Casas	153	
†3 J. C. Atkinson-Clark	b Benn, b Clive	19	
4 J. N. Hogg	c Clive, b Covington	17	
5 M. S. Gosing	not out	73	
8 A. M. Hedley	b Benn	15	
6 H. J. L. Aubrey-Fletcher			
7 A. M. Baerlein			
9 R. Page	...Innings closed.		
10 N. E. W. Baker			
11 T. F. Hanbury			
	B 25, l-b 11 w 4 n-b 2, 42		B , l-b , w , n-b
	Total	431	Total

FALL OF THE WICKETS.

| 1 208 | 2 238 | 3 296 | 4 299 | 5 431 | 6 | 7 | 8 | 9 | 10 |

ANALYSIS OF BOWLING.

Name.	O.	M.	R.	W.	Wd.	N-b.	O.	M.	R.	W.	Wd.	N-b.
Benn	65	2	28	1	3							
Clive	28	3	80	2	1							
Las Casas	20	1	78	1								
Hopton	17	1	84	0								
Covington	17	3	40	1								
Couper	18	1	54	0								
Blackmore	8	0	25	0	1							

HARROW.	First Innings.		Second Innings.	
1 K. Blackmore	c Hedley, b A. Fletcher	20	b Baker	53
2 M. Tindall	b Hanbury	16	c Baerlein, b Hogg	77
3 A. S. B. Gascoyne	b Page	22	c Baerlein, b Baker	6
†4 F. E. Covington	b Aubrey Fletcher	56	c A -Fletcher, b Hogg	7
5 G. F. D. Haslewood	c Allen, b Baker	10	l b w, b Baker	0
6 A. Benn	b Baker	12	b Baker	0
7 N. B. Clive	not out	44	c Atkinson-Clark, b Baker	4
8 D. O. Couper	c Page, b Baker	13	b Hanbury	1
9 E. J. E. de Las Casas	b Baker	2	b Hanbury	0
*10 W. E. Hennemann	l b w b Page	4	b Hanbury	4
11 J. G. Hopton	b Page	0	not out	0
	B 35, l-b 5, w 2, n-b 6, 45		B 10, l-b 4, w 4, n-b	18
	Total	245	Total	170

FALL OF THE WICKETS.

| 1-34 | 2 54 | 3-110 | 4-149 | 5 149 | 6 183 | 7-212 | 8-214 | 9-245 | 10 245 |
| 1-101 | 2-144 | 3 147 | 4-147 | 5 147 | 6 158 | 7 159 | 8-169 | 9-169 | 10 170 |

ANALYSIS OF BOWLING.

Name.	O.	M.	R.	W.	N-b.	O.	M.	R.	W.	Wd.	N-b.
Page	11.3	4	39	3	2	3	0	16	0		
Hanbury	11	3	48	1	4	11	2	36	3		
Aubrey-Fletcher	10	1	72	2		8	2	23	0		
Baker	10	2	46	4		14	3	14	6		
Hogg	8	5	8	0		13	7	32	2	4	
Atkinson-Clark	5	1	19	0		7	5	10	0		
Hotchkin	3	0	11	0		4	0	20	0		

Umpires—Hardstaff and Morton.

The figures on the Scoring Board show the batsmen who are in.

Play commences at 11 each day.

Luncheon at 1.30. †Captain. *Wicket-keeper.

Stumps drawn 7, half-an-hour extra on last day if necessary.

The scorecard of 1931 presented to Neil Hotchkin after his fine innings of 153 (see colour section).

2d. Lord's Ground

ETON v. HARROW.

FRIDAY & SATURDAY, JULY 8, 9, 1932. (Two-day Match.)

ETON.	First Innings.		Second Innings.	
1 N. S. Hotchkin	c Covington, b Simpson	109	b Simpson	96
2 A. N. A. Boyd	run out	32	c Gascoyne, b Borwick	18
3 J. O. J. Stevens	b Borwick	7	c Covington, b Borwick	44
4 G. H. Dixon	c Strange, b Borwick	44	l b w b Simpson	5
5 G. R. Branch	c Strange, b Borwick	16	b Borwick	10
6 H. J. Keigwin	b Clive	0		
*7 C. Bewicke	c Strange, b Borwick	7	not out	12
8 K. H. R. Johnson	not out	6	not out	20
†9 N. E. W. Baker	b Clive	2		
10 H. Birkbeck	b Clive	0		
11 J. Turnbull	b Clive	0		
	B 42, l-b 8, w 6, n-b 4, 60		B 1, l-b 4, w 1, n-b 5, 11	
	Total	283	Total	216

FALL OF THE WICKETS.

| 1 80 | 2-178 | 3-222 | 4 256 | 5 257 | 6-265 | 7-272 | 8-283 | 9 283 | 10 283 |
| 1-39 | 2 159 | 3 159 | 4-173 | 5-185 | 6- | 7- | 8- | 9- | 10- |

ANALYSIS OF BOWLING.

Name.	O.	M.	R.	W.	Wd.	N-b.	O.	M.	R.	W.	Wd.	N-b.
Strange	17	5	29	0	2	3	11	3	42	0		
Simpson	15	7	30	1		1	13	5	39	2		3
Covington	5	2	13	0			5	2	15	0		
Clive	10.3	10	54	4			19	4	44	0		2
Borwick	32	12	54	4	2		25	8	49	3	1	
Haslewood	4	0	10	0	2		3	0	5	0		
Peel							5	0	14	0		
Pulbrook							2	1	9	0		
Tindall							1	1	0	0		

HARROW.	First Innings.		Second Innings.
1 M. Tindall	c Keigwin, b Baker	21	
2 R. Pulbrook	c Boyd, b Birkbeck	104	
3 A. S. B. Gascoyne	c Dixon, b Hotchkin	50	
†4 F. E. Covington	c and b Turnbull	55	
5 G. F. D. Haslewood	b Turnbull	0	
6 N. B. Clive	b Turnbull	67	
7 P. M. Borwick	c Bewicke, b Turnbull	12	
8 E. B. Peel	b Baker	1	
9 S. Strange	c Bewicke, b Turnbull	0	
10 J. R. Simpson	not out	1	
*11 T. M. Heaton	c Branch, b Baker	19	
	B 7, l-b 1, w 5, n-b 6, 19		B , l-b , w , n-b
	Total	349	Total

FALL OF THE WICKETS.

| 1-38 | 2 98 | 7-212 | 4 212 | 5-292 | 6-320 | 7 329 | 8-329 | 9 329 | 10-349 |
| 1- | 2- | 3- | 4- | 5- | 6- | 7- | 8- | 9- | 10- |

ANALYSIS OF BOWLING.

Name.	O.	M.	R.	W.	Wd.	N-b.	O.	M.	R.	W.	Wd.	N-b.
Baker	35	5	119	3		1						
Turnbull	29	8	75	5	4							
Birkbeck	12	2	43	1		1						
Johnson	14	3	42	0								
Hotchkin	13	2	51	1	1							

Umpires—Morton and Hardstaff.

The figures on the Scoring Board indicate the batsmen who are in.

Play begins at 11 each day.

Luncheon at 1.30. †Captain. *Wicket-keeper.

Stumps drawn at 7, half-an-hour extra on last day if necessary.

TEA INTERVAL—During the Tea Interval (if any) spectators are earnestly requested to keep outside the ropes, which will be placed about 25 yards from the boundary line, and to pass off the ground when so directed by the Police. Otherwise delay cannot be avoided.

ETON WON THE TOSS

Scoreboard showing the record first wicket partnership of 208 before lunch on the first day. Hotchkin went on to score 153. Note the new grandstand completed in 1931.

N.S. HOTCHKIN'S MATCH

1932 July 8, 9   Match Drawn

Eton	283	(N.S. Hotchkin 109)
	216	(N.S. Hotchkin 96)
Harrow	349	(R. Pulbrook 104)

Harrow for the first time in years were favourites to win the match with only two of the previous Eton eleven left from 1931. Once again N.S. Hotchkin batted supremely to score 109 in the first innings and 96 in the second innings to save Eton from defeat. He was desperately close to equalling M.C. Bird's feat of 1907 as the only double centurion in this match and only a yorker from Simpson which took his stump out on 96 prevented it. R. Pulbrook, the Harrow left-handed rackets player, was the main feature for Harrow, scoring 104 out of a total of 349. Attendance on both days was at least 30,000 with 15,028 paying on Friday and 14,524 on Saturday.

1933 July 14, 15   *Match Drawn*

Harrow	237	(J.H. Pawle 96)
	146-6 dec.	
Eton	195	(N.S. Hotchkin 88)
	84-4	

M. Tindall, the Harrow captain, tried hard to force a result in this rather uneventful game. The two outstanding players on both sides, J.H. Pawle for Harrow and N.S. Hotchkin for Eton, both made significant contributions to their respective totals. Pawle with 96 out of 237 in the Harrow first innings and Hotchkin with 88 out of 195 in the Eton total. Harrow set Eton 189 to win in 95 minutes

Eton XI 1933 captained by Neil Hotchkin, the highest aggregate run getter in the history of the match. LEFT TO RIGHT, BACK ROW: *N.F. Turner, J.M. Brocklebank, A.B. Eccles (12th man), J.H. Cripps, R.C.L. Pilkington,* SEATED: *G.H. Dixon, C. Bewicke, N.B. Hotchkin, A.N.A. Boyd, J. Turnball,* ON THE GROUND: *A.T.G. Holmes, Hon. N.H. Villiers.*

(Left) M. TINDALL is the Captain of the Harrow Cricket XI. which met Eton at Lord's last week.

(Right) N. S. HOTCHKIN is the Captain of the Eton Cricket XI. which met Harrow in the 104th match at Lord's.

The two opposing captains in the drawn fixture of 1933. They were to join together at Cambridge, and both gained their blues in 1935.

J.H. Pawle, Harrow XI 1933/4, Cambridge 1936/7 and Essex. Scorer of 96 and 93 not out in 1933/34 respectively against Eton. He was a very fine striker of the ball, as befitted a top racquets player who was British amateur champion from 1946/9 and twice challenger for the world title. His career was interrupted by the war years and he afterwards played for Hertfordshire. After a long career as a stockbroker he became a successful artist in retirement.

but after losing wickets quickly including that of Hotchkin for 12, his only failure in five innings at Lord's, Eton put up the shutters and settled for a draw.

J.H. PAWLE'S MATCH

1934 July 13, 14   *Match Drawn*

Eton	306	(A.N.A. Boyd 100, Hon. N.H. Villiers 66)
	47-3	
Harrow	169	(J.P. Mann 5/66) (J.H. Pawle 93 not out)
	243-3 dec.	

Eton won the toss on a good batting wicket and scored 306 in 5¼ hours. A.N.A. Boyd, the Eton captain, distinguished himself with 100 but had three chances put down in his 3¼ hour innings, hitting nine fours. Harrow only made 169 in their first innings with J.P. Mann's slow leg-breaks taking 5/66. Harrow lost 10 wickets for 118 runs in 2hrs. 40 minutes and followed on 137 behind. J.H. Pawle, the Harrow captain, batted gloriously in the second innings to score 93 not out with one six and 14 fours and with G.A. Stogdon put on 130 in 80 minutes. He made the most unselfish and some would say foolhardy act of all, declaring 7 short of his century and setting Eton to get 107 runs in 50 minutes but after losing three quick wickets they declined to chase. Eton were never going to lose 10 wickets in 50 minutes but the glory of a century lasts forever.

P.M. STUDD'S MATCH

1935 July 12, 13   *Match Drawn*

Harrow	249	(W.R.Rees-Davies 5/66)
	204-6 dec.	(P.M.Studd 100 not out)
Eton	298	(M.A.C.P.Kaye 6/91)
	94-6	

An evenly matched contest resulted in another draw. W.R. Rees-Davies bowled well for Eton in the first innings and was compared favourably to another famous Eton fast bowler, Gubby Allen of Cambridge, Middlesex and England fame, in taking 5/66. Eton replied with 298 for a lead of 49 – M.A.C.P. Kaye bowling his medium pace shrewdly, making the new ball swing and producing a good off-cutter, took 6/91. Harrow replied with 204/6, the captain P.M. Studd playing particularly well to score

100 not out, and set Eton a target of 156 in 105 minutes. Eton after making a gallant attempt lost wickets quickly and finished on 94-6, 62 runs short. There was a strange incident in the Eton innings when F.G. Mann played a ball from A.H. Duveen just in front of him and when it came to rest tapped it back to save the wicket-keeper having to fetch it. The wicket-keeper however did not take the ball which hit the stumps and on appeal Mann was given out. Kaye finished with a match analysis of 9/125 for Harrow

---

.**1936** July 10, 11   *Match Drawn*

Harrow   180   (D.H. Macindoe 6/50)
Eton   26-0

In a severely rain affected match only one innings was completed. F.G. Mann, the Eton captain, put Harrow in and D.H. Macindoe with his late swing caused Harrow great problems and finished with 6/50. Only R.A.A Holt with 45 looked convincing. Eton were 26-0 when rain washed out the rest of play and could rightly say the moral victors.

	S.M.A. BANISTER'S MATCH	
1937 July 9, 10	*Eton won by 7 wickets*	
Harrow	118	(S.M.A. Banister 6/32)
	211-5 dec.	(R.A.A. Holt 111)
Eton	171	(J.F. Boughey 61, J.P. Mann 57)
	156-3	(F.F.T. Barnardo 62 not out)

In the first definite result since 1931 Eton were set 156 to get in 95 mins and won comfortably with 15 minutes to spare. There were several notable features in the match. S.M.A. Banister with his slow off-breaks bowled very well for Eton taking 6/32 off 16 overs, the last four in succes-

sive balls, a unique feat in this match. The Eton first innings started equally badly with five wickets falling for 39 runs. W. Stewart bowling his medium pace took 4/18 but after rain fell he had great difficulty with his foothold and bowled a series of loose overs. J.P. Mann, 57, and J.F. Boughey, 61., retrieved the situation for Eton and enabled them to reach 171, a lead of 53. R.A.A. Holt then played a brilliant knock for Harrow in their second innings to score 111, pulling, cutting and hooking superbly, enabling the Harrow captain to set a competitive declaration which Eton achieved with some ease, F.F.T. Barnardo scoring 62 not out and the Eton captain, J.P. Mann, unbeaten on 32.

The 1937 Eton XI led by J.P. Mann, brother of F.G. Eton achieved a fine win against the clock by 7 wickets. Left to right, back row: J.L. Darell, R.C. de Rougemont, M.W. Pragnell, (12th man), N.H. Huntingdon-Whiteley, P.A. Walker. Seated: J.F. Boughey, F.F.T. Barnado, J.P. Mann (capt), R.M. England, A.J.B. Marsham. On ground: D.L. Curling, S.M.A. Banister.

The losing Harrow XI 1937 led out by M.D. Watson. R.A.A. Holt who scored 111 is second on the left and W. Stewart (with sweater in hand) far left. C.J. Sage, Harrow XI 1936/8 is on the far right.

R.A.A. Holt, Harrow XI 1936/8. An exceptional schoolboy cricketer, he scored 111 in 1937 when Eton won by 7 wickets. He would have led Harrow to certain victory in 1938 had not rain intervened. The scorer of 910 runs in a Harrow season at an average of 101 in 1938 - a Harrow record, only beaten recently by Martin Walters in 2004. Holt played 5 matches for Sussex in 1938/9 and was also a fine racquets player winning both Amateur singles and doubles.

1938 July 8,9   *Match Drawn*

Eton	230	(P.H.Thomas 66)
	118	(J.F.Boughey 65, D.R. Hayward 5/40)
Harrow	200	(R.C. Fenwick 87)
	16-1	

Harrow were denied victory by the bad weather on both days. Play was postponed until 1 o'clock on the first day and on a slow wet wicket Eton, batting first, scored 230 with P.H Thomas top scoring on 66. Harrow replied with 200 and Eton were delighted to get R.A.A Holt, the Harrow captain and previous year's centurion, out for 22, but Fenwick, scoring 87 in two and a half hours, cutting, driving and hooking well, saved Harrow. Eton batted poorly in the second innings apart from J.F. Boughey who batted well for the second year running with 65 out of 118. D.R. Hayward with his slow right-arm leg-breaks and googlies took 5/40. Harrow needed 149 to win in 145 minutes but rain prevented any further play after 5.15 with Harrow on 16/1 robbed of near certain victory.

E. CRUTCHLEY'S MATCH

1939 July 14, 15   *Harrow won by 8 wickets*

Eton	268	
	156	
Harrow	294	(E. Crutchley 115, G.F. Anson 76)
	131-2	(A.O.L. Lithgow 67 not out, J.L. Paul 50)

Harrow at last achieved a famous victory, their first since 1908, largely due to the great batting of E. Crutchley and G.F. Anson, scions of two members of the last victorious Harrow eleven, G.E.V. Crutchley and the Hon R. Anson. Crutchley's knock in particular was magnificent, he scored 115 and batted in a stylish manner reminiscent of his father G.E.V., the Oxford and Middlesex cricketer. He played with easy grace, driving and forcing the ball off his legs, interspersed with the odd hook shot. D.F. Henley's medium pace turned the issue for Harrow in the second innings; he dismissed three Etonians in seven deliveries

This card does not necessarily include the fall of the last wicket

2d. Lord's ⟨CC⟩ Ground

ETON v. HARROW

FRIDAY & SATURDAY, JULY 14, 15, 1939. (Two-day Match)

ETON		First Innings				Second Innings	
1 B. D. Barton		b Byam	20		c P. Brune, b Henley	20	
2 D. W. J. Colman		b Boult	12		b Byam	5	
†*3 N. T. A. Fiennes		b Boult	26		c Anson, b Henley	43	
4 J. G. Mackeurtan		st Lithgow, b Cowley	14		c Byam, b Henley	0	
5 A. F. S. Coats		b Boustead	24		b Boustead	15	
6 Hon. R. F. Wood		c Crutchley, b Boult	26		b Byam	8	
7 M. B. Henderson		b Boult	45		b Byam	9	
8 J. A. Lyttelton		b Byam	5		c Boustead, b Cowley	22	
9 C. W. W. Gilmour		l b w, b Cowley	42		c Boustead, b Cowley	3	
10 I. McL. Pearson		st Lithgow, b Cowley	43		run out	13	
11 V. G. Wallace		not out	1		not out	7	
		B 6, l-b, w 2, n-b l,	9		B 9, l-b l, w l, n-b	11	
		Total	268		Total	156	

FALL OF THE WICKETS

1-34	2-36	3-53	4-92	5-102	6-162	7-181	8-185	9-263	10-268
1-6	2-66	3-66	4-69	5-79	6-95	7-116	8-135	9-137	10-156

ANALYSIS OF BOWLING

Name.	1st Innings				2nd Innings			
	O.	M.	R.	W. N.b.	O.	M.	R.	W. N.b.
Boult	23	2	69	4 2 1	12	2	38	0 1
Byam	20	3	82	2 ...	17	4	30	3 ...
Boustead	10	1	28	1 ...	11	1	35	1 ...
Cowley	5.5	1	26	3 ...	8.5	0	28	2 ...
Henley	11	1	54	0 ...	8	2	14	3 ...

HARROW		First Innings				Second Innings	
1 J. L. Paul		b Lyttelton	16		b Henderson	50	
2 R. M. Boustead		c Coats, b Wallace	11		b Wallace	4	
†*3 A. O. L. Lithgow		c Mackeurtan, b Wallace	16		not out	67	
4 E. Crutchley		c Barton, b Henderson	115		not out	9	
5 P. E. E. Prideaux-Brune		b Wallace	0				
6 G. F. Anson		b Lyttelton	76				
7 D. C. H. McLean		b Wallace	16				
8 L. E. W. Byam		run out	9				
9 D. F. Henley		c Mackeurtan, b Pearson	14				
10 J. L. Cowley		c Fiennes, b Wallace	4				
11 F. C. Boult		not out	1				
		B 15, l-b l, w, n-b	16		B , l-b , w , n-b l,	1	
		Total	294		Total	131	

FALL OF THE WICKETS

1-29	2-29	3-93	4-102	5-219	6-248	7-265	8-283	9-292	10-294
1-18	2-96	3-	4-	5-	6-	7-	8-	9-	10-

ANALYSIS OF BOWLING

Name.	1st Innings				2nd Innings			
	O.	M.	R.	W. N.b.	O.	M.	R.	W. N.b.
Henderson	16	3	46	1 ...	9	1	37	1 ...
Wallace	26.4	9	69	5 ...	10.4	1	35	1 ...
Lyttelton	21	5	72	2 ...	9	1	26	0 1
Pearson	10	0	58	1 ...	5	0	27	0 ...
Gilmour	7	0	33	0 ...	1	0	5	0 ...

Umpires—Hardstaff and Newman   Scorers—Mavins and Sweetland

The figures on the scoring board indicate the batsmen who are in.

Play begins at 11 each day

Luncheon at 1.30.   †Captain.   *Wicket-keeper.

Stumps drawn at 7, half-an-hour extra on last day if necessary.

TEA INTERVAL—During the Tea Interval (if any) spectators are earnestly requested to keep outside the ropes, which will be placed about 25 yards from the boundary line, and to pass off the ground when so directed by the Police. Otherwise delay cannot be avoided

ETON WON THE TOSS

The Harrow XI taking the field for Eton's 2nd innings 15th July 1939, led by A.O.L. Lithgow (wicket-keeper). LEFT TO RIGHT: *J.L. Cowley, J.L. Paul, R.M. Boustead, D.F. Henley, D.C.H. McLean, A.O.L. Lithgow, L.E.W. Byam, E. Crutchley (not seen), P.E.E. Prideaux-Brune and G.F. Anson.*

E. Crutchley, Harrow XI 1939/40. It was somewhat appropriate that his match-winning innings of 115 was the main reason why Harrow were victorious in 1939, their first win since 1908 when his father G.E.V. was the hero with both bat and ball. A wartime blue at Oxford, he was wounded in the war and afterwards became a stockbroker.

and finished with 3/14 off 8 overs in Eton's total of 156. Harrow needed 131 runs to win in 210 minutes. They were in the driving seat from the start and it was all over by 6 o'clock with J.L. Paul scoring 50 and A.O.L. Lithgow, the Harrow captain, appropriately finishing the match with three successive fours and 67 not out. Lithgow and Crutchley, who was batting with him at the end, were carried off the field by Harrow's delighted supporters into the pavilion. Not for over 20 years had the match ended with such frenzied scenes. Patsy Hendren, the old Middlesex and England cricketer and Harrow coach, appeared on the balcony, Harrow songs were sung and a free fight for top hats ensued. Before the 1920 match W.W. Hill-Wood, the Eton captain, issued a warning that any repetition of the fighting that followed the conclusion of the first game after the 1914-1918 Great War would lead to the match being taken away from Lord's. It was almost certain that a similar warning would have been issued had not the Second World War intervened in 1940.

1939 will be long remembered by Harrovians as Harrow's first victory at Lord's since 1908, winning by 8 wickets. A.O.L. Lithgow, Harrow's captain, chaired at the end. He himself had a great match, managing his team with good judgement, keeping wicket admirably and showing versatile stroke play in his second innings of 67 not out. He finished off the match with three consecutive drives to the boundary.

THE WARTIME MATCHES

As in the Great war these matches were not counted as part of the regular series between the two schools.

SIXTH FORM GROUND, HARROW

1940 July 13   *Eton won by 1 wicket*

Harrow	185	(A.V. Gibbs 7/43)
Eton	189-9	(D.W.J. Colman 92, A.F.S. Coats 61, D.F. Henley 6/38)

The first of the wartime matches produced an exciting win for the Etonians. After A.V. Gibbs, the Eton opening bowler, had bowled out Harrow for 185 with 7/43, a third-wicket partnership of 150 between the Eton captain, D.W.J. Colman, and A.F.S. Coats looked like producing an easy win. But D.F. Henley, the Harrow opening bowler, induced a sudden collapse and three wickets fell for one run and with the last pair at the wicket Eton still needed six runs to win. After an agonisingly long time they crept home to victory, Henley finishing with 6/38.

The first of the wartime matches in 1940 alternating at Eton and Harrow resulted in an exciting win for Eton by 1 wicket. D.F. Henley, seen bowling here for Harrow, played in the XI 1939/41, and gained Oxford blues for both cricket and golf in 1947, going on to play for Suffolk. His figures in this match were: 21 overs, 9 maidens, 38 runs, 6 wickets; he also scored 24 valuable runs.

C.M. WHEATLEY'S MATCH
AGAR'S PLOUGH, ETON

1941 July 12   *Eton won by 136 runs*

Eton	190	(D.W.S.S. Lane 51, C.M. Wheatley 48 not out)
Harrow	54	(C.M. Wheatley 7/31)

Eton were helped to an overwhelming win after the intervention of the weather. Shortly after the start of the Harrow innings a thunderstorm left the pitch very helpful to bowlers, particularly C.M. Wheatley, the Eton opening bowler, who with his medium pace in-swingers was at times virtually unplayable. He finished with 7/31 off 16 overs. He also performed well with the bat at No.9 scoring 48 not out.

T.H. MARSHALL'S MATCH
SIXTH FORM GROUND, HARROW

1942 July 11   *Eton won by 9 wickets*

Harrow	79	(T.H. Marshall 7/24)
Eton	80-1	

In an unwise decision Harrow decided to bat first on a damp wicket following overnight rain. Nevertheless Harrow batted very poorly, particularly against T.H. Marshall, the Eton slow left-arm bowler who kept a consistent length and turned the ball enough to beat the bat. He finished with 7/24 off 18.1 overs and only J. F. Leaf with the highest score of 22 in Harrow's 79 all out played with any confidence. Eton won the match shortly after 3 o'clock with the loss of one wicket with C.H.B. Pease 45 not out and the Eton captain, E.N.W Bramall, on 12 not out. Eton had a highly successful unbeaten season, very well captained by Bramall who went on to play for the Lord's Schools v. The Rest and the Public Schools v. Lord's XI. He was fortunate in having two very good bowlers to call on in C.M. Wheatley, who distinguished himself in the schools trial matches with 5/78 and 4/80, and Marshall, who was also highly effective as he showed in the Eton and Harrow match.

AGAR'S PLOUGH, ETON

1943 July 10   *Match Drawn*

Harrow   88-3   (Abandoned)

Cricket was played for two hours before lunch in a drizzle but no more play was possible after lunch due to the state of the ground, although play was not abandoned till after five o'clock. Harrow batted reasonably well during this period, especially C.C. Blount who hit freely for his 30. E.R. Flint, the Eton leg-break bowler, flighted the ball cleverly and accurately finishing with 2/7 off his nine overs.

A Fosh, the Harrow wicket-keeper, captained the side in the absence of I.N. Mitchell who was unable to play due to a poisoned finger. M.E.A. Keeling, the Eton opener, distinguished himself by scoring 129 and 65 for the Lord's Schools v. The Rest to provide the perfect finale to a fine season for him. W.G. Keighley, the Eton captain, also represented the Schools as did A. McCorquodale, the tall left-arm Harrow opening bowler who took 4/70 in the Rest's first innings and finished with 30 wickets at an average of 12.80 in 10 matches for Harrow.

SIXTH FORM GROUND, HARROW

1944 July 15   *Eton won by 5 wickets*

Harrow   147
Eton   151-5   (Hon. L.R. White 76)

Harrow batted extremely cautiously during their three-hour innings although only J.D.I. Stewart-Grey, the Eton opening bowler appeared difficult to play. J.F. Leaf batted two hours for his 47 with eight fours and only A. McCorquodale with 27 batted briskly in an undistinguished Harrow innings interrupted by rain for 90 minutes. Eton lost two wickets quickly for 8 runs but then the Hon. L.R. White took Eton close to victory with 76 out of 128 and C.R.D. Rudd finished it with 29 not out. Stewart-Grey, the Eton opening bowler, had the remarkable figures of 2/12 off 21 overs including 16 maidens. White who had a most successful season for Eton scoring 503 runs at an average of 50.30, achieved 102 for the Public Schools v. Lord's XI in a very fine innings including 15 fours. H.A. Hely-Hutchinson, the Eton captain, and A. McCorquodale, the Harrow opening bowler played for the Lord's XI.

AGAR'S PLOUGH, ETON

1945 July 14   *Eton won by 6 wickets*

Harrow   159   (M.N. Garnett 82 not out)
Eton   162-4   (P.D.S. Blake 76 not out)

M.N. Garnett, the Harrow captain, carried his bat through the Harrow innings lasting 210 minutes and saved his side from a far more ignominious defeat than would have otherwise been the case. He was given little support apart from P Wallis, 37, in a second wicket partnership of 58. B.P.M. Keeling with his cleverly flighted leg-breaks took 4/34 and at one point took four wickets in eight overs for nine runs. Eton lost three wickets for 44 runs but P.D.S. Blake, the Eton captain 76 not out, and W.N. Coles, 42, made it look easy, adding 88 together. Blake hit shots all round the wicket. and stayed till victory was achieved.

Summer 1945 Eton v. Harrow at Eton resulted in an easy win for Eton by 6 wickets. The two captains M.N. Garnett for Harrow with 82 not out and P.D.S. Blake 76 not out for Eton distinguished themselves.

RESUMPTION OF OFFICIAL MATCHES

The 1946 Eton XI. Eton had much the better of the first contest at Lord's after the War, and would probably have won if the Eton captain, C.R.D. Rudd, had enforced the follow-on. BACK ROW, LEFT TO RIGHT: *C.S. Woodall, J.A. Worsley, J.D. Lake, (12th man), Hon. P. Lindsay, F.P.E. Gardner.* SEATED: *R.A. Wellesley, R.G.T. Speer, C.R.D. Rudd, W.N. Coles, A.L. Cleland.* ON GROUND: *T. Hare, C.W.R. Byass.*

The 1946 Harrow XI captained by P. Wallis were fortunate to avoid defeat in a rather one sided contest. BACK ROW, LEFT TO RIGHT: *R.K.F.C. Treherne-Thomas, G.C. Hoyer-Millar, D.C. Prior, P.E. Reynard, P.S. Day.* SEATED: *J.R. Day, J.C. Thorne, P. Wallis (capt.) P.B. Blackwell, R.la.T. Colthurst.* ON GROUND: *T.J.M. Skinner.*

W.N. COLES' MATCH

1946 July 12, 13   *Match Drawn*

Eton	313-9 dec.	(W.N. Coles 107, C.R.D.Rudd 84)
	112-2 dec.	
Harrow	190	(Hon. P. Lindsay 4/31)
	191-7	

Official contests started again after the end of hostilities in 1945 and the Eton captain C.R.D. Rudd, younger son of the old Oxford and Olympic runner, after batting very well himself to score 84 with W.N. Coles, 107, aroused severe criticism by not enforcing the follow on when Harrow were 123 behind on first innings. Harrow were bowled out for 190 with H.P. Lindsay's fast medium bowling taking 4/31. Harrow set 236 to win in 220 minutes in their second innings went for the runs but eventually fell 45 short with seven wickets down.

1947 July 11, 12   *Match Drawn*

Harrow	266-5 dec.	(R.H. Thompson 71, R. La T. Colthurst 51)
	122-4	
Eton	394-8 dec.	(T. Hare 103, S.D.D. Sainsbury 100, C.W.R. Byass 78)

Eton enjoyed the best of the match with the batsmen overall having the advantage. Harrow batted first on a soft easy-paced wicket. D.C. Prior and R.H. Thompson opened the Harrow innings with a first wicket partnership of 68 and R. La T. Colthurst, who was badly missed at deep point on 55, went on to make 51 and helped Thompson put on 104 for the second wicket. T.J.M. Skinner hitting well to leg scored 49 not out and Harrow declared shortly after tea. Eton lost their first four wickets for 78 before S.D.D. Sainsbury and T. Hare put on 150 in 120 minutes on a very good wicket that made the Harrow attack look very ordinary on an outfield that had quickened up considerably. Eton overtook Harrow with five wickets down and C.W.R. Byass in a powerful innings of 78 in 90 minutes put Eton 128 ahead when the declaration came at teatime on the second day. Only 150 minutes of play remained and though Prior and Thompson put on 48 quickly together Harrow could only aim for a draw and the match finished tamely with Harrow six runs behind and four second innings wickets down. The game was watched on the Friday by the King and Queen, Princess Elizabeth, Princess Margaret and Prince Philip. The bowling on both sides was rather weak although the Harrow opening bowler, fifteen-year-old R.A. Jacques, performed well in his first year in the Harrow XI, taking 28 wickets during the term at 16.71 per wicket.

The Eton XI of 1948 captained by T. Hare who scored 103 well supported by S.D.D. Sainsbury 100 and C.W.R. Byass 78. The declaration was a little late otherwise Eton would have won. Harrow were captained for the second year running by G.C. Hoyer-Millar, the future Oxford Univ. & Scottish rugby international. LEFT TO RIGHT, BACK ROW: *A.S. Aird, I.R. Lomax, D.H. Clegg, C.E.A. Hambro, J.M.N. Rankin.* SEATED: *C.A. Impey, J.D.K. Barnes, T. Hare (capt.), A.L. Lutyens, S.D.D. Sainsbury.* ON GROUND: *J.A. Bailey, J.S. Guthrie.*

S.D.D. Sainsbury, Eton XI 1947/8, on his way to a fine century during Eton's first innings.

1948 July 9, 10   *Match Drawn*

Eton	205	
	205-8 dec.	(R.G. Marlar 5/78)
Harrow	160	
	209-9	(A.S. Day 66)

In the third contest at Lord's since the end of the war a fluctuating match resulted in an exciting finish with Harrow 42 runs short with one wicket in hand when time was called at 7 o'clock. Eton gained a first innings lead of 45 which seemed unlikely at one stage after Harrow's first wicket stand of 66, T.A.M. Pigott, the father of A.C.S., scoring 41 with some fine strokes. Poor light and cold

conditions on the Friday helped neither side, particularly the fielders and several important catches were dropped. J,D.K. Barnes and C.E.A. Hambro opened well for Eton in the second innings putting on 73 for the first wicket but R.G. Marlar, the right-handed Harrow slow bowler making the ball turn both ways, had Eton in some bother and finished with 5/78 off 29 overs Eton declared at three o'clock in their second innings on the same total as in the first innings. Harrow needing 291 to win in 210 minutes changed their batting order and quickly lost G.S.O. Colthurst and J.D. Thicknesse. A.S. Day, the son of S.H. Day the Cambridge and Kent cricketer, batted very well for his 66 with Pigott, 36, and A.A. Persse, 28, but finished well short. The last two Harrow batsmen, F.G.F. Richardson and R.E.C. Parkes, held out for the remaining five minutes to save the match. Both R.G. Marlar with 40 wickets and R.A. Jacques with 34 wickets bowled well for Harrow throughout the season.

The Eton XI of 1949, which triumphed by 7 wickets, led by J.A. Bailey. Other fine cricketers included I.R. Lomax to the right of the captain, and the 16-year-old Ingleby-Mackenzie, back row right. Alistair Aird, former private secretary to the late Queen Mother, is seated to Lomax's right.

1949 July 8, 9   *Eton won by 7 wickets*

Harrow	128	(M.G.C. Jeffreys 4/7)
	151	(J.S. Guthrie 6/56)
Eton	176	(R.G. Marlar 6/60)
	107-3	

In a low scoring match Eton gained their first victory since 1937, not counting the war years. The weather had a considerable part in this as dull morning conditions tended to give the bowlers help and there was awkward bounce with the odd ball keeping low. Harrow had a disastrous start from which they never really recovered when M.G.C Jeffreys, a fast right-arm bowler, took the first three wickets in 19 balls for no runs. Harrow had lost their first five wickets for 37 runs before the Harrow captain, A.S. Day in his fifth year in the eleven, made 29. R.G. Marlar, the Harrow slow right-arm bowler, hit J.S. Guthrie, the Eton slow bowler, for 20 in an over and with M. Kok, a South African pace bowler, put on 48 for the ninth wicket to take Harrow up to 128 with Marlar scoring 45 in 35 minutes. After Eton's good first-wicket partnership of 51 between D.H. Clegg and R.A. Brooks there was a considerable collapse to Marlar who troubled all the batsmen to take 6/60 in 19.2 overs. Eton's lead of 48 was much less than it should have been and M. Kok accelerated the collapse by bowling three Etonians in an over. Once again Harrow were put on the rack by the accuracy of Jeffreys with 1/15 off 10 overs to follow his 4/7 off 10 overs in the first innings and only a rearguard action by P.H. Ryan, 38, and M. Kok, 28 not out, enabled Harrow to reach 151. Eton had the relatively easy task of scoring 104 for victory but after losing two quick wickets I.R. Lomax,

31, and then M.D. Sellar, 32, not out and the 15-year-old A.C.D.Ingleby-Mackenzie, 24 not out, wrapped up an easy victory for Eton by 3.30. Marlar had an outstanding schools season for Harrow with 50 wickets at an average of 13.74 per wicket.

1950 July 14, 15   *Match Drawn*

Eton	237	(N.C. Wadham 87 R.A.Jacques 4/56)
	147	
Harrow	282-7 dec.	(A. Falcon 85 not out, W.J. Foster 77, B.C.G. Wilenkin 53)
	34-5	

Although the match was drawn for the fourth time since the war the game see-sawed excitingly. When Eton had lost five wickets for 66 runs after being sent in to bat by R.A. Jacques, the Harrow captain, on a damp wicket it appeared that Harrow had the advantage. However a fine partnership of 127 between N.C. Wadham, 87, and B.C. Gordon-Lennox, 46, restored Eton's position. Wadham scored his 87 in just over 90 minutes with well timed off-drives and skilful glances whilst his partner concentrated on defence in a stay of 160 minutes. Harrow batted well throughout with B.C.G. Wilenkin, hitting a solid 53, W.J. Foster, 77, and A. Falcon, 85 not out, being the main contributors. Falcon and Foster put on 148 for the fifth wicket in 130 minutes before the Harrow declaration came with a lead of 45. Eton collapsed in the second innings with Jacques again bowling well to take 3/44 after his 4/56 in the first innings off 23 overs. The loss of an hour's play for rain ultimately proved decisive and Harrow were left only 52 minutes to get 103. Harrow's desperate attempt to score the runs only succeeded in their losing 5 quick wickets before stumps were drawn. The 15-year-old R.V.C. Robins, son of the Middlesex and England captain R.W.V., took 41 wickets at 16.31 per wicket in an outstanding display of leg-spin bowling during the schools season. R.A. Jacques had an outstanding season for Harrow with 57 wickets and with M. Kok on 44 wickets formed a formidable opening attack. Harrow had a fine season only losing to M.C.C. on the stroke of time in their 14 matches with seven wins and Jacques was most unlucky not to be selected for the representative games. In his four years in the Harrow XI Jacques had taken 149 wickets, still the overall Harrow record.

The Eton XI of 1951 captained by N.C. Wadham who just failed to bowl out Harrow in the second innings. Two outstanding schoolboy cricketers A.C.D. Ingleby-Mackenzie and R.V.C. Robins (LEFT IN THE FRONT ROW) *distinguished themselves in this match and went on to represent their counties, Hampshire & Middlesex respectively. The captain N.C. Wadham, another highly talented cricketer, was tragically killed in the Fleet Air Arm a few years later.*
BACK ROW, LEFT TO RIGHT: *R.J. Carr, H.G. Impey, A.G.P. Leschallas, M.J. Beaver, T.H.M-S. Pilkington.* SEATED: *R.V.C. Robins, A.C.D. Ingleby-Mackenzie, N.C. Wadham, P.L. Eckersley, P.L.B. Stoddart.* ON GROUND: *W.G. Winter, T.J. Clegg.*

R.V.C. ROBIN'S MATCH

1951 July 13, 14   Match Drawn

Eton	203	(A.C.D. Ingleby-Mackenzie 81, M. Kok 5/43)
	172-4 dec.	(A.C.D. Ingleby-Mackenzie 52)
Harrow	105	(R.V.C. Robins 8/29)
	167-9	(R.V.C. Robins 5/62)

In the end Harrow just managed to avoid defeat, finishing 104 runs short with 9 wickets down largely due to an invaluable innings by W.J. Nokes who batted for 165 minutes for 43 not out. Eton were sent in to bat on a damp wicket and all except A.C.D. Ingleby-Mackenzie found the medium pace of M. Kok with 5/43 difficult to cope with. Ingleby-Mackenzie, a left-hander, drove effectively on the off and leg and scored 81 out of 97 in 70 minutes largely with N.C. Wadham, the Eton captain. Harrow were soon in desperate trouble to the deadly leg-breaks and googlies of R.V.C. Robins and were extremely fortunate to avoid the follow on by two runs. In an outstanding performance Robins took 8/29 off 16 overs to bowl Harrow out for 105. Once again fine batting by Ingleby-Mackenzie, 52, and Wadham, 45 not out, led to Eton declaring leaving Harrow to score 271 in 240 minutes. Despite resistance

from J.W.E. Bleackley, the Harrow captain with 49, and Nokes, Harrow were once again in desperate trouble to Robins who just failed to pull off victory for Eton with 5/62 off 34 overs. His match figures of 13/91 were the highest in the match this century and second only to H.W. Studd (Eton) in 1888 who took 14/99 (since proper bowling analyses were recorded from 1854 onwards). Ingleby-Mackenzie had an outstanding season for Eton, scoring 720 runs at an average of 51.42, and went on to play in the two schools representative games as did Robins and M. Kok, the Harrow opening bowler, played for the Southern Schools.

D.J. HULBERT'S MATCH

1952 July 12, 13   *Harrow won by 7 wickets*

Eton	153	(D.J. Hulbert 8/36)
	73	(D.J. Hulbert 4/31)
Harrow	159	(R.A. Eckersley 5/45)
	68-3	

Harrow achieved their first victory over Eton since 1939 and were indebted to D.J. Hulbert, the son of a Muswell Hill policeman, who bowled outstandingly throughout the match cutting the ball sharply either way at fast medium pace. He was so accurate that the Eton batsmen could not attack him and he took the first four wickets for 13 runs out of 44 and three after lunch on the first day in 11 balls for a single. Only A.G. Morris, a dour left hander with 28, R.V.C. Robins, 32, and D.A.C. Marr, 34, made worthwhile contributions with Robins and Marr putting on 60 together for the sixth wicket. Eton did better in the field and both R.A. Eckersley, the son of the Lancashire cricketer Peter Eckersley, a leg-break bowler, and Robins bowling off-breaks because of a hand injury contained Harrow to 159 in their first innings. Eckersley took a very creditable 5/45 off 16.3 overs and Robins bowled 13 overs for 9 runs and 1 wicket. R.L. Feather, the Harrow captain, was top scorer in the Harrow innings with 38 opening the batting. Hulbert was deadly again in the second innings on the rain affected turf after his 8/36 in the first innings. Eton lost their first three wickets for no runs and were all out in 95 minutes for 73 with Hulbert taking 4/31 off 11 overs and his opening partner H.A. Clive taking 4/18 off 9.4 overs. Hulbert's match analysis was the best for Harrow since 1848 and equalled only by R.C.S. Titchener-Barrett in 1961 and I. Coomaraswamy in 1968. When

The Harrow XI of 1952 which achieved the first victory over Eton since 1939 by 7 wickets. LEFT TO RIGHT, BACK ROW: A.R.B. Neame, R.M.N. Green, H.A. Clive, R.B. Bloomfield, R.J.R. Simpson, C.A. Strang. SEATED: C.R.J. Hawke, W.J. Foster, R.L. Feather (capt), J.M. Nokes, D.J. Hulbert.

Harrow batted a second time Robins rubbed the ball in the dust for Eton and sent back the first three Harrow batsmen for 9 runs out of 31. However W.J. Foster and C.R.J. Hawke, the Harrow keeper, confidently hit off the remaining 37 runs. Tremendous scenes of enthusiasm greeted Harrow's victory at Lord's and it was a long time before the ground was cleared. Eton lacked youthful support at Lord's because of a fatal attack of polio at college. Eton boys were not allowed to attend the game and both teams dined separately. R.L. Feather captained the Harrow eleven superbly throughout the season and C.R.J. Hawke, the Harrow wicket-keeper, kept very well and also scored 486 runs at an average of 48.60 which earned him a place in the two schools representative matches in which he performed creditably.

1953	July 10, 11	*Eton won by 10 wickets*
Eton	238	(R.V.C. Robins 102, D.J. Hulbert 5/73)
	3-0	
Harrow	82	(R.A. James 5/13)
	158	

After D.J. Hulbert, the Harrow captain and hero of their great win in 1952 had put Eton in to bat on a damp wicket, Harrow had only themselves to blame for letting Eton off the hook after the first four wickets had fallen for 70 runs. R.V.C. Robins, the Eton captain, took advantage of some poor Harrow catching when he was dropped five times to rescue Eton with 102 in 195 minutes hitting only five fours – and was considerably helped by P.D. Hill-Wood, the son of the old Oxford and Derbyshire player D.J. Hill-Wood, with 32 and D.R. Maclean with 47. Hulbert again bowled well for Harrow to take 5/73 in 27 overs, well supported by R.B. Blooinfield with 4/73 off 21.2 overs. Harrow were soon in great trouble against the Eton opening attack of R.A. James and D.R. Maclean losing their first five wickets

The powerful Eton XI of 1953 in traditional pose led by Charles Robins, son of the great Walter Robins, Middlesex and England who thrashed Harrow by 10 wickets.

for 29 runs. James in particular was very effective with his medium paced in-swingers and finished with the remarkable analysis of 5/13 off 14 overs, well supported by Maclean who finished with 4/32 off 17 overs. Harrow fared only marginally better in their second innings after following on 156 runs behind. After an opening partnership of 54 between R.J.R. Simpson, 38, and J.M. Parker, the Harrow innings fell apart unsettled by frequent changes of bowling by the Eton captain. Once again the back of the innings was broken by James when he bowled three Harrow batsmen for two runs in eight deliveries. After Harrow just avoided the innings defeat Eton had the formality of scoring three runs for victory. Robins had captained the side with great ability and for the first time in over twenty years had beaten both Winchester and Harrow in the same year although losing three fixtures in the season. Robins had a good season for Eton scoring 531 runs at an average of 40.84 and taking 31 wickets at 20.48 per wicket. R.B. Bloomfield had a most successful bowling season for Harrow with 42 wickets at 11.95 per wicket and the captain Hulbert, although selected for the Southern Schools, did not make enough impact to gain selection for the Schools v. the Combined Services match. He did not have as successful a season as 1952 because of the burdens of leadership and finished with 30 wickets at 19.46 per wicket.

C.A. Strang, Harrow XI 1952/4. Here seen batting in 1954, he scored 52 in Harrow's first innings. A fine racquets player, he won the public schools racquets with R.B. Bloomfield, Harrow XI 1952/4 gaining both racquets and golf blues at Cambridge in 1956/7.

A.R.B. NEAME'S MATCH

1954 July 9, 10   *Harrow won by 9 wickets*

Eton	168	(C.T.M. Pugh 76, R.B. Bloomfield 5/27)
	119	(A.R.B. Neame 7/30)
Harrow	221	(C.A. Strang 52)
	69-1	

A.R.B. Neame, the Harrow captain, decisively turned the tables from the previous year and had an outstanding match with bowling figures 11/77 and 49 runs in the first innings. In Eton's first innings C.T.M. Pugh, the future Gloucestershire captain, scored 76 out of 168 and R.B. Bloomfield bowled very well at medium pace to take 5/27. In Eton's second innings Neame had a match-winning spell of 7/30 with his off-breaks to bowl the light blues out for 119 and leave Harrow the simple task of scoring 67 to win, which was achieved with consummate ease. Boisterous scenes degenerating into rowdyism followed and water was poured down from the Harrow dressing room balcony onto the Eton supporters who were trying to tear down the colours of the victors and a clergyman had his hat knocked off and kicked about. This recalled similar occurrences in 1919 and 1939 when warnings were issued about the match being taken away from Lord's if such behaviour recurred.

The Harrow XI of 1954 captained by A.R.B. Neame which won decisively by 9 wickets, largely due to the outstanding performance of the captain who took 11/77 in the match. LEFT TO RIGHT, BACK ROW: *G.W.H. Stevenson, G.D. Massy, J.M. Parker, R.V.L. Sidley, N. Davies-Barker, R.S. Miller.* SEATED: *T.V.E. Lardner, C.A. Strang, A.R.B. Neame (capt), R.B. Bloomfield, W. Aldous.* ON GROUND: *R.D. Cole (12th man).*

1955 Edward Lane-Fox (Eton), c. Maydon, b. Neame, 6. The 15-year-old Harrow wicket-keeper is A.B. Cable.

The Eton XI of 1955 which won the low scoring match by 38 runs. LEFT TO RIGHT, BACK ROW: *S. Douglas Pennant, H.C. Blofeld, R.A. Head (12th man), E.J. Lane-Fox, A.R.B. Burrows.* SEATED: *A.M. Wolfe-Murray, C.T.M. Pugh, C.H. Gibson (capt), D.R. Stoddart, I.A.C. Sinclair.* ON GROUND: *A.P. Marsham, G.E.D. Mac L. Pearson.*

S. DOUGLAS PENNANT'S MATCH

1955 July 8, 9   *Eton won by 38 runs*

Eton	161	(C.H. Gibson 53)
	166	
Harrow	105	(E.J. Lane-Fox 5/33)
	184	(S. Douglas Pennant 7/33)

In a low scoring match Harrow outplayed in the first innings put up a good fight. A.R.B. Neame, the Harrow captain for the second year, again bowled very well taking 8/81 in the match and achieving only the second hat-trick since 1900 after S.W.A. Banister in 1937 for Eton who took 4 wickets in 4 balls. E.J. Lane-Fox with his slow left-arm bowling took 5-33 in Harrow's first innings to bowl Harrow out for 105. After Eton had made 166 in their second innings Harrow needed 223 to win the match. S. Douglas Pennant with clever variation, left-arm medium pace round the wicket bowled extremely well to take 7/33 to scupper the slim chance Harrow had of winning and take them to a 38 run victory. Neame, an outstanding schoolboy cricketer in his 4 years in the Harrow XI, went on to captain the Southern Schools and Public Schools and play a few games for Kent after his great success in the representative games.

FUTURE LOOKS BRIGHT FOR YOUNG ETON 2nd Day

Pennant's 7 for 33 Beats Harrow

By MICHAEL MELFORD

THE 120th Eton and Harrow match, won by Eton by 38 runs with 10 minutes to spare, was in many ways an excellent game of cricket.

There was much accurate and intelligently directed bowling, including a hat-trick by the Harrow captain, Neame, which almost turned the game, and a long, sustained effort by Douglas Pennant which did.

There was much fine fielding and throwing; and after many fluctuations, there was a finish to test the strongest light and dark blue nerves.

Only the batting, singularly lacking in quality and enterprise, failed to grace the occasion. On a good wicket Eton batted moderately, but still vastly better than Harrow. They also held several awkward and important catches and were well worth the victory won by an unusually young side. The future looks bright for them.

NEAME'S HAT-TRICK

Second in Match's History

Neame's hat-trick seems to be only the second in the long history of the match, the other being that of E. G. Whateley for Eton in 1900. It gave a welcome turn to the game which had seemed to be running all Eton's way.

At 12.45 Eton led by 169 runs and had six second innings wickets standing. Neame then had the left-handed Lane-Fox and Wolfe-Murray caught at short-leg and bowled Blofeld.

This famous feat by an off-spinner of guile and maturity, followed by the fall of another wicket almost at once, opened an entirely new possibilities. But the last three Eton batsmen—Marsham, Pearson and Douglas Pennant — handsomely justified their side's reputation for batting right down the order.

When morale must have been at its lowest, they kept their heads and added 51 for the last two wickets.

HARROW PANIC

Magnificent Pennant

Harrow set off to make 223 in four hours 10 minutes and for a short time the batting had confidence, if not elegance, 37 runs being made in 35 minutes. But once Neame was taken at the wicket, panic seemed to strike at Harrovian hearts—panic and the persevering Douglas Pennant.

This young man, not yet 17, left arm and above medium pace, bowled 24 overs between 2.30 and 6.50 taking seven for 33. He remained lively and accurate throughout.

He moved the ball both ways, with variations of pace, and kept the batsmen thinking all the time. It was a performance of stamina and character.

The Harrow batting between the fall of the first and the ninth wickets is best forgotten. Thoughts of victory seemed to be abandoned at an ingloriously early hour, and Champniss, a left-hander of prodigious patience and application, who had been bowled first ball in the first innings, spent 100 minutes over his first 12 runs.

Desperate Last Effort

When the ninth wicket fell with 40 minutes left he rose to loftier heights. Eton, on the evidence of his previous strokelessness, fed him with tempting slow spin. Champniss forthwith struck it boldly to all parts, actuated no doubt by the thought that this was the best and most honourable way to use up time.

He kept the strike with some skill from the faithful and equally resolute Maydon and they actually added 39 runs in half an hour. It was in an attempt to keep the bowling that Champniss fell at last, after batting 2¼ hours, to a simple catch at cover-point, fittingly off Douglas Pennant.

The Scoreboard

ETON.—First Innings: 161 (C. H. Gibson 53; A. R. B. Neame 4-45).

Second Innings

C. T. M. Pugh, b Champniss	22
D. R. Stoddart, c Miller, b Champniss	58
I. A. C. Sinclair, run out	5
A. R. B. Burrows, lbw, b Maydon	21
C. H. Gibson, b Neame	6
E. J. Lane-Fox, c Maydon, b Neame	0
R. M. Wolfe-Murray, c Miller, b Neame	0
H. C. Blofeld, Neame	0
A. F. Marsham, not out	20
A. Macl. Pearson, c Maidon	0
S. D. Pennant, b Champniss	10
Extras	33
Total	**166**

Bowling: Barker 2-1-5-0; Maydon 14-3-45-2; Miller 5-1-14-0; Champniss 14-3-3-51-3; Neame 18-5-58-4.

HARROW—First Innings: 105 (Lane-Fox 5-33).

Second Innings

J. M. Parker, c and b Pennant	21
A. R. B. Neame, c Blofeld, b Pennant	16
R. S. Miller, c Blofeld, b Pennant	0
D. J. Massy, b Pennant	0
A. S. R. de W. Winlaw, b Pearson	12
A. J. Champniss, c Sinclair, b Pennant	49
A. B. Cable, c Sinclair, b Pennant	3
J. C. T. Harvey, c Gibson, b Pennant	20
I. H. Stewart-Brown, c Burrows, b Pearson	3
N. Davies-Barker, not out	6
M. L. Maydon, not out	26
Extras	26
Total	**184**

Bowling: Pennant 24-12-33-7; Sinclair 22-8-51-1; Pearson 20-7-44-2; Lane-Fox 12-3-21-0; Gibson 1-1-0-0; Burrows 2-0-15-0.

Harrow in Trouble

Harrow's troubles began at 29, when Douglas Pennant, bowling over the wicket and from wide of the crease, got two good balls past the left-handers Parker and Miller, and Blofeld took his catch to remove the formidable Neame.

Winlaw, son of the late R. de W. K. Winlaw, of Cambridge and Surrey, held out with Massy for nearly an hour, but Lane-Fox's grip was not disturbed. As soon as Winlaw was caught at mid-on at 61, the decline was resumed, and the young bowlers passed triumphantly through to the end, delayed only by a last-wicket stand of 19 between Stewart-Brown and Maydon.

ETON BOWLERS ROUT HARROW 1st Day

GIBSON PLAYS BEST INNINGS OF DAY

From MICHAEL MELFORD
LORD'S, Friday.

The first day here has gone very definitely to Eton, though their passage was not wholly smooth. They batted well below reputation to make 161 but, after a still less glorious performance by Harrow, won a lead of 56 which they have increased without loss by 18.

The pattern to-day was curiously in accord with modern trends. On a good, hard wicket the bowlers of both sides revealed a control remarkable for their years, and were always on top. Batting was all desperately hard work.

The heroes of the day were the four young Eton bowlers, all under 17. Much depended on their getting among the seasoned Harrow batsmen early. This was done, largely by Douglas Pennant, left-arm medium pace, and the 15-year-old Lane-Fox, a left-arm spinner with disconcerting swing, dealt with the rest, ably assisted by Sinclair and Pearson.

On the day, Eton fielded the better and a touch of quality was supplied by their wicketkeeper, Blofeld, another 15-year-old. He made a lot of ground to catch the Harrow captain low down on the leg side and in all looked a cricketer of much promise.

Brilliant Setting

Whatever criticism could be levelled at the male attire during the University match, few could have cavilled at the graceful scene to-day. The ladies were of customary elegance, their escorts impeccably unscruffy. The sun shone, the breeze was enough to temper the heat, but not enough to imperil the top hats; and the cricket, fluctuating and eventful, was well worth the occasional glance ladies and escorts spared it.

This morning, however, an hour passed before a wicket fell. In this Pugh and Stoddart made 53, Pugh assaulting anything approaching a half-volley with vehemence.

At midday Harrow came suddenly into the game by taking three wickets in five balls. Maydon, aged 15, and already of good pace, had the left-handed Stoddart caught at the wicket aiming a pull towards square leg. The medium-paced Miller bowled Pugh and Sinclair with full toss and yorker.

A few minutes later Eton had Neame's off-spin to plague them, and Burrows, after one agreeable stroke through the covers, projected a horrifying thing towards mid-wicket and had his off stump knocked back.

Neame could turn the ball little, but he has the control and variations which were last seen in this match from R. G. Marlar. Soon he bowled Lane-Fox and Eton were 74 for five.

At this the resistance stiffened and Gibson, the Eton captain, the survivor of four left handers, fought back with stout heart, if somewhat crooked bat. Support was forthcoming in stands of 36 and 46 from Wolfe-Murray and Blofeld, a number eight of confidence and ability.

The last four wickets fell for five runs, Gibson being last out after an invaluable innings lasting two hours 10 minutes.

ETON.—First Innings

C. T. M. Pugh, b Miller	
D. R. Stoddart, c Cable, b Maydon	24
I. A. C. Sinclair, b Miller	
C. H. Gibson, b Maydon	24
A. R. B. Burrows, b Neame	53
E. J. Lane-Fox, b Neame	6
R. M. Wolfe-Murray, b Neame	18
H. N. Blofeld, c Champniss, b Neame	12
A. F. Marsham, c Massy, b Maydon	7
A. Mac L. Pearson, run out	0
S. D. Pennant, not out	0
Extras	17
Total	**161**

Bowling: Davies-Barker 7-3-16-0; Maydon 9.2-1-51-3; Miller 11-4-20-2; Champniss 14-7-54-0; Neame 20-6-45-4. Second Innings: 18-0 (C. T. M. Pugh 12 not, D. R. Stoddart 5 not, Extra 1).

HARROW—First Innings

J. M. Parker, b Pennant	
A. R. B. Neame, c Blofeld, b Sinclair	2
R. S. Miller, b Pennant	
D. J. Massy, b Lane-Fox	14
G. B. Massy, b Lane-Fox	
L. R. Winlaw, c Pennant, b Lane-Fox	14
A. J. Champniss, b Lane-Fox	
A. B. Cable, lbw, b Lane-Fox	10
J. C. T. Harvey, c Stoddart, b Sinclair	4
N. Davies-Brown, b Sinclair	1
I. Davies-Barker, not out	
M. L. Maydon, c Lane-Fox	12
Extras	
Total	**105**

Bowling: Pennant 11-9-23-2; Sinclair 10-5; Pearson 6-1-17-0; Lane-Fox 14-3-33-5.

The Eton opening pair in 1955, D.R. Stoddart and C.T.M. Pugh.

1955 - G.D. Massy, (Harrow) bowled by Edward Lane-Fox for 14. The Eton wicket-keeper is H.C. Blofeld and slip fielder C.T.M. Pugh. G.D. Massy, Harrow XI 1954/6, was a splendid all round sportsman. He scored 655 runs in 1956 at an average of 66 and took 29 wickets. He went on to represent England at squash racquets as No. 2, before being tragically killed in an air crash in 1966.

1956 July 13, 14   *Match Drawn*

Eton   157-8 dec.   (R.S. Miller 6/38)
Harrow   94-1   (J.M. Parker 51 not out)

The match was badly affected by rain and what looked a commanding position for Harrow was unable to be consolidated. R.S. Miller for Harrow bowled extremely well to take 6/38 off 22 overs with his medium pacers off the wrong foot and the Harrow captain, J.M. Parker, confirmed his outstanding promise with 51 not out. He went on to captain the Public Schools side scoring 73 in the second innings against the Services and afterwards playing for Surrey II. in this match also emerged an outstanding talent in H.C. Blofeld, the 16-year-old Eton wicket-keeper. He achieved a most remarkable feat in the Schools matches scoring 104 not out, and 41 run out in the Public Schools v. Combined Services match and only being once out for 179 runs in the two matches. G.D. Massy had a very good batting season for Harrow scoring 655 runs at an average of 65.50 hitting the ball very hard as befitted a top rackets and squash player. His medium pace bowling off the wrong foot also proved useful.

The Harrow XI of 1956. BACK ROW, SECOND FROM RIGHT: *J.D.C. Vargas, House Master & Second Master of Harrow, next to him, the tallest of the line is F.E.R. Butler now Lord Butler of Brockwell, former Chief Secretary to the Cabinet & Head of the Civil Service.* LEFT TO RIGHT, BACK ROW: *R.F.C. Webster, A.S.R. Winlaw, M.L. Maydon, F.E.R. Butler, J.D.C. Vargas, R.F.S. Miles.* SEATED: *L.J. Champniss, G.D. Massy, J.M. Parker (capt.), R.S. Miller, A.B. Cable.*

1957 July 12, 13   *Match Drawn*

Harrow   183-9 dec.   (J.D.C. Vargas 50, E.J. Lane-Fox 4/14)
Eton   204-6   (A.B..B. Burrows 68 not out,
                        W.G.A. Clegg 77)

Rain interfered with play on both days with Eton looking in a good position by the finish of the second day. Harrow had only scored 101/4 by the close of the rain affected first day. E.J. Lane Fox, who was leading Eton in the absence of H.C. Blofeld who had a serious road accident at Eton some weeks earlier, bowled cleverly to take 4/14 with his slow left-arm off-breaks in 17 overs, ten of which were maidens. J.D.C. Vargas, a stylish left-hander, batted well for his 50 in the Harrow innings and in their innings Eton had two good strikers of the ball in W.G.A. Clegg, 77, and A.R.B. Burrows, 68 not out, to take Eton into the lead before a further downpour on the second day finished any further play for the day.

Eton v. Harrow is Still Alive

Enjoyment at Lord's

Sir — I would like to assure Mr. Eliot Crawshay-Williams that the modern Eton and Harrow match, far from being "a shadow of what it used to be," is a thoroughly lively affair, well attended and obviously well enjoyed.

Peterborough, who cast an unusually malign eye over the proceedings on a wet and gloomy morning, might have seen and heard much to enliven his venerable spirit, despite the continued bad weather, if he had stayed a little longer.

In fact, if the entertaining is necessarily more modest, all the old accompaniments of the occasion are still to be found, including the rival cries and much salty comment from the seats above the Nursery sight screen

He wonders whether Lord's makes as ideal a setting as tradition would have us believe. Where else would he find accommodation, let alone the amenities, to accommodate 20,000 people, which is the total attendance over the two days to be expected in fine weather? The figure this year, despite the rain on both days, was 15,000.

The fact is that no fixture is more popular with M.C.C., whose receipts this year were £3,373 2s as compared with an average pre-war figure of £5,000. The two schools, I am assured, are equally anxious to play at Lord's.

All concerned are hoping that the match will not suffer unduly next year from it being played a week earlier because of the demands of the General Certificate of Education examinations. This will mean it coincides with Henley and the finals at Wimbledon. Yours faithfully,
E. W. SWANTON.
London, N.W.8.

Conjecture about the Eton and Harrow match at Lord's was a continuing debate. E.W. Swanton, the doyen of cricket journalists put the case for very succinctly in 1957.

1958 July 4, 5   *Match Drawn*

Eton   170
            110-7 dec.
Harrow   96
            81-7

In a rather dreary match between two ordinary sides Eton came out overwhelmingly the better side and had they shown more enterprise in their first innings, when they took 5 hours to score 170 against steady Harrow bowling, would easily have won. Harrow set to score 185 in 165 minutes made no attempt to go for the runs and in the event were lucky to play out time thanks to a dour eighth wicket partnership between D.E. Crowther and P.E. D'Abo when they were 69/7.

W.G.A. Clegg, the Eton captain, was the outstanding player on both sides, scoring 603 runs in the season and was to play in the schools side v. the Combined Services at Lord's. His opposite number, A.B. Cable, scored a double duck against Eton and with a weak side under his command did not inspire much confidence.

1959 July 3, 4   *Match Drawn*

Eton 270-5 dec.   (M.L. Dunning 79, J.Baskervyle-Glegg 75,
                    P. Wigan 59)
            106
Harrow   175
            157-8

Once again Eton had much the better of the match but could not quite push home their advantage. Harrow put Eton in to bat on a moist green pitch but the patience of their opening batsman wicket-keeper, J. Baskervyle-Glegg with 75, and the hitting of M.L. Dunning, the Eton captain with 79, left Eton in a strong position when the declaration came at 270/5. Harrow only just avoided the follow on by 5 runs against the effective seam bowling of T.C. Pilkington. Eton forced the pace in the second innings and set Harrow to get 202 in 165 minutes. Half the Harrow side were out for 48 and looked well beaten until P.A.McN. Boyd and M.J.B. Wood came together and put on 53 for the sixth wicket. At the close Harrow were

still 44 runs behind with two wickets standing. Baskervyle-Glegg and B.S. Raper, the Harrow opening bowler, both represented the Public Schools v. The Combined Services at Lord's. Baskervyle-Glegg scored 669 runs in the season for Eton and Raper took 41 wickets for Harrow. Earlier in the season, Harrow had a most remarkable match against a strong Winchester side including the Nawab of Pataudi and Richard Jefferson, the former a future captain of Oxford, Sussex and India and the latter a Cambridge and Surrey star which they won by 1 run off the last ball of the match, a truly epic game which could have had three different results. Mark Weedon the Harrow opening bowler bowled the last man out, hitting the middle stump. An amazing result!

1960 July 1, 2   *Harrow won by 124 runs*

Harrow   216
            143
Eton   153
            82   (C.B.N. Rome 4/26)

Harrow deservedly won a low scoring match, in which there was only one outstanding batsman, M.A. Rogerson of Eton, on either side, due to their strength in spin bowling on a turning wicket on the second day. C.M.S. Kaye, son of M.A.C.P. and grandson of H.S., C.B.N. Rome, son of D.A.M. and grandson of C.S., and N.A.R. Waterlow were too good for a generally poor Eton batting side. After hard hitting by B.S. Raper, the Harrow captain, 30, and P.A.McN. Boyd, 28, in the second innings Harrow left Eton to make 207 in 195 minutes. Eton were skittled out for 82 with 90 minutes to spare by good spin bowling on a sharply turning wicket from Rome, 4/26 and 6/28 in the match, Kaye, 3/12 off 14 overs, and Waterlow, 2/9. Raper failed to retain his place in the Public Schools representative side at Lord's but proved to be an inspiring captain of a good fielding side whereas Eton were undoubtedly very moderate apart from M.A. Rogerson who had an excellent season with 690 runs at an average of 58. This was a fine start for Jack Webster, the old Northants and Cambridge seam bowler who had taken over as master in charge of cricket at Harrow from Mark Tindall, the old Cambridge captain and Middlesex player.

Harrow won by 124 runs

4ᴰ LORD'S 𝑀𝐶𝐶 GROUND 4ᴰ

ETON v. HARROW

Friday & Saturday, July 1 & 2, 1960   (2-day Match)

HARROW	First Innings		Second Innings	
1 M. J. B. Wood	l b w b Ward	8	c Wagg b Ward	0
2 A. A. Denison-Smith	b Ward	39	b de Grey	10
3 I. S. R. Reynolds	c Cornes b Ward	5	l b w b Ward	6
4 H. T. Pelham	c Ward b Wigan	29	st Cornes b Nation	19
5 G. M. Reid	l b w b Ward	26	l b w b Christie	3
*6 I. H. Angus	c Dixon b Christie	20	b Christie	8
†7 B. S. Raper	b Christie	25	l b w b de Grey	30
8 P. A. McN. Boyd	b Milne b de Grey	32	l b w b Ward	28
9 C. M. S. Kaye	l b w b Christie	0	c Ward b Wigan	5
10 N. A. R. Waterlow	not out	6	not out	16
11 C. B. N. Rome	c Dixon b de Grey	7	b Wigan	11
	B 9, l b 10, w , n b ,	19	B 4, l-b 3, w , n b ,	7
	Total	216	Total	143

FALL OF THE WICKETS

1—20   2—28   3—82   4—107   5—128   6—158   7—175   8—175   9—207   10—216
1—0   2—14   3—16   4—22   5—40   6—61   7—99   8—104   9—124   10—143

ANALYSIS OF BOWLING

Name	1st Innings					2nd Innings				
	O.	M.	R.	W.	Wd. N-b	O.	M.	R.	W.	Wd. N-b
de Grey	23	6	49	2	...	17	8	35	2	...
Ward	29	5	66	4	...	19	5	46	3	...
Christie	15	3	29	3	...	6	2	15	2	...
Wigan	10	4	19	1	...	12.2	2	33	2	...
Nation	10	2	34	0	...	2	0	7	1	...

ETON	First Innings		Second Innings	
1 J. H. R. Loudon	c Angus b Reid	10	b Kaye	8
2 P. Wigan	l b w b Waterlow	24	c Reid b Raper	4
3 M. A. Rogerson	c and b Reid	21	c and b Rome	6
4 M. H. Dixon	b Kaye	21	b Kaye	7
5 G. P. Milne	c Angus b Raper	18	c Waterlow b Rome	6
6 A. R. Wagg	c Wood b Kaye	9	l b w b Rome	13
†7 R. D. Christie	b Rome	32	c Angus b Rome	1
8 M. J. de Grey	c Pelham b Raper	4	b Waterlow	13
9 D. P. C. Nation	l b w b Rome	0	b Waterlow	12
10 A. G. Ward	l b w b Kaye	0	l b w b Kaye	1
*11 J. A. Cornes	not out	0	not out	0
	B 7, l-b 5, w 2, n-b ,	14	B 9, l-b , w 2, n-b ,	11
	Total	153	Total	82

FALL OF THE WICKETS

1—17   2—45   3—100   4—100   5—104   6—123   7—152   8—152   9—153   10—153
1—6   2—14   3—26   4—35   5—39   6—54   7—61   8—77   9—82   10—82

ANALYSIS OF BOWLING

Name	1st Innings					2nd Innings				
	O.	M.	R.	W.	Wd. N-b	O.	M.	R.	W.	Wd. N-b
Raper	23.2	3	52	3	1 ...	11	4	18	1	1 ...
Reid	7	0	23	2	1 ...	3	1	5	0	1 ...
Kaye	22	9	49	2	...	14	10	12	3	...
Waterlow	8	2	13	1	...	4.1	2	9	2	...
Rome	2	1	2	2	...	19	12	26	4	...
Pelham					...	3	2	1	0	...

Umpires—B. L. Muncer & W. B. Morris   Scorer—A. Fowler

† Captain   * Wicket-keeper

Play begins at 11 each day   Stumps drawn at 6.30 each day
(Half-an-hour extra on the last day if necessary)
Spectators are requested not to enter or leave their seats during the progress of an over

Harrow won the toss

The 1960 Harrow XI which beat Eton convincingly by 124 runs on a wicket which turned sharply on the second day suiting Harrow's three off-spin bowlers. LEFT TO RIGHT, BACK ROW: *I.S.R. Reynolds, A.A. Denison-Smith, C.M.S. Kaye, C.B.N. Rome, N.A.R. Waterlow, J.R. Sheffield (12th man), I.H. Angus.* FRONT ROW: *M.J.B. Wood, H.T. Pelham, B.S. Raper (capt), G.M. Reid, P.A.McN. Boyd.*

R.C.S. TITCHENER-BARRETT'S MATCH

1961   *Harrow won by an innings and 12 runs*

Harrow 295-9 dec.   (J.R. Hodgkinson 94, C.J.A. Jamieson 72)
Eton   147   (N.C. Pretzlik 63,
                R.C.S. Titchener-Barrett 7/37)
       136   (R.C.S. Titchener-Barrett 5/39)

Harrow won by an innings for the first time since 1866 largely due to the magnificent fast bowling of R.C.S. Titchener-Barrett who moved the ball significantly both ways at a rapid pace. After Harrow had lost their first three wickets for 21 runs the left-handed Harrow opener C.J.A. Jamieson, 72, hit hard and J.R. Hodgkinson, 94, drove and pulled effectively, hitting 13 fours in 150 minutes at the crease. J.R.H. Loudon, the Eton opener who the previous week had scored a century against Winchester, lost his wicket first ball to a long hop, gliding the ball into gully's hands. Titchener-Barrett took four of the first six wickets for 19 runs out of 67 and finished the innings with 7/37 off 20 overs despite powerful hitting by N.C. Pretzlik, 63, with 10 fours. On the second day Eton followed on 148 runs behind but once again succumbed to the pace of Titchener-Barrett and the left-arm spin bowling of C.M.S. Kaye. The only real resistance came from Pretzlik once again with 36 and M.C.T. Prichard, 30, who was bowled by a vicious break back which took the leg stump out of the ground. Eton lost their first five wickets for 69 runs and were all out in three hours. Titchener-Barrett took 5/39 and 12/76 in the match and Kaye 3/48 to take Harrow home to an overwhelming win by an innings and 12 runs by 4.15 on the second day. Harrow had a highly successful season well led by their captain M.J.B. Wood, only just losing to Malvern of the schools. Both Kaye and Titchener-Barrett went on to represent the Southern Schools v. the Rest at Lord's but neither did enough to gain selection for the final XI which was the strongest for many years and included nine future first class cricketers.

LORD'S **GROUND**

ETON v. HARROW
Friday & Saturday, July 7 & 8, 1961 (2-day Match)

HARROW	First Innings		Second Innings
1 C. T. A. Jamieson	c Barber b Braithwaite	72	
2 C. M. S. Kaye	c Barber b Hazlerigg	4	
3 I. S. R. Reynolds	c Cornes b Ward	4	
4 L. G. R. Wood	c Barber b Ward	8	
†5 M. J. B. Wood	c Glyn b Braithwaite	32	
6 J. R. Hodgkinson	c Glyn b Hazlerigg	94	
7 H. T. Pelham	b Ward	30	
8 R. C. Maydon	b Ward	17	
9 J. C. Beard	c Loudon b Pretzlik	8	
*10 D. W. W. Norris	not out	7	
11 R. C. S. Titchener-Barrett	Innings closed		
	B 14, l-b 5, w , n-b ,	19	B , l-b , w , n-b ,
	Total	295	Total

FALL OF THE WICKETS
1—6 2—13 3—21 4—91 5—146 6—185 7—225 8—268 9—295 10—
1— 2— 3— 4— 5— 6— 7— 8— 9— 10—

ANALYSIS OF BOWLING

	1st Innings					2nd Innings				
Name	O.	M.	R.	W.	Wd. N-b	O.	M.	R.	W.	Wd. N-b
Ward	24	3	66	4	...	...	...	...	...	...
Hazlerigg	23.3	6	77	2	...	...	...	...	...	...
Pretzlik	12	2	41	1	...	...	...	...	...	...
Wigan	5	0	20	0	...	...	...	...	...	...
Braithwaite	11	1	49	2	...	...	...	...	...	...
Prichard	5	1	23	0	...	...	...	...	...	...

ETON	First Innings		Second Innings	
1 J. R. H. Loudon	c Kaye b T.-Barrett	0	c Kaye b Beard	4
2 A. J. Glyn	b Titchener-Barrett	0	b Maydon	0
3 M. C. T. Prichard	c L. Wood b Kaye	18	b Titchener-Barrett	30
†4 P. Wigan	c Hodgkinson b T.-Barrett	24	b Titchener-Barrett	19
5 M. H. Dixon	b Kaye	0	b Titchener-Barrett	0
6 G. W. P. Barber	b Titchener-Barrett	18	c Jamieson b Kaye	15
7 C. E. Braithwaite	not out	9	b Titchener-Barrett	1
8 N. C. Pretzlik	c Norris b T-Barrett	63	c Kaye b T.-Barrett	36
*9 J. A. Cornes	run out	2	c Jamieson b Kaye	0
10 A. G. Ward	l b w b Titchener-Barrett	0	c Jamieson b Kaye	13
11 R. H. Hazlerigg	b Titchener-Barrett	0	not out	0
	B 5, l-b 5, w , n-b 3,	13	B 8, l-b 4, w , n-b ,	12
	Total	147	Total	136

FALL OF THE WICKETS
1—0 2—11 3—23 4—56 5—60 6—67 7—140 8—147 9—147 10—147
1—10 2—20 3—56 4—56 5—69 6—83 7—85 8—94 9—184 10—136

ANALYSIS OF BOWLING

	1st Innings					2nd Innings				
Name	O.	M.	R.	W.	Wd. N-b	O.	M.	R.	W.	Wd. N-b
T.-Barrett	20	2	37	7	... 3	21	8	39	5	... ...
Beard	15	3	28	0	... ...	15	6	30	1	... ...
Kaye	16	9	33	2	... ...	16.4	3	48	3	... ...
Maydon	7	3	18	0	... ...	10	5	7	1	... ...
Pelham	2	0	18	0	... ...					

Umpires—H. P. Sharp & B. L. Muncer   Scorer—A. Fowler

† Captain   * Wicket-keeper

Play begins at 11 each day   Stumps drawn at 6.30 each day
(Half an-hour extra on the last day if necessary)

Luncheon Interval 1.30 p.m.–2.10 p.m.
Tea Interval 4.30 p.m. (may be varied according to state of game)

Harrow won the toss

Harrow Bowler takes 12-76 in Eton Defeat

By VIVIAN JENKINS—Lord's, Saturday

HARROW, for the second year in succession! At precisely 4.33 p.m. here today, the last Eton second innings' wicket fell, to give their rivals victory by an innings and twelve runs—and a sea of grey toppers, cornstalks and multi-coloured hats and dresses surged out in front of the pavilion to acclaim the winning team.

Most deservedly so, for this was Harrow's first win by an innings in this match since 1866, 95 years ago, and the first time since 1908 that they had won for two years in succession.

With Eton 129 for six overnight, in reply to Harrow's 295, their remaining four wickets fell for only 18 runs in 35 minutes and, with the follow-on being enforced, Eton then succumbed again, for 136, in spite of an hour lost through rain, in three and a half hours.

Wicket-taker

Harrow's hero, without a doubt, was their 17-year-old fastish right-arm bowler, R. C. S. Titchener-Barrett, whose match figures were 12 for 76. In the first innings he took seven for 37—three of them coming for only four runs in six overs this morning—and in the second innings he followed it up with five for 39.

What is more, the wickets he took were usually the best ones; and he broke the back of Eton's second innings by clean bowling their numbers three, four and five, Prichard, Wigan, the captain, and Dixon, the last two in successive balls.

Titchener-Barrett, who has

HARROW.— First Innings: 295-9 dec. (Hodgkinson 94, Jamieson 72: Ward 4-66).

ETON—First Innings

J. R. H Loudon, c Kaye, b Titchener-Barrett	0
A. J. Glyn, b Titchener-Barrett	0
M. C. T. Prichard, c Wood, L. G. R., b Kaye	18
†P. Wigan, c Hodgkinson, b Titchener-Barrett	24
M. H. Dixon, b Kaye	0
G. W. P. Barber, b Titchener-Barrett	18
C. E. Braithwaite, not out	9
N. C. Pretzlik, c Norris, b Titchener-Barrett	63
‡J. A. Cornes, run out	2
A. G Ward, lbw, b Titchener-Barrett	0
R. H. Hazlerigg, b Titchener-Barrett	0
Extras (b5, lb5, nb3)	13
Total	**147**

Fall of wickets: 1-0, 2-11, 3-23, 4-23, 5-60, 6-67, 7-140 8-147, 9-147.
Bowling: Titchener-Barrett, 20-2-37-7: Beard, 15-3-28-0: Kaye, 16-9-33-2: Maydon, 7-3-18-0: Pelham, 2-0-18-0

Second Innings

J. R. H. Loudon, c Kaye, b Beard	4
A. J. Glyn, b Maydon	0
M. C. T. Prichard, b Titchener-Barrett	30
†P. Wigan, b Titchener-Barrett	19
M. H. Dixon, b Titchener-Barrett	0
G. W. P. Barber, c Jamieson, b Kaye	15
C. E. Braithwaite, b Titchener-Barrett	1
N. C. Pretzlik, c Kaye, b Titchener-Barrett	36
‡J. A. Cornes, c Jamieson, b Kaye	0
A. G. Ward, c Jamieson, b Kaye	13
R. H. Hazlerigg, not out	0
Extras (b8, lb4)	12
Total	**136**

Fall of wickets: 1-10, 2-20, 3-56, 4-56, 5-69, 6-83, 7-85, 8-94, 9-134.
Bowling: Beard, 15-6-30-1: Titchener-Barrett, 21-8-39-5: Maydon, 10-5-7-1: Kaye, 16-4-3-48-3

Middlesex qualifications, hopes to go up to Oxford in a few years' time, and if he maintains the pace and life he showed today could become an asset in both quarters.

For Eton, the bravest batting came from N. C. Pretzlik, primarily a bowler, who was top scorer in both innings, with 63 and 36. He and Ward resisted the Harrow attack for three-quarters of an hour for the ninth wicket in the second innings after eight wickets had gone for 94, and added 50 together.

This was a noble last ditch effort; but by and large Harrow came out of the match better in all departments—batting, bowling and fielding alike, while their 15-year-old wicketkeeper, Norris, showed marked promise.

A pity, though, that, owing to examination calls, this match has to clash with Henley, Wimbledon and the like. In the two days only 7,443 paid for admission, the lowest attendance recorded yet. Surely some change of date is needed.

M.C.T. Prichard, Etonian grandson of famous author Agatha Christie, comprehensively bowled for 30 runs by R.C.S. Titchener-Barrett during Harrow's innings victory of 1961, their first by an innings since 1866.

1962 July 6, 7 *Match Drawn*

Harrow	247	(C.J.A. Jamieson 54)
Eton	110	
	262-7	(M.C.T. Prichard 95, J.A. Cornes 61)

For the third year in succession Harrow were in the driving seat and probably should have won this match if catches had been held. After winning the toss Harrow were given a good start by C.J.A. Jamieson, 54, and R.J. Pelham, 30, who put on 74 for the first wicket, aided by their captain J.R. Hodgkinson, 44, and a last wicket stand of 34, reaching 247. At the close of play on the first day Eton had lost five wickets for 59 in the face of hostile Harrow bowling from Titchener-Barrett, with 3/30 off 21 overs, and J.C. Beard, 2/33 and next morning lost their last five wickets for 51. When Eton following on lost five wickets for 134, Harrow looked in a strong position. However a simple dropped catch off J.A. Cornes, 61, and a more difficult one off M.C.T. Prichard the Eton captain, 95, at a vital time enabled Eton to recover and, deservedly in the end, save the game. Prichard drove and pulled attractively to add 123 for the sixth wicket with D. Calvert-Smith in two hours before he was brilliantly run out five short of his hundred. When stumps were drawn Eton were 125 runs on with three wickets standing. In a very good season for Harrow, Titchener-Barrett took 46 wickets and opened the bowling for the Public Schools at Lord's as well as representing Oxfordshire and Middlesex XI's in the holidays.

1963 July 5, 6 *Match Drawn*

Eton	202-9	dec. (R.C. Daniels 84)
Harrow	82-8	

In a match ruined by the weather Eton had high hopes of registering their first win for eight years. Eton won the toss and were indebted to R.C. Daniels, 84, in achieving a reasonable total. He drove forcefully and was particularly strong on the leg side in a stay of $2\frac{1}{4}$ hours. C.A. Holt and B.G.D. Blair both bowled well for Harrow in long spells. Harrow floundered from the start and were in deep trouble against the lively J.P. Consett, 3/17, and the flighted leg-breaks of G.R.V. Robins, younger son of the Middlesex and England cricketer R.W.V. and brother of R.V.C., who took 3/26 off 16 overs. Harrow were reeling on 79/8 at the end of the first day. Only 15 minutes play was possible on the second day when the game was abandoned with Harrow in deep trouble.

M.C.T. Prichard, Eton captain in 1962 scored 95 in Eton's second innings following on and saved them from a third defeat in succession. D.W.W. Norris Harrow XI 1961/4 went on to gain Cambridge Blues in 1967/8. Here he dives to stop a return to the wicket as Prichard just makes his ground.

R.C. DANIELS' MATCH

1964 July 3, 4

Eton won by 8 wickets

Harrow	134	(R.J. Clover-Brown 90)
	188	(R.J. Clover-Brown 51)
Eton	260-9 dec.	(R.C. Daniels 84, S.P. Sherrard 56)
	63-2	

Eton thoroughly deserved their first victory over Harrow for nine years despite Harrow having seven old flannels to Eton's two. Harrow were thoroughly disconcerted by the pace of J.P. Consett, 4/36 off 15.2 overs, and R.M. Witcomb, 3/32 off 14 overs, and but for the stylish driving of R.J. Clover-Brown, son of the Harrow captain of 1927 with 90 out of 134 and 14 fours, would have been in an even deeper crisis. At the end of the first day, Eton were 126 ahead, mainly due their captain R.C. Daniels, 84, who attacked with vigour, well supported by S.P. Sherrard the Eton opener with 56. Daniels declared at the overnight score and once again Harrow were undone by the pace of Witcomb, 4/28 off 18.2 overs, and the off spin of Daniels, 2/53 off 22 overs, despite another fine innings by Clover-Brown, 51, and M. Rahman, 43. Eton knocked off the 63 they needed for victory for the loss of two wickets with plenty of time to spare. I. Coomaraswamy, a 14-year-old Sri Lankan left-arm off-spinner, made the first of his five appearances for Harrow in this match, the first time since A.S. Day from 1945/9 (one of these war years), performing very creditably to take 5 wickets in the match including 4/80 in Eton's first innings. Daniels, the Eton captain, had an exceptional season scoring 713 runs at an average of 55 and taking 37 wickets at 19 per wicket and doing exceptionally well in the school's representative matches. By contrast D.W.W. Norris, the Harrow captain and wicket-keeper, had a disappointing season only averaging 19 with the bat and failing to score in the representative match for the Southern Schools, his fourth and last year in the Harrow XI.

The Eton XI of 1964, which deservedly won by 8 wickets, led by Rupert Daniels, their first victory over Harrow for nine years. LEFT TO RIGHT, BACK ROW: *A.S.T. Negretti, D.M. Smith, Hon. P.J.H. Inskip, C.A. Lawrie (12th man), R.M. Witcomb, P.M.M. Campbell, C.J. Wake.* FRONT ROW: *G.W. Pilkington, J.P. Consett, R.C. Daniels (capt), N.J. Selwyn, S.P. Sherrard.*

274

C.A. HOLT'S MATCH

1965 July 1, 2

Harrow won by 48 runs

Harrow	279	(A.H. Crawley 62)
	172-7	dec. (A.H. Crawley 73)
Eton	265	(S.P. Sherrard 93)
	138	(C.A. Holt 5/22)

In the best contested match since 1955 Harrow won a closely fought game with 5 minutes to spare, largely due to two splendid innings from A.H. Crawley, the Harrow opener and son of A.M. Crawley, the Oxford blue of 1927/30, and a deadly spell of medium fast bowling from C.A. Holt, the son of R.A.A. Holt the Harrow captain of 1938, in Eton's second innings. In Harrow's first innings Crawley shared a first innings stand of 100 with R.W. Evans, 41, hitting 12 fours in his 62, driving and pulling with gusto, reminiscent of his father. A last wicket stand of 65 by S.A.St.J. Miller, 21 not out, and I. Coomaraswamy, 34, proved crucial and enabled Harrow to reach 279. S P. Sherrard, the Eton opener, again batted well in this match following his 56 in 1964 to score 93 in Eton's reply of 265. Crawley was again the leading scorer in Harrow's second innings of 172/7 dec. with 73 including 11 fours, well supported by the Harrow captain R.I. Evans, 29 not out. Eton set 187 for victory in two hours collapsed dramatically to Holt, 5/22, who disposed of five Etonians in three overs for one run despite another impressive innings from Sherrard, 47. He was well supported by P.J. McSwiney, son of the Elmfield housemaster, with 3/25 off 10 overs.

D.M. SMITH'S MATCH

1966 July 1, 2

Match Drawn

Eton	227	(D.M. Smith 106)
	173-3 dec.	(G.E.N.S. Wilson 59 not out)
Harrow	149	(R.E. Lindsay 72 not out, C.A. Lawrie 6/31)
	141-5	(N.G. Stogdon 59)

A fine start by Eton's opening batsman and captain D.M. Smith with 106, the first century in this match since R.V.C. Robins in 1953, enabled Eton to make 227. He was aided by his opening partner P.M. Hodges, 43, and they put on 131 in 100 minutes for the first wicket and by lunch had reached 164. After Smith had batted for 170 minutes, hitting one six and 14 fours, came a collapse when eight

Coomaraswamy (Harrow) stumped by N.R. MacAndrew after hitting 34 runs quickly in a last wicket stand of 65. Harrow won a closely fought game in 1965 by 48 runs with five minutes to spare. Coomaraswamy, featured here, Harrow XI 1964/8, is the only player this century to have made five appearances at Lord's in peace time. He won the contest for Harrow in 1968 with 12/92. As a left-arm spinner he was unlucky enough to be at Cambridge during Phil Edmonds's residence - he would surely have gained a blue in other times.

Eton XI 1967 captained by Viscount Crowhurst (later Earl of Cottenham) which just failed to bowl out Harrow in the second innings.

V.A. Cazalet, Eton XI 1967/9, son of the Queen Mother's trainer during the 1969 match. Captain of Eton in 1969 when they were unlucky not to win. He finished creditably in the season with 683 runs. A hard hitter like his father, P.V.F. he played racquets for Oxford.

The Crawley brothers, Andrew and Randall pictured together at the 1967 match. Keen sportsmen, talented at both cricket and racquets. A.H. on the left, Harrow XI 1964/5, scored 62 and 73 in 1965 when Harrow won by 48 runs. R.S., Harrow XI 1966/7. Inseparable, they were tragically killed in an air crash in 1988.

wickets fell for 63 runs. Harrow's reply started adequately with 107/3 but the later Harrow batsman could not cope with C.A. Lawrie's pace and the innings collapsed to 149 with the Harrow opener, R.E. Lindsay, son of the 1928 Harrow captain William Lindsay, 72 not out, finding no-one to stay with him. Lawrie took his last five wickets for 13 runs in 11 overs. Eton forced the pace in the second innings scoring at well over four an over, Smith, 42, and G.E.N.S. Wilson, 59 not out, being the main orchestrators. Eton's declaration left Harrow to score 252 in 180 minutes and Harrow made no serious attempt to go for them, finishing on 141/5 with Lindsay once again carrying his bat for 27.

1967 June 29, 30   *Match Drawn*

Eton	274-6 dec.	(B.L.H. Powell 79, M.J.J. Faber 53)
	132-6 dec.	
Harrow	188	(P.J.E. Needham 53)
	151-7	(A.P. Webster 54)

A strong Eton batting side put the weak Harrow bowling attack to the sword on the first morning of the match, scoring 151 before lunch with some forceful batting by M.J.J. Faber, 53, and R.S.A. Paget-Stevenson, 39. Later B.L.H. Powell played sensibly for 79 in 135 minutes for the highest innings of the match, hitting eight fours and thus enabled the Eton captain, Viscount Crowhurst, to declare on 274 for 6. Harrow were doomed to follow on at 122/6 until the 15-year-old P.J.E. Needham saved the situation in a fine innings of 53 which included two sixes and six fours. After Eton had declared their second innings on 132/6, Harrow were left to score 219 in 135 minutes. Harrow were hard pressed to save the game and only an unbroken stand between R.W. Vinson, the Harrow wicket-keeper, and D.R. Herbert of 32 enabled them to achieve this against a far better all-round Eton side. B.L.H. Powell represented the Public Schools v. E.S.C.A. and M.J.J. Faber averaged over 43 with the bat during the season.

HARROW TAKE COMMAND AFTER FABER'S 100

COOMARASWAMY HAS 7-42

By HENRY CALTHORPE

LORD'S, Thursday.

AN innings full of fine attacking strokes by Webster gave Harrow the advantage at the end of a day of exciting, challenging cricket. After bowling out Eton for 210, Harrow are 159 for three, having lost Webster for 90 off the last ball of the day.

After Eton had lost two early wickets, Faber and Cazalet, batting extremely well, put on 126 in two hours and Faber went on to reach his century.

Then they collapsed against Coomaraswamy, who, flighting his left arm spin cleverly and bowling accurately, took seven for 42 in 21.2 overs.

Harrow lost one of their openers early on, but Webster then played some magnificent strokes all round the wicket against bowling which tended to be over-pitched. He batted 135 minutes and hit 14 fours.

The overnight rain delayed the start for an hour this morning. But when things got under way the Harrow supporters were soon cheering loudly as Eton lost two quick wickets.

Despite the empty stands, the coaches which used to be in front of the Tavern and were now behind the boundary rope at the Nursery end, gave atmosphere and colour to the proceedings.

THREE RUNS . . .

. . . two out

Webster, bowling fast, and Holland dismissed Woodd and Stewart in their second and third overs respectively, and Eton's two best batsmen, Cazalet and Faber, found themselves together with the scoreboard reading three for two.

But they responded splendidly to the situation in their pleasant upright styles. Two hooks by Faber gave the Eton supporters some cheer, and both batsmen played some line strokes in front of the wicket. At lunch Eton were 86 for two off 22 overs.

Twelve minutes after lunch Cazalet was lbw trying to force Coomaraswamy to leg, and in the same over Kinkead-Weekes was

The Scoreboard

```
ETON—First Innings
D. J. B. Woodd, b Webster ......... 0
J. B. W. Stewart, b Holland ......... 0
V. A. Cazalet, lbw b, b Coomaraswamy 62
M. J. J. Faber, c Vincent, b Holland 100
*†R. C. Kinkead-Weekes, b Coomara-
  swamy ......................... 0
G. M. P. Consett, b Coomaraswamy 3
A. P. R. Tomkin, st Vinson, b
  Coomaraswamy ................. 19
M. G. E. Hughes, b Coomaraswamy 4
C. H. R. Fortescue, c Harrison, b
  Coomaraswamy ................. 6
A. Douglas-Home, b Coomaraswamy 0
J. R. T. Barclay, not out ......... 0
  Extras (b 3, lb 9, nb 4) ....... 16
    Total ..................... 210
Fall of wickets: 1-3, 2-3, 3-129, 4-
129, 5-140, 6-184, 7-191, 8-206, 9-
206.
Bowling: Holland 12-3-50-2; Webster
12-2-40-1; Evans 3-0-22-0; Coomara-
swamy 21.4-8-42-7.

HARROW—First Innings
A. P. Webster, c Cazalet, b Barclay 90
A. H. Bruce, c Kinkead-Weekes,
  b Douglas-Home .............. 0
M. E. Harrison, c Hughes, b Barclay 42
T. M. Franks, not out ........... 15
  Extras (b 7, lb 4, nb 1) ..... 12
    Total (3 wkts.) ......... 159
Fall of wickets: 1-15, 2-111, 3-159.
  To bat: R. J. E. Needham,
*I. Coomaraswamy, S.G. French,
†R. W. Vinson, M. C. Dickinson, S. G.
Holland, M. T. A. Evans.
Umpires: N. Cooper & F. R. Parker.
```

yorked. Soon afterwards Consett went in the same way.

This did not deter Faber. He went on playing some strong leg-side strokes. Just after reaching his 100 he was caught behind, cutting at Holland, and none of the other batsmen stayed for long.

When Harrow were 15 Bruce followed a ball from Douglas-Home and was caught behind. Webster went for his shots from the start of the innings and, partnered by Harrison, pushed the score along until both were out to Barclay, the 14½-year-old off-spinner, in the last half hour.

Stewart was right out of luck. Apart from making nought in his first appearance at Lord's, he pushed his hand through the glass in the dressing room door when he returned to the pavilion and had to have seven stitches inserted.

The Eton XI of 1968 which lost by 7 wickets at Lord's but contained four top-class schoolboy cricketers - R.C. Kinkead-Weekes, Eton's wicket-keeper captain gained an Oxford blue in 1972, as did M.J.J. Faber in the same year. J.R.T. Barclay captained Sussex, and V.A. Cazalet played for Kent II and was good enough to have gone further. LEFT TO RIGHT, BACK ROW: *D.J.B. Wood, J.B.W. Stewart, Hon C.H.R. Fortescue, M.G. Horsfall (12th man), M.G.E. Hughes, G.M.P. Consett, J.R.T. Barclay.* SEATED: *A. Douglas-Home, M.J.J. Faber, R.C. Kinkead-Weekes (capt), V.A. Cazalet, A.P.R. Tomkin.*

J.R.T. Barclay in the first of his four Eton appearances at Lord's, justified his selection with 6/100 off 31 overs with well flighted off-spin. Eton were again flummoxed by Coomaraswamy in their second innings and only D.J.B. Woodd, the Eton opener with 69, made much impression. Coomaraswamy had match figures of 12/92 and Harrow needing only 92 in 120 minutes made it more difficult

I. COOMARASWAMY'S MATCH

1968 July 11, 12   *Harrow won by 7 wickets*

Eton	210	(M.J.J. Faber 100, V.A. Cazalet 62, I. Coomaraswamy 7/42)
	141	(D.J.B. Woodd 69, I.Coomaraswamy 5/50)
Harrow	260	(A.P. Webster 90, J.R.T. Barclay 6/100)
	92-3	(M.E. Harrison 48 not out)

After the first two wickets had fallen without a run being scored M.J.J. Faber and V.A. Cazalet batted well together putting on 126 in 105 minutes before, soon after making his 100, Faber was caught behind off the Harrow opening bowler, S.G. Holland. Subsequently the Harrow captain, I. Coomaraswamy playing in his fifth Eton and Harrow match, only achieved by five other Harrovians in the history of the match, bowled superbly with his well flighted slow left-arm bowling to take 7/42 off 21.4 overs. Harrow's better all round batting led by A.P. Webster, 90, and M.E. Harrison, 42, produced a first innings lead of 50.

The Harrow XI of 1968 which won against the odds largely due to a superb performance by their Captain. LEFT TO RIGHT, BACK ROW: *T.M. Franks, M.T.A. Evans, S.G. French, M.C. Dickinson, P.J.E. Needham, M.E. Harrison, R.A. Carr (12th man).* SEATED: *S.G. Holland, A.P. Webster, I. Coomaraswamy (capt.), A.H. Bruce, R.W. Vinson.*

Harrow stroll home after Eton collapse

By HENRY CALTHORPE

LORD'S, Friday.

A SURPRISING collapse by Eton here this afternoon left Harrow to score 92 runs in two hours, and, after a slow start, in which only 20 came in the first 15 overs, they won by seven wickets with 14 minutes of the extra half an hour left.

In the morning, Harrow were bowled out for 260, which gave them a first innings lead of 50. But Eton then batted badly and

---

More sport on Pages 6 & 7

---

their second innings was held together only by a patient innings from Woodd, who made 69 out of 141.

Harrow deserved their victory, for throughout the two days, they had looked slightly superior in every department. Their fielding was tidier, their bowling more penetrative and they batted more solidly than Eton.

The morning belonged to Barclay, who took another four Harrow wickets and finished with six for 100 in 31 overs. His control is remarkable for a boy of 14, and he should take a lot of wickets for Eton in the next three years.

Eton began their second innings, hoping to score enough runs to be able to leave Harrow a target. But these hopes disappeared when Cazalet and Faber were out soon after lunch.

Cazalet was lbw, playing back to a ball from Webster to which he would have been better forward, and Faber was brilliantly caught by

Note the pseudonym of Henry Blofeld, the well known Etonian writer and commentator. Calthorpe is his second initial, named after his grandfather the Hon. F.G. Calthorpe, the Warwickshire & England cricketer.

Barclay, 14, the youngest Etonian to win his colours for more than 30 years, took 6-100 in Harrow's first innings.

Webster at backward short leg. He turned Evans hard round the corner, and Webster took the catch when the ball seemed to have gone past him.

The later batsmen again had no answer to Coomaraswamy, who turned the ball more today and took five for 50. He had the splendid match figures of 12 for 92, and he thoroughly deserved them.

Douglas-Home and Hughes bowled throughout the final hour and three-quarters, and they both maintained their pace and length well. Harrow began cautiously and, for a time, they fell some way behind the clock.

Bruce was bowled swinging at Hughes, and Webster lost his off stump as he played across Douglas-Home. But, after Coomaraswamy had been bowled, driving at Hughes, some robust drives by Harrison saw Harrow home.

ETON—First Innings 210 (Faber 100, Cazalet 62; Coomaraswamy 7-42).

Second Innings

D. J. B. Woodd, c Holland, b Coomaraswamy	69
A. P. R. Tomkin, c Dickinson, b Holland	5
V. A. Cazalet, lbw, b Webster	16
M. J. J. Faber, c Webster, b Evans	12
†R. C. Kinkead-Weekes, c Dickinson, b Coomaraswamy	3
G. M. P. Consett, b Holland	0
M. G. E. Hughes, st Vinson, b Coomaraswamy	2
C. H. R. Fortescue, c Webster, b Coomaraswamy	16
J. R. T. Barclay, b Coomaraswamy	0
J. B. W. Stewart, b Webster	0
A. Douglas-Home, not out	0
Extras (b 10, lb 5, nb 3)	18
Total	141

Fall of wickets: 1-11, 2-35, 3-61, 4-89, 5-105, 6-119, 7-122, 8-122, 9-123.

Bowling: Holland 11-5-19-2; Webster 22-7-38-2; Coomaraswamy 24-11-50-5; Evans 4-2-16-1.

HARROW—First Innings

A. P. Webster, c Cazalet, b Barclay	90
A. H. Bruce, c Kinkead-Weekes, b Douglas-Home	0
M. E. Harrison, c Hughes, b Barclay	42
T. M. Franks, b Douglas-Home	21
B. J. E. Needham, b Barclay	5
I. Coomaraswamy, b Douglas-Home	34
S. G. Ffrench, c Hughes, b Barclay	19
†R. W. Vinson, c Barclay, b Douglas-Home	21
M. C. Dickinson, b Barclay	1
S. G. Holland, st Kinkead-Weekes, b Barclay	4
M. T. A. Evans, not out	1
Extras (b10, lb6, nb6)	22
Total	260

Fall of wickets: 1-15, 2-111, 3-159, 4-167, 5-191, 6-224, 7-230, 8-240, 9-258.

Bowling: Douglas-Home 32-9-... Hughes 8-1-27-0; Fortescue 10-3-...; Barclay 31-7-100-6; Faber 3-0-12-...

Second Innings

A. P. Webster, b Douglas-Home	
A. H. Bruce, b Hughes	
M. E. Harrison, not out	
*I. Coomaraswamy, b Hughes	
P. Needham, not out	
Extras (lb 4)	
Total (3 wkts.)	

Fall of wickets: 1-10, 2-36, 3-... Bowling: Douglas-Home 17-5-... Hughes 16-2-4-37-2.

Umpires: N. Cooper & F. R. I...

---

⑥ᴰ LORD'S Ⓜ GROUND ⑥ᴰ

ETON v. HARROW

Thursday & Friday, July 11 & 12, 1968 (2-day Match)

ETON	First Innings		Second Innings	
1 D. J. B. Woodd	b Webster	0	c Holland b Coom'wa'y	69
2 J. B. W. Stewart	b Holland	0	b Webster	0
3 V. A. Cazalet	l b w b Coomaraswamy	62	l b w b Webster b Evans	16
4 M. J. J. Faber	c Vinson b Holland	100	c Dickinson b Coom'wa'y	12
†*5 R. C. Kinkead-Weekes	b Coomaraswamy	0	c Dickinson b Holland	3
6 G. M. P. Consett	b Coomaraswamy	3	b Holland	0
7 A. P. R. Tomkin	st Vinson b Coom'wamy	19	c Dickinson b Holland	5
8 M. G. E. Hughes	b Coomaraswamy	4	st Vinson b Coom'wamy	2
9 Hon. C. H. R. Fortescue	c Harrison b Coom'wa'y	6	c Webster b Coom'wa'y	16
10 A. Douglas-Home	b Coomaraswamy	0	not out	0
11 J. R. T. Barclay	not out	0	b Coomaraswamy	0
	B 3, l-b 0, w , n-b 4,	16	B 10, l-b 5, w , n-b 3,	18
	Total	210	Total	141

FALL OF THE WICKETS

1—3 2—3 3—129 4—129 5—140 6—184 7—191 8—206 9—206 10—210
1—11 2—35 3—61 4—89 5—105 6—119 7—122 8—122 9—123 10—141

ANALYSIS OF BOWLING

	First Innings					Second Innings				
Name	O.	M.	R.	W.	Wd.	N-b	O.	M.	R.	W.	Wd.	N-b
Holland	12	3	19	2			11	5	19	2		
Webster	12	4	40	1		2	22	7	38	2		
Evans	3	0	22	0			4	2	16	1		1
Coomaraswamy	21.4	8	42	7			24	11	50	5		

HARROW	First Innings		Second Innings	
1 A. P. Webster	c Cazalet b Barclay	90	b Douglas-Home	22
2 A. H. Bruce	c K.-Weekes b D.-Home	0	b Hughes	6
3 M. E. Harrison	c Hughes b Barclay	42	not out	48
4 T. M. Franks	b Douglas-Home	21		
5 B. J. E. Needham	b Barclay	5	not out	8
†6 I. Coomaraswamy	b Douglas-Home	34	b Hughes	8
7 S. G. Ffrench	c Hughes b Barclay	19		
*8 R. W. Vinson	c Barclay b D.-Home	21		
9 M. C. Dickinson	b Barclay	1		
10 S. G. Holland	st K.-Weekes b Barclay	4		
11 M. T. A. Evans	not out	1		
	B 10, l-b 6, w , n-b 6,	22	B , l-b 4, w , n-b ,	4
	Total	260	Total	92

FALL OF THE WICKETS

1—15 2—111 3—159 4—167 5—191 6—224 7—230 8—240 9—258 10—260
1—10 2—36 3—49 4— 5— 6— 7— 8— 9— 10—

ANALYSIS OF BOWLING

	First Innings					Second Innings				
Name	O.	M.	R.	W.	Wd.	N-b	O.	M.	R.	W.	Wd.	N-b
Douglas-Home	32	9	72	4		6	17	5	51	1		
Hughes	8	1	27	0			16.2	4	37	2		
Fortescue	10	3	27	0								
Barclay	31	7	100	6								
Faber	3	0	12	0								

Umpires—N. Cooper & F. R. Parker   Scorer—A. Fowler

† Captain   * Wicket-keeper

Play begins at 11 each day   Stumps drawn 1st day at 6.30, 2nd day at 6
(half-an-hour extra on the last day if necessary)
Luncheon Interval 1.15 p.m.—1.55 p.m.
Tea Interval 4.15 p.m.—4.35 p.m. (may be varied according to state of game)

Eton won the toss

Eton XI 1969. LEFT TO RIGHT, BACK ROW: *T.J.P. Ramsden, R.B.P. England, A.E. Martin Smith, M.P. Powell, A.T. Fennell, J.M. Robertson, A.G. Dyer.* SEATED: *Hon. C.H.R. Fortescue, J.R.T. Barclay, V.A. Cazalet (capt.), G.M.P. Consett, A.G. Milne.*

than it should have been, scrambling home with only 15 minutes to spare. M.E. Harrison played another good innings of 48 not out to guide them home but undoubtedly the hero was Harrow's Sri Lankan captain. M.J.J. Faber scored 751 runs for the season in only 13 innings for Eton averaging 83.44 and went on to representative honours for M.C.C. Schools v. the Combined Services. A.P. Webster, the Harrow opening bat, averaged over 49 with the bat and took 31 wickets and also represented the Schools v. the Combined Services.

S.A.F. MITCHELL'S MATCH

1969 July 10, 11   *Match Drawn*

Eton	189	(A.E. Martin-Smith 60, S.A.F. Mitchell 5/61)
	158-8 dec.	(S.A.F. Mitchell 6/52)
Harrow	140	
	136-8	(S.A.F. Mitchell 50)

Eton's first innings was largely sustained by a dour innings from the Eton opener A.E. Martin-Smith who scored 60 in 200 minutes, aided by C.H.R. Fortescue, 44, who helped him add 82 and took Eton to relative respectability. The Harrow medium pace in-swing bowler S.A.F. Mitchell took 5/61 in 33.5 overs to restrict Eton with sustained accuracy. Harrow made no better fist of it and finished 49 behind on first innings with Fortescue taking 4/23 with his slow off-spin. Eton's captain, V.A. Cazalet with 49, led the second innings charge and the declaration came at 158/8 leaving Harrow to score 208 in 155 minutes. Mitchell had again bowled tightly to keep Harrow in the game and finished with 6/52 for match figures of 11/113. Harrow collapsed dramatically to 52/6 and were once again saved by an aggressive 50 from Mitchell which led Harrow to safety; they finished on 136/8 at the close. J.R.T. Barclay's outstanding display with the ball, 43 wickets at 13 during the season, earned him the first of his three appearances at Lord's for M.C.C. Schools v. the Combined Services and Cazalet, the Eton captain with 683 runs at an average of 57, was unlucky not to gain representative honours.

SIXTH FORM GROUND, HARROW

H.M. WYNDHAM'S MATCH

1970 July 9, 10   *Eton won by 97 runs*

Eton	165	(S.A.F. Mitchell 6/64)
	198-6 dec.	
Harrow	151	(J.C. Lepp 50, HM. Wyndham 4/44)
	115	(H.M. Wyndham 6/39)

This was the first occasion in peacetime since 1805 that the fixture was not played at Lord's. The ground had been reserved for Middlesex in case it was needed for a Gillette Cup tie but they had already been knocked out of the competition. There were some fine bowling displays on both sides and it was an even contest until well after tea on the first day. S.A.F. Mitchell, the medium pace in-swing bowler, took 6/64 off 26 overs and only J.R.T. Barclay, the Eton captain with 43, played him easily and Eton were bowled out for 165. When Harrow were 131/4 it seemed they were in a good position with J.C. Lepp 50 and the Harrow captain for the second year running, P.J.E. Needham, 36. But they were badly let down by their remaining batsman and the last six wickets fell for 20 runs in 40 minutes to give Eton a first innings lead of 14. H.M. Wyndham, 6ft. 4 ins tall, used his height effectively with his medium pace inducers to take 4/44 off 16 overs. More consistent batting by Eton on the second day enabled Barclay to give Harrow a competitive declaration, 213 to win at 76 an hour. They never looked likely to achieve this and Wyndham bowled even better than in the

A view across the 6th form Ground at Harrow with play in progress during the two-day match in 1970. This was due to the reservation of Lord's ground for a Gillette Cup match.

HARROW v. ETON

at Harrow

Thursday & Friday, July 9th & 10th, 1970

ETON	First Innings		Second Innings	
1 H. C. Birkbeck	b Mitchell	23	b Mitchell	6
2 A. E. Martin - Smith	c Needham b Mitchell	7	b J. Halliday	29
†3 J. R. T. Barclay	b Mitchell	43	c Stewart b C. Halliday	29
4 T. N. Heywood-Lonsdale	lbw b S. Halliday	7	run out	13
5 G. M. P. Consett	c Lepp b Mitchell	32	c Needham b Mitchell	36
6 M. A. Gibson-Watt	st Needham b Mitchell	11	b Mitchell	18
*7 N. C. W. Bramall	b Mitchell	1	not out	14
8 A. G. Dyer	c Needham b C. Halliday	20	not out	22
9 R. P. McCall	b C. Halliday	0		
10 H. M. Wyndham	not out	1		
11 N. J. Boustead	c Needham b C. Halliday	0		
	B 8, l-b 6, w 4, n-b 2,	20	B 12, l-b 6, w 4, n-b 9,	31
	Total	165	Total (6 wkts. dec.)	198

FALL OF THE WICKETS

1—16 2—34 3—66 4—100 5—126 6—136 7—137 8—149 9—165 10—165
1—11 2—61 3—90 4—106 5—147 6—165 7— 8— 9— 10—

ANALYSIS OF BOWLING

	First Innings						Second Innings				
Name	O.	M.	R.	W.	Wd.	N-b	O.	M.	R.	W.	Wd.	N-b
N. J. W. Stewart	7	1	24	0		2	18	4	47	0		6
S. A. F. Mitchell	26	8	64	6			28	10	82	3	4	
M. T. A. Evans	2	0	12	0	4		4	2	4	0		2
C. A. R. Halliday	6.1	2	8	3			13	7	25	1		1
J. Halliday	12	2	37	1			5	2	9	1		

HARROW	First Innings		Second Innings	
1 H. St. J. S. Corbett	b Boustead	0	b Boustead	8
2 J. C. Lepp	c Gibson-Watt b Boustead	50	c Bramall b Boustead	16
*3 P. J. E. Needham	c Martin-Smith b Wyndham	36	b Wyndham	24
4 O. M. L. Gough	c Boustead b Dyer	23	c Martin Smith b Wyndham	14
†5 T. M. Franks	b Wyndham	5	c Barclay b Wyndham	9
			c Heywood-Lonsdale	
6 E. J. D. Clarke	b Boustead	8	b Boustead	20
7 J. Halliday	st Bramall b Wyndham	7	c Gibson-Watt b Wyndham	0
8 C. A. R. Halliday	b Dyer	3	c McCall b Wyndham	5
9 S. A. F. Mitchell	c Boustead b Wyndham	1	c Bramall b Wyndham	8
10 M. T. A. Evans	c Wyndham b Dyer	3	c Gibson-Watt b Barclay	0
11 N. J. W. Stewart	not out	0	not out	0
	B 11, l-b 4,	15	B 9, l-b 1, w 1,	11
	Total	151	Total	115

FALL OF THE WICKETS

1— 0 2—55 3—117 4—122 5—131 6—138 7—141 8—141 9—151 10—151
1—23 2—52 3— 54 4— 90 5— 91 6— 99 7—101 8—110 9—110 10—115

ANALYSIS OF BOWLING

	First Innings						Second Innings				
Name	O.	M.	R.	W.	Wd.	N-b	O.	M.	R.	W.	Wd.	N b
N. J. Boustead	10.2	3	24	3			10	2	26	3		
R. P. McCall	5	1	25	0			5	2	13	0		
H. M. Wyndham	16	4	44	4			25	14	39	6		
J. R. T. Barclay	10	4	19	0			10.2	8	5	1	1	
A. G. Dyer	14	5	24	3			9	2	21	0		

Eton won the toss.

Umpires—S. H. Moore and L. D'Arcy

† Captain   * Wicket-keeper

Play begins at 11.30 a.m. each day   Stumps drawn at 7 p.m. each day

Luncheon Interval 1.30 p.m.—2.10 p.m.

Tea interval 4.30 p.m.—4.55 p.m. (may be varied according to state of game)

6D.

The Eton XI of 1970 led by Johnny Barclay which emerged victorious by 97 runs. This was the first time in peace time that the match was played on the Sixth Form Ground at Harrow; fortunately it returned to Lord's the following year.
LEFT TO RIGHT, BACK ROW: R.P. McCall, T.N. Heywood-Lonsdale, M.A. Gibson-Watt, H.M. Wyndham, W.R.S. May (12th man), N.J. Boustead, N.C.W. Bramall. SEATED: A.G. Dyer, G.M.P. Consett, J.R.T. Barclay (capt.), A.E. Martin-Smith, H.C. Birkbeck.

first innings to take 6/39 off 25 overs and Harrow were bowled out with six minutes to spare – Eton had won by 97 runs. P.J.E. Needham, the Harrow captain, had a useful season scoring 579 runs at an average of 44.53 and Eton's Barclay an even better one with 897 runs at an average of 64.07 and 28 wickets. Barclay went on to represent the Schools v. E.S.C.A. and had the rare distinction of taking all nine E.S.C.A. wickets that fell in their total of 199 with 9/57 off 28 overs. The declaration, when he had the once-in-a-lifetime chance of taking all ten wickets at headquarters seemed somewhat unchivalrous.

1971 July 8, 9   *Match Drawn*

Harrow	183	(J. Halliday 58)
	148-8 dec.	
Eton	195-9 dec.	(J.R.T. Barclay 66)
	70-4	

Compared to the previous year this was a rather lacklustre match. The two captains, J.R.T. Barclay, the Eton captain for the second year running, and J. Halliday, the Harrow captain, both played leading parts in the match. Halliday opening the Harrow batting kept the first innings together against useful bowling from the Eton opener N.J. Boustead, 3/40 off 21 overs, and H.M. Wyndham, who once again performed well in this match to take 4/49 off 35 overs. Barclay scored 66 in 150 minutes to take Eton to a first innings lead of 12 before he declared. G.W.H. Joynson's, 46 not out, was Harrow's best score before the declaration came, setting Eton 137 to score in 77 minutes. Somewhat surprisingly no attempt was made by Eton to go for the runs and the game finished tamely with Eton only having scored 70 off 29 overs. H.M. Wyndham's match figures of 8/86 off 57 overs was the feature of Eton's bowling. A back injury kept Barclay out of the Eton side for much of the term and he was unable to bowl his off-breaks. He still averaged 53 in his five innings and was able to represent the Schools v. E.S.C.A. along with the Eton opening bowler N.J. Boustead and M.C.C. Schools v. the Combined Services with some success scoring 30 and 39. Eton also missed the penetration of H.M. Wyndham who went down with jaundice for much of the term. Harrow went through an unbeaten season but found it difficult to bowl sides out with 8 draws in their 12 completed matches although Halliday, the captain, bowled and batted well throughout the year.

1972 July 13, 14   *Match Drawn*

Harrow	247-8 dec.	(J.C. Lepp 59, C.H.P. Lee 55)
	140-7 dec.	
Eton	195-9 dec.	
	106-6	

Harrow had much the better of this drawn match with the batting in general being stronger than the bowling. J.C. Lepp opening the batting for the third year running was the pick of the Harrow batsmen and scored 59 with stylish drives, well supported by C.H.P. Lee, 55, in their total of 247/8 before the declaration came. P.W.R. Leigh, the Eton opening bowler, took the first hat-trick in this fixture since A.R.B. Neame of Harrow in 1955, dismissing M.W. Hall, C.D. Gilliat and W.R. Worthy on 247. Eton started almost as well as Harrow in their first innings when H.W.A. Palmer, 42, and N.J.G. Stewart-Richardson put on 92 for the first wicket but the later Eton batsmen were unable to push the score along. Lepp, 40, again batted competently for Harrow in their second innings and with the declaration coming at 140/7 Eton were set 193 to win in 140 minutes. After five wickets fell for 35 Eton looked in danger of defeat but in a fine rearguard action they were saved by P.J. Remnant, 30 not out, and the wicket-keeper captain, I. MacDonald, 36, finishing on 106/6 at the close. W.R. Worthy, the Harrow medium pacer, bowled well in both innings to take match figures of 8/85 off 42 overs. R.J.R. Seligman kept wicket neatly for Harrow taking four catches and a stumping. J.C. Lepp had a fine season for Harrow with 601 runs at an average of 50.08 and W.R. Worthy took 44 wickets at 18.70 per wicket.

1973 July 14, 15   *Match Drawn*

Harrow	181-5 dec.	(C.H.P. Lee 83)
	98-1 dec.	
Eton	121-9 dec.	
	63-3	(Marquis of Bowmont 53 not out)

A fluent innings by C.H.P. Lee, 83, enabled the Harrow captain C.D. Gilliat, a cousin of the Hampshire captain Richard Gilliat, to declare the innings at 3.15 and his decision looked fully justified when Eton were 121/9 at the end of the first day. J.H. Morrison, the Harrow opening bowler, took 4/39 in 17 overs, well supported by J.S.B. Phillips 3/26. After play was lost on the second day Harrow hit hard, scoring 98 in 75 minutes with R.E.P. Lee, the twin of C.H.P., 59, and M.W. Hall, 42 not out, to the fore. After another long delay for rain Eton were eventually set 159 to get in 80 minutes and, despite a fluent innings by their captain, Lord Bowmont, were never seriously in the hunt and finished on 63/3. Morrison again bowled well to finish with 2/11 off 10 overs. Altogether over 2½ hours were lost to rain on the second day. C.D. Gilliat, the Harrow captain, had a fine season with his leg spinners taking 45 wickets at an average of 11.60 per wicket.

Harrow won by 8 wickets

5p LORD'S GROUND 5p

ETON v. HARROW

Saturday (no play) & Sunday, July 13 & 14, 1974   (2-day Match)

ETON	First Innings		Second Innings
1 R. G. Martin	l b w b Leaf	1	
*2 E. R. Moodie	st Hopton b Norman	27	
3 C. H. Ballantine Dykes	c Lee b J. Morrison	0	
4 A. J. E. Malcolm	b J. Morrison	13	
5 Hon. R. J. Remnant	l b w b Norman	4	
†6 J. E. H. Ward	b Norman	2	
7 J. O. Mbu	c Phillips b Norman	8	
8 A. N. E. Baxter	b J. Morrison	4	
9 R. H. M. Raison	not out	3	
10 J. N. C. Gaisman	b J. Morrison	10	
11 Hon. J. A. L. Boyd	b J. Morrison	0	
	B 3, l-b 8, w 1, n-b 6,	18	B , l-b , w , n-b
	Total	90	Total

FALL OF THE WICKETS
1—3 2—7 3—34 4—42 5—44 6—54 7—66 8—79 9—90 10—90
1— 2— 3— 4— 5— 6— 7— 8— 9— 10—

ANALYSIS OF BOWLING	First Innings						Second Innings					
Name	O.	M.	R.	W.	Wd.	N-b	O.	M.	R.	W.	Wd.	N-b
J. Morrison	14	4	25	5	1	4						
Leaf	8	2	12	1								
Pigott	6	2	9	0								
Norman	11	5	18	4								
P. Morrison	6	2	6	0		2						

HARROW	First Innings		Second Innings
†1 R. E. P. Lee	run out	29	
2 R. C. Compton	l b w b Boyd	6	
3 A. C. S. Pigott	not out	37	
4 M. K. Fosh	not out	10	
5 P. R. C. Morrison			
*6 N. C. Hopton			
7 R. A. D. Onslow			
8 N. L. Phillps			
9 J. H. Morrison			
10 J. M. Norman			
11 E. A. G. Leaf			
	B 4, l-b , w 1, n-b 2,	7	B , l-b , w , n-b
	Total	91	Total

FALL OF THE WICKETS
1—26 2—57 3— 4— 5— 6— 7— 8— 9— 10—
1— 2— 3— 4— 5— 6— 7— 8— 9— 10—

ANALYSIS OF BOWLING	First Innings						Second Innings					
Name	O.	M.	R.	W.	Wd.	N-b	O.	M.	R.	W.	Wd.	N-b
Gaisman	5	3	13	0								
Baxter	6	3	10	0								
Boyd	14	5	28	1		1						
Remnant	5	2	8	0		1						
Ward	5	0	21	0								
Raison	2.3	0	4	0								

Umpires—D. E. Collins & H. E. Robinson   Scorers—J. C. de Ferranti & P. Davis

†Captain   *Wicket-keeper

Play begins 1st day at 11 a.m., 2nd day at 12.30 p.m.
Stumps drawn at 6.30 p.m. each day
Luncheon Interval 1st day 1.15 p.m.—1.55 p.m., 2nd day 2.00 p.m.—2.40 p.m.
Tea Interval 1st day 4.15 p.m.—4.35 p.m., 2nd day 4.45 p.m.—5.05 p.m.
(Tea Intervals may be varied according to state of game)

Eton won the toss

J.H. MORRISON'S MATCH

1974 July 13, 14   *Harrow won. by 8 wickets*

Eton   90   (J.H. Morrison 5/25)
Harrow   91-2

The first day's play having been washed out by rain the match became a one innings contest. Eton collapsed most disappointingly and were all out for 90 in 43 overs. J.H. Morrison again bowled well at Lord's taking 5/25 off 14 overs. Harrow were able to amble to their target in 37 overs, R.E.P. Lee, the Harrow captain, played a classy innings of 29 before he was run out in a hopeless mix up with A.C.S. Pigott who went on to make a promising 37 not out to take Harrow to an easy victory.

M.K. FOSH'S MATCH

1975 July 12, 13   *Harrow won by an innings and 151 runs*

Harrow   303-2   (M.K. Fosh 161 not out,
         dec.   R.C. Compton 63)
Eton   96   (A.C.S. Pigott 5/31, F.J. McMullen 4/3)
         56   (F.J. McMullen 3/10)

This was the strongest Harrow eleven for many a year and Eton were duly overwhelmed by a side containing three future county cricketers in the largest margin of victory for Harrow since the start of the series in 1805. An outstanding batting display by their captain, M.K. Fosh who scored 161 not out, the third highest score in the history of the match, and a fine second wicket partnership of 125 with R.C. Compton, 63, the Harrow opener, put Harrow on the road to success. Fosh, a left-hander who showed excellent footwork and positioning to play a variety of attacking shots, batted only 145 minutes hitting four sixes and twenty-four fours. The declaration came at 303/2 and Eton were forced to bat the last eighty-five minutes of the first day after a shower of rain. They were never happy against the aggressive pace bowling of A.C.S. Pigott and finished on 46/5 at the end of the first day. Apart from R.H.M. Raison, the Eton captain, 41 in the first innings, there was little resistance in both innings from Eton's weak batting side and Pigott finished with 5/31 in the first innings off 19 overs and 3/28 in the second. F.J. McMullen, the medium-paced swing bowler and scion of the Hertfordshire brewing family, had even more remark-

M.K. Fosh, Harrow XI 1973/5, Cambridge Univ. 1977/8 and Essex. He captained Harrow in 1975 - he was Harrow's second highest individual scorer since the start of the series in 1805, with 161 not out in their overwhelming victory by an innings and 151 runs, the greatest margin of victory by Harrow in the history of the match. His 778 runs in the season was, until then, the highest individual total since the war for Harrow. He had the ability and natural talent to reach the highest levels of the game but not perhaps the will, nevertheless one of Harrow's two best batsman since the war.

The fine Harrow XI of 1975 who won by an overwhelming innings and 151 runs and were probably Harrow's strongest side since the war, ranking equally with the XI of 2005 and Harrow's greatest win since 1805.
LEFT TO RIGHT, BACK ROW: *T.D. Glennie, J.D.S. Fricker, D.R. Baucher, H.M.D. Jones, R.M. Tindall, F.J. McMullen.* SEATED: *A.C.S. Pigott, R.C. Compton, M.K. Fosh (capt), N.C. Hopton, P.D.M. Greig.*

A.C.S. Pigott, Harrow XI 1974/6, Sussex, Surrey and England. Harrow captain in 1976 when they narrowly failed to pull off a resounding hat-trick of wins. One of the three outstanding Harrow fast bowlers since the war.

able figures of 4/3 in the first innings and 3/10 in the second. Fosh, the Harrow captain, had a great year taking Harrow to nine victories and only one defeat in the season, scoring 778 runs at an average of 70.72 and also taking 33 wickets with his medium pacers. Pigott's wickets tally of 58 in the season at 10.55 per wicket was also outstanding and the Harrow record until 1985 when beaten by Jason Pethers with 59 wickets.

		R.M. TINDALL'S MATCH
1976 July 10, 11		*Match Drawn*

Eton	220	(M.R. Kary 63)
	112-9	(R.M. Tindall 5/39)
Harrow	328-9 dec.	(R.M. Tindall 151)

Harrow very nearly pulled off their third victory in succession and were unbeaten by a school since Eton last won this match in 1970. Eton knew what awaited them from 12 months ago and started their innings disastrously when H.L.A. Hood, the Eton opener, was bowled first ball for 0 by A.C.S. Pigott, the Harrow captain, and only a lively eighth wicket partnership between M.R. Kary, 63, and P.D. Whitby, the Eton wicket-keeper, 36, of 106 in 55 minutes kept Eton in the match. The left-handed R.M. Tindall played a superb innings of 151 in Harrow's reply

of 328 for 9 dec., reminiscent of his father M. Tindall, the old Harrow and Cambridge captain, striking 20 fours in an innings full of graceful drives. Extras of 49 did not help Eton's cause due to some wayward bowling. Despite fine spin bowling by R.M. Tindall, 5/39 off 18.2 overs, Eton just managed to hold out with one wicket left and only four runs ahead. Both Tindall and Pigott had very good seasons. Tindall with 601 runs at an average of 50.08 and Pigott with 57 wickets at an average of 12.21 to add to his 58 wickets in 1975 and an impressive 127 wickets in his three years in the eleven.

1977 July 9, 10		*Eton won by 6 wickets*

Harrow	225-7 dec.	(T.D. Glennie 84)
	94-5 dec.	
Eton	127	(J.L. Rawlinson 53)
	196-4	(R.H.M. Raison 73 not out, J.L. Rawlinson 61)

Harrow at one stage appeared to have this match for the taking when at the end of the first day they had scored 225 for 7 dec. and taken seven Eton wickets for 93. A fine opening stand by T.D. Glennie, 84, playing in his third Lord's match, and D.P. Wiggin, 22, of 109, set Harrow on

The fortunate Eton XI of 1977 which won by 6 wickets against the run of play due to a generous declaration by the Harrow captain Robert Tindall, son of Mark Tindall. LEFT TO RIGHT, BACK ROW: E.B.S. Farmer, R.J. Compton-Burnett, N.Y.J. Kirkpatrick, J. Boughey (12th man), Hon. J.P.C. Purnell, P.W. Morris, T.W. Prest. SEATED: P.D. Whitby, J.L. Rawlinson, R.H.M. Raison (capt), C.P.W. Buller, N.D. Burney.

the right path. Eton failed to make much headway against the accurate seam bowling of F.J. McMullen, 2/17 off 21 overs, and T.M.H. James, 3/34 off 22 overs, which left them in a weak position at the end of the first day, only J.L. Rawlinson, 53, prospering. After gaining a first innings lead of 98 Harrow made rather slow progress in the second innings with T.M.H. James's 34 not out being the best in Harrow's total of 94/5 dec. R.M. Tindall, the Harrow captain, set Eton a generous target of 193 in 160 minutes which after their first innings display they seemed unlikely to make. But Eton's R.H.M. Raison, captain for the second year running 73 not out, and J.L. Rawlinson, 61, in a stand of 101 confounded the Harrow supporters and took Eton home to victory with one ball to spare, their first victory for seven years although slightly fortuitous perhaps. J.L. Rawlinson had a very fine season for Eton scoring 728 runs at an average of 56.00 and R.M. Tindall the Harrow captain scored over 500 runs and took 37 wickets in the season showing the potential which persuaded Northants to offer him a contract.

T.M.H. JAMES'S MATCH

1978 July 15, 16   *Match Drawn*

Eton	112	
	219-9	(J.R. Boughey 73, P.J.R. Goulder 59)
Harrow	341-6 dec.	(T.M.H. James 112 not out, W.J. Haggas 65)

Eton were very fortunate to scrape a draw in a match Harrow dominated from start to finish. Good medium-pace seam bowling from the Harrow captain, T.M.H. James 3/32 off 20 overs and C.L. Feather, son of the winning Harrow captain of 1952 R.L. Feather, 4/35 off 15 overs, restricted Eton to 112 in their first innings. Harrow's formidable first innings total was dominated by an aggressive hard hitting innings of 112 not out from their captain James, son of the Cambridge blue R.M. James who scored a century against the 1956 Australians. He was well supported by W.J. Haggas, 65, E.C. Gordon-Lennox, 47, and D.P. Wiggin, 41, in Harrow's total of 341/6 dec. Eton looked doomed to defeat when they were 43/3 in their second innings but J.R. Boughey, 73 the son of Eton's 1939 captain, and P.J.R. Goulder, who had been dropped the previous year, with 59 in a partnership of 127 in 105 minutes, just saved Eton from an ignominious defeat. Eton were still 10 runs behind with the last pair together at the close. James, the Harrow

captain, had an excellent season scoring 560 runs and taking 45 wickets at a cost of 11.73. P.W. Morris, the Eton opener, scored 728 runs in the season at an average of 45.50 and C.G. Crace took 44 wickets at a cost of 11.04 with his medium-pace swing bowling.

W.J. HAGGAS' MATCH

1979 July 14, 15   *Match Drawn*

Eton	261	(R.J. Compton-Burnett 66, H.T. Rawlinson 50, J.P. Boden 50)
	138-7 dec.	
Harrow	211-2 dec.	(W.J. Haggas 87 not out)
	8-0	

Eton's first innings was based round a fluent innings of 66 from their captain, R.J. Compton-Burnett, son of Cambridge blue and Eton master A.C. Burnett, well supported by H.T. Rawlinson, 50, and J.R. Boden, 50. Harrow scored reasonably quickly and declared on 211 for 2 with four hours of play remaining. This was a very sporting gesture as the Harrow captain, W.J. Haggas, was only 13 short of joining the small number of Harrovians who have made centuries in this match. He was well supported by E.C. Gordon Lennox, 47 not out, and M.W.J. Ruffell, 46. Slow batting by Eton in the second innings, particularly the captain who spent half an hour on one, and defensive field placing and bowling by Harrow's battery of six seam bowlers resulted in stalemate and Eton were not able to get enough runs to set Harrow a sensible target. Harrow were left only 15 minutes batting at the end. W.J. Haggas, the Harrow captain, performed well throughout the season scoring 475 runs at an average of 52.77, taking 35 wickets at the low cost of 10.28 per wicket and leading them in an unbeaten season.

1980 July 12, 13   *Match Drawn*

Harrow	230-9 dec.	(S.E. Haggas 75, I.R.M.D. Bluett 6/55)
Eton	90	(O.F.O. Findlay 4/13)
	141-4	(O.F.O. Findlay 3/12)

Harrow had much the better of the drawn game which was affected by rain on the second day. S.E. Haggas, the 16-

year-old brother of Harrow's 1979 captain W.J. Haggas, batted well for his 75, supported by the Harrow captain, C.L. Feather, 48. Only I.R.M.D. Bluett was a threat to Harrow with his medium-pace swing bowling, taking 6/55 off 26.2 overs. Eton were bowled out by lunch on the second day for 90, largely due to some hostile medium-pace bowling from O.F.O. Findlay, 4/13 off 13 overs, and the leg spin of F.W.A. Horn, 4/25 off 21 overs. Eton showed much more resolution in their second innings, especially their captain H.T. Rawlinson 41, and were one run ahead with six wickets in hand when rain ended play two hours early. Findlay again bowled well to take 3/12 off nine overs and 7/25 in the match. He finished with 32 wickets in the season at the very low average of 8.37 per wicket.

1981 July 11, 12   *Match Drawn*

Harrow	209-8 dec.	(R.C. Patrick 56)
	148-2 dec.	(S.E. Haggas 63 not out)
Eton	126	(C.C. Birch Reynardson 66, R.C. Patrick 5/28)
	94-1	(C.C. Birch Reynardson 50 not out)

Eton put Harrow in to bat and when they had taken the first three wickets for 11 runs looked likely to dismiss Harrow for the first time in 10 years. But R.C. Patrick, 56, and A.M.H. Ford, 36, produced a fourth wicket partnership of 94 and Harrow were able to declare on 209/8 and at the close of the first day Eton were 93/3. However, after they had progressed to 111 with C.G. Birch Reynardson on 66, there was a total collapse and they were all out for 126 with some fine bowling from R.C. Patrick who took 5/28 off 20.2 overs, well supported by T.S.M.S. Riley-Smith, 3/24 off 16 overs. Although Harrow batted well in their second innings to score 148/2 with the captain S.E. Haggas 63 not out, the target was far too stiff for Eton, 232 to win in 150 minutes, and no attempt was made to go for them. Birch Reynardson scored 50 not out with Eton finishing on 94/1 at the close. Both teams had good seasons, Harrow were unbeaten in 14 matches and Eton only lost one match but appeared to be stronger in batting with Birch Reynardson scoring 698 runs at an average of 50 and M.V. Fleming, the future Combined Services, Kent and England one day player, scoring 563 runs at an average of 38. It was somewhat

surprising that Birch Reynardson did not get a trial in the schools representative fixtures.

1982 July 3 *Match drawn*

Eton	216-3 dec.	(M.H Brooks 71 not out, M.V. Fleming 52)
Harrow	108-5	

In the first Eton and Harrow fixture played as a one day match at Lord's except for the War years, Eton decidedly had the better of the contest. After Eton had been put in to bat they took full advantage of an easy-paced wicket to score freely off the weak Harrow bowling attack. M.V. Fleming, 52, and D.N. Gibbs put on 72 for the first wicket and M.H. Brooks, 71 not out, and J.P. Berry, 45, then added 114 for the third wicket before the declaration came and Harrow were left to score 217 to win in 150 minutes. Some tight bowling from Eton's seam attack of Fleming, 1/1 off 8 overs, E. Brassey and C. Pettifer, left Harrow on 45/5 facing defeat. But in the final hour J.D.R. Field, 19 not out, and D.R. Nirmalalingham, a 15-year-old Sri Lankan, 37 not out, defended well to put on an undefeated 63 to save the match for Harrow. Eton had an excellent season and were unbeaten with eight wins as were Harrow who were unbeaten for the second year running, although a lack of penetration in their bowling resulted in twelve drawn matches. it was again surprising that Fleming was not chosen for any of the representative matches since he had an excellent all-round season with 648 runs and 36 wickets.

1983 July 2, 1   *Match drawn*

Harrow	214-6 dec.	(J.M.H. Ford 73)
Eton	150-7	

In an evenly contested match Harrow probably had the edge. J.M.H. Ford, 73, and W.E. Peel-Yates, 45, put on 123 for the second wicket in Harrow's 214/6 dec. The medium-pace bowlers on both sides were constrictingly accurate and only F.P.E. Marsland, 49, was able to score reasonably freely against the Harrow attack but Eton still finished 64 short of the Harrow score with only three wickets left at the close. Eton once again had a good season only losing one match and winning seven whilst Harrow had an unbeaten season for the third year running but again with far too many draws, nine out of eleven completed Fixtures. J.W.S. Raper, the Harrow captain, played for the Rest v. the Southern Schools and had a good all round season with 503 runs at an average of 42 and 26 wickets at 12.38 per wicket whilst C.E. Pettifer, the Eton opening bowler, took 47 wickets at an average of 14.38 per wicket.

The 1985 Eton XI which scraped home in a thrilling game by 3 runs, the closest run margin in the history of the match. LEFT TO RIGHT, BACK ROW: *J.B.A. Jenkins, J.D. Norman, J.A.D. Carr, N.B. Squire, W.A.C. Pym, D.A. Clifton-Brown, T.M. King.* SEATED: *A.D.A. Zagoritis, F.N. Bowman-Shaw, S.R. Gardiner (capt.), T.R. Pearson, C.R. Erith.*

1984 July 7   *Match drawn*

Eton	166	(F.N. Bowman-Shaw 51, D.B.M. Fox 5/36)
Harrow	73-6	

In the 149th match between the schools the game ended tamely. The fine Harrow opening attack of D.B.M. Fox and J.J. Pethers had Eton in trouble from the start and only F.N. Bowman-Shaw, 51, aided by N.E. Evans-Lombe, 29, and J.B,A. Jenkins, a 14-year-old, 20, batted with any certainty. Fox finished with figures of 5/36 off 21.4 overs and Pethers 4/55 off 20 overs. An Eton score of 166 looked infinitely possible for Harrow with nearly 180 minutes to obtain them. However Harrow batted with such caution that they struggled to avoid an ignominious defeat, finishing on 73/6 at the close. C.G.M. Redmayne, the Eton opening bowler, took 3/22 off 17 overs, well supported by A.G. Butterwick with 2/18 off 14 overs. Redmayne had a fine season with the ball carrying the Eton attack and took 46 wickets at an average of 12.39 in twelve completed fixtures, nearly four wickets per match and a very fine performance.

The 1985 Harrow XI which lost a low scoring game by the narrowest of margins, the closest in the history of the fixture. LEFT TO RIGHT, BACK ROW: *A.W. Sexton, R.A.J. Hills, R.M. Wells, M.D.S. Raper, M.R. Middleton, D.C. Manasseh, P. Davis (Professional).* SEATED: *G.E.G. Waud, D.B.M. Fox, R.C. Wiltshire (capt.), R.A. Pyman, J.J. Pethers.*

1985 July 6   *Eton won by 3 runs*

Eton	141	(J.J. Pethers 6/87)
Harrow	138	(F.N. Bowman-Shaw 7/38)

In a low scoring match Eton achieved victory by the narrowest of margins, their 50th victory in the 150th contest between the two schools, largely due to an outstanding all-round performance from F.N. Bowman-Shaw with a vital 42 out of 141 and joint top scorer with W.A.C. Pym and 7/38 off 16.1 overs of medium-pace swing bowling. In his second fine performance at Lord's J.J. Pethers bowled fast and accurately to take 6/87 off 26.2 overs and achieve a new Harrow wicket-taking record of 59 wickets in the season, well supported by D.B.M. Fox, 2/24, and

M.D.S. Raper, 2/24, to bowl Eton out for 141. Harrow started confidently led by R.C. Wiltshire, the Harrow captain, and R.M. Wells but collapsed rapidly from 64/2 to 98/9 when it looked all over for Harrow. However R.A. Hills, the Harrow wicket-keeper, 46, bravely supported by the No.11, M.R. Middleton, put on 40 for the last wicket before Hills was caught on the boundary at deep square-leg, four short of the target, with what would have been the winning hit and 2.5 overs to spare. Pethers fine performance during the season gained him a place in the Rest side v. the Southern Schools although he did not progress further despite a reasonable performance with both bat and ball, competition for places was very fierce.

HARROW'S WORST OF CENTURY

By A. S. R. WINLAW

THERE WERE some unkind Etonian reminescences of the famous 1910 "Fowlers Match" on Saturday when Harrow were dismissed for just 37 runs—their lowest total this century in the 151st edition of the oldest fixture at Lord's.

Heavy overnight rain prevented any play until 3 p.m. and later, just as triumphant Eton were going out to bat, the bad weather returned and the match was abandoned

The smallest total ever recorded is Harrow's 24 in 1823; Eton were all out for 35 in 1855.

York, who conceded only six runs from nine overs, and Pettifer three for 22 dismissed the opening batsmen before Harrow suffered a cruel blow. Sexton was hit above the eye, attempting to hook a ball from York, and retired hurt, requiring nine stitches. He was unable to bat again.

HARROW

*R. A. Pyman, c MacLeay, b Pettifer ...	4
D. I. H. Greenall, c MacLeay, b York ..	0
A. W. Sexton, ret'd ht	5
M. D. S. Raper, c Teeger, b Pettifer	10
J. J. Pethers, c Winter, b Pettifer	5
B. W. M. Burgess, b Pym	8
D. C. Mannsseh, st Teeger, b Norman..	5
R. T. Brankin-Frisby, lbw, b Norman ..	0
A. C. W. Snow, c Lunt, b Pym	0
N. C. Morgan, b Norman	0
†A. K. C. Green, not out	2
Extras (lb 2)	2
Total	37

Fall of wickets: 1-1, 2-9, 3-21, 4-24, 5-31, 6-35, 7-35, 8-35, 9-37.

Bowling: York 9-5-6-1; Pettifer 9-2-22-3; Pym 6-1-5-6-2; Norman 6-5-1-3.

ETON: †J. A. Teeger, R. O. MacLeay, *A. D. A. Zagoritis, W. A. C. Pym, L. Fernandes, D. M. Pearson, C. E. C. Winter, A. R. G. Lunt, J. D. Norman, H. D. Pettifer, C. York.

1986 July 5 — *Match Drawn*

Harrow	37	
Eton		did not bat.

Overnight rain delayed the start until three o'clock in the afternoon when Harrow collapsed in desultory fashion and were all out for 37 in less than two hours and 30.1 overs, their lowest total since 1847*. All four Eton bowlers shared in the nine wickets that fell, J.D. Norman having the most remarkable figures of 6 overs, 5 maidens, 3 wickets for one run. A disastrous performance by Harrow was only mitigated by further rain in late afternoon which stopped the Eton formality of scoring 38 runs for victory and left the match abandoned as a draw. If ever there was a travesty of justice this must have been the ultimate. J.J. Pethers was unable to sustain his outstanding performance of the previous year but finished with 33 wickets in the season and an improved batting performance.

* *when Harrow scored 27 including 10 extras in their first innings and E.W Blore, the Eton bowler, took 15 wickets in the match, achieving the highest number of wickets ever recorded in the fixture.*

1987 July 4 — *Match Drawn*

Harrow	196-8	(H.Boralessa 68)
Eton	169-5	(R.D.O MacLeay 70 not out)

A record Harrow first-wicket stand in the 152 matches played between the two schools of 116, between H. Boralessa and M.B.T. de Souza Girao, was finally broken soon after lunch when Boralessa was run out for 68, after which there was a collapse of 5 wickets for six runs. T.P.M. Fleming, the Eton left-arm spinner and younger brother of Matt Fleming, was extremely accurate in a spell of 27 overs for 33 runs and 2 wickets but the Harrow total was boosted by 20 wides and no balls, mainly from the opening bowlers. Eton were set 197 runs to win in 140 minutes and although the Eton captain, R.D.O. MacLeay, played very well for 70 not out, they fell well short of the target. Eton received only 44 overs compared to Harrow's 74 and could be considered the moral victors. Eton had a most successful year and were undefeated for the first time since 1982, the captain MacLeay being the main success with 548 runs in the season at an average of 50. D.C. Manasseh, the son of Maurice Manasseh, the old

Middlesex and Oxford University cricketer and Harrow captain, played for the Southern Schools v. the Rest in the representative match at Oxford but failed to progress further. He was undoubtedly talented but suffered from an attitude problem rather like his father before him.

C. Keey, Harrow XI 1987/8 and Oxford 1992/3, Harrow captain and best player in 1988. This combative South African played for Durham University, and gained Oxford blues in 1992/3 batting with some success against the counties.

1988 June 25   *Match Drawn*

Harrow   215-7   (J.K.Bourne 67)
           dec.

Eton   197-6   (C.H.G. St. George 84 not out, J.E. Carr 51)

Harrow's innings was built around H. Boralessa who took more than three hours over 42, although C. Keey, 37, and J.K Bourne, 67, had both batted attractively and C. Raper scored 24 not out at the end of the innings. Eton left 48 overs to score 216, went bravely for the runs and when C.H.G.St. George, 84 not out, and J.E. Carr, 51, were together adding 123 it seemed Eton could do it. But once Carr was unluckily run out the momentum was lost and Eton finished 19 runs short of the target. C. Keey, Harrow's South African captain, had a most successful year scoring 703 runs in the season at an average of 44 and was unlucky not to get a trial in the representative matches. He later proved for Oxford that he had class in his batting.

1989 June 10   *Match Drawn*

Eton   226-5 dec.   (E.R. Lush 89, S.R.B. Martin 71)
Harrow   171-6

C. Raper, the Harrow captain, decided to put Eton in on a slow pitch. After A.G. Bignell, 41, and E.R. Lush, 89, had put on 112 for the first wicket and W. Edlin took 3 wickets with his medium pace swing, S.R.B. Martin set about the Harrow bowling with gusto, hitting nine fours in his 71 from 82 balls. J.T. Trusted, the Eton wicket-keeper and captain, declared minutes after Martin's dismissal leaving Harrow to score 227 in 175 minutes. After a good opening partnership between S.H. Aldous, 35, and C.J.A. Virgin, 37, Harrow lost five wickets for 98 after 37 overs to the contrasting spin of H. Chetwood's off-breaks and T.M. Fleming's slow left arm. J.A.R. Hill 47 not out, and M.E.D. Jarrett, 22, batted well in the last hour to save the day for Harrow on 171/6 at the close.

The Eton XI of 1990 which won by 7 wickets against the clock. LEFT TO RIGHT, BACK ROW: *J.A. Claughton (Master-in-Charge Eton cricket), B.K. Ssennyamantono, W.R.G. Sellar, J.M.S. Whittington, T.A.J. Jenkins, J.J.S. Larken, G.H.B. Lewis, S.C.E. Strickland, J.M. Rice (coach).* SEATED: *T.J. Stanley, N.R.J. Hagen, H.J.P. Chetwood, P.M. Eastwood, C.N. Ulvert.*

1990 June 9   *Eton won by 7 wickets*

Harrow   219-8. dec

Eton   221-3   (W.R.G. Sellar 57, P.M. Eastwood 53, N.R.J. Hagen 53 not out)

Eton achieved a convincing victory, the first result since 1985, by successfully chasing a target of 220 runs in 153 minutes. Harrow put in to bat made a very slow start, S.H. Aldous, 26, and M.A. Holyoake, 47, put on 77 for the first wicket in 32.3 overs but afterwards there was a good partnership from S.M. Guillebaud, 34, and E.M.S. Hewens to take Harrow to respectability on the declaration. J.M.S. Whittington bowled well in a long spell of slow left-arm bowling to take 3/78 off 25 overs for Eton. After a solid opening partnership P.M. Eastwood, 53, and W.R.G. Sellar, 57, added 50 for the second wicket in 38 minutes. Eton needed 121 off the last 20 overs but Sellar and N.R.G. Hagen put on 70 in 46 minutes to put Eton in the driving seat. Hagen aided by S.C.E. Strickland scored the remaining 54 runs in the last half-hour to take Eton home with four balls to spare. H.J.P. Chetwood, the Eton captain, represented the Rest v. the Southern Schools but unluckily did not go on to further honours.

1991 June 8   *Eton won by 3 wickets*

Harrow   142   (C.G. Hill 54)

Eton   146-7   (M.M.J. Hawkins 5/50)

Eton achieved a second successive win over Harrow, rather more narrowly this time and Harrow made them fight all the way. Harrow struggled in their innings, particularly against E.J.M. Amies who took 4/33 off 13 overs. After thirteen overs they had scored 30/3 and could well have lost another at 45 when R.J. Preece was caught off a no-ball. But C.G. Hill's dogged defence kept Harrow in the game and he and Preece built a stand of 62 before J.M.S. Whittington took 3/41 off 24.3 overs to finish off the Harrow innings. M.M.J. Hawkins bowled particularly well for Harrow with his left-arm round the wicket medium pace, ducking the ball into the Eton batsman at a lively pace and thoroughly deserving his five wickets. If Harrow had scored another twenty or thirty runs the result could well have gone the other way.

1992 June 24   *Match Drawn*

Harrow	209-3 dec.	(H.St.J.R. Foster 102 not out, J.A.J. Renshaw 80 not out)
Eton	137-7	(M.M.J. Hawkins 5/35)

Eton put Harrow in to bat and immediately had them in trouble with Harrow on 13/3 after nine overs with A.F. Douglas, the Eton opening bowler, dismissing N.G. Harrap and C.B.J. Danby for 0 and 1. H.St.J.R. Foster and J.A.J. Renshaw batted very cautiously and Harrow had scored only 81 by lunchtime. During the afternoon the partnership prospered and an unbroken stand of 196 was reached over nearly four hours before the declaration came, despite the tidy spin bowling of T.M.A. Wemyss and C.G.R. Lightfoot. Foster, the son of D.R.J., Harrow captain in 1959 and grandson of J.H.N, scored the first century for Harrow since T.M.H. James's 112 not out in 1978 and hit 13 fours in 239 deliveries received. In retrospect Harrow, who batted for 87 overs, went on far too long and set a stiff target of 210 in 44 overs against a very inexperienced Eton side. For the second year running M.M.J. Hawkins bowled beautifully to take 5/35 off 17 overs and at one stage Harrow came close to victory. Eton were steered to safety by the dogged defence of J.J. Walsh, the Eton wicket-keeper with 21 not out, and Eton finished on 137 with three wickets in hand. Eton made up for a disappointing season by winning the Silk Trophy for the first time and Harrow only won one match out of 14 with 10 draws, an indictment of the defensive nature of most of their cricket during the season.

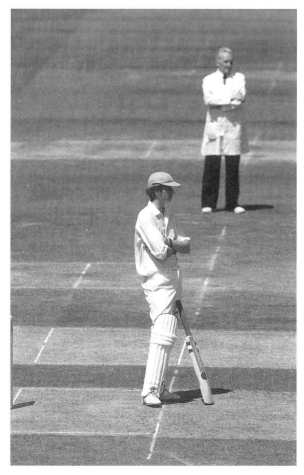

H.V. Machin, Eton XI 1993/4. His 150 not out in 1993 was the first Eton century at Lord's since M.J.J. Faber in 1968. A rather dour opener with some talent, he failed to improve in 1994 but played for Durham University later.

	H.V. MACHIN'S MATCH
1993 June 29	*Match Drawn*

Eton	254-2 dec.	(H.V. Machin 150 not out, T.A. Simpson 52)
Harrow	114-4	(J.A.J. Renshaw 57 not out)

On a good wicket Eton took advantage of some very poor Harrow bowling to lay waste to the Harrow attack. T.A. Simpson, the Eton captain, and H.V. Machin, the two openers, put on 149 for the first wicket and Machin scored the first century for Eton since M.J.J. Faber's 100 in 1968 and the sixth highest score for Eton in the history of the match. His innings included 13 fours from 193 balls received over nearly four hours but he was very fortunate to avoid an easy run out in the seventh over due to some inept fielding by Harrow in the covers. Thereafter he took advantage of a series of long hops, full tosses and rank bad bowling against the weak Harrow attack, M.P. Barker and B.A. Hollway being particularly guilty. Harrow set a target of 255 in 180 minutes were never in the hunt especially after losing their first three wickets for 21 runs. N.G. Harrap, the Harrow opener, failed for the second year running and was run out for 3 in the third over and A.I.H. McIntosh had to retire hurt when he was hit on the head by A.F. Douglas, the Eton opener. The Harrow captain J.A.J. Renshaw, who had hardly scored a run all season, came to the rescue and batted for 120 minutes for his fifty reached just before the close and was well supported by Barker and then S.D. Henson who batted an hour for 3 runs. By the close Harrow had only scored 114 runs in 55 overs and clearly Eton had been far too cautious against a modest Harrow side. If they had been more attacking Eton would have surely have won the day. Eton had an outstanding season and were unbeaten in their 17 matches with 9 wins and a team built around their two openers, Simpson and Machin. Simpson scored 835 runs in the season at an average of 52.18, the second highest total since the War after J.R.T. Barclay's 897 runs in 1970, and he went on to represent the Northern Schools v. Southern Schools in the representative match at Oxford. Machin also scored heavily and finished with 660 runs. The bowling was also effective and both Douglas and C.G.R. Lightfoot with 40 wickets performed well. Harrow fared less well and only Foster with 472 runs looked convincing with the bat and their bowling attack was the weakest for many years.

O. Chittenden, Harrow XI 1993/4. On his way to a fine 96 in a stand of 160 with Simon Roundell, 89.

1994 June 28   *Match Drawn*

Harrow	235-6 dec.	(O.H. Chittenden 96, S.F. Roundell 89)
Eton	230-7	(J.A.G. Fulton 112, J.C.S. Hardy 75, M.S. Rayner 4/47)

Eton won the toss and put Harrow in to bat in an attempt to force a result. After Harrow's first three wickets fell for 41 runs, O.H. Chittenden and S.F. Roundell regained the initiative and put on 160 together before being separated. Both looked likely to reach centuries but were dismissed by C.E. Steel's gentle spin on 96 and 89 respectively. When the declaration finally came after 81 overs Eton were set a demanding target of scoring 236 in 46 overs, a run rate of over five an over. After H.V. Machin, the previous year's centurion, was l.b.w to M.S. Rayner, the Harrow opening bowler, for nought, J.A.G. Fulton, a 16-year-old making his debut, and J.C.S. Hardy set about the Harrow attack with relish on a fast outfield. They especially 'went for a succession of leg stump half volleys and long hops from M.G. Hatcher whose six overs opening the bowling went for a disastrous 46 runs. S.F. Roundell's fourteen overs went for 82 runs, his analysis was only saved by two wickets in the last over. Fulton and Hardy made such good progress, putting on 179 in 23 overs, that coming to the last eight overs 60 runs were needed with 9 wickets in hand. Fulton reached the third successive century in a row in this match and in a very fine knock he hit three sixes and eleven fours from 138 balls and but for some superb fast bowling from M.S.

Rayner, a tall South African in his only year at Harrow, Eton would undoubtedly have won the match. He bowled Hardy and H.G. Duberly with successive deliveries and finally Fulton for 112. Nine runs were required from Roundell's last over and two wickets fell off the first two deliveries and for a wild moment any result was possible. Both sides had shot their bolt and honours remained even with Eton six runs short. Eton gained the plaudits however having had 35 fewer overs than Harrow. Eton had a most disappointing season after their previous record year with only two wins in their 13 completed fixtures and five losses. Only Fulton of the batsmen looked convincing, Machin had a poor year after his previous year's success and they suffered from a light-weight bowling attack unable to bowl sides out. Harrow fared no better and failed to win a match in their twelve completed fixtures, a sad indictment of their negative cricket. It was no surprise that the master in charge of cricket Bill Snowden resigned after 11 years in charge and was replaced by Mark Williams. It was hoped that this would engender a new more attacking spirit in Harrow cricket which had been lacking for some time.

1995 June 27 *Match Drawn*

Eton 219 (H.H. Dixon 100, T.D. de M. Leathes 6/19)
Harrow 176-7

Harrow with only two old flannels in their side finally convinced the sceptics that a new era of competitive, attacking cricket had begun. A young side had performed well throughout the season and gave Eton a real fight in this match. Eton were put in to bat and struggled against the Harrow seam attack of C.R.C. Parker, D.C.A. Titchener-Barrett, S.D.G. Engelen, the Harrow captain, and especially T.D.deM. Leathes with his out-swingers. Eton were dismissed for the first time in 10 years and but for a determined knock from H.H. Dixon, the Eton opener with 100, they would have been in dire straits particularly against Leathes who took 6/19 in 16 overs, the best analysis by a Harrovian since the match became a one-day fixture in 1982. Eton had used up 75 overs in accumulating their total and for once the boot was on the other foot. Harrow had a maximum 155 minutes to achieve a target of 220 and Eton's openers exacerbated the situation by bowling their overs very slowly with short, wide and bouncing balls on the quick Lord's wicket. Both Harrow openers were back in the pavilion after three overs and all hope appeared to be lost when R.G. MacAndrew, the Harrow wicket-keeper and son of the Eton keeper of 1965 N.R. MacAndrew, lost his wicket at 52. The final 20 overs began with Harrow needing 156 with 7 wickets in hand. A.N.L. Cox, 45, and W.A.T. Gillions 33 not out attacked aggressively well supported by a neat 31 from O.C.T. Spry, but it was a well nigh impossible task, Harrow finishing 43 runs short with 3 wickets in hand. Harrow had 30 overs less batting than Eton and came out with much of the credit. For the first time for many years Harrow had a more successful season than Eton and were only found wanting against a very strong Tonbridge side. R.G. MacAndrew finished with an aggregate of 775 runs, the second highest total by a Harrovian since the war only beaten by M.K. Fosh, the Harrow captain of 1975 with 778 runs. He also took 30 victims behind the stumps including five at Lord's. S.D.G. Engelen took 43 wickets with his medium-pace swing bowling at an average of 15.40 per wicket, well supported by Leathes with 34 wickets. D.C.A. Titchener-Barrett also represented Middlesex in the under 19's County Championship. Eton had some fine young batsmen particularly the captain J.A.G. Fulton, the hero of 1994,

R.G. MacAndrew, Harrow XI 1995/6, The scorer of 775 runs for Harrow in 1995, 3 runs off Matthew Fosh's total in 1975. He also took a creditable 30 victims with his useful wicket-keeping, including 5 at Lord's.

D.C.A. Titchener-Barrett, son of the author, opening the bowling at Lord's for Harrow in 1995. He represented Middlesex under 19s and was in the combined Oxford squad and has proved to be a more than useful all-rounder for Wimbledon.

Three generations of Etonian cricketers, H Dixon, Eton XI 1995/6, son of M.H., Eton XI 1960/1 and grandson of G.H., Eton XI 1932/4. Scored 100 at Lord's in 1995, the third century in successive years and the only time this has been achieved in the history of the match. Eton's leading scorer in 1995 and 1996.

H.J.H. Loudon and H.H. Dixon. The 15-year-old O.L. Barnett, the Eton opening bowler who was injured for most of the season, clearly had potential and was to make good progress in 1996. There were indications that the long period of Eton domination might be coming to an end with John Claughton, the Eton Master in charge of cricket for ten years, leaving at the end of 1996, the conclusion of a highly successful period for Eton cricket. Harrovians fervently hoped that a Harrow win was near, they would have to wait a while longer though.

1996 June 25   *Match Drawn*

| Harrow | 238-8 dec. | (J.R.W. Norris 56, N.A. Bailey 5/44) |
| Eton | 139-4 | (A.M. Lea 57) |

Harrow had the better of a match contested by two strong sides with Harrow's lack of a strike bowler being their one weakness. A.N.L. Cox and R.G. MacAndrew both batted well against some good Eton seam bowling led by O.L. Barnett and J. Bruce. Both were out shortly before lunch for 37 and 32 respectively to leave Harrow on 101/3 at the interval. After lunch there was a fine attacking stand of 85 between J.R.W. Norris, 56, and W.A.T. Gillions, 28, to take the initiative back to Harrow. The declaration came after 63.3 overs of what was rather a slow over rate by the Etonians with the occasional medium pace of N.A. Bailey finishing with the surprising figures of 5/44 off 13.3 overs. H.H. Dixon and H.J.H. Loudon, the two Eton openers of last year, found it somewhat hard to score off Gillions and the sometimes wayward seam bowling of C.R.C. Parker, who nevertheless captured the prize wicket of Dixon, last year's centurion, with an in-ducking yorker. S.D.G. Engelen once again bowled steadily from the pavilion end to capture the

All tips off

THE ECCENTRIC racing tipster John McCririck spent yesterday at Lord's oldest fixture watching his old school, Harrow, take on Eton at cricket. He was wearing a blazer to rival that of John Redwood's supporter, the maverick MP Tony Marlow. The match was drawn.

Surrounded by schoolboys, he took a good barracking about his sideburns. "I take them off at night and stick them on again in the morning to save shaving," he snarled at the whippersnappers. Quite what he was doing there, nobody could fathom. "I was one of the great failures at Harrow," he said. "No good at cricket and only three O-levels. The only person in the country with fewer than me was John Major."

John McCririck going to blazers at Lord's in 1995.

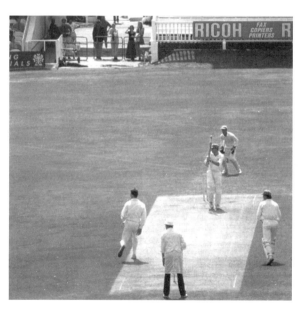

J.R.W. Norris, Harrow XI 1995/7. Son of D.W.W. 1961/4 on his way to a fine 56 in Harrow's 238/8 dec.

A.N.L. Cox, Harrow XI 1995/6, illustrating the style which made him the top scorer for Harrow with 672 runs in 1996. He captained the XI in 1997 with slightly less successful results.

wickets of Loudon and their captain J.A.G. Fulton for 0. Eton were now 23/3 and the shutters came down rapidly despite all Harrow's efforts to keep the game open. J.W.B. Neame, the 15-year-old Harrow leg-spinner and son of A.R.B. Neame, Harrow captain in 1954/5, bowled well on his debut match at Lord's to take 1/26 off 13 overs. A.M. Lea, 57, and Bailey, 36 not out, sons of two former Etonion cricketers saw their side home to safety. This capped a very fine sporting year for Bailey in which he achieved the unique treble of winning the singles Foster cup at rackets as well as the Schools doubles at Queen's and the Schools fives championship, a remarkable effort. Eton scored their 139 off 57 overs and it seemed incomprehensible that they did not make a greater attempt to achieve a result in what was John Claughton's last year in charge of Eton cricket. He left Eton cricket in good shape but the fear of losing marred his last appearance at Lord's. Always a challenging perfectionist, he will be remembered for improving the standard of Eton cricket markedly and making it more competitive. J.A.G. Fulton, the Eton captain of 1995/6, represented M.C.C. Schools v. Combined Services despite a moderate season and Dixon had a fine season with 702 runs. A.N.L. Cox scored 672 runs for Harrow in hard hitting style and proved a fine catcher. S.D.G. Engelen also performed well with 49 wickets and 472 runs in the Harrow season. Eton finished the season unbeaten and Harrow lost only to Tonbridge in the term and Millfield and the Antipodeans in the Schools festival.

S.D.G. Engelen, Harrow XI 1994/6. He captained Harrow in 1995 with success, winning eight matches. His all-round capabilities were shown to good effect in 1996 when he took 49 wickets in the season with his fine swing bowling and scored 472 runs.

1997 June 27 *Match Abandoned*

ETON

H. J. H. Loudon†, Hon. D. C. Kay-Shuttleworth,
A. F. S. Leslie, J. R. S. Redmayne, D. R. Vassar-Smith,
A. G. R. Loudon, J. T. A. Bruce, R. F. Horne*,
O. R. A. Shuttleworth, L. J. Rankin, P. A. Norman-Butler.

HARROW

W. J. L. Matthews, L. F. de Rougemont*, A. N. L. Cox†,
S. H. Stevens, J. R. W. Norris, D. R. Hepher,
A. T. R. Titchener-Barrett, J. S. Weston-Simons, J. R. F.
Cooke-Hurle, J. W. B. Neame, P. F. Bourke.

†Captain   *Wicket-keeper

This was the first match in the whole series that had been
totally abandoned. The wettest June for a century kept its
reputation to the end as the authorities declared the
ground waterlogged at 8.30 a.m. The match would have
been especially interesting as the two Captains, Hugo
Loudon of Eton, and Andrew Cox of Harrow, both came
from the same prep. school Wellesley House, Broadstairs,
to which Lord Cowdrey sent his three talented sons and
long a nursery for good cricketers. They had opened the
batting together in 1992 when Wellesley won the Prep.
Schools' Knockout Cup. There had been some concern
that the fixture would again end in a draw. A century ago,
after the 1897 match, the demand was for a third day. This
was declined by Eton. In 1997 it was agreed by the two
masters in charge – Simon Doggart at Eton and Mark
Williams at Harrow after much debate at both schools– to
play an experimental formula of 65 overs for the side batting first and 50 overs for the side batting second, with the
option of a draw.

In a very wet summer when seven matches were abandoned Eton went through the season unbeaten winning
six matches and drawing six. This was largely due to the
prolific form of the two openers Hugo Loudon, the
capatain and David Kay-Shuttleworth. The ten stands
they shared included one of more than 200, two over 100
and six worth 50 or more. Loudon averaged nearly 90 and
Kay-Shuttleworth 71. The bowling was always tight but
often less penetrative than it should have been. Harrow
also had a reasonable season winning seven matches with
Andrew Cox, the captain leading the way with 599 runs.
Although the bowling was tidy with Jack Cooke-Hurle
and Jasper Neame to the fore, again it was not always
incisive enough.

Eton 1998. LEFT TO RIGHT, BACK ROW: *G.G. Maan, S.J.R. Ross, R.J.B. Edes, W.S.L. Patrick, C.M. Matheson, C.I.C. Bond, O.G.C. Broome.*
SEATED: *S.E.S. FitzGerald, A.F.S. Leslie, A.G.R. Loudon (Captain), J.T.A. Bruce, S.L.J. McL. Hawke.*

Harrow 1998. LEFT TO RIGHT, BACK ROW: *S.H. Stevens, L.F. de Rougemont, L.C.L. FitzWilliams, J.R.F. Cooke-Hurle, A.M.A. Andjel, J.A.S. Dixon.*
SEATED: *J.M.G.S. Warman, W.J.L. Matthews, D.R. Hepher (Captain) A.T.R. Titchener-Barrett, J.S. Weston-Simons.*

1998 June 26 *Match Drawn*

Harrow	195-7 dec.	(L. F. de Rougemont 68, J. T. A. Bruce 6/40)
Eton	165-3	(A. G. R. Loudon 64 not out, G. G. Maan 47 not out)

A new format was tried in this match with a maximum of
115 overs in the match, with the side batting first allowed
up to 65 overs. Since rain accounted for 28 of these, it
might have been better to have had an even quota. It was,
however, a spirited contest with the features being the fine
batting of Luke de Rougemont 68, well supported by Sam

LORD'S GROUND

150 years of printing scorecards at

1848   1998

30p   30p

ETON v. HARROW

FRIDAY, 26th JUNE, 1998   (1-day Match)

HARROW   Innings
1 A. M. A. Andjel	c Maan b Bruce	14
2 A. T. R. Titchener-Barrett	c Ross b Bruce	14
*3 L. F. de Rougemont	c Ross b Bruce	68
4 S. H. Stevens	b Bruce	26
5 W. J. L. Matthews	run out	31
†6 D. R. Hepher	c Ross b Bruce	2
7 J. A. S. Dixon	c Bond b Bruce	8
8 J. S. Weston-Simons	not out	8
9 J. R. F. Cooke-Hurle	not out	6
10 L. C. L. FitzWilliams		
11 J. M. G. S. Warman		

B , l-b 6, w 6, n-b 6, 18

Total .... (7 wkts dec.) 195

FALL OF THE WICKETS
1—30 2—42 3—102 4—158 5—168 6—181 7—186 8— 9— 10—

ANALYSIS OF BOWLING
Name	O.	M.	R.	W.	Wd.	N-b.
Bruce	16	2	40	6	2	3
Patrick	5	0	26	0	1	4
Matheson	6	0	20	0	1	...
Maan	8	2	36	0	1	...
Bond	3	1	14	0	1	...
Loudon	2	0	14	0	...	...
Broome	8	1	39	0	...	...

ETON   Innings
1 S. L. J. McL. Hawk	b Cooke-Hurle	13
2 S.E.S. FitzGerald	st de Rougemont b Stevens	19
3 A. F. S. Leslie	c Hepher b FitzWilliams	14
†4 A. G. R. Loudon	not out	64
5 G. G. Maan	not out	47
6 O. G. C. Broome		
7 C. I. C. Bond		
8 J. T. A. Bruce		
*9 S. J. R. Ross		
10 W. S. L. Patrick		
11 C. M. Matheson		

B 2, l-b 4, w , n-b 2, 8

Total .... (3 wkts, 39 overs) 165

FALL OF THE WICKETS
1—28 2—36 3—50 4— 5— 6— 7— 8— 9— 10—

ANALYSIS OF BOWLING
Name	O.	M.	R.	W.	Wd.	N-b.
Warman	10	1	32	0	...	2
Weston-Simons	4	1	25	0	...	...
Cooke-Hurle	12	2	50	1	...	...
Stevens	5	3	8	1	...	...
FitzWilliams	8	0	44	1	...	...

Umpires—J. M. Tythcott & D. O. Oslear   Scorers—C. J. Hamilton & G. O. F. Pepys

†Captain   *Wicket-keeper

Play begins at 11.00   Luncheon Interval 1.15—1.55   Tea Interval 4.40—5.00

115 overs match with a maximum of 65 overs for the side batting first

Stumps drawn at 7.00

(Timings may be varied according to state of game)

Eton won the toss and elected to field

Match drawn

Luke de Rougemont, Harrow XI 1997/2000. Arguably Harrow's best wicketkeeper/batsman since the War, an outstanding talent but unlikely to be promoted in county cricket.

1999 June 29   *Match Abandoned*

ETON

C. A. W. Taylor, O. G. C. Broome, A. G. R. Loudon†, G. G. Maan, A. P. Noorani, D. C. Ferreira, A. E. Knight, P. S. S. Patrick, P. P. Evans*, G. E. Crofton, S. W. F. Collins.

HARROW

T. G. Dunbar, K. Motaung, L. F. de Rougemont*, S. H. Stevens†, H. W. Jack, P. C. B. Harmsworth, N. R. D. Compton, C. J. M. Cooke-Hurle, A. G. D. Minoprio, R. J. Wilcox, E. C. C. Chute.

Stevens and Will Matthews, and the pace bowling of James Bruce with 6/40 on a green wicket who was the outstanding bowler on both sides.

Eton had put Harrow in and were 17 without loss after 5 overs before the long stoppage for rain. On resumption, Bruce made the ball move sharply and removed the two Harrow openers, Titchener-Barrett and Andjel, when well set at 30 and 42. Afterwards de Rougemont batted beautifully during a stand of 60 in 14 overs with Stevens that forced Alex Loudon to reintroduce Bruce and de Rougemont was finally dismissed after a 77 ball innings in the declaration push.

Eton in reply found it difficult to score off Harrow's seamers and, with three wickets down for 52, made little attempt to reach the Harrow target until near the end, when it was rather meaningless. Both Alex Loudon, the Eton captain and former England under-15 captain, and Gurrick Maan, batted soundly in a fourth wicket partnership of 113, and fell only 30 runs short, but it was all too late and the draw inevitable.

The second Lord's match totally abandoned to the rain. This would have been the first limited overs match of 55 overs per side but we would have to wait another year for this to happen.

Eton had an impressive season with a record 10 wins and a tie v. Tonbridge. The captain Alex Loudon scored 772 runs and took 26 wickets and was an outstanding captain recognised by the E.C.B. who chose him as England under 19 captain for the World Cup in 2000. Gurrick Maan took 8/27 in 9.5 overs v. Winchester and had an excellent season taking 48 wickets at 10 and also scoring 406 runs. Harrow did less well and would have struggled against the strength of Eton if the match had been played. Luke de Rougemont stood out as a quality wicketkeeper-batsman and easily topped the batting averages whilst the bowling was steady but unspectacular.

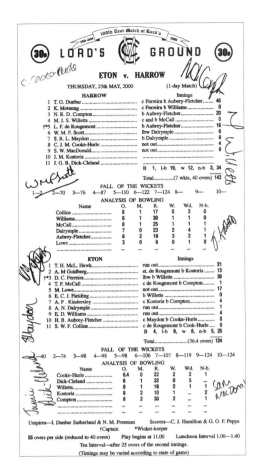

LORD'S GROUND
75th 2000 100th Test Match at Lord's 2000

ETON v. HARROW
THURSDAY, 25th MAY, 2000   (1-day Match)

HARROW

					Innings	
1	T. G. Dunbar				c Ferreira b Aubery-Fletcher	46
2	K. Motaung				c Ferreira b Williams	0
3	N. R. D. Compton				b Aubrey-Fletcher	20
4	M. J. S. Willetts				c and b McCall	0
†*5	L. F. de Rougemont				b Aubrey-Fletcher	16
6	W. M. F. Scott				lbw Dalrymple	6
7	S. R. L. Maydon				b Dalrymple	8
8	C. J. M. Cooke-Hurle				not out	4
9	S. W. MacDonald				not out	4
10	J. M. Kostoris					
11	J. G. B. Dick-Cleland					
					B 1, l-b 19, w 12, n-b 2,	34
					Total..........(7 wkts, 40 overs)	143

FALL OF THE WICKETS
1—2   2—70   3—76   4—87   5—110   6—122   7—124   8—   9—   10—

ANALYSIS OF BOWLING

Name	O.	M.	R.	W.	Wd.	N-b.
Collins	8	1	17	0	3	0
Williams	6	1	30	1	1	0
McCall	8	1	25	1	1	1
Dalrymple	7	0	23	2	4	1
Aubrey-Fletcher	8	2	19	3	2	1
Lowe	3	0	9	0	1	0

ETON

					Innings	
1	T. H. McL. Hawke				run out	21
2	A. M Goldberg				st. de Rougemont b Kostoris	13
†*3	D. C. Ferreira				lbw b Willetts	38
4	T. P. McCall				c de Rougemont b Compton	1
5	M. Lowe				not out	17
6	E. C. J. Fielding				b Willetts	0
7	A. P. Kindersley				c Kostoris b Compton	4
8	A. N. Dalrymple				run out	1
9	E. D. Williams				run out	4
10	H. B. Aubrey-Fletcher				c Maydon b Cooke-Hurle	0
11	S. W. F. Collins				c de Rougemont b Cook-Hurle	0
					B 4, l-b 8, w 8, n-b 5,	25
					Total..........(36.4 overs)	124

FALL OF THE WICKETS
1—40   2—74   3—98   4—98   5—98   6—106   7—107   8—119   9—124   10—124

ANALYSIS OF BOWLING

Name	O.	M.	R.	W.	Wd.	N-b.
Cooke-Hurle	6.4	0	22	2	2	1
Dick-Cleland	6	1	32	0	5	—
Willetts	8	1	18	2	1	1
Kostoris	8	2	10	1	—	2
Compton	8	2	30	2	—	1

Umpires—I. Dunbar Sutherland & N. M. Freeman   Scorers—C. J. Hamilton & G. O. F. Pepys
†Captain   *Wicket-keeper

55 overs per side (reduced to 40 overs)   Play begins at 11.00   Luncheon Interval 1.00—1.40
Tea Interval—after 25 overs of the second innings
(Timings may be varied according to state of game)

Eton 2000. LEFT TO RIGHT, BACK ROW: *F. Ackersley, E.C.J. Fielding, A.N. Dalrymple, A.P. Kindersley, E.D. Williams, T.P. McCall, A.M. Goldberg, A. England.* SEATED: *H.B. Aubrey-Fletcher, T.H.McL. Hawke, D.C. Ferreira (Captain), S.W.F. Collins, M. Lowe.*

Harrow 2000. LEFT TO RIGHT, BACK ROW: *S.W. MacDonald, M.J.S. Willetts, S.R.L. Maydon, J.G.B. Dick-Cleland, W.M.F. Scott, J.M. Kostoris.* SEATED: *C.J.M. Cooke-Hurle, N.R.D. Compton, L.F. de Rougemont (Captain), K. Montaung, T.G. Dunbar.*

2000 25 May   *Harrow won by 19 runs*

Harrow   143-7   (T G. Dunbar 46)
Eton   124

Harrow achieved their first victory over Eton for 25 years in the inaugural limited overs match between the two sides, reduced to 40 overs a side after heavy overnight rain and in unlikely style.

Play didn't start till 2 p.m. and then much to the chagrin of groundsman Mick Hunt and Harrow were put in to bat. They were indebted to Tom Dunbar, son of a Harrow housemaster, and Nick Compton, grandson of the great Denis, for a second wicket partnership of 68. Compton, who had come to the school on a sports scholarship from South Africa, looked the part until dismissed for 20, trying the sweep associated with his famous grandfather. What followed was not so impressive as Mike Willetts, promoted to swing the bat perished quickly for 0 and Luke de Rougemont was out for 16. A score of 143 did not look anywhere near enough especially as conditions favoured Eton with the outfield quicken-

ing up. The Eton spinners had bowled well, particularly Harry Aubrey-Fletcher with 3/19 off 8 overs. Eton looked comfortable at 98-2, particularly their captain, David Ferreira, with five boundaries in quick succession, who looked a class act. When he was out for 38, Eton needed 51 off the last 10 overs. Thereafter, they collapsed to 107-7 and eventually were all out for 124, not helped by three needless run-outs. An exemplary yorker from Willetts to bowl Fielding for 0 at an important stage of the innings was crucial, and he bowled well to take 2/18 off 8 overs as the Eton wickets were shared around. Harrow had gained their first win since the days of Matthew Fosh and Tony Pigott in 1974/5.

2001 June 16   *Match Abandoned*

ETON

A. C. H. Rudd, A. M. Goldberg, T. P McCall,
B. R. Thompson, R. C. Wallce, H. W. A. Clarke,
E. C. J. Fielding, H. E. F. Smith, S. W. F. Collins†,
J. H. Mathias*, F. P P. McN. Boyd.

HARROW

N. R. D. Compton†, S. W. MacDonald, S. R. L. Maydon,
P. R. Dunbar, A. W. Stileman, J. M. Kostoris,
R. V. G. Harmsworth, N. E. Defty, A. B. Mitchum*,
H. A. Fleming, P. D. Moseley.

The third match abandoned to the rain in five years was particularly sad as it was the only totally wet day throughout June. Eton were captained by Sam Collins, whose grandfather had captained Harrow in 1919, the first match after the Great War (see photograph) and Harrow by Nick Compton, grandson of Denis (Middlesex and England).

It was suggested there should be an unofficial game and this duly took place on Upper Club, Eton, on June 27th. It was a splendid occasion with lovely weather, parental support and a superb game of cricket. Eton scored 287/7 in their 55 overs, with Ben Thompson, a class act scoring 73 and Ainsley Barker 43. Harrow had given away too many runs in the last few overs, particularly Nick Compton, who had 30 runs taken off him in the last two overs of the Eton innings. Harrow looked to be in the driving seat on 254/4 with Nick Compton making 82 before being stumped. Harry Smith then performed the hat-trick with his off-spinners and despite a valiant 83 from Simon Maydon, Harrow finished 13 runs short. A very high quality match, but was some historian aware that Harrow had won a century earlier in 1900 and 1901 and fancied their chances once again?

Eton had a relatively moderate season with ten losses to seven wins in their seventeen completed matches. Ben Thompson and Tom McCall stood out as the two cricketers of class. Thompson scored 500 runs and took useful wickets and McCall scored 509 runs and took 29 wickets with his accurate off spinners. The consolation of narrowly beating Harrow by 13 runs in the unofficial match on Upper Club made up for other disappointments.

Harrow had their most successful season for a number of years including wins v. Wellington College and Bedford. Nick Compton stood out as the player of pedigree with 685 runs and the notable double of a century and hat-trick v. St. Edward's, Oxford. He later made a one day debut for Middlesex. Simon Maydon and Peter Dunbar also looked good and the bowling was sound enough with Hector Fleming, scion of the Fleming banking dynasty showing good form with the ball when fit.

		B.R. THOMPSON'S MATCH
2002 May 25		*Eton won by 66 runs*

Eton	221-7	(B. R. Thompson 98, J. H. Mathias 36 not out)
Harrow	155	(R. V. G. Harmsworth 48)

Eton won the toss and chose to bat first; and it was really the very fine innings of Ben Thompson, who batted through 40 of the 55 overs allotted for his 98 and firm hitting at the end by James Mathias, the wicket-keeper, who scored 36 not out off 30 balls, including a four and a six from the last two balls, that ensured a comfortable Eton victory. Thompson's sixth score of more than fifty that summer showed that it was no flash in the pan. His straight driving stood out, and an ability to roll his wrists and flick the ball through the on side, as did his judgement of a run. He eventually got out this way, only two short of a deserved century, caught by Maydon off Harmsworth.

Harrow had a disastrous start and lost their first three wickets for 12 runs and were, in truth, never in the fight. Simon Maydon, the Harrow captain, battled hard for 31 and towards the end Rupert Harmsworth batted well to keep the strike and score 48, aided by Charlie Reid 26. Amid increasing desperation, there were two sharp run-outs by Eton of these two batsmen and they were home and dry. The Eton bowling was tight all the way through, especially Will Dobson with his off-spinners, who took 2/17 off 11 overs of clever flight and change of pace. On this occasion Eton's fielding was sharper than Harrow's and a contributory factor in their defeat.

MARYLEBONE CRICKET CLUB

30p LORD'S GROUND 30p

ETON v. HARROW

SATURDAY 25th MAY, 2002   (1-day Match)

ETON

			Innings	
1	A. M. Goldberg		c Dunbar b Harmsworth	14
2	A. W. A. Barker		c Mahon b Kostoris	22
+3	T. P. McCall		run out	20
4	B. R. Thompson		c Maydon b Harmsworth	98
5	E. F. J. Nissen		b Moseley	8
6	H. W. A. Clarke		run out	7
7	C. P. A. Nissen		b Roditi	1
*8	J. H. Mathias		not out	36
9	A. E. M. P. de Lisle		not out	3
10	W. T. Dobson			
11	N. C. R. Westoll			
		B , l-b 7, w 3, n-b 2,	12
		Total .... (7wkts, 55 overs)	**221**

FALL OF THE WICKETS

1—34   2—49   3—97   4—115   5—132   6—142   7—198   8—   9—   10—

ANALYSIS OF BOWLING

Name	O.	M.	R.	W.	Wd.	N-b.
Moseley	11	3	26	1	3	...
Roditi	11	1	52	1	...	2
Harmsworth	11	0	53	2	...	...
Kostoris	11	0	35	1	...	...
Morrison	7	1	32	0	...	...
Defty	4	0	16	0	...	...
	...	...	...	...	...	...

HARROW

			Innings	
1	S. R. L. Maydon		c sub b Dobson	34-0
2	N. E. Defty		lbw b Barker	10
3	M. B. Mahon		b de Lisle	8-31
*4	P. R. Dunbar		c Nissen b de Lisle	0
5	J. M. Kostoris		c Nissen b Thompson	16
6	R. V. G. Harmsworth		run out	48
7	C. R. Reid		run out	26
8	A. W. Stileman		b Westoll	9
9	H. M. Morrison		lbw b Westoll	2
10	J. B. K. Roditi		lbw b Dobson	3
11	P. D. Moseley		not out	0
		B , l-b 4, w 6, n-b ,	15
		Total .... (48.3 overs)	**155**

FALL OF THE WICKETS

1—11   2—12   3—12   4—59   5—66   6—122   7—135   8—139   9—150   10—155

ANALYSIS OF BOWLING

Name	O.	M.	R.	W.	Wd.	N-b.
de Lisle	5	0	37	2	2	...
Barker	4	1	14	1	1	...
Thompson	6.3	2	16	1	1	...
Dobson	11	6	17	2	...	...
Goldberg	2	0	4	0	...	...
McCall	9	1	20	0	1	...
Westoll	11	1	43	2	1	...

Umpires—A. Patel & J. H. Mills   Scorers—R. J. E. Kerr & W. A. Blad

+Captain   *Wicket-keeper

55 overs per side   Play begins at 11.00   Luncheon Interval 1.00—1.40

Tea Interval—after 25 overs of the second innings.

(Timings may be varied according to state of game)

Eton won the toss

Eton won by 66 runs

Eton XI 2002. LEFT TO RIGHT, BACK ROW: *R.J.E. Kerr (Scorer), C.P.A. Nissen, W.I. Dobson, R.C. Wallace, P.E.C. Warner, E.F.J. Nissen, N.C.R. Westoll.* SEATED: *A.E.M.P. de Lisle, H.W.A. Clarke, B.R. Thompson, T.P. McCall (Captain), J.H. Mathias, A.M. Goldberg, A.W.A. Barker.*

Ben Thompson Eton's captain in 2003. Very unlucky not to score the century he deserved in winning the match for Eton by 66 runs in 2002.

2003 July 1   *Eton won by 36 runs*

Eton	211-8	(B. R. Thompson 50, G. D. G. George 42)
Harrow	175	(P. R. Dunbar 43, W. Dobson 3/19,
		J. P. Sherrard 3/32)
		50 overs per side

Eton went into the match firm favourites as one of the strongest school sides in the country, having had an exceptional season with notable victories against Millfield and Brighton, two schools with unmatched cricketing pedigrees in recent years. Strangely, Harrow won the toss and elected to field which, in hindsight, was a crucial mistake as the Harrow bowling was steady but nothing special. Eton were given a solid start by Guy George 42, and Ainsley Barker 30. At 105-1 Eton were in the box seat but a sudden rattle of wickets changed the game and 123-5 meant Harrow were back in the game. Some wayward Harrow bowling, particularly from Davidson, who had 48 runs taken off his 7 overs let Eton off the hook and 58 runs came in quick time from Thompson and Alex Ball 31 before Thompson was out at 181. Eton's total of 211 was certainly possible but only if Harrow batted positively.

After a short rain delay, Harrow batted and were soon in some trouble with the Eton opening bowlers, Ed Bruce and Ben Thompson, causing problems and Bruce removing the two openers for 1 and 12 respectively. Once again the Eton spinners James Sherrard and Will Dobson took a grip on the game and a further six wickets fell, Sherrard with 3/32 off his 10 overs and Dobson 3/19 off 10 overs. At 125-8 Harrow were in a mess and it would have needed a remarkable transformation to make a game of it. In truth it needed Harrow captain Peter Dunbar to show a lead and this he signally failed to do by batting nearly 40 overs for his 43 and not taking the quick singles. Davidson showed what could be done by scoring 35 in 8 overs and Harrow another 50 but it was all too late. Eton deservedly won by their more positive cricket but it was disappointing that so few Etonians turned up to watch at Lord's due to term finishing as Harrow had not yet broken up.

At the end of the match in 2003, Ben Thompson leading the Eton team off after their win by 36 runs.

Eton XI 2003. LEFT TO RIGHT, BACK ROW: *J.P. Sherrard, C.A.E. Bruce, A.H. Ball, A. Bruce, D.G.G. George, D.A.G. Scott-Hayward.* SEATED: *W.T. Dobson, W.A.A. Barker, B.R. Thompson (Captain), C.P.A. Nissen, F.J.E. Nissen, C.R.N. Westoll.*

E.F.J. NISSEN'S MATCH

2004 June 26   *Eton won by 20 runs*

Eton	239-6	(E. F. J. Nissen 124 not out)
Harrow	219	(H. M. Morrison 79)
		Match reduced to 40 overs per side

"Oh, God, if there be cricket in heaven, let there also be rain," the last O.E. Prime Minister, Lord Home, and a fine cricketer himself, once said. He would have enjoyed the weather forecast on the morning of the match. Torrential rain held off and, after a delayed start in spite of cloud and occasional drizzle, play was continuous from 1.40 p.m. in a reduced match till the close. It was worth waiting for; the most exciting and of the highest standard seen for many years.

Eton won the toss and elected to bat. The overcast conditions meant Harrow's seam bowlers had conditions in their favour and run scoring was difficult. The run rate hovered around four an over for the first 10 overs and Eton had reached 83 at the halfway stage with the openers and Bruce back in the pavilion. What took place after this was little short of astonishing. The Eton captain, Ed Nissen, played an innings of superb quality, which would have graced any arena. Finding gaps in the field at will and making the most of the short boundary on the Tavern side, he reached his 50 off 45 balls, including four boundaries, the next 50 in 27 balls, and finished the innings on 124 not out off a remarkable 82 balls. This, in spite of poor early season form and recurring injuries, must go down as one of the best in the history of the matches at Lord's and the eighth highest Eton score since 1805.

Eton finished on 239-6, a winning score on most occasions in 40-over schoolboy cricket, but Harrow had two match winners in Martin Walters, the 19-year-old South African, and Hamish Morrison, both prolific scorers through the season. Ed Bruce, the Eton opening bowler, bowled with aggression and control from the Pavilion End, but the bowlers at the other end struggled to find consistency and the Harrow batsmen capitalised. Morrison, who finished with 70 off just 72 balls, batted beautifully with Walters to take the score to 145-1. Two very fine diving catches by Bruce in the covers accounted for the dangerous Morrison and then Walters 36 off Gyles Scott-Hayward.

Eton XI 2004. Left to right, back row: *C.N. Lee, D.G. Taylor, H.G. Franks, E.C.A. Bruce, A.H. Ball, O.G. Williams, H.L.C. Rawlinson.*
seated: *G.O.A. Scott-Hayward, N.C.R. Westoll, E.F.J. Nissen (Captain), W.T. Dobson, D.G.D. George.*

Harrow XI 2004. Left to right, back row: *W.J. Spencer, S.A. Northeast, G.M. Harper, M. Habib, R.T. de Oliveira, E.J. Turner.* seated: *S. Crawley, G.C.M. Travers, H.M. Morrison, H.R. Howe (Captain), M.D. Walters, J.B.K. Roditi, R. Davidson.*

Ed Nissen (right) Eton XI 2002/4. His match winning innings of 124 not out won the day narrowly for Eton by 20 runs in 2004.

Chris Travers Harrow XI 2003/5, winning captain in 2005 and Hamish Morrison Harrow XI 2002/4, an outstanding performer in 2004.

Wickets then fell in quick succession, not helped by two needless run-outs and two outstanding stumpings from George, a high quality keeper. Eton eventually won by 20 runs in the 38th over, their third victory in succession not achieved by either side since Eton in 1921, and a tribute to their captain Nissen and the quality of their fielding. The atmosphere in the Mound Stand was lively and good-natured and the play of a quality to be proud of by both schools.

200TH ANNIVERSARY

R.G. QUERL'S MATCH

2005 June 18   *Harrow won by 7 wickets*

200th Anniversary of the first match at Lord's in 1805

Eton	176	(A. H. Ball 51, R. G. Querl 4/26)
Harrow	177-3	(R.G. Querl 65 n.o., S.H. Crawley 54 n.o.)

Harrow were undoubted favourites this year, coming to Lord's with an unbeaten record and all-round strength. They managed to lose the toss with an 1805 Irish penny specially bought for the occasion and fielded first on the hottest day of the summer. Querl and Harper bowled very good opening spells for Harrow and Eton found it hard work scoring, losing Farley and Bruce for 35 before Alex Ball, Eton's best player on his third appearance at Lord's, and Hugo Rawlinson began to make headway and take the score to 106. They took advantage of some much looser bowling from the Harrow support bowlers,

particularly Chris Travers, the Harrow captain, who had 36 off his 5 overs and some careless fielding.

A pivotal moment in the game when Travers put on Charlie Pelham, a third generation Harrow player, to bowl his leg-spinners just before lunch. Ball, who had played very well for his 51, walked inside a ball that pitched outside leg and was bowled. The match was well balanced at lunch with Eton on 107-3. The first few minutes after lunch decided the match; Rawlinson trying to sweep Pelham nicked it onto pad and was well caught by Matthey, the Harrow keeper, who was having a very good day and did not give away any byes in the innings. Querl then blew away George, the Eton keeper and Rowland Clark in successive balls. At 120-6 Eton were in serious trouble and Querl should probably have finished his overs. Pelham should also have been allowed to finish his spell, 2/16 in 8 overs was impressive and Eton didn't know how to play him. Harper's second spell was just as tight as his first and he finished with 0/22 off 11 overs and

---

LORD'S 🅼🅲🅲 GROUND

(50p)   **(50p)**

ETON v. HARROW
200th Anniversary of the first Eton v. Harrow match at Lord's

SATURDAY, 18th JUNE, 2005   (55 overs per side)

ETON	Innings		
1	E. J. Farley	lbw b Querl	2
2	A. H. Ball	b Pelham	51
3	E. C. A. Bruce	c Matthey b Coaker	11
4	H. C. L. Rawlinson	c Matthey b Pelham	34
†*5	G. D. G. George	b Querl	7
6	T. L. Redmayne	c Harper b Habib	15
7	J. R. Rowland Clark	b Querl	0
8	G. W. H. Reynolds	run out	2
9	R. J. Botros	c Jenkins b Querl	18
10	T. S. Annandale	c Habib b Travers	7
11	H. T. O. Brown	not out	5
		b , l-b 4 , w15, n-b 5, p ,	24
		Total (55 overs)	176

FALL OF THE WICKETS
1—4   2—35   3—106   4—120   5—120   6—120   7—125   8—148   9—160   10—176

ANALYSIS OF BOWLING
Name	O.	M.	R.	W.	Wd.	N-b.
Querl	11	2	26	4	4	1
Harper	11	2	22	0	3	1
Coaker	7	2	15	1	...	...
Habib	6	0	27	1	1	...
Spencer	7	0	30	0	1	...
Travers	5	0	36	1	2	2
Pelham	8	1	16	2	4	1

HARROW	Innings		
1	W. J. Spencer	c Rawlinson b Reynolds	17
2	S. H. Crawley	not out	54
3	S. A. Northeast	c Rowland Clark b Bruce	8
†4	C. G. M. Travers	c Ball b Botros	26
5	R. G. Querl	not out	65
6	M. Habib		
7	I. R. Jenkins		
8	G. M. Harper		
9	C. T. Pelham		
*10	G. I. Matthey		
11	T. J. C. Coaker		
		b 1, l-b , w 5, n-b 1, p ,	7
		Total (3 wkts, 39 overs)	177

FALL OF THE WICKETS
1—23   2—40   3—70   4—   5—   6—   7—   8—   9—   10—

ANALYSIS OF BOWLING
Name	O.	M.	R.	W.	Wd.	N-b.
Bruce	11	0	63	1	2	1
Reynolds	11	1	27	1	2	...
Botros	9	1	31	1	...	...
Annandale	5	0	30	0	...	...
Redmayne	2	0	16	0	1	...
Rowland Clark	1	0	9	0	...	...

Umpires—C. Pocock & J. M. Tythcott   Scorers—E. P. Agnew & O. G. L. Cohen
†Captain   *Wicket-keeper

Play begins at 11.00   Luncheon Interval 1.00—1.40   Tea Interval—after 25 overs of the second Innings

Eton won the toss   **Harrow won by 7 wickets**

REAL TENNIS
Old Etonians will play Old Harrovians for the Wellesley Trophy to-day on the Tennis Court between 10 a.m. and 6 p.m. Spectators are warmly welcome.

Glen Querl Harrow XI 2005. His superb all round performance won the match for Harrow. A tremendous talent for the future and a potential international in the making.

303

Reynolds was run out by a thundering throw from Habib. Harper also took a superb catch off a very wide half volley from Habib, which Redmayne only succeeded in spooning over extra cover, where Harper, running back, took the catch with a full-length dive inches above the ground. Eton's last three wickets added 51 runs but, in truth, Eton had not performed well since lunch, scoring only 69 runs for the loss of 7 wickets.

Eton needed to bowl tightly if they were to have any chance of winning. The first three overs produced 23 runs for Harrow, including a beamer that flew past the keeper for 5 runs, and two fours off Ed Bruce. It did not augur well for Eton and so it proved. Reynolds had Spencer well caught for 17 and Northeast caught at point off, Bruce for 8 and at 70/2 Harrow were well placed. Travers, the Harrow captain who had played attackingly for his 26, then succeeded in lofting a long hop from the leg spin of Botros straight to deep square leg. Spencer Crawley continued to concentrate well and Glenn Querl, fresh from his century at Radley, hit boundaries with impressive ease. Eton were struggling to find a fourth bowler, let alone a fifth, as Brown, their opening bowler, who was hit on the arm earlier in the day, was unable to bowl. The ancillary Eton bowlers were taken apart by Querl and at tea the score was 116 off 25 overs. The two Eton pace bowlers, Bruce and Reynolds, returned, but runs still came quickly and the game was over in 39 overs. An unbroken partnership of 107 between Crawley and Querl, with the winning runs being scored by Crawley was a perfect end to a deserved Harrow victory.

Eton XI 2005. LEFT TO RIGHT, BACK ROW: *J. Warren, H.T.O. Brown, O.G. Williams, T.L. Redmayne, J.R. Rowland Clark.* SEATED: *T.S. Annandale, E.J. Farley, A.H. Ball, G.D.G. George (Captain) E.C.A. Bruce, H.C.L. Rawlinson, G.W.H. Reynolds.*

The powerful Harrow XI 2005. LEFT TO RIGHT, BACK ROW: *I.R. Jenkins, W.J. Spencer, C.T. Pelham, T.J.C. Coaker, G.I. Matthey, S.A. Northeast.* SEATED: *G.M. Harper, S.H. Crawley, C.G.M. Travers (capt.), M. Habib, R.G. Querl.*

APPENDIXES

The scorer, by Thomas Henwood signed and dated 1842. A familiar sight at Lord's until the middle of the 1840's. It is often forgotten what an important part the scorer has played in the history of cricket and our records would not be so complete without them particularly so in the case of Eton and Harrow.

RESULTS OF MATCHES

168 matches have been played up to 2005 of which Eton have won 55, Harrow 47 and 66 have been drawn and 3 abandoned. This is the generally accepted record but Harrovians object to the first game in 1805 being treated as a regular contest between the schools, especially as the game in 1857 was rejected because of the age of the participants. For the purposes of this record I have included both, as the one in 1805 cancels out the Harrow win in 1857. The one day matches between the two schools during both World Wars of which Eton won ten, Harrow one and one drawn, are not treated as belonging to the regular series.

1805	Eton won by an innings and 2 runs	1867	Drawn
1818	Harrow won by 13 runs	1868	Harrow won by 7 wickets
1822	Harrow won by 87 runs	1869	Eton won by an innings and 19 runs
1823	Eton won by an innings and 33 runs	1870	Eton won by 21 runs
1824	Eton won by 9 wickets	1871	Eton won by an innings and 77 runs
1825	Eton won by 7 wickets	1872	Eton won by 6 wickets
1827	Eton won by 6 wickets	1873	Harrow won by 5 wickets
1828	Eton won by 6 wickets	1874	Eton won by 5 wickets
1832	Eton won by an innings and 156 runs	1875	Drawn
1833	Harrow won by 8 wickets	1876	Eton won by an innings and 24 runs
1834	Harrow won by 13 runs	1877	Drawn
1835	Eton won by 165 runs	1878	Harrow won by 20 runs
1836	Harrow won by 9 wickets	1879	Drawn
1837	Eton won by 8 wickets	1880	Harrow won by 95 runs
1838	Eton won by an innings and 30 runs	1881	Harrow won by 112 runs
1839	Eton won by 8 wickets	1882	Drawn
1840	Eton won by 31 runs	1883	Drawn
1841	Eton won by an innings and 175 runs	1884	Drawn
1842	Harrow won by 65 runs	1885	Harrow won by 3 wickets
1843	Harrow won by 20 runs	1886	Eton won by 6 wickets
1844	Eton won by an innings and 69 runs	1887	Eton won by 5 wickets
1845	Eton won by an innings and 174 runs	1888	Harrow won by 156 runs
1846	Eton won by an innings and 135 runs	1889	Harrow won by 9 wickets
1847	Eton won by 9 wickets	1890	Drawn
1848	Harrow won by 41 runs	1891	Harrow won by 7 wickets
1849	Harrow won by 77 runs	1892	Harrow won by 64 runs
1850	Eton won by 7 wickets	1893	Eton won by 9 wickets
1851	Harrow won by 8 wickets	1894	Drawn
1852	Harrow won by 71 runs	1895	Drawn
1854	Harrow won by 98 runs	1896	Drawn
1855	Harrow won by an innings and 66 runs	1897	Drawn
1857	Harrow won by ten wickets	1898	Harrow won by 9 wickets
1858	Harrow won by an innings and 7 runs	1899	Drawn
1859	Harrow won by an innings and 48 runs	1900	Harrow won by 1 wicket
1860	Drawn	1901	Harrow won by 10 wickets
1861	Drawn	1902	Harrow won by 8 wickets
1862	Eton won by 54 runs	1903	Eton won by an innings and 154 runs
1863	Drawn	1904	Eton won by an innings and 12 runs
1864	Harrow won by an innings and 66 runs	1905	Drawn
1865	Harrow won by an innings and 51 runs	1906	Eton won by 4 wickets
1866	Harrow won by an innings and 136 runs	1907	Harrow won by 79 runs

1908	Harrow won by 10 wickets	1964	Eton won by 8 wickets
1909	Drawn	1965	Harrow won by 48 runs
1910	Eton won by 9 runs	1966	Drawn
1911	Eton won by 3 wickets	1967	Drawn
1912	Eton won by 6 wickets	1968	Harrow won by 7 wickets
1913	Eton won by 9 wickets	1969	Drawn
1914	Eton won by 4 wickets	1970	Eton won by 97 runs
1916-1918	No regular matches during the war	1971	Drawn
1919	Eton won by 202 runs	1972	Drawn
1920	Eton won by 9 wickets	1973	Drawn
1921	Eton won by 7 wickets	1974	Harrow won by 8 wickets
1922	Drawn	1975	Harrow won by an innings and 151 runs
1923	Drawn	1976	Drawn
1924	Drawn	1977	Eton won by 6 wickets
1925	Drawn	1978	Drawn
1926	Drawn	1979	Drawn
1927	Drawn	1980	Drawn
1928	Eton won by 28 runs	1981	Drawn
1929	Drawn	1982	Drawn
1930	Eton won by 8 wickets	1983	Drawn
1931	Eton won by an innings and 16 runs	1984	Drawn
1932	Drawn	1985	Eton won by 3 runs
1933	Drawn	1986	Drawn
1934	Drawn	1987	Drawn
1935	Drawn	1988	Drawn
1936	Drawn	1989	Drawn
1937	Eton won by 7 wickets	1990	Eton won by 7 wickets
1938	Drawn	1991	Eton won by 3 wickets
1939	Harrow won by 8 wickets	1992	Drawn
1940-1945	No regular matches during the War	1993	Drawn
1946	Drawn	1994	Drawn
1947	Drawn	1995	Drawn
1948	Drawn	1996	Drawn
1949	Eton won by 7 wickets	1997	Match abandoned without a ball being bowled
1950	Drawn	1998	Drawn
1951	Drawn	1999	Match abandoned without a ball being bowled
1952	Harrow won by 7 wickets	2000	Harrow won by 19 runs
1953	Eton won by 10 wickets	2001	Match abandoned without a ball being bowled
1954	Harrow won by 9 wickets	2002	Eton won by 66 runs
1955	Eton won by 38 runs	2003	Eton won by 36 runs
1956	Drawn	2004	Eton won by 20 runs
1957	Drawn	2005	Harrow won by 7 wickets
1958	Drawn		
1959	Drawn		
1960	Harrow won by 124 runs		
1961	Harrow won by an innings and 12 runs		
1962	Drawn		
1963	Drawn		

CAPTAINS

Year	Eton captain	Harrow captain	Year	Eton captain	Harrow captain
1805	J.H. Kaye	J.A. Lloyd	1871	G.H. Longman	E.P. Baily
1818	W. Pitt	C. Oxenden	1872	E.O.H. Wilkinson	E.A. Stuart
1822	G.W. Barnard	G.L. Prendergast	1873	Hon. F.J. Bruce	H. Leaf
1823	G.W. Barnard	F. Calvert	1874	Hon. E. Lyttelton	A.J. Webbe
1824	J. Dolphin	C. Wordsworth	1875	Hon. A. Lyttelton	C.W.M. Kemp
1825	C. Chapman	C. Wordsworth	1876	W.F. Forbes	H.E. Meek
1827	H. Dupuis	Lord Grimston	1877	H. Whitfeld	H.E. Meek
1828	R.H. Wilkinson	C.J. Harenc	1878	C.M. Smith	C.J.E. Jarvis
1832	C.A. Wilkinson	J. Leslie	1879	C.T. Studd	J.H. Stirling
1833	C. Vance	J. Leslie	1880	P.J.de Paravicini	M.C. Kemp
1834	J.C. Ryle	R.J.P. Broughton	1881	P.J.de Paravicini	A.F. Kemp
1835	F.E. Long	R.J.P. Broughton	1882	H.W. Bainbridge	Hon. E.W.H. Ward
1836	R.W. Essington	C.W.A. Napier	1883	R.J. Lucas	H.E. Crawley
1837	W.P. Pickering	H.J. Torre	1884	R.J. Lucas	E.M. Butler
1838	W.P. Pickering	H.J. Torre	1885	F. Freeman-Thomas	E.M. Butler
1839	G.J. Boudier	W. Mills	1886	H.J. Mordaunt	M.J. Dauglish
1840	J.R.L.E. Bayley	E.M. Dewing	1887	T.W. Brand	J.St.F. Fair
1841	J.R.L.E. Bayley	E.M. Dewing	1888	H.R. Bromley-Davenport	J.A. MacLaren
1842	M.M. Ainslie	Hon. C.W.H. Agar	1889	H.R. Bromley-Davenport	F.S. Jackson
1843	G.E. Yonge	W. Nicholson	1890	R.C. Norman	A.C. MacLaren
1844	L.H. Bayley	J. Marshall	1891	R.C. Norman	C.G. Pope
1845	E.M. Macniven	C.S. Currer	1892	D.H. Forbes	M.Y. Barlow
1846	F.J. Coleridge	C.S. Currer	1893	G.E. Bromley-Martin	C.S. Rome
1847	J.W. Chitty	T.D. Platt	1894	G.E. Bromley-Martin	J.H. Bulloch
1848	H.M. Aitken	T.D. Platt	1895	C.C. Pilkington	J.H. Stogdon
1849	H.M. Aitken	H. Vernon	1896	C.T. Allen	Hon. F.R. Henley
1850	C.L. Norman	R. Hankey	1897	A.D. Legard	P.T. Maw
1851	C. Thackeray	Hon.E. Chandos Leigh	1898	H.C. Pilkington	E.M. Dowson
1852	T.D. Tremlett	W. Marillier	1899	W. Findlay	E.M. Dowson
1853	H.N. Hoare	K.E. Digby	1900	H.K. Longman	G. Cookson
1854	F.V. Northey	K.E. Digby	1901	E.G. Whately	E.W. Mann
1855	E.B. Fane	K.E. Digby	1902	R. Gregson-Ellis	C.H. Eyre
1857	F.H. Norman	H. Arkwright	1903	K.I. Nicholl	R.E.H. Baily
1858	J.B. Dyne	R. Lang	1904	G.C. Campbell	R.E.H. Baily
1859	J.B. Dyne	R. Lang	1905	W.N. Tod	E.H. Crake
1860	Hon. C.G. Lyttelton	A.W.T. Daniel	1906	C.E. Hatfeild	E.H. Crake
1861	R.A.H. Mitchell	H.R.T. Alexander	1907	H.S. Hatfeild	M.C. Bird
1862	S.F. Cleasby	I.D. Walker	1908	R.L. Benson	A.H. Lang
1863	A. Lubbock	I.D. Walker	1909	R.H. Twining	A.H. Lang
1864	W.S. Prideaux	C.F. Buller	1910	R.St.L. Fowler	G.F. Earle
1865	Hon.G.W.S Lyttelton	M.H. Stow	1911	C.W. Tufnell	T.L.G. Turnbull
1866	E. Lubbock	M.H. Stow	1912	D.G. Wigan	C.H.B. Blount
1867	C.R. Alexander	W.B. Money	1913	J. Heathcoat-Amory	G.L. Jackson
1868	C.I. Thornton	S. Pelham	1914	G.S. Rawstorne	G. Wilson
1869	W.C. Higgins	S.W. Gore	1916	N.A. Pearson	L.H.K. Gregson
1870	Hon. G.R.C. Harris	C.W. Walker	1917	H.F. Wilkinson	G.M. Butler

Year	Eton captain	Harrow captain	Year	Eton captain	Harrow captain
1918	C.H. Gibson	W.A.R. Collins	1964	R.C. Daniels	D.W.W. Norris
1919	C.H. Gibson	W.A.R. Collins	1965	G.W. Pilkington	R.I. Evans
1920	W.W. Hill-Wood	P.H. Gold	1966	D.M. Smith	R.W. Evans
1921	Hon. D.F. Brand	C.T. Bennett	1967	Viscount Crowhurst	I. Coomaraswamy
1922	G.K. Cox	H.J. Enthoven	1968	R.C. Kinkead-Weekes	I. Coomaraswarny
1923	M.R. Bridgeman	P.H. Stewart-Brown	1969	V.A. Cazalet	P.J.E. Needham
1924	D.M. Bateson	A.M. Crawley	1970	J.R.T. Barclay	P.J.E. Needham
1925	R.H. Cobbold	N.M. Ford	1971	J.R.T. Barclay	J. Halliday
1926	H.E.H.P.C. Hope	N.M. Ford	1972	I. Macdonald	H.R. Jenkins
1927	R.C.C. Whittaker	C. Clover-Brown	1973	Marquis of Bowmont	C.D. Gilliat
1928	E.R. Sheepshanks	W.O'B. Lindsay	1974	J.E.H. Ward	R.E.P. Lee
1929	A.G. Hazlerigg	D.A.M. Rome	1975	N.E Fane	M.K. Fosh
1930	K.F.H. Hale	A.S. Lawrence	1976	R.H.M.Raison	A.C.S. Pigott
1931	J.C. Atkinson-Clark	F.E. Covington	1977	R.H.M. Raison	R.M. Tindall
1932	N.E.W. Baker	F.E. Covington	1978	P.D. Whitby	T.M.H. James
1933	N.S. Hotchkin	M. Tindall	1979	R.J. Compton-Burnett	W.J. Haggas
1934	A.N.A. Boyd	J.H. Pawie	1980	H.T. Rawlinson	C.L. Feather
1935	B.M. Fisher	P.M. Studd	1981	N.A. Metaxa	S.E. Haggas
1936	F.G. Mann	B.D. Carris	1982	C.A. Watt	J.F. Turner
1937	J.P. Mann	M.D. Watson	1983	W.A.B. Russell	J.W.S. Raper
1938	J.F. Boughey	R.A.A. Holt	1984	R.V. Watson	R.G. Robinson
1939	N.T.A. Fiennes	A.O.L. Lithgow	1985	S.R. Gardiner	R.C. Wiltshire
1940	D.W.J. Colman	A.O.L. Lithgow	1986	A.D.A. Zagoritis	R.A. Pyman
1941	H.M. Chinnery	D.F. Henley	1987	R.D.O. Macleay	D.C. Manasseh
1942	E.N.W. Bramall	A.J.S. Griffin	1988	J.K. Erith	C. Keey
1943	W.G. Keighley	A. Fosh	1989	J.T. Trusted	C. Raper
1944	H.A. Hely-Hutchinson	T.G.H. Jackson	1990	H.J.P. Chetwood	M.E.D. Jarrett
1945	P.D.S. Blake	M.N. Garnett	1991	J.M.S. Whittington	S.M. Guillebaud
1946	C.R.D. Rudd	P. Wallis	1992	D.M. Trusted	C.G. Hill
1947	P.T. Lewis	G.C. Hoyer-Millar	1993	T.A. Simpson	J.A.J. Renshaw
1948	T. Hare	G.C. Hoyer-Millar	1994	C.G.R. Lightfoot	P.A.J. Montgomery
1949	J.A. Bailey	A.S. Day	1995	J.A.G.Fulton	S.D.G. Engelen
1950	J.S. Guthrie	R.A. Jacques	1996	J.A.G. Fulton	E.G.L. Maydon
1951	N.C. Wadham	J.W.E. Bleackley	1997	H.J.H. Loudon	A.N.L. Cox
1952	P.L.B.Stoddart	R.L. Feather	1998	A.G.R. Loudon	D.R. Hepher
1953	R.V.C.Robins	D.J. Hulbert	1999	A.G.R. Loudon	S.H. Stevens
1954	N.A.T. Winter	A.R.B. Neame	2000	D.S. Ferreira	L.F. de Rougemont
1955	C.H. Gibson	A.R.B. Neame	2001	S.W.F. Collins	N.R.D. Compton
1956	I.A.C. Sinclair	J.M. Parker	2002	T.P. McCall	S.R.L. Maydon
1957	E.J. Lane Fox	L.J. Champniss	2003	B.R. Thompson	P.R. Dunbar
1958	W.G.A. Clegg	A.B. Cable	2004	E.F.J. Nissen	H.R. Howe
1959	M.L. Dunning	D.R.J. Foster	2005	G.D.G. George	C.G.M. Travers
1960	R.D. Christie	B.S. Raper			
1961	P. Wigan	M.J.B. Wood			
1962	M.C.T. Prichard	J.R. Hodgkinson			
1963	C.E. Braithwaite	R.J. Pelham			

CENTURIES

There have been 49 centuries in the match, 29 by Etonians and 20 by Harrovians, listed below:

Eton			Harrow		
183	D.C. Boles	1904	173	G. Wilson	1913
159	E.W. Dawson	1923	161*	M.K. Fosh	1975
158	I. Akers-Douglas	1928	151	R.M. Tindall	1976
153	N.S. Hotchkin	1931	142	T.G.O. Cole	1897
152	J.R.L.E. Bayley	1841	137	C.H.B. Blount	1912
150*	H.V. Machin	1993	135	A.K. Watson	1885
135	J.C. Atkinson-Clark	1930	131	M.C. Bird	1907
124*	E.F.J. Nissen	2004	124	J.H. Stogdon	1895
120	B.J.T. Bosanquet	1896	115	E. Crutchley	1939
117	A.W. Ridley	1871	112*	A.W.T. Daniel	1860
114	C.P.Foley	1886	112*	T.M.H. James	1978
113	W.F. Forbes	1876	111	R.A.A. Holt	1937
112	J.A.G. Fulton	1994	108	R.B. Hoare	1888
112	A.W. Allen	1931	104	R.Pulbrook	1932
109	N.S. Hotchkin	1932	103	L.G. Crawley	1921
109	K.F.H. Hale	1929	102*	P.H.Stewart-Brown	1923
108	C.J. Ottaway	1869	102*	H.St.J.R. Foster	1992
107	W.N. Coles	1946	100*	M.C. Bird	1907
106	D.M. Smith	1966	100*	P.M. Studd	1935
103	T. Hare	1947	100	E. Crawley	1885
102	R.V.C. Robins	1953			
101	H.C. Pilkington	1896			
100	P.V.F. Cazalet	1926			
100	E.N.S. Crankshaw	1903			
100	H.H. Dixon	1995			
100	M.J.J. Faber	1968			
100	S.B.D. Sainsbury	1947			
100	R.H. Cobbold	1923			
100	A.N.A. Boyd	1924			

M.C. Bird of Harrow is the only player to have scored two centuries in the match with 100 not out and 131 in 1907. N.S. Hotchkin of Eton went desperately close with 109 and 96 in 1932.

* Not Out

PLAYED FOR ENGLAND

Eton	Harrow
G.O.B. Allen	M.C. Bird
Hon. Ivo Bligh	B.A.F. Grieve
B.J.T. Bosanquet	A.N. Hornby
H.R. Bromley-Davenport	F.S. Jackson
E.W. Dawson	F.A. MacKinnon
N.E. Haig	A.C. MacLaren
Lord Harris	A.C.S. Pigott
Lord Hawke	A.J. Webbe
Hon. Alfred Lyttelton	
F.G. Mann	
H. Philipson	
C.T. Studd	
G.B. Studd	
Hon. L.H. Tennyson	
N.C. Tufnell	
M.V. Fleming (One Day Internationals)	
A.M. Miller	
F.W. Milligan	
R.T. Stanyforth	
Hon. C.J. Coventry	
C. Heseltine	
(21)	**(8)**

21 Etonians have played for England and 8 Harrovians. A.W. Carr has not been included as he was only at Eton for one year before going to Sherborne.

PLAYED FOR SOUTH AFRICA

Eton
O.R. Dunell

BOWLING ANALYSES

of 10 wickets or more in the match

Up to 1854 before proper analyses were recorded

Eton wickets		
15	E.W. Blore	1847
14	E.W. Blore	1845
14	G.T. Lowth	1824
13	J.H. Kirwan	1835
12	H.M. Aitken	1846
11	W. de St. Croix	1838
11	W.B. Gwyn	1839
11	G.E. Yonge	1841
10	J.H. Kirwan	1834
10	W.P. Pickering	1837
10	H.M. Aitken	1848

Harrow wickets		
14	R. Hankey	1849
13	R. Broughton	1834
13	T.D. Platt	1848
11	A.H. Farmer	1843
10	Lord H.Y.A. Loftus	1840
10	Hon.H.W.E. Agar	1842

From 1854 proper bowling analyses were recorded and the following achieved analyses of 10 wickets or more till 1982 when the fixture became one day.

Eton wickets		
14/99	H.W. Studd	1888
13/91	R.V.C. Robins	1951
13/94	F.H.E. Cunliffe	1894
12/77	F.M. Buckland	1872
12/91	C.E. Hatfeild	1903
12/92	P.J. de Paravicini	1880
12/99	P.J. de Paravicini	1881
12/113	R.St.L. Fowler	1909
11/44	A.G. Pelham	1930
11/156	F.H. Mitchell	1897
10/83	H.M Wyndham	1970
10/137	E.G.Bromley-Martin	1885

Harrow wickets		
12/67	D.J. Hulbert	1952
12/76	R.C.S. Titchener-Barrett	1961
12/92	I. Coomaraswamy	1968
11/63	C.L. Arkwright	1864
11/66	H. Linton	1857
11/68	F.S. Jackson	1888
11/77	A.R.B. Neame	1954
11/113	S.A.F. Mitchell	1969
10/50	G. Macan	1870
10/63	R.C. Ramsay	1879
10/79	A.C.Raphael	1925
10/80	W.B. Money	1865
10/86	C.W. Walker	1868

Since 1982 the following have achieved analyses of 5 wickets or more

Eton		
7/38	F.N. Bowman-Shaw	1985
6/40	J.T.A. Bruce	1998
5/44	N.A. Bailey	1996

Harrow		
6/19	T.D.de M. Leathes	1995
6/87	J.J. Pethers	1985
5/35	M.M.J. Hawkins	1992
5/36	D.B.M. Fox	1984
5/50	M.M.J. Hawkins	1991

HAT TRICKS

In the Eton and Harrow match

Eton		Harrow	
H.E. Whitmore	1873	W.B. Money	1866
E.G. Whately	1900	A.R.B. Neame	1955
S.M.A. Banister	1937		
(4 wickets in 4 balls)			
P.W.R. Leigh	1972		

MOST WICKETS

In the Eton and Harrow match

Eton		
E.W. Blore	33 wickets	1845/47
H.M. Aitken	32 wickets	1846/49
P.J.de Paravicini	31 wickets	1878/81
C.E. Hatfeild	30 wickets	1903/06

Harrow		
E.M. Dowson	35 wickets	1895/99

HIGHEST
TOTALS

Eton		Harrow	
502	1923	388	1900
431-5 dec.	1931	385	1898
425	1903	382-8 dec.	1907
415-8 dec.	1928	376	1901
406	1904	376	1926
394-8 dec.	1947	349	1932
386	1896	341-6 dec.	1978
383	1913	328-9 dec.	1976
365	1906	326	1895
347	1929	324	1885
340	1912	324	1913
313-9 dec.	1946	322	1923

LOWEST
TOTALS

Eton		Harrow	
35	1855	24	1823
36	1843	27	1847
42	1866	32	1845
44	1858	35	1841
49	1836	37	1986
50	1834	41	1919
52	1822	44	1832
56	1975	45	1910
57	1848	47	1835
58	1853	48	1835
63	1864	49	1832
64	1881	52	1843
67	1910	53	1828
71	1908	53	1853
73	1952	55	1805
		56	1838
		56	1862
		58	1840
		59	1839

OXFORD

Eton

Ainslie M.M. (Capt. 1844-45)	1843-5
Aitken H.M.	1853
Aitken J. (Capt. 1850)	1848-50
Arkright H.A.	1895
Blake P.D.S. (Capt. 1952)	1950-2
Bligh E.V.	1850
Bosanquet B.J.T.	1898-1900
Boswell W.G.K.	1913-14
Bristowe O.C.	1914
Bromley-Martin G.E.	1897-8
Buckland F.M.	1875-77
Butler S.E.	1870-3
Buxton R.V.	1906
Cazalet P.V.F.	1927
Chitty J.W.	1848-9
Coleridge C.E.	1849-50
Coleridge F.J.	1847,1850
Colman G.R.R.	1913-14
Coote A. (Capt. 1838)	1838-40
Cunliffe F.H.E. (Capt. 1898)	1895-98
Denison H.	1829
Eden F.M.	1850-1
Faber M.J.J.	1972
Findlay W. (Capt. 1903)	1901-3
Forbes D.H.	1894
Forster H.W.	1887-9
Frederick J.St.J.	1864,1867
Fulton J.A.G. (Capt. 1998)	1997-8
Garnett C.A.	1860-2
Garth R. (Capt. 1840-1)	1839-41
Harris Hon. G.PL.C.	1871-2,1874
Haskett-Smith A.	1879
Hatfeild C.E.	1908
Hildyard H.C.T.	1845-6
Hill-Wood C.K.	1928-30
Hill-Wood D.J.	1928
Hollins A.M.	1899
Hollins F.H	1901
Honywood R.	1845-47
Jones R.T.	1892
Ker R.J.C.R.	1842
Keighley W.G.	1947-8
Kinkead-Weekes R.C.	1972
Lightfoot C.G.R.	1997-8

Harrow

Barnes R.G.	1906-7
Benn A.	1935
Bolitho W.E.T.	1883 1885
Brandt D.R.	1907
Butterworth E.E.C.	1927
Carlisle K.M. (Capt. 1905)	1903-5
Carpentier-Garnier J. (formerly Carpentier)	1858
Chandos Leigh Hon. E.	1852-4
Cherry G.C.	1841-3
Commerell W.A.	1845
Crawley A.M.	1927-30
Crutchley G.E.V.	1912
Currer C.S.	1847
Dauglish M.J.	1889-90
Des Voeux H.D.	1844
Digby K.E.	1857-9
Digby R.	1867-9
Dury T.S.	1876
Evetts W.	1868-9
Ford N.M.	1928-30
Gibbon J.H.	1869
Grimston Hon. E.H.	1836
Grimston Hon. R.	1838
Hadow W.H.	1870-2
Hankey R.	1853,1855
Henley D.F.	1947
Hewett H.T.	1886
Hodgkinson G.L.	1857-9
Jones M.	1849-50
Keey C.L.	1992-3
Kemp C.W.M.	1878
Kemp M.C. (Capt. 83-4)	1881-4
Law W. (Capt. 1874)	1871-4
Leslie J.	1843
Lewis W.H.	1827
Lindsay W.O'B.	1931
Linton H.	1858-9
Loftus Lord H.Y.A.	1841
Longe F.D.	1851-2
Maitland W.F.	1864-6
Mathews E.	1868-9
Medlicott W.S.	1902
Mills B.S.T.	1841/3
Napier C.W.A.	1838-9

OXFORD

Eton

Llewelyn W.D.	1890-1
Lowndes W.G.L.F.	1921
Napier C.W.A.	1838-9
D.H. Macindoe (Capt. 1946)	1937-9, 1946
Marcon W.	1844
Marsham A.J.B.	1939
Marsham C.H.B. (Capt. 1902)	1900/2
Martin E.G.	1903-6
Maude J.	1873
Mayhew J.F.N.	1930
Mitchell R.A.H. (Capt. 1863-5)	1862-5
Morgan P.G.	1997
Musters W.M.	1829
Newman G.C.	1926-7
Newton A.E.	1885
Ottaway C.J. (Capt. 1873)	1870-3
Patteson J.C.	1849
Peel H.R.	1851-2
Pepys J.A.	1861
Philipson H. (Capt. 1889)	1887-9
Pilkington C.C.	1896
Pilkington H.C.	1899-1900
Randolph C.	1844-5
Rawlinson HT.	1983-4
Redmayne J.R.S.	2000,2002
Ridley A.W. (Capt. 1875)	1872-5
Rudd C.R.D.	1949
Ryle J.C.	1836-1838
Scott Lord George	1887-9
Spencer-Smith 0.	1866
Teape A.S.	1863-5
Tritton E.W. (Capt. 1866)	1864-7
Twining R.H. (Capt. 1912)	1910-13
Vance G.	1836-1838
Walter A.F	1869
Ward, Lord	1841-42
Waud B.W.	1857-60
Wilkinson W.A.C.	1913
Wynne J.H.G.	1839-40
Wynne-Finch C.G.	1836
Yonge C.D.	1836
Yonge G.E. (Capt. 1848)	1844-8

TOTAL OXFORD BLUES: 86

Harrow

Monro R.W.	1860
Nethercote H.O.	1840-1
Oppenheimer J.E.	1991
Patterson W.H.	1880-81
Pelham S.	1871
Popham F.L.	1829
Rashleigh J.	1842
Russell H.S.	1839
Sibthorp G.T.W	1836
Simpson E.T.B	1888
Stewart-Brown P.H.	1925-6
Torre H.J.	1839-40
Walker R.D.	1861-5
Wallroth C.A.	1872-4
Watson A.K.	1889
Watson H.D.	1891
Webbe A.J. (Capt. 1877-8)	1875-8
Wordsworth C. (Capt. 1827,1829)	1827,1829
Wrigley M.H.	1949
Wyld H.J.	1901-3

TOTAL OXFORD BLUES: 64

CAMBRIDGE

Eton

Aird R.	1923
Allen A.W.	1933-4
Allen G.O.B.	1922-3
Anson T.A. (Capt. 1840-42)	1839-42
Baggallay M.E.C.	1911
Bagge T.E. (Capt. 1861)	1859-61
Bainbridge H.W. (Capt. 1886)	1884-6
Barnett W.E.	1849-50
Bligh Ivo F.W. (Capt. 1881)	1878-81
Blofeld H.C.	1959
Blore E.W. (Capt. 1851)	1848-51
Booth H.W. (Capt. 1836)	1836
Boudier G.J. (Joint Captain 1843)	1841,1843
Bridgeman W.C.	1887
Brocklebank J.M.	1936
Bromley-Davenport H.R.	1892-3
Buckston G.M.	1903
Burghley, Lord	1847
Bury L.	1877
Clissold ST.	1844,1846
Cobbold P.W.	1896
Cobbold R.H.	1927
Cooke C.R.	1858
Cookesley W.G.	1827
Dawson E.W. (Capt. 1927)	1924-7
De Grey Hon. T.	1862-3
de Paravicini P.J.	1882-5
de St.Croix W.	1839-42
de Zoete H.W.	1897-98
Deacon W.S. (Capt. 1850)	1848-50
Dolphin J.	1827
Douglas-Pennant S.	1959
Dupuis G.R.	1857
Dyke E.F.	1865
Ebden C.H.M.	1902-03
Foley C.P.	1889-91
Foley C.W	1880
Frere J.	1827
Gibson C.H.	1920-1
Gosling R.C.	1888-90
Hartopp E.S.E.	1841-2
Hawke Hon. M.B. (Capt. 1885)	1882-3,1885
Hazlerigg A.G. (Capt. 1932)	1930-2
Hill-Wood W.W.	1922

Harrow

Arkwright H.	1858
Bagnall H.F.	1923
Baily E.P.	1872-1874
Baily R.E.H	1908
Bennett CT. (Capt. 1925)	1923,1925
Blacker W.	1873-6
Blayds E.	1846-9
Boldero H.K.	1851-3
Broughton R.J.P.	1836,1838-9
Butler E.M.	1888-9
Buxton C.D. (Capt. 1888)	1885-8
Carris B.D.	1938-9
Cobden F.C.	1870-2
Crawley E.	1887-9
Crawley L.G.	1923-5
Daniel A.W.T.	1861-4
Dewing E.M. (Capt. 1844-5)	1842-5
E.M. Dowson	1900-03
du Cane A.R.	1854-5
Enthoven H.J. (Capt. 1926)	1923-6
Eyre C.H. (Capt. 1906)	1904-6
Falcon M. (Capt. 1910)	1908-11
Fitzgerald R.A.	1854,1856
Fosh M.K.	1977-8
Fryer F.E.R. (Capt. 1873)	1870-3
Gibson J.S.	1855
Grimston F.S.	1843-5
Handley E.H.	1827
Henery P.J.T.	1882-83
Hope-Grant F.C.	1863
Hopley F.J.V.	1904
Hopley G.W.V.	1912
Jackson F.S. (Capt. 1892-3)	1890-3
Jarrett M.E.D.	1992-3
Jarvis L.K.	1877-9
Jenner H.L.	1841
Kaye M.A.C.P.	1938
Lang A.H.	1913
Lang R.	1860-2
Lawrence A.S.	1933
Long R.P.	1845-6
Macan G.	1874-5
MacKinnon F.A.	1870
Mann E.W. (Capt. 1905)	1903-5

CAMBRIDGE

Eton

Hodgson E.F.	1836
Hone-Goldney G.H.	1873
Hotchkin N.S.	1935
Howard-Smith G.	1903
Hume A.	1841-2
Jenner C.H.	1829
Jenner H. (Capt. 1827)	1827
Johnson P.R.	1901
Kingdon S.N.	1827
Kirwan J.H.	1839
Knatchbull-Hugessen Hon. C.M.	1886
Koe B.D.	1838
Long F.E.	1836
Longman G.H (Capt. 1874-5)	1872-5
Longman H.K.	1901
Lyttelton 4th Lord	1838
Lyttelton Hon. Alfred (Capt. 1879)	1876-9
Lyttelton Hon. C.F.	1908-9
Lyttelton Hon. C.G.	1861-4
Lyttelton Hon. Edward (Capt. 1878)	1875-8
Lyttelton Hon. G.W.S.	1866-7
MacNiven E.	1846
Mann F.G.	1938-9
Manners-Sutton J.H.T.	1836
Marchant F.	1884-7
Meetkerke A.	1840
Micklethwait F.N.	1836
Mordaunt H.J.	1888-9
Mulholland H.G.H. (Capt. 1913)	1911-13
Norman C.L.	1852-3
Norman F.H. (Capt. 1860)	1858-60
Norris W.A.	1851
Oddie H.H.	1836
Pelham A.G.	1934
Pelham Hon. F.G. (Capt. 1866-7)	1864-7
Penn E.F	1899,1902
Pickering E.H. (Capt. 1829)	1827,1829
Pickering W.P.	1840,1842
Prest E.B.	1850
Rees-Davies W.R.	1938
Savile Hon. A.	1840
Savile G.	1868
Shirley W.R. de la C.	1924
Simonds H.J.	1850

Harrow

Marlar R.G. (Capt. 1953)	1951-3
Massey W.	1838-9
Middleton M.R.	1987
Mills W.	1840-3
Money W.B. (Capt. 1870)	1868-71
Nicholson J.	1845
Norris D.W.W.	1967-8
Northey A.E.	1859-60
Pawle J.H.	1936-7
Plowden H.M. (Capt. 1862-3)	1860-3
Ponsonby Hon. F.G.B.	1836
Pope C.G.	1894
Pyman R.A.	1989-90
Ramsay R.C.	1882
Richardson J.M.	1866-8
Robertson W.P.	1901
Rowe F.C.C.	1881
Royston, Lord	1857
Smith A.F.	1875
Southwell H.G.	1852-3
Spencer R.	1881
Spiro D.G.	1884
Stogdon J.H.	1897-9
Stow M.H. (Capt. 1869)	1867-9
Studd P.M. (Capt. 1939)	1937-9
Thornewill E.J.	1856
Tindall M. (Capt. 1937)	1935-7
Trevelyan W.B.	1842-3
Vernon H. (Capt. 1852)	1850-2
Weedon M.J.H.	1962
Wilenkin B.C.G.	1956
Wilson F.B. (Capt. 1904)	1902-4
Wilson G.	1919

TOTAL CAMBRIDGE BLUES: 77

CAMBRIDGE

Eton

Sivewright C.K.	1829
Stacey F.E.	1853
Studd C.T. (Capt. 1883)	1880-3
Studd GB. (Capt. 1882)	1879-82
Studd J.E.K. (Capt. 1884)	1881-4
Studd R.A.	1895
Tabor A.S	1872-4
Taylor C.G. (Capt. 1838-9)	1836,1838-9
Thackeray F.	1838-40
Thomas F.F.	1886-9
Thornton CI. (Capt. 1872)	1869-72
Townley T.M.	1847-8
Tremlett T.D.	1854
Tuck G.H. (Capt. 1865)	1863-6
Tufnell N.C.	1909-10
Webb R.H.	1827
H. Whitfeld	1878-81
Whymper F.H.	1849

TOTAL CAMBRIDGE BLUES: 106

Harrow

192 Etonians have gained cricket blues at Oxford and Cambridge and 141 Harrovians.

John Wisden (1826-1884) c.1850 by William Bromley fl.1844-70. Wisden was a fast right arm off-break bowler and his greatest achievement was to take all 10 wickets in the North v. South match at Lord's in 1850. He played for Sussex from 1845/63 and was Harrow's first professional in 1852. He initiated the system of professional bowlers at the school which continued until fairly recently but his main claim to fame was the founding of Wisden's almanack in 1864, the cricketer's 'bible' which still continues to this day. He went on the first ever overseas tour to North America in 1859 and to have observed that the ocean needed 10 minutes of the heavy roller!

MASTERS IN CHARGE
OF CRICKET

Eton

1866-1896	**R.A.H. Mitchell** (Oxford Univ., Leics. & Warwicks)
1897-1919	**C.M. Wells** (Oxford Univ. & Middx.)
1920-1928	**R.A. Young** (Cambridge Univ., Somerset & England)
1929-1937	**W.N. Roe** (Cambridge Univ. & Somerset)
1938-1941	**N.G. Wykes** (Cambridge Univ. & Essex)
1942-1948	**C.H. Taylor** (Oxford Univ. & Leics.)
1949-1960	**D.H. Macindoe** (Oxford Univ. & Bucks.)
1961-1965	**M.A. Eagar** (Oxford Univ. & Glos.)
1966-1969	**G.P. Marsland** (Oxford Univ.)
1970-1975	**E.M. Dyson** (Oxford Univ.)
1976-1984	**P.R.Thackeray** (Oxford Univ. & Devon)
1985-1996	**J.A.Claughton** (Oxford Univ. & Warwicks)
1997-1998	**S.J.G Doggart** (Cambridge Univ.)
1999-	**R.D. Oliphant-Callum** (Oxford Univ.)

HARROW

1890-1920	**M.C.Kemp** (Oxford Univ. & Kent)
1921-1922	**M.C. Bird** (Lancs, Surrey, & England)
1923-1929	**R.L. Holdsworth** (Oxford Univ. Warwicks & Sussex)
1930-36	**C.R. Browne** (Cambridge Univ. & Sussex)
1937-1939	**D.F. Walker** (Hampshire)
1940-1945	**G.R.McConnell**
1946-1959	**M. Tindall** (Cambridge Univ. & Middx.)
1960-1970	**J. Webster** (Cambridge Univ. & Northants)
1971-1982	**G.M. Attenborough** (Berks)
1983-1994	**W. Snowden** (Cambridge Univ.)
1995-1997	**C.M.B.Williams** (Staffordshire)
1998-	**S.J. Halliday** (Suffolk)

HEAD PROFESSIONALS

Eton	
1885-1919	**M.W. Wright** (Bucks)
1920-1938	**G.H.Hirst** (Yorks & England)
1939-1942	**A. Ducat** (Surrey & England)
1943-1959	**J. O'Connor** (Essex & England)
1960-1983	**V.H.D. Canning** (Hampshire, Warwicks, & Bucks)
1984-	**J.M. Rice** (Surrey, Hampshire & Wiltshire)

HARROW	
1901-1902	**D. Pollard** (Yorks)
1902-1915	**G.R. Baker** (Yorks & Lancs)
1916	**J.R. Gunn** (Notts & England)
1917	**G. Gunn** (Notts & England)
1918-1920	**J. Iremonger** (Notts & M.C.C Tour to Australia 1911/1912)
1921-1922	**E.W. Bale** (Worcs)
1923-1929	**J.T. Hearne** (Middlesex & England)
1930-1936	**W. Rhodes** (Yorks. & England)
1937-1947	**E.H. Hendren** (Middlesex & England)
1948-1965	**T.H. Barling** (Surrey)
1966-1985	**P.C. Davis** (Northants)
1986-2006	**R.K. Sethi** (Shropshire & East Africa)

INDEX OF PLAYERS

1805-2005

INDEX OF PLAYERS 1805-2005

ETON		HARROW		ETON		HARROW	
Bayley J.A.	1848	Bloomfield R.B.	1952-53-54	Bowden H.G.S.	1852	Burnett E.W.	1861-62-63
Bayley J.R.L.E.	1838-39-40-41	Blount C.C.	1943	Bowles T.G.	1952	Burnett J.D.	1858-59
Bayley L.H.	1841-42-43-44	Blount C.H.B.	1910-11-12	Bowman-Shaw F.N.	1984-85	Burroughes R.	1854
Bayly J.	1874	Blyth D.A.	1917	Bowman-Shaw G.A.	1981	Burton R.H.L.	1860
Bean H.L.	1839-40-41	Boissier P.C.	1941	Bowman Shaw J.B.	1987	Bushby J.S.	1842
Beaver M.J.	1951	Boldero G.N.	1846	Bowmont, Marquis of	1972-73	Butcher J.D.J.	1977
Benson R.L.	1906-07-08	Boldero H.K.	1850	Boyd A.N.A.	1932-33-34	Butler A.H.M.	1890
Benthall C.H.	1978	Bolitho W.E.T.	1880-81	Boyd Hon J.A.L.	1973-74	Butler E.M.	1883-84-85
Bernard A.C.	1899-1900	Bolton W.	1838	Boyd F.P.P.McN.	2001	Butler F.E.R.	1956
Berry J.P.	1983	Bolton W.S.	1902-03-04	Bradley R.	1805	Butler G.M.	1916-17
Best T.G.W.	1963	Bond R.N.	1934-35	Braithwaite C.E.	1961-62-63	Butler H.M.	1851
Bevan J.G.	1953	Booth J.E.J.	1983	Bramall E.N.W.	1941-42	Butler Lord J.H.H.T.	1865
Bevan T.	1918	Boralessa H.	1987-88	Braman N.C.W.	1970	Butterworth J.C.	1923-24
Bevan T.J.	1971	Borwick P.M.	1932	Branch G.R.	1932	Butterworth R.E.C.	1923-24
Bewicke C.	1932-33	Bosville G.W.B.	1843	Brand Hon. D.F.	1919-20-21	Buxton A.	1900-01
Bignell A.G.	1988-89	Bosworth-Smith B.N.	1891-92	Brand Hon. T.H.	1918	Buxton C.D.	1883-84
Bircham H.R.W.	1892-93	Bolt C.W.A.	1976	Brand T.W.	1885-86-87	Byam L.E.W.	1939
Birchenough W.T.	1909-10	Boult F.C.	1938-39	Brassey Hon. E.	1982	Byde J.P.	1818
Birch Reynardson C.C.		Boulton	1805	Brewis G.R.	1890-91	Byron, 6th Lord	1805
	1979-80-81	Bourke P.C.	1997	Bridgeman M.R.	1921-22-23		
Birckbeck H.	1932	Bourne J.K.	1987-88	Bridgeman W.C.	1884		
Birkbeck H.C.	1970	Boustead R.M.	1939-40	Broadhead A.	1827		
Blacker M.J.	1840	Bovill B.	1872	Brocklebank J.M.	1933		
Blackett B.J.	1905	Bovill G.B.	1885	Brocklebank T.A.L.	1917		
Blake P.D.S.	1943-44-45	Boyd P.A.McN.	1959-60	Bromley-Davenport H.R.			
Blake T.W.S.	1979	Boyson J.A.	1865		1886-87-89		
Blake W.N.S.	1980	Bradshaw J.	1894	Bromley-Davenport W.	1880		
Bligh Hon. Ivo	1876-77	Brand Hon.T.C.W.	1825	Bromley-Martin E.G.	1884-85		
Blofeld H.C.	1955-56	Brandt D.R.	1904-05-06	Bromley-Martin G.E.	1892-93-94		
Blore E.W.	1845-46-47	Brankin-Frisby R.T.	1986	Brooks M.H.	1982-83		
Bluett I.R.M.D.	1980-81	Brewer E.	1835	Brooks R.A.	1949		
Boden J.P.	1979	Bridgeman C.G.O.	1811	Broome O.G.C.	1998-99		
Boden T.W.	1918	Brigstocke G.O.	1923-24	Brown E.F.T.	1975		
Boles D.C.	1903-4	Brockman W.	1805	Brown H.T.O.	2005		
Bond C.I.C.	1998	Brooke F.C.	1827-28	Brown R.L.	1828		
Booth H.W.	1832	Brooke F.R.R.	1902	Brown W.T.	1851		
Bosanquet B.J.T.	1896	Broughton H.V.	1837	Browning C.H.	1896-97		
Bosanquet N.E.T.	1898	Broughton R.J.P.	1832-33-34-35	Brownlow J.R.	1882		
Boscawen J.P.T.	1925	Brown K.E.	1913	Bruce E.C.A.	2003-4-5		
Boscawen V.D.	1909	Bruce A.H.	1967-68	Bruce Hon. F.J.	1871-72-73		
Boswell W.G.K.	1910-11	Bucher F.M.	1923-24	Bruce R.W.J.	1994-95-96		
Botros R.J.	2005	Bourke P.C.	1997	Bruce J.T.A.	1996-97-98		
Boudier G.J.	1836-37-38-39	Buckingham W.	1834	Buckland F.M.	1871-72-73		
Boughey J.F.	1936-37-38	Bucknall G.R.C.	1988	Buckland W.L.C.	1983		
Boughey J.R.	1978	Bull R.H.	1929	Buckley A.	1848		
Boughey R.J.	1943	Buller C.F.	1861-62-63-64	Buckston G.M.	1900		
Boustead N.J.	1970-71	Buller E.T.	1911-12-13	Buckston R.H.R.	1927		
Bovill A.G.	1871	Bulloch J.H.	1893-94	Buckworth C.P.	1835		
Bovill E.P.	1863	Bullock L.	1923	Buller C.P.W.	1976-77		
Bowater E.D.	1953	Burgess B.W.M.	1986	Bullock A.J.	1938		

G / H

ETON		HARROW	
Forbes D.W.A.W.	1926	Fryer F.E.R.	1867-68
Forbes W.F.	1873-74-75-76	Fuller O.J.A.	1822
Forster H.W.	1883-84-85	Fulton T.R.	1992
Forster S.E.	1885		
Forsyth H.D.	1864		
Fortescue Hon. C.H.R.	1968-69		
Foster R.A.C.	1913-14		
Fowler RSt.L.	1908-09-10		
Fox G.H.B.	1919		
France-Hayhurst F.C.	1891		
Franks B.M.F.	1929		
Franks G.M.G.	1965		
Franks H.G.	2004		
Fraser T.O.M.	1994		
Frederick J.St.J.	1861-62-63		
Freeman-Thomas F.	1885-84-85		
Freeman-Thomas Hon.G.F.	1911-12		
Fremantle T.F.	1848		
Frere J.	1825		
Fulton J.A.G.	1994-95-96		
Fulton R.H.G.	1966		

G

ETON		HARROW	
Gardiner S.R.	1984-85	Gambier S.J.	1825
Gardiner Hill P.F.	1944	Gardner J.A.	1822
Gardner F.P.F.	1946	Garland L.	1823
Gardner J.A.	1822	Garlies, Lord	1853-54
Garnett L.	1860-61-62	Garnett M.N.	1943-44-45
Garnier E.H.C.	1938	Gascoyne A.S.B.	1931-32
Garth H.	1841-42-43	Gathorne H.	1842-43
Garth R.	1837-38	Geaves F.S.	1919-20
George G.D.G.	2003-04-05	Gibbon J.H.	1866
Gervais F.P.	1876	Gibson J.S.	1851-52
Gibbs A.V.	1940	Giffard W.J.F.	1888
Gibbs D.N.	1982	Giles A.B.	1876-77
Gibbs J.H.	1858	Giles C.T.	1868-69
Gibbs S.V.	1865	Gillespie R.W.	1861
Gibson C.H.	1916-17-18-19	Gilliat C.D.	1971-72-73
Gibson C.H.	1954-55	Gillions W.A.T.	1994-95-96
Gibson K.L.	1906-07	Gilroy C.E.	1888
Gibson-Watt M.A.	1970	Glennie T.D.	1975-76-77
Gilliat H.	1866	Glyn D.R	1838-39
Gilliat O.C.S.	1899	Glynne J.A.	1945
Gilmour C.D.D.	1939-40	Godsell J.F.	1940

ETON		HARROW	
Glyn A.J.	1961	Gold P.H.	1918-19-20
Goad F.E	1888	Goodchild R.C.R	1936
Gold C.A.	1905-06	Goodden C.P.	1899
Goldberg A.M.	2000-01-02	Goodchild R.C.R	1956
Goodhart H.C.	1876-77	Gordon A.G.	1972
Goodier W.F.	1958	Gordon J.	1941-42
Gordon D.S.	1945	Gordon P.J.	1989
Gordon-Lennox B.C.	1950	Gordon-Lennox E.C.	1978-79
Gore A.C.	1918	Gore G.P.	1893-94
Gore T.C.	1945	Gore S.W.	1867-69
Gosling C.H.	1927-28	Gorell-Barnes R.	1902-03
Gosling E.D.	1879	Gough O.M.L.	1969-70
Gosling G.B.	1889	Gowans J.	1889-90
Gosling L.D.	1893-94	Graham O.B.	1910
Gosling M.S.	1930-31	Graham R.J.	1867-68
Gosling R.C.	1885-86-87	Grant A.	1844
Gosling W.S.	1888	Greatorex J.E.A.	1881
Goulder P.J.R.	1976-78	Greatorex T.	1882-83
Green S.S.	1886	Greaves W.E.	1888
Greenwood J.	1825	Green A.K.C.	1986-87
Greenwood S.H.	1983	Green R.M.N.	1952-53
Gregson-Ellis R.	1901-02	Greenall D.I.H.	1986
Grenfell A.M.	1892	Gregson H.G.	1911
Grenfell C.A.	1883	Gregson L.H.K.	1914-16
Grenfell E.O.	1899	Greig P.D.M.	1975
Grenfell P.St.L.	1879-80	Grenfell W.H.	1873-74
Greville R.C.	1927	Grieve B.A.F.	1883
Grimston G.C.W.	1972	Griffin A.W.M.S.	1906
Gull F.W.L.	1908	Griffin A.J.S.	1941-42
Gull R.C.	1913	Grimston, Viscount	1825-27
Gurdon E.	1828	Grimston Hon. E.H.	1827-28
Gurdon W.	1822	Grimston Hon. F.S.	1838-39
Guthrie J.S.	1948-49-50	Grimston W.E.	1862-63
Gwyn H.N.	1838	Grundy C.G.S.	1875-76
Gwyn W.B.	1838-39-40	Gunning S.G.	1818
		Gurney –	1845

H

ETON		HARROW	
Hagen N.R.J.	1990	Habib M.	2004-05
Haig-Brown C.W.	1875	Hadow A.A.	1872
Hale J.H.	1942	Harlow E.M.	1880-81
Hale K.F.H.	1929-30	Hadow P.F.	1872-73
Halsey T.E.	1916		
Hambro C.E.A.	1948		

ETON		HARROW	
Hambro C.J.	1914	Hadow W.H.	1866-67
Hamilton D.M.	1972	Haggas S.E.	1980-81
Hamilton K.M.	1947	Haggas W.J.	1977-78-79
Hamilton M.M.	1973	Hall M.W.	1971-72
Hamilton-Fletcher G.	1912-13	Halliday C.A.	1937
Hanbury E.	1872	Halliday C.A.R	1970
Hanbury T.E.	1930-31	Halliday J.	1969-70-71
Hand H.G.	1827	Halliday J.A.	1893
Hand T.	1822-23	Halliday M.A.C.	1905
Hankey T.S.D'A.	1914	Hamilton Lord E.W.	1877
Harbord W.E.	1927	Hamilton R.C.	1987
Harding F.E.	1875	Handley E.H.	1822-23-24
Hardman J.M.I.	1984	Hankey F.A.	1850-51
Hardy J.C.S.	1994	Hankey R.	1849-50
Hare T.	1946-47-48	Hardinge C.	1876
Hargreaves J.	1881-82-83	Harenc C.J.	1827-28
Harris Hon. G.R.C.	1868-69-70	Hargrove G.C.	1934
Harrison H.R.E	1893	Harmsworth P.C.B.	1999
Haskett-Smith A.	1874-75	Harmsworth R.V.G.	2001-02
Hatfeild C.E.	1903-04-05-06	Harper G.M.	2004-05
Hatfield H.S.	1905-06-07	Harrap N.G.	1992-93
Hawk S.L.J. McL.	1998	Harrison H.A.	1852
Hawk T.H. McL.	2000	Harrison M.E.	1968
Hawke Hon.M.B.	1878-79	Hartley T.	1865-66
Hawtrey A.	1838	Harvey J.C.T.	1955
Hay J.W.	1840	Haslewood G.F.	1930-31-32
Hay W.H.	1867-68	Hatcher M.G.	1994
Hayter A.D.	1851-52-53	Hawke C.R.J.	1951-52
Hazlerigg A.G.	1927-28-29	Hawkins M.M.J.	1991-92
Hazlerigg R.H.	1961	Hay N.F.M.	1981-82
Heathcote U.	1836	Hay W.D.M.	1950
Heathcote W.G.	1854	Haygarth A.	1842-43
Heathcoat-Amory J.	1912-13	Hayward D.R.	1937-38
Heaton J.	1805	Heale W.H.	1878
Hedley A.M.	1931	Heaton T.M.	1932-33
Hely-Hutchinson C.C.	1944	Heinemann W.E.	1931
Hely-Hutchinson H.A.	1943-44	Henery P.J.T	1877-78
Henderson M.B.	1939	Henery R.W.P.	1903
Herbert M.R.H.M.	1901	Henley D.F.	1939-40-41
Hervey-Bathurst F.R.G.	1887-88	Henley F.R.	1895-96
Hervey-Bathurst F.T.A.	1849-50	Henley-Welch A.N.	1963
Heywood-Lonsdale T.N.	1970-71	Henriques D.J.Q.	1936-37
Higgins W.C.	1866-67-68-69	Henson E.G.	1996
Hill E.V.L.	1925	Henson S.D.	1992-93
Hill M.L.	1920-1	Hepher D.R.	1997-98
Hills P.H.L.	1943	Herbert D.R.Ap.G.	1966-67
Hill-Wood B.S.	1916-18	Hermon J.V.	1923-24
Hill-Wood C.K.H.	1925-26	Hewens E.M.S.	1989-90

ETON		HARROW	
Hill-Wood P.D.	1952-53-54	Hewett H.T.	1882-83
Hill-Wood W.W.	1918-19-20	Hewitt W.J.D.	1989-90
Hitchcock. W.L.	1879	Hewlett W.O.	1862-63
Hoare A.R.	1890	Hill C.G.	1991-92
Hoare E.B.	1917	Hill J.A.R.	1987-88
Hoare H.N.	1851-52-53	Hills E.H.	1874
Hoare H.W.	1860-61	Hills R.A.	1985
Hoare J.M.D.	1971	Hillyard J.M.	1909-10
Hoare M.D.	1943	Hoare H.S.	1868
Hoare R.H.	1901	Hoare R.B.	1888-89
Hoare V.R.	1890-91-92	Hoare S.	1858-59
Hoare W.M.	1858-59	Hodgkinson G.L.	1854-55
Hoare W.R.	1886	Hodgkinson J.R.	1961-62
Hodges P.M.	1966	Hodgson C.G.L.	1916
Hodgson E.T.	1888	Hodgson G.H.	1858
Hogg J.N.	1930-31	Hogarth J.U.	1916
Holland F.J.	1845	Holden E.A.	1824-25
Holland W.T.F.	1910-11	Holland C.J.T.	1971
Hollins A.M.	1894-95	Holland S.G.	1967-68
Hollins F.H.	1896	Hollway B.A.C	1993
Hollins J.C.H.L.	1909	Holmes G.A.	1854-55
Holmes A.T.G.	1933	Holmes N.T.	1886
Honywood R.	1843-44	Holt C.A.	1963-64-65
Hood H.L.A.	1975-76	Holt R.A.A.	1936-37-38
Hope H.E.H.P.C.	1925-26	Holyoake M.A.	1990-91
Horlick J.N.	1904	Holyoake R.G.	1992
Hornby C.R.	1859-60	Hopley F.J.V.	1901-02
Hornby E.G.S.	1857	Hopley G.W.V.	1909-10
Hornby J.J.	1845	Hopton C.J.	1973
Horne R.F.	1996-97	Hopton N.C.	1974-75
Horner M.	1867	Horn F.W.A.	1979-80
Horrocks C.	1833	Hornby A.N.	1864-65
Hotchkin N.S.	1931-32-33	Hornby C.L.	1862-63
Howard E.	1818	Howe H.R.	2003-04
Howard-Smitb G.	1898-99	Hoyer-Millar C.G.	1976
Hubbard R.A.	1927	Hoyer-Millar E.G.	1918
Hughes M.G.E.	1968	Hoyer-Millar G.C.	1946-47-48
Hughes-Onslow A.	1880	Hue Williams L.E.T.	1962
Hughes-Onslow A.C.	1975	Hulbert D.J.	1951-52-53
Hume A.	1836-37	Humphreys E.W.	1858-59
Hunloke H.P.	1925	Humphreys W.A.	1904
Huntingdon-Whiteley H.		Hurt S.F.A.A.	1897-98
	1937-38	Hutton C.F.	1886
Hurley J.E	1922-23	Hutton H.E.	1846-47
Hutchison C.K.	1896	Hyde-Thompson P.C.	1945
Hyde, Lord	1924-25		

I cc

ETON		HARROW	
Ilingworth J.H.H.	1953	Ingram J.	1834
Impey C.A.	1947-48	Ipswich, Lord	1805
Impey H.E.	1951	Isaac H.W.	1917
Incledon-Webber G.S.	1922-23		
Ingleby-Mackenzie A.C.D.			
	1949-50-51		
Inkin P.A.D.	1982-83		
Inskip Hon. P.J.H.	1964		

J

ETON		HARROW	
Jackson J.B.	1935-36	Jack H.W.	1999
Jafri A.R	1994-95	Jackson A.H.M.	1916-17
James J.A.	1844-45	Jackson R.S.	1887-88-89
James R.A.	1953	Jackson G.L.	1911-12-13
Jamieson GJ.E.	1940	Jackson G.R.	1914
Jardine J.I.F.	1880-81	Jackson T.G.H.	1943-44
Jeffreys M.G.C.	1949	Jackson T.R.	1978
Jelf R.H.	1928-29	Jacques R.A.	1947-48-49-50
Jenkins J.B.A.	1984-85-87	James S.A.	1983-84
Jenkins T.A.J.	1990	James T.M.H.	1976-77-78
Jenkinson D.J.	1972	Jameson T.O.	1909-10
Jenner C.H.	1825-26	Jamieson C.J.A.	1961-62
Jenner H.	1822-23	Jarrett M.E.D.	1989-90
Johnson C.W.	1839	Jarvis C.J.E.	1876-77-78
Johnson E.B.J.	1988	Jarvis L.K.	1876
Johnson K.H.R.	1932	Jenkins H.R.	1969-71-72
Johnson P.R.	1897	Jenkins I.R.	2005
Johnstone F.L.J.	1913-14	Jessopp N.A.	1914-16
Jones R.T.	1988-89	Jodrell F.B.	1827
Jowett C.R.J.	1996	Jones F.P.	1852
Judd F.S.H.	1873-74	Jones H.M.D.	1975
		Jones M.	1845-46-47
		Joynson G.W.H.	1971
		Joynson W.R.H.	1934-35

K

ETON		HARROW	
Kary M.R.	1975-76	Kaye C.M.S.	1960-61
Kavanagh W.	1832-33	Kaye H.S.	1899-1900
Kay-Shuttleworth Hon. D,C		Kaye M.A.C.P.	1933-34-35
	1996-97	Keey C.L.	1987-88
Kaye J.H.	1805	Kemp A.F.	1880-81
Keate R.W.	1832	Kemp C.W.M.	1874-75
Keeling B.P.M.	1944-45	Kemp. H.F.	1885-86
Keeling M.E.A.	1942-43	Kemp M.C.	1879-80
Keighley W.G.	1941-42-43	Kemp M.F.	1923
Kekewich J.	1909	Kennaway C.R.	1898
Kennerley-Rumford R.G.M.		Kenyon E.	1827
	1922-23	Kinahan G.C.	1921
Kenyon-Slaney R.O.R.	1908-09	Kindersley C.E.	1884
Ker R.J.C.R.	1840	Kington P.O.	1851
Kerrison R.G.G.	1935	Kinnison R.C.A.	1981-82
Kettlewell H.W.	1893-94-95	Knight P.H.	1853
Kindersley A.P.	2000	Kok M.	1949-50-51
Kindersley R.H.M.	1947	Kortright M.C.W.	1912
Kingsborough, Viscount	1916	Kostoris J.M.	2000-01-02
Kinkead-Weekes R.C.			
	1966-67-68		
Kirkpatrick N.Y.J.	1977		
Kirwan E.D.G.M.	1832-33		
Kirwan J.H.	1834-35		
Knatchbull-Hugessen Hon. C.M.			
	1881-82-83		
Knight A.E.	1999		
Kynaston R.	1825		

L

ETON		HARROW	
Lambert A.F.	1903	La Fontaine W.E.J.	1895
Lambert C.E.	1899-1900	Lambert J.A.	1834
Landale O.D.F.	1923	Lambert R.E.	1901
Lane D.W.S.S.	1941	Lang A.H.	1906-07-08-09
Lane O.J.M.	1991	Lang G.L.	1854-55
Lane-Fox E.	1891-92	Lang R.	1855-58-59
Lane-Fox E.J.	1955-56-57	Lardner T.J.E.	1953-54
Langham R.N.	1858-59		
Larken J.J.S.	1991		

ETON		HARROW	
Lascelles Hon. D.H.	1881	Laverton G.A.	1906-08
Lawrie C.A.	1965-66	Law W.	1867-68-69-70
Lawrie P.E.	1920-21	Lawrence A.S.	1928-29-30
Lea A.M.	1995-96	Lawrie A.W.	1963
Lea T.N.	1962	Lawson E.M.	1877-78
Lee H.R.	1892	Lawson-Smith T.E.	1908
Legard A.D.	1894-95-96	Layard A.J.	1873
Leggatt L.C.	1912-13	Leaf E.A.	1974
Legge P.B.	1952	Leaf F.W.	1878
Legh W.P.	1827	Leaf H.	1871-72-73
Leigh P.W.R.	1972-73	Leaf J.E	1942-43-44
Leonard J.W.	1957-58	Leaf J.G.	1918
Leslie A.F.S.	1997-98	Leathes T.D.de M.	1995
Letts F.C.	1914	Lee C.H.P.	1972-73
Lewis A.R.	1995	Lee E.H.	1971
Lewis G.H.B.	1990-91	Lee R.E.P.	1973-74
Lewis P.T.	1947	Le Marchant E.H.C.	1913
Lightfoot C.G.R.	1992-93-94	Lepp J.C.	1970-71-72
Lindsay C.P.	1941	Leslie J.	1832-33
Lindsay Hon. H.P.	1946-47	Lewis A.J.	1818
Lister-Kaye K.A.	1910-11	Lewis W.H.	1825
Little R.T.K.	1973	Lewis-Barclay C.L.	1942-43
Llewellyn-Davies N.	1922	Leyland F.D.	1873
Llewelyn W.D.	1886-87	Liddell C.H.	1929
Lofft C.P.	1825	Lindsay M.J.	1927
Lomax.D.	1925-26	Linday P.A.R.	1936
Lomax I.R.	1948-49	Lindsay R.E.	1966
Long F.E.	1833-34-35	Lindsay W.O'B.	1926-27-28
Longman G.H.	1868-69-70-71	Linton H.	1854-55-57
Longman H.K.	1898-99-1900	Litherland J.P.	1994
Loraine P.	1898	Lithgow A.O.L.	1938-39-40
Loudon A.G.R.	1997-98-99	Lithgow W.S.P.	1937-38
Loudon H.J.H.	1995-96-97	Lloyd F.O.G.	1920-21-22
Loudon J.R.H.	1960-61	Lloyd J.A.	1805
Low H.H.	1917-18	Lloyd-Jones A.T.C.	1983
Lowe M.	2000	Lloyd-Jones J.F.P.	1978-79
Lowndes P.G.	1965-66	Lockett J.B.	1957
Lowndes W.G.L.F.	1916	Loftus Lord H.Y.A.	1840
Lowth G.T.	1824	Long R.P.	1843-44
Lubbock A.	1861-62-63	Long W.H.	1873
Lubbock A.B.	1894-95	Longe F.D.	1847-48-49
Lubbock E.	1864-65-66	Loring E.H.	1841
Lubbock. M.	1859	Lucas A.C.	1870
Lubbock R.	1896-97	Lucas F.G.L	1880
Lubbock R.H.	1909-10	Lyon H.F.	1900
Lucas C.E.	1903		
Lucas R.J.	1881-82-83-84		

ETON		HARROW	
Luke R.J.F.	1983		
Lunt A.R.G	1986-87		
Lush E.R.	1989		
Lutyens A.L.	1947-48		
Lutyens C.B.	1945		
Lyle I.A. de H.	1928		
Lyttelton Hon. A.	1872-73-74-75		
Lyttelton Hon. A.T.	1870		
Lyttelton Hon. C.E.G.	1965		
Lyttelton Hon. C.G.	1858-59-60		
Lyttelton Hon. E.	1872-73-74		
Lyttelton Hon. G.W.	1900-01		
Lyttelton Hon. G.W.S.	1863-64-65		
Lyttelton J.A.	1939-40		
Lyttelton Hon. N.G.	1862-63-64		
Lyttelton Hon. R.H.	1871-72		

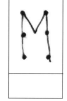

ETON		HARROW	
Maan G.G	1998-99	Macan A.H.	1902
MacAndrew N.R.	1965	Macan G.C.	1869-70-71
Macdonald A.R.	1979	MacAndrew R.G.	1995-96
Macdonald I.	1971-72	MacDonald S.W.	2000-01
Machin H.V.	1993-94	McCorquodale A.	1943-44
McCall R.P.	1970	McCorquodale E.G.	1899-1900
McGoughan A.N.J.	1989	Maclean A.S.	1944
Macindoe D.H.	1935-36	Maclean D.C.H.	1939-40-41
Mackeurtan J.G.	1938-39	McLinlock W.K.	1914
Maclachlan L.C.	1886-87	MacGregor C.E.E.	1828
Maclean D.	1818	McInroy J.P.H.	1874
Maclean D.R.	1952-53	McIntosh A.I.H.	1993
Macleay R.D.O.	1986-87	Mackenzie A.	1844-45-47-48
McLeod J.R.C.	1978	Mackenzie D.	1850
McCall T.P.	2000-01-02	Mackenzie H.	1845-46-48-49
Macnaghten C.M.	1898	Mackie E.D.	1886
Macniven E.	1843-44-45	MacLaren A.C.	1887-88-89-90
Magill M.D.P.	1934	MacLaren G.	190I-02
Makhija R.	1971	MacLaren J.A.	1886-87-88
Malcolm A.J.E.	1974	McMullen F.J.	1975-76-77
Mann F.G.	1934-35-36	McNeill A.J.	1860
Mann J.P.	1934-35-36-37	McNeill R.J.	1880
Manners Hon. J.N.	1910	McSwiney P.J.	1965
Marchant F.	1882-83	Magnay C.B.W.	1903
Marcon W.	1841-42	Maitland W.F.	1860-61-62-63
Marillier C.H.	1853	Makant A.V.	1907-08
Marr D.A.C.	1952	Makant R.K.	1913-14
Marriott W.B.	1842		

ETON		HARROW	
Marsh W.A.	1832	Manasseh D.C.	1984-85-86-87
Marshall T.H.	1941-42	Mann E.W.	1899-1900-01
Marsham A.J.B.	1936-57	Mann E.W.E.	1925
Marsham A.P.	1955	Manning H.E.	1825
Marsham C.H.B.	1897-98	Mardenborough C.	1827
Marsham F.W.B.	1901	Marillier W.	1850-51-52
Marsland F.P.E.	1983	Marlar R.G.	1947-48-49
Martin E.G.	1898-99	Marsden-Smedley G.F	1914
Martin R.G.	1973-74	Marshall J.	1842-43-44
Martin S.R.B.	1988-89	Massey W.	1835-36
Martin-Smith A.E.	1969-70	Massy G.D.	1954-55-56
Matheson C.M.	1998	Marten G.N.	1859
Mathias J.H.	2001-02	Martin R.	1822-23
Matthews L.W.	1877	Martineau P.H.	1880-81
Maude J.	1861-62	Mathews E.	1866
Mayes C.M.A.	1942	Matson J.R.M.	1917-18
Mayhew J.F.N.	1928	Matthews E.S.	1890
Mbu J.O.	1973-74	Matthews H.L.	1895-96
Meeking H.F.	1893	Matthews W.J.L.	1997-98
Metaxa N.A.	1979-80-81	Matthey G.I.	2005
Metaxa P.A.	1950	Maw P.T.	1895-96-97
Methuen Hon. P.A.	1905	Maydon E.G.L.	1995-96
Meyrick G.C.T.C.G.	1959	Maydon M.L.	1955-56
Micklem L.	1865	Maydon R.C.	1961
Micklethwait F.	1834-35	Maydon S.R.L.	2000-01-02
Miles A.C.	1873-74	Maynard E.A.J.	1879
Miles C.N.	1871-72	Medlicott W.S.	1897-98
Miles C.F.W.	1837	Meek A.G.	1861
Miles G.W.	1842	Meek H.E.	1874-75-76-77
Millar M.J.F	1992	Menpes-Smith W.A.	1982
Millar P.M.C.	1989	Mercer J.F.	1851
Milne A.G.	1969	Merivale C.	1824
Milne G.P.	1959-60	Merivale R.	1827
Mitchell F.H.	1896-97	Methold J.W.	1818
Mitchell J.H.	1823	Michell E.J.	1871-72
Mitchell R.A.H.	1858-59-60-61	Middleton M.R.	1984-85
Mitchell R.H.	1893	Miles F.H.H.	1912
Mitchell R.W.	1894-95	Miles P.E.	1847-48-49
Moodie E.R.	1974	Miles R.F.S.	1956
Moffatt J.N.P.	1993	Miles W.S.	1918-19
Monroe-Hinds L.	1928-29	Millbourn R.L.	1962
Montagu J.D.	1950	Miller R.S.	1954-55-56
Montgomery A.J.	1975	Miller S.A.St.J.	1965
Monypenny R.J.	1818	Mills B.S.T.	1840
Mordaunt H.J.	1884-85-86	Mills W.C.	1837-38-39
Mordaunt J.M.	1854-55	Minoprio A.G.D.	1999
Mordaunt O.	1860	Mirehouse W.E.	1863
Morgan G.E.A.	1989	Mitchell I.N.	1941-42
Morgan P.G.	1991	Mitchell S.A.F.	1969-70
Morris A.G.P.M.	1952	Mitchum A.B.	2001

ETON		HARROW	
Morris P.W.	1977-78	Monckton W.T.	1910
Morrison Hon. A.G.	1979	Moncreiff H.J.	1857
Morton A.H.A.	1854	Moncreiff R.C.	1862
Mostyn T.E.L.	1848	Moncreiff R.	1881-82
Mott W.K.	1857	Moncreiffe T.G.H.	1877-78-79
Mulholland A.E.S.	1901	Money W.B.	1865-66-67
Mulholland G.J.A.M.	1911	Monro R.W.	1857
Mulholland H.G.H.	1907	Montgomery H.H.	1864-65-66
Murdoch C.E.G.	1884	Montgomery P.A.J.	1994
Murray J.	1901-02	Moolman F.E.M.	1920
Murray-Willis J.H.	1967	Morewood W.F.P.	1840
		Morgan H.E.	1840-41
		Morgan N.C.	1986
		Morier G.	1840
		Morrall C.	1873
		Morrice F.F.J.	1836
		Morrice F.L.H.	1874
		Morris R.O.	1904-05
		Morrison J.H.	1972-73-74
		Morrison K.B.	1911
		Morrison H.M.	2002-03-04
		Morrison P.R.C.	1974
		Moseley P.D.	2001-02
		Motaung K.	1999-2000
		Mumm J.E.	1907
		Munro R.M.C.	1893
		Murly-Gotto H.T.	1918-19
		Murray A.R.G.	1977-78
		Murray P.R.G.	1982

N

ETON		HARROW	
Napier R.S.	1949	Napier C.W.A.	1834-6
Nash R.S.	1839	Napier D.R.	1889-90
Nation D.P.C.	1960	Nash L.C.F.	1901
Naylor J.M.	1906-07	Neame A.	1889
Naylor R.E.	1912-13	Neame A.R.B.	1952-53-54-55
Negretti A.S.T.	1964	Neame J.B.	1981
Neville L.	1844	Neame J.W.B.	1996-97
Nevinson J.H.	1928-29	Needham P.J.E.	1967-68-69-70
Newman G.C.	1923	Neeld J.	1822-3
Newton A.E.	1879-80-81	Nelson R.D.	1987-88
Nicholl K.I.	1902-03	Nethercote H.O.	1835-36
Nickerson W.L.G.	1976	Neumark T.V.	1934
Nissen C.P.A.	2002-03		
Nissen E.F.J.	2002-03-04		

ETON		HARROW	
Noorani A.P.	1999	Nicholson J.	1840-41
Norman C.L.	1848-49-50	Nicholson N.F.	1957
Norman D.M.	1959	Nicholson W.	1841-42-43
Norman F.H.	1854-55-56	Nicol F.W.	1995-96
Norman H.G.H.	1855	Nieboer J.C.S.	1958-59
Norman J.D.	1985-86	Nirmalalingham D.R.	1982-83
Norman P.	1859-60	Nobbs M.B.A.	1966
Norman R.O.	1890-91	Nokes J.M.	1951-52
Norman-Butler P.A.	1997	Norman J.M.	1974
Norris G.W.	1924	Norris D.W.W.	1961-62-63-64
Norris W.A.	1848-49	Norris J.R.W.	1995-96-97
Northey C.H.	I891	Norris R.M.W.	1994
Northey F.V.	1852-53-54	Northeast S.A.	2004-05
Novis R.A.	1956	Northey A.E.	1857
Nugent T.E.G.	1913-14	Norton J.B.	1832-33

ETON	
Ottaway C.J.	1867-68-69

ETON		HARROW	
Packe C.W.C.	1927	Page A.	1894-95
Page R.	1930-31	Paget C.	1827
Paget-Steavenson R.S.A.	1967	Paine A.I.	1891-92
Palmer Sir G.C.J.	1954	Palmer R.H.	1925-27
Palmer H.W.A.	1972	Palmer T.W.	1861
Palmer R.H.R.	1916	Parbury E.P.	1870
Parker A.E.	1883	Paris T.C.	1837
Parkyns T.M.F.	1872	Park A.W.	1853
Parnell J.H.	1828	Parker C.R.C.	1995-96
Parnell Hon. J.P.C.	1976-77	Parker J.B.	1841
Parry S.D.R.	1975	Parker J.M.	1953-54-55-56
Patel S.K.	1995	Parkes R.E.C.	1948
Patrick P.S.S.	1999	Partridge H.C.	1824
Patrick W.S.L.	1998	Paterson W.S.	1835-36
Patteson J.C.	1843-44	Patrick R.C.	1979-80-81
Payne-Gallwey W.T.F.	1900	Patterson H.G.	1916
Peacock H.St.G.	1891	Patterson W.H.	1877
Pearson D.E.	1986	Paul J.L.	1939
		Paul M.J.L.	1979
		Pawle J.H.	1933-34

ETON		HARROW	
Pearson G.E.D.McL.	1955-56-58	Pearson T.M.	1951
Pearson I. McL.	1939	Pease M.W.R.	1917
Pearson N.A.	1916	Peasgood R.A.H.	1991
Pearson-Gregory P.J.S.	1906	Peebles H.M.	1889-90
Pease Hon. C.H.B.	1941-42	Peel E.B.	1932
Pechell C.A.K.	1888	Peel R.	1838-39
Peebles A.R.T.	1966	Peel R.	1916
Pelham A.G.	1930	Peel Yates W.D.	1983
Pelham Hon. F.G.	1863	Pelham C.H.	1965
Pelham T.H.W.	1866	Pelham C.T.	2005
Pemberton R.H.	1882-83	Pelham E.T.	1933-34
Penn. E.F.	1897	Pelham H.T.	1958-59-60-61
Pennant S.D.	1955-56	Pelham R.J.	1962-63
Pepys A.	1863	Pelham S.	1867-68
Percival L.R.	1924-25	Pember F.W.	1880
Persse R.A.	1911	Penn W.	1867
Pettifer C.E.	1982-83	Pennefather G.E.M.	1926
Pettifer H.D.	1986	Perry C.	1822-23
Petre H.R.E.	1988	Perry J.W.	1841
Philips G.H.	1849	Persse A.A.	1947-48
Philipson H.	1884-85	Peterken L.E.	1950
Phillips L.G.	1850	Pethers J.J.	1984-85-86
Phipps T.H.	1865	Phelips G.A.	1902-03
Phipps W.W.	1864-65	Phelps T.T.	1891
Pickering E.H.	1824-25	Philcox E.A.	1892
Pickering F.P.U.	1869-70	Phillips J.S.B.	1973
Pickering J.H.	1834	Phillips N.L.	1974
Pickering W.P.	1834-35-37-38	Phipps H.G.	1863-64
Pilkington C.C.	1892-93-94-95	Pidcock C.A.	1868
Pilkington F.C.	1890	Pigott A.C.S.	1974-75-76
Pilkington G.W.	1964-65	Pigott T.A.M.	1948
Pilkington H.C.	1896-97-98	Pike G.	1905
Pilkington R.A.	1962-63	Pix T.S.	1824
Pilkington T.C.	1957-58-59	Plasket T.H.	1834
Pilkington T.D.	1894	Platt T.D.	1844-45-46-47-48
Pilkington T.H.M.	1951	Plowden H.M.	1858
Pinney J.C.	1853-54	Ponsonby Hon. F.G.B.	1832-33
Pipe-Wolferstan F.S.	1845	Ponsonby J.H.	1866
Pitt W.	1818	Pool J.L.	1989-90
Pocklington D.	1860	Pope C.G.	1889-90-91
Polhill-Turner A.T.	1879-80	Popham F.L.	1825-27
Polhill-Turner C.H.	1878	Porter A.M.	1892
Pollard R.C.	1824	Powell M.	1922
Ponsonby Hon. F.J.W.	1865	Pratt J.G.H.	1977
Portal G.H.	1876-77	Preece R.J.	1991
Porter J.M.	1954	Prendergast G.L.	1822
Post J.M.	1875	Prichard E.C.	1858
Powell B.L.H.	1966-67	Prideaux-Brune P.E.E.	1939
Prest T.W.	1977	Pringle M.	1828
Prest W.P.	1849-50	Prior D.C.	1945-46-47

ETON

Pretzlik N.C.	1961-62-63
Price H.W.F.	1992
Prichard J.C.	1988
Prichard M.C.T.	1961-2
Prideaux W.S.	1862-63-64
Primrose Hon. A.R.	1928-29
(Lord Dalmeny 1929)	
Proudlock N.G.D.	1943
Pugh C.T.M.	1954-55
Pym W.A.C.	1985-86

HARROW

Prior J.D.	1983
Proctor P.D.	1924
Prothero G.	1835
Pulbrook R.	1932-33
Pyman R.A.	1984-85-86

Q

Querl R.G.	2005

R

ETON

Raison R.H.M.	1974-75-76-77
Ralli E.P.C.	1873-74
Ramsden T.J.P.	1969
Randolph C.	1841-42-43
Rankin A.M.	1952-53
Rankin H.D.P	1945
Rankin J.M.N.	1948
Rankin L.J.	1997
Rawlinson H.C.L	2004-05
Rawlinson H.T.	1979-80
Rawlinson J.L.	1976-77
Rawlinson R.	1857
Rawson R.H.	1881
Rawstorne G.S.	1912-13-14
Read T.F.	1828
Reay T.O.	1850-51-52
Redmayne C.G.M.	1983-84
Redmayne J.R.S.	1997
Redmayne T.L.	2005
Rees-Davies W.R.	1934-35
Reikey J.C.	1866
Remnant Hon. P.J.	1971-72
Remnant Hon. R.J.	1974
Rhodes F.W.	1869-70
Richards A.C.	1881-82-83
Richardson S.B.	1963

HARROW

Radford S.J.	1977
Rahman M.	1962-63-64
Ramsay A.D.	1884-85-86
Ramsay M.F.	1878-79
Ramsay N.	1887-88
Ramsay R.C.	1879-80
Ramsay R.O.	1918-19
Raper B.S.	1957-58-59-60
Raper C.	1988-89
Raper J.W.S.	1981-82-83
Raper M.D.S.	1984-85-86
Raphael A.C.	1925
Raphael E.G.	1887
Raphael G.L.	1926-27-28
Rattigan C.S.	1903
Rattigan T.M.	1929
Rattigan W.F.A.	1896-97-98
Rawlinson T.	1842-43
Rayner M.S.	1994
Reade C.W.	1833
Readman I.R.	1941-42
Reid C.F.	1861
Reid C.R.	2002
Reid G.M.	1959-60
Reid H.V.	1958

ETON

Ridley A.B.	1877
Ridley A.W.	1870-71
Robarts A.	1839-40
Robarts G.	1897
Robertson F.B.	1895
Robertson H.G.	1892
Robertson J.M.	1969
Robins G.R.V.	1963
Robins R.V.C.	1950-51-52-53
Robins T.R.V.	1980
Robinson A.C.E.	1959
Rodger J.P.	1869-70
Rodwell R.E.H.	1965
Rodwell R.H.	1936
Roe W.N.	1916
Rogerson M.A.	1960
Rolle M.G.K.	1853-54
Ross S.J.R.	1998
Ross W.H.M.	1962
Rosseter R.G.	1839
Round J.	1860
Rowe C.V.F.	1898
Rowland Clark J.R.	2005
Rudd A.C.H.	2001
Rudd B.J.B.	1944
Rudd C.R.D.	1944-45-46
Rudd M.J.B.	1980
Ruggles-Brise E.J.	1875-76
Russell D.C.E.	1980
Russell W.A.B.	1981-82-83
Russell-Scarr A.M.K.	1967
Ryle J.C.	1833-34

HARROW

Rennie J.K.	1847
Renshaw J.A.J.	1992-93
Renton H.N.L	1914
Reunert C.	1904-05
Reunert J.	1904-05
Reunert J.M.	1936
Reynard P.E.	1946
Reynolds I.S.R.	1960-61
Richards E.J.	1919
Richardson F.G.F.	1948
Richardson J.M.	1864-65
Richardson M.K.O.	1976
Richardson W.	1865
Riddell W.J.	1928
Ridgeway C.S.C.F.	1891
Riley-Smith T.S.M.S.	1980-81
Rivett-Carnac G.C.	1870
Robertson W.P.	1896-97-98
Robinson C.T.	1818
Robinson J.F.	1926-27-28
Robinson J.P.	1918
Robinson R.G.	1983-84
Roditi J.B.K.	2002-03-04
Roffey G.W.	1888
Rogers H.M.	1859
Rogerson J.R.	1982
Rome C.B.N.	1960
Rome C.S.	1891-92-93
Rome D.A.M.	1926-27-28-29
Ross E.	1846-47-48
Rothschild N.M.V.	1929
Roundell S.F.	1993-94
Routledge L.A.	1881
Routledge V.	1908
Rowe F.C.C.	1877-78
Rowe R.P.C.	1940
Royle J.S.	1906-07
Rudd C.J.L.	1890-92
Ruffell M.W.J.	1978-79
Russell H.S.	1837-38
Rutherford M.J.	1976-77
Ryan P.H	1949

S

ETON		HARROW	
Sainsbury S.D.D.	1947-48	Sage C.J.	1936-37-38
St.Croix W. de	1837-38	Sanders A.T.	1918
St. George C.H.G.	1988-89	Sanderson J.T.	1885
Sampson D.D.	1822-23	Sanderson L.	1882
Sandeman G.A.C.	1901-02	Sanderson L.	1950-51
Sanders T.	1827	Sandilands J.W.	1893
Savile A.	1836-37-38	Saunders W.C.	1862
Scarlett R.W.	1827-28	Saurin D.E.	1847
Scholfield R.B.	1903	Scott R.S.G.	1940
Scott E.J.R.	1956-57	Scott W.M.F.	2000
Scott-Hayward G.O.A.	2003-04	Sealy C.T.	1834
Scott, Lord F.G.	1898	Sealy M.L.	1978-79-80
Scott, Lord George	1884-85	Seligman R.J.R.	1972
Scott-Chad G.N.	1917	Seligman R.M.	1936-37
Secker I.O.	1818	Sexton A.W.	1985-86
Sellar M.D.M.	1949-50	Sexton R.E.	1990-91
Sellar W.R.G.	1990-91	Seymour C.F.	1834
Selmon G.P.F.	1987	Shakerley G.A.	1951
Selwyn N.J.	1964	Shakerley G.H.	1881
Severne E.C.W.	1904	Shakespear A.	1805
Seymour G.A.	1835	Shand F.L.	1872-73
Shaw R.W.	1822	Sheffield J.R.	1959
Sheepshanks C.E.W.	1930	Sheriffe T.B.	1838
Sheepshanks E.R.	1927-28	Shewell H.P.	1823
Sheldon H.D.	1921	Shuckburgh C.G.	1927-28-29
Sherrard J.P.	2003	Sibthorp G.T.W.	1832-33
Sherrard S.P.	1964-65	Sidley R.J.L.	1953-54
Shirazi S.H.	1987	Simpson J.R.	1932
Shirley W.R.De la C.	1917-18-19	Simpson R.J.R.	1952-53
Shuttleworth O.R.A.	1997	Skinner T.J.M.	1946-47
Simpson J.	1832	Smith C.J.	1866
Simpson T.A.	1992-93	Smith F.W.	1864
Sinclair I.A.C.	1955-56	Smith M.A.	1941
Sivewright E.	1823-24-25	Smith R.H.	1834-35
Slingsby J.	1805	Smith T.C.	1837
Smijth-Windham S.	1852	Snow A.C.W.	1986-87
Smith C.M.	1876-77-78	Soames C.	1844
Smith D.M.	1964-66	Southwell H.G.	1848-49
Smith G.J.S.	1861	Spencer R.	1878-79
Smith H.E.F.	2001	Spencer W.J.	2003-04-05
Smith J.	1838-39	Spiro D.G.	1881-82
Smith M.G.	1836-37	Spiro R.M.	1949
		Spring-Rice Hon.G.	1944
		Spry O.C.P.	1995

ETON		HARROW	
Smith O.S.	1861	Stancomb F.W.	1879-80
Snow H.	1825-27-28	Stanhope E.	1859
Soames F.A.	1884	Stanley E.	1818
Somers-Cocks J.V.	1940	Staveley W.C.	1882
Southby A.R.C.	1928-29	Stevens S.H.	1997-98-99
Speer R.G.T.	1946	Stevenson G.W.H.	1954
Speke C.C.	1978	Stevenson-Moore N.S.	1916-17
Spooner E.H.	1940-41	Stewart A.F.	1875-76
Sprot H.M.	1906-07	Stewart J.A.G.H.	1979-80
Squire N.J.	1985	Stewart N.J.	1970
Ssennyamantono B.K.	1990-91	Stewart Hon. R.H.	1853-54
Stacey F.E.	1848-49	Stewart W.G.	1937
Stanley T.J.	1990	Stewart-Brown H.	1882
Steel A.I.	1910-11	Stewart-Brown I.H.	1955
Steel C.E.	1993-94	Stewart-Brown P.H.	
Steel H.C.	1992		1920-21-22-23
Stevens J.O.J.	1932	Stewart-Brown R.D.	1930
Stewart J.B.W.	1968	Stileman A.W.	2001-02
Stewart-Grey J.D.I.	1944	Stirling J.	1913
Stewart-Richardson N.G.J.		Stirling J.H.	1877-78-79
	1972-73	Stogdon G.A.	1933-34-35
Stock A.B.	1910	Stogdon J.H.	1893-94-95
Stoddart D.R.	1954-55	Stogdon N.G.	1966
Stoddart P.L.B.	1951-52	Stow J.M.	1930
Stone W.H.	1858	Stow M.H.	1863-64-65-66
Story J.B.	1851	Straker A.C	1909-10
Streatfeild N.W.	1844-45-46-47	Strang C.A.	1952-53-54
Strickland S.C.E.	1990-91	Strange S.	1932
Stubbs A.R.P.	1942	Streatfield-Moore J.E.A.	1967
Studd A.H.	1882-83	Strong C.I.	1857
Studd C.T.	1877-78-79	Strutt H.	1859
Studd G.E.B.	1877-78	Stuart D.W.	1936-37
Studd H.W.	1888-89	Stuart E.A.	1871-72
Studd J.E.K.	1876-77	Stuart R.B.	1942-43
Studd R.A.	1890-91-92	Studd E.B.T.	1896-97-98
Studley-Herbert D.H.	1926	Studd P.M.	1933-34-35
Sudbury S.G.D.	1981	Surtees H.E.	1836-37
Sullivan J.P.	1988	Swan C.A.S.	1983
Surtees H.R.C.	1920	Symes-Thompson F.	1894
Sutherland C.L.	1855-58		
Sutherland H.B.	1861-62-63		

T

ETON		HARROW	
Tabor A.S.	1869-70-71	Tabor A.	1868
Tabor R.M.	1864	Talbot A.	1834-35

ETON		HARROW	
Talbot J.E.	1889	Taylour, Lord R.C.	1844
Taylor C.A.W.	1999	Templer F.G.	1867
Taylor C.G.	1834	Thatcher M.	1971
Taylor D.G.	2004	Thicknesse J.D.	1948-49-50
Taylor P.G.E.	1828	Thomas D.J.G.	1978
Taylor S.B.	1827	Thomas G.M.D.	1943
Teape A.S.	1862	Thompson G.E.	1913
Teape C.A.	1863	Thompson R.H.	1947
Teeger J.A.	1986	Thompson V.	1883
Tennyson Hon. L.H.	1907-08	Thorne J.C.	1945-46
Tew. J.E.	1924	Tindall D.F.	1973
Thackeray C.	1849-50-51	Tindall M.	1931-32-33
Thackeray F.	1834	Tindall R.M.	1975-76-77
Thesiger A.H.	1857	Titchener-Barrett A.T.R.	1997-98
Thomas P.H.	1938	Titchener-Barrett D.C.A.	1995
Thompson B.R.	2001-02-03	Titchener-Barrett R.C.S.	1961-62
Thompson H.M.	1864	Torre H.J.	1836-37-38
Thornhill G.	1828	Torrens A.	1848-49
Thornton C.I.	1866-67-68	Torrens A.A.	1892
Throwley, Lord	1880	Torrens H.A.G.	1930
Thursby W.P.	1922-23	Tower A.R.S.	1944-45
Tod A.A.	1899-1900	Tower H.J.B.	1839
Tod W.N.	1903-04-05	Travers C.G.M.	2003-04-05
Tollemache M.A.	1870-71	Tregoning D.C.L.	1996
Tollemache M.G.	1887-88-89	Tregoning G.R.	1993
Tomkin A.P.R.	1967-68	Trehearne-Thomas R.K.F.C.	
Townley T.M.	1841-42-43		1946-47
Townsend C.H.	1818	Trench F.C.	1823-24
Trasenster M.W.de C.	1972	Treveleyan W.B.	1837-38-39
Travis C.M.D.	1973	Trew V.P.	1911-12
Trefusis Hon. C.J.R.	1881	Tudway H.G.	1845-46
Tremlett E.J.	1853-54	Turnbull M.T.	1935
Tremlett T.D.	1850-51-52	Turnbull T.L.G.	1909-10-11
Trenchard-Cox A.D.	1942	Turner E.J.	2003-04
Tristram M.H.	1889	Turner Hon.J.F.	1981-82
Tritton E.W.	1862-63	Tylden-Wright G.M.	1917
Tritton W.F.	1867-68	Tyssen C.A.D.	1875
Trusted D.M.	1992		
Trusted J.T.	1987-88-89		
Tryon G.T.L.	1896-97		
Tuck. G.H.	1861-62		
Tucker W.H.	1818		
Tufnell C.W.	1910-11		
Tufnell K.E.M.	1920		
Tufnell N.C.	1904-05-06		
Tunnard J.	1832		
Turnbull J.	1932-33		
Turner A.G.	1904		
Turner N.F.	1933		
Turnour, Lord	1855		
Twining R.H.	1907-08-09		

U

ETON		HARROW	
Ulvert C.N.	1990	Upcher G.	1860
		Upcher H.M.	1858
		Upcher H.R.	1828
		Upton P.V.	1921

V

ETON		HARROW	
Vance G.	1832-33	Vargas J.C.D.	1956-57
Vane-Tempest C.S.	1914	Verney H.A.	1938
Vassar-Smith D.R.	1997	Vernon H.	1845-46-47-48-49
Venables-Llewellyn C.M.D.	1917	Vibart R.F.	1893-94-95-96
Villiers A.G.C.	1902	Vigne G.T.	1818
Villiers Hon. N.H.	1934	Vinson R.W.	1967-68
		Virgin C.J.A.	1989

W

ETON		HARROW	
Wadham N.C.	1949-50-51	Walker A.H.	1850-52
Wagg A.R.	1959-60	Walker C.H.	1852
Wagg R.M.	1991	Walker C.W.	1868-69-70
Wagner G.	1835	Walker G.B.	1873-74
Wagner H.M.	1818	Walker I.D.	1860-61-62-63
Wake C.J.	1964-65	Walker J.H.	2003
Wakefield J.	1874-75	Walker R.D.	1859-60
Wakeman E.M.	1865	Walker V.E.	1853-54
Walker P.A.	1937	Wallis P.	1944-45-46
Wallace R.C.	2001	Wallroth C.A.	1870
Wallace V.G.	1939	Walsh J.	1867
Walrond W.H.	1866-67	Walters M.D.	2004
Walsh J.J.	1992	Ward E.W.H.	1881-82
Walter A.F.	1864-65	Warman J.M.G.S.	1998
Walter H.M.	1866-67-88	Waterlow N.A.R.	1960
Walter J.	1836	Wathern S.W.J.	1966-67
Ward A.G.	1960-61	Watson A.K.	1884-85
Ward A.S.	1895		
Ward Hon. G.E.F.	1896		

ETON			HARROW	
Ward J.E.H.	1973-74		Watson C.P.	1929
Ward Hon. J.H.	1889		Watson G.H.	1905
Ward M.S.C.	1926-27		Watson H.D	1887-88
Ward Hon. R.A.	1888-89		Watson M.D.	1935-36-37
Watney D.C.	1950		Watson M.J.	1964
Watson R.V.	1983		Waud G.E.G.	1984-85
Watt C.A.	1981-82		Webbe A.J.	1872-73-74
Waud B.W.	1855		Webster A.P.	1966-67-68
Wear G.	1818		Webster R.F.C.	1956
Webb R.H.	1825		Weedon M.J.H.	1957-58-59
Webber A.H.	1972		Wegulin C.	1857
Wellesley R.A.	1945-46		Welch R.C.	1871
Wemyss T.M.A.	1992-93		Wells R.M.	1984-85
Wendell J.	1942		Welsh W.M.	1928-29-30
Westoll N.C.R.	2002-03-04		Wenn J.B.	1846-48
Whately E.G.	1900-01		Weston-Simons J.S.	1997-98
Wheatley C.M.	1941		Whetherly R.E.	1935
Whitby P.D.	1976-77-78		Whistler L.G.	1916
White Hon. L.R.	1943-44		Whitaker A.I	1876
Whitfeld H.	1875-76-77		Whithers M.H.	1943-44
Whitmore H.E.	1872-73-74		Wiggin D.P.	1976-77-78
Whitmore W.W.	1872		Wilcox R.J.	1999
Whittaker R.C.C.	1925-26-27		Wilenkin B.C.G.	1949-50-51
Whittington J.M.S.	1990-91		Wilkes J.F.	1897-98
Whymper F.H.	1846-47		Wilkinson M.G.	1875
Wigan D.G.	1910-11-12		Willetts M.J.S.	2000
Wigan P.	1959-60-61		Williams C.D.	1893-94
Wigram A.J.	1851		Williams C.E	1990-91
Wild V.L.	1934-35-36		Williams C.L	1823
Wilkinson C.A.	1832		Williams F.V.	1862
Wilkinson E.O.H.	1871-72		Willock C.W.	1837
Wilkinson H.F.	1916-17		Wills C.P.	1889
Wilkinson R.H.	1828		Wilson C.S.	1911-12
Willey S.J.	1984		Wilson C.T.	1833
Williams E.D.	2000		Wilson F.B.	1899-1900
Williams M.V.C.	1962-63		Wilson G.	1912-13-14
Williams O.G.	2004		Wilson G.R.R.	1935
Williams P.F.C.	1902-03		Wilson T.B.	1909-10-11
Wilson C.J.	1916-17		Wiltshire R.C.	1984-85
Wilson G.E.N.S.	1965-66		Winlaw A.S.R.de W.	1955-56
Wilson R.R.P.	1950		Winthorp B.	1855
Windsor-Clive A.	1908-09		Withers M.H.	1943-44
Winter C.E.C.	1986-87		Wood L.G.R.	1961
Winter N.A.J.	1852-53-54		Wood M.J.B.	1959-60-61
Winter W.G.	1951		Woodhouse W.H.	1842-43
Witcomb R.M.	1964		Woodroffe H.G.P.	1916
Witts W.F.	1836-37		Woodward K.A.	1892-93
Wodehouse E.R.	1852-53		Wordsworth C.	1822-23-24-25
			Wormald D.	1925
			Worthy W.R.	1972

ETON			HARROW	
Wolfe-Murray A.M.	1954-55		Wrigley M.T.	1942
Wolfe-Murray J.A.	1954		Wrigley N.H.T.	1973
Wood Hon. R.F.	1939		Wroughton W.M.	1868
Woodall C.S.	1946		Wyld H.J.	1896-97-98-99
Woodd D.J.B.	1968		Wyndham G.	1818
Wormald E.	1867			
Wormald J.	1899-1900			
Worsley J.A.	1946			
Worsley W.A.	1908-09			
Wright H.F.	1889			
Wyndham H.M.	1970-71			

ETON			HARROW	
Yate-Lee C.	1888		Yarrow D.E.	1930
Yeo W.A.	1854		Yates F.S.J.	1990
Yonge G.E.	1841-42-43		Young W.A.R.	1883-84-85
York C.	1986			
Yorke G.J.	1918-19			
Yorke J.R.	1852			
Yorke-Long R.A.	1971			
Young H.	1822-23			
Young W.	1834-35			
Young W.M.	1859			
Younger H.W.	1851			

ETON		
Zagoritis A.D.A.	1985-86	

1200 Etonians and 1134 Harrovians have represented their schools in the Eton and Harrow match.

*Edward Chandos Leigh
(aged 28) pictured in 1860
by Robert Allan Fitzgerald
(Harrow XI 1852 and MCC
Secretary 1864/76).
Copyright MCC/Fitzgerald.*

THE HON. SIR EDWARD CHANDOS LEIGH
Harrow XI 1850/1, Oxford University 1852/4 & M.C.C.(1832 -1915)

Edward Chandos Leigh started playing cricket at Stoneleigh Abbey, the Leigh family home in Warwickshire after his father Chandos Leigh, who was a contemporary of Byron's at Harrow, established a ground there in 1839. He managed to get into the Harrow XI of 1850/1 scoring 42 as Harrow captain in 1851, and gained Oxford blues in 1852/3/4. Although his record was mediocre, he only scored eight runs in three matches, Oxford won on all three occasions. He was a founder of the famous Oxford Harlequins Club, well known for their colourful cap, and a fellow of All Souls, Oxford until 1871. He was a long serving member of the M.C.C. Committee, a close friend of Bob Fitzgerald, M.C.C. Secretary, from 1863/76, and his brother-in-law, Secretary of the prestigious I. Zingari and M.C.C. President in 1887 its centenary year, but he had a somewhat inflated opinion of his ability as a player. His highest score in first-class cricket was 62 for M.C.C. v. Kent at Canterbury in 1861. On congratulating his nephew H.D.G. 'shrimp' Leveson-Gower, the Winchester, Oxford University, Surrey and England player, on his fine 73 in the 1895 varsity match with the words "Well done Schwimp, (he could not pronounce his 'r's) capital, capital, you played just like I used to" met with the reply from his nephew "Heaven forbid Uncle Eddy!" He was, however, a very popular and well respected man who was knighted in 1901 after being Recorder of Nottingham from 1881/1909 and Counsel to the Speaker from 1883/1907.

Lord Hawke, he was left handed (see shooting pose below) but batted right handed.

THE AUTOCRAT
WHO PLAYED THE GAME
TO HIS OWN AGENDA

In May 1896 Yorkshire scored 887 v. Warwickshire without declaring. It is the highest total ever scored in a county match. It left Yorkshire no time to dismiss Warwickshire twice and occupied 274 overs. What was the object of such a useless record? Well seven wickets had fallen for 448 when Lord Hawke came in at no. 9. The Warwickshire bowlers were already very tired and his Lordship saw the opportunity for some fun. Hawke hugely enjoyed his slaughter of the weary bowlers scoring 166 with Bobby Peel (210 not out) taking the score to 740. When he was out he decided to continue and George Hirst at no.10 plundered another 85 runs. After the innings was completed he even had the temerity to ask for the ball as a souvenir! His plans did not always go so well. In 1898 at Chesterfield v. Derbyshire he thought he would like an innings. So irrespective of merit he put himself in at no. 3 after Brown and Tunnicliffe the Yorkshire openers and went to put his pads on. He did not expect to have to wait long. Poor 'Long John' Tunnicliffe had had a series of disasters on his way to the ground. He had had nothing to eat since tea time the day before. He had booked in at a dirty inn, found the bedclothes damp and sat up all night in a chair. Obviously he was exhausted and in no state to bat long. But Brown and Tunnicliffe scored 554 for the first wicket and it was 12 o'clock on the second day before his lordship got his bat!

A CROSS SECTION OF
FINE ETON CRICKETERS
LOST IN THE GREAT WAR 1914-1918

G.A.C. Sandeman Eton XI 1901/2, Hampshire 1913.

C.W. Tufnell Eton XI 1910/11 (captain in 1911), a very fine all round athlete.

F.O. Grenfell V.C. Eton XI 1899 (the first officer to gain the V.C. in the Great War).

H.B. Chinnery Eton XI 1894/5, Surrey and Middlesex 1897/1904.

F.H.E. Cunliffe Eton XI 1893/4, Oxford University 1895/8 and Middlesex 1897/1903.

G.W. Cattley Eton XI 1908, a well known Eton cricketing family.

W.G.K. Boswell Eton XI 1910/11, Oxford University 1913/14.

R. Gregson-Ellis Eton XI 1901/2 (captain in 1902).

C.E. Hatfeild Eton XI 1903/6, Oxford University 1908 and Kent 1910/14.

G. Howard-Smith Eton XI 1898/9, Cambridge University 1903.

R.W. Mitchell Eton XI 1894/5, Oxford University golf blue 1896. One of R.A.H's three sons in the Eton XI.

C.G.E. Farmer Eton XI 1904, M.C.C. (first class matches).

Their names will never be forgotten

5 July, 2005

Dear Robert,

I thoroughly enjoyed the Eve of Eton v Harrow Cricket Match Dinner and was most touched by the kind presentation, including your excellent book.

I simply wanted to write and say how much I have enjoyed reading it and how pleased I am to add it to my collection.

With all good wishes,

Yours sincerely,

John Major

Robert Titchener-Barrett Esq

P.O. BOX 38506, LONDON SW1P 1ZW
TEL. +44 (0) 20 7793 9292   FAX. +44 (0) 20 7793 9293

THE DREAM OF CRICKET

THE GAME THAT'S NEVER DONE

Soft, soft the sunset falls upon the pitch,
The game is over and the stumps are drawn.
The willow sleeps in its appointed niche,
The heavy roller waits another dawn —
Bowled is the final ball again,
Hushed is the umpire's call again,
The fielders and the batsmen cease to run —
But memory will play again
Many and many a day again
The game that's done, the game that's never done.

In happy dreams we'll see each re-bowled,
And mend the fault that robbed us of some prize,
In dreams we'll hold the catch we failed to hold,
And see our duck's-eggs swell to centuries —
In dreams we'll take the field again,
In dreams the willow wield again,
And set the red ball spinning in the sun —
Ah, memory will play again
Many and many a day again
The game that's done, the game that's never done.

THE MEANING OF CRICKET

THE CAPTAIN'S ROLE

'When you win the toss – bat.
If you are in doubt, think about it – then bat.
If you have very big doubts, consult a colleague – then bat.'

W.G. GRACE

'If everything else in this nation of ours were lost but cricket –
her constitution and the laws of England of Lord Halsbury –
it would be possible to reconstruct from the theory and practice
of cricket all the eternal Englishness which has gone to the
establishment of that Constitution and the laws aforesaid'.

NEVILLE CARDUS. CRICKET (1930)

AS THE GREAT LORD HARRIS, CAPTAIN OF ETON, KENT AND
ENGLAND SAID OF CRICKET A YEAR OR SO BEFORE HE DIED IN AN
EIGHTIETH BIRTHDAY MESSAGE TO THE TIMES IN 1931:

'You do well to love it, for it is more free from anything sordid,
anything dishonourable, than any other game in the world.
To play it keenly, honourably, generously, self-sacrificingly, is a
moral lesson in itself, and the classroom is God's air and
sunshine. Foster it, my brothers, so that it may attract all who
can find the time to play it; protect it from anything that
would sully it, so that it may grow in favour with all men.'

ETON v. HARROW

SATURDAY, 23rd, JUNE 2012   (55 overs per side)

	ETON	Innings	
1	J. B. Abbott	lbw b Boyd	72
2	E. James	b Turner	43
†3	H. L. Hayes	c Bond b Patel	83
4	J. S. D. Gnodde	c White b Macintyre	8
5	J. M. Hubbard	b Boyd	5
6	M. J. Roy	not out	34
7	M. H. P. Carleton-Smith	st White b Macintyre	6
8	R. N. MacDonagh	not out	5
9	G. H. J. Fitzroy		
10	J. O. Tugwell		
*11	F. A. N. Thorpe		

b , l-b 7, w 8, n-b 2, p , 17

Total ....(6 wkts, 55 overs) **273**

FALL OF THE WICKETS

1—94 2—181 3—216 4—220 5—225 6—242 7— 8— 9— 10—

ANALYSIS OF BOWLING

Name	O.	M.	R.	W.	Wd.	N-b.
Bose	10	1	51	0	...	...
Macintyre	9	0	49	2	1	...
Boyd	11	1	61	2	4	2
Fosh	8	0	31	0	2	...
Turner	6	1	22	1	1	...
Patel	11	0	52	1	...	...
	...	...	...	...	...	...

	HARROW	Innings	
*1	R. G. White	c Tugwell b Roy	8
2	L. Bose	run out	118
3	M. E. Cousens	st Thorp b Hayes	26
†4	N. M. T. Castleman	run out	3
5	A. W. Boyd	lbw b MacDonagh	6
6	V. M. Patel	c Thorp b Carleton-Smith	11
7	H. W. D. Whitrow	not out	80
8	A. R. G. Turner	run out	4
9	M. P. Ward	b Carleton-Smith	3
10	H. D. L. Macintyre	not out	4
11	M. A. Fosh		

b , l-b10, w 5, n-b , p , 15

Total ......(8 wkts, 54.1 overs) **274**

FALL OF THE WICKETS

1—29 2—84 3—99 4—106 5—130 6—216 7—241 8—269 9— 10—

ANALYSIS OF BOWLING

Name	O.	M.	R.	W.	Wd.	N-b.
Tugwell	10	1	63	0	2	...
Roy	7	0	45	1	1	...
Fitzroy	6.1	0	43	0	1	...
MacDonagh	11	2	26	1	...	...
Hayes	11	0	42	1	1	...
Carleton-Smith	8	0	38	2	...	...
Gnodde	1	0	7	0	...	...

Umpires—P. E. McKenzie & G. Pearson

Scorers—J. Jarvis & M. P. Carter

†Captain   *Wicket-keeper

Play begins at 11.00   Luncheon Interval 1.00-1.40   Tea Interval – after 25 overs of the side batting second

(Times may vary according to the state of the game)

Eton won the toss

Harrow won by 2 wickets

ETON v. HARROW

SATURDAY, 22nd JUNE, 2013   (55 overs per side)

HARROW	Innings	
1. F.W.A. Ruffell	c Carleton-Smith b Mould	9
2. L. Bose	c Russell b Eckett	35
3. R.G. White	lbw b Mould	12
†*4. M.E. Cousens	c Russell b Griffin	47
5. A.W. Boyd	run out	24
6. V.M. Patel	c Mould b Eckett	4
7. M.G. Kellock	b Griffin	0
8. A.R.G. Turner	lbw b Griffin	0
9. S.J.S. Assani	lbw b Carleton-Smith	7
10. M.P. Ward	not out	21
11. M.A. Fosh	b Griffin	3
	b 1, l-b 6, w 29, n-b 3, p ,	39
	Total .... (51.5 overs)	201

FALL OF THE WICKETS

1—38   2—60   3—99   4—145   5—149   6—161   7—161   8—161   9—178   10—201

ANALYSIS OF BOWLING — Innings

Name	O.	M.	R.	W.	W.	N-b.
Roy	10	2	45	0	5	3
Griffin	10.5	2	32	4	4	...
Mould	11	1	44	2	4	...
Eckett	10	1	35	2	2	...
Carleton-Smith	8	1	26	1	3	...
Blake	2	0	12	0	...	...

ETON	Innings	
†1. E.W.R. James	lbw b Kellock	54
2. J.A. Langen	c Fosh b Boyd	9
3. J.S.D. Gnodde	not out	65
4. J.F.G. Halstead	c Cousens b Boyd	37
*5. A.D.L. Russell	c Ward b Boyd	0
6. H.A.S. Blake	run out	3
7. M.J. Roy	not out	15
8. M.H.P. Carleton-Smith		
9. T.K.M. Eckett		
10. P.H.A. Mould		
11. C.R.D. Griffin		
	b 1, l-b 5, w 13, n-b 1, p ,	20
	Total .... (5 wkts, 49.2 overs)	203

FALL OF THE WICKETS

1—14   2—100   3—164   4—167   5—179   6—   7—   8—   9—   10—

ANALYSIS OF BOWLING — Innings

Name	O.	M.	R.	W.	W.	N-b.
Boyd	11	2	36	3	2	1
Assani	8	0	37	0	3	...
Turner	8.2	0	46	0	4	...
Fosh	4	0	20	0	1	...
Ruffell	4	0	20	0	1	...
Kellock	11	2	25	1	1	...
Ward	3	0	13	0	1	...

Umpires—J.G. Reed & M. Watton   Scorers—J.G.E. Jarvis & C.P. Coghlan
†Captain   *Wicket-keeper

Play begins at 11.00   Luncheon Interval 1.00-1.40   Tea Interval – after 25 overs of the side batting second
(Times may vary according to the state of the game)

Harrow won the toss   **Eton won by 5 wickets**

The Gentlemen of
Eton.